THE
MEDIEVAL FOUNDATIONS
OF ENGLAND

THE MEDIEVAL FOUNDATIONS OF ENGLAND

by

G. O. SAYLES

M.A., D.LITT.

PROFESSOR OF MODERN HISTORY IN THE
QUEEN'S UNIVERSITY OF BELFAST

Philadelphia
UNIVERSITY OF PENNSYLVANIA PRESS
1950

First published in Great Britain in 1948
First American edition, revised, with
new preface and introduction, 1950

PRINTED IN GREAT BRITAIN

TO
MY WIFE

FOREWORD

AMERICAN scholars of the intellectual calibre of Haskins, McIlwain and Lunt, to name but a few, have devoted themselves to a study of the medieval way of life, particularly in England, knowing that thereby they were getting a closer and firmer understanding of the traditions and modes of thought that have helped to fashion their own contemporary society. But the fruits of their work and of that of their fellows in England have too long confined within a narrow circle of specialists. There would be no point in writing this book if it could not claim to meet a need which has so far been inadequately satisfied. Too few efforts have been made in the last quarter of a century to bridge the gap between the monograph and the textbook. If, however, a thousand years of historical development—social, economic, ecclesiastical and cultural as well as the strictly political—are to be discussed in short space and the results of recent scholarship to be incorporated, then a special approach is necessary which demands omissions. Anything like a chronological narrative has been avoided: should it be wanted, there are many books already in print to supply it. Indeed, the recital of too many facts is apt to clip the wings of imagination and suppress that lively curiosity without which history has no vitality. Here the stress is laid upon the interpretation of the facts. And only on rare occasions has it been possible to state opposing views to those advanced here or to provide the nuances of meaning that are known to be desirable: the factor of limited space permits no more than a personal evaluation of the evidence. However, in the last analysis there is no other worth-while way of writing on history. But if this book is regarded as a working-book, which endeavours not only to ask questions but, more important still, to ask the right questions, and to give an answer to them, however much it may have to be in the nature of an interim report, it will have served its purpose. Therefore, whilst much has been read that can find no place in so short a treatment, and views have sometimes been put forward which venture to be at variance with received opinion, there is no *apparatus criticus* and no *pièces justificatives*. Instead, short reading-lists have been inserted at appropriate places, which will help the reader to test conclusions for himself and reach, as he should, his own independent judgements. 'Be not like the empiric ant which merely collects, nor like

r*

the cobweb-weaving theorists who do but spin webs from their own intestines; but imitate the bees which both collect and fashion.' Reference is usually made to recent publications only, since it is here that assistance is most needed; these themselves will provide a guide to the wisdom of the more distant past, for all historians stand upon the shoulders of their predecessors. My citation of authorities will itself express my gratitude to the historical world at large. To Mr. H. G. Richardson, in particular, who read my manuscript in the bits and pieces in which it was written in the night-watches of war, I remain indebted for criticisms so searching that it would require many books, and different books from this, to appraise them properly.

G. O. S.

THE QUEEN'S UNIVERSITY OF BELFAST

NORTHERN IRELAND

3 *September* 1949

CONTENTS

ABBREVIATIONS

The following books are cited in the reading-lists by the surname of their author or authors only:

R. G. Collingwood and J. N. L. Myres, *Roman Britain and the English Settlements* (1936).

F. M. Stenton, *Anglo-Saxon England* (1943).

R. H. Hodgkin, *History of the Anglo-Saxons* (Second Edition, 1939).

E. T. Leeds, *The Archaeology of the Anglo-Saxon Settlements* (1913).

E. Lipson, *Economic History of England: The Middle Ages* (1937).

F. Pollock and F. W. Maitland, *History of English Law* (1895).

Z. N. Brooke, *The English Church and the Papacy* (1931).

R. W. Chambers, *England before the Norman Conquest* (1926: a source-book in translation).

C. Stephenson and F. G. Marcham, *Sources of English Constitutional History* (1937: in translation).

Am. H. R.: American Historical Review.

B. J. R. L.: Bulletin of the John Rylands Library.

C. Med. H.: Cambridge Medieval History.

Econ. H. R.: Economic History Review.

E. H. R.: English Historical Review.

T. R. H. S.: Transactions of the Royal Historical Society.

INTRODUCTION

BRITAIN ON THE EVE OF THE ANGLO-SAXON SETTLEMENTS

IN its geological formation the island of Britain presents two sharply contrasted parts: a line drawn from the mouth of the Tees to the mouth of the Exe represents roughly the division between them. This basic divergence largely explains the different course of development in each region until the eighteenth century, when the Industrial Revolution introduced the new factor of mineral exploitation and altered the traditional economic balance. In particular, it explains the limits of the Roman Occupation of Britain during the first four hundred years of that country's history and the varying degree of romanization to which it was subjected.

I. THE LOWLAND ZONE TO THE SOUTH AND EAST

In a remote prehistoric age Britain had formed part of the northern plain of Europe, and it was a geological accident that had turned a river bed into the English Channel. Consequently, the lowlands of Southern England have their counterpart in the lowlands of Northern France and, historically if not geologically speaking, they have never been separated. Far from being a barrier, the Channel has always formed an easy means of communication, far simpler to traverse than mountain ranges or forest lands or swamps. And it must be borne in mind that, to those who came from the eastern shores of the North Sea, the Channel gave access equally to the lands on either side. The successive waves of Celtic peoples crossed the narrow seas, as before them some of the Neolithic peoples had done. On both sides of the Channel the Belgic Celts had made their settlements before Cæsar made his two 'armed demonstrations' in 55 and 54 B.C., ostensibly to prevent collaboration between them in resistance to Rome. To the German tribes who assaulted and finally occupied the north-west provinces of the Roman world, both north and south coasts of the Channel were similarly exposed. Many Britons, driven from Britain, found refuge in Armorica, and the language spoken in Brittany was basically that which was spoken in Cornwall until the eighteenth century. Even when Britain thereafter almost disappeared from recorded history, recent investigations are compelling us to realize more and more the influence that contact with Merovingian Gaul had upon the commercial, cultural and even administrative developments in at least the south-eastern corner of Britain.

It is not, therefore, surprising that, in their schemes of conquest, the Romans should cast their eyes past the Channel to the lowlands beyond. In the event this gently undulating country, carrying few hilly districts above six hundred feet, accessible in most of its parts, fertile in its soil, presented no serious obstacle to the Roman armies after the Claudian invasion of A.D. 43. So quickly was resistance overborne and the work of pacification completed that the forts that were presumably constructed here and there in the first stages of conquest must have been abandoned at an early date, and they have left only slight traces of their existence. So the lowland zone became an area of essentially civil occupation, in which the processes of romanization could exert their full influence.

II. THE HIGHLAND ZONE TO THE WEST AND NORTH

The mountain chain from Cornwall to North Scotland presented an entirely different problem, to which an entirely different answer had to be given. Very probably Claudius, and certainly Agricola, had thought that the subjugation of the whole of Britain was a quite feasible project, and for a time it must have seemed that success did not lie beyond their grasp. The Dumnonian peninsula of Devon and Cornwall gave no trouble and, as we now know, the Romans did not hesitate eventually to establish villa estates around the coast, though they left the inhospitable hills and moorlands to the Celts. And Wales had been brought firmly under control by the time Agricola became governor in 77 and on the whole it remained quiescent thereafter, so much so that the score or so forts, erected to keep it under supervision, were apparently denuded of their garrisons some time in the second century. Nor did the Pennine Dales impede for long the northward thrust of Rome: once the hill-fortresses of the native tribes had been overthrown, the surrounding countryside could keep up no prolonged resistance. The advance beyond the Cheviots, however, met with vacillating fortune. Agricola in 83 marched into Perthshire, defeated the Caledonians at Mons Graupius, and constructed garrison-forts at those strategic points where the Grampian passes debouched upon the Scottish plain. Whatever further plans he had made to conquer Caledonia, as Wales had been conquered before it, we can only surmise, for imperial politics brought about his recall. No succeeding period proved to be so suitable and favourable for such an enterprise, and the northern frontier of Roman Britain shuttlecocked between the later constructed Walls: it retreated from the Scottish lowlands in 122 to Hadrian's Wall, which formed a seventy-three mile cordon from the Tyne to the Solway Firth; it went forward again in 139–142 to the Antonine Wall, stretching thirty-seven miles across the other slender waist of Britain between the Forth and Clyde; it returned about 180–185 to Hadrian's Wall, where it remained until that line of defence finally collapsed or, more probably, was abandoned on strategic grounds in 383.

The highland zone could not be assimilated and the Romans were forced to construct in its northern section a military area of defence to screen the lowland zone. They found themselves committed for many generations to policing it with armed forces. To do this effectively demanded a permanent military establishment of 30,000 to 40,000 troops as well as an elaborate series of forts and an intricate network of roads.

The Romanization of Britain

The absorbing interest of the Roman Occupation lies in watching the Roman political genius at work in the shaping of provincial government: it was Mommsen rather than Gibbon who threw this truly magnificent achievement into proper relief. The northern military zone can be left out of the argument. It is not that romanization did not there take place. A certain measure was inevitable, for the army bases and depots attracted many hangers-on and called for a busy commerce which was evidently not restricted to the south side of the Wall alone. Furthermore, as the practice of drafting troops from abroad was dropped gradually from the beginning of the second century in favour of local recruitment, the native soldiery on their discharge from service carried their knowledge of Roman ways with them to the farms on which they were settled outside the forts. Nevertheless, urban life proper did not and could not flourish, and only recently has there been found near Durham the remains of a Roman villa beyond the neighbourhood of York. Romanized life remained necessarily superficial and, associated as it was with the army, it disappeared with the army. Rome could be no more than an alien intruder in a predominantly Celtic environment.

The position was far different in the civil zone of Southern Britain. We cannot appreciate the principles that directed Roman policy unless we first ask ourselves how many foreigners were brought into the country and what proportion of the total number of inhabitants did they form. Obviously neither question can be answered except in the broadest way: still, however much the experts may vary in their estimates, the general conclusion seems to be beyond cavil. Including the soldiers, who were early drawn away to guard the northern frontier, and the administrative and financial officials of the central government, and the traders, the immigrants did not exceed a total of 100,000 in an area whose native population has been placed at round about a million. The Romans were too wise and experienced to believe that they could remain for long simply a ruling class, holding down resentful subjects by force. That could be no more than an initial stage if their regime was to endure. Therefore, after they had as it were advertised their wares by showing the Britons four examples of romanized life on a level comparable with that in other parts of the Empire by building the 'coloniae' of Colchester, Lincoln, York and Gloucester, they set themselves to seek the co-operation of the Britons. Roman influence had been strong in the south of Briton before the invasions, and the rapid development of Roman civilization would have been impossible except on the basis of co-operation, and this co-operation, accepted for their part by the Britons, permitted them to make their own contributions so that the final result was not purely Roman but distinctively Romano-British.

The relative distribution of population and romanization was settled by geography, and the Romans made no determined effort to become the masters of their physical environment. When the sites of excavated villas are plotted on a map, it is plain that they lie mainly in a U-shaped tract, extending from Lincolnshire through Northamptonshire, Cambridgeshire and Essex to Kent, westwards along the counties between the Thames and the Channel coast as far as Dorset, and northwards through Somerset and along the Cotswolds into the Severn valley. Within this tract lay the Midlands, covered with forest lands and marshlands, which was the most thinly inhabited part of the lowland zone. It is evident that, though the lands already laid under contribution in pre-Roman times were more intensely cultivated to meet Imperial demands, little attempt was made to extend the acreage of arable and pasture, and the long and arduous fight against nature was left to be the unspectacular and magnificent achievement of the Anglo-Saxons. Apparently only in the Fenlands did the Romans apply their engineering skill to constructing great catchwater drains to reclaim land for the plough. The region of Norfolk and Suffolk, isolated by the Fens; the forest of the Weald in Kent; the swamps of the Lower Ouse and Upper Trent around the Humber estuary: such continued always to repel settlement.

The Impact of Roman and Celtic Civilizations

I. URBAN BRITAIN

As a natural outcome of the Mediterranean tradition of city states, the Roman conception of the political unit was the urban community administering its own affairs and those of the territory around it. But when the Romans came to Britain they found no towns. Instead the tribal community was the unit of political organization. It was their imperative task, therefore, to adapt the Celtic system to their own: the romanization of Britain was akin to that of Flanders and the Rhineland rather than Gaul or Spain. After the first fierce revulsion from the strange new ways and, especially, their repressive government, they encountered little difficulty. The aristocrats who ruled a tribe proved willing to form a civil magistracy and let themselves be called senators, and they continued to exercise under new names the authority they had previously wielded. Therefore a dozen tribal strongholds were converted into tribal capital cities in control over the extensive tribal lands round about, and it was not long before they imitated the higher civilization presented by the four Roman model towns. These had been termed 'coloniae' because they were the direct product of the Roman state and inhabited straightway by Roman citizens, presumably time-expired legionaries. The tribal capitals were not so much Roman in their origins as Romano-British, and the difference was marked by the use of another word, 'municipium'. Though according to our literary texts only St. Albans

(Verulamium) received a chartered constitution which placed it on terms of equality with the 'coloniae', it is reasonable to assume that it was only the early period of its establishment that distinguished it from its fellows and that Canterbury, Cirencester, Caerwent, Leicester, Aldborough and others came in time to enjoy corresponding rights. And, in addition, there was an anomalous group of some fifty lesser towns, placed here and there over the countryside, which derived their importance usually from some particularized purpose: centres of manufacture like Castor on the edge of the Fens, posting towns on the roads like Chesterton on the Fosse Way, or health resorts like Bath. London stands somewhat apart in its development: as the hub of six convergent roads, it became a focus of commercial life which was more continental than insular in its character; it formed the obvious centre of the Imperial financial administration; it became the headquarters of a Christian bishop. It grew into the most extensive and wealthiest of the cities in Britain and, in fact, it was the fifth largest in the north-western provinces of the Empire.

And yet we shall distort the picture if we place too much emphasis upon towns and town-life. For when we take into account the acreage of the built-up areas within the walls and the number of houses they contained, we realize that they did not expand very much during the long years of the Roman Occupation and that the population within them remained relatively small. It has been calculated that the sum total of urban Britain could not have been much more than four square miles, and even if London could boast of some 15,000 inhabitants, most towns barely averaged a tenth of that number. Nor with our modern conceptions in mind ought we to over-stress their economic role. There would undoubtedly be the activity of a market town with its retail trade as well as small-scale industry, but the failure to expand throughout the centuries indicates that there could have been no perfervid enthusiasm for urban life. Their *raison d'être* continued to be what it was at the beginning: as centres of administration. It was official encouragement as much as local support that kept them vital, and they were no more than pale reflexions of the cities of Gaul. They seem to dominate the life of southern Britain in the first two centuries because they were earliest developed as centres of romanized control and the villa estates in the countryside were slow in establishing themselves. Thereafter, various economic factors were influential in depriving town life of its advantages and conferring popularity upon villa life. Yet we should remember that the native Briton, even when romanized, remained a countryman at heart, and the late appearance of the villas must not obscure that fact.

II. RURAL BRITAIN

As we have already observed, the Celtic way of life had no place for towns, and the preference of the native British aristocrats for the country caused the villa system to be a spontaneous development, needing no stimulus from outside. Whether or not, as has been suggested, they had town houses where they could stay when their administrative and magistral duties brought them in from the country, they normally resided as gentlemen of leisure on villa estates, which were usually in close proximity to the towns. And practical motives combined with personal predilections, for unless the estates, farmed by semi-servile tenants and slaves under a bailiff's supervision, were properly managed, they could not have sustained the regular impositions of tribute in money and in kind for the Imperial treasury.

Beyond the villa estates lay the Celtic villages wherein the bulk of the peasantry lived, continuing the cultivation of great open fields which had made South Britain known abroad as a corn-producing country long before the Roman invasion. The villagers could not have remained immune from the general influence of romanization: they were to some extent under the supervision of the Imperial civil servants for the payment of Imperial dues; they were conscripted for service in the Roman army; they were visited by pedlars of Roman merchandise and used Roman pottery and Roman ornaments of personal decoration; they presumably visited on occasion the market towns. Yet they were not absorbed, the pattern of their way of life was not much altered, and, though many communities put up a stout fight against the invaders in the fifth century, to the peasantry at large the end of Roman rule in Britain was no overwhelming calamity.

Since the production of food had to be the primary consideration in the grim battle of life, since the province must be self-supporting and, in particular, feed a permanent defence force, it followed that agriculture was the main occupation. The Romans introduced no new methods and no new tools, for the heavy plough was known to the Belgic peoples before Cæsar's invasions, though perhaps the spread of Roman control made its use known all over the country and in that respect stimulated and improved the agricultural yield. And settled life and good communications must surely have increased the area of arable land, whatever implements were used. At all events, there was a sufficiency of corn in the fourth century to permit its export to the Rhineland. Activity other than agricultural, though it was naturally to be found in the towns, was mainly associated with the villas, which formed the numerous centres of small, localized and frequently specialized estate industries. The rule of Rome saw a vast development and exploitation of provincial resources. All mines became the property of the state, though on occasion they were apparently leased to the enterprise of private individuals. Mineral wealth came from the tin-mines of Cornwall, the copper mines of Anglesey, the lead mines of the Mendips, Flintshire, Shropshire, Yorkshire and Derbyshire. So abundant was the supply of lead that it could be used lavishly at home in, for instance, the use of forty pounds to the square foot for the bath floors at Bath, and enough was produced to form an important export abroad. Iron smelting was done, as in later medieval times, mainly in the Weald and the Forest of Dean. Silver was somewhat laboriously extracted from lead in refineries such as that at Silchester. Outcrop coal was made available not only for smelting but for domestic purposes as well: bunkers of it have been found on Hadrian's Wall and it served to stoke the fires of temples at Bath. Manufactured goods grew steadily in quantity during the long comparatively peaceful years to meet an ever-growing demand at home and abroad, and British craftsmanship produced work of high quality, particularly in metal. Bricks and flooring tiles provided by the kilns, glass for windows, Whitby jet for decorative brooches: these do not exhaust the list of native processes. The potteries, however, found all over the countryside, were content to turn out mass-produced utility ware, like the Castor drinking-cups, which had no artistic pretensions. The raw wool from the extensive sheep-farming could be whitened in fulling mills, like those of Darenth in Kent and Chedworth in Gloucester, dyed at Silchester, and woven at Winchester, and the Diocletian price-control Edict of 301 shows that British woollen cloths were held in high repute even in Eastern Europe.

The busy commerce in and out the country would have been impossible without the medium of an abundant coinage of wide denominations and, still more so, of transport facilities. The Roman roads, built primarily for the purpose of military strategy and not

economic needs, formed a new system of communications, which in
its five thousand mile extent and its general effects should be compared in the imagination with the twenty thousand miles of rail-
roads in twentieth-century England. The *Itinerarium Antonini* of
the third century, one of the many road maps compiled for the
guidance of government officials in their travels through the Empire,
describes fifteen routes in its British section and names more than
a hundred of the British posting stations. But we do not know what
the Romans themselves called their roads, and the names they now
bear are of Anglo-Saxon origin. Such roads, carried over bridges on
stone or wooden piers and through paved fords, meeting ferry
services across the Severn, the Mersey and probably the Wash, bore
heavy traffic of Bath stone to Colchester, of Purbeck marble to St.
Albans, of bricks, tiles and pottery everywhere. And, apart from the
need in times of emergency to carry military forces and military
supplies easily to and from Britain, exports and imports demanded
the provision of harbours, quays and lighthouses.

So the Britons of the upper classes entered enthusiastically into
the heritage of a high material civilization: the town-planning with
the streets running at right angles to one another in a 'grid-iron'
lay-out, the advanced ideas of sanitation, the town halls, public
baths and shops; the central heating, the mosaic floors, the frescoed
walls, the glazed windows. And though the peasantry, that is the
bulk of the population, continued to speak their Celtic dialects, the
knowledge of Latin must have been widespread in towns and the
higher sections of society. A useful parallel is to be found in the
use of English in Celtic Ireland after the Tudor Conquest. Furthermore, the native language was useless for the conduct of Imperial
government or the interplay of commerce or the command of the
army, in which so many Britons spent twenty-five years of conscripted service. Tacitus informs us that not only did Agricola give
special encouragement to the teaching of Latin but that the Britons
were not averse from learning it. However much it may have been
the colloquial Latin of the barracks, the market square and the
factories rather than the classical Latin of the schoolroom, it represented a means whereby the thought of Greece and Rome could be
transmitted to a new part of Europe. It would have been surprising
in the circumstances if Latin had not been taught and learned on
the cultural as well as the military and commercial levels, and though
the evidence is meagre, it is nevertheless convincing. Thus, already
in Agricola's day a grammarian, Demetrius of Tarsus, was teaching

in Britain; in 96 Martial could affirm that what he wrote was being read there; in 120 or thereabouts Juvenal stated that Gallic teachers were giving Britons instruction in Roman law and that teachers of rhetoric were also present in the country. Scenes from Vergil form a motif in the decoration of country houses. Whether or not the reason lies in the mischance of survival, it is true that Britain apparently contributed nothing to the stock of Latin literature during the next three centuries. Yet at the end, when Rome had abandoned the province, there were men in Britain so highly educated that they could understand the theological disputations of Pelagius and adopt his heretical views in sufficient numbers to compel the pope to send a special representative to win them from their errors. And Gildas had at his command a wide vocabulary and could quote the Latin classics and the Scriptures with ease.

We do not know much about the means whereby the Christian religion made its way in a country which had accepted the official cult of Emperor-worship and fitted the Celtic deities into the Roman pantheon of gods. The literary evidence tells us little: there are traditions that small Christian communities were to be found in Britain in the second century; there was some recognizable form of episcopal government in the fourth century when British bishops attended the Council of Arles in 314 and the Council of Ariminum in 360; there were British martyrs like St. Alban and British heretics like Pelagius; according to Bede St. Augustine found in 597 the sites of churches in Kent waiting to be used again. The archæological evidence tells us less and, incidentally, discloses its limitations thereby: an undatable church at Silchester; three or four tombstones that signify Christian burial; the monogram for the name of Christ incorporated in fourth-century mosaics and pewterware. The paucity of archæological remains has been explained away, if not explained, by the argument that Christianity may have made little appeal to the romanized aristocracy, who adhered to their paganism and regarded the new cult as unsettling and vulgar. It was to the lower classes that it breathed a message of hope at a time when peace and security were vanishing from the world, urging them to lay little stress upon the things of to-day and promising them compensation for their afflictions in the Kingdom of Heaven: such adherents were too poor to leave permanent memorials behind them. A minority religion it very probably was but, at least, it was firmly enough established to survive the approaching disasters.

We must end this discussion of the romanization of Britain where it began by stressing the interfusion of Roman and native thought. Celtic art, delighting in the abstract patterns of flowing curves, had reached a high standard in the pre-Roman age, but it had degenerated thereafter, being overwhelmed by Roman art with its naturalistic representation of human and animal forms. Nevertheless it did not die and, along with other expressions of the Celtic way of life, it continued to exert a very real influence: for instance, the native temples built to a Celtic architectural plan; the houses with the Celtic pillared halls; the pottery with its Celtic decorations; the brooches with their Celtic enamelling in vivid polychrome effect.

The character of Roman administration and military organization had not remained static throughout the whole period of the Occupation, and many crises had come and gone before early in the fifth century the trained soldiers and experienced officials were finally recalled. Often Britain had seen her military resources diminished by the Roman Emperors in order to relieve pressure elsewhere or to serve their personal ends. Often British governors had left the island denuded of troops in pursuit of their ambitions: in 197 Clodius Albinus had led most of the legions from Britain to their destruction on the continent in his schemes to wear the imperial purple and thus permitted the northern tribes to cross the defences of the Wall and spread devastation as far south as York and Chester; between 287 and 296 Carausius, and his murderer and successor, Allectus, had sacrificed British soldiery in Northern Gaul to promote their plans for independent rule. In each instance a reorganization of Britain had followed in order to lessen the authority of the governors: first into the two divisions of Lower Britain and Upper Britain, then into the four provinces of Diocletian's altered arrangements. Nevertheless, in 383 Magnus Maximus again sacrificed the army of Britain abroad in a bid for the Western Empire, and Hadrian's Wall, stormed and devastated and already become obsolete as a means of defence as a result of altered conceptions of strategy, was not manned again. In 407 Constantine weakened the garrison troops for a similar end. And, however much the deficiencies in manpower were later made good, the position grew increasingly complicated as the dangers from outside changed their nature. The Picts (a comprehensive term for all the 'painted people' who lived north of the Scottish Lowlands) became sea raiders and could circumvent the Roman Wall, which was equally useless against the onslaughts of the Scots, Saxons and Franks from overseas. Something equivalent to it had, therefore, to be constructed round the coasts instead. The result was the defence-system of the Saxon Shore in the last quarter of the third century: first seen in Kent and then extended from the Wash to the Solent, the forts were placed in sheltered harbours at all the vulnerable entrances into the country. They not only served as naval bases, for the 'classis Brittanica', formerly based at Boulogne to guard both sides of the Channel, was split up into a dozen or so coastal patrols for home waters, but they acted also as military garrisons. The northern and southern coasts of Wales were similarly protected against the Scots, whilst sometime after the great combined raid on Britain in 368 by Picts, Scots and Saxons, strong watch towers were erected on the Yorkshire coastline. The 'Commander of the Saxon Shore' (*Comes Litoris Saxonici*) in the south and the 'Commander in chief of the British Provinces' (*dux Britanniarum*) in the north disposed calvary and infantry forces to meet such invaders as managed to penetrate the outer defences.

But when the Emperor Honorius, face to face with the Goths at Rome, left the Britons to their own devices, they could not solve a problem which was baffling the wisdom and experience of Rome itself. Without central direction and supervision their attempts to collect Imperial revenues and customs-duties and carry on the routine of day-to-day government must have degenerated into the most diverse regional activities. The new fifth-century office of the 'Commander of the British Provinces' (*comes Britanniarum*), mentioned in the controversial document of the 'Notitia Dignitatum' in 428, may represent an attempt to replace the system of legions and auxiliaries by a new military organization, based on a single mobile field force for the civil area, but it is hardly likely that Rome sent reinforcements to the assistance of the Britons after 410. However that may be, nothing could change the fact that the army in Britain, like the Imperial armies on all frontiers, was made up, not of foreign drafts, but of local recruits, whose interests drew them more and more away from those in authority over them and attracted them to the side of the invaders. Furthermore, the Romans had been compelled to resort in Britain, as elsewhere in the Empire, to the practice of settling barbarians on lands inside the frontiers in return for their acceptance of responsibility for military defence, i.e. as *foederati*. It should be noted that Tacitus in his *Germania* asserts that the 'Aestii' on the south-east coast of the Baltic (the modern Esthonia) spoke a language similar to that of the Britons. Some authorities have rejected this statement, and it would seem impossible that the bulk of the Britons spoke a Germanic dialect. Yet it is difficult to dismiss it out-of-hand, for the information Tacitus collected about the Germanic peoples is substantially correct and has been remarkably corroborated by archæological and such other sources as there are. A first-century infiltration into Britain, the presence of some German-speaking inhabitants, does not seem out of the question: whether they came as settlers or as mercenaries does not much affect the issue, for the two things meant much the same. Certainly in the fourth century a Germanic tribe from the middle Rhine had been transported and settled somewhere in Britain in a vital defence area. The same practice had been employed in north-west Wales and along the Wall. Already before the fifth century Angles had been brought in to defend East York-shire. It is probable that Saxons, settled on the south-east and south coasts, served a similar purpose and thus gave point to the term 'Saxon Coast', which referred to its defenders and not to its polyonymous attackers. Indeed, perhaps the isolated frontier groups of Germanic peoples of post-Roman days, such as the Hwicce, derived from *foederati* who had been established in Britain long before the intensification of settlement in and after the fifth century. This gradual barbarization was not peculiar to Britain, and thereby all the frontiers of Rome were laid open to its enemies. There was no special incapacity on the part of the Britons when they failed to maintain the Roman traditions and Roman institutions of govern-ment. Romanized life went on after a fashion for a long time after the Romans had gone; to outward view Britain remained prosper-ous; but the romanized Britons were forced to realize that their only hope of safety lay in their ability to adapt themselves and their interests to the new conditions arising around them. They might wish to remain Romans: they had in practice to become Celts.

SELECT READING

Collingwood and Myres, 302–24, 425–56; Hodgkin, i. 154–83; Ian Richmond, *Roman Britain* (1947), 7–48; H. Haverfield, *Romanization of Roman Britain* (1923), 9–88; R. E. M. Wheeler, *London and the Saxons* (1935), 15–113; S. E. Winbolt, *Britain under the Romans* (1947); *Tacitus on Britain and Germany* (trans. H. Mattingly: 1948).

CHAPTER I

THE SOURCES OF HISTORY BEFORE 871

It should be said at once that the evidence on which we must rely for our knowledge of what was happening between the fifth and the ninth centuries is, with few exceptions, fragmentary and equivocal and presents an easy target for destructive criticism. This is particularly true of the period after 400, once termed the 'two lost centuries' of British history, when our sources are so scanty that we cannot reconstruct with confidence even a rough chronology of developments. And since so often we have doubtful information about still more doubtful events, it is inevitable that speculation and even invention should find free rein. Furthermore, when we do have facts at our disposal, what is most disturbing is the numerous occasions when one type of evidence seems to come into direct conflict with another. Fortunately, as we shall see, new approaches to the problems are now showing great promise that they will in time illumine the darkest places to an extent undreamed of only a generation ago. And the endeavour to compel all sources to yield every atom of evidence is not mere antiquarianism, for we are studying the birth and childhood of a nation when its physical type, the basis of its speech, its economic and social ways of thinking and, thanks to the happy accident of insularity and freedom from alien domination, even its political genius were being formed in readiness, as it happened, for a tremendous future. To understand things as they are we must understand how they came to be what they are, for such is the main justification of the work of historians.

The establishment of the Anglo-Saxon settlements and their varied fortunes must be given as a connected story with few of the modifications and qualifications that strict scholarship demands. It is, however, imperative that we draw attention to the fact that we are making bricks with little straw, that our generalizations are based on slight foundations, and this can be most usefully done by discussing whence our information comes.

Literary Evidence

It is unjust to the memory of those great scholars of the nineteenth century, whose gigantic labours have ever since provided the indispensable groundwork of our knowledge, to assert that they did not appreciate the value of anything but written evidence: a hundred years ago J. M. Kemble drew careful attention to the significance attached to the study of place-names and to archaeological discoveries on the Continent; J. R. Green, even if he described the landing of the Anglo-Saxons as though he stood on the seashore watching them, was convinced that one of the chief clues in tracking the invaders across country from the coast was provided by the physical geography of the land. But such lines of investigation were rarely followed up and historians as a rule were content to rely on literary texts. In doing so, they fell somewhat naturally into the danger of placing an excessive value upon the statements of their authorities, for they had nothing else whereby to check the conclusions they reached: much of the course of early West Saxon history is still distorted by the treatment it received at their hands.

The literary sources can be conveniently grouped under three heads.

I. CONTINENTAL WRITERS

Those who compiled the chronicles of the time had little interest in the remote province on the northern frontier, far distant from the Mediterranean centre of civilization. Their parenthetic allusions are simply the *obiter dicta* of men who had in no instance first-hand information, and they amount to very little. Still, they cannot be disregarded: they represent the nearest we can get to contemporary writing when native sources are totally lacking; they occasionally provide a date to form a *terminus a quo* for the discoveries of the archaeologist; they are assuming greater importance in the light of recent research. The *Gallic Chronicle* (*c.* 450), erroneously attributed to Prosper Tiro, a contemporary and friend of the great St. Augustine of Hippo, alludes to the early attacks of the Saxon pirates and the terrible plight of the Britons; the *History* (*c.* 500) of the Greek Zosimus records the warning of the emperor Honorius in 410 to the cities of Britain that henceforth they must look to their own salvation; another Greek historian, Procopius (*c.* 550), deriving his information from Angles who accompanied a Frankish mission to Constantinople, asserts that Frisians were amongst those who invaded Britain—a warning against accepting too easily Bede's simple classification of them as Angles, Saxons and Jutes—and emphasizes the close interest of the Franks in what was taking place across the Channel—this we shall have to bear in mind when we come to consider the recent arguments that the 'Jutes' were in reality Franks. Most important of all is the *Life of St. Germanus*, written about 480 by his old pupil Constantius, a priest of Lyons. Amongst the accumulation of miracles usual in hagiographical writings throughout the Middle Ages, we are told that St. Germanus (418–88), bishop of Auxerre in Gaul, visited Britain twice, in 429 and again in 447, in order to suppress the heretical views of Pelagius on the doctrine of the freedom of the will as opposed to the orthodox doctrine of the grace of God. Having held high military command before entering the Church, Germanus was able during his first visit to teach the Britons the rudiments of tactics and to help them to rout a combined army of Picts and Saxons somewhere in the Midlands by shouting 'Hallelujah' as a war-cry to give the impression of great numbers. This information may seem of no great moment, yet it is the first hint we have that by 429 the Saxons had got past the sea coast well into the interior, that on occasion they were acting in concert with the Picts, and that the Picts had come so far south, presumably by sea. And this biography indicates that right throughout the fifth century Britain was still regarded as 'a most wealthy island', still peopled by Britons, still romanized and still Christian. We shall have to set this evidence against the view that they were easily defeated and either exterminated or driven to wholesale flight into the west.

II. CELTIC WRITERS

These help us to understand the outlook of the descendants of the vanquished. Gildas, a British priest who was born about 500, provides in himself a picture of the romanized Briton still under the spell of Rome and still clinging obstinately to the belief that his country continued to be part of her great empire. His education was on a level with that of a cultured Roman provincial of his day; he was conversant with Latin classics like Virgil and the works of the Fathers of the Early Church like St. Jerome, and he wrote Latin with ease. We would expect, therefore, that his book *On the*

Destruction and Conquest of Britain, written some time before 547, would constitute our most trustworthy authority. Here is a man almost contemporary with the conditions he sets out to describe, certainly in touch with first-hand information, and with a gift for writing. Unfortunately Gildas's work is the 'literary tragedy' of the sixth century. He made it his object to denounce with all the fervour of a Hebrew prophet the moral shortcomings of the Britons which had brought their distress upon them, and therefore he wrote a book of lamentations, a 'tract for the times', and not a history. The little information he gives us is merely incidental to his main theme, it is limited in its interest to the west of England, it is exasperatingly vague and ambiguous. He it is who tells us of the important battle of Mount Badon without giving us its location or its date, save that it was in the 'forty-fourth year': as this number can be calculated backwards or forwards from some conjectural and undatable event according to one's personal choice, it is little wonder that the British victory has been variously put between 490 and 516. Nevertheless, it is foolish to criticize him for not doing what he never had any intention of doing, and it is equally foolish to imagine that an educated and intelligent man, highly respected by his own and later ages for this very work of his, could produce arrant rubbish. However difficult it may be to detect it, vital truth lurks among his diatribes, and it is already clear that, as we get to know more about the period, his meaning will become plainer and more valuable.

Alongside Gildas may be placed the still more irritating Nennius (*recte* Nemnius), a Welsh antiquary, who compiled the *History of the Britons* shortly after 800. The part he actually played in writing the seventy-six short chapters has been differently estimated. Mommsen, the great historian of the imperial provinces of Rome, believed that at the back of them lay a late seventh-century source (*c.* 680) which Nennius simply adopted, adding a preface and intruding here and there odd bits of information of his own. On the other hand, Liebermann, the German scholar who worked out for us the text of our Anglo-Saxon laws, thought that Nennius put the whole work into shape from unknown written authorities and oral traditions. Whatever the truth of this, it is certain that Nennius had no trained and disciplined mind: no matter the palpable contradictions in chronology, he sets everything down without any attempt at discrimination or interpretation. In his own words he 'made a heap of all he found' and in the process he accumulated much that is pure fantasy. However, he has given us unique references to the resistance of Arthur to the Saxons at the close of the fifth century, and valuable jottings on the early history of Northumbria, and, though what he has to say may be distrusted as the product of Celtic imaginativeness, it ought not to be ignored.

III. ENGLISH WRITERS

These provide the views of the descendants of the victors. The Venerable Bede of Jarrow (c. 673–735) is incomparably the greatest authority we have for the early centuries of the English settlements. Of his eminent position in the world of European scholarship, for no Englishman had greater influence there for many centuries, we shall have to speak later. Here our interest lies with that product of his mature years, the *Ecclesiastical History*, completed in 731. It stands in a class by itself, for by his time the art and practice of writing history had well-nigh died away in Western Europe and he had, so far as we know, no precursor in England, and not until William of Malmesbury began his *Gesta Regum* in the twelfth century was Bede to have anyone to rival him. Yet Bede would have been surprised to learn that his fame would rest upon his history, for to him it was his theological works that were all-important. It was, indeed, through them that he was led to history: his biographies of Christian saints like Cuthbert and Benedict Biscop, together with his studies in Christian chronology to settle the bitterly contested problem of the correct date of Easter, combined to produce a truly historical attitude of mind. Though the *History* ranges the centuries from Caesar until almost his own death, there is a clear division within it. Only one-tenth is devoted to the years before 597, partly because Bede was interested in the conversion of the English and not in the course of their settlements, partly because he was aware of the thoroughly unsatisfactory material at his disposal. He had to depend mainly on Gildas and the *Life of St. Germanus* and a lost 'Passion of St. Alban' and was clearly so sceptical of their reliability that he abandoned any attempt to date events. For the sixth century he gives only half a dozen trifling items of information. Apart from a few fresh details such as the identification of Gildas's 'proud tyrant' as Vortigern and the names of the pirate brothers as Hengist and Horsa, he provides very little fresh light, and it is significant of the destructive turmoil in which the invasions had involved Britain that so conscientious a historian should be unwilling to add to what his predecessors had written: evidently not many traditions of real value had reached him. After 597 we pass from acknowledged speculation to authentic history, to what has been the recognized basis of our knowledge ever since King Alfred had it translated from Latin into the vernacular for his people to read.

Three points particularly impress us: (a) The conscientious efforts Bede made to accumulate information and to be accurate about his facts. He obtained his knowledge about the ecclesiastical reforms of Theodore of Tarsus from an abbot of Canterbury who had been one of Theodore's pupils; a bishop of Winchester supplied him with the somewhat meagre details of the conversion of the West Saxons; even the papal archives at Rome were searched at his request for copies of letters written by Gregory the Great to the missionaries he had sent to Kent. His precision and accuracy have been curiously vindicated: though he alone declared that Jutes had landed in the Isle of Wight and South Hampshire, archaeology has confirmed that these districts shared with Kent a common culture distinct from that of the rest of England. Moreover, every word he wrote was carefully scrutinized and weighed: when he relied on rumour he was careful to note it with a 'they say' or 'it is reported'; when he made use of 'the sure testimony of men of good credit' he named them; when a written source was available, it was his wish that it should be mentioned in the margin; when a document was important, he cited it in full so that the text of precious papal letters and synodal decrees have been permanently preserved for posterity. This is indeed real research, revealing an awareness to the responsibilities of scholarship. (b) The essential impartiality with which he interpreted his facts. He had the credulities of his age and his prejudices such as his aversion from the British (not the Irish) Church and Celtic rites, nevertheless he sought to give justice where justice was due and did not permit his own convictions to distort his judgment: he paid generous tributes to Aidan and defended the monks of Iona from grave charges brought against them. It is sometimes said that his tolerance was derived from his being midway between two churches, 'a disciple of Rome inspired by the intellectual passion of Ireland', but this in no way smoothed the bellicosity of his contemporary, bishop Wilfrid of Ripon, and it is perhaps better to attribute his extraordinary freedom from bias pre-eminently to his cast of mind and then to the mental training and discipline of his studies. (c) The literary quality of his writing. In the arrangement of his material we can see the artist consciously at work pruning, revising and rearranging until each passage and even each separate book had its dramatic value. His Latin style had the lucidity and flexibility of a living language and is altogether free from the precious pomposity of Aldhelm, the contemporary West Saxon man of letters, which makes his writings almost unintelligible and certainly unreadable.

So Bede is rightly acclaimed the first historian of English blood, writing a clear and connected story informed by good sense, with little prejudice or distortion, and revealing a critical power to which his age can nowhere show a parallel.

Next to Bede the most important narrative source is the *Anglo-Saxon Chronicle*, written in the vernacular for two hundred and fifty years at a time when Latin was the language of scholarship in the West, and therefore the oldest chronicle in one of the modern languages of Europe. With the *Anglo-Saxon Chronicle*, properly speaking, we are not here concerned. Whatever part King Alfred may have played in its inception, there is no room for doubt that it took shape under his inspiration during the literary renaissance of his reign and that in its first form it was completed about 892. All manuscripts contain much the same version of pre-892 events, but thereafter they develop into semi-independent accounts stamped with their own individuality so that we should with greater truth speak of the 'Anglo-Saxon Chronicles'. The part dealing with the four centuries before 892 is therefore so distinct that it is worth while referring to it under a separate name as the 'Early English Annals'. Our major problem is to discover what materials were at the service of the Alfredian scribe for his account of the conquest and early settlements. Bede was naturally laid under contribution, but there is much in these 'Annals' which does not come from his pages: for example, whereas he evidently knew little more about the conquest than he could obtain from Gildas and the *Life of St. Germanus*, the compiler of the 'Annals' provides a summary account with the names of many kings and many dates. The ultimate source of this information remains very largely a mystery and has formed the centre of varied speculation. As the invaders had no written records, it follows that there could be no written evidence that was contemporary, and oral traditions must lie at the back of what we are told about the fifth and sixth centuries and the royal pedigree in particular. It seems certain that these traditions had been committed to writing long before Alfred's time: it has, indeed, been contended that the West Saxon 'Annals' represent such high antiquity that they reach back to *c.* 550 and forward to *c.* 754. If this be true, then the writer who mentioned the West Saxon kings Cerdic, Cynric and Ceawlin must have written 'within living memory' of these men and their doings, and the value of his statements is correspondingly increased. However this may be, it is reasonably certain that the 'Early English Annals' rested on the basis of a much earlier and now vanished written source.

Though these 'Annals' are of immense value in recording a genuine body of tradition which in its general drift is right, they have been accepted too literally and too uncritically in the past. This point will have to be developed when we consider the origin of the West Saxon kingdom. Here it is sufficient to say that the Celtic names of the early kings, the possible creation of unhistoric persons to explain the origin of historic places, the apparent invention of dates on an arbitrary plan of eight or four years, the propaganda element which seems to suppress anything which might enhance the credit of West Saxon opponents like the Britons or the Mercians: all these present difficulties which make us less ready to place implicit trust in the 'Early English Annals'.

Such in the main is the literary evidence prior to the reign of Alfred. It is not, of course, exhaustive of all that was written: we have notable biographies of St. Columba, St. Cuthbert, and St. Wilfrid; the correspondence of St. Boniface and Alcuin; the laws of Ethelbert of Kent and Ine of Wessex; royal charters from the seventh century granting land to churches; but these must await separate treatment in their proper places.

Archaeological Evidence

As a scientific study this is essentially the contribution of the present century towards finding a solution to the problems of the early settlements raised by the literary sources. We have only to read the chapter in the *Cambridge Medieval History* on 'The Teutonic Conquest of Britain', written in 1911, to appreciate the revitalization of our conceptions which was begun by the survey of archaeological evidence by E. T. Leeds in 1913. There is a danger that too much may be claimed for its authority: after all, it cannot give us a political narrative of events, it can tell us little about the fate of the Britons or the course of affairs after the seventh century when there is little or nothing for the spade to un-earth. But for the 'lost centuries' of our history it is a source of information which has been little more than tapped, and it has much yet to add to our knowledge of economic, social and even intellectual developments.

Sometimes, as in the case of the continental homes of the in-vaders, archaeology is the only adequate evidence we now possess. Frequently it provides a brilliant vindication of the otherwise un-supported statements in our literary texts: as we have seen, it has confirmed Bede's assertion that there was a cultural association between Kent and the Isle of Wight and South Hampshire. At other times, however, archaeological discoveries seem partly to contradict the written word. To take the most notable instance: according to the 'Early English Annals' the West Saxon leaders landed in 495 somewhere at the head of Southampton Water and drove the Britons back before them. A few years later they were reinforced and thereby enabled to extend their power over South Hampshire and Wiltshire and to capture the Isle of Wight. Then for half a century they stood still, content with their conquests, and made no attempt to reach north to the Thames until after 550. Many archaeologists, however, insist that the West Saxons entered England by the Wash, proceeding up the rivers to the Cambridge district and thence across country by the Icknield Way to the Upper Thames. How else are we to explain the cultural connexions be-tween the Cambridge region and the district round Oxford and Dorchester; or the Saxon remains that denote an extensive occupa-tion of this district, the very nucleus of the West Saxon folk, not long after 500 when, according to the 'Annals', the Saxons were still well south of the Thames; or the scarcity of pagan Saxon cemeteries in North Hampshire and Wiltshire which suggests no serious attempt at settlement at any early date? This conflict of evidence will have to be considered later.

What concerns us here is the methods of the archaeologists, and these can be usefully illustrated in connexion with the problem: from which parts of the Continent did the invaders of England come? Historians once had to do the best they could with the descriptions of West Germany at the close of the first century, given by Tacitus in his *Germania*. But though he names peoples who were then settled there, including the Angles, he somewhat surprisingly fails to refer to the Saxons, at least under that name, and there is serious doubt about where he intended many of the peoples to be located. In any case, he was writing more than three hundred years before the migrations occurred, and in the meanwhile many changes must have, and in fact had, taken place. Bede, on the other hand, was writing nearly three hundred years after these migrations when he inferred (but did not actually say) that the Jutes came from Jutland, the Angles from Eastern Schleswig and the Saxons from 'Old Saxony', apparently the north German coastland between the Elbe and the Rhine; these three distinct peoples, occupying exclusive areas on the Continent, migrated overseas as units to occupy their own areas in Britain—the Jutes in Kent, South Hampshire and the Isle of Wight, the Angles in East Anglia, Mercia and Northumbria, the Saxons in Sussex, Essex, Middlesex and Wessex. This is an obvious over-simplification of the problem, based on Bede's personal deductions from the political geography of England as it had developed by his own day.

Since the literary evidence is defective, enigmatic or suspect, we must depend for our knowledge on archaeology and we are not disappointed. The method employed is simple: the excavation of cemeteries to bring to light the pagan grave goods and, in the case of cremation, the burial urns; the sortation of pottery, jewellery, and weapons into classes according to their distinctive fashions so that they can be plotted on a map to reveal the directional spread of the various cultures; the dating of these objects, especially the personal trinkets of women, by their fashions and styles to provide a chronology of culture expansion. Christianity with its insistence on inhumation and its discouragement of heathen burial cults breaks the sequence of cultural objects which form the material for archaeological studies. As with the literary evidence, the stumbling-block is dates. In the absence of coins and inscriptions, so indispensable to the student of Roman Britain, the archaeologist is forced to date his materials according to analogy, the 'association of correlated finds', and typology, the development in styles. This is delicate work in which the margin of error may be serious: the sequence can be reconstructed but there is nothing to show exactly at what time it begins or what speed of progress it involves—a long-cherished heirloom, an alien importation, the interpolation of a single craftsman's genius, may introduce serious errors in the inferences made.

Nevertheless, valuable results have been obtained and the evidence for the continental homes of the invaders amounts to this: (*a*) The Saxons spread westwards from Holstein in the third century to occupy the Elbe-Weser region, vacated by the south-going Lombards, and afterwards extended themselves along the Frisian coastlands and across the Rhine: some apparently colonized the district around Boulogne. It is perhaps correct to conjecture that the Saxons formed the dominant component of a loose tribal confederation, to all members of which its name was loosely applied: so in later times the Scots termed all their southern neighbours, despite their origins, 'Sassenachs' and the identity of the Norwegians in England was submerged in that of the Danes. (*b*) The Angles had their original homeland in Schleswig but before the migrations took place many of them had moved southward and mingled with the Saxons, thereby losing their distinctive tribal characteristics. That there were in modern parlance 'Anglo-Saxons' on the Continent before they made their appearance in Britain goes far to explain the vagaries of the literary evidence in which well-known Angles call themselves Saxons whilst Saxons call themselves Angles and speak 'English'. Whatever differences in culture and vocabulary may be traced between them, it is certain that in England there was much inter-penetration and confusion. (*c*) The Jutes were not to be found in Jutland when the migrations began. Even Bede does not categorically place them there. Burials in the western part of the peninsula ceased towards the close of the second century, and the only reference, apart from Bede, which speaks of them as Jutes in the sixth century, places them in the Elbe-Weser region, populated by Saxons. And tradition never connected the Kentish royal family with Jutland, nor do the place-names of Kent reveal any ties with that country. Whether or not the Jutes were in fact at the beginning of the fifth century settled in Frisia, it is certain that they did not come to Britain directly from Jutland. It is, however, curious that, if Jutes had ceased to live in Jutland, their name should have survived there after the conquest by the Danes about the fifth century.

Archaeological studies of a similar kind to those which have provided this evidence also give us a truer picture of the early settlements in England: where they began, what direction they followed, what limits they reached and, very roughly, at what times all these things took place. Furthermore, the discovery in 1939 of the Sutton Hoo burial ship in East Anglia, with its amazing store of gold and silver objects and its evidence of contact with the

Eastern Mediterranean by way of Sweden or, more probably, Gaul, has forced us to revise drastically our conception of the standard of civilization attained in the opening decades of the seventh century.

An important auxiliary to archaeology is air-photography, which was introduced in 1922. Soil disturbances can be seen from the air though they are quite invisible to an observer on the ground, and attention can thus be directed as by no other means to the sites of cemeteries, villages, earthworks, roads and the like. Nevertheless, air-photography by itself points only to possibilities and its conclusions must not be uncritically accepted. For example, it was enthusiastically claimed that air-photography had disclosed the outline of distinctively Celtic fields—small rectangular plots of arable land, bundled together in upland villages away from the river-beds—which had long preceded the Roman invasion that they were long to survive; they were, however, allowed to go back to pasture and waste by the Saxons, who preferred to settle down in the valleys and there cultivate the heavier, deeper soil in large, oblong, open strips. This sharp contrast between Celtic and Saxon agricultural systems is a delusion, and other evidence suggests that open-field agriculture had no necessary connexion with the use of a heavy plough, that in any case such a plough was known in southeast Britain possibly before and certainly not long after the Roman occupation, and that Britons and Saxons did, in fact, face their problems the same way and work with the same kind of ploughs and the same methods.

Linguistic Evidence

In other countries of West Europe like Gaul, Spain and Italy, which the barbarians overran and subdued, they very largely abandoned their own language and adopted that of their subjects so that the Roman speech remained to form the foundation on which the 'Romance' dialects were built. In Britain, however, which was only superficially romanized, Latin in the circumstances of the time ceased to have any utilitarian value for the landowning and trading classes, who may often have ceased to exist as such: it is precisely because Latin was still useful to them that the clergy will come to retain it. The Celtic-speaking lower classes were overwhelmed. Therefore our language became basically Germanic and nothing proves so well the forcefulness with which the German occupation must have been carried out. The philological study of surviving documents and of local dialects sometimes throws unexpected light upon dark places, but the most remarkable assistance comes from the work that has been done, largely since the First World War, on the history of place-names, field-names and personal names. By laboriously tracing them back through the centuries until their earliest forms have been detected, we come to realize the historical reasons why such-named places should be found in this or that district, and we are given valuable information about the distribution of the newcomers and an indispensable check upon the inferences drawn from other sources. For example: (*a*) Literary evidence receives confirmation when we discover that Bede's statement that the Jutes made a settlement on the extreme south of Hampshire is proved again by the remarkable parallel between the very old place-names there and those in Kent. The early devastation and desolation of the land described by Gildas in such vivid and exaggerated language has certainly left its mark in the almost complete obliteration of British names of any kind in the coastal districts from the Solent to the Humber. (*b*) Archaeological evidence is supported at every turn. The English place-names ending in -ing tell a consistent story of primary settlements by small and self-sufficient groups of adventurers (Haestingas: Hastings; Goring; Worthing; Wittering). There is a remarkable concentration of such names in the south-east: indeed, it has been calculated that four-fifths of them are to be found roughly south of a line from the Wash to the Solent and half of these within short distance of the sea coast. Again, whilst archaeologists are rarely able to find early Saxon objects in any of the scores of Roman villas they have excavated, it is noticeable that the Romano-British villas have not bequeathed their names to later villages, as they so often did in Gaul. And in primitive Wessex, whilst British names survive in Central Hampshire and Wiltshire, it is difficult to find early English place-names except in the tiny Jutish area in the south and in the northern parts: this is at least some corroboration of the thesis that the West Saxons, who entered the country by way of Southampton Water, were not numerous enough to displace the natives and lived as a ruling warrior class upon tribute and that the real colonization resulted from a movement southwards from the district of the Upper Thames. And, finally, we have noted the probability that the Saxons and Angles had merged while on the Continent, and that it is not easy to distinguish their cultures after they had come to Britain: the evidence of the place-names indicates that in their new homes the ordinary economic forces resulting from unsuitable locations, overcrowding in relation to resources, lack of water or too much water—in brief, the whole system of trial and error—were still active, urging bands of them to leave the district and their own people and to settle in the territory of others. These local migrations and inter-tribal penetrations resulted in a confusion of dialects, vocabularies and artistic developments which modifies the impression given by Bede of completely distinct races. On one subject where we might reasonably have expected place-names to be helpful we receive no assistance: though it is significant that names ending in -ham are found in plenty in north-west Germany and are confined in England mainly to the south-east, it is apparently impossible to trace a group of English place-names back to a district on the Continent. Here, as we have already said, the archaeologists have the field to themselves. (c) Place-names have, however, their own unique contributions to make. Archaeology has revealed no traces of the pagan worship and rites which were practised for many centuries, and it is place-names alone that can lead us to the holy places of the invaders. But it is on the vexed question of British survival that they are of paramount importance. On the face of things their evidence supports the old theory of extermination. We are not perhaps surprised to find no place-names of British origin remaining in Sussex, Bedfordshire or Huntingdonshire and few in Kent or Buckinghamshire. But why should only one per cent remain in Dorset and less than one per cent in Devon, why should there be so few in Devon and in Worcester when we know that these districts were conquered late, that no question of massacre was involved, that the present inhabitants have a strong British strain in their blood, that Cornish was still spoken until the late eighteenth century, and that a process of absorption and not of extermination had taken place? If the evidence leads us astray in the west, is it not likely to have done so also in the east? As we shall see later, the West Saxon laws show quite clearly that the Britons (or Welsh) had their acknowledged place in the West Saxon social system, not only as slaves but also as men of fair substance and importance. A possibly too ingenious explanation lies in the theory that the Germanic invaders adopted British names but assimilated them so much in sound to their own form of speech that they seem to be Germanic in origin. This took place occasionally but so rarely that such a conjecture still awaits substantial proof. The evidence for British survival is to be found but rarely among the place-names of towns and villages (though even here if the names die the inhabitants may continue to live): it abounds, however, in those of hills, rivers and woods where little isolated communities of Britons remained safe from the fury of their enemies. These names could not possibly be with us at the present day unless there had come to be a long and close inter-course between victor and vanquished.

Geographical Evidence

To treat at length of the influence of physical geography upon historical development is here impossible. Fortunately the facts speak for themselves in the atlas. At a time when man had not yet made himself the master of his environment, geographical factors, taken together with the practical farming experience of the invaders, provide an excellent clue to the history of the early settlements. Though only five per cent of the British Isles is now wooded, a proportion threatening rapidly to decrease, then great forests as well as fens and marshes divided the plains into isolated districts. So Sussex, separated from the Thames by the almost impenetrable forest of the Weald and cut off from Kent by the Romney marshes and repelled on the west by the low eroding coastline, pursued its destiny in isolation and was not converted for more than a hundred years after St. Augustine had established his see at Canterbury thirty or so miles away. The barrier of the Fen District goes far to explain the individual characteristics of East Anglia. The heavy clay, always so much avoided, of the Midlands is sufficient to account for the thin population there. The rise and fall of the Northumbrian, Mercian and Wessex kingdoms is meaningless unless such factors as these are brought into the reckoning. All the same, there seems no physical reason why Durham should have remained so long a waste and desolate land. From the point of geography it is important to note that the very early place-names ending in -ing are exactly where from the physical formation of the country we should expect them to be and that no support is forthcoming for the view that the invaders conducted large-scale connected operations rather than piecemeal attacks.

The sources for the history of the Dark Ages that precede Alfred's reign may seem at first simply to make darkness visible:

the literary authorities fail to agree, the archaeological discoveries flatly contradict them, the linguistic material apparently proves what could not be the case. A new fact, a new date, may alter the trend of all our arguments. Yet this is superficial criticism, for what commands respect is the remarkable way in which scholars, approaching the same problems from entirely different angles, have ultimately reached the same conclusions. Anything like a final synthesis is at the moment beyond us, but there is reason to believe that it lies in the not too distant future.

SELECT READING

Literary Evidence

Collingwood and Myres, 292–4, 326–30; Stenton, 1–31; Hodgkin, i. 54–83, ii. 624–8, 706–8; Chambers, chs. ii–v; *Cambridge History of English Literature* (1907), i. ch. v; C. Plummer, *Bede* (1896), i. ix–lxxix; A. H. Thompson (ed.), *Bede: His Life, Times and Writings* (1935), 1–38, 111–51; A. M. Sellar, *Bede's Ecclesiastical History of England* (1907: trans. revised 1912); A. W. Wade Evans, *Nennius's 'History of the Britons'* (1938: translation); C. E. Stephens, 'Gildas Sapiens' in *E.H.R.* lvi (1941), 353–73.

Archaeological Evidence

Collingwood and Myres, 335–51; Hodgkin, i. 1–19; Leeds, 9–41, 83–98; J. N. L. Myres, 'The Present State of Archaeological Evidence for the Anglo-Saxon Conquest' in *History*, xxi (1936), 317–30; Grahame Clark, *Prehistoric England* (1940), 1–116; T. D. Kendrick, *Anglo-Saxon Art to 900* (1938), 92–221; G. C. Brooke, *English Coins* (1932), 1–115; *Antiquity*, xiv (1940), 1–87, xx (1946), 21–30 (for description of Sutton Hoo burial ship).
O. G. S. Crawford, *Air Survey and Archaeology* (1924), *Wessex from the Air* (1928), and *Air-Photography for Archaeologists* (1929).

Linguistic Evidence

A. Mawer and F. M. Stenton, *Introduction to Survey of English Place Names* (1924), ch. i; Mawer and Stenton (eds.), *English Place Name Society Publications* (1925–); F. M. Stenton, 'The Historical Bearing of Place Name Studies' in *T.R.H.S.*, 4th Series, xxi–xxv (1939–43: five papers); E. Ekwall, *Oxford Dictionary of English Place-Names* (1936).

Geographical Evidence

Collingwood and Myres, 1–15; Cyril Fox, *The Personality of Britain* (1932); E. W. Gilbert, 'The Human Geography of Roman Britain' in *Historical Geography of England* (1936: ed. H. C. Darby), 30–87; S. W. Wooldridge, 'The Anglo-Saxon Settlement' in *ibid.*, 88–133.

CHAPTER II

THE EARLY CONQUESTS AND SETTLEMENTS

WHEN the peoples of the north-west coastlands of Germany between the Elbe and the Rhine crossed the sea in their long, shallow, undecked boats, manned by twenty-eight oars, to settle in Britain, they acted partly under the pressure of necessity, partly on account of their own desires. It seems dubious guesswork to argue that their own homelands had become too small to contain them because their prolific breeding had produced an overcrowding which was intensified by the slow sinking of the coastline and the inroads of the sea, which were to culminate in forming the Zuyder Zee about the ninth century. It is quite clear that population in Europe in general was very thin and its increase was normally met, as in later centuries, by clearing forests, draining marshes and more intensive cultivation in general. The abnormal factor in the situation was that they were subjected to a growing pressure from the Huns and the Avars as they pressed their way from Asia into West Europe, and they could not escape them by moving inland or farther westward without coming into conflict with German peoples already there. Roman Britain presented a means of escape from acute discomfort. It was sparsely inhabited, for a recent authoritative estimate of its population has placed it at a round million only. It had many vacant sites for settlement, as the traditional account of the British offer of land in Kent to the invaders indicates. The Germans had been raiding Britain for at least five generations: they well knew its comparative wealth and the fertility of its soil; they were aware that it no longer lived under the protection of the Roman legionary; as habitual deep-sea fishermen they had no fear of a sea-passage.

About the year 450, when the raiders began to make Britain their permanent abode, the Romano-British civilization had long passed its noon and was sinking into a Celtic twilight: it was definitely sub-Roman. The causes are not far to seek.

(i) The attacks of the barbarians. The danger to Britain had come from three sides: the Picts harried the north, the Scots from Ireland assaulted the west, the Saxons raided the south and east. In 367 the three foes happened to combine their attacks and the whole of the area where Roman civilization flourished most was so devastated that this year may with reason be taken as marking the real beginning of the end of Roman rule. Thereafter Rome, facing similar perils much nearer home, gradually withdrew her legions and relinquished her hold until by 429, when St. Germanus first visited the island, even the civil service had ceased to operate.

(ii) A changed attitude upon the part of the ruling classes of society. As they were gradually deprived of Roman military assistance and had to depend upon their own resources for protection, they found that they had not the wherewithal to meet their problems. They could not repair the damage done by the raids and, in addition, conduct the work of defence. That is why the ravages wrought by such early attacks as that of 367 were not made good: towns and villas then destroyed were not rebuilt and thus shared the fate of many others which were coming to the end of their history simply by desertion and decay. And only by continuing something like the system of the 'Saxon Shore' could there be any likelihood of repelling the invaders. But it was beyond them to improvise the skill in organization and training men that the Romans had acquired over many centuries. They therefore ceased to live the lives of Roman provincials and reverted to Celtic ways. We should be chary of describing this inevitable readjustment as a sign of decadence, of a *malaise d'esprit* that destroyed vitality.

(iii) A Celtic revival. The pioneer students of Roman Britain were induced by their enthusiasm to claim a far wider influence for Latin thought and culture than these actually possessed. The great mass of the population continued to speak Celtic, to live in villages made up of groups of huts in a formless arrangement, to inhabit single-roomed and hive-shaped houses. The Celts were not uncivilized: the practice and persistence of their curvilinear art is proof enough of that. Round about the fourth century a Celtic renaissance occurred. The fact we know, the reasons and methods are not unnaturally quite obscure, though some have argued that it was responsible for the migration of Celts from Ireland to Scotland and South Wales and in the early sixth century from Britain to Brittany, which was apparently largely empty and could receive them without conquest being necessary and where their culture was certainly vital enough to survive the centuries. Very probably too much has been made of a desire to spread Celtic traditions and ways of life: it may be more than coincidence that the Celtic element in Britain came to the surface only when the veneer of romanization was wearing thin. Thus the appearance of one resulted from the disappearance of the other. Certain it is that by 450, when the Roman system of government had crumbled to pieces, the romanized Britons called to their assistance the chieftains of half-romanized tribes who with their mobile forces took command of the situation. Among such as these was Vortigern, the 'king' of Kent.

The romanized Britons, however, did not realize that the story had ended. They could not believe that a political, economic and social system which had lasted for nearly four centuries had collapsed beyond repair, and they sought to keep their heads above water until the time should come when the Romans would return to help them. In spite of their inability to construct a co-ordinated scheme of defence which would not leave individual towns and districts to their own devices, these Britons fought a long and bitter fight which was not without its successes. The 'Hallelujah' battle of 429 was an early phase of the struggle which showed the imperative need of leadership. That need was to some extent met when Ambrosius Aurelianus, clearly a romanized Briton of distinguished lineage, came to the front about 470 after the Saxons had wrought their havoc as far west as the Irish seas. He instilled such confidence into his countrymen that after a period of indecisive fighting they gained a temporary ascendancy at Mount Badon a generation later. The association of this battle with the name of Arthur was made only by Nennius; Gildas does not state to whom the credit was due, and it is at least surprising that his veneration for Rome did not compel him to mention this 'last of the Romans' who figured as so great a warrior and leader of the Britons. There is, however, no reason to doubt the historicity of Arthur despite his uncommon Roman name. It is clear that towards the close of the fifth century resistance was stiffening in the west: the sepulchral inscriptions found in Wales, written in Celtic runes with accompanying Latin transliterations, testify to the concentration of Britons there. It has been suggested that Arthur's notable contribution to success was his remembrance and recognition of the signal part played by cavalry in the campaigns of the late Empire: he organized and led a force of mounted soldiery ready for service anywhere and with its aid struck terror into the Saxon foot-soldiers and defeated them in battles in every part of the country until his noteworthy victory at Mount Badon, dated variously between 490 and 516 and sited with some probability in the Upper Thames valley near Swindon. On this basis of fact was built the great Arthurian legend which converted the military commander into a 'king' and his cavalry into 'knights' and identified his roving commission to aid local resistance at any point with deeds of chivalry. However that may be, Mount Badon marked a turning-point in the course of events, for it compelled the invaders to settle down: they realized that the age of easy and irresponsible spoliation was ended, that their expansion farther to the west was likely to be too expensive in face of the British counter-movement, and therefore for some forty years they turned to the task of consolidating their bases along the coastlands and the rivers. But by the time they resumed their penetration of the country about 550 the Romano-British provincials as such had disappeared: they had become indistinguishable from Welshmen. The influences brought to bear upon the Anglo-Saxons will be Celtic: the glory that was Rome's had finally faded away.

It has seemed advisable to stress at the outset the resistance of the Britons, for it is a fact which is often under-estimated. Nevertheless, the destruction of civilization was more complete in Britain than in any other part of Western Europe. This country was the victim of much more barbarous peoples than those who attacked Italy, Gaul and Spain, for these had lived a long time on the imperial frontiers, had gained a knowledge and acquired an appreciation of the Roman way of life, so that they were not widely different from the people on the inside of the border, and in Gaul, for example, a great part of the 'conquest' resembled simple penetration. Furthermore, the strife in Britain went on for some hundred and fifty years and proved far more disastrous to the natives. In the words of Tacitus, 'the German people revelled in war', and no one can read the horrors described by Gildas and reconcile them with the activities of the 'commonwealth farmers' of Victorian imagination. The Britons fought gamely for a long time, but their civilization was completely overwhelmed.

The course of the conquest and settlements is most intelligibly and most historically considered in relation to the three great river-systems used by the invaders to penetrate deep into the country: the Thames, the Wash and the Humber.

I. The Thames and the Settlement of the South-East

If the tremendous difficulties of transport do not settle the problem, then the evidence of place-names and of archaeological distinctions, especially in burial customs, would make it probable that the early invaders crossed over in small groups of adventurers, bent on living on the spoils of war, and not as whole tribes intent on immediate colonization.

I. KENT

The literary evidence for the foundation of this kingdom is bound up with the 'legend' of Vortigern. The story is first given by Gildas without names or dates; on the strength of eighth-century traditions of Kent, Bede calls the 'proud tyrant' Vortigern and the enemy chieftains Hengist and Horsa and he identifies the latter as Jutes, not Saxons; the 'Early English Annals' are content to copy Bede; by the time of Nennius the affair is embroidered with romance of a vivid but quite incredible nature. Put briefly, the story goes that Vortigern, a king of Kent, when hard pressed by the attacks of the Scots from Ireland and the Picts from the north, operating presumably by sea, turned in desperation to the Saxons and offered them the island of Thanet on condition that they assisted him in his measures of defence. Once given a footing, they consolidated their position, obtained reinforcements from abroad, provoked a quarrel with Vortigern, overthrew him, and mercilessly looted and destroyed the Romano-British towns and devastated the countryside over a wide area. According to Gildas their raiding in time 'licked the western ocean with its red and savage tongue'.

In spite of the thorough-going scepticism of some historians the story is not improbable, based as it is on genuine folk-tradition. The romanized municipalities had felt that they could no longer cope with a deteriorating situation and in 446 had made their frantic but unsuccessful appeal for help to Rome (the letter mentioned by Gildas and generally known under the title of 'The Groans of the Britons'). The dissolution of traditional government provided throughout the Empire an opportunity for native tribal chieftains to seize the power into their own hands: so Vortigern came to dominate the country on both sides of the Thames and not simply

Kent alone. When the perils seemed likely to overwhelm him, he adopted a device commonly practised at the time: he negotiated with some of the barbarian attackers, admitted them within the frontiers and gave them land in return for their support. But, as happened time and time again elsewhere, the *foederati* grew restless, enlarged their ambitions and shook off the control of their patron. From that point there began the settlement of the whole south-eastern area.

When we consider the character of these early settlers in Kent— their former associations and their customs and culture—we are faced with the most perplexing problem of the period. It is therefore wise to state at once the facts that are not greatly in dispute before venturing into a veritable maze of conjecture. Kent has always seemed to be a district apart and its inhabitants a peculiar people. Geographically it is practically a peninsula and from the earliest recorded times it stood out in marked contrast to the rest of England: the men of Kent were freer to live their own lives as they desired, they early engaged in cross-channel commerce, they had a higher standard of living, they had their own ways of doing things which eventually received comprehensive acknowledgment as the 'custom of Kent'. Distinctions are noticeable from the very start, and historians are at least of one opinion that the early archaeological remains in Kent are closely parallel to those of the Frankish Middle Rhine and quite unlike any to be found either in the north-west of Germany or in any other part of Britain. But there agreement ends, for various explanations have been advanced to explain how Frankish culture came to establish itself in the south-east. If in the discussion we continue to use the term 'Jutes', it is because the authority of Bede has sanctioned the usage, but we are abandoning his ingenious and unfortunate afterthought, based on a similarity of names, which associated a Germanic people called the 'Jutes' with a district called 'Jutland'.

(*a*) It has been vigorously argued that the whole coastal area from Kent as far west as Hampshire was settled about the middle of the fifth century by people of one kind and one custom. The individual property-rights of the Kentish peasants, signalized throughout the centuries by the special practice of 'gavelkind' whereby land continued to be divided among all heirs instead of passing to the eldest son only, the agricultural self-sufficiency of their hamlets, the organization of their larger territorial units called 'lathes' to make easier the systematic and equitable exploitation of the forest land of the Weald and ultimately to serve as divisions for fiscal and government purposes: all such characteristics, it is claimed, can be traced outside Kent throughout the south-eastern counties. Since this area has a close relationship with the Middle Rhine and shows remarkable points of resemblance to the Frankish practices there in its methods of burial by inhumation, its system of agriculture, its customary laws and, in particular, its artistic achievements in fine wheel-made pottery, precious jewels for personal adornment, and the filigree and enamel work of the expert jeweller's craft, it is contended that the Jutes were Ripuarian Franks who had moved to the Lower Rhine and crossed the sea to Britain. Their wanderings in that case were part and parcel of the Frankish migrations which had earlier resulted in their occupation of north Gaul. Thus both sides of the Channel came into their hands, and the eventual marriage of King Ethelbert of Kent to a daughter of the Merovingian king of the Franks before 597 might be interpreted as an attempt to maintain and emphasize the identical interests of the same Frankish people. So a Jutish colonization had taken place fully a generation before the Saxons, especially the West Saxons, began to expand, and to do this these had to subdue what was, so far as they were concerned, an 'alien civilization'. They never succeeded in obliterating its impress, though their own Saxon ideas naturally predominated in time. This thesis leaves too much unexplained and goes too far out of the way to explain the rest. We know that the Saxons had been raiding the shores of Britain for many generations but we have not a scrap of evidence about the sea adventures of the Franks or of the immense preparations required to transport a whole people on their novel journey over-seas. Furthermore, whether we call them Jutes or Franks, they have left no memorial of themselves in place-names: British and Irish Celts, Saxons and Angles will all express their racial origin in this way and it is at least noteworthy that the inhabitants of Kent style themselves 'men of Cantware' and in so doing recognize their early association with the Britons of this highly romanized district, for they have adopted a British name. It is by no means impossible that some of the Kentish distinctions are based in part on Romano-British influence, for we have already observed that the future conquerors lived for some time with their destined victims on negotiated terms and must have acquired some knowledge of their ways. It is difficult in any other manner to account for the fact that Kent alone preserved a resemblance to its Roman past in the pattern of the early settlement. We may therefore justly suspect that the 'consolidated fields' of the Kentish hamlets, so opposed to the 'strip' system elsewhere, may hold a memory of pre-Saxon agricultural arrangements, that the unusually detailed classifications of society are due to the presence of peasants of Romano-British descent, that British craftsmen remained to preserve and improve the native arts they had cherished so long. Whatever truth there is in this, the theory that the early settlement was made by a homogeneous people with customs in common cannot easily be reconciled with the archaeological evidence of the existence of another culture which was as early, much lower and quite different—for example, the practice of cremation in north Kent and Surrey. As for the presence elsewhere of customs obtaining in Kent, we might explain them by inter-tribal penetration radiating from Kent: the Jutes did not settle in the south of Hampshire and the Isle of Wight until after 491, by which time the Saxons had seized hold upon Sussex and thereby compelled them to sidestep them and to use the sea as a by-pass. In other words, it was the similarities and not the differences which were late in appearing. We can but receive with caution an explanation which raises as many problems as it solves.

(b) Some of the difficulties have been avoided by the presupposition that there were two groups of settlers, bringing with them their distinctive cultures: first, Anglo-Saxon immigrants from the Elbe-Rhine region of the same type as elsewhere in the southeast; then a second wave of invaders, Franks from the Middle Rhine, about 500, who broke the dynasty of Kentish kings founded by Hengist, of which we hear no more after 512, and finally obliterated all British names.

(c) The simplest, but not therefore erroneous, view sees one body of settlers who in the course of five or six generations exhibited two cultural types, but two only in the sense that they had in that time moved from the primitive to the more advanced. Although the links with the Empire had been snapped, it appears doubtful whether the connexion between Britain and Gaul was ever broken. It is necessary to regard the invasion and settlement of the two sides of the English Channel as a single movement or at most a series of related movements: the 'Saxons' raided both coasts and as far south as Aquitaine. Those who came as a Saxon tribe from the neighbourhood of Frisia had the same primitive customs and appreciations as their fellow-wanderers and, because the connexion with the mainland continued firm, they remained subject to Frankish influence which was clearly strong in Kent before the arrival of St. Augustine. Moreover, Kent has always been most favourably situated for commerce with the Continent, and in the course of business the 'men of Kent' acquired *objets d'art* that were Frankish in their characteristics and eventually came to mould their art on Frankish models: as it has been put, 'the Jutes were made in Kent'. However, trade alone is not sufficient to explain the Frankish culture of Kent. It cannot account adequately for other than cultural affinities: social and economic conditions and institutions have usually a wider basis for their origin than business influences, and the solution must be sought in the fact that the influences at work were common to both sides of the Channel.

It will be observed that the crux of the problem of the Jutes in Kent could be resolved if only we could date precisely the archaeological discoveries: we can merely place them in their typological order and confess that we do not know how long the intervals were between the making of one object and the making of another. For the moment it is safer to believe that the flowering of Kentish culture with its Frankish traits occurred about 600 when Ethelbert was at the height of his power.

II. SUSSEX

According to the 'Early English Annals' Aelle at the head of groups of Saxon adventurers landed in 477 somewhere near Selsey Bill and slowly made his way eastwards along the coast until British resistance was finally and mercilessly broken with the capture of the old Roman garrison town of Pevensey in 491. His kingdom remained a coastal settlement, hemmed in by natural boundaries: it was so isolated and remote from contact with the outside world that it remained heathen until a hundred years after its neighbour Kent had been converted. According to Bede, Aelle was the first 'Bretwalda' to dominate the country south of the Humber, but this can only be a recognition of his military abilities and can have no territorial significance: we certainly know nothing of his successors for the next two centuries.

III. ESSEX

The origins of this kingdom are obscure. The district with its heavy clay had not been colonized much by the Romans and did not prove attractive to the early settlers. Its population was therefore scanty and its development late. One important point, however, we know: its associations were with Kent across the Thames estuary and not with East Anglia to the north. By the early seventh century it had worked its way into prominence.

IV. SURREY AND MIDDLESEX

They may well at one time have been component parts of one unit of early settlement on both sides of the mouth of the Thames. Surrey, by derivation the 'southern district' (*Suthrige*) considered in relation to Middlesex, was colonized by Saxons who expanded there from north Kent. Of Middlesex we know little or nothing. It is somewhat surprising to find that London with its superb situation and established importance was apparently ignored and did not form the core of a strong kingdom. Instead Surrey came under the control first of Kent and later in 568 of Wessex, whilst Middlesex became dependent on Essex.

Probably the campaigning which culminated in Mount Badon, whatever its date, ends the first phase in the history of the south-eastern district. The resistance of the Britons in the west indicated the limit for the invaders' available resources for the purpose of conquest and thereafter they tended to fall back upon their bases, concentrate on colonization instead of campaigning, summon their countryfolk to their sides and go their own ways, regardless of any further co-operative effort, to found their kingly dynasties and their territorial states.

II. The Wash and the Eastern Midlands and South-Western Districts

The Wash and the magnificent river system connected with it made it easy for groups of Angles and Saxons to make their way into the country. We have no written evidence of their activities. However, they left behind them the largest collections of archaeological remains so far discovered. And not only the largest but the very earliest, so that we can properly surmise that penetration occurred long before the close of the fifth century and probably at the same time as the immigration by way of the Thames. With the rivers radiating in all directions the invaders spread out from the Wash like a fan. The Fenlands, which had been in Roman and prehistoric times a fertile and populous district, were not settled, at all events permanently, for it seems likely that, as in Frisia, the land was beginning to sink below sea-level and become an uncultivable swamp. It was, however, a simple matter to move inland along the rivers to drier gravel soils. Apart from a short advance north of the Wash along the Witham to colonize South Lindsey (Lincolnshire), the efforts of the invaders succeeded in laying the foundations of three kingdoms.

I. EAST ANGLIA

Here a number of independent folks made their homes and in the course of time united themselves into some sort of confederation. It must have been quite loosely organized, for the establishment and consolidation of the royal dynasty were not enough to make the North Folk and the South Folk forget their differences: they were placed under separate bishoprics after they were converted, and they retained their own forms of administration to such an extent that in the distant future they became the separate shires of Norfolk and Suffolk. The kingdom of East Anglia reached its highest importance under Redwald, whom Bede hailed as 'Bretwalda' after 616. If the treasure of the Sutton Hoo burial ship belonged to him, there would seem to be every justification for such a title.

II. MERCIA

Driving their way along and between the rivers Welland, Wreak and Soar, the invaders at last reached the Middle Trent, which was to become the heart of the Mercian kingdom with Tamworth as its royal headquarters and Lichfield and Repton the centres of its ecclesiastical organization. It is very probable that in this region they met and mingled with Angles who had entered the country by the Humber and come southwards along the Trent valley, peopling North Lindsey on the way. It is a moot question which outnumbered the others, those from the Fens or those from the Humber; the answer depends largely upon how much significance is attached to the political events that happened later. However this may be, during the unbroken silence of many generations the colonists lived a hard life on the heavy clay land of the Midlands and, unless they trekked elsewhere, there was nothing to be done but to tackle the formidable task of clearing the forests and draining the marshes. That was sufficient to take up all their energies: history knows little or nothing of them before the appearance of their first authenticated king, Penda, in 632.

III. WESSEX

The area around Dorchester in the Upper Thames was the nucleus of the West Saxon folk. There can be no doubt upon this point, for the evidence seems irrefutable: nowhere else has archaeology brought to light as many or as early West Saxon remains. On the evidence of cremation and brooches alone there must have been a settlement on an extensive scale round about 500. This is not surprising, for this district had always been able to support a heavy population. It is worth noting that Dorchester itself became the residence of Birinus when he evangelized the West Saxons and the centre of the first West Saxon bishopric.

What is puzzling is the conflict of evidence about the way in which the West Saxons arrived there. Three routes have at various times been suggested. (a) Along the Icknield Way. This was not a Roman road but a line of communications between the Fens and the Thames valley already some two thousand years old when the Germanic invasions began. The argument that the Saxons entered by the Wash, went south along the Bedfordshire Ouse to the area around Cambridge, and thence travelled along the Icknield Way to where it reaches the Thames near Goring, is strongly supported by archaeology: grave goods, dated early by the cremation rites, and pottery and jewellery lie along the route, and the Cambridge and Dorchester districts have remarkably close cultural affinities. From the point of view of geography there are no natural obstacles to make such an advance even slightly difficult. (b). Along the Thames valley. There is no good reason, speaking geographically, why the Saxons should not have travelled along the whole line of the Thames, and cremations and place-names bear witness to a connexion between North Kent and Surrey and the Upper Thames district. There is certainly a sudden break in the settlements along the Thames before the Goring gap is reached: perhaps it was because there the woodlands and heathlands pressed too closely upon the river banks to make habitation advisable. But though this prevented colonization, it constitutes no bar to an advance through it to the district beyond. However, the ties of the Dorchester area with the Lower Thames are by no means as strong as those with the Ouse. (c) Overland from the south coast. This was the route hallowed by tradition, recorded in the only literary evidence we have and therefore naturally accepted by historians who had no other sources of knowledge. In 495 two Saxon chiefs, Cerdic and his son (more correctly grandson) Cynric, landed at the head of Southampton Water, went north-west as far as Charford (Cerdicesford, Cerdic's Ford)-on-Avon and then struck north to Old Sarum in Wiltshire. The important point to notice is that it was not until a generation later, not until after 550, that these Saxons are said to have reached and to have established themselves in the district of the Upper Thames.

Though most historians have been reluctant to abandon this story as the foundation of the West Saxon people, some have rejected it in its entirety, and there can be no doubt that it will not stand detailed criticism: the artificial scheme of the chronology; the suspiciously British names of the leaders and the artificial names of their colleagues; the two distinct and contradictory versions provided; the disagreement between an early genealogical table of West Saxon kings and that contained in these 'Early English Annals'; the ignorance (or suppression) of the British victory at Mount Badon; above all, the evidence of archaeology which finds slight, if any, early West Saxon occupation of Hampshire and Wiltshire (and this is corroborated by the scarcity of early West Saxon place-names) but overwhelming proof that West Saxons were settled in large numbers on the Upper Thames many years before the 'Annals' place them there.

There is, however, no reason to jettison the folk traditions so ruthlessly. It is not the 'Annals' that are at fault so much as their modern interpreters: what is wrong is not the story so much as the importance attached to it. If we adopt the suggestion that the chronicler was not interested in the history of the West Saxon *people* but of the West Saxon *royal dynasty*, then the evidence becomes all of a piece. Cerdic and his retainers were one among several groups of adventurers who made their home in South Hampshire and Wiltshire without being numerous enough to settle down as farmers. They therefore remained a nomadic fighting force, spoiling and levying tribute from the Britons around them. That is why Gildas does not record their achievements as worthy of mention; why there is such a dearth of archaeological remains and place-names; why there had to be intermarriage with the Britons, thus introducing a British element into the pedigree of the future Saxon royal house and establishing a tradition of conciliation between West Saxons and Britons which is a most notable feature of their future policy; why the Wansdyke, a protective barrier constructed by the Britons, horizontally from Newbury nearly to the Bristol Channel, envisaged attack from the Thames valley and not a westward drive from South Hampshire. In course of time Cerdic's group, possibly the 'Gewisse', asserted its predominance over its fellows and in Ceawlin's time (560–91) extended their banditry to the Upper Thames, overcame the Saxons who for half a century had been there leading more or less peaceable lives, and brought them into subjection. Ceawlin had wider ambitions than merely this superimposition of a royal dynasty by armed force. For he inaugurated a policy of expansion towards the north and west: in 568, possibly near Wimbledon, he brought the menacing advance of Ethelbert of Kent along the Thames valley to a halt and included Surrey within his kingdom; in 571 at Bedford he broke the resistance of the Britons in the Chilterns and extended his authority across the Thames to the north-east; in 577 at Dyrham near Bath he drove the Britons from the Cotswolds and inserted a West Saxon wedge at the Severn estuary between them and their fellows in Devon and Cornwall. The military despotism of the second 'Bretwalda' named by Bede was, however, short-lived: it must have aroused hatred and resentment and certainly before 600 it had collapsed. Indeed, about 661 the Mercians were able to annex the district of the Upper Thames, which had been the focal centre of the West Saxon people. In consequence, their fortunes became associated with the home of their dynasty in Hampshire: Winchester displaced Dorchester in 662 as the ecclesiastical centre and became the royal headquarters as well.

Thus two courses of development, originally quite distinct, had become inseparably merged to the mystification of historians.

III. The Humber and the North

Geography made the Humber, as it had made the Wash, a centre of distribution from which the invaders spread out in all directions in the late fifth century: it was politics that snapped the connexions later so that by Bede's day it had become a dividing line. The earliest settlers were called the 'Humbermen', the 'Humbrenses'. The name possibly came from the 'Ambrones', an Anglian people living in Frisia: Bede certainly identified all of them with the Angles and archaeology has revealed connexions with Frisia. The 'Humbermen' went south to colonize North Lindsey (Lincolnshire) and along the Trent valley to the heart of the future Mercia; they penetrated north to the Tyne and Tees. But a few generations later a different future befell the two halves of this Anglian area of settlement, for the warrior Penda and his followers brought under their control all the men of the Mercian lands and then the men of Lindsey. In consequence, a distinguishing name was required for the Angles left beyond the Humber, and it has been suggested that it was Bede himself who coined and gave vogue to the new descriptive term 'Northumbrians', for he often goes out of his way to explain what he means when he uses it.

NORTHUMBRIA

The foundations of this kingdom had been laid before Penda's intervention. It was constituted by the union of two curiously distinct territories: Deira, settled in the fifth century and stretching from the Humber to the Tees; Bernicia, occupied later, possibly about 547 at the beginning of Ida's reign, and extending from the Tees to the Forth.

These two provinces, even after they were joined together, revealed so many dissimilarities and remained so antagonistic that it has been argued that Bernicia did not owe its existence to any colonization from Deira but to a completely new invasion from the Continent. This view is now generally discarded: the year 547 is too late for any such migration; though it is true that the Deirans were unable to make their way through the forests of Durham, they reached Bernicia by sea, where early remains are to be found confined to the coast; the cultural differences arose because the soil of Bernicia was too poor to attract many settlers and those who arrived formed simply a ruling class and left the Celtic ways of life unchanged, whereas Deira was heavily colonized and had, unlike Bernicia, been profoundly romanized.

By the end of the sixth century, therefore, a century and a half of confused struggles had produced the political geography of the Heptarchy, the division of the country into the seven more important of the numerous barbarian kingdoms: Kent, Essex and Sussex; East Anglia, Mercia and Wessex; Northumbria. These territorial monarchies will have a curiously shifting pre-eminence, but for the future the work of expansion will lie in the hands of those who have settled in the country and not of fresh hordes of immigrants from overseas.

At this point we may fittingly pause to contrast the picture of Britain about 600 with what it had been in the last years of Roman rule two centuries before. We can profitably concentrate our attention on the two major problems: to what extent did the invaders destroy all traces of the civilization of Rome and, further than that, drive the native inhabitants out of the land? To do one is not necessarily to do the other, and the way in which we answer these questions will decide our conception of the social and economic developments of the future.

For over three hundred years Britain had been part of the Roman Empire and subjected to its government. The military area of occupation, covering the uplands from Yorkshire to the Tyne and Solway, may have had only such contacts as were obtainable from garrison towns like Carlisle, but the civil area of the lowlands south and east of a line from York to Chester and down to Exeter knew the civilization of Rome in all its political, material and cultural aspects. In considering its fate we shall guard ourselves from hasty assumptions if we bear in mind that in Western Europe as a whole the attacks of the barbarians did not produce a *tabula rasa*. They wrought fearful havoc but before the invasion period they had learned to appreciate the high civilization into which they entered and they sought in their eager and clumsy way to copy it. That is why it is said that Rome, apparently defeated, overcame her conquerors. Are there any influences at work among the invaders of Britain which can be traced back to the Roman occupation? Or, to put the matter more specifically, can we, for example, find any connexion between the 'villa' system of agriculture as practised by the Romans and the later 'manor' system, and was the Christian church, the real inheritor of the achievements of Rome, so firmly established that it could withstand and mitigate, however unobtrusively, the barbarism of the Germans? Now, the civilization of Rome will undoubtedly count for much in our history: medieval England will lie under the shadow of its traditions, and medieval men will often seek to achieve their dreams by resurrecting the past. Nevertheless, it is plain that the permanent influence of Rome came to this country, not with the Roman soldier, but with the Roman priest. For nearly two centuries there was a greater break with the past in Britain than there was on the Continent. After all, the country was primarily an advance-guard of the Empire against barbarism: it had been the last province of importance to be acquired, it was far distant from the centre of Mediterranean culture, it was only partly romanized. Furthermore, it was attacked by enemies who, whilst on the Continent, had been least in touch with Rome: it will be more than a hundred years after other despoilers of the Empire have been converted that they themselves will accept Christianity. So the distinctive signs of the civilization of Rome vanished. The art of political government, denoted by Roman institutions, administrative machinery and civil service, was forgotten, and political consciousness was dead. Latin was no longer the language of military and official life, of urban communities and villa estates. Town-life disappeared from sight: thus Silchester was not rebuilt, and London, Canterbury and Rochester are heard of no more for nearly a hundred and fifty years after 457. We cannot prove the continuity of habitation of any Roman town: that such there was is probable, for the advantages of walled protection and geographical situation still remained. But to what extent 'urban life' in the sense of organized life went on remains an open question. We can say little more than this: that Canterbury was the centre of King Ethelbert's court when the Roman missionaries arrived in Kent and that the traditional attraction of Roman urban centres for the Imperial Church would presumably give an additional fillip to urban development. The country villas, those self-contained and self-supporting farmhouses and farms which were owned by country gentlemen of leisure and cultivated by semi-servile tenants and slaves, fell victim to the disorders of the times and, though numbers of them have been excavated, they show few signs of ever having been inhabited by Anglo-Saxons. The high material civilization, which set a standard of living which was not to be reached again for well over a thousand years, left only the magnificent network of roads as a direct and tangible legacy to posterity. And finally the Christian Church, whatever may have been the extent of its influence, saw that influence sadly diminished and the character of its organization changed. Episcopal administration could no longer centre itself in the towns and, if we can judge from the later structure of the Celtic Church, the episcopate may well have entered upon the course of a closer association with monasticism and monastic developments. At all events, Christianity survived in the west of Britain and kept its lamp bravely burning to light the torches which St. Ninian carried to Galloway and St. Patrick to Ireland and St. Columba to Scotland and St. Aidan from there back to England. So the Roman roads and the Roman Church alone remained standing among the debris of a ruined civilization.

When a civilization decays, the rot invariably starts at the top: until the machine age arrived, civilization in its higher developments rested on slaves or at least the unfree, no matter what form, lay or ecclesiastical, it took. Though the world of the Romano-Britons with its wealth, privileges and amenities had gone and with it the upper-class possessors of the culture of Rome, though cities and villas had been abandoned or destroyed, all this is no indication that the Celts had also disappeared. For they had lived their lives outside it and largely independent of it, and in a catastrophic age it is the poor who have nothing to lose and little to fight for in a mere change of masters who are most likely to survive. Their poverty will leave us no archaeological proof of their existence. But it is evident that we must jettison completely the old belief in their extermination. Even outside Strathclyde, Wales and the south-west peninsula there was a considerable British survival. As we have already seen, the proof is not to be looked for in place-names, for the Celtic villages were either abandoned or, what seems to be quite as probable, passed to other owners, but it may be seen in the field-names of hills, woods, and rivers and in that personal nomenclature which argues strongly for a large degree of intermarriage. Furthermore, it is to be found in the history of art. For the Celts must not be regarded as uncivilized. Their art had flourished long before the birth of Christ. It was a geometric art of decoration which concentrated on formal patterns of spirals and curving lines and drew no inspiration from nature, finding no pleasure in the naturalistic depiction of animal forms. This form of abstract art had been overwhelmed by the mass-production methods of Roman capitalist enterprise, but it had evidently not been destroyed, for when the Roman occupation came to an end Celtic art proved that it had been vital enough to persist and hold its own: the curious and important point is that the revival took place, not in the Celtic west but in the very heart of the romanized area, in Kent and the Home Counties. It is to this miracle of survival that we owe the Hiberno-Saxon art of the glorious manuscripts and crosses of seventh-century Northumbria.

SELECT READING

General

Collingwood and Myres, 291–324; Hodgkin, i. 37–74, 118–25; H. M. Chadwick, *Origin of English Nation* (1907), 1–90; E. K. Chambers, *Arthur of Britain* (1927), 1–19, 168–204; O. G. S. Crawford, 'Arthur and his Battles' in *Antiquity*, ix (1935), 277–91; R. V. Lennard, 'The Character of the Anglo-Saxon Conquests' in *History*, xviii (1933), 204–15; Ordnance Survey Map, 'Britain in the Dark Ages' (1935); J. N. L. Myres, 'Britain in the Dark Ages' in *Antiquity*, xi (1935), 455–64.

Thames Settlement

Collingwood and Myres, 352–82 and map; Hodgkin, i. 74–108; Leeds, 42–9; J. E. A. Jolliffe, *Pre-Feudal England: The Jutes* (1933); J. H. Round, 'The Settlement of the South- and East-Saxons' in *Commune of London* (1899), 1–27; E. T. Leeds, *Early Anglo-Saxon Art and Archaeology* (1936), 99–138.

Wash Settlement

Collingwood and Myres, 383–410 and map; Hodgkin, i. 108–18, 125–37, 184–94; Leeds, 49–82; F. M. Stenton, 'Lindsey and its Kings' in *Essays . . . to R. L. Poole* (1929), 136–50; E. T. Leeds, 'The West-Saxon Invasion and the Icknield Way' in *History*, x (1925), 97–109.

Humber Settlement

Collingwood and Myres, 411–24; Hodgkin, i. 147–53, 194–200; J. N. L. Myres, 'The Teutonic Settlement of Northern England' in *History*, xx (1935), 250–62.

CHAPTER III

THE CONVERSION OF ENGLAND

THE barbarian invasions had destroyed the Roman Empire as a territorial unit and had, in particular, cut the ties binding Britain to the Continent and forced her into comparative isolation. The collapse of civilization all over the romanized world was a fearsome tragedy, but the darkness was relieved by one glimmer of light. For the empire had left behind it its 'ghost', to use Hobbes's phrase, 'sitting crowned upon the grave thereof'. The Church never forgot that the bounds of Christendom were once identical with the frontiers of the far-flung empire: when it emerged from the catacombs, it utilized the framework of the empire because at first no other basis of organization was available, and it had continued to reflect Rome in its ecclesiastical geography, its machinery of government and its grades of officials from archbishops and bishops to priests and deacons; even the language of its services was in every country Latin; and it had retained and preserved the culture of Rome. Though the Roman bureaucracy had already disappeared in the provinces in the late Empire, an ecclesiastical hierarchy remained to keep the memory of its traditions alive. Now, on the Continent the Church came to be respected by the barbarians to whom it gave instruction in the arts of peace. For example, Theodoric, the king of the Ostrogoths in Italy, desired to get on friendly terms with it and obtain its support in his efforts to find a *modus vivendi* between his warriors and his Italian subjects: that he failed in the long run was largely because he adhered to the Arian sect of Christianity which denied the divinity of Christ, and for that reason the Church would not place the indispensable strength of its traditions at his service. Indeed, it was partly because Clovis, the king of the Franks, happened to become a Roman Christian when he was converted and could therefore be given the support of the Church that he was able to found what happened to be the one barbarian kingdom that survived on the Continent. Nevertheless, the facts compel us to remember that, though Gaul suffered far less than Britain from the fifth-century invaders and the Christian Church did not cease to exist there, yet in the long run it was England and not France that first attained political unity. The Church was not, and could not be, the first and the main factor in this work. Indeed, from the ecclesiastical standpoint, England came to be regarded not as a single unit but as two provinces; for a time, when Mercia was predominant, there were three. Similarly, Ireland was to be the home of four. And the archbishops of Canterbury and the archbishops of York later sat together in common deliberation only under a papal legate and on no other occasions. Furthermore, the inhabitants of England saw no reason why their traditional loyalties should be altered by nominal conversion to Christianity. Unity had to be enforced by the sword and was not achieved by the book. The Church, however, could in favourable circumstances act as a powerful auxiliary to the secular authority in the establishment of an ordered society. It is from that limited point of view that we should regard the conversion of England as a major event in *political* development.

The conversion of England was accomplished by two distinct movements, one a mission deriving its inspiration indirectly from Wales and Ireland and operating from the north-east, the other a mission from Rome working in the south-east.

I. The Celtic Church

Whether it is to be explained by the growth of religious feeling in a time of affliction or the concentration of christianized Britons in the west under the pressure of attack or the willingness of the Celts to be converted as another means of expressing their racial antipathy to the heathen invaders, it is certain that the Church in the Celtic-speaking parts of the country comes much more prominently into view. We may call it for the sake of convenience the British Church. Its centre was Wales where it had evolved a regular diocesan system in the simple sense of an organization based upon the rule of bishops, though by the early sixth century it was falling under the influence of monastic ideas from the East. It produced great saints like Illtud (died *c.* 540), who established the first monastery and the first monastic school in Wales, and like David (*c.* 520–88), who left such a reputation for godliness and austere devotion that he came to be adopted as the patron saint of Wales. It produced great missionaries like St. Patrick (*c.* 389–461), who evangelized Ireland, just as St. Ninian before him had spread the gospel among the Picts of Galloway from his monastic foundation of Whithorn on Wigton Bay, and St. Kentigern (or Mungo:

527–612) had later evangelized Strathclyde from his centre at Glasgow. It will be noticed, however, that the British Church, though it was eager to work among the Celts, was deliberately refusing to convert those Anglo-Saxons who had inflicted such horrors upon the Britons: the invaders deserved eternal damnation and should not be saved from it. In consequence, we must leave the British Church in its voluntary isolation and divert our attention to the Irish Church, that off-shoot of the British Church which came to overshadow its creator and took a more generous view of its responsibilities.

The establishment of the first organized Church in Ireland was the brave achievement of St. Patrick. It is not accurate to say that he was the first to introduce Christianity to the island, for a few small Christian communities had been in existence there ever since the early years of the fifth century, but nothing had been done to compare with his thirty years of tireless devotion. He was the son of a romanized Briton who had been both a member of the governing class and a Christian deacon. At the age of fifteen Patrick was captured with many others by raiding Scots from Ireland and carried off to Ulster. Some years later he managed to escape, made his way to Italy, resided for a while in the island of Lérins (near Cannes) which had become a noted centre of monastic life, studied with St. Illtud of Wales at Auxerre, where he was probably ordained priest by St. Germanus, and with some difficulty persuaded the British Church in 432 to authorize his going back to the land of his captivity as a missionary. As such his work had a twofold importance. (a) He preached Christianity throughout Ireland as far as the western seas, instituted a diocesan organization in which the jurisdiction of each bishop coincided with a tribal area, fixed his ecclesiastical headquarters at Armagh, and even convoked synods to formulate rules of discipline. It was evident that he intended simply to reproduce in Ireland the system of church government with which he was familiar as a boy and in which he had been trained at Auxerre. (b) He linked the Church in Ireland with the Church Universal of the Roman Empire and made Ireland part of Western Christendom. It is not merely that Ireland was given its first real contacts with the Continent, but it was the first occasion that the Church of Rome had crossed the old imperial frontiers to attempt a conquest of its own. He made Latin the language of the Church: fortunately so, for Gaelic would have proved a serious obstacle later on when reconciliation and absorption became necessary. He was eager to get advice upon his ecclesiastical problems from the bishop of Rome. The point is of interest because the Irish and Roman Churches were to come into collision in the distant future.

St. Patrick, however, like all his contemporaries looked upon the world as a Christian unity and, indeed, there never were any fundamental differences in doctrine. The divergences resulted essentially from the problem how the Church in Ireland was to be organized and governed, and they made their appearance during the dark century after St. Patrick's death. At its close we see that the Irish Church was no longer the Church of St. Patrick in close communion with the Church on the Continent. His work was largely undone and many of the churches he founded were dwindling in importance or completely gone. Celtic Christianity stood in the place of Roman Christianity: a monastic church had supplanted an episcopal church. Many circumstances had combined to produce a system which was quite peculiar.

(i) The barbarian invasions had completely disrupted communications between Ireland and the Continent and left her isolated. This dealt a mortal blow to the Patrician Church, for Ireland had not known what it was to be romanized and St. Patrick's work could hardly survive there when there was no guarantee of a stream of recruits from overseas to maintain it.

(ii) When the influence of the Church of the Continent was thus violently removed, it was replaced by that of the Celtic-speaking districts of Britain. There had always been much coming and going on the Irish Sea between the peoples of similar race, and language and geography had made the connexion between Galloway and the north-east coast of Ireland particularly close. These parts of Britain had never been romanized and, as their inhabitants had been christianized not much longer than the Irish, they had gained no firm knowledge of the system and practices of Western Christendom.

(iii) In consequence, monasticism came to occupy a preponderant position. This important change resulted chiefly from the influence of the monastic foundations of St. Ninian in south-west Scotland. Born the son of a British king near the Solway Firth, Ninian had been sent to Rome as a hostage and there he was educated in the Christian faith. About 395 he was encouraged to return home to convert his fellow-countrymen. On his journey northwards he paid a visit to the greatest ecclesiastic of his generation, St. Martin, who had established his famous monastery at Tours, and he was so impressed by what he saw that, when he arrived in Scotland, he set up monasteries rather than dioceses. His foundation of 'Candida Casa' at Whithorn enshrined in stone his memories of Tours and formed the starting-point of those missionary journeys which established daughter-houses elsewhere. Now, Ninian and his disciples formed contacts not only with the British Church in Wales but also with heathen Ireland: according to tradition it was Ninian himself who came there a generation before St. Patrick's arrival to preach and to found a few small churches and, after St. Patrick's death, many of the prominent saints of Ireland received their training at Candida Casa. It is not surprising, therefore, that the monastic and missionary organization established among a Celtic and heathen people in south Scotland should have become the prototype of a similar organization in similar conditions in Ireland: the work of St. Patrick on diocesan lines was obliterated and Roman traditions were submerged beneath Celtic novelties.

The growth in isolation explains the peculiarities of the Irish Church which were to make agreement with the Roman system difficult. Too much must not be read into the phrase 'diocesan system'. It will be several hundred years before a Roman ecclesiastical diocese means a congeries of parishes under archdeacons and a bishop. If we were to use strictly contemporary language, we should have to designate the area of a bishop's authority by the purely ecclesiastical word 'parish' and reserve the civil term 'diocese' to describe the districts on the fringe of the territory under his supervision. The point is important because it draws attention to the fact that the early ecclesiastical administration of England was conducted through the bishop's *familia*, the group of clerks who lived a communal life with him and were associated with the countryside rather than rigidly attached to a single urban unit. In consequence, the difference between a bishop's *familia* and a monastery was not at first stressed in England, and it is difficult to draw a firm line between them. Furthermore, the Anglo-Saxon world was quite as tribal as the Celtic and the early Anglo-Saxon bishoprics were largely tribal in basis. It follows, therefore, that we ought not to regard the Irish Church as having developed a special organization of its own, tribal and monastic, which stood in the sharpest contrast with conditions in England. Its ecclesiastical system was necessarily dictated by the political and social system of Ireland. Each Irish king or chieftain founded a monastery for his own tribe, endowing it with land and retaining the office of abbot for a member of his own family. So each tribal kingdom tended to be identified with the sphere of influence of a great monastery. Nor was any objection raised to the admission of women, and mixed monasteries became a common sight: Candida Casa itself was one before the close of the sixth century, whilst Whitby in Northumbria, Repton in Mercia and Ely in East Anglia were to be noteworthy examples in England. Where the Irish Church parted company from the Roman Church was not in its tribal character so much as in its monastic organization. The authority of the abbots was supreme and the bishops came to be of lesser importance. However hard it may have been in England to distinguish between the position and activities of an episcopal *familia* and a monastery, in Ireland the confusion had gone so far that the same man might be both abbot and bishop, and priests were frequently monks in Holy Orders. So out of touch with Western Christendom had Ireland become that the pope himself was regarded and addressed as simply an abbot. The bishops ceased to govern a diocese, lived as anchorites within the confines of a monastery under the rule of abbots and even abbesses, were given their dignity as a token of respect for saintly living and were restricted in their duties to essentially episcopal functions such as ordination. Moreover, their number was great, for each monastery wanted a bishop of its own so that it would not have to be dependent on one belonging to a rival establishment. The typical Irish monastery like that of Iona was large: its members lived like hermits in their separate cells and lived a real community life only when assembled together for prayer and food.

As a consequence, the Irish Church had no effective centralized organization. It had, indeed, many different centres, for the abbots of great monastic foundations, for example, Iona, remained the head of all their daughter-foundations. And even that headship gave little more than a moral authority, for each monastery was apt to be a law to itself and develop on its own lines with its own special rules of discipline and devotion. And there was nothing to prevent monks from wandering from one monastery to another as the spirit moved them.

Nor is it surprising that the Irish Church retained usages that had been changed or altogether abandoned on the Continent. Its archaic method of calculating the date of Easter allowed a variation of as much as a week, the tonsure of the Irish monks, extending over the head from ear to ear rather than round the crown of the head, was Druidical and not Roman, the rites in the ceremony of baptism were different. These seem trivial matters of disputation but they served to signalize a clash of fundamental principles and they were accordingly put forward prominently in the later controversies with the Roman Church.

When we remember that the Irish Church of the post-Patrician age had derived its origin from the half-civilized peoples living on the edge of the Roman world, we can but marvel at its achievements. Helped by the fact that it had not to face the onslaughts of barbarian invaders until the coming of the Northmen in the late eighth century, it conducted at once missionary enterprises of unparalleled courage and zeal and came to make Ireland a centre of scholarship and culture.

THE IRISH MISSIONS

The severe and self-tormenting life of the ascetic had become associated with the Irish Church through the influence of Egyptian monachism by way of the island of Lérins, and it played its part in encouraging Irish monks to obey the divine commandment to 'leave all and follow Me' and to venture on their fearless journeys into the heart of heathendom. Save for the exceptional outlook of Gregory the Great, the Roman Church had little enthusiasm for missionary undertakings, and it did nothing to compare with the Irish journeyings from Iceland to Lombardy and from Bavaria to Brittany. The mission of immediate concern to us is that of St. Columba (c. 521–97) from Ireland to Scotland. He himself was of royal descent and a kinsman of the king of Dalriada (the modern Argyll), to whom he came with his twelve disciples in 563 to revive the faith of those fellow-countrymen of his, the Scots, who had emigrated from Ireland half a century or more earlier. The island of Hy (Ioua: later mistranscribed as Iona) became a centre from which radiated missions to the Picts of north Scotland and eventually to the Angles of north England. St. Columba, it should be noted, was never a bishop, simply an abbot, and the Scottish Church was in organization only a collection of monasteries.

THE IRISH SCHOOLS

A scholastic and literary renaissance was set on foot at the great monastic schools of Clonard (c. 520), Clonmacnois (548) and elsewhere which made Ireland renowned in Europe for two centuries. So liberal an education could there be obtained that it was even remarked in the ninth century that if anyone in western Europe knew Greek he must be an Irishman or the pupil of an Irishman. For with all the ramifications of its missionary efforts the fame of Irish learning spread far and wide: the Irish monks took their scholarship with them everywhere so that to-day there are Irish manuscripts of the seventh and eighth centuries to be found in all great Continental libraries. We may take as a typical figure St. Columbanus (died 615) who left the monastery of Bangor on Belfast Lough in 590 to preach to the Burgundians, the Alemans of the Upper Rhine, and the Lombards of North Italy, and at the same time to establish such famous monasteries as Luxeuil in the Vosges, St. Gall in Bavaria and Bobbio in Lombardy.

II. The Roman Church

The very year St. Columba died a mission from Rome reached the Isle of Thanet. It must not be regarded as though it were an isolated expedition, the result of the whim of the moment. It was one small part of a general policy, for the first time clearly outlined and defined for the Church of Rome by Pope Gregory the Great. When this Roman noble resigned the high office of Prefect of Rome and entered the Church to become Bishop of Rome, there was illustrated in his career the way in which the gap between the old secular and the new spiritual Rome was so often to be bridged. And Gregory took with him ideas which made the Church more clearly imperialist and propagandist. His work anticipated many of the ways by which the medieval Papacy was to enlarge its authority until six hundred years later it had attained political and spiritual pre-eminence in Europe. For circumstances combined to compel the Papacy to act as an independent authority, unrestricted by any temporal control, and Gregory frequently ignored his nominal overlord, the Emperor at Constantinople, and negotiated his own treaties with the Lombard kings in Italy. He established his own position firmly within the Patrimony of St. Peter by a vigorous programme of reform. He strengthened the claim of his bishopric to universal authority in the Church by his activities abroad: he condemned the current evils in the Frankish Church, he had the satisfaction of seeing the Visigoths turn from their

Arianism, he set on foot the conversion of the English, and in all cases he drew the ties with Rome theoretically tight. So after a long silence the voice of Rome was being heard again in the West, but speaking through the Church. The conversion of the English was destined to prove of greater benefit to Rome and of more profound significance to Europe than Gregory could have imagined, for the Anglo-Saxons knew no Emperor and they knew the claims of no other bishop than the Bishop of Rome. Their clergy were far more enthusiastic supporters of the Pope than the clergy of either Italy or Gaul and consequently, when they took Christianity back to the Continent and carried through the evangelization of Germany where the Roman soldiery had failed to penetrate, they bound the newly converted territories to obedience to the Roman see.

The efforts of Rome to convert England proceeded by two stages.

I. THE MISSION OF ST. AUGUSTINE, 597

Gregory entrusted the enterprise to his own monastery of St. Andrew: the prior, Augustine, and forty monks traversed Gaul in 596, overcame the fears that nearly caused the mission to be abandoned altogether, and landed at Thanet just before Easter 597. Their friendly reception belied all their fears. Ethelbert of Kent (c. 560–616) had married a Christian, Bertha, daughter of the Merovingian king of the Franks, who had never given up the practice of her faith, and no doubt used skilful persuasion upon her husband to reject his pagan beliefs. In any case, Kent had for so many years imported the chief things of its material civilization from Gaul that it was not likely to look upon the religion of Gaul with any disfavour. It was customary for Rome to make its first appeal to the rulers and work its way downwards to the common people; still, it is probable that superstitious loyalty and habits of obedience would urge the men of Kent to go over to Christianity with their king. And as Ethelbert had at this time a vague authority over the lands south of the Humber and certainly exercised control over his nephews, Sebert, the king of the East Saxons, and Redwald, the king of the East Angles, it was not difficult after his conversion to carry the new religion to both these kingdoms.

Augustine was thus able to found Christianity in the three kingdoms of Kent, Essex and East Anglia. Though himself a monk, he instituted a diocesan organization under Gregory's directions. So far as Britain was concerned, Gregory evidently believed that its political geography was unchanged: he had only the surviving literary works of the Empire to guide him and was quite ignorant of what had been taking place. Therefore he ordered Augustine to make London the centre of his own metropolitan see and to consecrate twelve bishops to serve under him for the southern province; for the northern province he was to consecrate a metropolitan with his headquarters at York, who after Augustine's death was to rank equal in authority with his successor, and he also was to have twelve bishops to assist him. Christianity was not, however, at all firmly rooted, for Augustine was a man of limited capabilities, essentially one who could obey rather than initiate and lead. It was fortunate that his lack of statesmanship and tact was compensated to some extent by the wisdom and continued guidance of the Pope who, for example, advised him not to suppress the pagan feasts but to turn them into Christian festivals, to make the pagan temples into Christian churches, and not to bother about the correct liturgy to use but to take the best part out of all the liturgies he knew. It was, however, unfortunate that Augustine failed to reach a working agreement with the representatives of the British Church in the two conferences he held with them: he should have known that the Church of St. Alban, St. Illtud and St. David, with its old traditions and achievements, was not likely to obey his arrogant demand that it should submit itself to the rule of a newly arrived foreigner with a precarious hold upon one small district. The British Church, for its part, looked with suspicion upon anything emanating from among the Anglo-Saxons and would not let its Christianity overcome its natural antipathies. That typified a racial surrender which it could not bring itself to consider. Therefore the British Church made its great refusal and lost a great opportunity for ever. After Augustine's death in 605 and Ethelbert's in 616, there was a return to paganism in the south-east. Since acceptance of Christianity was at this time and later purely formal and made little or no practical difference to the lives of the people at large, apostasy (if a term of such definite meaning can be used at all) was easy.

II. THE MISSION OF PAULINUS, 625

Once again the introduction of Christianity was made possible through a woman, for Ethelbert of Kent's daughter married King Edwin of Northumbria (617–33) and took Paulinus north with her

as her chaplain.   In 627 Edwin was converted and made himself
the champion of Roman Christianity in the north.   Once more the
future seemed bright, for this Christian monarch became the most
powerful of the English kings.   But the time of his conversion was
also the time when that remarkable man Penda came to the throne
of Mercia, and for a generation his political rivalry with Northumbria was to have as its sequel the retarding of Christianity,
whether of the Roman or the Celtic type.   His defeat and slaying
of Edwin at the battle of Hatfield near Doncaster in 633 caused a
temporary pause in the rise of Northumbria and a corresponding
eclipse of Roman Christianity in the north of England.   Paulinus
felt it necessary to desert his bishopric and take refuge with the
queen in Kent, leaving James the Deacon to battle alone in Deira
for another generation.

The ground lost in Northumbria was soon more than regained,
but the victory was not that of the Roman but of the Celtic Church.
We must here slightly anticipate our discussion of political events.
Edwin of Deira had gained the throne of Northumbria only by
slaying Ethelfrith, the representative of the Bernician royal house,
in 617 and driving his two sons, Oswald and Oswy, into exile.   For
seventeen years they found refuge in Iona and there became earnest
and sincere Christians.   Shortly after Edwin's death in 633, Oswald
returned to Northumbria, managed to defeat the forces of Penda's
ally, Cadwallon, the king of the Welsh Britons, at Heavenfield in
the Tyne valley, and was eagerly accepted as king in both Deira
and Bernicia.   It was at his express invitation that Iona sent Aidan
(d. 651) to him in 634 to help in the christianization of his realm.
Aidan fixed his headquarters at Lindisfarne, or Holy Island, a few
miles from the royal castle of Bamborough: cut off from the mainland at high tide, it gave tangible expression to the Celtic habit of
withdrawing from worldly activities when the desire for solitude
was uppermost, but it would have been considered a totally useless
centre by any representative of Roman Christianity.   Oswald and
Aidan worked in harmonious co-operation to win the north from
paganism.   Once again, however, the political rivalries with Mercia
intervened.   Penda defeated and killed Oswald at 'Maserfield' in
Shropshire in 642, and it was not until the pagan warrior was himself slain by Oswald's brother Oswy at the Winwaed (near Leeds)
in 655 that the work of conversion could follow a comparatively
uninterrupted course.

Before the century was ended, the remaining kingdoms of the Heptarchy had formally adopted Christianity and in nearly all cases the credit is due to Celtic inspiration. Mercia was evangelized by the two brothers, Chad and Cedd, disciples of Aidan: Penda had been no persecutor, no fighter of purely religious wars, and with the tolerance of a polytheistic pagan had left his subjects to do as they pleased. There were no Christian martyrs and he even permitted his own son to become a Christian in 653, from which date there began the steady conversion of the Middle Angles. Some two years later Cedd reconverted Essex, which had apostasized from Rome forty years earlier. East Anglia was not evangelized directly from Lindisfarne but by a Burgundian, Felix, who reached the country about 630, but here again the work was aided by the perfervid preaching of Fursa, an Irish monk. Wessex presents some difficulty. If Bede's account is trustworthy, the conversion of Wessex is unique in that it was set on foot neither from Canterbury nor yet from Lindisfarne but directly by the Pope in Rome, who authorized one Birinus to be given episcopal consecration and sent to England to preach the gospel 'in the furthest inland regions'. It is quite plain that Bede had no trustworthy account and the details he gives are open to destructive criticism: Birinus was the bearer of no Roman name, he flatly disobeyed the papal orders by deciding to stop his journey short and reside among the West Saxons, he apparently had no relations with the Roman mission in Kent and he walked out of history as mysteriously as he entered it. It has been suggested that Birinus was an Irishman, possibly named Byrne, who had wandered like so many of his countrymen over the Continent, been consecrated in Italy and decided to make the West Saxon territory the scene of his missionary activities; he reached Wessex some time after 635, converted its king and baptized him in the presence of Oswald of Northumbria, the supporter of the Celtic Church, made Dorchester the centre of his activities and later retired in the usual Celtic way from the world. Whatever the truth may be, Wessex was won from its paganism. Sussex alone remained in its geographical isolation, curiously untouched by any Christian influence from Kent, until in 681 the Northumbrian bishop Wilfrid sought refuge there from his enemies and spent five years converting the South Saxons.

The Celtic Church had made a truly magnificent contribution to the sum of the world's good: it had maintained itself in Wales and Ireland entirely on its own merits, it had preached the gospel in remote parts as it had never been preached before, it had espoused the cause of civilization and education in a still barbarous society. There can be no two opinions that in the actual work of converting England it had played much the larger part, for the Roman Church could claim credit for little more than Kent, East Anglia in part and possibly Wessex. Nevertheless, the Celtic Church had no power to remain on the heights and its decline was quite inevitable. It depended for its success entirely upon an emotional enthusiasm and zeal which in the nature of things must be transient. In its monastic and missionary system too much was left to individuals and there was no effective means of co-ordinating their efforts and controlling their activities. Discipline was so lax that any monk who desired to 'peregrinate' could leave his monastery when it pleased him and even abbots would abandon their charges to lead the life of a solitary. The lack of any adequate centralized authority meant that churches would be founded by individual fervour and no steps be taken to see that they remained vital and prosperous. We can see the result best in those parts of Germany which the Celtic Church evangelized: Christian communities were established but they were not united to form a provincial church but left in isolation. It is quite clear that the Celtic Church was taking its stand upon its traditions rather than upon any clear principles for future action and, ill-organized and ill-disciplined as it was, it could not hope to surmount periods of doubt and danger. On the other hand, the system of the Roman Church was so designed as to avoid these precise defects of the Celtic Church. It might not keep the ideal so perfect: even Bede commented on the disappearance of spirituality when lordly abbots took the place of humbler men who had the common touch and a genuine contempt for values founded on money. But it guaranteed that the ideal would be preserved, for its centralized organization, based upon episcopal sees and not upon monasteries, made for durability, long-term planning, co-ordination and discipline. The future lay with the Roman Church.

For this reason it is a mistake to exaggerate the importance of the so-called Synod of Whitby in 664, to describe it as 'one of the great turning-points in the history of the English race', and to speak of its immense political significance as though, if the decision had been given in favour of the Celtic Church, England would have been side-tracked from European developments and remained outside Latin Christendom, unable to share in the cultural legacy of

Rome. For the Celtic Church was already losing ground everywhere, even in its own home: Southern Ireland itself had fully a generation earlier accepted the Roman Easter; many of the leading representatives of the Irish Church in Northumbria, like St. Cuthbert, St. Cedd and St. Hilda, the abbess of Whitby, were quite willing to do likewise when Oswy announced his decision in favour of Rome for personal and political rather than religious reasons. It is far from the truth to imagine that the two Churches had been growing more hostile. For in fact there was a fair measure of co-operation between them: Aidan and James the Deacon in Northumbria, Felix and Fursa in East Anglia, found it possible to work together, and Aidan was held in honour by the Roman bishops in the south. The Council of Whitby was designed to resolve difficulties and promote harmony, not to precipitate strife. The confusion caused by two rival church systems at work over the same ground was borne home upon Oswy when he found in 664 that, owing to the different methods of calculating Easter, he would soon be celebrating the feast whilst his wife, a Roman Christian, was still engaged on her Lenten fast. Moreover, his son, whom he had made an under-king of Deira, had also embraced the Roman form, and there was the immediate danger that religious divergences might be added to the political differences that already existed between Deira and Bernicia. When Oswy withdrew his adherence to 'one remote corner of a most remote island', as Wilfrid, the protagonist of the Roman cause, described Iona in the course of the debate, and transferred it to Rome, he did not decide the current of events, he simply recorded its direction. The choice had settled itself, he did not make it; the result would have been the same whatever decision he had made. Thereafter the end was quick in coming: Iona itself submitted in 716, and by 768 even the British Church, despite its isolationism and racial antagonism, had come to acknowledge the supremacy of Rome.

The Synod of Whitby signalled that the field was clear for action, and the Church of Rome had the chance to show what contribution it could now make to the political as well as the religious life of England.

It is really remarkable that there should have come immediately to the front three men whose work was to exemplify in the fullest possible manner all that the conversion of England and the connexion with the Church of Rome involved. These were Benedict Biscop, Wilfrid of Ripon and Theodore of Tarsus.

BENEDICT BISCOP (628–90)

A member of a Northumbrian noble house, he illustrates in his work the value to be obtained from a close connexion with the Continent. Six times he made the arduous visit to Rome, and he never returned from his travels without bringing back with him foreign craftsmen, like glassmakers, and foreign teachers, like the arch-chanter of St. Peter's, Rome, and pictures, manuscripts and other treasures. All these made their contributions to the building and reverent adornment of those twin monasteries of stone at Wearmouth (674) and Jarrow (681) which he founded and placed under the Rule of St. Benedict. He realized that the most dangerous obstacle to the rapid spread of Roman Christianity lay in the fact that education was provided in England only by the Irish Church: Roman usages could not hope to prevail unless a native clergy was produced which knew them. Therefore Benedict set up his monasteries to offer an education equally good but decidedly not Celtic. It was Benedict's library that made Bede's learning possible. Furthermore, as befitted one who had received the tonsure at Lérins and been trained as a Benedictine monk, he was determined that his foundations should not be vitiated by Celtic monastic thought but subjected to Roman conceptions of organization and discipline: there should be no attachment to a locally powerful family, no bishops living within their walls, no lax views about residence. So Wearmouth-Jarrow remained to perpetuate the influence of Rome long after its great champions had died, leaving no one competent to carry on their labours, and to stand like Roman fortresses inside a community which continued, despite the decision at Whitby, to be largely Celtic in its outlook.

WILFRID (634–710)

Like Benedict, he was a Northumbrian noble who had turned ecclesiastic, becoming abbot of Ripon about 661 and bishop of the Northumbrians in 664. He had been the uncompromising spokesman on behalf of Rome at Whitby, and his fame was always to rest upon the fact that, first among Englishmen, he perceived and insisted upon the unity and solidarity of Latin Christendom and on England's part therein. Very early in his life he had made a pilgrimage to Rome and that had fired his imagination and enlarged his vision: henceforward he stressed the importance of the connexion with the Continent and fought hard against provincialism in all its forms. In his stormy life of quarrels with his superiors, he created precedent by making frequent appeals direct to Rome. And he was particularly determined to have no truck with the peculiar customs of the Irish Church but to extirpate them ruthlessly. The educational methods of Benedict Biscop might be effective in the long run but they were too slow for Wilfrid's impetuous temperament. Therefore he attempted a short cut: he reached his objective but only at the cost of much bitter feeling. The purposeful magnificence of his way of life, with his scores of retainers and elaborate feasts and emphasis upon ceremony and ritual, impressed the name of 'Rome' upon the minds of the illiterate populace as he made his tours of his diocese and deliberately dissociated the Roman from the Irish Church with its frugalities and austerities. He concentrated on architecture and sculpture, both of them arts to which the Irish Church had paid little attention: he obtained the services of foreign masons and craftsmen to build his stone churches at York, Ripon and Hexham, and furnished their altars with embroidered cloths and their lecterns with illuminated service-books. Furthermore, he countered the distinctive monasticism of the Irish Church by being, according to his own boast, the first man to introduce into English monastic life the Rule of St. Benedict, which was by this time normally accepted on the Continent. Only a man of great force of character could have influenced his contemporaries as he did, and there is no reason to doubt that it was Wilfrid who gave the Roman Church the position it so rapidly reached in Northumbria and to that extent, at all events, he made simpler the organizing work of Theodore.

Nevertheless, to many historians Wilfrid can make no appeal. They deplore his lack of Christian humility and patience, his love of pomp, and the accumulation of wealth by this seventh-century Wolsey which was setting the Church upon its most dangerous course. They point out that, though Wilfrid's chaplain, Eddi, writes a panegyrical biography of him, Bede is strangely reluctant to extol his praises. In his constant bickerings with his archbishop, Theodore, and the Northumbrian king this man, they assert, was fighting personal quarrels for personal advantages; he was opposing a much-needed reform when he fought against Theodore's division of the great sprawling bishopric of Northumbria into four sees, because it would lessen his own authority at a time when he was possibly hoping to persuade the Pope to make York the seat of a separate archbishopric; he was furnishing an almost unique example of conflict between Church and State when he went almost out of his way to irritate the king of Northumbria. Conduct such as this was surely not compatible with the traditions of Roman Christianity which always stressed as absolutely essential obedience to authority and friendly co-operation with temporal powers. On the other hand, his supporters rebut these charges by contending that without wealth the culture and civilization of Rome, as expressed in architecture, art and other amenities of life, could not have been established, that Theodore acted arbitrarily and certainly tactlessly in not first consulting Wilfrid concerning the splitting of his diocese, that in fighting his king Wilfrid was contesting the supremacy of State over Church, a very timely protest when ecclesiastics were regarded as little more than the docile servants of local kings. Whatever the right and wrong of it all, Wilfrid was forced three times into exile, during which he began the evangelization of the Frisians (678), converted the Saxons of Sussex and the Isle of Wight (681–6) and worked with good result among the Mercians (692–702).

THEODORE OF TARSUS (669–90)

When Theodore landed in England, the Church, far from providing an example of unity to the State, presented an inevitable picture of confusion. It could not have been otherwise in the process of conversion, for the country had been divided among many peoples and each had had to be converted by itself. This piecemeal work, however, meant that the boundaries of a kingdom became the boundaries also of a bishop's diocese and that the bishop was apt to identify his interests closely with those of his king. Not only were many such dioceses far too large for effective administration but, under the influence of the monastic system of the Irish Church, there was a danger that the bishop might be left with no authority at all and that the diocesan system might perish in England as it had already done in Ireland. Thus in 669 Theodore found only three bishops in the country: Wini who had been expelled from the see of Winchester and had actually bought the see of London; Chad and Wilfrid, who were both claiming to be bishop of the Northumbrians. This was the result of King Oswy's confused ideas, for though he was now a Roman Christian he did not understand that a bishop ought to have a properly defined area of authority; so he still retained the views of the Irish Church concerning episcopacy and saw no harm in appointing two bishops. Moreover, the throne of Canterbury had been vacant for three years so that the English Church had no one at its head.

Into this ecclesiastical chaos entered Theodore of Tarsus at the age of sixty-six to become the real founder of the Church in England. Until this time the English Church had had only the loosest ties with Latin Christendom, and as long as the Irish Church was operating successfully in the country little could be done to tighten the connexion. But when its authority began to decline, the advantages of being a member of a Universal Church were seen at once. Two men came from abroad to give invaluable service: Archbishop Theodore was a Greek, and his close friend and colleague, Hadrian, made abbot of Canterbury, came from Africa. None but the Roman ecclesiastical system could in these times have been able to place the advanced knowledge and experience of Mediterranean civilization at the service of a northern country only two generations removed from 'heathendom'. In all their work we can detect the influence of Rome passing through the medium of the Church.

Theodore is the first man in English history to whom we can fittingly give the name of 'statesman'. He saw the foolishness of coming into direct conflict with Irish customs, for if he had alienated all those who had been educated in the Irish Church he could not have found others to take their place and the resultant disorganization might well have thrown the country back into paganism. Therefore he followed the wiser course of conciliation: he appointed as bishops prominent members of the Irish Church who had accepted the supremacy of Rome, like St. Chad and St. Cuthbert; he left Lindisfarne to its own devices; he allowed the 'mixed monasteries' to continue. On the main issues of government, however, he allowed no compromise.

(i) The work of organization

Theodore was undoubtedly a genius in a task of this kind and he provided the Anglo-Saxon Church with the permanent framework of its administration. (a) He placed the diocesan system of government upon a firm basis, not only by carefully choosing as bishops men of ideas like his own whenever opportunities occurred, but also by splitting up the quasi-tribal bishoprics. It was in the course of this work that he fell foul of Wilfrid, but he kept stubbornly to his policy and at his death the number of bishoprics had been raised from seven to fifteen. (*b*) He insisted that all bishops must look to the archbishop of Canterbury as their spiritual superior and their guide in matters of perplexity. (*c*) He convoked national synods, like those at Hertford in 672 and at Hatfield in 679, at which the presence of all the bishops was expected, though not obtained. Thereby he emphasized the unity of the Church: no longer should there be a collection of well-nigh independent local churches, but one church which should deliberate upon its affairs as one body. And by presiding at these synods Theodore stressed the precedence of Canterbury. (*d*) Theodore used to be given the credit for the creation of a system of parishes. However much a parochial organization fell in line with his ideas, there is no evidence at all that he did anything either to institute it or encourage it. Rather was it a much later and a slow and unobtrusive development, springing from the requirements of bishops and private landowners: the first came to need auxiliary centres from which they could administer far-off parts of their dioceses, whilst the second erected chapels on their estates and nominated priests to act as their private chaplains. These priests were, of course, under the jurisdiction of the bishop, but the right of appointment, that is of lay patronage, remained with the founder's descendants to indicate how strong the proprietary principle was in the foundation of parish churches. The evolution of parishes in charge of a resident priest had begun before the Norman Conquest but it did not reach its culmination until the twelfth century and it continued until the nineteenth century: it was to be a work of obviously great social importance. (*e*) Theodore introduced order and discipline and set a standard of morality. By the nine canons published at the synod of Hertford—applicable, it is to be noted, to the Church in every part of the land and hence described with misleading exaggeration as 'the first constitutional measure of the collective English race'— he ordered bishops to keep to their dioceses, monks to their monasteries, and priests to their charges. This contrasts sharply with the freedom and individualism allowed by the Irish Church. His *Penitential*, a collection of his decisions on moral points made apparently after his death, contains one novelty in the matter of discipline. So far the Roman Church had known only the public confession of sins. The Irish Church, however, had seen the difficulty of getting sinners so to humiliate themselves, especially if they were people of high social standing, so it introduced the practice of private confession. The broad-minded Theodore saw the value of this and did not hesitate to adopt it from the rival Church and thereby bring about its transmission to the Church Universal.

In Theodore's work for the Church we see the political implications of the conversion of England. Out of disruption and chaos Theodore had brought unity and order. He had founded a great corporation that transcended local boundaries and ignored local patriotisms. It owed allegiance to one man, the archbishop of Canterbury, who might be a West Saxon or a Mercian or a Northumbrian. The bishops had come from all corners of the land to deliberate together in the first quasi-national assemblies England had known and had published decrees affecting the whole Church over the whole country. A country in political disintegration had been presented with the picture, however faint, of a unified church. If we change ecclesiastical into political terms and speak of a national kingdom, an all-powerful king, a national council and national legislation, we shall find all these faintly mirrored for the moment in the Church. And when secular government expanded the scope of its own influence and devised its own machinery of administration out of the traditional institutions of its Germanic past, it called upon the assistance of the Church to put its plans into operation, for it included within its ranks learned and competent men who took their place among the principal advisers of the lay rulers. So the ideas of unity, of centralization and of imperialism that were Rome's passed into the Church in England and through it fortified the State. Political unification will be slow work, but without the union with Latin Christendom England would have found it harder to achieve, and certain it is that the disorderliness of the Celtic-Irish Church would have been no help but, in fact, a serious obstacle. For these reasons we can rightly speak of Theodore of Tarsus as a man of great political as well as ecclesiastical importance.

(ii) *The work of civilization*

It is not surprising that this student of Athens established a school at Canterbury. It was carefully nurtured by him with the assistance of Hadrian and, in its first two years, by Benedict Biscop who had escorted Theodore to England, that is to say, by men who had come personally into contact with the civilization of the Empire and could bring the culture even of the Eastern Mediterranean directly into England: thus at Canterbury the principles of Roman law could be studied and Greek was taught as well as Latin. Theodore's school contributed much to Benedict's famous foundations at Wearmouth and Jarrow which played so notable a part in the cultural pre-eminence of Northumbria. Moreover, by the emphasis he placed upon education Theodore helped the monks to get rid of that unhealthy introspection which resulted in fasts, flagellations and other crucifixions of the flesh: they could turn their zeal outwards to the study of theology, to the illumination of manuscripts, to the building of churches to the greater glory of God. Indeed, in many cases it was the educational side of things which attracted avid Irish scholars into the Roman Church.

SELECT READING

Celtic Church

Stenton, 118–127; Hodgkin, i. 245–57; *C. Med. H.* ii. (1913), 496–513; J. B. Bury, *Life of St. Patrick* (1905); J. A. Duke, *The Columban Church* (1932), 1–138; John Ryan, *Irish Monasticism* (1931), 57–190; Felim ó Briain, 'The Expansion of Irish Christianity to 1200' in *Irish Historical Studies*, iii (1942), 241–66, iv (1943), 131–63; M. L. W. Laistner, *Thought and Letters in Western Europe* (1931), 104–29; A. Gardner, *Handbook of English Medieval Sculpture* (1935), 20–39.

Roman Church

Stenton, 96–118, 130–99; Hodgkin, i. 257–311, 341–7; Chambers, ch. iv; *C. Med. H.* ii (1913), 514–32; A. H. Thompson, 'Northumbrian Monasticism' in A. H. Thompson (ed.), *Bede* (1935), 60–101; B. Colgrave (ed.), *Eddius Stephanus, The Life of Bishop Wilfrid* (1927: trans.); R. L. Poole, 'St. Wilfrid and the See of Ripon' in *Studies in Chronology and History* (1934), 56–81; W. Stubbs, 'Theodore' in *Dictionary of Christian Biography* (1877–87); M. Deanesly, 'The Familia at Christchurch, Canterbury' in *Essays . . . to T. F. Tout* (1925), 1–13; M. Deanesly, 'Early English and Gallic Minsters' in *T.R.H.S.*, 4th Series, xxiii (1941), 25–52.

CHAPTER IV

THE MOVEMENT TOWARDS POLITICAL UNITY

THE inter-related history of several kingdoms is apt to confuse the reader with its intricate detail and its picture of appalling confusion. It is well, therefore, to remember that the two main themes before 900 on which we should concentrate our attention are the political unification of the country and the conversion and christianization of England, with a practical rather than theoretical assessment of the political, social, economic, and cultural consequences. Though for the sake of clarity it is better to discuss them separately, they were never so divorced in fact and depended so much upon each other that the graph of their success and failure is the same.

During the seventh and eighth centuries the political centre of England moved from Northumbria into Mercia and thence into Wessex. There were other kingdoms in the south-east of the country where settled conditions of life were more easily attained so that the first rulers to whom the title of 'Bretwalda' was accorded came from that quarter: Aelle of Sussex at the close of the sixth century, Ethelbert of Kent until his death in 616, and Redwald of the East Angles for some ten years afterwards. These south-eastern kingdoms had a serious defect: they had no room for expansion as Northumbria had into Strathclyde and Scotland, and Mercia into Wales, and Wessex into Devon and Cornwall, and therefore, unless by going to war, not with the Celts but their own more formidable kinsmen, they could not enlarge the small scope of their authority. It soon became evident that it was just a question which of the three greater powers was going to absorb them.

I. The Kingdom of Northumbria

The seventh century is acclaimed as the 'golden age' of Northumbria when there seemed a possibility, though it never became an actual fact, that it would lead the country to unity, and when it was without doubt the home of a finer culture than was to be seen elsewhere in contemporary Europe. Why it should have first attained fame is largely bound up with events elsewhere in the country, with which it is preferable to deal separately, but naturally it made its own contributions towards its own success.

I. THE EARLY ATTAINMENT OF NATURAL FRONTIERS

It is evident that the Anglian settlers were involved in a long and fierce struggle with the Celtic people. In its political geography Northumbria included at first the two provinces of Deira, occupying central and eastern Yorkshire, and Bernicia, lying to the north of it as far as the Forth. For many years they had gone their own ways and been ruled by separate dynasties: of these the first satisfactory notice we have is from Bede, who refers to the House of Ida in Bernicia (547) and the House of Aelle in Deira (560), but neither of these kings has left any permanent traces of his activities. The first ruler to begin the consolidation of the Anglian kingdom in the north was Ida's grandson Ethelfrith (593–616): though his domination was transient, based as it was solely on military prowess, yet he gave clear definition to the twofold task to which his successors were to address themselves throughout the seventh century. First he turned to the work of defence against outside enemies in the north and in the west. In 603 he gained the victory of Dawston in Liddesdale over a coalition between the Scots of Dalriada (Argyll) and the Britons of Strathclyde. In this, the first of the Anglo-Scottish conflicts, he secured his position south of the Forth. In, or shortly before, 616 he defeated near Chester the Britons of the region between the Upper Severn and the Dee, extending his authority to the Irish Sea and driving a permanent wedge between the Celts of Wales and the Celts of Strathclyde. It would have been extremely dangerous if the attempt to divide the enemies' forces had been longer postponed, for there were indications that the Celts, confronted by a common foe, were discovering unity and patriotism, as expressed in the name they adopted of the 'Cymry' or 'companions', which has left its memorial in the modern 'Cumberland'. And secondly, he began the work of union within Northumbria. Ethelfrith married the daughter of Aelle of Deira and managed, about 605, to dispossess Aelle's son and heir Edwin, thus for a time getting the two provinces under his own control. The military might of Ethelfrith was overcome in 616 by Redwald of the East Anglians during his brief period of aggression and Ethelfrith himself was slain; still, he had provided his kingdom with not unsatisfactory or indefensible frontiers: the

Humber in the south, the North Sea and the Irish Sea to east and west, and the narrow land-frontier of the Forth and Clyde in the north. This was, at least, a satisfactory position as compared with the vague and fluctuating frontiers of Mercia and Wessex at this time. It meant that the rulers of Northumbria would have an opportunity to settle down and face the problem of how to organize the work of government and force their subjects into unity.

II. THE OUTSTANDING ABILITY OF THE NORTHUMBRIAN KINGS

In the seventh century Northumbria was fortunate in her line of kings: Edwin (617–33), Oswald (634–42), Oswy (643–70). Their military exploits can be briefly summarized. Edwin was that son of Aelle of Deira who had been driven into exile by Ethelfrith. He took up the policy outlined by his predecessor, strengthening his northern frontier against the Picts and his western frontier against the Britons and absorbing at home the British principality which had so far held out successfully in the forests of Elmet. Never again was Northumbria to claim so widespread a predominance, for Kent alone had apparently not acknowledged his paramount position. His overthrow at Hatfield in 633 by a combined force of North Welsh under Cadwallon and Mercians under Penda was a melancholy event: it divided Bernicia from Deira again, it caused the kingdom of Northumbria to split up among petty princes and to fall a victim to the ravages of the revengeful and remorseless Celts, it almost blotted out the newly founded Christian faith. Later Northumbrian kings were not to press their claim to authority in the south and it was really an advantage to limit territorial ambitions: there was little lost when Oswald could not dominate the Mercians and when Oswy's power did not pass the Humber. Oswald came back from Iona to fight both for his royal rights and for his religious convictions: he defeated and killed Cadwallon at Heavenfield near Hexham in 634 and restored discipline and unity to Northumbria. But his death at the hands of Penda of Mercia at 'Maserfield' (probably Oswestry in Shropshire) in 642 again brought political disintegration in its train: indeed, for several years Deira came under Penda's supervision. Oswy with undaunted courage worked in Bernicia to restore the fortunes of his dynasty and his defeat of Penda at the battle of the 'Winwaed' (a stream near Leeds) in 655 at last placed him securely on the throne. The rise of Northumbria to pre-eminence had been chequered with misfortune, and even the patriotic utterances of the Northumbrian Bede cannot conceal the fact that after Edwin's death Mercia was growing at its expense. Nevertheless, only rulers of strong character and firm resolve could in those days, when the power of the sword was everything, have snatched victory so often from the teeth of disaster.

III. THE INFLUENCE OF THE CHURCH

For the first time we have an opportunity to observe the action of Christianity, both Celtic and Roman, upon political life. We can view it best from two angles: (a) The ideal of an ordered and settled government. We can appreciate how novel this conception was after so many weary generations of warfare when we read the description in Bede of how 'a weak woman might have walked with her new-born babe over all the island, even from sea to sea, without any harm or danger'. Now, the three great kings had been very closely associated with Christianity. Edwin had welcomed a Roman missionary and been converted, and his death had been followed by a relapse into paganism and, along with it, into anarchy. Oswald had been the staunch friend of a Celtic missionary and for his virtues had been canonized the first of the Anglo-Saxon saints. The voice of Oswy had been decisive in the council at Whitby. It would be to deny the record of history to assert that it was only with the advent of Christianity and only through its influence that men could rise above the mere idea of military triumphs and learn and appreciate the art of civil government. Nevertheless, the Church was always on the side of authority and could do much to assist. It is noticeable that the Northumbrian kings began to adopt some of the practices of Rome in their court life and in their journeyings through their realms, and there seems to be dawning the conception of an autocracy that must be exercised for the public good. At all events, a tradition had been established and, though it was destined not to remain steadfast in Northumbria, it was remembered and followed elsewhere and never died again in England. (b) The work of civilization, especially in the remarkable development of learning. We have only to contrast the scholarship in Christian Ireland with the illiteracy of pagan England to realize the part that the Christian Church was to play in this respect. For in much less than three generations the Church had helped to make Northumbria, which had been completely provincialized for a century and a half, one of the most famous centres of learning in Western Europe. Yet again we perhaps too readily use the language of superlatives. So far as intellectual life is concerned, there is no doubt that Christianity was the channel by which the barbarians in Britain obtained access to classical culture. But this was not intentional on the Church's part: it was incidental and, because it was incidental, its effect was small. We have only to try to put into numbers the proportion of those who could read and write Latin and the still smaller proportion of those who were acquainted with Latin literature to place the matter in its proper perspective. And the phenomenon of such men as Bede and Alcuin would be inexplicable unless we accept the position that the mental outlook of the society from which they sprang closely resembled that of the rest of Western Europe and that it only needed a certain form of education to produce men of high culture if their mental endowments were sufficient. Later on we shall see this truth exemplified again when the pagan Northmen in two generations produced an archbishop of Canterbury in Oda and a cultured reformer in Bishop Oswald of Worcester. And not many years are needed to separate the post-Conquest Norman churchmen from heathendom. Northumbria happened to be the fortunate meeting-place of two streams of culture. The influence which came from Ireland by way of Iona and Lindisfarne has already been discussed: it is, however, the influence of Latin Christendom that permeates most strongly the work of the great Northumbrian scholars like Wilfrid, Benedict Biscop and, above all, Bede, the monk of Jarrow, to whom the Franks a century later gave the respectful title of 'Venerable'. Brought up under the care and instruction of Benedict Biscop, living all his days in one monastery with but few visits to the outside world, his was the life of the complete scholar. His intelligence was encyclopaedic and could easily embrace all known branches of learning, and his output of work was truly prodigious: most of the thirty-six volumes he wrote on varied subjects still survive. He was first and foremost the theologian and Biblical scholar, studying the Latin and Greek versions of the Bible and the writings of the Early Fathers of the Church and producing voluminous commentaries upon them. He was the scientist whose curiosity led him to study and write upon natural phenomena, chronology and grammar. He was the historian who in his mature years wrote with infinite care the immortal *Ecclesiastical History*. The fame of Bede, the most remarkable man of letters of his day, spread far and wide throughout civilized

Europe and his writings were accepted for centuries as standard authorities. And his influence was perpetuated, however indirectly, in the great school of York, which was founded by his friend and perhaps pupil, Egbert, when he became archbishop of York, and which instructed the celebrated Alcuin who was summoned by Charles the Great in 782 to organize his famous Palace School in Gaul.

Northumbria was the home of more than literature, which has no monopoly of culture, and we shall under-estimate the diversity of her achievements if we do not bear in mind the artistic talent which wrought the glorious illuminations of the 'Lindisfarne Gospels' (c. 721) and carved the Ruthwell Cross near Dumfries and the Bewcastle Cross on the moorlands north of Hadrian's wall.

A tentative advance towards the political unification of England had been made. Such an ideal was as yet far from even partial achievement but the first great step had been taken towards it. For men began to look to Northumbrian kings for guidance of their own motion and not because a conqueror had forced them to do so. In Bede's phrase, 'the nobility of all countries frequented their courts and coveted to be received in their service'. The ideal of political unity will disappear in the north of England but it will never vanish from men's minds: it has come at last into the sphere of practical politics. That is the ultimate gauge by which we should measure the permanent contribution of Northumbria to political progress.

The decline and fall of Northumbria had begun long before Bede's death. Its beginnings reached back to Oswy's successor Egfrith (670–85), whose army was routed by the Picts at the overwhelming disaster of Dunnichen Moss (Nectansmere) near Forfar in 685. It was a blow from which there was to be no recovery. Aldfrith (686–704), another son of Oswy's, was a learned prince, the best educated of all the Northumbrian kings, and a staunch friend of the Church, but he found it impossible to keep his kingdom intact and he had to be content to rule firmly a more restricted realm. His death signalled a relapse into anarchy which was only occasionally suppressed: a long list of short-reigning kings who reached the throne through bloodshed and revolutions, the emergence of turbulent subjects strong enough to lord it over the puppet monarchs. Indeed, the physical geography of Northumbria made it difficult for the kings to keep their subjects in order, and rebellion was made easier there than anywhere else in England. Then

Northumbria had no further contribution of permanent value to make, and we must shift our attention southwards.

That Northumbria did no more than show the promise of political unification is not surprising, for too many obstacles barred her way to the final goal. Among them physical geography was not the least. Furthermore, it was from the north that she received her early vital stimulus and, as the history of Northumbrian monasticism shows, her life was interwoven inextricably with Celtic traditions and Celtic thought. It was a most curious situation, for never again did the phenomenon appear of a predominant stream of culture flowing from the north of Europe southwards. The maintenance of Celtic inspiration was essential to the greatness of Northumbria and it was inevitable that they should dwindle together. King Oswy's decision at Whitby to get into closer touch with the alternative southern culture not only went against the current of development but it was foredoomed to failure as a means of preserving Northumbrian ascendancy. For his kingdom did not pass the Humber and the only means of communication with the south-east of England and the Continent was an old Roman road in a narrow coastal plain, which was extremely vulnerable to Mercian attacks. The future obviously lay with kingdoms more happily situated in the south. Political weaknesses and follies contributed their share to the dismal collapse. For there was a lamentable lack of cohesion within Northumbria itself. Bernicia and Deira had been founded separately under different dynasties and were more than ready to fly asunder when an opportunity came: they fell apart on Edwin's death and again on Oswald's death, when Deira placed itself, with Penda's consent, under the rule of one of its own princes until Oswy removed this last representative of the House of Aelle in 655. Even then the two provinces pulled in opposite directions: they seemed likely to favour different churches and, whereas Deira kept her eyes to the south, Bernicia was intent on extending northwards against the Picts. Furthermore, if the Northumbrian kings were not to be content with their natural frontiers and to identify themselves with Celtic traditions and ways, they should have concentrated on a drive to the south. Instead they over-expanded in other directions and this ultimately proved their undoing. Even Edwin had assembled a fleet at Chester to conquer Anglesey and the Isle of Man. His successors dreamed of the conquest of Wales and actually sent an expedition to ravage northern Ireland. Full retribution came under Egfrith when he advanced past the line of the Forth and Clyde into Forfarshire to meet disaster at Dunnichen Moss. Thereafter there came into full view the fatal weakness of Germanic monarchy, seen elsewhere but nowhere so prominently as in Northumbria: the lack of any settled principle of succession to the throne. The custom of choosing the fittest member of the royal house to be king, though admirable in times of peril, implied that all members of the royal family could put forward their claims, and endemic civil war was the result: in the eighth century seven different families were competing against each other and local hatreds and feuds were given free play. In the circumstances the Church was powerless, especially because the rule of bishops had never managed to oust monastic control and monasticism was falling into grave abuses: many monasteries were such only in name, for they were founded and endowed to become the homes of married laymen, their families and retainers, protected by the Church and free from all obligations to the State. Bede himself issued a warning that such fraudulent piety was depriving the temporal power of resources in men and money which were badly needed to preserve it from disaster. Before the close of the eighth century his prophecy was fulfilled, for the attacks of the Northmen with their destruction of the monasteries, genuine and sham, marked the end of a cultural pre-eminence which had outlived political greatness.

II. The Kingdom of Mercia

How it came about that a small community of Angles, settled in the late fifth century round the Middle Trent, should have been able to win its way to unchallenged predominance two centuries later is a problem that must be left largely to the historian's imagination. For little of whatever the Mercians recorded about their achievements has survived: apparently no Mercian chronicle or annals were compiled and all that we have is a short list of kings and a puzzling fragment called the 'Tribal Hidage': so named because it is a catalogue, compiled apparently in the century after Penda's reign, of tribal units in the Midland area with the number of hides attributed to each of them and therefore presumably serving some purpose in connexion with the imposition of tribute. Nor did others do for her what she failed to do for herself. The rise of Mercia may well have been so spasmodic and irregular that no trustworthy traditions were preserved for incorporation in the accounts of later writers, but it is evident that these were hindered by their own local patriotisms from any desire to do justice to Mercia in the century and a half of her greatness. Bede passes over the rebuilding of a Greater Mercia by Penda's son Wulfhere and, like a good Northumbrian, awards the title of 'Bretwalda' to Oswy, who had control of a much more limited area of England. His *Ecclesiastical History* stopped in 731 before Mercia experienced the benefits of the rule of her two greatest rulers. Beyond Bede there is a great darkness which is illuminated only by the 'Early English Annals'. And in this case also the light is dim and biased, for the West Saxon compiler had no desire to minimize the importance of Wessex by extolling the praises of a rival: Mercian expansion at the expense of her southern neighbours is belittled or even ignored, the small triumphs of Wessex arms are magnified into great victories, the first 'Bretwalda' after Oswy is not Ethelbald or Offa of Mercia, although they dominated their century completely, but Egbert of Wessex who came after them. However, if we wish to redress the balance we can but go to the correspondence of Boniface, a West Saxon, or Alcuin, a Northumbrian. Mercia continues to say little on her own behalf except through the medium of royal charters which from the eighth century onwards form the basis of such knowledge as we have. It follows, therefore, that the early history of Mercia must be told with great caution and its later history be freed from misleading arguments founded on prejudiced evidence.

For some reason unknown to us the early settlers who had congregated round the Middle Trent lost their cohesion more completely than the invaders elsewhere and split up into the small-scale regions denoted by the 'Tribal Hidage'. More than a hundred years will go by before they enter into history with Penda, and it is not easy to see how we are to recover the story of these years. Of one thing we can be certain from the fact that the Middle Anglians had by this time pushed their way gradually to the borders of Wales. These hardy folks had undertaken a task from which the Britons had always flinched: they had with undaunted courage waged a long and relentless war upon nature, overcoming their superstitious terrors to overthrow the impenetrable forests and drain the marshes and cut down the reed-beds. The military victories of their neighbours pale into insignificance beside this economic triumph. It was unobtrusive work which no one at the time would think it worth while to record: the story may some time be revealed by tracing the history of the monasteries established in the clearances as they were made.

The powerful character and military talents of Penda (632–55) forced the Midland tribes into some kind of confederation and made them for the first time the nucleus of a 'Greater Mercia' lying between the Humber and the Thames. In the west he brought the Hwicce, a group of West Saxons and Angles settled about the estuary and middle reaches of the Severn, under his control; on the east his victory over the Northumbrians at Hatfield pushed his frontiers through Lincolnshire (Lindsey) to the coast; and before he died he had brought the West Saxons and East Anglians to acknowledge his supremacy. For twenty years his kingdom stood firm across the middle of England. The Britons of Wales, though Christian, found no difficulty in forming a friendly alliance with the pagan and tolerant Mercian. Northumbria could offer no effective challenge until the very end; Wessex was politically negligible. Great as these achievements were, they were outdone by those of his Christian son, Wulfhere (658–75). Fully recognizing the strategic value of controlling the south-east of the country he asserted his suzerainty over Essex, thereby making London a Mercian town, annexed Surrey, dominated the men of Kent, and compelled even the obscure and distant Sussex to accept his overlordship. At the same time Wulfhere had made certain that Wessex would neither threaten his security nor compete with his ambitions, for about 661 he overran her territory, adding Oxfordshire to his own territories to make the Thames a natural frontier, handing southern Hampshire and the Isle of Wight over to Sussex to make of her a counter-balance to Wessex and allowing the rest of that kingdom to fall into disruption among sub-kings. For fifty years after his death in 675 Mercia was prevented from consolidating her position in the south-east by the unexpected and short-lived triumphs of Wessex under Cadwalla and Ine, which took Sussex, Kent and Essex from her grasp, but thereafter she resumed her 'forward' policy in what may still be called with justice the 'Age of Mercia'.

There has been a tendency among historians to react against this description as an exaggeration. To one it is 'an age of little men, of decaying faith, of slumberous inaction' during which Mercia engaged in 'perpetual objectless war, not ennobled by any great names or chivalrous deeds'; to another it is 'a period of dullness

and gloom'. It is said to exhibit that most sterile of political conditions, a balance of power, and to show no real desire for political
unity: since the Mercians established merely a leadership by force
of arms, there were few signs that it would have any permanence.
Furthermore, since Mercia did not emulate the cultural progress
of Northumbria and provided no scholars and only one saint of
note, St. Guthlac, the eighth century was a period of stagnation, a
barren age. The comparison with Northumbria to the detriment
of Mercia is misleading. Northumbria could not sustain her own
position: in the last resort her unity was enforced only through the
power of the sword and it perished with her armies; her culture
was premature and abnormal, fostered as it was by a group of
brilliant men who had the inestimable advantage of two sources of
inspiration, Roman and Irish, one of which had dried up before
Mercia reached the height of her power.

The facts must be left to speak for themselves, and it is well to
group them around our two main themes of development in discussing the two eminent rulers of Mercia whose reigns cover
practically the whole century, Ethelbald (716–57) and Offa (757–96).

I. THE WORK OF POLITICAL UNIFICATION

Nothing reveals the advance in the general conception of unity
better than the regnal titles those kings thought fit to adopt. Ethelbald found the 'king of the Mercians' an inadequate description of
his hegemony and styled himself 'king of the South English', 'king
not only of the Mercians but of those neighbouring peoples over
whom God has set me', even 'rex Britanniae'. Offa for his part
speaks of his 'kingdom of the whole land of the English' (*regnum
totius Anglorum patriae*). His contemporaries, though they did not
confirm what was a most unusual claim to authority over territory
rather than men, so far fell into line as to address him by his normal
title of 'king of the English'. It was without precedent for one man
to be so described, and these rulers well deserved their title for at
least their territorial policy.

The details of Ethelbald's activities are hidden from us, but in
the last pages of his history Bede wrote: 'All the southern provinces
up to the boundary of the Humber with their respective kings are
subject to Ethelbald, king of the Mercians'. We know only that
he extended his rule westward past the Severn estuary into Somerset (733), made a devastating raid upon Northumbria (740), and

towards the end of his reign was faced by a revolt among the West Saxons, who repulsed his forces at Burford in Oxfordshire (750). This success received inordinate praise from the propagandist writer of the 'Early English Annals', but it certainly did not remove the Mercian control from Wessex. Of Offa, his third cousin, we learn much more. Towards the greater powers on his frontiers, he adopted a wise policy of conciliation: in the north he married his daughter to the king of Northumbria but made no attempt to interfere there, for in its state of chaos it was no menace; in the south he married another daughter to the king of Wessex after he had crushed a revolt of the West Saxons in 779 with a heavy hand at Bensington in Oxfordshire and had thrown them back definitely south of the Thames; in the west he brought the Lower Severn valley securely within Mercia and signalized the end of the period of conquest in that direction by constructing Offa's Dyke between the Dee and the Wye, which was not intended to be a fortification like the Roman walls but an earth-line drawn according to physical contours to delimit a quasi-national or racial frontier. It was his drive towards the south-east of England, towards that part of the English Channel which came closest to the Continent, that reveals his vision and proves his ability to achieve his ambitions. As we have seen, the idea was not original to him and it is the most constructive one we meet within the whole of the period of Mercian predominance. To bring it into effect Offa incorporated Sussex and Essex into Mercia and, overcoming a rising of the men of Kent at Otford in 776, kept that territory as a dependent province. And in 794, in the last years of his life, he ruthlessly executed the last king of the East Angles and probably annexed their land to Mercia. So the control of London, the natural political centre of England, and of Canterbury, the ecclesiastical centre, came into his hands.

Furthermore, the epochal advance was measured by the fact that Offa was the first of the Anglo-Saxon kings to have a foreign policy, based on relations with both the future emperor of the West and the pope. So high did his reputation stand in Europe that he could remain firm in his claim to be the equal of Charles the Great and seek to bring about a marriage between his son and a daughter of the Frankish king and, though the negotiations broke down, yet trade relations with Gaul continued unimpaired, and in 796 the two rulers concluded a commercial treaty which guaranteed government protection for the merchants of England and Gaul in their mutual trading and subjected the length of English woven cloth for export to government supervision. And to him came from Rome in 786 the first papal mission to visit England, and as a result he agreed to mark his membership of the comity of Christian peoples by sending each year to Rome a gift of money for the benefit of the Church. As Offa tried to bind his successors to do the same, this has somewhat doubtfully been regarded as the origin of 'Peter's Pence'. It will not be until the time of Edward the Confessor that another mission from the heart of Roman civilization is sent to this country.

It can surely not be doubted that the 'imperium', the vague overlordship of the 'Bretwalda' over his neighbours, was on its way to being displaced by the political conception of the 'regnum', the direct rule of their lands. The royal dynasties that had ruled so long over the whole of Sussex, Essex, East Anglia and Kent vanished. Where, as in Kent, lesser princes lingered on, it was as sub-kings only. Offa evidently claimed that he could dispose of lands as he pleased and that before his underlings could do so they must obtain his consent. 'England' as a political fact was now emerging under the direction of a king whose political vision far transcended provincial limits and local interests and revealed a remarkable conception of the duties and the potentialities of king-ship.

Unfortunately Offa was not fully consistent in his striving to-wards unification: his local patriotism was still strong. He made the greatest mistake of his career when he followed an ecclesiastical policy which went dead against his territorial policy. He was apparently afraid that an archbishop of Canterbury who became hostile might weaken his authority in the south-east; therefore, instead of allying himself closely with the head of the Church, he set up a rival to him. He weakened the position of Canterbury by demanding that Mercia should have an independent archbishop of its own, such as Northumbria had already obtained in 735. The fact that the Pope consented should prevent us from speaking too uncritically about the cause of political unity being fostered by the cohesive force and centralized system of the Church. In 787 the bishop of Lichfield became the metropolitan of Mercia and seven of the twelve bishoprics previously under Canterbury were placed under him. This manifestation of provincialism was clearly a retrograde step, and it was not likely to assist Offa in his drive towards the Channel. Fortunately, after his death the archbishopric of Mercia was allowed to lapse in 803 and the primacy in the south remained indisputably with Canterbury.

Cenwulf (796–821), a far distant relative of Offa, continued to exercise a real overlordship over Sussex, Essex and East Anglia, and his wars against the Welsh princes resumed the Mercian policy of expansion westwards which Offa had abandoned. But he had to repress savagely a revolt of the men of Kent and that district remained uneasy under his authority, and Northumbria and Wessex were left free from Mercian influence as soon as Offa's sons-in-law died. In 825 the West Saxon victory over the Mercians at Ellendun brought the 'Age of Mercia' to a decisive close.

II. THE WORK OF CIVILIZATION

We have already noted the care with which cross-Channel commerce was fostered in the late eighth century. It was presumably the needs of foreign trade especially that urged Offa to strike a new coinage, broader and heavier and finer in execution than anything that went before it, with the result that his silver penny served as a model until the twelfth century. The pejorative criticisms of the 'Age of Mercia' are, however, mainly concerned with learning and literature, and it is true that we shall find no outstanding scholars who can be compared with those who flourished earlier in Northumbria or during the later renaissance under Alfred. Nevertheless, as our knowledge becomes more exact, our appreciation of Mercian contributions to culture is steadily increasing. Doubtless our estimation of Offa's importance might be immeasurably increased if we could recover the lost code of laws he issued, for it would tell us whether he held enlightened theories about the functions of kingship, whether, for example, he stressed his position as the dispenser of justice and the protector of the weak, as the Northumbrian kings had done. Certain it is that the Mercian royal charters must have been the work of a group of royal clerks at headquarters, professionally expert in drawing up written instruments of government. Sculpture, once ascribed to the twelfth century, is now acknowledged to belong to the period of Offa. And Cynewulf, who was after Caedmon the only one we hear of who continued writing religious poetry in the vernacular, is now identified with Mercia and the late eighth century. Existing manuscripts are proved to have originated at Lichfield and, even after the Danish wars of conquest nearly a hundred years later than Offa's reign,

Alfred could still call upon the services of Mercian men of letters to assist him in the intellectual revival in Wessex.

The processes of civilization are of particular interest in their connexion with the history of the Church, which provides one test of their strength or weakness. If it seems that the eighth century saw a lower level of religious life, this should occasion little surprise, for the first raptures of fervent emotionalism could not continue for ever, the age of the saints had to give place to the age of administrators, the ideal had to lose some of its attractiveness when it was institutionalized. Before his death Bede had commented with apprehension upon the decay of religious feeling. And, indeed, the reaction was to be seen at Canterbury as soon as Theodore was dead: his successors could not sustain his commanding position and Bede makes hardly any reference to them or their work at Canterbury. In the circumstances general criticisms were levelled against the Church, as by St. Boniface and Alcuin from abroad, which were often no more than indictments of the sins of the flesh—the acquisitive spirit of avarice, drunkenness, gluttony, excessive luxury in dress. There were two specific evils, however, and these the Church set itself to redress: the slackness of the bishops and the ill-discipline of the monasteries. Among the fifty canons published at the ecclesiastical councils at 'Clovesho' near London in 747 and Chelsea in 787, it was laid down that synods were to meet every six months for the regular supervision of the Church's work, that bishops were to visit every part of their dioceses at least once a year, that monasteries were to be placed under the control of the bishops, who were to be consulted in the appointment of new abbots and abbesses and to see that the monastic rules were observed, thus regulating though not suppressing the open frauds of the lay monasteries which Bede had so sternly denounced. The indictment brought by the Church against itself is not grave and certainly, when compared with the scandals and disorders of the contemporary Frankish Church, it seems trifling. And the work of these and other ecclesiastical councils of the Mercian Age is clear evidence that the Church had a conscious desire and the vitality to correct abuses. And all the time the parishes were being unobtrusively established round churches and chapels served by single priests, and the penitential system, despite the abuse of the practice of allowing money payments in lieu of penance, was imposing something of monastic discipline upon the outside world and procuring some improvement in social as well as religious life. Viewed in the proper contemporary perspective the Church of the eighth century was flourishing rather than stagnant, vital rather than lethargic.

When we ask ourselves what kind of relations existed between the Mercian kings and the Church the answer is not unfavourable. Wulfhere co-operated amicably with Theodore in the division of Mercia into bishoprics. Wulfhere's brother and successor became the patron of many churches and eventually retired from the throne to a monastery, and at his invitation Wilfrid of Ripon spent many years preaching and founding monasteries among his subjects. The next king, Wulfhere's son, likewise abdicated to end his days in Rome. Ethelbald, though scandalously immoral in his private life, made many pious benefactions and in 749 exempted all churches from the burden of secular taxation, and it is not without significance that three Mercians in succession sat on the throne of Canterbury. Offa, though he acted ruthlessly and unscrupulously at times, was in turn a liberal benefactor, presided like his predecessors at the councils which regulated the affairs of the Church, authorized the payment of tithes in 786, and opened the first direct communications between an English temporal ruler and the Pope at Rome.

The eighth century, therefore, cannot with justice be termed a barren age nor, dominated as it was by Ethelbald and Offa whilst Northumbria and Wessex fell into disruption, can it be characterized as a period when there was a balance of power. Mercia, like all other kindgoms, was dependent for its pre-eminence on the abilities of its rulers and, if Offa had been followed by a line of competent successors, Mercia might well have brought about the unification of England. Centrally situated with command over the south-east, it would have sloughed off its provincialism and, however venerated Lichfield might be for its traditions, as Winchester was, geography and commerce were enough to bring London into its own. As it was, Mercia's contribution to the future rested in the fact that it had removed the ruling dynasties in the south and cleared the field for action by Wessex.

III. The Kingdom of Wessex

If we discount the propagandist views of the West Saxon compiler of the 'Early English Annals', dismiss from our minds the knowledge of later events, and base our judgment solely upon what the West Saxons had achieved before the raids of the Northmen began, we must acknowledge that there was little reason to believe that England would owe its unification to Wessex. Three notable kings occupied her throne but each reign was separated by a century, during which the country became politically of no account and for most of the time under the dominance of Mercia.

Of these rulers we have seen that Ceawlin (560–91) was the first to wage a large-scale attack upon his fellow-invaders and that he gained considerable success in his policy of aggrandisement. But shortly after his death his work was more than undone: in 628 the Mercians took from the West Saxons the territory of the Hwicce on the Lower Severn and about 661, under Wulfhere, they annexed the district of the Upper Thames which had been the main original settlement of the West Saxons, forced them to remain in the south-west and even handed the south of Hampshire and the Isle of Wight over to Sussex. Meanwhile there was little unity within Wessex itself, for she followed her usual custom of splitting up among under-kings whenever the occupant of the throne was too weak to exercise authority: this may have been a reflexion of the days when the Gewisse lorded it in Hampshire and Wiltshire, for the word means 'companions' or 'confederates'. Despite these political disasters the men of Wessex slowly and quietly went on colonizing Somerset, Dorset and Devon.

Wessex reached the nadir of its political fortunes when it lay under the supremacy of the Mercian Wulfhere. Then for exactly forty years she leapt unexpectedly into the front rank to establish a temporary political equilibrium with Mercia and Northumbria. Though Cadwalla (685–8), an obscure descendant of Cerdic, did much, before he abdicated to go on pilgrimage to Rome, to rebuild the kingdom of Wessex by removing the under-kings and forcing the Isle of Wight, Sussex, Surrey, and even Kent to recognize his overlordship, it was his successor, Ine (688–726), who revealed the latent capabilities of the West Saxon people. He recognized the wisdom of abandoning the imperialism of Ceawlin which had extended northwards, and he concentrated on expansion along the south coast: on the east he kept Sussex, Surrey and Kent in his allegiance, on the west it would appear from his Laws, which very reasonably regulate the relations between West Saxon and Briton, that he was giving royal encouragement and support to the colonists in Devon and East Cornwall. The real significance of Ine's reign, however, is in the indication that he was constructing his united kingdom on a basis that was not purely military and therefore transient. For about 690 he issued his most valuable collection of customary laws. He has not the credit of producing the first of a remarkably long series of such collections, for that belongs to Ethelbert of Kent who drew up in 602, probably under Merovingian influence as much as through the inspiration of the Church, a series of regulations to protect person and property. Ine's legislation, however, represents a great advance in the declaration of law and its seventy-six clauses, dealing with the Church, the landed aristocracy and the Britons, throw a light upon the nature of Anglo-Saxon society and its economic and, particularly, agrarian problems, for which we shall look elsewhere in vain. And we can see Roman Christianity at work a half-century after its introduction into Wessex by Birinus, for the code is riddled with ecclesiastical thought: for example, all children must be baptized within a month of their birth and Sunday must be kept as a holiday. And the influence of Roman Christianity is portrayed in other directions at this time, for St. Aldhelm (c. 640–709), student of an Irish monk at Malmesbury as well as of Theodore and Hadrian at Canterbury, was writing Latin prose and verse, though in a deliberately fantastic style and vocabulary, whilst Wynfrith, better known as St. Boniface (c. 675–754), left his native Devon at the age of forty to become, with the constant assistance of his fellow-countrymen who sent him both assistants and books, the great evangelizer of Germany and the reformer of the Frankish Church. It must, however, be regretted that for piety's sake Ine, like Cadwalla, abandoned his throne to seek personal salvation at Rome, for once again Wessex relapsed into disorder, resurrected its sub-kings and bowed to the supremacy of Mercia. It says much for the strength of Ine's work that the two great Mercian kings, Ethelbald and Offa, sought to conciliate Wessex rather than subdue her and rule her directly, and evidently the West Saxons had learned sufficiently how to act together to be able to preserve their right to live, if not in an independent, at least in a separate kingdom where they could maintain their political identity.

Almost a century after Ine order came once again hard on the heels of chaos with the accession of her third great ruler, Egbert (802–39), a descendant from Ine's brother. Expelled by Offa from Kent where his father had been a sub-king, he spent some years in exile in Gaul where he had at least the opportunity to study at first hand the imperialistic ambitions and military organization of

Charles the Great. For some twenty years after his return to England as king of Wessex we hear little of his activities, and we may well imagine that he occupied these uneventful years of subjection to Mercia with armed preparations which afterwards gave him four years of astounding success. The death of Cenwulf, the last great king of Mercia in 821, followed as it was by a series of insignificant and short-reigning kings, provided him with his chance to attain predominance. In 825 he turned to the west and overwhelmed the Britons at Galford, placing immediately East Cornwall and eventually all Cornwall permanently within the frontiers of Wessex. During his absence there, the Mercian king crossed the Thames, was met by Egbert at Ellendun, south of Swindon in Wiltshire, and completely routed. That was the death-knell of Mercian supremacy. Sussex, Surrey, Kent, Essex and East Anglia eagerly placed themselves under the rule of a one-time Kentish prince. In 829 he overran Mercia and for a year took the title of King of the Mercians: it was the first time that Mercia had been dominated by a rival power since Penda's defeat nearly two hundred years before.

What Egbert did was undoubtedly a further advance towards political unification, but we must not with the West Saxon chronicler exaggerate his strength. He found it advisable not to continue the annexation of Mercia and was content to watch Mercia regain its independence in 830 under its own dynasty and to treat it on terms of equality. Though the king of Northumbria is said to have come voluntarily to meet him at Dore (near Sheffield) to do him homage, that act certainly had no political consequences. Egbert's achievements had solid worth enough without needing dubious laudation: he had brought the whole of the south coast from Cornwall to Kent into a single and, as it proved, permanent kingdom and he had altered the balance of power definitely in favour of Wessex. It was fortunate that he was followed by an uninterrupted line of brilliant successors for a century and a half, for the great testing-time had come. The last years of Egbert were marked by the first serious Scandinavian raids on England. The new attack from outside was terrible and ferocious, and it seemed very likely that it would smash to pieces all that had been so painfully accomplished since the Conversion. The Anglo-Saxons found themselves brought sharply up against the question of political leadership against the Scandinavian pirates. A leader could not be found among the rivals of Wessex, for very soon Northumbria,

Mercia, and East Anglia were all desolated by the Northmen and their dynasties came to an end. Wessex stood alone. If she could weather the storm successfully despite the enormous odds, then she would be left the unchallenged head of the Anglo-Saxon community, receiving, not enforced, but voluntary recognition from Englishmen in general, and her rulers would be given the opportunity to construct a national rather than a provincial monarchy. For the moment, however, we have to abandon the two principal themes of the slow progress towards political unity and the advance in civilization in order to observe once more the descent of the barbarians upon West Europe.

SELECT READING

Stenton, 201–36; Hodgkin, i. 312–68, ii. 383–446; W. J. Corbett, 'England and English Institutions' in *C. Med. H.* ii (1913), 543–74; Chambers, ch. v; F. M. Stenton, 'Offa' in *Encyclopaedia Britannica* (14th ed.); W. Stubbs, 'Offa' in *Dictionary of Christian Biography* (1877–87); F. M. Stenton, 'The Supremacy of the Mercian Kings' in *E.H.R.* xxxiii (1918), 433–52; A. Gardner, *Handbook of English Medieval Sculpture* (1935), 39–46; T. D. Kendrick, *Anglo-Saxon Art to 900* (1938), 205–210; G. C. Brooke, *English Coins* (1932), 21–9; M. L. W. Laistner, *Thought and Letters in Western Europe* (1931), 130–46; Ephraim Emerton, *Letters of St. Boniface* (1940: trans.); S. J. Crawford, *Anglo-Saxon Influence on Western Christendom* (1933); W. Levison, *England and the Continent in the Eighth Century* (1946), 15–44, 94–173.

CHAPTER V

THE SOURCES OF HISTORY, 871–1066

It is broadly true to say that about the year 900 the age of speculation is coming to an end and we are reaching at last a period of
comparative certainty when our imagination can be bridled by
authenticated facts. We can appreciate the difference most clearly
when we realize that we can for the first time write with reasonable
confidence the history of administration and governmental institutions. Indeed, all the main branches of history—legal, social,
economic, ecclesiastical—are beginning to stand out in their own
distinctiveness in the records of the time. No longer need we exalt
the subsidiary sources of information like archaeology, place-names
and geography into primary sources and base our conclusions upon
them, for they fall into their proper place as affording confirmation
to deductions drawn from written documents. There is one great
exception to this generalization: the literary and documentary
evidence for what was taking place in the Danelaw is so defective
that place-names and personal names have there to be pressed into
service. But, on the whole, evidence in writing is adequate enough
to let us piece together a coherent political history of England in
the two centuries before the Norman Conquest.

Literary Evidence

I. CHRONICLES

The main obstacle to our knowledge of the early centuries has
been the lack of a chronological survey except for the period
597–731 covered by the invaluable *Ecclesiastical History* of Bede,
for after him, as before him, no one else attempted to write a
narrative history. The reign of Alfred, however, saw the beginning of the Anglo-Saxon Chronicle which provides the indispensable
framework of developments before 1066. Indeed, it is only in
England that a nation's history has been set down more or less year
after year over such a long period of time (892–1154). The part
played by Alfred himself in the work of compilation is a matter of
debate that is of slight consequence: the important fact is that
it was the product of the literary activity of his reign and was

completed shortly after 891 so far as the earlier history of the West
Saxon people is concerned. To this part, based on earlier annals, now
vanished, on Bede, on royal genealogies and on traditions, we have
preferred to give the name of the 'Early English Annals' and to
reserve the term Anglo-Saxon Chronicle for the later continuations
of it. For copies were immediately made and circulated throughout
the country and in their respective homes they became so independent in their account of events that it might be better to make the
Anglo-Saxon Chronicle a plural noun: indeed, the only complete
edition of it has had to be printed in six parallel columns. Seven
different MSS. have survived and they provide us with four distinct chronicles and, though the details are controversial, the
explanation of the main divergences is fairly simple.

The Winchester Chronicle (MS. 'A': otherwise called the
'Parker' Chronicle). Essentially a Wessex record, this is the oldest
of the MSS. and is well-nigh contemporary writing. For seven
scribes at Winchester kept the story up to date after 891 until the
close of Edward the Elder's reign in 924. Then for some unfortunate reason interest in it died away and the MS. lay untouched
until 955, by which time the next scribe could apparently remember
remarkably little about the intervening period. The work was
continued until 1001, when the MS. was again neglected for seventy
years. During that time it was removed to Canterbury where ten
short entries were added for the years 1002 to 1070, when the
Winchester Chronicle in Anglo-Saxon ends.

The Worcester and the Peterborough Chronicles. Another copy
of the Alfredian work was sent north, very probably to Ripon.
There it was re-copied and in it was included additional information relating to northern affairs. The Northumbrian 'Gesta' cover
the years 733–806, that is from the time that Bede is no longer of
service to us, and therefore, although mainly a list of assassinations
and depositions, this is our sole authority for the history of that part
of the country at that time. Between 800 and 900 we know practically nothing of what was taking place there, but then a series of
'Northumbrian Annals' for 901–66 was also added by the northern
scribes. Copies of this augmented chronicle were then distributed
elsewhere. One must have been sent into Mercia and there it
received another accretion, the 'Mercian Register', or the 'Annals
of Ethelfleda', which gives a brief description of the warfare with
the Danes between 902 and 924. Eventually this version reached
Worcester abbey, where it was re-copied about 1100 to give us our

present MS. 'D', which goes up to 1079 and contains the best English account of the battle of Hastings and subsequent events. Another copy came from the north down to Canterbury shortly after 1022. Its entries were continued there, and about a century later a copy was made of it at Peterborough abbey to form MS. 'E'. This one alone carried the story on in the vernacular to Stephen's reign.

The Abingdon Chronicle (MS. 'C'). A version which included the 'Mercian Register' and ended at 977 was copied at Abingdon abbey about 1050 with a continuation until 1066.

Although Latin was at the time acknowledged to be the language of scholarship, these chronicles were written throughout in the vernacular Anglo-Saxon, a remarkable event in the literature of Europe. From the point of view of the historian three characteristics call for particular attention: (*a*) The chronicles are annalistic in form, giving simply a date and a comment. There is no attempt to write a connected story or to correlate the facts, and we are at least free from the perplexities and irritations which the scribes in a credulous age might have caused in their efforts to write history. Nevertheless, only too often there is the barest record of events, and the knowledge of the details which these mnemonics recalled to those living at the time has disappeared with them. The meagre notes expand into long and splendid pieces of historical narration only occasionally—the reigns of Alfred and Edward the Elder, of Ethelred and Edmund Ironside, of Edward the Confessor and Harold, and of Stephen. (*b*) The chronicles are unequal in their value, written as they were by many scribes at various times and in various places and under the influence of different traditions. In general, they are more interested in the southern part of the country, and they are fuller records in periods of misfortune. When peace, security and prosperity blessed the kingdom, they are so surprisingly inadequate and fragmentary that they have let whole periods sink into oblivion. The most glorious age of the Wessex Monarchy between the death of Edward the Elder and the accession of Ethelred the Unready is passed over almost in silence. Thus for Athelstan's reign only four events of general interest are recorded: the accession and death of the king, an expedition against the Scots which is dismissed in two lines, the battle of Brunanburh which is described in spirited verse that never divulges where the battle took place; indeed, only too often metrical passages of no historical or even literary value are inserted in this way to fill serious gaps. Again, the chronicles will tell us wonderfully little about the reign of Cnut. (c) The chronicles are local in their outlook, interested in the details of the neighbourhood and reflecting its opinions. They can therefore give quite a different version of the same events. For example, the scribe of the Peterborough Chronicle, whilst it was at Canterbury, was living within the territories of earl Godwin and gave him partisan support in his contest with the king, as also did the writer of the Worcester Chronicle. On the other hand, the Abingdon Chronicle is firmly anti-Godwin, accusing him of taking part in the atrocious massacre of 1036, stressing the evil deeds of his sons, and recognizing in 1066 that William the Conqueror had a certain legal title to the throne. Nothing can better reveal the danger of citing the Anglo-Saxon Chronicle as though it represented a single historical source.

In comparison other chronicle material adds little to our knowledge. Ethelweard (died c. 998), who has the distinction of being the first layman to compile a chronicle in Latin, might have gained the undying gratitude of historians. For he was a member of the Wessex royal family, he held a high official position as ealdorman of the south-western shires, and though he depended on a version of the Anglo-Saxon Chronicle for the earlier part of his narrative to 892, he brought his account as a largely independent record up to Edgar's death in 975 and therefore was writing of events within his own lifetime. Unfortunately his laboured Latin and puerile pomposities and confusing chronology have made him frequently unintelligible. The post-Conquest chroniclers are occasionally useful: Florence of Worcester, writing in the time of Henry I, had in his hands a different version of the Chronicle from those now extant; his contemporary, Simeon of Durham, supplies a few bits of information about Northumbrian affairs after the Danish invasion of 875; William of Malmesbury eked out the jejune details about Athelstan's reign with extracts from a panegyrical poem which tells us something about his wars with his neighbours and his diplomatic marriage alliances. However, even the addition of the 'Annales Cambriae', our best authority for early Welsh history, and Anglo-Welsh relations, and the 'Tigernach' Annals, the basis for most of the accounts of Irish affairs, do not provide a body of historical material of any considerable bulk. The Norse sagas whose preservation in written form we owe to the Icelandic scholar Ari (d. 1148) and his thirteenth-century editor, Snorri Sturlason, portray very vividly the conditions of life, the ambitions and wanderings of the Vikings and, though they are largely legendary, they have actual historical events embedded in them. Handled cautiously they throw light upon the dark period of the Scandinavian raids upon England, Scotland and Ireland in the tenth and eleventh centuries: for example, the relations of Harald Fairhair with Athelstan, the exploits of Eric Bloodaxe in Northumbria, the expeditions of Cnut and Harald Hardrada, the battle of Stamford Bridge.

II. BIOGRAPHIES

The regrettable gaps in the Anglo-Saxon Chronicle are fortunately filled to some extent by a series of contemporary biographies. Among these the most valuable and the most remarkable is the life of Alfred written by Asser, a Welsh ecclesiastic who for his learning's sake was summoned to Alfred's court about 884, became bishop of Sherborne and died in 910. This first biography to take an English layman as its subject was incorporated in the chronicles of later writers, one of whom was the early twelfth-century compiler of the 'Annals of St. Neots' whose imagination went riot in furbishing it with spurious and anachronistic details. Unfortunately for Asser's reputation it was not his real work which came to be printed but these derivative 'Annals' because it was believed that they also came from his pen and provided a fuller account. Further disaster occurred when the only MS. containing his biography proper was destroyed by fire in 1731. No historian could accept the printed version as it stood, and it was left to the fine scholarship of Mr. W. H. Stevenson in 1904 to prune it of its accretions, reveal the authentic contemporary writing which underlay it and clearly identify its author with Asser himself. The biography has many irritating shortcomings: it does not go past the year 887, though it was apparently compiled in 893 and Asser survived Alfred by ten years; it is most inartistically arranged, being a mixture of annalistic notes copied from the Chronicle and biographical details of the greatest value; it is written in a rhetorical style with all the involved verbosity of Celtic Latinity. Nevertheless, when all that is said, Asser has added flesh and blood to the bare bones of the Anglo-Saxon Chronicle and painted with all the perfervid enthusiasm of a Celt a vivid picture of the great West-Saxon king at a time when monastic scriptoria could not or did not produce biographies.

Happily the longest period about which the Chronicle is silent coincides with the revival of monastic life, and the contemporary biographies of the three great men, Dunstan, Ethelwold and Oswald, who introduced the reforms, illumine not only the history of the Church but also, however faintly, the social and intellectual life of the time. It must be confessed, however, that they are not very helpful for the reconstruction of political events; still, their occasional allusions to secular matters are all the more valuable because we have so little else. The scanty notice in the Chronicle of Cnut's reign can be augmented by the 'Encomium Emmae', dedicated by its monastic writer to the queen, the widow of Ethelred the Unready and the wife of Cnut. It yields disputable evidence and the writer's personal knowledge of events is offset by his obvious manipulation of the facts to please his patroness. The anonymous and certainly contemporary life of Edward the Confessor is quite indispensable for any understanding of the position of the Godwin family in English politics and acts as a counterbalance to the myths that after the Norman Conquest gathered round the last of the Wessex royal dynasty and were embedded in later biographies of little value.

III. DOCUMENTARY EVIDENCE

The most striking difference in the sources at our disposal before and after 900 is the increasing availability of the written documents, which tell us much about classes of people and developments where the literary evidence tells us nothing at all. It is true that at this time and, indeed, throughout the Middle Ages this information is embedded in legal records mainly, but we shall look in vain elsewhere for a proper insight into the structure of government, society and economic arrangements, and the nature of ordinary routine life which that structure encased.

(i) *The Laws*

Stretching as they do over the centuries from Ethelbert of Kent to Cnut, they constitute a monument which is unique in Western Christendom. It must be borne in mind, however, that they do not give us a codification of the customary law of the people: that remained unwritten and we have no means of recovering it as a whole. The Laws represent collections of articles made at different times to elucidate, interpret and emphasize the customary law at points where it was vague, little understood and ineffective. It follows from their fragmentary nature and the absence of the background to them that we must be extremely cautious how we fit the pieces together when we try to form a coherent and undistorted picture. Still, the Laws stand as an indispensable witness upon the rights of the king, the position of the witan, the shire and hundred courts, the boroughs—in brief, the machinery of central and local government—and upon the social stratification and economic life of the people at large.

(ii) *The Charters*

Reaching back to the seventh century, these do much to fill the gaps left by the Laws and to test the conclusions drawn from them. Very few of them survive in their original form, even for the later years. Most of them—and they run into many hundreds—come to us at second-hand in the monastic cartularies compiled between the eleventh and fifteenth centuries. Thus St. Augustine's abbey at Canterbury records its title deeds back to Ethelbert of Kent, Abingdon monastery to 687, Hyde monastery to Alfred's reign, Ramsey abbey to the late tenth century. There is need for expert discrimination, for many of the charters are patently spurious, concocted by monastic forgers, not to obtain something to which they had no legal claim but to provide a written guarantee that the rights they had they could continue to hold. The charters, issued only by the king, the Church and the very great men, exhibit a great diversity of subject-matter. Grants of land and privileges, leases and mortgages, show the land law in operation and therefore form an essential supplement to the Laws, disclose the powers of the king and the influence of the Church, reveal the extent of the approach to a feudalized society, and sketch the faint details of the litigation to which the charters were often the procedural end. Wills, marriage contracts and manumissions help us to some understanding of such matters as domestic family arrangements, the disposition of personal estates, the position of women and of slaves.

(iii) *Domesday Book*

Though it served a fiscal purpose and provided detailed information for the assessment of the land tax, its chief value for the historian is social and economic. It is of the greatest importance for pre-Conquest England because it describes the conclusion of the Anglo-Saxon developments. 'A result is given to us; the problem is to find cause and process.' By working backwards from the known to the unknown, we may learn the nature and direction of what has happened in the past. Moreover, within Domesday Book itself we have preserved for us the relics of a forgotten age, of institutions and conditions which by 1086 had become archaic. The method is dangerous, for we may in our imagination see in the past the shape of things we are looking for and tend to interpret the evidence wronglv, but there can be no two opinions about the value of the material itself.

Linguistic Evidence

As we shall see later, the settlement of Scandinavians caused a cleavage in the country between the Anglo-Saxon south and west and the Anglo-Scandinavian north and east, which was of fundamental importance in the later course of events, especially the work of political unification. But of what was happening in the Danelaw for two centuries before the Norman Conquest we know extremely little. The normal sources of information fail us. For the Scandinavians brought no chroniclers in their train to recount their exploits, and the Norse sagas were not put into writing until the thirteenth century and lack the value of contemporary evidence. The Anglo-Saxon Chronicle takes no interest in the Scandinavian districts save to catalogue the stages in its gradual recapture. Few contemporary Danelaw charters survive to reveal the slow and unspectacular rise of a new community. Even the graves of the newcomers will not yield to the archaeologist the kind of evidence on which he mainly depends, and few monuments and inscriptions remain for his inspection. In such circumstances the evidence of place-names, field-names and personal names continues to be a primary authority for the history of half the country. They have been studied so well and to such purpose that we can speak with fair confidence upon the extent of penetration and colonization; without this knowledge we could have no proper appreciation of the fact that the Danelaw was peopled by aliens who lived their lives in traditional ways and under traditional institutions.

Archaeology and geography call for no extended discussion. It is not that they have ceased to be important but, speaking generally, they have been relegated to their proper place as auxiliaries to the written material. Their evidence within their specialized limits continues, of course, to be valuable. Archaeology will show us examples of the arts and crafts, the boats and weapons and tools, and, in particular, the coins with their testimony to the growth of trade. The physical aspect of the countryside, especially the fields, will tell us much about agrarian arrangements and the formation of parish boundaries and compel us to bring common sense to bear upon our deductions from legal records.

SELECT READING

Stenton, 679–84; Hodgkin, ii. 624–7, 706–8; Chambers, xii–xx, 201–2; R. L. Poole, *Chronicles and Annals* (1926), 40–55; F. M. Stenton, 'The South-Western Element in the Old English Chronicle' in *Essays . . . to T. F. Tout* (1925), 15–24; A. H. Smith, *The Parker Chronicle* (1935), 1–14; C. Plummer, *Two of the Saxon Chronicles Parallel* (1896), i. xvii–xxii, cii–cxxii; A. Campbell, *Battle of Brunanburh* (1938), 43–80; E. V. Gordon, *Battle of Maldon* (1937), 1–40; R. A. S. Macalister, 'The Sources of the Preface to the "Tigernach" Annals' in *Irish Historical Studies*, iv (1943), 38–57; W. H. Stevenson, *Asser's Life of King Alfred* (1904), xi–cxxxi; M. Ashdown, *English and Norse Documents relating to the Reign of Ethelred the Unready* (1930, trans.), 107–195 (Norse documents); F. E. Harmer, 'Anglo-Saxon Charters and the Historian' in *B.J.R.L.* xxii (1938), 339–67; F. W. Maitland, *Domesday Book and Beyond* (1897); G. C. Brooke, *English Coins* (1932).

CHAPTER VI

THE INVASIONS OF THE NORTHMEN

We shall not appreciate the tremendous influence of these invasions on the course of events in England unless we resolutely remove from our minds two misconceptions which still distort our view of developments. These invasions were not local in their incidence but merely one part of a vast movement which did not confine itself to Western Europe or indeed to Europe itself but reached out to parts of the world, of which nothing so far had been known. Furthermore, they were not episodic in character, raising a problem which was solved within a hundred years and could afterwards be ignored: in England, for example, the Northmen did not enter the sphere of practical politics with Egbert and depart again with the reconquest of the Danelaw under Edward the Elder and Athelstan, for these people made their homes permanently in this country and their different traditions and alien customs altered the social and economic life of half the land, thus conditioning the policy of all Wessex kings and even of the early Norman rulers.

This last great migration of Nordic peoples westwards before the seventeenth-century descent upon North America placed the romanesque civilization of Western Europe in imminent peril of extinction. That simple fact must not be forgotten if we are to realize the European significance of what was done by the English king Alfred in preventing his country from becoming a dangerous base of operations against the Continent. It is inevitable that we should compare the devastations of the heathen warriors in the ninth century with those occurring four hundred years earlier, and it is indisputable that the havoc wrought by the Northmen was more terrible and much more dangerous to the future of the type of civilization then established. Though the German invaders had erased the work of the Roman occupation in England itself, this was an exception to what had taken place on the Continent where, after the inevitable initial destruction, they had come under the influence of Rome and sought as best they could to preserve its civilization, if only by imitation. All the same, there had been a great relapse and only by the ninth century was Europe beginning to recover her strength. The Carolingian Empire was in no way as powerful as the Roman Empire had been, even in its last days, and the artificiality of its unity was to be openly displayed by squalid succession disputes, whilst the intellectual and cultural renaissance it had evoked, however promising it was, was far from reaching the standard known even in the fifth century. Against this weaker structure the Northmen, though fewer in numbers than the Germans, hurled their fiercer and more destructive assaults for generation after generation. Effective resistance of some kind might have been made against a land offensive but against the novel attacks from the sea there was no means of defence whatever. The Northmen came in course of time to make piracy a professional business, planned their expeditions carefully, trained and armed themselves with deliberate purpose, and could land at will an army of several thousand warriors. The dominant feature of their raids was the rapidity with which they were executed. Their long narrow boats, sixteen-oared and masted, and holding forty fighting-men apiece, were strongly enough built to sail the open seas and yet were very fast, easily beached or navigated far up the rivers, and if occasion arose could be easily carried overland to another water-way. An exact model of one of their boats, fortunately preserved as it was constructed about 900, crossed the Atlantic comfortably in 1893 in four weeks. Their usual procedure after landing was to round up the horses in the neighbourhood and thereby convert themselves into a mounted infantry, extremely mobile and elusive, like the dragoons of the seventeenth century. When they appeared at the great river-mouths of the European coastline, they met with little or no resistance. There were no hostile boats to meet them at sea or to cut off their retreat. All that could be opposed to them on land were local levies of men who had no adequate military training and no proper equipment and who were desperately slow and cumbrous in their movements: often they could not find the invaders who carefully avoided pitched battles; when they did so they could not defeat them. It is hardly possible to exaggerate the hopeless misery created by the raids. They occurred in the summer and autumn months when the peasants were endeavouring to extract their bare subsistence living from the fields, and the loss of crops, especially for more than one year at a time, meant starvation, and undernourishment in its turn facilitated the ravages of those plagues which were so frequent a feature of life in the Middle Ages. Moreover, the main objects of attack were the wealthy monasteries and churches, the main centres of culture and the homes of literary treasures which disappeared at this time for ever. The Atlantic coastlands of Europe were dissolving into political disintegration and social chaos: when commerce and industry were brought to a standstill, when even agriculture on which life itself depended was made impossible, it is little wonder that a new verse was introduced into the Litany of the Church, 'From the fury of the Northmen, O Lord, deliver us'.

We know very little that is certain about the Northmen before their descents upon Western Europe. Their own historians are vigorously and with justice disputing the assumption that they were then little removed from savages. Archaeological discoveries indicate that they had always been in close relations with the German lands south of the Baltic and along the coastline facing the North Sea and that they were not merely fishermen and hunters but merchants conducting a lively trade, especially in furs. Except for the Frisians, they were without rivals in the art of shipbuilding and they showed no mean skill in wood-carving and metal work. They were certainly, however, illiterate or, if we take into account the fact that they used the curious characters of the Runic alphabet, at least without written literature (for the sagas, as we know them, do not go back beyond the thirteenth century) and they were heathens who offered human sacrifices to their gods. We should not simply assume that Christianity and civilization are interchangeable terms and that the second cannot flourish in the absence of the first. The colonization of Iceland after 860, where conditions were most unfavourable and where we can see Scandinavian life *tout pur* and not, as elsewhere, commingled and confused with the way of life of other peoples, serves to remind us that they could construct a quite satisfactory type of civilization. It is not easy to say why they took to the high seas when they did and began their careers of looting and exploration. The Norwegians, shut in their narrow fiords by dense forests and mountain ranges, were probably confronted then as now with the problem of over-population. The lack of land, if not of inclination, prevented a more extensive agriculture from providing a remedy. The only solution, as in more recent times, was to emigrate, and the only outlet and highway for these hard-living and courageous people was the sea. Such considerations can hardly have affected the Danes, but eventually they as well as the Scandinavians were stimulated to leave their homelands by political grievances, for about the middle of the ninth century a strong king, Horik, at last managed to establish effective control

in South Scandinavia and Denmark: those chieftains who chafed
at the restrictions on their freedom of action had to look outside
their own countries for means to satisfy their ambitions and
energies and the profession of Viking was already indicated as
a sure source of adventure with large profits. However we may
account for them, we must in the end regard the onslaughts of the
Northmen as beyond full explanation.

Physical geography supplies the reason for the two courses the
Northmen followed in their raids.

I. THE NORTHERN ROUTE

The Norwegians naturally went along a northern route. Quite
early in the ninth century many of them had migrated to the
Shetlands and the Orkneys where they made genuine settlements.
From there they worked their way down both sides of Scotland,
on the east to Fife, Northumbria, and even as far as Lincolnshire,
on the west to the Hebrides, the Isle of Man (sacking Iona frequently on the way) and Ireland. In that island they wrought their
most lamentable destruction, for Ireland had escaped the fury of
the barbarian invasions of the fifth century and had been allowed
to pursue its own more or less peaceable way for three hundred
years. The wealth of the Irish monasteries and the genial climate,
so different from their own sub-Arctic conditions, drew the Norwegians like a magnet and it was the first foreign country to be
threatened with deliberate conquest. As early as 795 they began
to make it their happy hunting-ground. From 850 onwards, after
capturing Armagh, the political and ecclesiastical centre of the
country, they stayed permanently in Ulster; shortly after 840
they established their coastal colonies at Dublin, Wexford, Waterford and Limerick; by 853 Olaf had founded his Dublin kingdom. These were by no means ephemeral conquests. The Norwegians dominated Ireland for a hundred and fifty years until the
victory of Clontarf in 1014 guaranteed the native Irish the preservation of their racial distinctiveness, although the power of the
'Ostmen' was not effectively broken until the Anglo-Normans in
their turn set off to conquer Ireland in Henry II's time. The Isle
of Man and the Hebrides were not surrendered to the kingdom of
Scotland until 1266, the Orkneys until 1468, and the Shetlands till
1462, and Norwegian was still spoken in the Shetlands until the
close of the eighteenth century.

II. THE SOUTHERN ROUTE

The Danes for their part sailed directly across from their own shores and thus followed a southern route. It brought them first of all to the east and south-east of England, then through the Channel, spreading devastation on both sides, round Brittany into the Bay of Biscay, past Cape Finisterre and through the Straits of Gibraltar to ravage the Mediterranean coasts of Spain, France and even Italy, where Rome narrowly missed discovery and pillage. No important river of that long European coastline escaped them and they sailed far into the interior: up the Thames to sack London, up the Seine to besiege Paris four times, up the Loire to Nantes, up the Gironde to Bordeaux. It is often evident that the Danes were not always working haphazardly: they went out with large fleets and, like the Elizabethan adventurers, they were supported by business interests at home.

During the havoc and desolation of these calamitous years the Northmen made one constructive contribution to knowledge which is without parallel in history before the fourteenth and fifteenth centuries. For the Swedes about the middle of the ninth century sailed eastwards to the Gulf of Finland, used the magnificent river system to penetrate to the Black Sea and to bring it into commercial contact with the Baltic, gave the country its name of Russia and established a dynasty of rulers under Rurik which lasted until the thirteenth century, and compelled the Emperor in Constantinople itself to make treaties of peace and marriage alliances. And the Norwegians and Danes were the first people who ventured to make transoceanic voyages of exploration which immensely extended the boundaries of the known world. The ancient world, of course, had known much of seafaring life, but it was chiefly centred within the Mediterranean and outside that sea navigators had not cared to sail far out of sight of land and had been content with coasting. The Northmen were a hardier people. In boats which had little room for water and food and no decks or shelter, they put out into Arctic seas and sailed westwards with no hope of return if they did not discover land. Thus about 860 they stumbled upon Iceland where they came across a few even more intrepid Irish monks, and began in 874 to colonize it so vigorously that two generations later there were 20,000 or more Norwegians settled there, and it became the meeting-place of their famous Althing, the annual assembly of the people, and the home of the sagas, which were a medium not merely for story-telling as such but for preserving a narrative account of the family-origins and exploits of the Scandinavian heroes. From Iceland as a base they went farther afield. Under the leadership of the great adventurer Eric the Red they undertook the colonization of the coasts of Greenland about 985, though not on a very extensive scale: the descendants of the settlers dragged out a precarious existence there until the close of the fourteenth century when, forgotten by their home country, they dwindled away, with the result that Martin Frobisher in Elizabeth's reign came to what was virtually a newly discovered land. Still more amazing in the annals of exploration was the discovery of the American continent. Leif, son of Eric the Red, sailed from Greenland to reach Labrador and Nova Scotia and eventually to camp either at the mouth of the Hudson or, as some would have it, as far south as Virginia on Chesapeake Bay. A second voyage was made in 1004 and a third, this time by a merchant, about 1020, but no practical use was made of the tiny settlements and therefore they had no permanence. Nevertheless, it was never forgotten in Scandinavia that land did exist in the far west, though Western Europe paid so little attention to these traditions that, when Columbus rediscovered America, he believed that it was India.

It will be observed that England was completely encircled by the waves of invasion and suffered accordingly. The assaults proceeded by two distinct stages:

(i) *A period of raids*

The Anglo-Saxon Chronicle states that the first descent of the Northmen upon English shores was round about 787 when they harried the Dorset coast. In 793 they pillaged and destroyed Lindisfarne, the cradle of Northumbrian Christianity, and a year later Jarrow. There followed a generation of comparative peace, but afterwards the raids were almost continuous and came with ever-increasing violence. Egbert of Wessex fought one successful pitched battle at Hingston Down in 838 against a band of Norwegians which was operating in Cornwall, but for the most part the Northmen acted with impunity: in the 840's they sacked London and ruthlessly pillaged Lincolnshire and Northumbria. Egbert's successor, the pietistic but none the less virile Ethelwulf (d. 858) just managed to hold his kingdom together—he even defeated a group of raiders at the unidentified 'Aclea', south of the Thames, in 851, and then in 855, sincerely believing in the efficacy of prayer as well as deed, he sought to avert the peril by going off for a year on a pilgrimage to Rome.

(ii) *A period of conquest and settlement*

The year 850, when a Scandinavian host with a fleet of 350 ships did not return home after looting Canterbury but wintered in the Isle of Thanet, marks an epoch in the history of England. It signalized the end of pirate raids and their supersession by campaigns of conquest with a view to permanent colonization. And so successful were the Northmen in their object that in the long run they altered the character of half the country. Before they could settle down they had to undertake the conquest of England, and it was this peril that the four sons of Ethelwulf were called upon to face—Ethelbald (d. 860), Ethelbert (d. 866), Ethelred (d. 871) and Alfred (d. 899). In 865 there appeared the largest combined host that had ever set foot in the country. The 'Great Army', as it was called, operating under a surprisingly unified command and exhibiting remarkable discipline, landed in East Anglia, spent the winter there, and then began its terrifying and destructive marches through the land. In 866 it went north to York: Northumbria, torn asunder by political feuds, could offer no resistance and collapsed; its dynasty, its religious establishments and its culture were completely overwhelmed and it fell back into obscurity and comparative barbarism. In 867 the 'Great Army' turned its attention to Mercia and had to be bought off by payment of tribute. In 868 it returned to York. In 869 it concentrated on East Anglia, plundered the rich monasteries and removed that area from the records of history for many years. In 870 it began its thrust towards the south-west, against Wessex, and established its base of operations at Reading, where it could hold the line of the Thames and be in a position to receive reinforcements from the Continent along the Icknield Way and strike at Winchester directly to the south. Its deliberate and carefully planned preparations for a conclusive campaign against Wessex, the last independent kingdom, coincided with the coming of Alfred to the throne.

The crisis of his reign is invested with a double significance—for the future of Wessex and the future of Europe. In 871, when most of England lay prostrate before the Northmen and its type of civilization was rapidly vanishing as it had done in the fifth century, there seemed very little chance that Wessex could survive the attack of the 'Great Army'. If by some miraculous means she could withstand the terrible odds against her, then the Wessex royal house might become the English Monarchy: there will be no Northumbrian, Mercian, East Anglian, Kentish or Sussex rival dynasties to make war on that issue as during the last four hundred years. But Alfred was not fighting simply an English battle. For Europe was face to face with the same menace, and the civilization of Christendom was quite as much in danger of extinction as was the civilization of Northumbria. The decisive theatre of operations was the land on both sides the English Channel, and for the time being Wessex had become the danger-point of that vital area. Alfred's contemporaries abroad realized quite clearly how much depended on what he did and rightly acclaimed him one of the great deliverers of Europe from the last 'barbarian' invasion of the West.

SELECT READING

Hodgkin, ii. 473–509; H. Shetelig and H. Falk, *Scandinavian Archaeology* (1937: trans. E. V. Gordon), 252–304, 345–76; E. V. Gordon, *Introduction to Old Norse* (1927), xv–xxxv, xlv–lvii; G. M. Gathorne Hardy, *The Norse Discoverers of America* (1921); T. D. Kendrick, *History of the Vikings* (1930), 1–87; W. G. Collingwood, *Scandinavian Britain* (1908), 7–81.

CHAPTER VII

THE SALVATION OF WESSEX

It is extremely fortunate that we are not solely dependent for our knowledge of the great man, produced in the hour of crisis, upon a bare recital of his deeds. For the first time we are able to see the mind of an English king at work, defining for us what he considered to be the political and moral duties of both ruler and ruled. We have at our disposal the self-revelations contained in the prefaces and notes to his Laws and the translations into Anglo-Saxon of standard literary works in Latin and, in addition, the intimate details supplied by Asser in one of the earliest historical biographies written in the Dark Ages. In many ways Alfred greatly resembles the men of the Renaissance with their insatiable curiosity about all phases of human life: he corresponds with the Patriarch of Jerusalem, he follows up his own early visits to Rome with the dispatch of missions and alms, he invites the Norwegian Arctic explorer Ohthere to his court to describe his adventures. And this eagerness for knowledge was allied with a remarkable versatility which ranged from the invention of a storm-proof reading lantern to the construction of a new type of ship. Alfred could, however, be no dilettante when the times were so much out of joint, and we shall miss the all-important side of his character if we do not perceive the extreme practicality which lay beneath all his schemes and the power of co-ordination which forced all men and all things to work together for the preservation and welfare of his realm. To the modern mind he may often seem credulous and imitative like his contemporaries and somewhat priggish and platitudinous, but the genius which can see to the heart of a problem seems only too often to a later generation to be providing glimpses of the obvious.

What at all events in his own estimation was his greatest asset was the deep religious faith which constrained him, however reluctantly, to accept the crown of Wessex, sustained him when all other weapons had broken in his hands, brought him to long deferred but ultimate victory, and inspired his efforts at reform.

Alfred's first and imperative task was to preserve his kingdom from subjugation by the Danes and it was only in the intervals of three major campaigns that he could turn his thoughts to constructive government.

(i) *The attack in 871 from the east, based on the Thames Valley at Reading*

The resistance to the 'Great Army' consisted in continuous skirmishes and at this time, when Wessex was badly disorganized, it speaks well for the work of Alfred's predecessors that the kingdom did not become demoralized like Northumbria and Mercia and that local patriotism should have emerged sufficiently strong to prevent any easy capitulation. Alfred, indeed, had ventured just before his accession to the throne to attack and managed to scatter a detachment of Danes advancing south of the Thames in the open country of the Berkshire Downs and resistance, such as this battle of Ashdown implied, must have made it so evident to the Danish leaders that the conquest of Wessex was not going to be as simple as that of the rest of the country that they consented to negotiate. Alfred for his part knew that he was in no position to fight and win, and therefore, following the precedents set by the men of Kent and the Mercians, he agreed to pay the Danes tribute on condition that they evacuated Wessex. He knew quite well from events elsewhere that he had bought no more than a temporary relief, but the ignominy of surrender concealed purposeful statesmanship, for he obtained a respite of five valuable years, during which he carried out a reorganization for war which determined the course of future events. Meanwhile, as perhaps Alfred had shrewdly surmised, the 'Great Army', after moving away to London and then transferring itself first for a few weeks to Northumbria in 872, and the following year to Mercia to complete its subjection, failed to maintain its unity any longer. In 874 it made its first split into two parts which divided up the country so far overrun: a northern kingdom was established under Halfdan in Deira with its centre at York and a vague supremacy over Bernicia, and the Danes began at once to settle down and till the ground and bring into existence the region of the Danelaw; a southern kingdom was set up under Guthrum in the Midlands, including East Anglia.

(ii) *The attack in 876–8 from the west, based on the Bristol Channel*

These were the most critical years of the reign, when Guthrum renewed his onslaughts with an army reinforced by bands from all over northern and eastern England and by large contingents from abroad. At first Guthrum moved his army with surprising secrecy and mobility through his enemy's lines to the Dorset and Devon coast, where he operated from the fortified camps of Wareham and Exeter and maintained close co-operation with Danish naval forces in the Channel. The engagements with the West Saxons were, however, quite inconclusive, and Guthrum marched north towards the Lower Severn to make in 878 his most formidable campaign. His army advanced on Wessex from its headquarters at Chippenham while a fleet moved from South Wales to land auxiliaries in North Devon. It can only be surmised that Alfred was taken unawares in that it was mid-winter when Guthrum struck his blow. His defeat was undoubtedly complete, for he himself sought refuge in the Athelney fens, many districts of Wessex were overrun by the enemy and their terrified inhabitants sought safety in exile overseas. What made the tide of victory turn so quickly in Alfred's favour we do not know, and we can only conjecture that the preparations of the last five years now proved their effectiveness, for Alfred found it possible to reassemble his army and overthrow Guthrum at Edington, a few miles south of Chippenham. This victory became the turning-point in the Scandinavian attacks. (*a*) It resulted immediately in the Treaty of Chippenham, 878, whereby Guthrum agreed to depart from Wessex and, along with his followers, to be baptized. This last stipulation was not a mere religious gesture originating in the piety of Alfred but an important political move. It was by no means an unusual condition to impose upon a heathen foe: for example, Charles the Great had always insisted that the Saxon tribes he overcame should accept Christianity. If that condition, however often it was broken, could be finally asserted, it meant that the forces of Christendom, mysterious and awe-inspiring, would be brought to bear upon the Scandinavian districts of England. Indeed, not many years will pass before the superstitious Scandinavian settlers begin to rebuild and re-endow the ruined churches and monasteries, and thus become the guardians of the civilization they had so nearly obliterated. (*b*) It led eventually in 886, for local skirmishes with Danish raiding parties still went on, to what was called 'Alfred and Guthrum's Pact', the text of which has come down to us. It delimited the Scandinavian territory by fixing the frontiers of Guthrum's East Anglian and Mercian kingdom as being very roughly the Roman Watling Street from London north-west across the Midlands to the Upper Severn. As it was not a natural boundary, border feuds and trade disputes were certain to arise, therefore provision was made to avoid them by placing an embargo on migration from one kingdom to the other. At the same time Alfred was able to make arrangements on behalf of the English who were resident in Danish-controlled territory which left them entitled to the same legal status as was enjoyed by the Danish soldier-settlers themselves. (c) It left Alfred with a period of fourteen years' comparative peace to go on with his work of reorganization and reform. The 'Pact' itself had been largely the result of his success in 886 in forcibly regaining possession of London and, knowing its long association with Mercia, he handed it over to Ethelred, a Mercian who had risen from obscurity by his talents to rule over that western part of Mercia which remained outside the zone of Scandinavian occupation, and shortly afterwards he gave him his daughter Ethelfleda in marriage. Whilst Alfred himself was content to exercise a tactful and amiable overlordship, the union of Ethelred and Ethelfleda was to produce its greatest effect on political developments after his death.

(iii) *The attack in 892–6 from the south-east, based on Kent*

Two great hosts, one of them being under the leadership of a redoubtable warrior, Haesten, sailed across from France and landed on both sides of the Kentish peninsula. Three times the Danes marched across the country into West Mercia, hoping to receive assistance from their resident countrymen. The danger was acute but not so great as in Guthrum's time. Alfred had given the Scandinavian settlers no reason for anxiety about their position and, though many could not resist the attractions of adventure and spoil, most remained faithful to their fields. Alfred's defences stood firm to keep Wessex safe and the enemy was resolutely attacked on the sea as well as on the land. Without any major decisive engagement being fought, the Scandinavian army broke up, part of it going to Northumbria, part to East Anglia and the remainder back to France.

THE MILITARY ORGANIZATION

Many factors contributed to the successful resistance of Alfred, not least of all the force of his own personality, but many of them are really imponderabilia. One, however, his military dispositions and the organization of his forces, lends itself to fairly definite assessment.

(i) *The Army*

This was strengthened through the reorganization of the thegns and of the fyrd. It was plain that the Danish army had two tremendous advantages over its opponents: it was composed of men who were warriors by trade, professionals with specialized training and superior equipment and, furthermore, men who had no other distractions and were prepared to fight the whole year round. If they were to be effectively resisted, then in Alfred's opinion they must be met on their own ground. Whatever the Anglo-Saxon fyrd may have been in the earliest times, by the ninth century it was certainly not the host of all tribal freemen. Military service had become connected with the ownership of land, and already before Alfred's succession the fyrd had as its all-important nucleus a small group of experienced soldiers, able to constitute a mobile force of mounted infantry and made up of the household retainers of both the king and the ealdormen as well as of the thegns of the shires. At their side stood the ordinary soldiers, the farmers and villagers of the countryside, who came to war as the personal followers of their lords rather than as members of any popular militia. Alfred reshaped the material at his disposal. Although it is pure fiction to assert that he either founded the social class of thegns or decreed that all men who possessed five hides of land were to become members of it, he undoubtedly encouraged the development of a special military class, distinguished from the peasantry by its greater landed estates, its greater expertness in war and its greater privileges. The heterogeneous body of thegns ranged in its members from the great nobles to the county gentry, its essential motive was public service, and it was destined to exert a powerful influence on government and society in the future. Alfred himself appreciated that fact when he made his famous statement in his Laws that society had three sections: those who prayed, those who fought, and those who worked. The mobilization of the peasantry for war presented serious difficulties. It was not so much the slowness with which this could be brought about but the need to see that crops were sown and harvested and vital food supplies maintained. Since the lives of all depended on this being done, it is little wonder that the peasants, after a few weeks' service or a slight victory, wished to get back to their farms. The problem of desertion had to be overcome without running the risk of famine. Alfred therefore adapted to the fyrd a principle which was followed at his court. Bearing in mind the fact that his personal retainers were permitted to alternate periods of service with the king with periods spent at their homes, he divided the fyrd into two parts: one constantly under arms, one constantly in the fields, each changing place with the other at regular intervals. It is possible that his law forbidding anyone from going from one shire to another without the permission of the ealdorman of his shire was also designed to prevent any evasion of military service. In the end, therefore, Alfred could counter the Danes with the support of professional soldiery and a standing army.

(ii) *The Navy*

It is foolish to imagine that the Saxons in the south of England, with their trade connexions with the Continent and Ireland, had no ships at their command with which to face the Scandinavian attacks by sea. For example, in the reign of Alfred's father, the Kentish fleet had met the Danes in the Channel and routed them in 851. The Saxon ships, however, were too few to cope with armadas and presumably their number dwindled every year. It is to Alfred's credit that he realized the meaning of sea-power, which was allowing the enemy to transfer his troops and concentrate his attacks when and where he pleased without observation or obstruction, and that he took steps to redress the balance. By 897 his naval programme had resulted in the construction of a new fleet of 'long ships', which it was claimed were original in their design and larger, swifter and steadier than the foreign craft. It would have been a miraculous achievement if within a few years he had been able to outdo the Scandinavians with their long inheritance of experience and skill, and in actual fact Alfred's ships did not meet with much success. The Frisian sailors who had to be hired to man them seem to have found them difficult to manage and they gained no victory of any great importance. The significance of Alfred's work, therefore, lay not in what was accomplished but in the creation of a precedent which was followed by his successors like Edward the Elder, who could assemble a fleet of a hundred ships in 911, and thus the south coast of England was guarded successfully for a hundred years.

(iii) *The Burhs*

All vulnerable points on the frontiers of Wessex—on the south coast as well as on the Thames—were protected by the provision of fortified strongholds. Their names and sites have come down to us in the document called the 'Burghal Hidage', which tells us the area of the military districts protected by burhs. Their maintainance was a responsibility laid upon the local people, who had to see that every hide of land provided one garrison soldier in time of war. They served their purpose well as a deliberately organized means of defence, and under Alfred's successors the system was extended to other parts of the country as it was reconquered from the Danes, and ultimately it found a permanent place within the framework of civil government.

THE RECONSTRUCTION OF SOCIETY

Alfred would have earned enduring fame for his military achievements alone, but his view of the responsibilities of kingship was not limited to leadership in war. Around him lay the ruins of a war-stricken and demoralized society: untilled fields and wasted villages, burnt monasteries and churches, lawlessness and illiteracy. In his eyes it was the imperative duty of a king to face the highly complicated problems of reconstruction, for the Christian kingship he had in mind was a divine trust to be exercised for the benefit of the community in giving peace, protecting the poor and oppressed, and punishing the evildoer. Alfred's reforms in their varied spheres were remarkably well co-ordinated and integrated in their aim to place society once more on a secure basis. His first task was to make respect for law and order the foundation on which he could build. In compiling his collection of laws he did not restrict his attention to the usages of Wessex alone, for he combined Kentish, Mercian and West Saxon law together by using all that he considered best in the legal codes of Ethelbert, Offa and Ine. It is noticeable that he laid particular stress upon the position of the aristocracy, the class of overlords which was unquestionably the main pillar of society, for death was to be the penalty for treason either to him or to them. A similar emphasis was placed upon the sacredness of oaths, for this was an essential safeguard of the rights of property. To issue laws is one thing, to enforce them another, and Alfred made it his special concern to supervise the judicial system by listening to complaints of injustice and punishing the corrupt acts of his officials. And all the time he was impressing upon the public consciousness his own conception of a high and exalted monarchy.

Nowhere does Alfred stand so much in advance of his contemporaries and at the same time show the sane practicality of his views as in the educational system he strove to introduce. Learning had by no means disappeared everywhere but it had decayed, and the knowledge of Latin had well-nigh disappeared in those districts ravaged by the Northmen, so much so that it was necessary for him to attract to his court scholars from outside the borders of his own kingdom—four representing West Mercian scholarship, Asser of Wales, Grimbald of St. Bertin from Flanders, John the Old Saxon. His zeal for education and culture had the utilitarian object of training his subjects to assume responsibilities in the work of government. His 'Palace School', to use a convenient term, was intended to educate the sons of nobles as well as his own so that they could fit themselves for administrative duties and guarantee the permanence of his work. In the same spirit he decided that classical works of instruction must be translated from Latin into Anglo-Saxon. It was not so much that he regarded the vernacular as 'second-best', on which he had to fall back on account of the general ignorance of Latin. He regarded the two languages in different lights: for advanced education and culture Latin was essential; for the prosaic work of government the language of the governed was equally necessary, and in one of his prefaces he mildly reproved his predecessors for not having issued translations from the classics long ago, when presumably Latin was better known. The *Pastoral Care* of Gregory the Great was a handbook which gave the clergy practical advice about their duties, the *Ecclesiastical History* of Bede, pruned of a quarter of its matter which Alfred considered no longer of interest, informed his people of their origins and Christian traditions, a lesson repeated later in the propagandist Anglo-Saxon Chronicle; the *History of the World* of Orosius enlarged their vision and showed them the Christendom of which their country was a part. Except for the *Consolation of Philosophy* of Boethius, it was not literary appreciation so much as practical expediency that guided Alfred's decisions. Whatever the reasons, the result was a body of literature in the vernacular which has no counterpart in the contemporary world. Unfortunately the renaissance was short-lived and established no enduring traditions: his 'Palace School' vanished and none of his successors, so far as we know, troubled to develop this side of his work.

It is somewhat surprising that, despite his piety and his awareness of how much the Church could help in strengthening the

secular arm, Alfred did so little in a practical way to assist the
revival of religious life. For the monks observed no recognized
'rules', the clergy were undisciplined and unlettered. Alfred contented himself with founding a monastery at Athelney and a
nunnery at Shaftesbury with his daughter as abbess and with
making preparations for the new minster at Winchester. Cluny
was not yet founded to send a new reforming inspiration through
the Church, and Alfred may well have thought that an educated
clergy must first precede and then be responsible for a reinvigorated
Church.

The full results of Alfred's superb achievements are seen in the
reigns of his successors, but we shall not appreciate the nature and
extent of their problems until we realize fully the significance of
the Scandinavian colonization that was taking place.

SELECT READING

Stenton, 237–73; Hodgkin, ii. 537–695; Chambers, ch. vi; W. J. Corbett,
'The Foundation of the Kingdom of England' in *C. Med. H.* iii. (1922),
340–70; C. H. Plummer, *Life and Times of Alfred the Great* (1902);
W. H. Stevenson, *Asser's Life of King Alfred* (1904).

CHAPTER VIII

THE CONVERSION OF THE WESSEX KINGSHIP INTO AN ENGLISH MONARCHY, 899-975

THE four sons of Ethelwulf had saved the kingdom of Wessex from extinction. Still Alfred, the last and by far the greatest of them, had in spite of his victories no direct rule over any part of the country north of the Thames, and the Scandinavian invasions of England, as elsewhere on the Continent, struck a blow at the work of political unification by increasing the number of independent rulers: Bernicia and Deira had fallen apart, West Mercia stood alone, the Midlands, East Anglia and Essex lay under the control of separate Danish 'armies'. It was left to Edward the Elder (899-925) and the three sons who succeeded him on the throne to start Wessex on the offensive and to make it the basis of an English kingdom wherein all rulers, whether English or Danish, submitted themselves to one man who alone had the acknowledged and un-disputed right to call himself 'king'. This was a stupendous achievement in little more than half a century. Nevertheless, the work of expansion did not proceed as smoothly as might have been expected. After all, Alfred had firmly established the royal power in Wessex, the ruler of West Mercia was his son-in-law and a loyal colleague, the Anglo-Saxon peoples elsewhere were overwhelmingly superior in numbers to their Danish conquerors and presumably willing to acclaim a West Saxon conqueror as a deliverer from a foreign and irksome yoke. In fact, however, the armies of Wessex, though brilliantly led, did not sweep their victorious way rapidly throughout the country, and the subjected districts were always apt to break out into rebellion whenever a petty crisis occurred in the politics of Wessex itself. For the Wessex kings found them-selves confronted by a new factor: the presence of an alien race in England which had strong fighting traditions and had settled down so determinedly in the country during the last thirty years that it could not be removed. Furthermore, the Danes within England were constantly made restless by the activities of their fellow-country-men outside: Danish fleets still infested the English Channel and made periodic raids; Norwegian hosts frequently crossed over from Ireland to support the claims of the royal house at Dublin to rule at York as well: thus in 919 one of its representatives, Ragnald, became the Norwegian king of York and the first of a series of such princes, who were not finally expelled from the country until 954.

The peril which lurked beneath the surface was revealed quite early. The death of Alfred was the signal for an attempt to upset the arrangements made in 'Alfred and Guthrum's Pact'. Though Edward the Elder's right to the Wessex throne had been partly secured through his father's action in allowing him to co-operate with him in the duties of kingship in the last years of his reign, yet Ethelwold, the son of Alfred's elder brother Ethelred, chose to put forward his own claims and, failing to inaugurate a rebellion in Hampshire, fled to the Yorkshire Danes who agreed to accept him as their king. Shortly afterwards he entered East Anglia, made an alliance with its Danish king Eric, and started a campaign against the district of the Upper Thames. Edward met this Danish threat by the bold counter-stroke of a direct invasion of the Danish territories and compelled the enemy to turn back to meet him. The resulting battle in 902, though not a victory for the West Saxon arms, resulted in the deaths of both Ethelwold and Eric and made possible a peace with the Danes of Northumbria and East Anglia on the basis of the *status quo* of 886.

THE WORK OF TERRITORIAL UNIFICATION

It was quite evident that Edward's immediate task was military: he had to guarantee the security of his kingdom and that meant that he must first of all quietly reorganize and train his forces and then adopt a clear-cut policy towards the Danes, who could not be left unmolested and an ever-present menace to his position. Eventually, therefore, he passed from the defensive to the offensive and undertook the conquest of the country beyond the Thames. Presumably with his father's conception of fortified burhs and their military purpose in his mind, he conducted a series of regular but strictly limited campaigns into enemy territory, always consolidating his position as he advanced by erecting strongholds in all strategic places. His methods were not designed to be spectacular, but they were quietly and eminently successful and constituted one of the masterpieces of military strategic campaigning in the early Middle Ages.

The work of constructing burhs actually began with the rulers of West Mercia, who gave Edward assistance of the utmost value. After the Treaty of Chippenham in 878 which turned the Danes away from Wessex, Guthrum's army apparently decided to expand from the Midlands they already dominated towards the west, not expecting to receive opposition from the puppet Mercian king they had allowed to remain in West Mercia. However, the Mercian magnates, with Ethelred, the future ealdorman at their head, ignored their royal lord and sought the assistance of the recently victorious Alfred, and the negotiated 'Alfred and Guthrum's Pact' of 886 was the result. That approach marked the virtual end of Mercian independence, surrendered as it was to Wessex by the Mercians themselves, and the beginning of a period of happy co-operation between Alfred and Ethelred, who about 886 married Alfred's eldest daugher Ethelfleda and ruled West Mercia with a separate administration in nominal dependence upon Wessex. The danger from the Scandinavians pressed most urgently upon Mercia: her vulnerable frontiers ran side by side with those of the Danish territories to her east, while on the west she was subject to constant invasion from abroad by way of the Bristol Channel and the estuaries of the Dee and Mersey. Already in 907, therefore, Ethelred had fortified Chester to command the Lower Dee, check the influx of the Norwegians from Ireland along the coast of North Wales, and cut their communications with the enemy in the interior. In 909 he called in the assistance of his royal brother-in-law and together they inflicted the following year a heavy defeat upon the Danes at Tettenhall in Staffordshire when a remarkable number of the enemy leaders were killed. Henceforward the Danes in Northumbria were too weakened to give any further assistance to their kinsmen south of the Humber; yet at the same time their lack of strength left them an easy victim to Norwegian contingents from Ireland, who established in Yorkshire a new and stronger kingdom by 919. When Ethelred died in 911, his wife Ethelfleda, styled the 'Lady of the Mercians', continued with remarkable competence erecting garrison towns to guard the principal routes leading particularly from the west into Mercia: Bridgnorth (912) commanded the Middle Severn; Stafford (913) and Tamworth (913), Watling Street; Warwick (914), the Fosse Way, which might have been used by the Danes from Brittany who landed in South Wales in that same year; Runcorn (915), the Mersey estuary. Before her death in 918 Ethelfleda felt secure enough to advance across country towards the east where she received the submission of the Danes of Derby (917) and Leicester (918).

It is quite evident that Ethelfleda was following a plan of operations carefully concerted with her brother: for example, when she came to power in 911 she handed over London and Oxford and the surrounding districts to Edward because it was so much easier for him to watch over their interests from Wessex. And while she looked to the west he was slowly and cautiously driving his way to the north: the fortification and deliberate colonization of Hertford (911–12) protected the passage of the River Lea to London; Maldon (912) and afterwards Witham (912, 916) and Colchester (917) guaranteed the subjection of Essex; Buckingham (914) and Bedford (915) controlled the Lower Ouse; Towcester (918), Nottingham (918) and Bakewell (920) eventually connected the defences of the Ouse with those of the Dee and Mersey. In 917 began the voluntary submission of the Danish 'armies' of Northampton, Huntingdon, Cambridge and East Anglia on condition that they should be permitted to retain their land and continue to live in their traditional ways. On the death of his sister in 918 Edward at last incorporated Mercia into Wessex with apparently little trouble, and in 919 he crossed the Mersey-Humber line which marked the southern frontier of Northumbria and fortified Manchester to stand between the Norse in Ireland and the Danes in Yorkshire. In 920, when he was king over all England south of the Humber and Mersey, his high authority was acknowledged by the other independent rulers around him who 'took him to father and lord' and personally commended themselves to their stronger neighbour: Constantine, king of the Scots, who governed a small kingdom on the east of Scotland between the Forth and the Moray Firth; Ethelred, the English-born high reeve of Bamborough, who had been left in control of the old district of Bernicia between the Tees and the Forth which was not actively settled by the Danes; Ragnald, the first of the Norwegian kings accepted by the Yorkshire Danes in 919; Donald, the king of Strathclyde Britons between the Mersey and the Clyde; and the princes of West Wales.

Athelstan (925–39) wielded an even wider authority than that of his father and added great prestige to the Wessex dynasty, but few men of such outstanding ability can have been so meagrely commemorated in the writings of their contemporaries. These content themselves with references to three campaigns and we must eke out their information with conjectures from charter evidence, which is fortunately again available after a mysterious gap in the reigns of Alfred and Edward the Elder. In 927, on the death of the Norwegian king of the Yorkshire Danes to whom Athelstan had married his sister the year before, he annexed the kingdom of York and sternly repressed all disorder. About the same time he fixed the line of the Wye as the boundary of the Welsh princes, and drove the Cornish Britons west of the River Tamar and fortified Exeter to keep them in order. In 934 he conducted a punitive expedition by land and sea against Constantine, king of the Scots, for daring to support a Norwegian claimant to the kingdom of York, and he penetrated as far north as Fordun in Kincardineshire. In 937 he was called upon to undergo the supreme test of facing a grand alliance of the Scots, the Strathclyde Britons and the Irish Norse: only a general feeling of fear, born of the recognition of a mighty power in Athelstan, could have leagued such divergent elements together. He overthrew them in the celebrated Battle of Brunanburh, possibly in the valley of the Annan some nine miles north of the Solway Firth. The renown of so great a warrior was noised abroad in Europe, and Athelstan was prompt to make himself the first English ruler to bring his country into really close diplomatic contact with the Continent. To his court came Constantine from Scotland, and Howell the Good from Wales, and embassies from Harold Fairhair, the first king of Norway; from the English court went one sister to marry the Carolingian King Charles the Simple, another to marry Otto the Great, who was to found a new line of Holy Roman Emperors, another to marry Hugh, the great Duke of the Franks, whose son was to originate the new Capetian dynasty of French kings, another to marry a German prince, possibly the Duke of Burgundy.

And yet the reigns of the next two short-lived kings show that the work of conquest was by no means completed and that success depended largely on the characters of individual kings. The Danes still provided the stumbling-block in the way of unification. The accession of Athelstan's half-brother Edmund (939-46) was made the occasion of another attempt by the Yorkshire Danes to achieve independence by welcoming the king of Dublin as their ruler. The revolt spread quickly into the Midlands where Northampton was besieged and Tamworth was destroyed. There was apparently nothing that Edmund could do except negotiate a truce which removed all England to the east and north of Watling Street from his allegiance. But within the next four years he had regained control of the situation: in 942 he won back the loyalty of the 'District of the Five Boroughs' whose Danish inhabitants had no love for the rule of a Norwegian, and in 944 he was able to expel the Norwegian dynasty and once more bring Yorkshire into subordination to himself. He recognized, however, the difficulty of keeping the northern parts of England under proper discipline and, therefore, after his invasion and devastation of the kingdom of Strathclyde for the support it had given to the Norwegian immigrants from Ireland, he gave the district to the king of the Scots: the cession was not derogatory to English kingship, for the territory had in no sense been English or under English government and, if the king of the Scots was thereby made a friend and turned from any alliance with the Danes in Yorkshire and proved willing to undertake the responsibility of controlling the Norwegian colonists around Carlisle and elsewhere, then a great step had been taken to assure the peace of England proper. Edred (946–55), his brother, had thrice to face rebellions in Yorkshire where once again Norwegian rulers from Ireland were accepted, until in 954 the death of the formidable Eric Bloodaxe allowed Edred in obscure circumstances to resume authority in the north and to break the connexion with Dublin for all time. The Scandinavian kingdom of York disappeared and the district was given to the high reeve of Bamborough to hold under the English king.

The year 955 may well be regarded as ending both the first phase of the Scandinavian invasions and settlements and also the work of territorial unification which had brought into existence a single kingdom stretching from the English Channel to the Forth. The West Saxons, the East Anglians, the Mercians, and the Northumbrians as well as the Danes had all been subjected to the political government of the royal dynasty of Wessex. It is noteworthy that no rebellions followed the death of Edred when a divided succession temporarily split the realm between his two nephews, Edwy, who, after inheriting the whole kingdom, came to rule only in Wessex until his death in 959, and Edgar, who ruled in Mercia and East Anglia and the Danelaw from 957 and over the whole kingdom from 959 to 975. The success attained by the remarkable succession of great West Saxon kings can be gauged by the tranquillity of the reign of Edgar the Peaceable, when attention could be focused completely on reforms in the Church and the machinery of administration and scarcely a sign of political discontent or revolt made itself known.

THE ORGANIZATION OF GOVERNMENT AND SOCIETY

When Edward the Elder and his successors embarked upon a policy which made them the direct rulers of a mixed population of

Anglo-Saxons and Danes, they were quite well aware that this would force them to grapple with novel problems of government. For the Danes were strangers to the traditional customs and unwritten laws which cemented Anglo-Saxon society together and could not be expected to jettison their own ways of life. Inasmuch as they could be neither exterminated nor expelled from the regions which they had colonized for more than a generation, it was a question of finding a *modus vivendi* which the two races could accept. It was this fact more than anything else which gave a wider significance to the conception of kingship and urged the West Saxon kings to realize that government meant more than the mere continuance of age-long methods and called for conscious statecraft and the deliberate shaping of institutions to deal with the new conditions of the time. An artificial scheme of local government, which ignored the old boundaries, was introduced and spread in a comparatively short time over the whole country and proved its value by enduring nearly a thousand years. In correspondence with previous arrangements in Wessex, the 'District of the Five Boroughs' was divided into shires in Athelstan's reign, and these, along with East Anglia and Essex, were by Edmund's reign sub-divided into the smaller units of the hundred for the purposes of justice, taxation, and police. At the same time the responsibilities of the kindred were being supplanted by the obligations of overlords and neighbours: thus Athelstan decreed that all men should be compelled to find lords who would agree to stand as surety for their good behaviour, and he encouraged the promotion of 'frith-gilds', or peace-associations, which united men in groups, each of which agreed to hand over to justice any of its members charged with wrongdoing or else to pay a fine collectively. Edmund for his part sought to suppress the blood-feuds and to reduce the scope of self-help by stating that the kin of a murdered man was to wreak vengeance only on the slayer, who was to be universally regarded as an outlaw, and that the slayer's kin was no longer to be regarded as liable to make compensation for the crime. It is such developments as these that deserve to be specially stressed, for they show vividly that in the tenth century the old conceptions of government and society were rapidly yielding ground to a new and better order, which owed its firm establishment to the wisdom and statecraft of the Wessex kings.

THE ADVANCEMENT OF RELIGION AND LEARNING

So far as the evidence at our disposal permits us to form a judgment, it cannot be said that the first part of the tenth century witnessed an enthusiasm for religion and learning at all commensurate with political achievements. Edward the Elder certainly sanctioned in 909 the sub-division of the two Wessex bishoprics of Winchester and Sherborne into five, thus creating the dioceses of Ramsbury, Wells, and Crediton to look after the interests of Wiltshire and Berkshire, Somerset, and Devon and Cornwall respectively. Athelstan formed the see of St. Germans for Cornwall when he took it firmly within his kingdom. This was a notable reconstruction when we compare it with the great sprawling sees of the archbishopric of York, though it may have been carried too far to permit the small dioceses to remain financially self-supporting. And just as Edward the Elder founded New Minster at Winchester as a house of clerks which was to become Hyde Abbey, so his sons and grandsons became the founders of other monastic houses. It was not, however, until Edmund came under the influence of Oda, a remarkable Dane who became archbishop of Canterbury, and Edred and Edgar consented to be guided by Dunstan that an attempt was made to bring the secular priests to an awareness of their spiritual duties and the monks to a compliance with monastic discipline. Similarly, though Edward was a well-educated man and Athelstan a magnificent donor of manuscripts and an indefatigable collector of relics, though the charters of Athelstan's reign are the literary, almost too literary, productions of a group of professional clerks in the king's service, the promising renaissance of Alfred's reign was seemingly allowed to collapse through default of royal patronage. The vernacular writings of the great Aelfric towards the close of the century were to show, however, that learning and scholarship had by no means perished in England.

SELECT READING

Stenton, 315–66; Chambers, ch. vii; R. L. Poole, 'The Alpine Son-in-Law of Edward the Elder' in *Studies in Chronology and History* (1934), 115–22; W. G. Collingwood, *Scandinavian Britain* (1908), 119–144.

CHAPTER IX

ST. DUNSTAN AND THE REVIVAL OF THE CHURCH

As elsewhere on the Continent the Scandinavian invasions had impoverished and demoralized the Church and thrown the machinery of its administration out of gear. Dioceses which had been long established in Northumbria and East Anglia no longer survived. Churches had been pillaged and destroyed everywhere. The clergy with their wives and families and secular interests were scarcely to be distinguished from their parishioners and only too often stood for no higher standard of morality than theirs. The laity were untended and left in their ignorance. The fearful havoc wrought can be best illustrated from the conditions to which the monasteries were reduced, since about them we have more precise information. Where they were not burned ruins or deserted or hopelessly crippled through the loss of their endowments, they had in general failed to stress the prime principles of monasticism which emphasized community life, celibacy, and personal poverty. Indeed, it is difficult to distinguish them from the colleges of clerks, that is groups of men in holy orders, who were usually married and therefore not resident within the minsters they served and who were owners of private property. Only too often they exhibited the worst vices of ordinary lay society. In particular, the Rule of St. Benedict, which Benedict Biscop and Wilfrid of Ripon had tried so enthusiastically to introduce into the country, had not taken root to supplant the influence of the type of monasticism associated with the Irish Church, and therefore the English monasteries were governed, if they were governed at all, by the most diverse regulations. It is sufficient to recall that Alfred and his immediate successors made little or no attempt to revive monastic life and discipline and that there were no English monks to assist the literary renaissance.

The revitalization of the Church is associated mainly with Dunstan and his circle during the peaceful years of Edgar's reign, but it is a serious mistake to imagine that for the first half of the century the leaders of the Church had viewed religious stagnation with complacency and done nothing to bring about improvements. The reputation and achievements of Oda as archbishop of Canterbury (942–58) have in particular been unfairly overshadowed by those of his younger contemporaries who were fortunate enough to find biographers. Yet we know enough of what he did to realize that his influence must have been widespread and powerful. He instructed his episcopal colleagues to set to work to repair the ruined churches in their dioceses. He promulgated a series of canons to bring the clergy and the laity to a sense of their spiritual responsibilities and duties. And, as befitted one who had himself been a monk at Fleury on the Loire and in contact with Continental tendencies, he was interested in monastic reform and laid great emphasis upon the need for the strict observance of vows.

It was his successor, Dunstan, however, who caught the popular imagination. Born about 909 in the neighbourhood of Glastonbury Abbey in Somerset, he was educated there and came to show in later life a remarkable versatility as an artist and musician. So powerful were his family connexions in both State and Church that he rose quickly into prominence: he joined the household of his uncle, Ethelhelm, who was archbishop of Canterbury until 923, and soon became on terms of personal friendship with the Wessex kings. About 936 he became a professed monk and about 940 he was created abbot of Glastonbury by King Edmund and worked there for some fifteen years to make it a model of a true and disciplined monastic life by insisting on the use of a common refectory and a common dormitory and by refusing to sanction the admittance of married men to the precincts. He did not come prominently into political life until Edred made him his principal adviser, and on that king's death the jealousy of a group of Wessex magnates, who resented the royal preference for an ecclesiastic, drove Dunstan into exile at St. Peter's monastery, Ghent, from which he returned on the accession of Edgar to the throne. Edgar wisely identified the monarchy with the cause of ecclesiastical reform, with a forward-looking and progressive movement, and appointed Dunstan as bishop of Worcester in 957, bishop of London in 959, and archbishop of Canterbury in 960.

It is natural to assume that Dunstan wielded a great political influence and was the real power behind the throne, for it is indisputable that his personality and forceful character, his genuine piety and learning, made a deep impression upon his contemporaries. Yet it is impossible to say exactly what was done by him in the sphere of administration and government. The Anglo-Saxon Chronicle is at this time extremely meagre in its information, and the five biographies of Dunstan, two written by men who knew him personally, and three which incorporated Canterbury traditions about him after the Norman Conquest, are riddled after the fashion of the time with legends and miracles and contain only incidental allusions to anything outside the scope of monastic affairs, which alone interested those for whom these works were compiled. Of Dunstan's own writings nothing survives. We can but judge from his place among the witnesses to royal charters and from the secular laws and ecclesiastical canons of the time, one of which begins with the significant words, 'I and my archbishop decree . . .' Similarly, we know as much, or as little, of his activities after Edgar's death in 975 and before his own in 988. This is a slender basis on which to found a claim that he was the first of that long line of ecclesiastical statesmen who were going to dominate so much of the history of the later Middle Ages. This may well be true despite the lack of evidence. And there is no doubt that by the people at large he was greatly admired, and his memory as a saint of the English Church was sedulously preserved.

Dunstan's chief fame, however, lies in the part he played in re-forming the English Church. The most striking result was the reintroduction and firm establishment of the reformed Rule of St. Benedict. The ills that beset the Church in England were not peculiar to it: they were much more injurious to the Church on the Continent. In consequence, a reform movement had begun in 910 at Cluny in Burgundy to recapture and reassert the lost ideals of monasticism. It did not draw up a new 'rule' or series of regulations but adopted and adapted that of St. Benedict of Nursia in Italy (480–543), as revised by his namesake St. Benedict of Aniane in France (c. 750–820), and the resultant Cluniac Rule met with wide acceptance in Europe until the twelfth century saw the inception of new monastic orders like the Carthusians and the Cistercians. From Cluny the zeal for reform spread rapidly outwards and reached the abbey of Fleury near Orleans in 930. The extent to which Fleury directed the course of monastic reform in England has become a controversial question. It has been argued that the drastic changes made by Dunstan at Glastonbury represent a native and indigenous movement which owed nothing to influences from abroad and that the first effective contact between the separate developments in England and on the Continent occurred when Dunstan himself was exiled in Flanders and at St. Peter's abbey, Ghent, came into touch not with the Cluniac school of thought but the different influences of Lorraine. This contention savours of special pleading. For, now that the Danish raids had ceased, there was much coming and going between the lands on both sides of the Channel; Oda, the head of the English Church whilst Dunstan was abbot of Glastonbury, had been a monk of Fleury; Ethelwold, the most vigorous of the reformers, had been Dunstan's chief colleague at Glastonbury, yet there he did not find an inspiration that was sufficient and deliberately looked for it at Fleury; and to the same place Archbishop Oda's nephew, Oswald, another prominent reformer, went in person to study for some years. Certain it is that it was not until the ties with Fleury had been tightly drawn that monastic reform progressed rapidly in England, and by that time Dunstan was not its most zealous advocate. That role was filled by Ethelwold (d. 984), whose life was written by his pupil Aelfric, the most famous of the eleventh-century Anglo-Saxon scholars. Prevented from going himself to Fleury, he acquired the new monastic learning vicariously by sending his assistants there and applied it to the ancient and derelict monastery of Abingdon. When he became bishop of Winchester in 963, he had a larger scope for his reforming zeal and he was determined to restore monasticism in the South Danelaw, and Peterborough, Thorney, and particularly Ely, of which he was a most generous benefactor, were the more famous establishments he reorganized. He followed exactly in the footsteps of the Cluniac reformers, who concentrated their energies on monasticism first and foremost, and it was his energy which made it possible for the reform party to gain its main objectives. The work was neither easy nor pleasant, for the reformers came up against the vested interests of those who were accustomed to personal freedom and lax supervision and had no intention of changing their old ways for the austerities and strict discipline of the new order of things. Nevertheless, victory was eventually achieved. The monasteries were subjected to the Rule of St. Benedict: they did not, however, become part and parcel of the Cluniac Order. The solemn and regular conduct of divine services was stressed as never before, especially by the *Regularis Concordia*, drawn up by Bishop Ethelwold with advice from both Cluny and Lorraine, authorized by a council summoned by King Edgar at Winchester, and issued to all monastic houses in the king's name: this phase represents a direct borrowing from Cluny which became famous (and later discredited) for its attention to ritual and ceremonial. A curious development was the arrangements which tended to bring the English cathedrals under the control and government of monks in preference to secular priests. The policy of turning a house of clerks into a monastic community succeeded in Winchester and Worcester and was followed later about 1000 at Canterbury and Sherborne and elsewhere. It was a very complicated process and one difficult to follow: we have a good illustration of it at work at Worcester, where Oswald did not supplant the secular clerks but placed a community of monks side by side with them and, later on, the foundations came to coalesce. The pattern of cathedral organization remained confused until after the Norman Conquest and was not finally settled until the close of the twelfth century. The conception of monastic cathedrals never met with universal acceptance, and whilst some of the cathedrals were served and administered by monks, others remained under the care of secular clergy, who were, however, persuaded to live together under their own, and not monastic, regulations (*canones*) and thus to form a community or chapter of canons. The new ideals of monasticism stirred the imaginations of many landowners, who made large endowments to enable what could have been nothing more than quite small communities to continue their lives of devotion and study. Quite often the secular as well as the monastic foundations found themselves harassed by the problem of looking after the estates granted to them, and it is to this period that we can attribute the great landed power of the Church before the Norman Conquest. Oswald (d. 992), the nephew of Oda, who became bishop of Worcester in 961 and archbishop of York in 972 and continued to hold the two sees together until his death, did much to promote reforms in his dioceses in a more tactful and gracious way than his colleague, Ethelwold, and he is particularly remembered as the careful restorer of the fortunes of Ramsey Abbey.

It is noticeable that Dunstan, though doubtless sympathetic to the extension of monasticism, did not himself play a very active part. Apparently he had a more balanced view of his duties than Ethelwold and rightly considered that the monasteries were only one part of the Church Universal, and that the secular clergy and the laity called for at least equal consideration. For though he had been a monk his contact abroad had been with the Lorraine Reformers, who did not work in isolation but in close collaboration with the bishops. Therefore he gave his attention to the Church in general, convoking ecclesiastical councils of his province, ordering the regular summons of diocesan synods, encouraging the restoration of dilapidated churches, urging, through with little practical result, that the country priests should become celibate, preaching regularly to the people and in general endeavouring to raise the standard of morality. Bishop Oswald likewise did not neglect his episcopal duties: he made frequent visitations to all parts of his dioceses and his careful administration of Church lands is revealed by a remarkable and quite unique collection of charters issued by him. It is true that the leaders of reform were all monks and that monks supplied for many years the archbishops and bishops of the Church, but it is a mistake to let the accident of monastic biographies blind us to the work that was being done outside the monasteries altogether. And it was inevitable that the ecclesiastical revival should be followed by a literary revival which saw the establishment of schools of learning at Glastonbury, Winchester, and Canterbury, and brought Anglo-Saxon prose to a high mark of vitality and practical usefulness.

SELECT READING

Stenton, 427–62; J. A. Robinson, *The Times of St. Dunstan* (1923); D. Knowles, *Monastic Order in England* (1940), 31–56; W. Stubbs, *Historical Introductions to the Rolls Series* (ed. A. Hassall: 1902), 1–34.

CHAPTER X

THE AGRICULTURAL FOUNDATION OF ENGLAND

HISTORIANS have for a long time past ceased to believe that a 'mark' system, whereby every free man had an inalienable right to an equal share in the land owned by the community of which he was a member, actually existed in north-west Germany in and before the fifth century: it represents a figment of the imagination created by the bias of nineteenth-century liberalism and democracy. Unfortunately the hypothesis has not been rejected outright but still lurks in the mind to distort the picture of what actually happened when the emigrants from Germany set foot in Britain and began to lead a settled life. For it is still too often assumed that they were politically minded, intensely conscious of their social equalities and determined to reproduce them in their new homes. This predominant consideration dictated the way in which the land to be tilled was divided among them: all men were to have their holdings in strips scattered here and there, not in one compact block, and thereby take their share of poor soil as well as good soil and have the same advantages and disadvantages of accessibility. It is most unlikely that these newcomers to a strange land sought to express political and social ideas in terms of agriculture. Apart from the fact that there is no proof that the principle of equality was at work at all and that such meticulous arrangements were quite unnecessary when the early settlers were not numerous and had far more land at their disposal than they needed, this explanation does not tell us why each owner of a strip did not follow his own inclinations and farm it as he pleased but conformed to a common system whereby all sowed precisely the same crops at precisely the same time and left the same field fallow; or why the strips should be of widely varying extent and lie at all sorts of angles to one another instead of being uniform in size and orderly in arrangement.

This traditional account of the origin of the medieval fields, accepted by Seebohm, Vinogradoff, and surprisingly even Maitland, is now properly discredited. The problem must be approached not from the point of view of the political theorist but of the practical farmers. The Germans who had uprooted themselves from their homes on the Continent were obsessed, like their descendants for hundreds of years, by the fear of hunger, and their main preoccupation lay with the grim business of keeping alive. They had to engage themselves in a hard and unceasing fight with the land and with nature. Therefore the agricultural arrangements they made were the result of common-sense farming and had nothing to do with political organization or social status. They faced the problems of husbandry with expert knowledge and with expert implements: nowadays labour has been made easier, wastage less necessary and products more varied by the discoveries of science, but no new radically essential instrument has been invented.

It must not be imagined that, when the Anglo-Saxons chose of their own accord to come to Britain, they expected to find it a wilderness. Even before Caesar's expeditions, at least the south-eastern districts had been known on the Continent for their agri-culture, and throughout the period of the Roman occupation the sod-turning plough was employed in the production of corn, even for export. Therefore, since we may safely assume that the Anglo-Saxons dispossessed the Britons, they found cultivated land ready at their disposal. There was no need to settle immediately on virgin soil: they could till the British fields. Furthermore, we should hesitate to accept without question the common assumption that they found in Britain a specifically Celtic type of agricultural fields—the 'closes', or enclosures, of small size and rectangular shape. These they are said to have supplanted by the large and oblong strips of the open-field system. Such an antithesis is an illusion, for Britons and Anglo-Saxons used the same kind of plough and let their methods be dictated simply by the layout of the ground: as practical farmers they all knew that the technique of ploughing could not be the same for the flat lands of Lincolnshire and the narrow valleys and hill-sides of Devon.

The Anglo-Saxons tackled the work as small communities living close together, in what is usefully termed 'nucleated' villages, for the sake of protection and companionship. They ploughed just suffi-cient land to feed themselves and themselves alone and, faced by a common need, indeed, a common peril, they worked as a common body. The layout of the arable was settled by three dominating factors: (a) The mould-board plough. It did not differ in essentials from that used to-day with its coulter, share and, most particularly, its mould-board which makes it possible not merely to cut the sod but to turn a furrow. In effect, that all-important action of the mould-board made it convenient for the farmer, then as now, to

arrange his ploughing so that his day's work consisted of two contiguous strips, all the furrows in one lying in one direction and all
the furrows in the other lying in the opposite direction. The length
of the furrow was limited by the need to rest the plough-team to a
furlong (furrow-long), which is now standardized in our measure-
ments of length at 220 yards. The width of these strips was determined by the capacity of the teams working a full day. They were
turned round upon the head-land, and the plough re-entered the soil
at a distance which ensured that the two contiguous strips should be
completed before the end of the day. The total width of these two
strips was reckoned at four roods or twenty-two yards in relation to
a furrow of 220 yards in length. So we arrive at our present acre of
4,840 square yards. (*b*) The physical contours and soil characteristics. All strips, however, did not work out at just an acre in extent,
for the result of a day's work naturally depended on whether the
land was flat or sloped and whether the soil was dry and porous or
wet and clayey, and the length and width of the strips varied
accordingly. The 'acre', therefore, is what it was, for example, to
the compilers of Domesday Book, a conventional term for a day's
ploughing and not a standard and uniform measurement. Furthermore, the direction of the ploughing altered with the lie of the land
to obtain natural drainage, and for that reason the blocks of strips
point in all directions. (*c*) The system of co-aration. A self-contained
and self-sufficing society, which was not greatly animated by the
motive of profit and had no desire to engage in commercial farming,
had no reason for not adopting the same methods, which, indeed,
were dictated by the limited range of crops and by the seasons. It
is to be supposed that very few of the cultivators possessed a full
plough-team and that these were made up by beasts contributed by
several owners. This co-aration presumably determined the distribution of the acre plots among the cultivators: they were handed
over in rotation, with the result that each man had his strips
scattered among those of his neighbours and, quite incidentally,
shared the good and the bad, the near and the distant land. Thus
the patchwork appearance was not the consequence of previous
planning but of the technique of farming. Once the layout had
been fixed, there would be no need for constant re-allocation and
each man would retain the same strips year after year and would
cultivate them as his own.

Presumably in the early days, with so much land at their disposal,
the settlers could break fresh ground whenever they thought it

advisable: the limiting factor was the distance from the settlement. Still, the Anglo-Saxons had apparently passed the stage of extensive cultivation by the time they crossed to Britain; although it was not until the eighteenth century that the scientific principles of manuring and rotation of crops showed how land could be used all the time without a serious decline in productiveness, yet they were accustomed to keep the same block of arable continually under contribution. Thus, after cropping one field they left it fallow the next year to allow the soil to recover its strength, and they ploughed a second field beside the first and divided it between spring and winter corn. The two-field system, as it was called, seems to have been normal until and throughout the twelfth century, and it is obvious that the evolution of the three-field system soon afterwards was an easy and natural transition from the arrangements of its predecessor: in fact, both are found in operation at the same time.

Most villages in England could show their 'open fields', so called because they were without permanent fencing, and it was the practice after harvest to leave the ground as common pasture. They stood, therefore, in contra-distinction to the permanent 'closes', or enclosures, which were to be found in every part of England. Outside the 'open fields' were the meadow lands, usually fenced permanently and shared out each year in due proportion among the members of the settlement, and the wastelands, upon which all could turn out their cattle to graze at any time of the year. Though the arable is the most conspicuous part of the village lands, pastoral pursuits were vitally necessary in rural economy: there was an imperative need for live-stock to produce milk, butter, cheese, and wool and to carry out the natural manuring of the fallow before it was broken up. The meadows did not produce a large quantity of hay and its value was accordingly high, and the right of common pasturage was always jealously guarded.

This is the basic groundwork of agriculture and agricultural life throughout the Middle Ages in the greater part of England. We must bear in mind, however, that the 'open field' system was not universal. It will for special reasons rarely be found in Kent in the east, or along the west from Devon to Lancashire. The pastoral village, with its isolated homesteads scattered over the countryside, rather than the agricultural village in its 'nucleated' form, will predominate in northern England and in Wales because much of these regions, while fit for stock-raising, was not suitable for arable cultivation and therefore communal services and communal life were less imperative. The general picture, however, is not altered. Corn had to be grown practically everywhere or else there would be no bread. And co-aration in all its elements was not restricted to the 'open fields' but was just as possible in the case of the closes and scattered fields to be found, for example, in Kent, East Anglia, and Wales. It is left to our imagination to visualize the old village communities slowly pushing their way farther and farther afield and other village communities establishing themselves in new clearances in forest and fen. The work of subjugating nature, though begun before by the Britons, is being tackled for the first time in all parts of the country: it will be hard and laborious, it will take many centuries to achieve, it will leave little trace of its steady and unspectacular advance; still, by 1066 many of the villages of to-day, especially south of the Humber-Mersey line, had already taken firm root in the soil of England.

The principle of equality and the contrary principle of lordship have not entered into the discussion because they are irrelevant to it: the method of ploughing would have been precisely the same whether operations were conducted by a community or on behalf of an individual. So developing disparities and social distinctions did not alter the layout of the medieval fields and the system of agriculture, for these were dictated once and for all by the requirements of practical farming. In this respect the assertion of lordship and even the manorialization after the Norman Conquest changed nothing because no improvement could be suggested.

SELECT READING

Lipson, i (1937), 1–31; C. S. and C. S. Orwin, *The Open Fields* (1938), 1–64.

CHAPTER XI

THE STRUCTURE OF ANGLO-SAXON SOCIETY

GERMANIC society, both before the migrations and after the settlement in England, was marked by two prominent characteristics: the folk-law and the kindred. Whenever people begin to associate together in some kind of communal life, rules of conduct have to be devised to maintain peace and order. Such rules are rarely committed to writing, but they are faithfully remembered and handed down from one generation to another as the 'folk-law' or 'custom' of the people. Whilst it is impossible to believe that folk-law was completely immutable, it is clear that any irresponsible alteration or adjustment to a particular case was little removed from impiety. Therefore the early assembly-courts concentrated simply on one task, to see that, before the mystic ordeals of fire, water and the like were called upon to proclaim guilt or innocence, there had been no mistake in the hallowed preliminaries. That is why Anglo-Saxon law placed all the emphasis upon procedure with all its elaborate formulas and formalities. Folk-law protected all men's persons and property by imposing upon wrongdoers a fine in accordance with a fixed tariff of compensations: the 'wergild' was the sum paid to the kin of a slain man and varied in its rate with the victim's social status; the 'bot' was the sum paid to the injured man himself and varied with the parts of his body outraged and the kind of property damaged. For its enforcement, folk-law depended largely upon the kindred. Should a man do wrong or be wronged that was not a matter which concerned himself alone, for his kinsmen were involved in either suffering revenge or in having to carry out retaliation. Hence the assembly-courts would pay no attention to a mere individual and do nothing on his sole behalf. They required every litigant to be accompanied by his kindred to vouch for him. Even then his personal and unsupported statement was of no value: his kindred must swear a confirmatory oath with him; how many 'compurgators', as they were called, were necessary depended on the social status of the parties to the litigation and the seriousness of the offence. And, finally, to make sure that he would accept the findings of the court, whatever they might be, he had to rely upon his kindred to furnish a guarantee, to act as his sureties or 'borh'.

After the main stages of conquest and settlement had been completed, Anglo-Saxon England appeared as a mosaic of many independent 'folks'. The territorial area, occupied and developed by each 'folk', whether it constituted a large or a small community, was frequently termed a 'province'. These 'provinces' precede the division of the land into the later 'shires', and we know nothing of their boundaries and they are certainly disappearing from sight in the charters of the ninth century. Though some evidently underlie shires like Dorset and Somerset and sub-divisions of shires like the lathes of Kent and the rapes of Sussex, we should remember that there is no evidence at all to show that the 'provinces' themselves had ever been regarded as administrative units, and it is wiser to look upon them as simply the tribal and economic units they undoubtedly were.

We must not imagine, however, that Anglo-Saxon society was moulded simply by the influence of 'folk' and 'kindred' or that it was essentially static, for other factors were always at work in its midst. To appreciate the dynamic impulses of society we must turn from the legal evidence of laws and charters to the literary evidence of epic poetry like the *Beowulf* and the historical work of Bede and other narrative writers.

I. The Development of Lordship and Dependency

It is beyond all dispute that the Anglo-Saxons introduced into their new home the principles of Germanic society simply because they were the only ones they knew. This does not, however, imply either that such principles tallied with those described by Tacitus three hundred years earlier or even with those which prevailed among them before they left the Continent. The Anglo-Saxons had a long history before the settlement in England and ranks of society were a very real thing in pre-migration days. Even kinship had already seen at work the disruptive effects of the personal relationships between chieftain and warriors. Then their social order was presumably disturbed by the circumstances of their settlement, which meant a cataclysmic sundering of the old ties. Furthermore, the British had to be fitted in to some kind of subordinate relation, and all the subsequent wars among the Anglo-Saxons themselves meant further captives and unfreedom: it was

English slaves in Rome who caught the attention of Pope Gregory the Great and the slave-trade was still flourishing in Bristol in the eleventh century.

So society formed a pyramid of many stages. The highest under the king was occupied by the *athelings*, members of the royal family, who were frequently placed in control of some part of the kingdom. Next to them came the *eorls*, the gentle-born, who as warriors were men of considerable importance: the term is not frequently used in records except in Kent because this old nobility of blood was soon augmented and then eclipsed by a new nobility of service, by men who had attached themselves to the king and gained rewards in lands and privileges and were known as *gesiths*, and, still later, as *thegns*. Much lower down were the *ceorls*, the typical free men, the farmers who had a high wergild of 200 shillings to mark their place in the community as the solid basis of society. The *laets* formed a social group only in Kent apparently and were semi-servile in that they had to do labour-services for a superior and semi-free in that they shared in the rights and obligations of the free. It has been suggested that they constituted a class of British peasantry surviving under the domination of the Jutes. Lowest of all were the *theows*, the slaves who were outside the folk and therefore had no existence in law. They comprised the enslaved Britons and Welsh and also Anglo-Saxons who had sworn false oaths and been outlawed or fallen on evil days and been forced down into servitude. It should be observed that these are only the main gradations of rank, for within them were further sub-divisions: for example, in Kent there were four classes of eorls, three of laets and four of theows.

Society, however, was not so confined as it were to hermetically-sealed compartments that movement from one to another, either higher or lower, was impossible. The long adventurous years of settlement and conquest had from the outset made social and economic advancement both possible and rapid to those who had the strength and vigour to take advantage of the situation. And it is quite clear that the principle of 'lordship', the superiority of one man over another, was firmly rooted and openly acknowledged in the Anglo-Saxon system as soon as written evidence comes to hand: the kings, by their charters, have granted royal rents and services to bishops and nobles and made them the lords of many peasants. The numbers of the aristocracy grew steadily with each succeeding generation: this was inevitable in the progress of civilization, for, although a primitive society may share its poverty equally, it cannot advance either in wealth or what then was largely its derivative, culture, at an equal pace. Some will always forge ahead and by that fact acquire a privileged position they had not held before, and the gap between lords on one side and tenants on the other was always widening. The laws of Ine speak much of such matters as lords who have granted lands to dependents and receive services in return for them, and of dependents who have dared to forsake their lords and must return to them and pay them compensation.

The broad line of social division is seen when we examine the history of the two all-important groups.

I. THE GESITHS

The gesiths, a word meaning 'companions', were men who voluntarily abandoned their kindred and entered the service of the king, took him as their lord and entered within the protection of his 'peace'. As members of his household they became legally and economically dependent on him. Their service was primarily military and their official status gave them a far higher wergild (1,200 shillings) than that of the ordinary ceorl (200 shillings). The development was quite natural and goes back beyond recorded time: it reflected the relationship between a chieftain and his warriors described by Tacitus. In return for their services they were given grants of lands and thereby their social prestige was raised still further: their oath became of greater value and their houses more sacrosanct. Such free men were set apart from their fellows and were placed in responsible control of the free men who cultivated the lands they had received. The term 'gesith' disappears from the records in the ninth century. For some time it had been yielding place to that of *thegn*. There was little practical difference between their positions: in each case they held what was essentially an office at first, though in time it became an hereditary status; for the most part they performed military and administrative services; they entered the households not only of the king but of any important dignitary.

II. THE CEORLS

The ceorls included all free men below the rank of gesith, and as a class they were losing ground. For if war could create an aristocracy, it could also depress free men simply by drawing a line between those who fought and those who farmed, to the disparagement of the tillers of the soil. The ceorls gradually lost the full measure of economic freedom, and the development of inequalities went on steadily throughout the centuries. (*a*) Royal action made depression possible when the king rewarded services or conferred favours by granting away to others the food-rents and other dues that had been payable to himself. If for some reason those responsible for them could not render them, then it would be easy for their new lord to demand that they should make compensation by working for him on his own land in accordance with some agreed contract. (*b*) Economic forces were always at work to depress part of the peasantry. The catastrophe of illness, the occurrence of bad harvests, the crushing burden of a land-tax like Danegeld, spelt ruin to many people and, eager to sell some of their independence for their lives, they sought lords and put themselves under obligations to others, which they could pay only in terms of their labour or their land. Or else rich landowning classes, especially in the Church, settled tenants on their estates upon conditions of service. Whether it was through the surrender of land or the acquisition of land makes no difference to the fact that conditional tenures were making their appearance with growing frequency. (*c*) Motives of security were working in the same direction with other peasants who had once found protection in their groups of kinsmen; as the ties of kinship weakened, they were left to look after their own interests, especially in the courts of law. Many of the peasants were in no position to assume so heavy a burden and voluntarily placed themselves under the protection of a powerful neighbour and paid him for it in money or services. Usually, however, it was not only the safety of their persons about which they were anxious, for in extremity they could always go into hiding: it was their landed property which was the difficulty, for it stood still, exposed to whatever violence and danger might occur. So, very slowly and very obscurely, they began to put their holdings also under the care of a lord. This process of 'commendation' of person or land or both together was at first an individual matter, a private contract between the parties concerned, but soon the monarchy saw its advantages in the sphere of police administration. A man for whom no one was responsible, like the 'sturdy beggar' of Tudor times, was an object of distrust and it was essential that he should be produced in court to answer for any wrongdoing on his part:

therefore royal decrees came to insist that men of no substance and standing should find a lord who would guarantee their good conduct.

The ever-changing character of society can be traced in the altered attitude to kindred as a social bond. Its defects in the process of the courts were manifest. For instance, the natural bias in favour of an accused kinsman might defeat the ends of justice. In some of the earliest Anglo-Saxon laws we possess, the Laws of Wihtred of Kent which go back to the last years of the seventh century, an accused ceorl was ordered to clear himself, not by kinsmen but by three oath-helpers of his own class, while the Laws of Ine a hundred years later required anyone charged with homicide to include a man of high rank among those who testified for him and thus some impartiality was ensured. Again, the lack of knowledge often made the testimony of kindred worthless. The commonest offence in the Middle Ages was theft, normally taking place in secret, and as the kindred could know nothing about it, no confirmatory oath came to be demanded from them. Instead, the accused was required to accept the assistance of oaths sworn by non-kinsmen, by neighbours who were at first selected by himself and later nominated for him by the court, provided that he suffered no disparagement thereby, for the notion of peerage in its primary sense of trial by equals seems to have been present quite early. Furthermore, if offences were committed against the king, he was not disposed to trust the word of any automatically functioning group of kinsmen but preferred to secure the more reliable services of neighbours chosen by his officials.

How far kinship weakened during the Anglo-Saxon period is a difficult question, but as soon as neighbours began to take the place of kin, it was essential to define the territorial limits from which they could be drawn and, by the time we have explicit information, Anglo-Saxon society is being organized in territorial units which can assume responsibility for the reporting of crime and the production of wrongdoers for judgment.

Though the operations of a developing feudalism are clearly visible in England before 1066, they have acted in a very haphazard and incomplete way: each district had reached a different stage in its growth and, in fact, localism was so deep-rooted that each village had its own peculiar customs and agricultural arrangements. The village community always remained the essential form of rural organization and the lowest unit of organized political life: though the common round of village life did not vary and the extraordinary was rarely to be met with, though it is in the nature of things that we should have little or no record of their activities, it is presumable that village meetings could be convoked to assert discipline where necessary, settle the current problems and draw up regulations which were the laws, the by-laws, the 'custom' of the village. There was, however, no economic or social uniformity among the villages themselves: many of them were quite independent and knew no lords; others were completely under lordship and knew no free-holders; others represented a middle stage in which many peasant proprietors existed alongside those who no longer had their lands free and unattached. A most bewildering confusion was seen in some villages where the inhabitants had entered into ties of 'com-mendation', not to one but to many lay and ecclesiastical lords, and quite often placed their persons under the patronage of one man and their lands under the protection of another. Out of this chaos of relationships one general principle holds broadly true: commendation in all its forms had not meant that the peasantry was deprived of its free status. It is wrong to assume that dependence is necessarily abject. The ceorl who was the typical peasant remained under the protection of the customary law: what other law was there to take its place? He might pay rent in money (*gafol*) or in kind (*feorm*) or in labour-services for the land he held, but his obligations were regulated according to custom. Economic dependence did not necessarily mean the loss of his personal rights and the degradations of serfdom. This curious blend of freedom and dependence in one and the same person com-pletely baffles any attempt to produce a clear-cut and logical analysis of Anglo-Saxon society.

II. The Expansion of Monarchy

The influence of the rapidly developing conception of kingship was early at work to alter social organization. For before they left the Continent the Anglo-Saxons had passed the stage of tribal society where a patriarchal type of government, based upon the heads of families and an aristocracy of blood, held sway. The Angles already knew a dynasty of strong kings, presumably elected in time of military crisis to act as leaders in war and possessing in peace a vague and ill-defined authority. And after the migrations to England war and conquest created more kings, for the Germans had well-recognized leaders like Aelle in Sussex, Cerdic in Wessex, and Ida and Aelle in Northumbria, from whom lines of descent were unbroken to prove that pagan monarchy was no ephemeral and weak institution.

The early kings were undoubtedly stronger in prestige than in actual power. As divine origin was usually attributed to them, they were regarded as the mystical embodiment of their people who made them the focus of their racial life and racial enthusiasms and accorded them a reverent and devoted obedience. Appointment to the kingship was not so much elective as selective. In other words, the office was kept within the narrow circle of the royal kindred, but within that limitation the choice was free and it did not follow that the eldest son or any son would succeed his father. Much depended upon the urgency of the times, since war would hardly tolerate the accession of a minor, upon the will of the reigning king, maybe upon the wishes of the witan whom it would be usually wise to consult, even though this was not essential. In its potentialities, at least, monarchy inevitably grew stronger. (a) As war begat kings, so it enlarged their authority. Success meant an increase in the area under their control and in their wealth until the narrow borders of tribal settlements had become the frontiers of large kingdoms. The Heptarchy of the seven more important of these kingdoms was but one stage in a process which went on until, for example, the kingdom of East Anglia had become merely the two districts of Norfolk and Suffolk in the realm governed by the Mercian and then the Wessex dynasty. The advance to unrivalled supremacy must have been difficult—the 'Early English Annals' speak much of the sub-kings of Wessex and indicate how unprecise the overlordship of the Wessex kings could be—but it was undoubtedly made. Military force by itself, however, was unlikely to found an enduring kingdom, and stability was promoted by another development. (b) Pagan monarchy was not weak and we ought not to seek an explanation of its expanding authority solely in the influence of Roman political ideas and traditions as incorporated in the Church. For the knowledge of those ideas must have been very feeble round about the time of Gregory the Great, and yet it is evident that before the mission of St. Augustine the king was exercising the important function of interpreter of tribal custom, of folklaw, as exemplified in the 'Laws' issued in consultation with the witan. Thus in a vague manner he was on the way to being recognized as the fountain-head of justice. And it is very likely that it was under Merovingian influences that an imperialist conception comes to light quite early in the period of Mercian greatness in the eighth century when Ethelbald bestowed upon himself the regnal title of 'rex Britanniae'. His cousin Offa went still further: as a consequence of his military campaigns he deposed or executed the kings of neighbouring states like Sussex and East Anglia, he degraded sub-kings to the position of royal officials, and he included all newly acquired territory with his own in the *regnum Anglorum*. His death cut short this imperialist development so far as Mercia was concerned, but the idea did not die and was resumed later by the Wessex line of kings. (*c*) When pagan kingship in England became christianized, the Church and the Monarchy entered upon a long, harmonious, and fruitful co-operation, in the course of which their interests became closely identified: the partnership between them has never since been dissolved. The Church could not hope to do its work properly unless peace and order were guaranteed, and therefore in its own interests it found it essential to support the king and increase his authority. Hence it encouraged obedience to Caesar in the things that were Caesar's as a religious duty and gave him trained and educated advisers from its bishops and abbots. As early as 787 Offa's son had been anointed during his father's lifetime as king of the Mercians and such consecration carried with it a special sacrosanctity.

Thus by the close of the ninth century Monarchy had already formed strong traditions and acquired authority enough to maintain them; it was no colourless institution but a powerful and dominating force. What this was to mean in the evolution of administration the last century and a half of the Anglo-Saxon Monarchy was fully to disclose.

SELECT READING

Stenton, 274–314; J. E. A. Jolliffe, *Constitutional History of Medieval England* (1937), 1–55; Jolliffe, 'Era of the Folk in English History' in *Oxford Essays . . . to H. E. Salter* (1934), 1–32; Jolliffe, 'Northumbrian Institutions' in *E.H.R.*, xli (1926), 1–42; G. Lapsley, 'Mr. Jolliffe's Construction of Early Constitutional History' in *History*, xxiii (1938), 1–11; P. E. Schramm, *History of the English Coronation* (1937), 12–27.

CHAPTER XII

THE IMPACT OF SCANDINAVIAN AND ANGLO-SAXON CIVILIZATIONS

IT is little more than a generation ago that it was customary to discuss in detail the contributions made by the Romans, the Anglo-Saxons and the Normans to the development of England and to dismiss the irruptions of the Scandinavians as a regrettable incident of a fortunately transient character. It was argued that few Danes and fewer Norwegians settled in the country, that in consequence they were quickly absorbed by the native population and lost their racial distinctiveness, and that the paganism and backwardness of their civilization meant that they could 'contribute nothing because they had nothing to contribute'. In any case, so it was said, by Edgar's time the Wessex kingship had become an English monarchy with political control over all parts of the country so that a Scandinavian influence was of little or no account during the following half-century, whilst any later reassertion of it by Cnut was equally short-lived and impermanent. Within recent years, however, attention has been diverted from the destructive and purely negative aspect in an attempt to vindicate and appreciate the positive and therefore more lasting effects. As generally happens, the new orientation, though most valuable in itself, has been adopted so uncritically that we are now informed that 'institutional development among the Anglo-Saxons in the tenth and eleventh centuries was largely a matter of adopting and assimilating Scandinavian elements' and that the Scandinavian influence was more important on the course of future events than that of the Norman Conquest itself.

In comparison with the darkness which covers the Anglo-Saxon infiltrations of the fifth and sixth centuries, we have a fair amount of evidence to throw light upon the Scandinavian settlements. This does not mean that we shall ever be able to make a proper reconstruction of what took place in the tenth and eleventh centuries, for we have very little contemporary witness: no Scandinavian chroniclers, few charters, the meagre entries in the Anglo-Saxon Chronicle and the Laws, and the ambiguous statements of Norse folklore. Nevertheless, though direct information is lacking on the fundamental problems, we can work backwards from the unique memorial of Domesday Book and from the remarkably numerous and varied charters made in the twelfth century by small land-holders in the Danelaw and draw deductions and make interpretations with reasonable confidence.

The first problem for attention must be the extent of the country into which the Scandinavians penetrated: this must be largely determined by the evidence of place-names. The 'Great Army', which had ravaged England so mercilessly after 865, finally broke up into three parts: one division under Halfdan marched north into Yorkshire in 874 and settled down on the land between the Humber and the Tees, another in 877 occupied the eastern part of Mercia, the third in 879 chose East Anglia as its home. The Danes, who formed the major part of what was doubtless a composite host of adventurers, naturally found it necessary to continue to organize themselves on military lines. Thus part of eastern Mercia was split into five areas, each under an independent jarl and each having as its centre a fortified camp to which the foreigners could retire for protection in times of emergency. From these strategically placed burhs the Danes did not spread themselves haphazardly over the surrounding countryside but worked their way outwards on each side of the Roman roads, which permitted them to get back rapidly into safety and to concentrate their forces: with them it was the roads and not, as in the case of the Anglo-Saxons, the rivers which governed the direction of expansion. What happened in what was called the 'District of the Five Boroughs' of Lincoln, Derby, Nottingham, Leicester, and Stamford was repeated elsewhere, and the reflexion of a military organization can be seen generations later: for example, in 962 Edgar sent a writ to Yorkshire addressed to 'Earl Oslac and all the Army which dwells in his ealdormanry' and the 'Army' of Northamptonshire is mentioned in the reign of Ethelred II. Indeed, the fortified burhs were so much the heart of the Danish organization that Edward the Elder's main efforts were concentrated on reducing them to submission, for he knew that that implied the automatic subjugation of the surrounding districts, and they were made later the centres of the shires created in the Midlands. By the eleventh century, when England was viewed according to the law—West Saxon, Mercian, or Danish—which prevailed within it, the Danish law was said to cover fifteen shires, and on that basis we can conveniently consider the area of Danish influence as comprising three districts, each affected in different degree: (a) The Southern Danelaw between the Thames and the Welland which flows into the Wash. (*b*) The Eastern Dane-law of East Anglia. (*c*) The Northern Danelaw between the Welland and the Tees, which was the essential Danelaw, covering an area larger than Normandy where other Danes were at the same time forming another distinctive community within a foreign land.

The Norwegians for their part operated mainly from Ireland and penetrated north-west England into Cheshire, especially the Wirral peninsula, the coasts of Lancashire, Westmorland, and Cumberland, particularly round Carlisle, and made small settlements in North and South Wales, whilst the numerous places called 'Normanby' elsewhere in England show that at some time or other they had co-operated with the Danes and settled down among them.

The reality of the presence of the Danes in England is adequately witnessed by the place-names: there is no escape from the fact of the ubiquitous towns and villages ending in '-by', the hamlets ending in '-thorpe' and '-toft', and the comparatively late clearances in forests, moors, and fens which were marked by '-thwaite'. It has been calculated that by the end of the eleventh century nearly eight hundred place-names ending in '-by' were in existence south of the Tees. But, as in the case of the Anglo-Saxon settlers in the fifth century, much depends on the fundamental question of the size of the invading armies, the number of warriors who decided to remain in their new country, and the likelihood of further immigrations. In this connexion it is well to remember that the motley collection of Normans, Bretons, Flemings and others who fought in the battle of Hastings was no more than 7,000 strong, whereas the native population of England, conjecturally estimated on the statistics of the Domesday survey, numbered between one and two millions. These newcomers from France were doubtless reinforced later, yet there can be no question that, so far as they were concerned, they made their pre-eminence secure by monopolizing high office in administration, the Church and the army, and thereby were able to superimpose their own language and customs and ways upon the numerically superior English, though without affecting the lives of the lower classes fundamentally. We are therefore compelled to ask ourselves whether the place-name evidence should be interpreted to mean simply that the Danes enjoyed a political, social, and economic predominance without necessarily having anything approaching equality, much less superiority, in numbers.

We cannot rely upon the figures given by contemporary chroniclers about the size of the Scandinavian fleet and armies, for they are notoriously prone to exaggeration. In any case, it was not the numbers but the exceptional mobility and superior training and equipment which wrought the downfall of the English and kept them quiescent. Presumably, many of the warriors had no desire to settle: some would prefer to return home, many to continue their piracy in Normandy and elsewhere. To begin with, therefore, we must assume that the Scandinavian settlers were not numerous, that there was no serious displacement, let alone extermination, of the English, and that in the main there was only a change of owner-ship resulting from the superimposition of Danish warriors upon native farmers.

There must have been, however, though we know nothing of its details, a continuous flow of Danish immigrants into the northern and eastern parts of the country before the Norman Conquest. There was certainly no lack of opportunity, for Yorkshire was, as often as not, under the rule of a Scandinavian king until 954, Scandinavian armies were again in the country in the early eleventh century, and three Danish kings sat on the English throne itself. The exceptionally valuable clue to the relative numbers of English and Danes is provided by a study of personal names. We have no early lists, but the evidence of Domesday Book and the twelfth-century charters suggests that some sixty per cent of the Lincoln-shire peasantry, forty per cent of the East Anglian peasantry, and roughly fifty per cent of the population of the Northern Danelaw as a whole, were then bearing names of Scandinavian origin, and the records of the thirteenth-century royal courts reveal that hosts of such names were still in common use four hundred years after the first settlements had been made. The large proportion of women's names at least implies that, just as Haesten, the leader of the last invasion of Alfred's reign, and his followers were accom-panied by their wives and families, so in some way or other the Danish soldier-settlers got their womenfolk to join them and give their venture the character of a genuine colonization. Furthermore, the history of personal nomenclature shows quite clearly that the colonists kept their own traditions strong and vital: otherwise their names would not have survived the competition with English and Norman rivals for more than twelve generations and have gone on preserving rare forms which were forgotten even in Scandinavia itself, or have continued to exhibit changes and varieties in contra-distinction to English names which, though still in frequent use, had by the twelfth century begun to decline in number and simply repeat themselves. By the fourteenth century, however, Scandinavian as well as English names were going out of fashion because the peasantry began to mark its social advancement by adopting the French names of their masters, like William, Robert, Maud, and Joan.

The evidence of place-names and personal names, taken together, suggests to us the extent, the intensity, and the permanence of Scandinavian colonization. The Southern Danelaw exhibits the conditions which must have prevailed in the earliest stages of settlement, when there was little more than a change in ownership. For the Scandinavian names belong not so much to the peasantry as to the official or landowning classes, and presumably because such men controlled for a time the administration and the dispensation of justice in the local courts, therefore counties as far south as Middlesex and Essex could once be regarded as within the scope of the Danelaw. However, this region was soon brought under the direct rule of the Wessex monarchy, any great influx of the Scandinavian folk was prevented, and assimilation was brought about without difficulty or long delay. The eastern Danelaw saw a more vigorous colonization of Norfolk than of Suffolk and produced a complex society, neither stable nor coherent. The Northern Danelaw knew the presence of Scandinavians so numerous that they could not be quickly submerged, so independent that they could not easily be assimilated, so predominant that they could at first lord it over the native English, impose many of their customs upon them, and, in doing so, change the general character of a great part of the country.

We are not, therefore, surprised to find that the Danelaw shows a divergence from the rest of England in many aspects of life.

I. SOCIAL DIFFERENCES

The comparatively late influx of free warriors, to whom the conditions of war had given a rough equality or at least the chance of rapid social advancement, resulted in the establishment of a peasant population which retained its personal liberty and independence. The compilers of Domesday Book, whose primary concern was with the ways in which lands were held and not with the social rank of individuals, were confronted with the existence of men who were neither lords nor tenants of lords, by men who owned their small tenements and could do what they liked with them. They gave special recognition to these small proprietors under the name of 'sokemen'. These presumably represented the rank and file of the Danish soldiery who had settled on the land but remained still in close touch with their military leader. The connexion between them remained personal and did not degenerate into a servile relationship: that is to say, though the 'sokemen' acknowledged his superiority, his 'lordship', and were bound to attend his court (the fundamental meaning behind 'soc' and 'soc-man' or 'sokeman'), and in return for his military protection paid him dues which became sooner or later identified with rents in kind or, quite frequently, in money or occasionally in light labour services, yet he was not and never became the lord of their land. They owned it themselves, however small it might be, and they paid the taxes on it direct to the king. At the time of the Domesday survey, 'sokemen' made up a half (11,000) of the population in Lincolnshire, one-third (2,000) in Leicestershire, and nearly one-third (1,500) in Nottinghamshire. In the charters and court records of the twelfth and thirteenth centuries, we see large numbers of freemen with Danish names transacting business and disposing of their property quite freely: they bought and sold among themselves and made innumerable gifts to monasteries without needing to refer to any lord. Freedom such as this did not, of course, belong to the villeins and bordars who lived beside them in the Danelaw and who probably represented the depressed Anglo-Saxon peasantry; yet even in their case, though they had no power to alienate their tenements, the labour-services demanded were not grievously heavy. All this represents a greater measure of independence than is to be found among the peasantry outside the Danelaw: many, though by no means all, had been subjected there to feudalizing influences so that they could rarely part with land without a lord's permission and in consequence have left us comparatively few charters like those so commonly made in the districts of heavy Scandinavian settlement. The 'sokemen', therefore, formed an integral and a dominant class in society which had no counterpart in other parts of the country.

II. ECONOMIC DIFFERENCES

The continued existence throughout many centuries of a free peasantry in the north and east of England gave to the practice of agriculture a distinctive character. For, unlike the Anglo-Saxons who reckoned the arable of their open fields in 'hides' of roughly a hundred acres, they divided the soil into 'ploughlands' (latinized as 'carucates') of some hundred and twenty acres. And, despite the opportunities presented by the ability to buy and sell, the normal unit of a peasant's holding in the twelfth century remained the 'oxgang' (or 'bovate') of fifteen acres, one-eighth of a single 'ploughland', which could normally be kept cultivated by a team of eight oxen. It may, therefore, be conjectured that in the early days there was a uniform scheme whereby each settler received an oxgang of land as his share. And just as the Scandinavian system of agrarian economy differed from that of the Anglo-Saxons, so also a new method of counting was introduced, whereby reckonings were made in twelves instead of tens: thus what came to be called for clarity's sake a 'long hundred' comprised a hundred and twenty acres. And, along with new terms of measurement, came new terms, though not new coins, for financial calculations: sixteen silver pennies went to an 'ora', a hundred and twenty of which made the 'hundred' of silver.

III. LEGAL DIFFERENCES

The very name of 'Danelaw' emphasizes a diversity which William the Conqueror recognized when he confirmed the use of the customary laws of the West Saxons, the Mercians, and the Danes. The distinctive usages, mainly in procedure, have not yet perhaps been given adequate attention and assigned their proper place in the general developments of later times: the twelve 'lawmen' who were concerned with civil administration and could declare and interpret the Danish customs and usages; the severe penalties for wrongdoing which disturbed the public order and were regarded as definitely anti-social acts, not lightly to be atoned for; the new rules like that which committed stolen cattle to a third party until the rightful ownership had been determined, or compelled the seller of property to produce witnesses to swear that it had not been stolen. It is little wonder that Edgar the Great in 962 openly acknowledged that the Danes were a law to themselves when he imposed regulations about cattle-stealing upon both northern and southern England but left the Danes to decide for themselves the nature of the punishment to be inflicted 'according to such good laws as they may best choose'.

IV. LINGUISTIC DIFFERENCES

Among the three main sources—Scandinavian, Latin, and French —which have affected the grammar and enriched the vocabulary of the English language, the Scandinavian was the earliest to exert a clearly formative influence. When we view the nature of the Danish settlements, we might well expect that influence to be considerable and, in fact, a peculiar vocabulary did arise among the peasantry of the Danelaw and many loan-words were contributed which are in common and indispensable use at the present day. Nevertheless, the borrowings never reached the same importance as those from Latin or French, partly because Anglo-Saxon, Danish, and Norse were languages of common descent with so many kindred words that they could pass freely from one language to another, partly because the races were so similar in character and institutions that there was not the same need for loan-words as when the Normans introduced a latinized civilization into a Germanic country. Still, when the conservative country folk came to adopt the forms of speech of their one-time enemies and to abandon even their personal pronouns ('hie', 'him', 'hiera' yielding place to 'they', 'them', 'their'), the implication is that there was a complete fusion, an intermixing on a fairly equal footing. But that did not take place at once, otherwise the repercussions on language would hardly have been so persistent and the results so durable: we know that place-names, given in their Anglo-Saxon forms in Domesday Book, will even after 1087 be subjected to Danish influences and emerge finally scandinavianized.

V. ADMINISTRATIVE DIFFERENCES

It is altogether too fanciful to believe that the 'District of the Five Boroughs' evolved a quasi-federal government: their common assembly was no more than a supreme court for the interpretation and application of custom in the whole region where that law was considered valid. There is, however, no denying the geographical permanence of the tri-sectional divisions of the 'trithings' (thirds) or 'ridings', as in Yorkshire, which were once units of local government, the 'wapentakes' which came to correspond with the Wessex 'hundreds', the 'sokes' which might include as many as thirty villages, clustering round the capital town where suit of court was paid and dues rendered, and which survived as territorial units into the thirteenth century.

It has been necessary to go into detail to show that the Danelaw was not a mere geographical expression, that the Danish settlements were firmly established and their influence so permanent that it could survive the shock even of the Norman Conquest, to emphasize that England was not one homogeneous society but the home of two types of civilization with different racial composition, institutions and laws and with social and economic structures of their own. This does not mean that within the Danelaw the English and Danes remained completely isolated from one another. The fortunes of war were quickly accepted by the mass of the people: clearly by Edward the Elder's reign land was being purchased from Danes by Englishmen, and the fundamentally common Germanic origin of their race and speech, the incentive to unity of a common religion, and the absence of great physical barriers to shut the Danes, as they shut the Welsh, from the rest of England, made it soon possible for them to live in peace side by side, and, though only after the lapse of centuries, to become properly assimilated. There was no underlying bitterness to prevent the ultimate production of an undivided community.

Nevertheless, though there was a difference, it did not make all the difference. We must not attribute to the perpetuation of Scandinavian influence a significance that it did not possess, for it was in no way decisive for the future course of events. If in our imagination we can subtract it from the history of England, we shall appreciate the fact that it scarcely affected the broad current of evolution, for England did not develop on Scandinavian lines. The Romans, the Anglo-Saxons, the Normans were conquerors who produced what was in many ways a new country and an altered, if not a new, civilization. The case was far different with the Danes who achieved military success in only a limited area, and an area which was ever decreasing in size throughout the tenth century. Nor were the triumphs of their arms followed by signs of any ability for political reorganization. They were clearly not a politically conscious or ardently propagandist people and to that extent the old doctrine of their 'inertia' is not without justification: the traditions of effective government under a monarchy remained with the Anglo-Saxons. And though the Danes left their mark on law and society, it was not more than a mark, it was just sufficient to remain recognizable, and English law and English society were not diverted to new courses. The newcomers undoubtedly gave an added and appreciable stimulus to trade, especially with the

Baltic, and to town life, but it was simply a stimulus, for before they settled in England commerce with Western Europe had long been in operation, and market towns in the south-east were already showing many of the essential features of later urban developments. And there can be no doubt that, Danes or no Danes, physical geography was itself sufficient to guarantee economic advance in the future. In the ecclesiastical sphere the damage done was such that the old organization of the Church was never re-established. A century after the Danish spoliations the losses to the see of York had not been made good and it had been a struggle to maintain even the continuity of the northern archbishopric: during the years 972–1016 the administration of York by the bishops of Worcester showed the dire straits to which the Church had there been reduced. In East Anglia the see of Dunwich was never revived, and it was not until about the middle of the tenth century that Norfolk and Suffolk were combined to form a single diocese. Most anomalous of all was the vast bishopric of Dorchester, which had to be extended to incorporate the see of Lindsey centred at Lincoln and the see of Leicester, and thus became responsible for the extensive district between the middle Thames and the Humber. Nor was there much improvement in this regrettable state of affairs even after the Norman Conquest. And even monasticism in the Danelaw fared no better, for monasteries were far fewer in number in 1066 than they had been two hundred years earlier.

Therefore the vital impulses in State and Church still came from the southern parts of England. We must remember that, though there are two races and two civilizations in the country, the Anglo-Saxons have not lost their virility. In fact, even so far as the Danelaw itself is involved, the fact that the number of Danish settlers was considerable should not blind us to the fact that Anglo-Saxons went on living there in even greater numbers and kept numerous place-names completely unchanged. It would, however, have been most impolitic and, indeed, out of accord with contemporary thought to interfere with the traditions and ways of life of the Danes. The decree of Edgar in 962, which permitted them to follow their own customary procedures, must not be viewed as a concession wrung from a weak king or as a confession of his inability to dominate the Danelaw. Edgar was neither a weakling nor a fool, and he realized that the suppression of the age-hallowed practices of the Danes was a task as difficult as it was purposeless. Since they had by that time settled down and were no longer a force actively disturbing the peace of his realm, he simply issued instructions and left them to carry them out in their own way. This was statesmanship and not weakness, and any different course of action, if such were ever imagined, would have aroused quite needless antagonism. Similarly in 997 the validity of Danish custom was openly acknowledged and there is no evidence that any Wessex king attempted to alter it. The Norman kings were to give it a similar recognition.

The contribution of the Danes to the history of England was made immediately the settlements occurred rather than in the centuries that followed. It was something more vital than anything their legal or social distinctiveness could or did provide, something which lives on unobtrusive and unnoticed. They contributed themselves. It is here that the historical proof of a folk-migration is of high importance, for never again will there be a displacement of population in England such as took place in the areas of Danish occupation. And it was all to the good that the sparsely inhabited and undeveloped northern regions beyond the Humber and in the Lake District should receive large additions to their population to till the soil. Comparatively little Norman-French blood flows in English veins, but the Scandinavian element in the racial composition cannot be slight. What England and other countries in the long run gained, Scandinavia lost: she was deprived of the most daring, enterprising, and dynamic part of her population. What this meant to her is shown by the political incapacity and economic distress of the Baltic states in the later Middle Ages and the brilliant achievements of the southern lands their one-time inhabitants did so much to people.

If we can rely on the conclusions drawn from later evidence, we can make a more intelligent approach to the two last centuries of Anglo-Saxon history. For if we may assume with confidence that after Alfred's reign England was neither a racial nor a social unity, that there was a well-recognized cleavage between the Anglo-Saxon south and the Anglo-Scandinavian north and east, then we can more easily explain some curious facts in the history of the political unification of the country which would otherwise remain puzzling.

I. THE FLUCTUATIONS IN THE POSITION OF THE WESSEX KINGS
BETWEEN THE REIGNS OF ALFRED AND ETHELRED

It might well be thought that, when the hour of crisis in the history of the Wessex Monarchy had been safely passed under Alfred and followed by a remarkably successful assertion of its political ascendancy throughout the length and breadth of England, there only remained the relatively easy task of reorganization and consolidation.   In fact, however, the tenth century is not one of even development but of confusion, stumbling, and faltering.   For the Wessex kings were no longer confronted with the problem of conciliating Anglo-Saxons but of absorbing aliens.   Though there was a semblance of political unity in the person of a single ruler, the fundamental and more important social unity had vanished. The Wessex kings realized the difficulty and seemed willing to acquiesce in being simply overlords beyond the Welland.   The 'District of the Five Boroughs' and Yorkshire were not incorporated within their kingdom in any effective sense.   For, though they had the right to appoint ealdormen and bishops and to receive the usual profits of overlordship, they had little interest in the north, where they had few estates and rarely went on tour with their court.   Even the Church found it necessary to concentrate its energies in the south: the Age of Dunstan saw no reformed monasteries established in the Danelaw, and the archbishopric of York was administered by the bishop of Worcester who was more interested in his own diocese.   The simple truth is that the Wessex kings, like the Danish and the Norman rulers after them, had not the machinery of government which could cope with the administration of distant provinces and, whether they liked it or not, they had to leave local magnates in charge and allow them to appoint their subordinates, to let local customs prevail and to hope for the best.   In consequence, whenever the opportunity presented itself, especially during a minority, there was a danger that the particularist elements in the country would get out of control and show themselves openly on the surface: thus Athelstan's magnificent reign was followed immediately by a revolt which spread from Yorkshire into the Midlands and temporarily placed the Northern Danelaw under a Scandinavian king from Ireland; the minority of Edwy resulted in the strife of discordant regions and the elevation of different West Saxon kings upon the thrones of Wessex and Mercia.   Only with Edgar the Peaceable was there ushered in a short period of almost unruffled tranquillity.

II.   THE RAPID DECLINE OF THE WESSEX DYNASTY UNDER ETHELRED THE UNREADY

As it happened, England had passed through her direst peril by Edgar's time.   Whatever the future might hold in store for her, she would not have to fear again a total relapse such as the late ninth century had threatened. The outlook for the Wessex dynasty itself, however, was not reassuring. Its time of trial was upon it and, after the most brilliant period in its history, it collapsed a generation later, and the line of kings that had held sway in the south for five hundred years came to an inglorious and apparently lasting end. Since England was not united it could not be expected that there would be any single-hearted devotion or unswerving loyalty to purely West Saxon rulers. They could maintain their hold upon all their subjects only upon the condition that they were resolute and strong enough to guarantee peace and security which would allow the mass of their people to have a chance to earn their daily bread. If this condition were not fulfilled, the disruption of the kingdom was inevitable and men would give their support to someone more capable. The essential factor was the personality of the ruler. For if the representative of the Wessex royal house were reasonably competent, then he had it within his power to become the strongest king in Christendom, for his difficulties were slight as compared with those of any contemporary rulers of Western Europe or the Scandinavian north: no rival kingdoms or dynasties menaced his position which was firmly based on an increasingly effective administration and experienced officials, on the support of the Church, on a fleet, fortified burhs and, as the Danegeld was to show quite clearly, great wealth. The personal king could make the impersonal monarchy what he pleased: he could place it on the heights or reduce it to the depths. That fact is fundamental throughout the whole of the Middle Ages.

It was unfortunate that the death of Edgar was followed by two unhappy reigns. The accession of a lad in his early teens, Edward the Martyr (975–79), who was crowned and supported by Dunstan, was the signal for all parties of discontent, particularly magnates resentful of the recent munificent grants of land to religious foundations and the decline in their own political influence, to express their own dissatisfaction under the mask of an anti-monastic reaction. What can have been but little removed from civil war ended with Edward's assassination, procured according to a late and perhaps untrustworthy source at the instigation of the queen, who, as Edgar's second wife, wished her own son Ethelred to supplant his half-brother. The minority of Ethelred (979–1016), a boy of ten when he came to the throne, was apparently uneventful; he was crowned by Dunstan, and that ecclesiastic seems to have been in regular attendance at court until his death in 988. The unlucky fact that the reign of the first thoroughly incompetent king for over a hundred years should have coincided with the unexpected resumption of Scandinavian raids and plans of conquest brought the oldest royal stock in Europe to an end.

So far the tenth century had been almost free of the dreaded Vikings. But once again the assertion of strong kingship in Scandinavia caused the export of turbulence, and in 980 the Danes began a series of inconsequent raids for plunder along the south and west coasts. Ten years afterwards the attacks became far more serious, for Olaf Tryggvason, later king of Norway, and then Swein, later king of Denmark, began operations in the country with resident armies. The situation rapidly deteriorated after the turn of the century: English cities were sacked all along the coast from Exeter to Norwich; the maritime counties were ravaged and the interior penetrated until by 1011 fifteen shires had been laid waste; the shameful culmination was reached in 1012 when Canterbury was looted and the head of the English Church murdered. All this ruin and devastation was wrought with impunity, for Ethelred proved inexcusably futile and made every possible mistake that a weak man in power could make. The Anglo-Saxon Chronicle, which becomes as usual voluminous in time of trouble, charged the king with having no clear principles of action and it is, indeed, his pursuit of the expedient and his shiftlessness that leave the deepest impression. A bad judge of character, he relied upon the advice of men like Aelfric, ealdorman of Hampshire, and Edric Streona, ealdorman of Mercia, who played him false, and anything he attempted to do in occasional fits of energy was ruined by the divided counsels offered him. As early as 991 he adopted the palliative of the ominous Danegeld but, having rightly bought off the Danes in a moment of supreme peril, he did not, like Alfred, use the breathing space to reorganize his forces and instead committed the folly of continuing to purchase immunity with bribes until by 1014 the fabulous sum of 158,000 lb. weight of silver had been demanded by the enemy. He used the old device of taking some of the raiders into his pay in order to protect him from the rest. When his mercenaries betrayed his trust, he sought revenge in 1002 by the insensate 'Massacre of St. Brice's Day' of the Danes in his service. When this criminal blunder brought full retaliation in its wake, the king avoided the consequences by going away to the west country to reside there.

It is not surprising that even the people of Wessex, virtually leaderless for over twenty years and leaderless in fact when Ethelred saw fit to fly to Normandy in 1013, submitted to Swein when he entered Danish England at the Humber, deliberately bent on conquest, and marched unopposed through the Danelaw and south to Winchester. His death in 1014 before he was crowned king of England resulted in the revival of English opposition, the recall of Ethelred from Normandy on condition of reformed behaviour, the heroic and strenuous resistance of his son and successor, Edmund Ironside, to Swein's son Cnut, which ended in the agreement of 1016 to divide the country on the lines of Alfred and Guthrum's Pact, leaving Edmund with authority over Wessex alone. His death a few months later at the age of twenty-two settled the issue. The surviving representatives of the Wessex dynasty were Edmund's infant sons, Ethelred's twin boys of about twelve years of age by his second wife Emma of Normandy, and Edwy, the son of his first marriage, who was still a minor. In the circumstances further resistance was thought useless. Everyone was weary of disorder and, however ready to continue the fight under a competent leader, realized only too well the uselessness of a merely nominal ruler. Therefore Cnut was received as king by the whole country.

III. THE READY ACCEPTANCE OF THE DANISH DYNASTY OF CNUT

If a Scandinavian element was in control in half of England and acted as a counterpoise to the Anglo-Saxon element elsewhere, it needed only a reinforcement and a fresh stimulus from the Baltic to tilt the balance in favour of the Danes. For a time they dominated the situation and, instead of the English claiming superiority over the northern Danes, it was the Danes who lorded it over the southern English.

The reign of Cnut caused remarkably little disturbance. Though he had won his throne by the might of the sword, to many of his subjects he was no foreigner, and there was, in fact, no break in the continuity of traditions and policy. Becoming king of England in 1016 at the age of twenty-two, succeeding his brother in Denmark in 1019, winning his way in 1028 by bribery and war to the throne of Norway, to which were attached the dependencies of Greenland, the Orkneys and the Shetlands, the Hebrides, and the Isle of Man, Cnut had risen to be the head of a vast Scandinavian empire, which in the way in which it was divided by the great seas might be called a colonial empire. This northern confederacy had nothing more than the formal acknowledgment of the same ruler to keep it together; anything like imperial organization was inconceivable at a time when Cnut could hardly rule directly over all the English provinces, and signs of disruption were already apparent before Cnut died; by 1049 England, Denmark, and Norway were once again under different dynasties. Except for a very appreciable quickening of trade and commerce with the Baltic, England showed no signs that her position as the centre of the Scandinavian empire altered in any way her normal development.

For Cnut chose England, the earliest and wealthiest part of his dominions, as his permanent home and the headquarters of his government. And he made it his main object to continue and foster the English traditions he had inherited. It is a remarkable fact that Cnut, on becoming king, developed dramatically from the leader of a marauding host like Guthrum or Haesten into a statesman genuinely interested in the art of government, from one who was indifferent to the Christianity he had formally embraced into a zealous supporter of it, anxious to associate himself closely with the civilization into which he had entered. In view of what is often said about the value of the Norman Conquest in saving England from political bankruptcy and ecclesiastical stagnation, it is imperative to draw attention particularly to two points.

(i) *The strength of the conception of monarchy*

Nothing shows more clearly the unwisdom of regarding the weakness of an individual king like Ethelred as indicative of the bankruptcy of the institution of monarchy itself than the speed with which Cnut seated himself on the throne, dismissed his Scandinavian warriors, left the country to go abroad for many months and returned to find that his confidence had not been mistaken. All this happened within the first three years of his reign. The country was certainly not held down by force and cowed into submission, rather did it react readily and eagerly to the reassertion of the traditions of good government laid down by the Wessex line of kings and accorded to monarchy the respect in which it had been disciplined for a century.

The primary consideration of the new king was to make his position secure and to safeguard the interests of the dynasty he hoped to found. He therefore sought in one way or another to eliminate any possible danger from the few remaining members of the Wessex royal family: he sent the two baby sons of Edmund Ironside into exile abroad where, instead of being killed, they were brought up at the court of the king of Hungary and did not come into contact with their native land again until the question of a successor to Edward the Confessor urgently arose; he murdered Edmund's brother Edwy, the last adult son of Ethelred; he married Ethelred's widow, Emma of Normandy, though she was thirteen years his senior, presumably with the hope of restraining the Normans from giving any support to the claims of her two sons, one of whom was the future Edward the Confessor, whom she left behind her in the Duchy. There was more than a distinct possibility that those who had helped him to the throne might later turn against him and seek to remove him: therefore he levied by far the heaviest Danegeld yet extracted to pay off the warriors of the Scandinavian host and sent them back to Denmark; he executed the double-dealing Edric Streona, whom he had thought fit a few months before to reward with the earldom of Mercia; he even removed from his service in England Thorkell the Tall, who as earl of East Anglia had done much to get the machinery of administration and justice started again in the first three difficult years of the reign. Cnut was not so stupid as to forget that what had been won by the sword must, at all events for a time, be preserved by the sword, and he retained a standing army of 'housecarls', picked warriors from the Scandinavian army placed under strict discipline, to protect his own person and to suppress any signs of revolt. Nevertheless, this was not the factor which guaranteed his supremacy for nearly twenty years. His rule remained unquestioned because his ability to govern firmly brought about the restoration of that peace, order, and security which was the main desire of his subjects in all parts of the country. Furthermore, he not only carefully refrained from antagonizing the English but deliberately set himself to conciliate them: his accession was not followed like that of William the Conqueror by a systematic forfeiture of estates and a depression of the peasantry; as early as 1018 he declared in an assembly at Oxford his intention of enforcing the laws of his English predecessors, and two years later he issued a proclamation, asserting that he would govern his kingdom in accordance with the advice of the bishops of the Church; the lengthy code of laws he eventually issued was based deliberately on the enactments of his English predecessors; he appointed Englishmen to command the most important of his earldoms. There is no doubt that England prospered greatly under him. There is equally no doubt that that prosperity depended on the preservation of order and that the people at large would accept as their ruler one who was not of direct descent from the Wessex line if he fulfilled that condition, especially when there was no Wessex representative who could for reasons of age or character comply with it. As it was with Cnut, so later would it be with the Norman William. The reign of Cnut showed that, despite the anarchy of Ethelred's time, the strength and the potentialities of monarchy in England remained unimpaired.

It was the division of the country into earldoms that most influenced the course of developments after Cnut's death. Already by the early decades of the previous century there was a tendency to concentrate authority in fewer hands: ealdormen were being placed in charge not of a single shire but of a combination of shires. The problem was essentially one of government. At this time it was quite impossible for any king to rule the country directly from centralized headquarters: to do that would have required a system of state departments and law-courts and the assistance of a great staff of experienced servants. Such an organization was to be the product of many centuries of experimentation, and it was out of the question for any Anglo-Saxon, Danish or Norman ruler and, indeed, it was not completely achieved even under the Tudors. The delegation of the royal authority could not be avoided by a medieval king: he had to be content with seeing that his subordinates recognized that the ultimate control remained in his hands. Success or catastrophe was therefore conditional on his character. Cnut, like his Wessex predecessors, accepted the main historical boundaries and traditions of local autonomy and continued to make them the basis of his government. He established a series of earldoms which were not limited to merely four or five, for nearly a dozen different earls are mentioned in his early charters. His first appointments doubtlessly resulted from his wish to reward those who had assisted him to the throne and, indeed, he was responsible for the formation of the small Scandinavian aristocracy which was attached to his royal person by ties of kinship or marriage. Later, however, prompted partly by the desire not to leave his former companions in war too strong or independent, partly by his determination to bring about a political conciliation with his English subjects, he appointed native-born Englishmen to the southern earldoms. Wessex he kept in his own hands until apparently in 1018 he bestowed it upon Godwin, a Wessex man of no distinguished aristocratic origins, who owed his rapid rise to his own energies and abilities and to the personal favour of Cnut, into whose family circle he entered through marriage. Mercia was first given to Edric Streona and after his execution in 1017 to Leofric, a member of an old Mercian noble family. Bernicia, shorn of the district of the Lothians (which was ceded to Kenneth, king of the Scots, early in Edgar's reign long before Malcolm, king of the Scots, won his victory at Carham in 1018) and therefore restricted to the land between the Tees and the Tweed, was left in the care of the native high reeves of Bamborough under the general supervision of the Danish earl of Northumbria. But East Anglia, Yorkshire, Worcester, and Hereford and possibly other districts passed into the hands of Scandinavians. This method of controlling the provinces had its obvious dangers, and Cnut would have done well to anticipate William I in retaining scattered portions of them as crown lands to yield him indispensable revenue. Under Cnut the establishment of these administrative divisions worked admirably, but it was no more exempt from danger under a weak king than any other system of local government that could have been devised at the time. Several new families had been founded, intent on converting their appointments as earls into hereditary offices and increasing their authority and wealth.

(ii) The continued vitality and influence of the Church

No more striking single proof that the Age of Dunstan was not followed by the steady decline of the Church into stagnation is to be found than Cnut's proclamation in 1020 that he would govern his kingdom in close co-operation with the bishops. Though Cnut was baptized in Germany before he became king in England, we must be on our guard against accepting uncritically the laudation of the Most Christian King provided by the monastic writers of the time. For the Scandinavian sources reveal him in an entirely different light: like other Christian monarchs, he was consumed with political ambition rather than religious devotion and could commit brutal murders at any period of his career to obtain his objects. His attitude to the Church was what we should expect in the case of a man who had the usual powers of adaptation and assimilation of his race. Having submitted himself to the profession of Christianity, he grew afraid of retribution for his own and his fellow-countrymen's past misdeeds and sought to escape it by acts of reparation, like the endowment of the abbey of Bury St. Edmunds in honour of the king of East Anglia martyred by the Danes as long ago as 870, and the translation to Canterbury of the body of the archbishop of Canterbury, murdered in 1012. So later Henry II sought to make retribution for the murder of Becket by the establishment of religious foundations. Cnut became a most generous benefactor of monasteries which could pray for him in life and after death. This ostentatious religiosity was interwoven with much shrewd calculation. He quickly appreciated what the Church could do to contribute to the stability of his dynasty, the government of his kingdom and the peace of his realm. The prosperity of his reign lay, therefore, not in any innovations—we shall find little that is new in his series of laws regulating the affairs of Church and State—but in the assertion and maintenance of Anglo-Saxon practices and traditions. Cnut's close alliance with the Church was spectacularly demonstrated in his pilgrimage to Rome in 1027: nearly a thousand years will go by before another English king pays a visit there. He came into contact not only with papal but also imperial traditions, for he was an honoured guest at the coronation of Conrad II, the founder of a new line of Holy Roman Emperors, who were soon to fight a long and stern duel with the popes over the intractable problem of lay investitures, and a few years later Cnut's only daughter was married to Conrad's son, the future Emperor Henry III. And it was from Rome that Cnut addressed his famous open letter to his people in England, doubtlessly intended to be read in every shire court, which has come down to us, not in the Anglo-Saxon original but in the latinized versions of two twelfth-century monastic chroniclers. What it contains is not remarkable: the pope had promised to reduce the heavy charges imposed upon archbishops before they were granted the pallium and in return Cnut had agreed to pay promptly to the Church what was its due, especially tithes; the emperor and other lay rulers had consented to remove unjust tolls from northern merchants and pilgrims; royal officials in England were enjoined to refrain from extortion and to deal equal justice to all men. The main significance of the letter lies in the public pronouncement by the king of the principles of good government.

Cnut's death in 1035 at the age of forty showed once again that, although the English machinery of government was unrivalled in Europe, it needed the dynamic force that a strong king could alone provide. His empire broke up into its component parts; his two sons Harold (1035–40) and Harthacnut (1040–2) were untrue to his principles and regarded their office as a means of exploitation, and in 1042 the failure of direct heirs made it possible to restore, after an interval of twenty-five years, the line of Wessex kings in the person of Edward the Confessor, the sole surviving son of Ethelred the Unready.

SELECT READING

Stenton, 367–426, 495–518; Chambers, ch. viii; W. J. Corbett, 'England: 954–1066' in *C. Med. H.*, iii (1922), 371–89; F. M. Stenton, *The Danes in England* (1927), 3–46; E. Ekwall, 'The Scandinavian Settlement' in *Historical Geography of England* (1936: ed. H. C. Darby), 133–64; W. G. Collingwood, *Scandinavian Britain* (1908), 144–81.

CHAPTER XIII

THE LAST ENGLISH KINGS

WHEN the Danish dynasty came to its sudden and miserable end with the death of its last direct representative, Harthacnut, there were only three possible candidates for the throne, and two of these had such slender chances of succession that their claims were not seriously pressed and were passed over without difficulty. Edward the Exile, the son of Edmund Ironside, who had been removed from the country in infancy, was still at the court of Hungary and to all intents and purposes a foreigner; Swein Estrithson, king of Denmark, the nephew of Cnut, was caught up in the throes of a long and bitter war with Norway, and it soon became clear to all concerned that he was in no position to come and rule in England. There remained Edward, the son of Ethelred II and Emma of Normandy, who had already returned to his native land in 1041 and apparently been acknowledged by Harthacnut as his heir, and the restoration of the Wessex line was peacefully secured when Godwin wisely ignored the family connexions which made him the uncle of the Danish claimant and gave Edward his full support.

It was a tragedy that Edward should have proved himself from the outset completely incapable of governing. This was very largely the result of his education and environment, for he had lived not in England but in Normandy for the previous thirty years and had been brought up by monks within the monastic cloister. In consequence, he remained all his life a monk at heart. He clearly viewed secular politics and the strain and stress of worldly affairs with repugnance and preferred a life of quiet contemplation in which he could attend to his devotions, his alms-giving, and his plans for constructing Westminster Abbey. Therefore, though conscientious, well-meaning, and sufficiently saintly to be given half-canonization as 'confessor' by papal bull a hundred years after his death, he was not fitted to bear the responsibilities to which he had been summoned. Inexperienced, unadaptable, uninterested, he lacked strength of character himself and was a poor judge of the character of those whom he chose to be his closest friends.

Furthermore, he had a far greater affection for Normans, their speech and their customs, than he had for his English subjects, whose habits he thought in comparison coarse and unrefined. So uncomfortable did this man of forty with his fixed ideas find himself in his English surroundings that he immediately reproduced about him the conditions of his life in Normandy: he had his household administered by Norman officials, he invited his Norman friends to stay with him, he habitually spoke French himself and insisted that it should be the language of his court, he introduced the French way of life. It was not difficult for those living at the time to see the dangers ahead. Though the institution of monarchy had far stronger traditions of power and influence in England than anywhere else on the Continent, the driving force of a strong king was imperative. If Edward was to be as ineffective and colourless as his father, then the intrigues and jealousies and general disorder of Ethelred II's time would certainly be repeated. And, indeed, Edward not only failed to take the reins of government firmly into his own hands, but he laid the country he could not govern open to a disruptive influence from the Continent by drawing tight a valueless connexion between his new country and a Norman duchy which was at the time on the verge of political anarchy and civil war, and by introducing a group of dangerous, cunning, and unprincipled Normans into English political and ecclesiastical life.

Nor did the future hold any promise that catastrophe could be more than held at bay during the Confessor's own lifetime, for it was early realized that, though he had consented to marry, he was determined to maintain a vow of chastity. Since there was no hope of an heir, the problem of the eventual succession to the throne cast its shadow over the whole reign and forms the fundamental issue to which all else must be related.

If we examine the family policy of the House of Godwin against the background of the king's incompetence and the failure of heirs, then it becomes not only intelligible and explainable but also justifiable. It has been subjected to severe criticism on purely theoretical grounds which had not the slightest meaning for those at the time and are therefore, as we should expect, flatly contradicted by the facts. Only twenty-seven years had passed since the reign of Ethelred the Unready had brought ruin upon a prosperous country, and it was generally agreed that his chronic indecisiveness could only have been balanced by the acceptance of good advice. When a similar threat to stability arose with Edward the Confessor, a similar remedy was proposed, and since a power behind the throne

was imperatively necessary, the Godwins were determined to supply
it. And, when the lack of heirs to the throne made it possible for
William of Normandy quite early to put forward his candidature,
it is not surprising that they should stress their superior claims and
work to obtain the crown themselves. They had constantly before
their eyes the example of Hugh Capet, the greatest earl in northern
France, who fifty years before had advanced from behind the
throne to the throne itself by excluding the male heir of the worn-out
Carolingian dynasty, and had founded the Capetian line of rulers
which was to survive the danger of extinction by powerful feudatories and at long last create the strongest monarchy in Europe and
bring about the political unification of the country. In acting as
they did, the Godwins were not neutralizing the power of the monarchy: the character of Edward did that without their help. Far
from representing a disintegrating force which cared nothing for
the preservation of law and order, the main function of monarchy,
and far from fostering political disunity and anarchy for their own
ends, they stood between the country and disruption. The alarm-
ing feature, when so useless a king as the Confessor was at the head
of affairs, would have been not the presence but the absence of the
strong House of Godwin. For the existence of several noble houses
of approximately equal strength would certainly have encouraged
separatism, provincialism, and political disintegration. Against
such tendencies there stood the obstacle of the might of the earls
of Wessex: they might choose to ignore the king but they had no
intention of destroying the power and tradition of the monarchy
which they hoped themselves to inherit. This fact was appreciated
by the most saintly and wise ecclesiastics in the kingdom like Archbishop Ealdred of York and Bishop Wulfstan of Worcester, by the
men of Wessex and the Londoners, and in the hour of crisis of
1066 by all other earls and the king himself. And, in fact, the Godwins were not unmindful of responsibilities which coincided so
exactly with their interests, and the accession of Harold saw England strongly protected on her frontiers, free from civil war, far
ahead of any other country in political unification, as a glance at
a map will readily reveal, and possessing in the strength of its monarchical traditions and in its machinery of administration a means
of advancement unrivalled in contemporary Europe.

The personal ambitions of the Godwin family, therefore, lie at
the heart of domestic policy in England before 1066. It was
English in its origins, though it did not appear prominently in

history until the eleventh century, and it owed its rapid advancement to a close connexion with the Danish kings, beginning with the personal favour of Cnut and the marriage of Godwin into the royal family circle. After we have indicted the Godwins as an ambitious, self-seeking, and acquisitive clique, we must still recognize that they were as a whole vital and dynamic men, distinguished always by their courage and usually by their abilities. But just as William I fathered the spineless Robert and the avaricious and lustful William Rufus, and Henry II his brood of rebellious children ending with John, so among the five sons of Godwin appeared two unworthy men whose lawless Viking blood brought scandal and disaster to their family. Yet if their relatives could not control them, they did not at any rate prevent the application of the full rigours of the law to their wrongful deeds: Swein was outlawed and eventually died on pilgrimage to Jerusalem, Tostig was removed from power and exiled by his own brother Harold. Though the Godwin connexion was easily predominant, it had to take into account the natural jealousies and resentments of other noble families, particularly the House of Siward in Northumbria between Humber and Tweed and the House of Leofwine in Mercia. Still, there is very little evidence to suggest that either of these families desired to take the place of the Godwins in the direction of national affairs. The dangers resulting from the existence of four or five earldoms to the political unity of the country has been exaggerated out of all proportion. Localism was not a new phenomenon in the reign of Edward and it was to continue long after 1066, for no medieval kings were able to rule directly all the territory under their nominal control, and the Norman and Angevin kings could not do without their palatinates in Kent and Cornwall and along the Welsh Marches and on the Scottish Borders. Nor need the localism in England be a serious danger to the centralized authority vested in monarchy: indeed, if even the Confessor in the first and last exhibition of energy he showed could compel the great earl of Wessex and his sons to fly the country, it is not likely that a forceful ruler would have had much difficulty in keeping lesser magnates in order after the fashion of Cnut. For the English earls were not identical in their position and powers with the dukes and counts of France who for long made monarchy in France a powerless institution. Their earldoms might perpetuate the names but they did not, as is so often loosely stated, perpetuate the old tribal divisions and boundaries of Northumbria, Mercia, and Wessex:

Wessex no longer stood entirely behind the Thames, Mercia no longer ranged beside the Welsh frontier and over to the North Sea, Northumbria no longer stretched to the Forth. Racial particularism did not survive the Danish conquests. Nor had the title of earl progressed so far towards an hereditary dignity that the earls had consolidated themselves as necessarily the greatest landowners with an administration and officials peculiarly their own. For they had newly entered into society and Cnut's conception of their earldoms as an office had by no means disappeared. Earldoms were created, enlarged, reduced, destroyed: it was not because the king owned great estates to give away that new earldoms arose but because he was granting what was essentially an office with duties and responsibilities. All the earls remained the representatives of the king in a military and administrative capacity: the levies they raised for war were popular levies, not armies of their private retainers; the courts over which they nominally presided were popular courts and not private courts; the organization they supervised was based on royal hundreds and the officer they used was the essentially royal sheriff. Such men can hardly be described without misleading exaggeration as powerful and independent enough to thrust the country into political chaos and social anarchy so long as monarchical authority could be enforced either by the king or by someone acting in his name.

The reign of Edward is divided into two distinct parts by the crisis of 1051 when the great trial of strength took place between king and earl. It is at this significant moment that we can estimate the might of the traditions of monarchy, the use that the Confessor made of his short-lived triumph, and the extent of the respect with which the Godwin family was regarded by the country in general.

In the years 1042 to 1051 Earl Godwin moved rapidly towards making himself the mightiest subject in the realm. He had thrown the weight of his authority on to the side of Edward at the time of a disputed succession and he immediately claimed and obtained his reward. It was probably in acknowledgment of his indispensable assistance that Edward agreed in 1045 formally to marry his daughter Edith: Godwin could have obtained no greater precedence than as father-in-law of the king, and Edith herself made no small contribution to the early fortunes of her family in the estates with which she was dowered and in her ability to influence the weak-willed king to bestow dignities upon her kindred. Swein, the eldest of Godwin's sons, was given authority as earl in the Severn valley; another son, Harold, in East Anglia, a nephew Beorn (brother of Swein of Denmark) in an undefined region north of London, so that by permission of the king and the witan the Godwins ruled over a great belt of land reaching from the Wash down to and along the south coast and north to Hereford.

Meanwhile Edward gathered a French rather than an exclusively Norman coterie around him at his court. We must not too readily attribute to him a conscious and deliberate policy. He acted as he did, not so much with the intention of building up an anti-Godwin party, for he continued to sanction the increase of their authority all the time, but simply because he was a stranger in a strange land, probably bullied by Earl Godwin, and therefore turned for comfort to his former friends whom he could understand and patronize. No one could or did object to his giving his household offices to Normans or to welcoming his sister's relatives to his court: her son Ralph the Timid was made earl of Hereford and created an ominous precedent by erecting the first private castle in England; her second husband, Eustace of Boulogne, was a frequent and honoured guest. Two Breton nobles were given large estates in Essex and East Anglia. It was naturally within the Church that the pietistic monarch could most easily promote his friends: in 1044 Robert of Jumièges, a political intriguer with few qualifications for spiritual office, was brought over from his Norman abbey to become bishop of London and the king's closest associate; in 1049 another Norman, Ulf, was made bishop of Dorchester and was perilously near being suspended the same year by a papal council for the complete worthlessness of his character. It speaks much for the cosmopolitanism of the Church in England and its unquestioning recognition that it was part of the Church Universal that such appointments as these apparently aroused no more active protest than the scathing words of the Anglo-Saxon Chronicle.

Sooner or later the native and foreign influences which surrounded the king were bound to clash, and conflict arose as soon as the evil deeds of Swein, in seducing an abbess and murdering his cousin Beorn, deprived his father of much of his prestige in the eyes of the saintly king, the Church, and the nobility.

(i) In 1051 the archbishopric of Canterbury fell vacant. It was essential for the fulfilment of Godwin's ambitious policy that the head of the Church should be favourably disposed to him, and he persuaded the monks of Christ Church, Canterbury, with whom the formal right of election lay, to choose a relative of his. Ignoring this action, the king arbitrarily appointed Bishop Robert of Jumièges, who journeyed at once to Rome and received papal confirmation. Furthermore, the king and Robert would not permit the consecration of the bishop-elect of the vacant see of London, who was a close friend of Godwin's, and secured the appointment of another Norman, William of London. This contest has been overloaded with ecclesiastical significance, and Godwin has been charged with the intention of subordinating the Church to the control of lay magnates of the realm, keeping it isolated from Continental influences and immune from the activities of a reform party, represented by Robert of Jumièges, and a reform movement, inaugurated by the papacy. It is sufficient to note that the lay control of episcopal appointments lay without questioning with the king himself, that the papacy by its history gave little promise to Englishmen in 1051 of leading the way in reform, and that certainly Robert of Jumièges would have been almost the last person with whom they, laymen or ecclesiastics, would have identified reform. It is imperative to relate the incident to the hard facts of secular politics to which it belongs and to remember that Godwin, unblessed with the historian's knowledge of later events, acted according to the situation as he saw it. He was well aware that Robert of Jumièges was intriguing against him and would as archbishop be openly obstructionist to his plans. He may well have suspected that his appointment was made by the king in order to prepare the way to the throne of Duke William of Normandy, who was soon to visit the English king and receive the promise of his support in his designs on the throne. In his own interests, therefore, Godwin sought to forestall the king's intentions and in so doing revealed himself not as anti-clerical but as anti-Norman.

(ii) A personal quarrel occurred between Godwin and the king's brother-in-law, Eustace of Boulogne, during one of his visits to England. As his servants were journeying back to the south coast, they were assaulted and several of them killed by the men of Dover. Eustace returned to lay a complaint before the king who, without examination of the facts, at once sent word to Godwin that he must punish the English offenders inasmuch as they were within his jurisdiction as earl of Wessex. Godwin's point-blank refusal represented the general feeling of hostility to foreigners and favourites shown in the Dover riot and formed an uncompromising challenge to the Normanophile attitude of the king. Edward revealed an unexpected capacity for action and, calling on the help of the Earls Siward and Leofric, prepared to march to battle against his rebellious subject. The results are highly significant. For it is doubtful whether in any other country in Europe civil war could have been avoided in such circumstances. Actually Godwin and his family gave way and submitted to a royal sentence of banishment imposed upon them: Godwin went with Swein, Tostig, and Gyrth to Flanders, Harold and Leofwine sailed to Ireland, while their sister Edith was placed in a nunnery. It is impossible to reconcile this débâcle, this complete victory over the most powerful man in the kingdom, with a belief in the weakness and bankruptcy of the English monarchy.

For a short time the Norman influence was in the ascendant and the fact was marked by the only visit paid by William of Normandy to England before 1066. Edward welcomed him with enthusiasm and in the exhilaration of his triumph he apparently gave William a vague promise to nominate him as his heir. As early as 1051, therefore, William had shown his hand and revealed himself as an aspirant to the English throne and a completely new factor in a sufficiently troubled situation.

Though the Godwins had gone from the country, the anti-Norman feeling had not gone with them. The estates confiscated in the south were bestowed upon arrogant and greedy Normans who hastily crossed the Channel, the whole country was seemingly to go eventually to a Norman, and it was not easy to see any benefit that the banishment of the Godwins had conferred upon their fellow-countrymen. The English instinct was sound. Knowing quite well that a Norwegian army might land in the country at any moment to enforce the claims of the Norwegian king to the throne and comparing the ineffectiveness of Edward with the weakness of his father, Englishmen viewed the return of Godwin not as a preliminary to civil war but as a safeguard against a foreign invader. There was no one else capable of defending the country, and the repulse of a Norwegian expedition against England as early as 1058 proved the wisdom of their attitude. In 1052 the exiled family took advantage of the consequent reaction in their favour to return with armed force to England and were welcomed with enthusiasm in the south and especially in London. Archbishop Robert and Bishop Ulf immediately deserted their sees and fled with other Normans overseas.

The king, mortified by the rejection and the eclipse of his friends, lost whatever interest he had in secular politics and devoted himself to his religious projects. The second part of his reign saw the kingdom under the control of Harold Godwin, who succeeded his father as head of the family in 1053. Even hostile chroniclers admit that he was a remarkable personality. Highly expert and courageous in war, and cautious, conciliatory, and generous in peace, he was a close friend of an equally remarkable man, Wulf-stan, bishop of Worcester, and exhibited his interest in the Church by his foundation of the community of secular canons at Waltham Holy Cross in 1061. The general peacefulness and growing pros-perity of the country during the next twelve years is the best gauge by which to measure the wisdom and popularity of his government. Freed from a foreign connexion which had nothing to give which could not be obtained by other and less dangerous means, the kingdom was carefully guarded from external foes: Harold's two campaigns in 1056 and 1063 dealt firmly with the aggressions of Griffith ap Llewellyn, who had made himself su-preme in Wales, and guaranteed the absence of further trouble in the west. And all the time Harold continued the policy of family aggrandizement which had the throne as its final end. He himself took over the earldom of Wessex, which was soon afterwards ex-panded to include the counties of Gloucester and Hereford on the Welsh border. The death of Siward of Northumbria in 1055 was followed by the elevation of Harold's brother Tostig as earl in his place: the choice of Tostig proved to be a mistake, still it would certainly have been dangerous to leave the north, exposed as it was to an impending invasion from Scandinavia and to an attack by the king of the Scots in revenge for the Northumbrian campaign against him in the previous year, to the charge of Siward's son, Waltheof, who was a mere child. In 1057 the death of Leofric of Mercia resulted in a complicated redistribution of earldoms: his son Aelfgar succeeded him and surrendered the earldom of East Anglia, to which he had been appointed when Harold left it four years earlier to become earl of Wessex; East Anglia thereupon was bestowed upon Harold's brother, Gyrth, and at the same time another brother, Leofwine, was given an earldom made up of the counties north and south of London, which had been in part detached for him from Mercia. Thus the four brothers had in their possession all the earldoms save Mercia, which was itself consider-ably reduced in size and on Aelfgar's death in 1062 came into the young and inexperienced hands of his son Edwin. This remark-able family solidarity did not, however, remain unbroken, for eight years later it suffered a severe blow when Northumbria revolted against the rule of Tostig, despising him as a southerner and resenting his misgovernment and his absenteeism at the royal court where he was high in the Confessor's favour. The Northumbrians secured the assistance of Aelfgar's young sons, Edwin who had become earl of Mercia in 1062 and Morcar who was now chosen by the rebels as their ruler, and marched south towards the Thames. Faced in November 1065 with the need to choose between his family and a prospective kingdom, Harold did the only wise thing possible in adopting a conciliatory attitude: he concurred in the removal of Tostig, who fled to the Continent to become his brother's evil genius; he agreed that Morcar should remain earl of Northumbria and that Siward's son Waltheof should be given in compensation an earldom in the Midlands. Two months later the Confessor lay dead, and Harold had his reward in an unopposed accession to the throne.

The death of Edward did not mean the complete extinction of the Wessex dynasty. Until late into his reign there had been still alive other representatives in the descendants of Edmund Ironside and, indeed, the Confessor must have considered the possibility of their succeeding him, for he formally invited them to return from their long exile in Hungary and stay in England. But Edward the Exile died shortly after setting foot in the country in 1057 and his son Edgar the Atheling was left as the last of the line of Cerdic. In 1066, however, he was a mere boy, sickly in health, foreign in upbringing, and incapable of guaranteeing law and order, and, as the old English monarchy, like the Norman monarchy after it, had evolved no hard and fast rules of succession, his legitimist claims were passed over. There was, in fact, a good precedent for this action, for the Wessex line had within living memory been sharply and effectively broken by the interpolation of three Danish kings. In the eyes of the English the successor to the throne was obvious, for at home Harold's claims were quite undisputed. He was the brother-in-law of the late king and, though this constituted no blood-relationship with the royal house of Wessex, yet the royal blood of the Danish dynasty ran in his veins, for he was first cousin to the king of Denmark. Furthermore, there is really good authority for his assertion that Edward had on his death-bed named him as his heir: the wishes of a reigning monarch had much to do in deciding upon a successor and it is a pity that the Confessor did not follow the example of some of his predecessors and leave a written will to remove all doubts and scruples. And for twelve years Harold had been the real protector and ruler of the kingdom and had proved his strength of character, his abilities as a statesman, and his appreciation of the true line of English traditions. He had presumably made careful preparations for his succession before Edward died: he claimed the throne immediately, and like Cnut in 1016 and Edward in 1042 obtained the consent of a witan comprising such members as happened to be in the neighbourhood of London at the moment. There could have been no feeling that his haste implied the methods of a *coup d'état* for the simple reason that there was to Englishmen in general no other candidate and, indeed, there was little or no sign of any opposition to his enthronement and the ensuing months saw the voluntary assistance and collaboration rather than the hostility of the young earls of Northumbria and Mercia, whose sister became at this time his wife. Nor was there the slightest sign of any disruption in the administration of the country. Harold was no more a 'usurper' than Cnut and those who describe him as such are speaking the language of later Norman monks and not that of Englishmen living at that time.

For the claims of William of Normandy were not considered. A strong anti-Norman feeling had revealed itself in 1051–2 and nothing had happened since to cause a change of opinion. If there were no national antipathies in the eleventh century, it is impossible to deny that there were racial antipathies, and not an English voice was raised on William's behalf in January 1066 and not an English hand was lifted to help him when he landed in the country in the following September. For William had little he could advance on his own behalf. He was a cousin of the Confessor, but this relationship arose from marriage-connexions only and was without precedent in England as the basis of a claim to kingship. There was neither royal English nor simple English blood in his veins. He was essentially a Dane and a Dane of bastard origin. He also asserted that, when he visited England in 1051, the Confessor had agreed to regard him as his heir and there is no reason to doubt his word. But Edward could not have laid much store by his promise, for it was six years later that he summoned Edward the Exile from Hungary and fifteen years later that he supported the cause of Harold. And, finally, William stressed the fact that in 1064 Harold had bound himself to him by an oath when the accident of shipwreck had placed him in the hands of the Norman duke. What kind of oath it was we do not know: English writers say nothing about it, Norman writers say too much and most of it contradictory. When the story is stripped of all its unnecessary legends and accretions—the deliberate mission to bring William the English king's assurance that he would make him his heir, the hidden relics, the promise to marry William's daughter—it can hardly be doubted that the oath had something to do with William's designs on the English throne. What would have happened to Harold if he had not taken the oath or whether he adopted the perfectly legal view that an oath extracted under duress had no validity we cannot say. He evidently obtained his release on conditions which William argued he did not fulfil and therefore denounced him as a perjurer who, by breaking his oath, had struck a blow at the very foundations of society. It is plain that William could present only an artificial plea and that he would have to turn from the force of argument to the argument of force and submit the issue to the typically Norman ordeal by battle.

William skilfully sought to conceal the stark fact that he was proposing to embark on the unprovoked conquest of a neighbouring country by laying his case before the papal curia, arguing that England was in the control of a perjured king and a schismatic archbishop, and urging the necessity of allowing him as a devout son of the Church to bring the country back to orthodox communion with Rome. The case for Harold was not presented, and it was only after acrimonious discussion that judgment was given for the Norman duke. However, papal politics allowed William to fight under a papal banner, and this fact is given great prominence by post-Conquest Norman chroniclers and clerks. But the pseudo-sanctity of the expedition was openly revealed in the preparations made for it, and no one could have doubted that, like the Norman conquests in Sicily, it was undertaken to obtain the spoils of war.

The Battle of Hastings provided a dramatic finale to the old English monarchy, but the victory of the Normans was by no means a foregone conclusion. The stars in their courses fought for William.

(i) Precisely in 1066 he found it possible to obtain either the support or the neutrality of his neighbours: Flanders was ruled by his father-in-law, Baldwin; his old opponent, Henry, king of France, died in 1060 and his new overlord, Philip, was a minor, aged seven, and the government was under Baldwin's control as regent; his bitter and traditional enemy, Geoffrey of Anjou, also died in 1060 and left his country involved in a dynastic struggle. The death of the Confessor either a few years earlier or a little later would have found Flanders, France, and Anjou his enemies, but in 1066 they were most unusually friendly or untroublesome, and this fact alone made it possible for him to act.

(ii) It was fortuitous circumstances which allowed William to assemble an army and transport it across the Channel. For the Normans would not commit the Duchy to the enterprise: they recognized no feudal obligation to serve overseas, and no feudal host therefore could be enlisted. His Norman vassals would join his expedition only for specific bribes and a share in the plunder, and it was by similar inducements that he augmented their numbers with adventurers from Brittany, Flanders, Aquitaine, and even South Italy. This motley host had a ready incentive in the success with which the Norman family of the Guiscards had recently carved a kingdom for themselves in Southern Italy by the power of the sword alone.

But William was then faced with a problem over which he had no control: a favourable wind to carry his ships to England. Of his army of some five thousand men nearly a half were knights, and to transport their horses across the Channel in open boats was an undertaking with hazards that are insufficiently appreciated. He waited a month before the south wind of the equinox brought them to Pevensey on 28 September. If it had come earlier, he would have found the English fully prepared awaiting his arrival on the south coast, and Harold, fine general as he was, was convinced that William would not make good his landing. If, on the other hand, it had been much longer delayed, it is very doubtful whether the Norman duke could have kept his composite army together: he had done marvels already in the past months in feeding it and disciplining it, but to do so much longer was out of the question.

(iii) At the critical moment Harold was compelled to remove his troops from the south and to march north to cope with the last Scandinavian invasion of England. William landed unopposed. For since his exile Tostig had been wandering from country to country—Flanders, Normandy, Norway, Scotland—seeking revenge upon the brother who had chosen not to stand in the way of his banishment. For the moment an unusual peace had descended upon the Scandinavian world, and Tostig had managed to persuade Harold Hardrada, king of Norway, to try his fortunes in England. For Hardrada was an experienced and renowned man of war:

commander of the Varangian Guards at Constantinople, brother-in-law of the Russian king of Novgorod, successor to the throne of Norway in 1047, which he kept out of the Danish clutches by a long war with Swein of Denmark until 1062, he was a most formidable enemy. The Northumbrian levies had already driven Tostig from their shores before he joined forces with Hardrada's Scandinavian fleet. Together they sailed up the Humber, overthrew the local force that the earls Edwin and Morcar brought against them at Fulford, captured York and retired seven miles from the city to Stamford Bridge. The English king was caught in a dilemma: it was his royal duty to protect his kingdom in the north, yet he dared not leave the south. He sought a compromise in an amazing and unparalleled exhibition of rapid marches. Five days after the battle of Fulford on 20 September, Harold had arrived at York, pressed on to Stamford Bridge to come upon the Northmen unawares and completely rout them, both Tostig and Hardrada being killed. Three days later, on 28 September 1066, the Norman duke landed at Pevensey, and about four days after that the news reached the English king. With extraordinary energy he took the two hundred mile road to the south, reached London about 6 October, and was facing William on the field of Hastings on 14 October. But it was with tired and depleted forces, for many of his soldiers could not have stood the strain of his marches. Indeed, though the northern earls were not at Harold's side on the fateful day, it must be borne in mind that their forces had suffered disaster just three weeks before and that, though they were marching south to the help of their king, they had neither the inspiration nor the skill nor presumably the knowledge of Harold's plans to galvanize their actions.

The battle a few miles north-west of Hastings was one between cavalry and the long-range weapons of archers on the attack and massed infantry on the defensive. Harold had chosen his own ground for the engagement to such good purpose that not only did his troops command a slight hill on the Downs but they barred William's advance northwards and made it essential for him to attack. The day was decided not so much by the superiority of William's seasoned warriors as by the one serious mistake that the English should not have made. For six hours they had maintained an unbroken front. At last, deceived by the Danish stratagem of a feigned flight from the field of battle, they themselves broke their own lines to pursue the enemy. That was the end, for they could not restore formation and were in isolated groups at the mercy of the cavalry. By the evening there was not left alive in England an adult member of the Godwin family: with Harold perished his brothers Gyrth and Leofwine. The throne of England was vacant. There was no one suitable left to occupy it but William. The country accepted what was now inevitable and reached the greatest turning-point in its history during the Middle Ages.

SELECT READING

Stenton, 552–72; W. J. Corbett, 'England: 954–1066' in *C. Med. H.*, iii (1922), 389–99.

CHAPTER XIV

THE ADMINISTRATIVE HISTORY OF ENGLAND
899–1066

THE Anglo-Saxon period cannot from this point of view be adequately studied as a whole, and it is well to remember that the death of Alfred or thereabouts marks a dividing line which cannot be ignored. Until 900 we are in the obscure realm of speculation and conjecture where a single new and authenticated fact may prove sufficient to destroy what had previously been accepted as unquestionably true. Despite all the difficulties and dangers we cannot ignore these early centuries of English history if we would study the birth and infancy of a nation and observe the formulation of its ways of life and its attitude to government. After 900 and before 1066 the darkness lifts sufficiently to indicate that the character of that nation has been already set and to show in firm outline the machinery of administration by which the country was ruled. It will then be seen that Anglo-Saxon England has made many magnificent contributions, particularly in providing instruments of government, which are ever afterwards to affect the whole course of history and to become part and parcel of English life as we now know it.

Fundamentally we are observing the outcome of the clash between a Latin civilization and a Germanic civilization with their differing conceptions and traditions. The Romans taught the world to look upon law as the legislative act of a supreme and sovereign authority in the state: the Germans regarded law as the ancient and unchangeable custom of the people, equally binding upon all members of the community, whether king or not. The Roman Empire saw the evolution of principles which paved the way for absolute monarchy: the German peoples looked upon kingship, however divine in origin and hereditary in its nature, as essentially an office created to be of service to themselves, particularly in war, and they emphasized the close personal relationship between themselves and the king who was their tribal chieftain, their leader in battle and their protector in peace. Such divergent ideas in the sphere of law and government had to find a reconciliation. Latin civilization, with its stress upon political unity, centralized authority and disciplined order inter-penetrated and gradually fused with Germanic civilization with its emphasis upon local independence, decentralization and personal liberty, and what we regard as our own civilization is the result of that fusion which left it neither Latin nor Germanic. It is obvious that we cannot exactly assess the relative contributions made by each one of them as they operated in their individual ways from above downwards or from below upwards, and for that reason the controversies of 'Latin' and 'Germanic' schools of thought are hardly likely to subside.

Administrative history divides naturally into the two topics of Central Government and Local Government. The first brings us to consider the king, his household, and the witan: what was the nature of monarchy and what were its rights and duties? what organization was there at headquarters to put its will into effect and make its centralized authority increasingly strong? to what extent did the witan represent the people at large and act as a counterbalance to the power of the king? It is often said that the Anglo-Saxon political system was so weak in central government that it became bankrupt of power and that the Norman Conquest was necessary for the restoration of control. Such a view underestimates to the point of caricature the achievements and potentialities of Anglo-Saxon monarchy. But, leaving that question on one side for the moment, there is general agreement that even the strong line of Norman rulers would have found it impossible to govern the whole country if it had not been that they found a remarkable system of local government ready to hand for their use. The shires, the hundreds, the boroughs, with all their administrative officers and regular assembly-courts, constitute a unique legacy from the Anglo-Saxon age and to it the newcomers, knowing previously only the extremely confused institutions of Normandy, had little they could add.

Central Government

I. THE MONARCHY

After the death of Alfred in 899 the Wessex monarchy found itself in a position to make a great and rapid advance towards becoming the unquestioned ruler of a unified state. Wessex stood alone as the symbol of Anglo-Saxon unity and the rallying-point of Anglo-Saxon resistance. Alfred's great descendants—Edward the Elder, Athelstan, Edmund, Edred, Edgar the Peaceable—could call upon a fund of loyalty and devotion and real affection from their fellow-countrymen which was the direct response of an admiring and grateful people to vigorous leadership in periods of anxiety and strain. The territorial expansion, slow but sure, for which they were responsible, itself enhanced the prestige of kingship. For political unification was very largely the work of tenth-century kings and was superimposed by them from above: it did not spring from any innate consciousness of national unity among the Anglo-Saxons themselves. Greater political strength and increased stability at home inevitably led to a larger interest in the affairs of the Continent, the beginning of a foreign policy, and the achievement of European fame by Anglo-Saxon monarchs. And now the close alliance of State and Church produced its full effects. The royal patronage of the Church was accompanied by the action of the Church in giving monarchy a powerful sanction for its rule. Monarchy was ordained of God and must be endowed with high powers with which to do its work, including the uncontested right to appoint bishops and abbots. The sacred character of the king's office was given public expression when the rites of consecration and anointment became an integral part of the coronation ceremony with the accession to the throne of Edgar: indeed, the coronation office was apparently modelled upon that for the consecration of a bishop. Thereafter kingship became invested more and more with an abstract authority so that it no longer remained as intensely personal as it had previously been.

The political advance of monarchy is naturally reflected in legal charters and legal developments.

(i) New regnal titles

No longer were the Wessex kings content to regard their title as simply a racial one, as indicated in the phrase 'rex Anglorum' used by Offa. They were determined to give it a territorial content. Thus Alfred's successors are found adopting such grandiloquent titles as 'rex Britanniae' or 'Basileus' or 'imperator Britanniae' until with Cnut, whose claim to kingship certainly could not be viewed as racial, we have the modern 'rex Angliae', an anticipation of a regnal title which was not regularly used before the reign of John. To accompany imperialist titles there were imperialist witans containing Welsh kings, Danish magnates and Northumbrian ecclesiastics.

We must not, of course, read very much into these practices, for they did not accord with realities; nevertheless, the Anglo-Saxon laws show us that the kings were enlarging the area covered by their enactments. Edgar legislates for the men of Wessex and Mercia but, so far as the Yorkshire Danes are concerned, he simply makes recommendations and asks them to provide adjustments according to their own customs and traditions. Ethelred has no hesitation in issuing regulations for the famous 'Five Boroughs' of the Danes. Cnut makes decrees applicable to all people within the borders of his kingdom. What all this came to in actual practice may be disputed, but there can be no gainsaying that the theoretical conception of kingship had developed rapidly.

(ii) *The idea of fealty*

The Germanic conception of kingship had always emphasized the close personal relationship between the king and his subjects. However, the notion that all men in the realm, whatever their racial origins, owed personal allegiance to a West Saxon king was naturally a slow growth. Already under Alfred it had been laid down that he who plotted against the king's life or harboured his enemies was to lose his life and property. As early as Edmund's reign everyone was required to swear fealty to the king 'as a man ought to be faithful to his lord'. This is a notable advance, though everything depended on the character of the king for its fulfilment, and the Norman kings were glad to avail themselves of the Anglo-Saxon tradition of fealty to overshadow the narrower bonds of feudal homage.

(iii) *The 'king's peace' and the administration of justice*

We must make a clear distinction between two meanings of the phrase, the 'king's peace'. Used in a general way, as when kings refer to trespasses against their 'peace' (*frith*), it denotes a political conception of public order, a general state of peacefulness, and it does not indicate a legal conception because a breach of that 'peace' could not form by itself the basis of an action by any known form of legal procedure. But in a very limited way the 'king's peace' (*mund* or *grith*) has a technical significance in law and offences against it were punished by the imposition of special payments (*wites*) to the king. (*a*) The king's *mund*. It should be observed that there was attached to the house of every free man a 'peace' which was violated if, for example, strangers fought within it.

The more exalted a man's rank and the greater his authority, the more grievous the breach of that peace was, until at last there comes the king, whose 'peace' is the highest and widest of them all. As the king travels farther afield and as his household increases in size, naturally a larger and larger area becomes acquainted with the protection of his peace and is, however temporarily, covered by it until, to anticipate a little, in Henry I's reign it becomes the whole county in which he is resident. At the same time the 'king's peace' in this sense of a *general* protection was beginning to be associated with the county courts and the hundred courts, that is with courts popular in origin but royal in their reorganization, at which the king was theoretically present in person. For this reason we hear in Edward the Confessor's reign that the sheriff can proclaim the king's peace as well as the king himself. Moreover, the king took within his peace particular places like high roads, great rivers, churches, and monasteries, and special periods of the year like Christmas, Lent, Easter and Whitsuntide. The king's *mund*, therefore, was not all-embracing, for it did not include all his people, and it was frequently only temporary in its cover. (b) The king's *grith*. If the king's peace was to operate on behalf of individuals beyond the king's presence, then it was a very special gift made by word of mouth or by his hand (the first recorded instance being found under Ethelred) or under his seal: once given, it placed an individual in his protection at all times and in all places and made anyone who assaulted him liable to extremely heavy penalties. The king's *grith*, therefore, was a protection which looked to individuals only, and it could be brought into effect not for trifling misdeeds but only when violent assaults which might result in death had occurred. It cannot be too strongly emphasized that in these circumstances the 'king's peace' is a highly exceptional privilege: it covers only a few people and it applies only to serious offences, but it alone is legally guaranteed in that it can be enforced by process in the courts. So the 'king's peace' has no meaning in law until there has been a specific breach of either his general *mund* or his particular *grith*. We must therefore discard the classical theory that from at least the days of Cnut there was a group of major crimes like murder, arson, house-breaking and the like which were completely reserved to the royal jurisdiction and the royal financial profit; that this group was gradually enlarged until by Henry I's reign a long list of some forty 'pleas of the crown' (*placita coronae*) had been drawn up to form the basis

7*

of a criminal jurisdiction that belonged peculiarly to the king. This is a misconstruction of the evidence, for not until the first Angevin king, Henry II, introduced his extraordinary innovations did the crown have any intention of monopolizing the jurisdiction over certain crimes *wherever and against whomsoever they were committed*. All it had done previously was to expand the general protection of its *mund* to places where the king and his household were only theoretically present and to give the special protection of its *grith* to special persons in special circumstances.

For as yet the Crown in Anglo-Saxon and in Norman times concentrated not on the acquisition of a direct jurisdiction but on the enforcement of law wherever it happened to be dispensed. For example, it gradually obtained the exclusive right to out-law and to in-law a man, and this royal prerogative of mercy will remain throughout the Middle Ages the only means of stopping the law from operating harshly and unjustly. It began from Edward the Elder's reign to impose what were called *oferhyrnes*, that is, special *wites* to be paid to the king for disobedience to his orders, and thus corrupt or inefficient officials who gave wrongful decisions or failed to perform their duties could be punished. It began to encourage appeals to itself when courts failed to deal justice and thereby it supervised their activities. Strong weapons lie in the king's hands but he has not yet learned how to use them to the best and fullest advantage.

II. THE KING'S HOUSEHOLD

The geographical difficulty of communications implied as a direct consequence that the amount of governing done at headquarters could not be very great: therefore a very simple and a very personal organization was all that was required. Nevertheless, it must not be underestimated, for it shows the embryo of a civil service, the origin of many offices of state and public departments, and it represents, however crudely, an administrative system which could cut right across provincial and local boundaries.

The king's household was essentially domestic both in its nature and in the way it worked. Private servants like the chamberlains and the steward and the butler were responsible for its running. They grew in importance with it, and by Athelstan's reign, before which we know little or nothing about them, they had become sufficiently dignified to witness the royal charters, and by 1066 they were well on their way to being transformed into public officials. From the point of view of future developments the household administration is most usefully considered according to its functions rather than its officials.

(i) *The Chamber*

This was the king's private apartment, his bedroom, placed in the care of the chamberlains. Off it was the wardrobe where were placed the royal robes as well as the treasure-chest which contained the bullion and important records such as papal bulls, charters and other diplomatic documents. It is probable that Winchester, the capital town of Wessex, was already in Cnut's time being regarded as a fixed and permanent repository for the treasure-chest, and it may well be that the office, even if not the name, of Treasurer was already known. The Chamber, the Wardrobe, and the Treasury were all destined to expand into high departments of state. Sooner or later finance came to underlie all their activities. Under the Anglo-Saxon kings, as for many generations later, the public revenue of the kingdom was identical with the private income of the king. Much of it was paid to the king in kind in the form of food-rents (*feorm*) as he travelled from one to another of his estates. Still, constant cash payments were made in connexion with the various kinds of royal income—tenants' rents; profits of jurisdiction like *wites* and *oferhyrnes*; the land tax which had taken the place of the extraordinary levy of the Danegeld in time of war before 1012 and become thereafter a regular contribution in time of peace for the upkeep of a standing army; miscellaneous dues from such sources as tolls, sea-wreck, and treasure-trove. Before 1066 there had grown up tentatively the practice for the sheriffs to pay each year a fixed sum to cover the profits from the royal estates in their shires. Though the evidence is slight, we can hardly doubt that the assessment and collection of the royal revenues could not have been carried out effectively unless a skilled financial bureau had been at work.

(ii) *The Chancery*

This writing-office developed from the organization of the royal chapel, for it seems clear that the royal chaplains, responsible for the daily mass, were doing the king's secretarial work, and we can ascertain who they were by the early tenth century when they began to add their names as witnesses to charters. The Anglo-Saxon chancery exhibited an inventiveness to which there was no parallel in Western Europe except in Merovingian and Carolingian

Gaul and, apart from the many official copies of new laws for transmission to the shire courts, it issued a truly remarkable number of documents. (a) The charters. These reach back as far as the seventh century and more than a thousand, issued before the Norman Conquest, are still known to us. With all their elaborate and solemn formulas they were highly technical productions, but they had a serious defect in that they could not be regarded as properly 'authenticated'. For not only did they bear no seal but the royal clerks themselves wrote out in their stereotyped monastic book-hand the names of the witnesses. In consequence, it was very easy for anyone to copy such charters and, indeed, the forgery of charters was, if not a common offence, at least a common practice. (b) The chirographs. These were indentures, clearly devised as far back as the early tenth century, to get over this difficulty of authentication. Two copies of a document, written out on a single sheet of parchment, were separated and cut out by a wavy, zigzag line. Any collation of the separate pieces would afterwards testify to their genuineness. (c) The writs. These were brief, simple and informal notes, contrasting sharply in this respect with the charters with their crosses and curses, for the purpose of making a grant of land or transmitting information to the shire courts. Furthermore, they solved the problem of authentication by being sealed, and the earliest surviving example from the Confessor's reign carries a two-faced pendant royal seal. These sealed writs were apparently far in advance of continental usages, for they provided an instrument of administration which for the first time made effective government possible. Freely used before the tenth century was over, they were the parent of the multitudinous types of royal missives in medieval England—charters, letters patent, letters close, warrants and fines—and came to exert a simplifying influence upon continental secretarial practices. Evidently, therefore, the work of chancery was being done by a group of highly trained clerks and, though it is not until Edward the Confessor's reign that we find the chief clerk apparently styled 'chancellor' and have our earliest surviving specimen of the royal seal, the first 'great seal' known in the West, it is evident that the Anglo-Saxon chancery was by then 'an ancient and sophisticated institution', the product of a hundred and fifty years' organized development. The frequent appointment of king's chaplains to bishoprics in and after Cnut's reign is sufficient witness to the great importance the chancery had assumed.

It is a noteworthy fact that the writs were written in Anglo-Saxon and not in Latin. For the use of the vernacular as the language of government was remarkable and it must have done much to stimulate the political consciousness of laymen as distinct from clergy when government was carried on directly in a tongue they could understand and without the post-Conquest need and habit of translation. It has been suggested that Anglo-Saxon was used with reluctance *faute de mieux* because the decay of learning which resulted from the Scandinavian invasions had made the preferable use of Latin impossible, but this does not account either for the constant promulgation of laws in Anglo-Saxon long before those invasions began or the continued use of Anglo-Saxon in the charters and writs of Norman kings for more than a generation after the Norman Conquest.

(iii) *The Council*

The king's deliberations about affairs of state could not have been restricted to such few occasions as the formal meetings of the witan: an administrative group in continuous existence was indispensable and inevitable. Though it is rare to find evidence of the everyday activities of the king's household court, yet there is more than the presumption, raised by analogies with Frankish practices and with later developments in England itself, that the king and his intimate advisers formed a small body, constantly supervising the work of government and controlling the administration of justice as they journeyed through the country.

III. THE WITAN

The old views of the witan, which saw it as a kind of democratic parliament, deliberately devised to limit the king's power and to act as a constitutional check upon his authority, very largely make a botch of the evidence. For all the instances we come across of a concourse of people assembling together and making common acclamation occur at the time of coronations when we should expect them, and there is nothing to link them with the witan. Moreover, attendance was not so much a right or even a privilege, it was a troublesome duty which would be shirked whenever the chance occurred.

(i) *Its composition*

It is of very little real value to discuss the democratic, aristocratic, or monarchical theories of its origins, for all are based upon the chronologically unsatisfactory statements of Tacitus, and it is wiser to acknowledge a hiatus in our evidence and speak only about the tenth century onwards when there is precise information. By that time it is plain that the witan reflected an aristocracy of birth —the male and female representatives of the royal house and of the families of the old nobility, itself possibly degraded often from minor kingship; an aristocracy of wisdom—the bishops and abbots who were so prominent in discussions that it is often difficult to say whether the meeting was a lay or an ecclesiastical assembly; an aristocracy of service—the king's ministers or, to use an Anglo-Saxon term, the king's thegns who attended as his nominees and played no unimportant part in what was done. Membership of the witan depended, therefore, on wealth and influence. It has been estimated that an average of thirty to forty persons attended its meetings, which were held at least once and frequently three times a year.

(ii) *Its work*

This was not carefully differentiated. In the dispensation of justice the witan was a court of first instance, dealing with pleas affecting the king and the great men of the day, and its judicial work, therefore, was not heavy. It was not a court of appeal, for the local assembly courts could hear to a finish all cases that came before them, and resort to the witan was not encouraged and, indeed, only permitted if proper justice was not forthcoming locally. A more important part of the witan's work was to sanction grants of land, particularly those accompanied by privileges accorded by the king: in these times the transfer of valuable property needed all the solemnity possible and it was just as well to get the great men to give their formal consent to it by acting as witnesses to the deed of gift and to get the charter strengthened by the anathema that could only be pronounced by such great ecclesiastics as were members of the witan. Other miscellaneous business was transacted, including politics—foreign relations, war, taxation, the prosecution of traitors—and ecclesiastical affairs.

One of the witan's functions calls for consideration by itself. No dooms or laws were issued by the king on his sole authority: this was done always with the assent of his advisers because the preservation or alteration of unwritten custom was something which vitally affected the community as a whole which had evolved that custom. It has been argued that the dooms were not legislation as the Romans would have understood that term, because Anglo-Saxon custom was regarded as fundamental law, unalterable law, law that had existed from time immemorial and could not be tampered with by man. Therefore the dooms were no more than 'official memoranda' of custom and simply clarified and adjusted it. We ought, however, to remember that the Anglo-Saxons made no attempt at codification, at setting down the existing laws in full, and we are, in consequence, in no position to decide whether the dooms were or were not the deliberate making of law as distinct from its mere 'remembrance'. Furthermore, when Ethelbert of Kent promulgated his laws, which gave special protection to foreign missionaries who had entered Germanic society as strangers and were therefore not covered by Germanic custom, he could not have been far from legislating in the Roman sense of that word. And nothing is more certain than that 'custom' was never rigid and unchanging: as long as society was vital and remained able to change its character in response to new developments like feudalism, so long would it be at work adjusting and amending its 'customary law' till the point was reached when it was, indeed, radically altered.

The Anglo-Saxon laws provide a unique series of records of tribal customs. In Kent the ninety dooms of Ethelbert (*c.* 602) are 'the first laws of a Teutonic people in a Teutonic language', and they were revised and enlarged by his successors, Hlothar and Edric (685–6) and Wihtred (695–6). In Wessex the dooms of Ine (688–95) were perhaps evoked, not as in Kent by the appearance of Italians, but by the inclusion of Welsh Britons within Germanic society and the need to define their position. In Mercia the dooms of Offa (757–96) are unfortunately lost and known only through the use made of them by Alfred. From Northumbria and East Anglia no collection of dooms has come down to us, though we have reason to believe that this is no more than the mischance of survival.

The legal renaissance of Alfred's reign caused a tentative approach to codification in that he proceeded to select the best he could find among the enactments of Ethelbert, Ine and Offa, and incorporated them in his own series of laws. The tenth century was the golden age of Anglo-Saxon laws: two series from Edward the Elder, six from Athelstan, three from Edmund, four from Edgar, and nine or ten from Ethelred. Presumably they were largely called forth by the need to accommodate the alien Scandinavians, and for a similar reason Cnut was responsible for a long and comprehensive series of dooms in two parts, secular and ecclesiastical. As the preservation of peace was naturally the paramount necessity, all these dooms were primarily concerned with enforcing the law against evildoers—hence the meticulous tariffs for compensatory wergilds and bots—and with establishing police duties like the hue and cry, the borhs and the tithings. There is little private law, that is to say, regulations concerning such matters as the conveyance of property, the rules of inheritance and the enforcement of contracts.

(iii) *Its so-called constitutional rights*

The crux of the problem is whether the witan had the right to elect or to depose a king and to give him advice. The king certainly recognized restraints upon his power: for example, the powerful force of customary law which he could not ignore and the coronation oath which bound him to keep the Church in peace, to rule justly himself and to prevent injustice being done by others. Can we say, however, that the witan had an acknowledged right to control the king? Did he ever come to hold his position by election and could he be deposed if he governed badly? When the Germans entered the Roman Empire, they brought with them an elective principle in connexion with monarchy, whereas the late empire had seen the hereditary principle at work. In the later Anglo-Saxon period the facts suggest that both principles were in use. Generally speaking, son succeeded father and, if this did not occur, the new occupant of the throne was at least a member of the royal family. The rule of strict primogeniture was unknown and in time of crisis the strongest royal candidate might ascend the throne. Thus Alfred was the last of four brothers to become king of Wessex in perilous conditions, his elder brother's children being passed over. Often it was the last will and testament of the king that settled the question, or the open association of the heir-to-be in the work of government before his actual succession. There are in the eleventh century a few instances of what looks like election, but it is unwise to see in them the advent of any elective monarchy, for they do no more than lay special emphasis in special circumstances on the ancient custom of making a formal acceptance of a new king. Thus Edmund Ironside was the son of a king who had abdicated, and he was challenging the claims of the son of a recently accepted Danish king; Edward the Confessor succeeded in spite of the Danish candidate; Harold in his turn broke the

West Saxon succession again, as Cnut had done before him: all realized the wisdom of getting the witan to express formal recognition of the validity of their title. Indeed, it is unlikely that monarchy would have survived as the effective institution it was if it had been mainly elective, for this would have opened the way to such civil war and anarchy as was to come later in Stephen's reign. Nor have we any warrant for saying that the witan could depose a bad king: the practical check upon the king was evidently might and not right.

Nor had the witan an acknowledged right to tender advice. However, if the king was politic, he secured the support of all those influential magnates whose aid was necessary in enforcing his decisions. It would have been folly to issue orders that might infringe custom or to declare a war that might be unpopular unless he had first made certain that his great subjects agreed with him. So, though the witan had no right to offer advice or to give consent and though the king had no obligation to consult them, in practice they generally acted in concert in serious matters. The witan was therefore a check, but a political and not a constitutional check.

So, though the witan served an undeniably useful purpose in providing an opportunity for men from all parts of the kingdom to meet frequently to discuss topics of common interest, though it had founded an invaluable tradition of co-operation, it had not consolidated its position by obtaining a fixed place in the scheme of government: it had no regular time and place of meeting, no fixed personnel, no stereotyped procedure, no definite business. Such matters were all left to the decision of the king: if he was powerful, the witan became largely his creature.

Local Government

The institutions established for governing the country districts by the close of the Anglo-Saxon period provided a unique gift to posterity. For though similar institutions are met with on the Continent among other Germanic peoples, these did not for various reasons develop—or were not developed—in the same fashion and they ceased to be important.

In Anglo-Saxon times government was very largely local government, and so it essentially remained throughout the whole of the Middle Ages so far as the daily administration of affairs was concerned, for there was no possible alternative. It was carried out through shires and hundreds with their courts and officials, through organs which always bore the traces of tribal influences and are as old as any political institutions in the land. They formed almost self-sufficient sub-divisions of authority and were so firmly established that they came to be for many centuries an indispensable part of the machinery of government. Yet it would be foolish to attribute to the Anglo-Saxon people in general an innate and irresistible urge to govern themselves, for if these popular assemblies had not been remoulded under royal influence it is more than doubtful if they would have survived to any effective purpose. There was always a measure of self-government, but it was at the king's command that government frequently functioned, its dynamic came to it increasingly from above instead of from below, and the contribution made by the monarchy was imperative to its development.

I. THE SHIRE

As a *territorial* unit in the south and east the sub-division called a shire had many diverse origins: it might be, for example, an early kingdom like Kent, Essex and Sussex, or simply a tribal division within a kingdom, like Norfolk and Suffolk which made up East Anglia, or an area round the nucleus of a large town which produced Dorset (Dorchester), Somerset (Somerton), Hampshire (Southampton) and Wiltshire (Wilton) within Wessex. It may have been left intact in the control of the descendants of the old ruling houses as sub-kings, or these may have been removed in favour of members of the dominant royal family. However this may be, the first unequivocal evidence for territorial shires occurs a hundred years or so before Alfred's reign. As an *administrative* unit in the scheme of government the shire seems to have begun as a burghal district and to have been the creation of Wessex kings. In this sense it was comparatively late in emerging and it is only under Alfred that we can see it in full operation as a political unit —for no one must leave one shire to go to another without permission; as a military unit—for the levies are raised and assembled by shires; and as a judicial unit—for the shires have their own moots. In some way or other, the Wessex monarchy has accepted traditional territorial divisions and created others—all having the common factor that they gathered round about an important town —and deliberately adapted them to the purposes of government.

When the Eastern Midlands had been methodically released from the Scandinavian grip, the Wessex shire system was applied to them. This was easy to do, for the Danes in their settlements had completely ignored already the ancient internal boundaries, and the shires were comparatively modern creations, based upon the military districts round the Danish boroughs. For, since the chief towns of the new shires lie usually right in the centre of them and the shires bear the same name as these towns, like Northampton, Bedford, Derby and Nottingham, it is evident that the shires have been formed round the pre-existing towns in order to create a neat scheme of political government: they are, in fact, very much like burghal districts. Indeed, these Midland shires seem to represent a round number of hides of land deemed sufficient to support the fortified burh at effective strength. It was possibly Edward the Elder in the closing years of his reign who proved strong enough to ignore the traditional boundaries of the West Midlands, which had never been occupied by the Danes, and to create new artificial shires such as Shropshire and Warwickshire represented. The north of England beyond the Tees was not 'shired' until after the Norman Conquest. — *shire court* —

The first reference we have to the shire court under that name is in Edgar's reign when it was ordered to meet twice a year. It is clear that it was the direct descendant of the old folk moot, a term sometimes applied to it. Yet royal influence had certainly come to restrain and direct the popular will. To give a simple illustration, the chief officials of the court were the creatures of the king, though the judgments of the court were made by all free men who attended it. Supervision of its work was exercised by three presidents. (*a*) The ealdorman, meaning by derivation the 'chief man'. The ealdorman was associated with the shire from the very beginning. Whether or not he was in his origins a tribal representative, he always figures in the records we have as a royal official. It is very likely that he was often of royal descent, nevertheless he held what was essentially an office, subject to whatever alterations the king desired and forfeitable for neglect of duty. He had great privileges: a high wergild on his life, a special peace upon his house, a landed property attached to his office. In return he had to bear heavy responsibilities as leader of the shire levies, president of the folk moots, executor of the royal commands. In Alfred's reign the ealdormen were not numerous: there was one to each shire in Wessex and less than half a dozen all told in Mercia. It is not, however, until the tenth century that we know much about them. Then, as the Wessex kingdom expanded its frontiers, their ambitions grew with it, and the practice began with Edward the Elder of grouping three or four shires under each of them so that by Edmund's time, for instance, there were only three for the shires south of the Thames and five for those of the Midlands and East Anglia to the north.   Under Cnut they became virtually viceroys in their districts under the new name of 'earls'.   Nevertheless, they held what was still regarded as first and foremost an office and not a firmly established hereditary dignity; though the title was naturally likely to become a monopoly of the same prominent local families, the scope of their authority was expanded or restricted as it seemed best to the central government.   The earls succeeded to the ealdormen's privileges, notably the right to the 'earl's penny' or third penny from the judicial profits of the shire court, but they eventually took little active part in the work of the court.   (b) The sheriff.   When the ealdorman ceased to devote his attention to a single shire, the most prominent of the king's reeves, the shire-reeve, took his place there. His office originated somewhere round the middle of the tenth century, he was certainly the active president of the shire court by the close of Edgar's reign, but strangely enough the name 'sheriff' does not appear in surviving records until the time of Cnut.   (c) The bishop.   He attended the meetings of the shire court to look after the interests of the clergy and to propound the law of the Church. For the shire court dealt with ecclesiastical as well as lay affairs and we must remember, therefore, that it formed an important part of the organization of the Church.

The shire court met to exercise all the functions of government. It was a popular assembly, convoked to execute the orders of the king, as well as a judicial tribunal, and so much was it the shire in action that the same Latin word 'comitatus' came to be used to describe them both.   Its jurisdiction, in particular, was limitless, it could hear all actions—criminal, civil, and ecclesiastical—and from its decisions there was no technical appeal elsewhere.   The suitors of the court were once all the free men, but it is presumable that in time the court knew the presence of only a few of the more important and wealthy and leisured men, and by Edward the Confessor's reign the once personal duty of attendance may have been territorialized and attached to specific tenements of land.   Whoever the suitors may have been, they were the doomsmen who declared the customary law and prescribed the manner of proof, that is, which party should submit to it and what kind, ordeal or compurgation, it should be. They did not go further than this 'medial' judgment: the final judgment was left to the inscrutable wisdom of God who might be for the defendant though his neighbours were against him.

II. THE HUNDRED

Just as the kingdom was cut up into shires, so the shires came to be divided into districts called hundreds. All Germanic peoples on the Continent were acquainted with what was evidently a tribal unit called a 'hundred': it is, for example, to be found in the kingdom of the Franks. But whether it originally represented a hundred persons or a hundred householders or a hundred hides or the district which supplied a hundred warriors to the tribal host is mainly an academic problem. There was clearly a calculation by 'hundreds' of hides at the back of such fiscal and administrative schemes as were devised before the tenth century, but it is not until then that the term 'hundred' makes its appearance in any English record and that an institution called a 'hundred' enters into the plan of royal government.

Before that time it is quite clear that local government found its centre in the royal 'tuns' or vills and depended for its working upon the royal reeves. We obtain our first glimpse of these officials in the laws of Ine in the seventh century, when they were the bailiffs in charge of the king's private estates, and thereafter they were brought more and more prominently into the public life of their districts in supervising financial levies, punishing criminals, keeping order, collecting tolls from traders, and generally executing the king's orders. In Edward the Elder's time they were commanded to hold moots every four weeks: this is the first clear statement that local courts were being held for areas less than a shire. The local administrative unit, therefore, was the royal vill with its adjoining and dependent territory, normally assessed as a hundred or some multiple of a hundred hides of land, and ruled for all purposes, whether fiscal, administrative or judicial, by a royal reeve. A similar method of government is found in Northumbria and Cornwall, and it is apparently of remote antiquity, reaching far back before the tenth century and, it has been suggested, finding its origins in Celtic arrangements.

It was this unit of government, for which our records give us no convenient descriptive name, which provided the basis for what was later called a 'hundred'. We have, therefore, to find an explanation for the introduction of the new term in Edgar's reign. It is well to state at once that the reasons which prompted the Wessex kings to manufacture the hundred as a territorial unit of government can only be conjectured. One ingenious explanation has been put forward for many years and has recently been given authoritative support. In the time of Athelstan, when a strong desire for law and order was evident after the strain of the Danish wars, the people of London as well as of other districts formed voluntary associations to undertake police duties, especially against cattle thieves. These frith-gilds or gilds of peace arranged for their gildsmen to be grouped in tens to make up a hundred under a chief called a hundred man. They were put under royal patronage by Athelstan, who allowed their members to share in the profits from any convicted thief. This scheme of self-help was so successful that Edgar's 'Law relating to the Hundred' adopted it, extended it compulsorily over the country and gave it an official and legal basis by allowing the gilds not only to arrest but also to try suspects with full use of the ordeal. So the moot at the royal vills acquired the name of the hundred court, and the territory covered by the jurisdiction of the hundred was defined in accordance with pre-existing areas of administration. Since these varied in accordance with the density of population, that is why the hundreds came to be so widely different in their size: there were, for instance, seventy-one hundreds in Kent but only five in Lancashire; and they ranged between one-eighth of a square mile and eighteen square miles. By Cnut's reign every free man was ordered to be within the supervision and jurisdiction of a hundred.

The hundred court met every four weeks under the presidency of the hundred reeve, a bailiff of the sheriff, who was himself already before 1066 holding those occasional and special sessions of the courts which were later to be known as the 'sheriff's turn'. The hundred court had a jurisdiction as extensive and final as that of the shire, and it was, in fact, the place where most judicial, police, and commercial business was done.

III.   THE BOROUGHS

In the midst of the shires and hundreds there appeared distinctive communities which, under the name of 'boroughs', came in the early twelfth century to claim the privilege of looking after their own affairs and appointing their own officials and thereby constituted themselves as quite separate units in the framework of government. For what reasons and by what processes did a few among so many townships and villages obtain this unique recognition? That question must be answered, for boroughs were destined to play a highly important part in the national life, so much so that they were permitted special representation in the parliaments of the king. The Anglo-Saxon boroughs have aroused controversy for many years and theory after theory has been put forward only to be instantly destroyed. We must abandon the conjecture that the boroughs arose simply out of the garrison towns established by Alfred and his successors in rural areas, for fortification alone never assured the future for them and many failed to develop and went back in their prosperity. Evidently other factors were at work. Nor is the suggestion more acceptable that the test of a borough is its possession of a court of law of its own, for it is now recognized that the 'borough court' of the Anglo-Saxon laws might not be a municipal institution but a hundred court which sat within the borough and had jurisdiction over a district extending far beyond the walls of the borough itself. Nor can we accept as convincing the recent argument that the Anglo-Saxon boroughs had no independent and exclusive life of their own in that their inhabitants lived a mainly agricultural life, depending for their livelihood on the arable fields attached to the boroughs; that there was little trade save in a few market-towns; and that it required the settlement of French traders and the stimulus provided by energetic and avaricious Norman barons to produce the borough proper.

We have really to consider two things: a 'town' as a trading centre and a 'borough' as a municipal institution. Given fairly continuous prosperity the first will in time normally become the second, though this is not invariably true: Cornwall, for example, possessed five market-towns but no boroughs. Nevertheless, the economic factor is all-important. Though the civic life and the civic institutions of Roman Britain had completely vanished, the advantages of physical geography which had then determined the sites of cities could not be destroyed as well, and archaeology and numismatics amply testify to the vigorous trade which had sprung up between south-east England and the Frankish kingdom, restoring their commercial importance to London, Canterbury and

Rochester and penetrating far behind the coastal districts. This resuscitation of urban life, though it may not have been sufficient to relieve the urban communities from their dependence on agriculture, had occurred before the Scandinavian invasions began in real earnest to put a temporary check upon its development. As soon as the Danish threats to peace and security had been removed, a great revival of trade followed, associated particularly with the fortified towns which had been placed by Alfred and Edward the Elder for strategic reasons on the main lines of communication. To them the term 'burh' was applied, and it came later on naturally to be transferred to other equally well situated and populous places: most of them will find entrance in Domesday Book under the headings of 'boroughs'. As we have already noticed, they were used by the Wessex kings in the governmental scheme they devised, and it is indicative of how much the boroughs owed to royal protection and care that they are still found under royal control when the Normans arrived. Nevertheless, it was not the military and administrative factors that produced the municipalities of the future: it was essentially economic forces. Foreign trade flourished with France, the Low Countries, the Rhineland and the Baltic, even, for over a century before the Norman Conquest, with Italy; the organization of the Cinque Ports looks back before 1066 for its beginnings; the men who crossed the sea three times were deemed worthy of the status of thegns. Internal trade is signalized by the presence of numerous royal moneyers, the great amount of good coinage in circulation, the commercial legislation upon such matters as weights and measures, the tolls on imported goods, and the punishment of forgers of money. Commerce of such dimensions encouraged the large populations of such places as London, Norwich, Lincoln, and York, and invited the heavy geld laid upon them which could not have been paid from the profits of mere agriculture. Still more, it meant the creation of those distinctive characteristics which promoted a civic consciousness. (a) The great majority of the inhabitants of boroughs were free men. Indeed, had they not been their own masters, it is difficult to see how trade could have been carried on at all. (b) The term 'burgess' had already obtained a technical content; it did not cover all the inhabitants of the borough but was a term applied to those whose property was held by what is called 'burgage tenure' or 'borough tenure', under which their tenements—that is their houses, shops, and booths—paid a fixed money rent, were regarded as heritable, and could be freely mortgaged and sold. This tenure was peculiar to boroughs, and in its freedom from the agricultural and other types of services demanded elsewhere, it engendered a different social spirit and a different social attitude. (*c*) Whatever the original purpose of the Anglo-Saxon gilds, whether they were simply convivial clubs or mutual benefit societies, it is quite clear that they had come to include the leading merchants and were acting as a trade organization after the fashion of the later merchant gilds. (*d*) Special rules were indispensable to the conduct of trade and commerce and there were already forming before 1066 a little body of special laws which grew into the 'borough customs' of the later Middle Ages. (*e*) Though the borough courts of which we read mostly in the surviving records are usually hundred courts held within a borough, there are some grounds for believing that courts peculiar to the boroughs alone did exist as early as the tenth century for the regulation of merchant business, and this is a development which, despite the understandable meagreness of the evidence, we should naturally expect. At all events, the burgesses had full opportunities to learn the habit of co-operation and there is no doubt that self-government, however inchoate it may have been and however restricted to matters of trade, was already present in the boroughs in the later Anglo-Saxon age. They had all the essentials necessary for their later progress, and the central government had for many years been giving them signs of special recognition. Indeed, Edward the Elder and Athelstan had attempted to confine all buying and selling to boroughs and, though the plan broke down, yet the privilege of being the official centres of the royal mints remained with them. The West Saxon kings had a personal interest in their growth because from them they drew a steadily increasing income through tolls and fees of various kinds. The high point of co-operative bargaining was reached in Edward the Confessor's reign when the king conceded that Dover should be exempt from paying any local tolls on the merchandise it sent throughout the country. The time had not come yet—and it will hardly come even in the twelfth century—when boroughs will claim to be responsible themselves instead of the sheriff for collecting the crown rents, tolls and fees and making a composition payment to the king (*firma burgi*), and obtain the privilege of choosing their own officials; nevertheless, they had prepared the way for future further advances and, indeed, had already progressed far on the way to a real municipal status.

IV. THE 'TUN' OR 'VILL'

This was the smallest and lowest unit of local government. Although no direct evidence can be found for it, it is difficult not to believe that the ever-present need to discuss in common and to see to the execution of projects connected with the common agriculture of the time resulted in the establishment of village moots to make and enforce by-laws: the 'hall-moots' mentioned in the twelfth century must surely have been their lineal descendants. At all events, the primary importance of the vills in governmental life lay in the police duties which came to be imposed upon them. The most serious problem of everyday administration was to discover and punish those evildoers whose deeds struck at the roots of an orderly society. All that the kings could do was to throw responsibility upon the people themselves, and this was done in two different ways: (a) The 'borh', meaning a 'surety'. All persons had to find others who would undertake to produce them in court in the event of their misconduct and the failure to pay their debts: thus members of a family could become the 'borh' for one another, a master for his servants, a lord for his tenants. (b) The 'tithing'. The later Anglo-Saxon laws required every male person over the greater part of the country, unless excused through high social position or great property, to be enrolled for police purposes in a group of 'ten', that is a 'tithing', headed by a tithingman. If a member was involved in wrongdoing, the others produced him for trial or else they were fined for dereliction of duty and were called upon to make compensation to the injured party. In some quite mysterious way the tithing eventually became in some places identified not with a personal group of ten but with a territorial unit of the vill. So for the purpose of producing and punishing criminals the vill became a sub-division of the hundred.

Before the Norman Conquest the lords disliked being held responsible for their tenant's acts and shuffled out of their obligations. For very often the king granted them the fines imposed in the hundred courts, whereupon they found themselves in the irritating position of being themselves the guarantors that fines would be paid to themselves. Therefore they put pressure upon their tenants to seek their 'borh' among their neighbours instead. In some such way the ideas of the 'borh' and of the 'tithing' came to combine to produce what the Normans called the system of 'frankpledge', the most important police institution of the Middle Ages, whereby the whole body of the peasantry was placed in tithings without being allowed themselves to choose their own pledges. All members of the community were then compelled after some fashion to serve the common weal.

The Contact between Central and Local Government

From what we have already said, it will be observed that the Wessex kings had for over a century and a half been occupied with the task of devising a system of local government which could function efficiently. It was no even course of development: much tentative experimentation took place and many schemes were abandoned before a workable plan was evolved. The paucity of evidence about experiments which came to nothing should not blind us to that fact. Certain it is that the shires and the hundreds were deliberately remoulded under the direction of the monarchy and bear firm witness to its intention to exert a directive, though in the circumstances of the time necessarily remote, control over local government. It is difficult, therefore, to believe that the governmental ties between headquarters and the localities were as tenuous as is often stated. And indeed, there is much else to convince us to the contrary. The royal chancery grew in importance mainly through the demands made upon its time in sending information and instructions to the local courts. The numbers of the thegns were deliberately increased from the time of Athelstan to help the Wessex monarchy in the essential work of maintaining public order. Those in constant service at court were sent as commissioners to the local assemblies to see to the execution of some particular business; those who had established themselves through the king's patronage as a landed aristocracy in the provinces were called upon to act as the local agents of his will and to co-operate with his reeves in the routine work of administration and justice in the shire and hundred courts and in the villages they controlled, to assume responsibility for the military service of others and to serve themselves on summons. The royal authority was thus extended over the country, for the king's thegns are to be found not merely in Wessex but in Mercia and East Anglia as well. Such thegns of the shire, acting under the king's direction, were a powerful factor in the deliberate work of unified government.

So the sheriff represents but one part of the same far-reaching development in the tenth and the eleventh centuries, however dual in character their office may have been originally in that they were the deputies of the ealdormen and earl in military and judicial matters and the deputies of the king in fiscal and police matters. It is not true that the earl exercised a more powerful, because more immediate, influence, with a consequent decentralizing effect. For the earls as well as the sheriffs were the nominees of the king who could and did appoint them and remove them as occasion demanded, and the steady increase in the control exercised by the sheriff reflected a parallel increase in royal authority. The Anglo-Saxon kings through centuries of efforts and in face of strong racial feeling at home and of prolonged invasion from outside had brought together the widely diverse peoples of England—Celts, Angles, Saxons, Norwegians and Danes—into a unity. Solely through their efforts was England a developed entity rather than a collection of separate and perhaps stunted growths. There is no acknowledged theory or uniform practice behind what they did: the basis of the unity they produced was simply traditions, strong traditions, monarchical traditions. And they had built up their England on the old free institutions of the folk-moots and therefore there was little of that sacrifice of liberty which the centralization of government so often exacts: it was, indeed, fortunate that central government lagged behind local government so that this danger was avoided. So the voice of the king was heard throughout his realm, a co-ordinated system of administration had been formed which had no peer in Western Europe, and England was comparatively a much-governed country. In comparison with this achievement the task of the Normans was to be simple: the period of barbarian invasions was over, the field was clear for action, the machinery stood ready: all it needed was a dynasty of strong rulers to supply the drive. This the Normans provided, but in political concepts and administrative agencies they had little to offer in advance of what they found.

SELECT READING

Stenton, 518–36; Pollock and Maitland, i. chs. i, ii; Stephenson and Marcham, 1–32; F. Liebermann, *National Assembly in the Anglo-Saxon Period* (1913), 1–90; F. W. Maitland, 'The Laws of the Anglo-Saxons' in *Collected Papers*, iii. 447–73; Maitland, *Domesday Book and Beyond*

(1897), 220–356; V. H. Galbraith, *The Public Records* (1934), 15–20; H. M. Cam, *Liberties and Communities in Medieval England* (1944), 64–90; J. Tait, *Medieval English Borough* (1936), 130–8; C. Stephenson, *Borough and Town* (1933), 47–72; R. R. Darlington, 'Early History of English Towns' in *History*, xxiii (1938), 141–50; W. Morris, *The Medieval English Sheriff to 1300* (1927), 1–39.

CHAPTER XV

CHURCH AND CULTURE IN THE ELEVENTH CENTURY

THE first half of the eleventh century was not one of the greatest periods in the life of the Church in England: to give any other impression would be misleading. But we must not go further and condemn the Church because it had not remained on the heights of the Age of Dunstan: the emotion which produces a revivalist movement must inevitably lose its intensity. Nevertheless, the post-Dunstan Church was by no means lacking in vitality and worthily maintained its ancient and honoured traditions of service. It has been severely and unjustly criticized with regard to three points and it is well that we should let them form the centre of discussion.

I. SUBORDINATION TO THE STATE

Neither in Anglo-Saxon England nor anywhere else in Western Europe had any serious challenge yet been made to the belief, ratified by many centuries of practical experience, that the Church was an integral part of the State and that the clergy were subordinate to the lay rulers of the world, who were expected by the divine character of their authority to act piously and take the lead in the work of regeneration. The political conception universally held was that of a royal theocracy, the government of the world by God through emperors, kings and princes who act as his agents. To condemn the lay control of the Church as such before 1066 is to anticipate the revolutionary concept of society enunciated by Gregory VII and to become hopelessly entangled in anachronisms. The absorption of churchmen into secular affairs was in theory wholly justifiable and in practice largely justified, and their dependence on a devout prince was not regarded as either derogatory or undesirable. Thus the five centuries of Anglo-Saxon rule exhibited a close co-operation between State and Church, a union between throne and altar, which made strife between them of very rare occurrence. As we have seen, they grew together and they flourished together. This close identification of State and Church resulted, if not in the disappearance from the records of ecclesiastical councils such as Theodore of Tarsus had envisaged, at least in the rarity of the occasions when it is possible to be certain that it was definitely a Church assembly that was meeting. For since royal control was taken for granted and bishops and abbots were royal nominees and formed an influential part of the witan, it was a convenient custom to allow the witan to legislate for the Church: ecclesiastical laws were often published in the king's name. Nevertheless, it must be borne in mind that the witan was not exclusively a lay body which completely dominated the Church. It was, indeed, a highly important part of the machinery of Church government. And from one point of view it could be argued that it represented an ecclesiastical body legislating for the laity rather than a lay body legislating for the Church. The same merging of authority and interests was seen in the local shire court, to which clergy and laymen were alike subject: there the bishop sat to propound the law of the Church and enforce a penitential system for the improvement of general morality. Diocesan synods were certainly not unknown in the eleventh century, a differentiation between lay and Church assemblies could be recognized when convenient, but there was no need to define carefully the limits of secular and ecclesiastical authority and therefore no hard and fast line was ever drawn between them.

II. TIES WITH THE CHURCH UNIVERSAL AND THE POPE

It would have been strange if the eleventh century, which saw foreigners in possession of English estates in the reigns of both Cnut and Edward the Confessor and foreign trade rapidly growing in its range and volume, had not also felt the cosmopolitan influence of a universal Church. And, in fact, whilst foreigners, men of Lorraine as well as Normandy, occupied English episcopal sees and found homes in English monasteries, Englishmen were becoming bishops in the Scandinavian countries of the Baltic, and Ealdred, later archbishop of York, was making his pilgrimage to Jerusalem. It is, however, the relations with the papacy that demand particular attention. The Anglo-Saxon ecclesiastics never forgot their debt of gratitude to the popes who had sent St. Augustine with the message of Christianity and given them organizers such as Theodore and teachers such as Hadrian. Kings like Cadwalla, Ine and Ethelwulf, bishops like Wilfrid of Ripon, and abbots like Benedict Biscop had all made pilgrimages to Rome; representatives of the English Church had attended councils of the Western Church, and papal legates had visited the court of Offa, and the same king had sanctioned payment of regular contributions to the papacy; a 'Saxon school' had been established at Rome itself. The Scandinavian raids had broken communications and caused a rupture, and the disrepute into which the papacy fell, when it became a prize of Roman political factions, bid fair to make the breach irreparable. Nevertheless, the ties were never broken. From Canterbury English archbishops had been going to Rome to receive the pallium since at least 925 and from York since 1026; English bishops were present at the great papal councils at Rheims in 1049 and Rome and Vercelli in 1050. Cnut made his famous journey to Rome in 1027, and apparently only England continued to send Peter's Pence there without a break from Alfred's reign until 1066. And in 1061, when Harold was the power behind the throne, appeals were going from England to Rome and legates from the pope were being received in England, and the bishop of Wells was at Rome as envoy to the pope. Not only was there no perceptible desire to limit papal authority but, instead, that authority was visibly on the increase in the more favourable conditions that the eleventh century produced. The elaborate theories that the English Church was slowly falling away from its obedience to Rome and lapsing into isolation are constructed solely from the unfortunate position of Stigand. Bishop of Winchester in 1047, he was elected archbishop of Canterbury in the place of the fugitive Robert of Jumièges. According to the strict letter of the canon law no such successor should have been appointed, inasmuch as Robert was still living and could be deposed by papal decision alone. The problem, however, of an archbishop who deserted his charge was novel in England and it was felt that his flight was equivalent to resignation: as one chronicler put it, 'thus did he according to the will of God leave his pallium here in this land and that archiepiscopal dignity which, not according to the will of God, he had here obtained'. Therefore the Church proceeded to elect a leader and, in the circumstances of 1052, it was natural that it should choose a partisan of the Godwins. The reasons for what followed are quite obscure. Stigand may well have thought that it was tempting Providence too much to expect the same pope Leo IX, who had given the pallium to Robert, to consent to bestow it upon him. At all events, he did not go to Rome for it until 1058 when he received it from Benedict X, a friend of Leo IX and of the reform movement, who was not an anti-pope inasmuch as he was the only pope formally elected and in power when Stigand arrived, and who evidently agreed with the English Church in regarding the archbishop's election as quite valid. Unluckily for Stigand, the course of papal politics led to the later deposition of Benedict and the elevation of Nicholas II, who refused to regard his predecessor's confirmation as canonical. Only then was Stigand's position in England viewed as in some measure irregular: he was not deprived of his nominal dignity but he no longer exercised the right of a metropolitan to consecrate bishops and to officiate at ceremonies of state. Harold evidently shared the general feeling of dubiety and refrained from using the services of his partisan at his coronation. Therefore, when William I later was crowned by the same archbishop of York, he was not so much slighting Stigand as a schismatic as following a well-established precedent. And, indeed, the king who came to England with a papal banner did not remove Stigand from his archbishopric until 1070 and had even permitted him in 1067 to resume the consecration of bishops. That being so, it is preposterous to regard the ambiguity of Stigand's position as a proof that the English Church was provincial, isolated and schismatic.

III. THE PROGRESS OF REFORM

The influence of Dunstan and his colleagues reached out into the eleventh century and inspired others to continue their labours. The movement for reform may well have slackened; it certainly did not suddenly stop. It is no accident that the four immediate successors of Dunstan to the see of Canterbury were monks who were closely identified with the work that their predecessor had at heart; that new Benedictine houses like Bury St. Edmunds and Burton-on-Trent were founded and were destined to be among the most famous in the country; that parish churches were repaired or built by great landowners and by groups of humble free men to make good the recent Scandinavian ravages. And no one can read the tracts and pastoral letters of Wulfstan, archbishop of York, sternly rebuking the abuses of the secular clergy and instructing the priests on the orderly fulfilment of their duties and providing them with a collection of sermons to expound to their congregations, or the 'Manual' of Byrhtferth of Ramsey with its exposition of all points first in Latin and then in Anglo-Saxon as a deliberate concession to young clerks and country clergy, without realizing that there was no willingness to condone unspirituality among the clergy or to leave the laity uninstructed. Nor was this work confined to the early decades of the century. For Cnut continued to make appointments from reformed monasteries to episcopal office and openly expressed his dependence on the Church for the efficient government of his kingdom. And the eve of the Conquest saw Ealdred, archbishop of York, recognizing the administration and busily supervising the affairs of his see, and Wulfstan, bishop of Worcester, perpetuating in his diocese the inspiration of his famous predecessor, Oswald, and worthily earning his future canonization. Nothing perhaps exhibits in such practical fashion the virility of the Anglo-Saxon Church in its last years as the conversion of the Scandinavians: not only did it proselytize those who had settled within the borders of England, but it undertook and carried through remarkable evangelizing missions to Norway, Sweden and, to a lesser extent, Denmark. To lay stress upon the prominence of ecclesiastical politicians like Stigand and Robert of Jumièges is to misrepresent entirely the character of the old English episcopate, of which they formed but a small section. A need to remove abuses existed in England and even more so on the Continent but, as we shall see later, the accusation that the Church was riddled through with simony and pluralism rests on the slenderest basis of fact, and a highly coloured picture of ignorant and worldly prelates and illiterate and even vicious priests and monks is drawn from post-Conquest Norman sources which stress only the exceptional and the scandalous. This was no period of ecclesiastical sterility and the spirit of reform was neither dead nor dying.

We have stressed the fact that general culture was in these days closely connected with the Church: they could not go different ways. A dependable index of vitality is to be found in literature and art and, should they command respect, we can be sure that the Church was not barren that produced and nurtured them.

When it is summarily and loosely stated that the late old English period witnesses a literary decline and even decadence, it is evident that an unfair and really valueless comparison is being made with the age of Bede or of Alfred, who are, it should be noted, themselves witnesses to the restricted circle of Latin culture in their day. It is apparently assumed that an unbroken and continuously progressive development should have occurred throughout nearly five hundred years, and it is dismissed as of little importance that for a generation after 980 there had been an invasion of half the country by heathen foreigners who sacked and destroyed many of the centres of learning and culture. Despite these catastrophes

English scholarship survived to resume its activities, and we can but marvel at its resilience and the positive value of its achievements.

The knowledge of Latin was not merely present among the cathedral and monastic clergy, for it is evident that a serious attempt was being made to extend it to the lower clergy as well. For not only were new manuscripts of Bede, Aldhelm and others being produced to meet an increasing demand for them, both at home and abroad, but treatises were written expressly to assist in the teaching of Latin: for example, Aelfric, abbot of Eynsham (955–1020), compiled the earliest medieval Latin grammar and wrote for his pupils a charming Latin colloquy with an English rendering. But the literature in the vernacular is of predominating interest. There was clearly to be no restriction of learning to a narrow circle, for the practical wisdom of Alfred in using Anglo-Saxon as an instrument in educating the people at large in Christian ideals and raising the general standard of the moral life of the community continued to be acknowledged, and it is indicative of a praiseworthy intimacy and sympathy between teachers and taught. Aelfric, 'the great master of prose in all its forms', wrote his cultured 'Catholic Homilies' to explain the mysteries of theology in simple language for the understanding of ordinary people, and in his Anglo-Saxon version of the Lord's Prayer, the Creed and parts of the Bible he is authoritatively declared to be 'more enlightened than any other translator before Tyndale'. The Anglo-Saxon Chronicles still had no rival in vernacular historical prose. In all its forms Anglo-Saxon prose, which a long process of civilization had alone made possible, revealed both its vigour and its versatility, its unshaken confidence in its future, and its promise of a rich development. Just as many of the old Anglo-Saxon laws are known to us only through a single twelfth-century manuscript, so the mischance of survival has preserved for us only a small fraction of all that was written; nevertheless, that fraction is unique among the contemporary literatures of Europe.

The same paucity of material evidence makes it difficult to appreciate properly Anglo-Saxon achievements in architecture and the minor arts. There was an extensive revival of ecclesiastical building in the time of Dunstan, and Cnut's reign saw many churches and monasteries either constructed or repaired. And we have still with us substantial remains of over two hundred pre-Conquest churches. It is sufficiently evident that England had a developed 'romanesque' architecture of her own which reached a high standard, survived many years after the Norman Conquest and won the unstinted admiration of the pro-Norman William of Malmesbury, familiar though he was with the products of a later age. Unfortunately the great churches often disappeared during the Norman period of construction, and we are left to judge by secondary productions, the smaller and cruder village churches, among which Earls Barton in Northamptonshire stands apart in stateliness. We are more happily placed with regard to manuscripts, many of which are still extant in continental as well as English libraries, for they were in great demand by churches abroad. In the fineness of their script and the beauty of their illuminations they were not surpassed in Europe. Of minor arts like the work of the goldsmith, the armourer and woodcarver, few examples remain, but the artistry which went to the designing of the royally controlled coinage before the Conquest was not to be rivalled again in England for a hundred years.

The literary and artistic memorials of the eleventh century may be safely left to bear testimony to the quality of the spiritual resources of the Anglo-Saxon people.

SELECT READING

Chambers, ch. viii; D. Knowles, *Monastic Order in England* (1940), 56–83; R. W. Chambers, 'On the Continuity of English Prose from Alfred to More' in *N. Harpsfield's Life of More* (Early English Text Society: 1932), lvii–lxxxi (published separately: 1932); *Cambridge History of English Literature*, i (1907), 108–48; R. K. Gordon, *Anglo-Saxon Poetry* (1927: translation); R. R. Darlington, 'Last Phase of Anglo-Saxon History' in *History*, xxii (1937), 1–13; Darlington, 'Ecclesiastical Reform in the Late Old English Period' in *E.H.R.*, li (1936), 385–428; Arthur Gardner, *Handbook of English Medieval Sculpture* (1935), 47–78; A. W. Clapham, *Romanesque Architecture in Western Europe* (1936), 138–153; Clapham, *English Romanesque Architecture* (2 vols.: 1930, 1934); G. C. Brooke, *English Coins* (1932), 56–90.

CHAPTER XVI

THE FEUDALIZATION OF SOCIETY BEFORE THE NORMAN CONQUEST

WITHIN the last few years it has been plainly stated that feudalism had not made its presence known in England before the advent of continental influences in 1066. This problem cannot be faced squarely unless we first make up our minds what exactly we mean by feudalism. It will never be possible to give a precise definition: that is the reason why the general treatment of the subject is so frequently confusing and why historians reach apparently different conclusions. For the word 'feudalism' was not used by medieval men: the term has been invented for the convenience of historians in describing the social structure of Europe from roughly the eighth century onwards. Feudalism is therefore no more than a comprehensive term to describe the roughly similar arrangements made by society both inside and outside Europe in accommodating itself to changes of a similar kind which were everywhere taking place. It follows, therefore, that feudalism must remain in its meaning somewhat vague, indeterminate, elastic, if it is to cover the activities of many peoples of diverse origins and traditions over a period of half a thousand years: it will mean something different in different places, something different in the same place at different times. It is only a rough and ready summation of medieval society, a useful generalization to which exceptions are legion. Unfortunately, once having invented the term as one of general significance only, historians have been apt later to invest it with a specialized meaning in accordance with their own regional or particular interests: the date of the appearance of feudalism will then depend upon whether the aspect of development in which they are interested comes to the fore early or late. Thus the social or economic historian with his stress upon inequalities of status or the methods of working the land will trace feudalism back to the days of the later Roman Empire; the constitutional historian with his emphasis upon the transference of political authority from the central government to great landowners will concentrate his main attention on the later Merovingian age; the military historian with his preoccupation with mounted knights and castles will date the advent of feudalism later still.

Nowhere is it more obvious than in the study of feudal developments that the history of England cannot and must not be studied in isolation. They will be quite meaningless to us until we have firmly grasped the reasons why the structure of European society, as it had been known for centuries under the Roman Empire, should have undergone drastic alteration. And inasmuch as it has been contended that feudalism was a direct and late importation into England from the Continent, it becomes all the more essential to understand what had been taking place in Europe in general and in France in particular.

Feudalism represents quite a natural phase in the development of society when we take into consideration the conditions of the time. It must not be unfairly judged as a form of life which was, in comparison with the past, perverted, corrupt and decadent, for the old past could not have coped unchanged with the new circumstances; nor must it be condemned as anarchic, for it was deliberately fostered and encouraged by authority itself. The principal reason for its growth was the breakdown of centralized government, which could no longer protect society as it had done under the Empire. The inevitable collapse began with the incursions and settlements of barbarian peoples within its frontiers, and the pace was accelerated tremendously in the ninth and tenth centuries when, for example, the Northmen plundered Europe from the Baltic to the Mediterranean and, in particular, wrested half of England from the Anglo-Saxon kings and the province of Normandy from the kings of France. The arrangements, therefore, that we call 'feudal' came to be viewed as a means whereby society protected itself when protection was no longer forthcoming from emperors and kings; they provided for the deliberate organization of society on a war basis and supplied the only method of effective resistance to the deadly peril which hemmed European civilization round about. That is the all-important fact. Too wise in our knowledge of later, much later, events, we must not allow them to colour our views of what occurred before. Ever since the 'pax romana' had vanished completely in the fifth century, every country in Western Europe had seen war as the normal state of affairs within it. Certainly under feudalism society had been purposively built for war and, when there were no external foes to defeat, men still went on fighting, but among themselves: the right of private warfare was almost universally recognized and the superfluity of military force prolonged dispeace. Still, the twelfth century, when the social structure of Western Europe remained feudalized, was a distinct improvement on the tenth. That is the only valid comparison. To compare the feudal age with the state of Europe in the second and early third centuries and to conclude, in consequence, that feudalism was an anti-social and anarchic force may be sociology: it is certainly not history.

Feudalism made no sudden appearance in history. It had its roots firmly embedded in the past. It was, indeed, partly a result of the fusion of two ways of life, the Roman and the Germanic, and it was because each of them was predisposed towards it that they were able to amalgamate so smoothly. The feudalization of society originated in simple and understandable causes.

It is not difficult to find developments within the Roman Empire analogous to those which were to take place in the barbarian kingdoms which supplanted it.

I.   THE PERSONAL CONCEPT OF SOCIETY

The idea that one's loyalty should be given to a person was a notion common to both Roman and non-Roman peoples. The ordinary citizen of the empire owed a duty to the emperor, who was in some sense a sacred person; the Carolingian kings demanded an oath of fealty from all their subjects. Furthermore, Roman emperors and Roman generals alike had had their personal bodyguards, and this practice can be compared with the Celtic clan system which was based on personal devotion to chieftains, and with the Germanic 'companionry' (*comitatus*), known to both Caesar and Tacitus, which saw warriors voluntarily gathering round a chosen leader. And in Roman social life the practice of 'patronage' (*patrocinium*) had seen the weak seeking the protection of the strong and even placing their property under their patron's care. What the early Middle Ages called 'commendation' was, as we have seen, prompted by not dissimilar motives; the practice developed and extended through all grades of society. The central government raised no objection, for it was a normal phase in social development which it found useful to encourage: the result came to be a pyramid of tenants and tenures. In all these instances the arrangements were founded upon a personal oath of faith, fidelity, fealty.

II.   THE LEGAL CONCEPT OF PROPERTY

Roman law permitted an individual to have complete control over land and transmit it by inheritance, will or contract. It had also elaborated the highly technical 'precarium', land bestowed at the 'prayer' of the grantee and revocable at the will of the grantor, which differentiated the ownership of land from the mere possession and use of it. Such legal concepts did not die a sudden death among, for example, the romanized people of Gaul. Some retained lands which descended by simple inheritance, and a new and philologically obscure term, 'allodial' property, was used by the Franks to describe what they did not understand until it was eventually lost to sight among feudalized tenures. And the 'precarium' had obvious similarities with the later 'benefice', which was also a 'precarious' tenure: the lord granted the use of his own lands on condition that the grantees rendered service. The word 'benefice' was used to indicate that the holding of the tenements was by an act of grace, a 'benefit' or boon, which depended on the good will of the grantor and could be withdrawn. Such benefices were common in the seventh century and the practice was extremely useful to the Merovingian Church which could thus get round the Church law which decreed that no ecclesiastical lands were to be alienated in perpetuity.

However, when all is said and done, we shall be approaching the problem of a feudalized society from a very misleading angle if we concentrate our attention on the decay of the Roman state instead of the creation of new states which owed little to Roman law and Roman practices until the twelfth century. For if we keep the legal and sophisticated concepts of Rome in the forefront of our minds, we shall be led into social theorizings and grave anachronisms which will make the facts grotesque. The deliberate and subtle thinking, of which the Romans were capable, vanished. The barbarians did not start with the principles of Gaius: they did not know or acquire the Roman concept of the sovereign state and they were ignorant of the Roman law of property.

If we imagine ourselves in the place of the barbarian intruders, we shall realize that they came as conquerors into lands where the humbler folk still lived on but whence many of the propertied and ruling classes had fled, if they had not already been killed. They made the best of the situation. They retained their own practices, but they had to recognize many local practices with which they were not familiar and make what compromise they could. Society in Gaul, which we must take as the vital theatre of developments, passed by very slow gradations from romanized provincial life to the Merovingian and the Carolingian state. Different peoples existed side by side and for generations they lived their lives apart: each preserved its own customs and was judged according to its own 'law'.

The Franks, however, dominated the situation, and it is upon their actions that we must fix our attention. The Frankish kings remained leaders in war, they kept an armed band around them, they owned vast territories. They could not maintain the conditions on which the civilization of Rome depended, and the reigns of Clovis, his sons and grandsons show how completely engrossed they were in the waging of war. The *comitatus* with its emphasis upon personal service, particularly in war, was the prototype of vassalage with its personal relationships, marked by the oath of fealty, and with its mutual obligations of protection and service. Personal loyalty and personal service called for their reward, and this usually took the form of a grant of land from the royal estates: being revocable and dependent on the fulfilment of services, it came into the general category of a 'benefice'. All vassals, however, did not have a 'benefice', and all 'benefices' were not, as we have seen, held by vassals. The close tie between 'vassalage' and 'benefice' was drawn mainly under the Carolingians when their dominions were harried by Scandinavians and Saracens, Slavs and Magyars. A struggle for survival needed the full-time services of military experts who possessed horses, equipment and technical skill: the tactical value of cavalry was, it has been suggested, first appreciated in West Europe in warfare against the Saracenic horsemen in the eighth century. It signalled a military revolution with a tremendous rise in the cost of warfare, and the mounted knight had to be reimbursed for expenditure by the grant of a 'benefice'. Such a military 'benefice' came to be called a 'fief': it could be held only by a vassal who took an oath of homage to indicate the bond involved, and by the ninth century it was to all intents and purposes regarded as hereditary property. To begin with, therefore, the fief was a special 'fee' conditional on the rendering of specialized services. In the dangerous circumstances of the time the tenure of a fief by military services ranked far above all other forms of tenure, it gave both name and vitality to a new social structure, and eventually it did not matter whether the subject of a grant was land or a chattel, an office or an 'immunity', it came under the general concept of a fief However, the presence of stipendiary knights in royal and noble households as late as the twelfth century, who had no fiefs and were paid wages, is a reminder that feudalism in its essentials goes back past the fief to simple vassalage and the Germanic *comitatus*. In its development to meet the needs of a society continuously at war it was a Germanic, not a Roman, institution.

 We have mentioned 'immunities' without defining them. It was these which gave to feudalism its political colour. The delegation of the political authority of the Frankish kings can be traced to their very earliest days, because it was the only way in which an extensive realm could be governed at all. They sent to every city a representative under the Roman title of 'count' to rule in their name and assume full local responsibility: their own supervision could only be what the power of the sword could make it. The Franks, far removed from the royal household, and retaining their ineradicable tradition that service must be personal, could have been governed in no other way. When the Carolingian Empire was shaken by the storms of the ninth century and centralized government of any kind could no longer function, its rulers were compelled to allow their public servants in the provinces to wield independent authority. (For quite practical reasons they were granted 'immunities' from all government control and government interference: they could raise troops, levy taxes, dispense justice, fulfil police duties.) As the position grew worse and more and more districts had to be left to look after themselves, these 'immunities' were granted to other than royal servants and were bestowed upon local magnates in general, either as an emergency measure or as a direct bribe to obtain military assistance. As it has been put, the kings abdicated in order to remain kings. And often 'immunities' were simply quietly assumed. However it happened, the fiefs were in consequence brought into the framework of government.

For long the series of relationships remained ill-defined and amorphous. But the nearer society came to collapse, the faster the processes towards feudalism worked. The tenth century saw the feudal régime: the rule of lords or 'seigneurs', the presence of innumerable small lordships, self-contained, independent, intensely jealous of their neighbours and conducting private war against them. But when the Scandinavian and the other menaces were past, the feudal régime was gradually pruned of its excesses and it was bound to the observance of specified regulations, and there came out of it that structure of society, to which modern historians have given the general descriptive term of 'feudalism'.

Nevertheless, the notion of sovereignty did not altogether vanish.

In fact, it found a place for itself within the very scheme of feudalism: the perfect pyramid must have an apex where there is room for one and one only. The king was in feudal practice the 'lord of lords', the general lord of the kingdom: it was feudalism itself which kept him paramount in unique isolation until he was strong enough to discard it. Moreover, the kingly office remained an institution supported by divine sanctions for the furtherance of divine purposes. These conceptions were never questioned throughout the Middle Ages, and therefore monarchy stayed pre-eminent in the feudal world which had formed beneath it. It is true that in practice it had become paralysed and shorn of most of its power. Nevertheless, it still retained within its armoury for use at an appropriate time the weapon of the 'prerogative': it had not lost all interest in the lands it had given to others, for it could claim that it still possessed all the political rights which it had not very specifically given away. Therefore monarchy will eventually grow again in strength in the very midst of feudalism by developing political forces which were older than feudalism and which had never been eliminated. There would be no limit to the elasticity of the prerogative as soon as the right time and the right man came together.

We are now in a position to supply a yardstick with which to measure roughly the comparative extent of developments as essential to feudalized life.

I. THE PRIVATE RELATIONSHIP BETWEEN LORD AND MAN

This lies deep at the roots of feudalism. The bond between them was made as unbreakable as possible, for unless the mutual obligations entered into were strictly observed, then society would inevitably disintegrate. Therefore every possible religious and social sanction was placed upon the maintenance and enforcement of the solemn oath of 'homage', sworn by the man (*homme*) to his lord. Nevertheless, we must remember that the contract was indeed a contract, a bargain in which each side had rights and duties, and that if one party broke it then the other, whether lord or man, was *ipso facto* released from his own obligations. It was not considered that the lord, whether he were king, duke, count or lesser magnate, had unfettered and irresponsible authority: he was tied by whatever the terms of his contract might be. In theory, at least, feudalism was not synonymous with tyranny. Indeed, feudal custom came to bestow upon the 'man' the legal right to make a formal 'defiance' (*diffidatio*), a withdrawal of 'faith' (*fides, foi*).

II. THE PRIVATE CONTRACT BASED ON LAND

As soon as this occurred, then lordship became confused with landlordship and landowning with landholding. And there was a natural transition of thought whereby a man's personal status, his position in society and in political life, was settled entirely by the kind of services he had to render in return for his land. All depended upon whether his tenure was military or freehold or servile.

III. THE WORK OF GOVERNMENT CARRIED ON THROUGH LANDLORDS

With the growth of immunities from control and the consequent decentralization, feudal domains, both great and small, became miniatures of a state. The tenants became, as it were, their landlord's subjects, swearing allegiance to him, performing quasi-public duties at his command, and giving him counsel when he asked for it. The landlord for his part took the role of their political ruler with military, fiscal, judicial and police rights over them.

IV. THE MILITARY ORGANIZATION FOUNDED ON THE TENURE OF LAND

This specialized development requires individual notice because round it has gathered much of the argument that feudalism was unknown in Anglo-Saxon England. The military service demanded from tenants was scrutinized and systematized in the eleventh century as, for example, in Normandy, and each parcel of estates had to guarantee to supply a definite number of knights so that there should be no doubt about the military resources available in a time of crisis.

We can now approach the hazy problem of Anglo-Saxon feudalism along clear-cut channels of investigation. Were these four salient characteristics of feudalism present in England before 1066? A *prima facie* judgment would agree that they were, simply because it would have been more than strange if she had remained completely isolated from the changes which were transforming the character of the whole of European society. Since the law of the land was rapidly becoming little more than the land-law, since the ways and conditions of holding land and, to use a technical phrase, the system of dependent tenures form the crux of the whole matter, we must needs grapple with the intricacies of Anglo-Saxon methods of holding property.

(i) *The private relationship between lord and man*

We have already observed that the principle of lordship was clearly at work in England as soon as written evidence comes to hand. The theme of personal devotion and attachment runs through the relationships between lords and their gesiths and thegns, and the idea of patronage underlies the process of 'commendation'. It should be remembered, however, that at the time of the Norman Conquest there still remained in England, chiefly in the Midlands, East Anglia and Yorkshire which had received a comparatively recent influx of Scandinavian settlers, large numbers of free men who recognized no lords.

(ii) *The private contract based on land*

The private contract with a lord need not be based upon land at all: he might receive payment for his favours in the form of a moneyed rent or labour services. Nevertheless, obligations were commonly associated with the possession of land in some way or other. The Anglo-Saxons were aware of three methods of holding property: (a) *Folkland*. A recent attempt to resurrect the old view that folkland represented, as it were, state property, that is property belonging to the Anglo-Saxons as a community in contrast with the king's personal property, has not met with acceptance, and it is generally agreed that it means land held in accordance with the customary law of the folk and hence subject to all public burdens, from none of which it had gained exemption. It was held by individual landowners and it normally reverted only to kinsmen, but they had no written title to their property and any disputes concerning it were naturally settled in the folk or popular assembly courts. Since no written documents were needed, we hear little about folkland: it is mentioned only four times in surviving sources. (b) *Bookland*. This, on the other hand, represents land or rights over land held by written title, by a land-book or charter. It was an ecclesiastical practice, the way in which the Church, itself a stranger to Germanic customary law, held most of its property, but it was soon adopted into lay practice as well, so far as great men only were concerned: thus from the seventh century the kings were making liberal grants of bookland to the Church and from the eighth century to thegns. Bookland had many advantages to give its recipients: no folk court had any jurisdiction over it, and any discussions concerning it took place before the king and witan who took it under their special care; a genuine charter was indisputable and no evidence could be led against it; it provided a way for the formation of large estates and for this reason had a tremendous influence upon the development of society. The point of significance for us, however, is that bookland was a gift outright and therefore its recipient was an owner, not a tenant: he had property, not simply tenure, with full freedom of alienation. There is frequently the notion that services, like the saying of masses, ought to continue being performed for it, and both sides must have taken this for granted. And the heriot, the primitive form of death duties, which the recipient's heir had to pay on the succession to the estate, is there to suggest that the donor had not parted with all his interests in the land he had given away. Still, the bookland was in essence a reward for services in the past, it was not a retaining fee for services in the future. (c) *Loanland.* So far land, whether folkland or bookland, had been held and granted without the imposition of conditions binding in the future. The Anglo-Saxons realized the difficulties of this disability and they evolved a practice which came very close to the continental 'benefice' or 'fief'. The land was not alienated so that property rights were lost; it was loaned for generally the period of three lives and within that period it was heritable and bequeathable. 'The loan is a gift for a time.' Services could therefore be laid upon the land and it could be lost if they were not performed: dependent tenures had come into existence. Though the conception of leasehold tenure can be traced back to the laws of Ine in the late seventh century, nearly all our precise evidence about loanland comes from the activities of Oswald, the great reforming bishop of Worcester, who granted some seventy such leases of episcopal lands and defined the terms on which they were to be held: hospitality and escort duties during his visits, the delivery and execution of his messages, repairs to bridges, payments to the Church. Unfortunately we do not know whether loanland was spread more widely over the country. However that may be, the grants of loanland bear a close resemblance to feudal enfeoffments and, indeed, they come very close to having feudal incidents connected with them: for example, by Edward the Confessor's time the grantor of loanland was claiming the right to marry the heiress to his own nominee. Yet, though we have here conditional tenures, we have not quite reached the finality of a feudal enfeoffment: the services are too miscellaneous in their character, too vague in their form, too little specialized and, most important of all, loanland is not fully hereditary and therefore the relations between grantor and grantee are not regarded as being perpetually fixed between all succeeding heirs.

(iii) *The work of government carried on through landlords*

There is no doubt that from the seventh century lords had been given powers of police: it was their duty to present their men in court. And the strong kings of the tenth century had deliberately made much use of them in the routine work of administration. The serious problem, however, is whether they ever obtained the right to hold a court of law, a private court where the king's officials could not interfere. It has long been accepted doctrine that by the tenth and eleventh centuries the king was rewarding his servants by granting away his rights of jurisdiction along with what was in all probability more attractive, the financial profits which came from exercising them. Many hundred courts thus passed from royal control into the hands of private persons. The arguments put forward on behalf of this thesis could be used to indicate the growth of private jurisdictions as far back as the seventh century. As this is unlikely, it has aroused doubts about the validity of the arguments themselves, and it has been recently vigorously contended that there is no express statement in any surviving charter that the king had given judicial immunities and permitted private jurisdictions. He had done no more than permit a lord to have those profits of a hundred court which would otherwise have gone to the crown and perhaps to act as its presiding officer. That is the full meaning of that mysterious phrase 'sac and soc', 'cause' and 'suit', which occurs for the first time in the middle of the tenth century. The king gave away fiscal rights but not judicial rights and, that fact apart, the hundred courts continued as before. We may reasonably suspect, however, that the king would retain little active interest in the execution of justice that brought no financial profits. However, even if we contend that private courts were established in Anglo-Saxon England, it is evident that they owed their origin to an explicit grant from the crown, that they represented a delegation of royal justice. There is apparently no knowledge of any feudal doctrine that a lord had a right to hold a court for his tenants as a direct result of the relationship between them. There is no feudal justice in England, there is only essentially royal justice.

(iv) *The military organization founded on the tenure of land*

When we ask ourselves the question whether we can see in England before 1066 a group of military experts who had been given grants of land on the express condition that they would fight their lord's battles, we immediately think of the Anglo-Saxon thegns and the Danish housecarls. The obligation to perform military service was understood to lie upon both these groups. Together they formed a landed aristocracy, bound to serve the king in war, and they were to outward view not unlike the tenants-in-chief of the Norman régime. If they failed in their military duties, they were liable to forfeit their property. This represents an approximation to military tenures, yet the association of military service and land was still vague. Though the thegns in general were required to fight, yet fighting was not their only nor even their main business: their work in the routine of administration was more prominent. Furthermore, thegnship was essentially a rank in society: a merchant who crossed the sea three times or a prominent priest in attendance on the king might attain it. It was because of the ancient traditions and duties connected with their social rank, and not because of the lands they held, that the thegns rendered service in war. The obligation is purely personal and not territorial. They could break their bond with their lord if they so desired, they could give away their lands without in any way altering their military commitments: military service has therefore not been essentially and inextricably tied up with land. The reason is simple: England was part of an island and was not called upon to face the attack of specialist cavalry, for the finely trained horses or destriers, as they were called, would have had to be transported by sea. Since there was no call to breed such destriers and to learn a new technique in fighting, the costs of warfare remained comparatively low and it was unnecessary to make further arrangements to meet them.

It is evident, therefore, that society in England was not sharply dissimilar from society in France: it knew the private relationships between lord and man in hierarchical form; it knew an inchoate seignorial régime in the self-contained estates worked by the peasantry on behalf of lords; it knew dependent tenures like loan-land, hardly to be distinguished from the fief; it knew a nobility with military duties; it knew a monarchy which had granted mon-archical privileges away to its subjects. The mere fact of conquest will permit the ready application of the more developed form of feudalism to be found in France. It is essential that we state a truism: we do not find Norman feudalism in England before the Normans came. But we do find a social system cognate to it and cognate still more to the feudalism of other parts of France, notice-ably Brittany. To deny the descriptive term of 'feudal' to the changes which had produced the Anglo-Saxon social structure on the ground that it did not fully resemble the social structure in Normandy is begging the question: it could equally well be argued that Norman society was never feudalized because it did not reach the still more developed form of feudal society in the Latin king-dom of Jerusalem. Feudalism is an unsatisfactory word: however, if what went on in England before 1066 was not feudal, even though it was no more than tentative in military and political aspects, the word to describe it will have to be invented.

SELECT READING

Stenton, 563–93; F. L. Ganshof, *Qu'est-ce que la Féodalité?* (1947); C. Stephenson, *Medieval Feudalism* (1942); C. Seignobos, *History of the French People* (trans. 1933), 36–88; C. Stephenson, 'Origin and Signifi-cance of Feudalism' in *Am. H.R.*, xlvi (1940), 788–812; C. Stephenson, 'Feudalism and its Antecedents in England' in *Am. H.R.*, xlviii (1942), 245–65; D. C. Douglas, 'The Norman Conquest and English Feudalism' in *Economic History Review*, ix (1938), 128–43.

CHAPTER XVII

THE IMPACT OF THE NORMANS UPON ANGLO-SAXON CIVILIZATION

THE remarkable historical continuity and the even development of the political life of England have become a commonplace of history. It is not perhaps surprising in a country whose geographical position permitted easy contact with the main centres of civilization and yet prevented foreign domination from radically altering its indigenous growth. The evolutionist interpretation of the course of events governed the minds of Victorian historians like Kemble, Freeman and Green, whose generation did more than any other to dissipate the darkness which overhung the Anglo-Saxon people and their achievements. Unfortunately they could not escape the bias of their times, when British supremacy in the world was attributed to the beneficent workings of nationalism and democracy. Therefore, fully accepting the current perverse historical doctrine that the past could only be understood in the light of the present, they became preoccupied with tracing modern principles backwards. As a result they were led to eulogize the Anglo-Saxon age, in which they detected the seeds of all later freedom, and contended that the incursions of the Normans did no more than put fresh life into the old institutions and intrude a foreign element which was absorbed and assimilated.

The disappearance of the Victorian illusion of progress meant the end of what had been little removed from unconscious propaganda masquerading as history and exposed to the scholars of the early twentieth century the aberrations of the evolutionist doctrine. It was not difficult to show the absurdity of these historical preconceptions and to tear them derisively to pieces. The new interpretation of the Norman Conquest placed a great emphasis upon the influence of continental innovations. This fresh orientation of outlook produced a changed attitude to the Anglo-Saxon age and, most regrettably, in order to counterbalance the previous excessive veneration for what had been accomplished before 1066 and in order to extol and magnify the part played by the Normans in the making of the English nation, it became customary to dwell at length upon the shortcomings and faults of the Old English state, especially in the twenty years before the Conquest. Just as elaborate theories of the institutional weakness of the Old English monarchy were constructed from no better evidence than the character of the Confessor, so equally elaborate theories about the isolation of the English Church were constructed from the unfortunate position of Stigand. A highly coloured picture was painted of a completely decadent state, face to face with political anarchy and social disintegration and tied for its future to the culturally backward countries of the Baltic, and of a provincial and stagnant Church, cut off from communion with Rome and even the Church Universal. From all these evils, it was asserted, the Norman Conquest freed the country immediately by introducing Latin influences into State and Church in England for what is inferred to be the first time, thus bringing it into contact with Western Europe at a moment when the great constructive ideas, inherited from the Roman Empire, were coming once again to the forefront through an ecclesiastical reform movement and an intellectual and cultural renaissance. The evolutionist conception was thus displaced by that of cataclysmic change, and the Conquest came to be openly regarded as a revolution which signalled the real starting-point in the unbroken development of England. Extreme opinions are superficial opinions and, plausible as this explanation of events may appear to be, it dissolves completely when removed from the realm of theory and submitted to the acid test of fact: it has, indeed, less of the essential truth in it than the account of the Victorian historians it ridicules when it regards the Old English state, not as rich in its promises for the future, but evil in its portents.

Pre-Conquest Normandy

It is impossible to approach a subject of so much controversy without first clearing the ground of some statements which have been a frequent cause of stumbling. It has been said, and said recently, that 'the miserable history of England forms the most striking of contrasts to the civilization of Normandy', that in turning from the history of one to that of the other 'one is conscious at once of passing from decadence to growth'. It is the simple truth that we know and can but know very little about the history of the duchy of Normandy before 1066 because there is a great dearth of information. The position has not altered since it was authoritatively remarked fifty years ago that 'the great tendency to ascribe to the pre-Conquest Normans the organization of later times and to exaggerate their civilization would be checked if it were more generally recognized how exceedingly slight is the information that has come down to us as to their administrative, legal, fiscal, military and other organization, and that in many cases we have absolutely no information'. Since these words were written, the history of the duchy has been studied with remarkably minute care and the paucity of evidence has been fully confirmed. To take one important point, the Normans had no written laws to bring with them to England and were slow to produce their first legal treatise, the *Très Ancien Coutumier*, which in its present form can scarcely date before the opening of the thirteenth century, though it apparently contains earlier elements. It is hardly open to argument that the Normans were less literate and less civilized than the Anglo-Saxons, and we can say nothing with certainty about the processes whereby the Danish heathen pirates became a French-speaking and christianized people. The obvious parallel is with the settlement of their fellows in England, where also they quickly adopted the language, the Church and the civilization of the people among whom they dwelt, leaving little trace of that transformation. Where all is inference, it is with justified scepticism that we read the language of superlatives which describes the Normandy of William I as the most advanced and progressive European province.

The Scandinavians, mostly of Danish extraction, had already been settling between the Somme and the Cotentin peninsula when the almost unknown Rollo made the quite unknown treaty, allegedly at St. Clair-sur-Epte, in 911 with the king of France, which presumably settled the limits of conquest like the almost contemporary Pact between Alfred and Guthrum on the other side of the Channel. Thereby a small duchy, less than Wessex in size, became a dependency of the French crown. The Norse element was small and the bulk of the population unchanged in racial composition. It was not strange that Normandy should come to exhibit a more consistent and logical form of feudalism than was to be found elsewhere in France: the stern work of a conquest had done much to destroy the old ways of life and to dissociate the province from its past, while the agreement of 911 introduced into it at once the feudal ideas as they stood in that year and without the multifarious exceptions which a gradual evolution from old traditions had left in other provinces of France. Thus the Normans, borrowing their institutional framework from their neighbours, especially from their Capetian overlord in the early eleventh century, gave greater defini- tion to feudalism as a political system and used it as an instrument of government. The greater lay lords and ecclesiastics held heredi- tary fiefs of the duke on condition of military service and divided their estates into knights' fees to provide it: their knightly tenants accompanied them to battle in groups of five or multiples thereof. Both the duke and the barons claimed such feudal incidents as reliefs, wardships, marriage and aids. The ultimate supremacy of a powerful duke was acknowledged, but the strength of the Norman state was no more than the strength of its rulers, for it was not reinforced by an administrative system which could function when the head of the state was incompetent. At the centre was the ducal court with its household officials after the style of the Capetian model; we hear nothing of a chancery and little of writs, and there are only a few instances of the dispatch of commissioners into the country districts. In local government some four or five counties, entrusted to the duke's kin or most trusted friends, looked after their own affairs; the rest of the duchy was split up among some twenty necessarily small 'vicomtés', administrative units common to all France and not unlike the English shire, which were under the control of 'vicomtes', public officials who were the nominees of the duke and undertook all the duties of civil government; there is no sign of municipal institutions. Though a strong duke could enforce political order through the jurisdiction of his court and insist upon his sole right to coin money and licence castle-build- ing, not even William I could abolish the ancient custom of private warfare. How much this direct negation of authority, coupled with the absence of a firmly established routine of government, could mean under a weak ruler was shown immediately after the Con- queror's death in 1087 when the horrors of anarchy returned to Normandy for twenty years, during which its greatest historian can discern only 'a dreary tale of private war, murder and pillage, of perjury, disloyalty and revolt'.

The greatest hope of permanent progress that the Norman duchy could show was provided by its enthusiasm for the Church. It was not of very long standing, for it does not go back much earlier than Duke Richard the Good, the brother-in-law of Cnut. Nor did it much assist the secular Church, the Church of bishops and priests who dwelt among the laity: we know almost nothing of their activities, but the few references we have indicate the serious

need of discipline and reform—the ecclesiastical decrees condemning Norman bishops who were converting Church lands into lay
fees for their relatives, the ecclesiastical baronies held by military
tenure, the disclosure of grave clerical abuses at the Council of
Lillebonne in 1080. What appealed most of all to the recent con-
verts—the conversion of the Normans does not seem to have been
complete even in Duke William's time—was the monastic Church
with its emphasis upon the world to come and its constant prayers
for its benefactors, alive or dead. The revival of monasticism on
the Cluny model in Normandy had to be mainly the work of others
than the Normans themselves: the abbey of Le Bec, founded as
recently as 1034, owed its first distinction to the Italian Lanfranc,
who undertook the direction of its school in 1042, and its greatest
fame to another Italian, Anselm of Aosta, and, indeed, in 1066
nearly all the greater abbeys of Normandy were ruled by 'foreign'
monks. It was, however, the financial support of the zealous
Normans which had made it possible to raise the number of abbeys
founded from four in 1001 to twenty-one in 1066, eight under royal
and the rest under noble patronage. Still, it is well to remember
that there could have been hardly more than five hundred monks
all told and that their fundamental purpose was defeated if they
had contact with society or engaged themselves in social reform.
The Norman Church as a whole was in complete subordination to
the duke, who appointed and deposed its bishops and abbots as he
pleased, settled all problems about the scope of its authority, and
kept a firm control over its councils and their decrees.

Just as the history of Normandy before 1066, especially under
Duke William, has been marked by quite unwarrantable eulogy,
so William himself has been endowed with qualities which it is
hardly likely that he possessed. However carefully we study his
career as duke, we fail to discern more than a masterful man,
determined to have his own way, no matter the means or the cost
either to himself or to others. A bastard succeeding his father in
1035 at the age of eight, he lived in obscurity for twelve years
among intrigues, wars and assassinations: all four of his guardians
met deaths by violence within the first five years of his nominal
rule. It was not until 1047 that he comes into history when his
overlord, the king of France, won for him the battle of Val-ès-
Dunes when he was faced by a rebellion of still largely unassimilated
Scandinavians in the western parts of Normandy. Thereafter
he slowly and resolutely set about consolidating his position by

every means possible. In 1053 he took as his wife Matilda, daughter of the count of Flanders, in open defiance of the Church which had solemnly banned the marriage at the General Council of Rheims four years earlier: after Normandy had lain under an interdict and William himself had deposed the archbishop of Rouen for excommunicating him, a long delayed reconciliation between duke and pope was brought about by Lanfranc in 1059 on the basis of a dispensation for the marriage. The same act which led him to fall foul of the pope was the cause of his disregarding his oath of fealty to his Capetian overlord, who resented and feared the union of Norman and Flemish interests, and the victories of Mortemer, 1054, and Varaville, 1058, rendered him for all practical purposes independent of his lawful suzerain. In 1063 William took advantage of circumstances to make himself, by force and trickery and pitiless intimidation, the lord of the neighbouring province of Maine.

Before 1066 there is disclosed the unattractive picture of a friendless man, suspicious, grasping and hard in his nature, unscrupulous and ruthless in his methods, formally devout in his religion, yet withal indomitable in the pursuit and attainment of his ends. There is, however, no indication that William was equipped with high powers of constructive statesmanship or advanced theories of government when he made the gambler's throw and invaded England. It is the way of conquests to make great changes, and there certainly followed a reconstruction of upper society on a new and feudal basis, but it is more than doubtful if William acted with deliberate intent and looked into the future and foresaw the momentous results of what he was doing. He asserted strong monarchy because he was determined to be master in his own house and tolerate no opposition; he introduced the military tenures of feudalism because military necessity compelled him to introduce the only system of defence he knew; he patronized the Church for the sake of his superstitious conscience and his immortal soul rather than for any religious or moral convictions, for these at no time bridled his actions. From the point of view of character and abilities it is wiser to regard William as the successor of the Scandinavian Cnut rather than as the predecessor of the Angevin Henry II.

The work of the Norman conquerors of England can nearly all be traced to the operation of two factors, Norman monarchy and Norman feudalism, which are brought to bear upon every phase of

English life. Despite their intricate inter-relations, the changes in government, society, Church and culture, and foreign policy are most intelligibly considered apart.

I. The Impact upon Government

THE ESTABLISHMENT OF NORMAN MONARCHY

After 1066 the cardinal point in development is the monarchy, from which the institutions of the past were to continue to draw their strength and the institutions of the future to derive their origin. The change made in 1066 was severely practical: it placed a stronger emphasis upon the part that kingship should play in the routine of government, and the vigour of all three Norman kings, autocrats with 'institutionally unlimited' authority, supplied the drive to machinery which was already in existence. It is easy to forget how much the Norman monarchy owed to the Old English monarchy and how little it differed from it. When William landed in England the only rights he had over his Norman followers were as duke of Normandy. From Christmas Day 1066 these followers became the subjects of a king, not a self-appointed king but one who claimed to be the successor of Edward the Confessor and the inheritor of the rights and privileges he had enjoyed, and the whole power of the royal prerogative became his to develop and extend. That the Norman rulers made a far wider use of it than the Anglo-Saxon kings does not alter the fact that the prerogative came to them directly from the Anglo-Saxon age.

Furthermore, the Norman kings did not come to a land which knew neither unity nor government. In the basic work of terri-torial unification their work was done for them, for only the north-western districts remained outside the territories ruled by English kings. Assailed on every side by Scandinavian invaders for more than two hundred years, England had remained a bulwark of Christendom and obstinately retained her political integrity and, though the Danelaw stood somewhat apart with its own laws and customs, it is a tremendous tribute to the Anglo-Saxon monarchy that the two parts of the country, north and south, had learned to live peaceably together. Nowhere else on the Continent was the groundwork of the state so firmly laid. There is little need to do more than look at a map of the political geography of the different countries of western and northern Europe to test the truth of this statement: by comparison the kingdom of France was a collection of independent provinces gathered round a tiny royal demesne, each one of them a potential victim of anarchy. And nowhere else was there a comparable framework of administration, as the Normans acknowledged by the free borrowings they made. The Norman royal household offered no fundamental contrast to the Anglo-Saxon, for both had a common parent in that of the Carolingian rulers of France; there was naturally a substitution of Norman officials. The Norman curia did not greatly differ, save in its feudal aspect, from the witan: though once more there was a Norman preponderance, the position and functions of its members were so similar that contemporary English writers saw no reason for discontinuing the use of the Anglo-Saxon word. The Anglo-Saxon chamber had developed traditions of financial administration. The Anglo-Saxon chancery, the Anglo-Saxon writ, the Anglo-Saxon seal were taken over or copied by the newcomers, and it is curious to observe that the services of English clerks were retained in the Norman secretariat and that official documents continued to be written in the vernacular: not for another generation was Latin to be used instead as the single written language of government. The unique system of Anglo-Saxon local government—the shires and hundreds and townships—was incorporated in the Norman state almost unchanged and remained so vital and so vigorous that it never succumbed nor merged with its feudal rival. The sheriff found his already growing powers as the agent of centralized government vastly increased. The so-called danegeld, as a regular tax on land, represented fiscal rights and a far-reaching scheme of fiscal organization which were quite novel to William and immediately welcomed by him. Except for the addition of feudal revenues there was little financial change: the sources of profit were made more productive rather than their number increased. It is undeniable that the Conqueror found a vigorous English state already in existence.

The danger of his position in England largely explains why William was determined at all costs to uphold the English traditions. The kingdom had to be safeguarded against the attacks of English rebels, against recurrent threats of invasion from Scandinavia, against the turbulence of the Normans, Bretons, Flemings and others who had joined him for the spoils of war, whilst the duchy overseas must be defended and governed. His supporters were a comparatively small group of alien adventurers among the

English people. He had not the resources to be a dictator who could afford to disregard the susceptibilities of his subjects. If he wished to establish himself as king he must not ride roughshod over England. It is inconceivable in these circumstances that he could have undertaken any drastic reorganization, even if he had so desired: it would have brought chaos and disruption rather than the settlement of England he needed for the establishment of himself and his dynasty. Wisely he accepted the past. He claimed to be the legal heir of the Confessor, he secured the formality of election by the witan, he was consecrated by an Anglo-Saxon primate. He accepted the laws of the Anglo-Saxons, he accepted their institutions. He sought to attach to his person that habit of loyalty which had unostentatiously been the mainstay of the Anglo-Saxon monarchy for centuries and to keep in active operation in England a tradition which had died in France.

How successful he was is sufficiently shown by the relative ease with which William managed to accomplish the suppression of all English resistance in less than six years after his accession. If powerful forces making for anarchy had been latent in the country before 1066, then the disaster at Hastings was surely the signal for them to come openly into action. Yet what actually happened was that the responsible leaders of Anglo-Saxon opinion recognized the plain truth that there was no native claimant to the throne round whom they could rally: the House of Cerdic was represented only by the incompetent Edgar Atheling whose claim had already been rejected once; the House of Godwin had been obliterated. Therefore they came quickly to give their support to the only candidate left and to make the best of what must have seemed to them a bad job. William's rule was accordingly accepted in many shires like Staffordshire, Gloucestershire and Worcestershire a few weeks after Hastings and long before a Norman army was seen at all; by the time of his coronation he was the acknowledged ruler of England at least south of the Humber; by March 1067 he felt sufficiently secure to leave England for a visit to Normandy: by the end of 1067 Archbishop Ealdred of York and Bishop Wulfstan of Worcester had put themselves at the head of a native group determined to support him; by 1068 the English fyrd was fighting on his behalf. It is not surprising, therefore, to find that the salient characteristic of native opposition was its utter lack of coherence and its fitfulness, which allowed William to deal with each insurrection separately. The two revolts of the Saxon Edric the Wild on the borders of Wales in 1067 and 1069; the defiance of Exeter for three weeks in 1068; the two rebellions of the Earls Edwin of Mercia and Morcar in Northumbria in 1068 and 1069, made ominous by the co-operation of the last Danish fleet to ravage the coasts of England; the opposition of the legendary hero of the common people, Hereward the Wake, in 1070: this was the sum and the nature of the resistance movement.

William adopted a deliberate and ruthless policy of terrorization, such as he had already put into execution in Maine and elsewhere, by the mutilation of hostages and the devastation of large areas of arable land. There is, for example, a fearsome connexion between his movements after Hastings and the lands returned as 'waste' to the Domesday commissioners twenty years later: his journey to Dover and thence towards London and his circuit round the north of London can be traced to-day by simply plotting the entries of 'waste lands' in Domesday Book. If such destruction can be justified as the stern necessity of war, even the Norman chroniclers were scandalized when he spent a year in laying waste the north of England from the North to the Irish Seas. Having no solution for a problem which had confronted the Anglo-Saxon kings, he resorted to a barbarity which has no equal in the whole history of England. He turned one thousand square miles and more of land into a wilderness and imposed upon it the peace of death: not a single inhabited place remained between York and Durham and, for example, of the sixty-two villages in the district of Amounderness in 1066 forty-six had been completely destroyed three years later and the remaining sixteen were barely occupied; in Staffordshire and Derbyshire a tenth of the places recorded in Domesday Book are described as 'waste'; the same record of devastation marks Cheshire and the district to its north. The deliberate burning of farm implements and food stores meant starvation and death to numberless families if they could not escape by selling themselves as serfs. William had gained a more stable throne and paid the price of a province: generations were to pass before his criminal act, committed when victory was already his, was forgotten and its consequences made good.

THE CO-OPERATION OF MONARCHY AND BARONAGE

It is clear that the Norman monarchy took up the reins where the Anglo-Saxon monarchy had laid them down. The new kingship did not differ fundamentally from the old in any essential save one: the new position of the king as feudal suzerain through universal landlordship and tenurial bonds.

The transportation of Norman feudalism into England was of great importance in the work of administration inasmuch as it entered into the structure of government and constituted a means through which the Norman monarchy operated. For the intruders from France formed a minority which was constantly afraid of bitter retaliation. Therefore there was for fully a generation after the Conquest a very close co-operation between the king and his Norman followers in defence of their common security and interests. The barons needed the king to support them; the king for his part had to trust them and, indeed, there is no evidence that either William I or William II lived in fear of them. The strong government seen after 1066 was not made possible by the monarchy alone, it needed the indispensable assistance of the barons in their estates throughout the country.

The simple fact that England was a conquered country cleared the field for action and permitted the easy imposition of a new order upon the old society. Apart from William's implicit claim to be the ultimate owner of all the land, the proprietor as well as the ruler of England, a great part of it came directly into his hands, either immediately through the acquisition of the vast property of the Godwins and all others who had fought at Hastings or eventually through the confiscation of the estates of later rebels. His notorious avarice, however detestable in his private character, was as laudable in his public capacity as that of the first Tudor. Since the king's private income was roughly identical with the public revenue of the state and had to pay the expenses of government, it was well for the future that all three Norman kings laid great store upon the acquisition of private wealth. It has been calculated that the Conqueror kept to himself some fourteen hundred manors, from which he drew a large proportion of the country's total landed rents, bringing in about £11,000 a year, more than double the income of the Confessor. The royal demesne lands are found more regularly distributed throughout the counties than before. It is apparent that the rents were sharply raised and not all was spent, for a fair proportion found its way to the treasury in bullion. There was more than enough land left over with which to reward the motley host of Normans, Bretons and Flemings, who had crossed the Channel for the sole object of gaining the spoils of victory.

The oft-repeated statement that William gave them lands scattered in many different counties rather than in one compact block in order to weaken their power is a good illustration of the inveterate tendency to attribute deliberate policy to the Conqueror when in fact he only fell in line with the habits of his time. Such grants as that of Cornwall to his half-brother, Robert of Mortain, and of the palatine earldoms indicate that, when he thought it desirable, William had no strong objection to granting a great fief all together in one place and, as we have pointed out, effective government could not have been built upon a foundation of distrust among the invaders. Nor does it seem likely that scattered estates resulted simply from the piece-meal nature of the Conquest, so that each time a new district was subdued there was a new division of territory among the victors, for estates were granted away long before they were physically taken over and fiefs on the same principle of dissipation were bestowed by Henry I when a matter of conquest did not arise at all. It was a common practice in the Middle Ages to have scattered estates: it was a reasonable precaution, just as to-day it is wise to place one's money in many and not one single investment, for then the ravages of invaders or of private war or of bad weather or of plague were less likely to destroy the prosperity of all estates at one fell blow. Therefore it is probable that the Saxon nobles had their property dotted about here and there and that the Norman lords took it over from them as it stood.

Military feudalism always contained the potential seeds of civil war, and it is more than likely that the Norman conquest of England would eventually have been followed by anarchy and a feudal dismemberment after the example of France, if it had not been for the happy accident of a succession of strong kings for a period of sixty years. And fortunately the common interests and mutual dependence of king and barons made it certain that he would always receive the support of the responsible members of feudal society. Nevertheless, the latent threat to law and order was always present, especially among the second generation who had not known the insecurity of their fathers. We must not, however, be led to exaggerate the menace of the few insurrections that William I and William II were called upon to face. The insurrection in Kent of the dissatisfied Eustace of Boulogne in 1067 and the drunken plot of Ralph, earl of East Anglia, and Roger, earl of Hereford, hatched at the 'Bridal of Norwich' in 1075, were neither serious enough in the support they gained to bring the Conqueror back from Normandy to deal with them. William experienced no difficulty in thwarting in 1082 the obscure machinations of his ambitious half-brother, Bishop Odo of Bayeux, despite the fact that by his appointment as earl of Kent and warden of Dover Castle he had become second in importance only to Lanfranc among the king's subjects. William Rufus, though faced in 1088 with a league comprising such powerful magnates as the recently released Odo of Bayeux, Roger Bigod, Roger Lacy, Roger of Montgomery, Robert Mowbray and the warlike bishop of Durham, could nevertheless count on the help of the greater number of the barons and the high-placed ecclesiastics as well as of the native English who, knowing that the throne alone stood between the country and civil war, rallied round him as they had come to rally round his father before him.

Common interests and a common danger bound the king and the barons, lay and ecclesiastic, closely together and prevented a general conflict which would assuredly have been suicidal to them all. To present the few manifestations of Norman indiscipline as a serious menace to the position of the monarchy before 1100 is to misread the evidence and to misinterpret the spirit of the times.

THE FEUDALIZATION OF GOVERNMENT

William applied to England, and applied more uniformly and rigorously, the only system of government he knew whereby his relations with the barons could be regulated. In considering the Norman feudalization of government it is well for clarity's sake to gather our arguments together around the four factors which we have previously suggested were the essentials of feudalism.

(i) *Military organization through private contracts based on land*

We have already observed that the condition of things in the late Old English period was in no way hostile to the changes which the Normans were to introduce. Indeed, the practice of holding lands of a lord, of owing him services (albeit of an indefinite and unspecialized kind), and of assisting him in war could not have seemed as fundamentally different from the Norman system as it has appeared to historians searching for institutional distinctions. Moreover, the transition was made all the smoother because the Norman landowners, in order to attain the full rights enjoyed by their English predecessors, chose to regard them as their 'ancestors', as though they had succeeded them in the ordinary way of family inheritance, and in some cases they consolidated their positions by marrying the heiresses of the Anglo-Saxons they had displaced.

Nevertheless, we must not minimize the Norman innovations. To one in William's precarious position the vital function of feudalism still remained as the organization of society on a war basis and the provision of an adequate military force. For that purpose he instituted the system he had known in Normandy, a system which had no special distinctive features from that in France as a whole, a system which converted what had before been casual and haphazard, vague and fluctuating, into a precise and definite scheme of organization. In short, he introduced the full conception of a feudal fief. The Anglo-Saxons had on the whole been acquainted only with the conception of property over which they had full property rights, and the services expected from them were connected with their persons rather than their estates; therefore they could, if they wished, part with their lands during their lifetime and split them up by their wills after their death. Thus their estates did not need to be kept heritable and indivisible as a permanent guarantee that their successors would always continue to perform the services they owed. They did not know the fief, that is the 'fee', or the feudal tenures which kept lords and tenants and the heirs of lords and the heirs of tenants bound closely together in perpetuity. Therefore the introduction of knight service, the most characteristic of the feudal tenures, did not arise out of Old English custom and was the most revolutionary conception that the Normans brought with them.

About 1070 the Conqueror made a drastic arrangement whereby a professional army was constructed and based firmly on the soil. The whole emphasis was placed upon the mounted knight who was to dominate the field of battle for three hundred years, upon one who had to serve a military apprenticeship and who rested his claim to knighthood upon his military skill. William made no attempt to fix the amount of land which should be able to provide a knight. What he wanted to be certain about was that he could call upon the services of some five thousand suitably equipped knights whenever necessary. Therefore he simply bargained with his tenants-in-chief individually. The only common factor seems to have been that the knights were to be provided in fives or multiples thereof, apparently in conformity with the normal unit of the Norman army called the 'constabularia'. With what happened afterwards it seems that he rarely concerned himself. His tenants for their part had by the end of the reign naturally adopted the plan of leasing or sub-infeudating part of their estates to as many others as there were knights demanded from them. In such circumstances the knight's fee was not a uniform territorial unit, and it was not until Henry II's time that there was a recognizable tendency to consider that it should represent land yielding an income of £20 a year. And eventually it came to be understood that the knight's period of service should be limited to forty days a year. Even if active service in the field did not become necessary, knights were needed in regular rota for 'castle-guard', garrison duty at those three score or more castles which had been erected during William's reign at strategic places to form the key-points of defence. All enfeoffments, however far down they went from the king, were normally hereditary and thus there had been created on behalf of one person and his heirs a perpetual right in the lands of another person and his heirs.

So the principle that the king was the owner of the land and therefore the lord of lords was of great significance. For when he made a grant of lands, the conditions of tenure he imposed were passed down through society and were thus reflected in the similar contractual relationships between the king's tenants-in-chief and their own under-tenants. This position was in a real sense new to England. The great subjects of the Anglo-Saxon king had sworn an oath of fealty, but they were not tied to him in this feudal sense because the king had entered into no formal reciprocal agreements with them. Thus the relationship between the Norman king and his great subjects was profoundly changed. The Norman tenant-in-chief held his lands on a direct and clear-cut agreement to provide the king with a specific number of fully-equipped knights for a specific time when called upon to do so; the Anglo-Saxon earl's military obligations were more vague and more liable to fluctuate, his land was a reward for past service rather than a gift with an express condition of service in the future. Land tenure and military service were not, in consequence, connected in the same intimate way as for a Norman baron. Similarly, whilst the knight's military service usually issued straight from his enfeoffment, the thegn's service sprang from his personal loyalty to the king and his thegnly rank.

In short, public service, personal relationships and tenure of land were all fairly easily distinguishable in Anglo-Saxon England: in Norman England they were combined into a coherent system in which public service arose directly out of private contracts and private contracts were based securely and permanently on land tenure.

It follows that, without possession of the land, the services attached to it could not be properly performed. Hence logically emerged those rights of the king, viewed as overlord, which are comprehensively called the 'feudal incidents'. (*a*) *Relief*, or the sum of money payable by the heir of one who held a military fief. Death broke the contract and, as the fief was by nature an express grant, a 'benefice' which the donor could withdraw, and was theoretically not inheritable, it became customary for the heir to pay the lord a 'relief' for permission to renew the ties and for the lord to re-invest the heir. Thus the fief was in practice made hereditary. It should be noted that the curious and arbitrary and apparently unfair privilege of the eldest-born derives its origin from feudal practices when it was presumably imperative for a lord to get the services due to him rendered immediately or at the earliest possible moment: the principles of primogeniture find no place in either Roman law or in Germanic custom. (*b*) *Primer seisin*. Until relief was paid the lords took 'first possession' of the land. (*c*) *Wardship*. If the heir was a minor, he was physically incapable of performing the services due to his lord; therefore that lord administered his estates for him and appropriated the revenues and looked after the fulfilment of the services until the heir had come of age. This also applied, of course, where the heir under age was a woman. (*d*) *Marriage*. If the heir was a woman, she might marry someone quite unfitted to perform the services properly or, indeed, she might marry the lord's enemy and take the services away from him at a critical time and convey them to her husband. To guard against such possibilities the lord had the right to choose the heiress's husband, provided that she suffered no disparagement thereby. On the whole feudalism kept a tight grip upon women and their liberty of action. (*e*) *Escheat*. If the holders of the land ceased to be able to perform the services, either because they had been outlawed or imprisoned for a heinous offence or because the line of succession had come to an end, then the contract lapsed and the land returned to the lord. (*f*) *Fine on alienation*. Naturally, no one could sell or give away any of his land in case it should prejudice the proper fulfilment of services. Therefore the permission of the lord must first be obtained and an appropriate fee or 'fine' paid. (*g*) *The Aids*. At first it was thought that a man should aid his lord not only with his person but also with his money whenever that lord felt himself

9

in financial need. How exactly this worked for many years we do not know, but the position had ultimately to be regularized and by the time of the Great Charter the occasions had been reduced to three: the ransoming of the king's body, the knighting of his eldest son, the marrying of his eldest daughter once.

For the sake of intelligibility it has been advisable to draw the picture of feudal organization in England in firmer outline than is strictly correct. It should not be imagined that either the reign of William I or that of William II saw any uniform system in operation over the whole country. It was not so much that the newcomers were few in number or that communications were difficult: the main cause of confusion lay in the fact that Normans, Bretons, Flemings and those who came from other parts of France knew different feudal laws and customs and applied them to their different estates in England. In consequence, we shall find many exceptions to any ideal conception of feudalism we may unwisely hold, and from that we shall better understand the ease with which Anglo-Saxon feudalism accommodated itself to the new order of things. Thus enfeoffed knights did not always hold by hereditary tenure but might be given a life-tenancy only: they were therefore not dissimilar to the Anglo-Saxon loanland tenants. William Rufus himself was not averse from slurring over the hereditary nature of feudal tenures. Many knights received no grants of lands and attached themselves for personal and continuous service to royal and baronial households: in this respect they were not unlike housecarls and thegns. They were really little more than military adventurers, hired mercenaries, and as such they were for long a curse to society. The Bretons who had at home regarded knighthood as a social rank rather than a military qualification would find no problem in the Anglo-Saxon thegn. So the systematization of feudalism was the work of the twelfth and not of the late eleventh century: it was a slow process and only recently have some of its details become known to us.

(ii) *The work of government carried on through landlords*

So long as it was clearly understood that ultimate control lay with the king, the Conqueror left his tenants-in-chief perfectly free to make their own arrangements for the full administration of their estates. In this he fell in line with the normal practice of his times but in any case there was no alternative: like all medieval kings he had neither the organization nor the money for the work of local government. So the lords of great fiefs set to work to produce machinery wherewith to control the life of their tenants in all its forms. Their previous experience, provided by other provinces besides Normandy, dictated the lines of feudal administrative development, and we should not therefore expect to find anything but diversity of practice. The times are much too early to speak of feudal uniformity: a tentative approach to that must await the legal sophistication of the late twelfth and thirteenth centuries. The main units of the feudal geography of England had, however, made their appearance within a few years of the Conquest.

(a) The earldoms

These were not created lavishly but given only to those who could claim close kinship or intimate friendship with the king: the English earl was equated with the Norman count. The four earldoms which were instituted by William I in or before 1071 issued from military necessity: two of them, Hereford and Kent, had ceased to exist before the close of the reign; the other two, Chester and Shrewsbury, remained as 'palatine' earldoms outside the scope of royal administration and were a law to themselves. It is quite clear that Old English and Norman earls were alike in this, that they owed their position to a royal grant and had administrative duties to fulfil. The Norman earl, however, was not brought into the scheme of government as prominently as his Saxon predecessor, and his title mainly conveyed a personal honour and a social superiority like that indicated in the three new earldoms formed by William II.

(b) The honours

'Honour' was the term of art eventually applied to the collection of estates scattered here and there over the counties of England which made up the fief of a great lord. He ruled it as a single and independent unit, and his duties and his system of administration—his council, his court of tenants-in-chief, his exchequer, his justiciars and other officials—came to mirror those of the king as lord of the greatest 'honour' of all, the honour of England.

(c) The baronies

It has been estimated from Domesday Book that some one hundred and seventy baronies of varying values above £10 a year were to be found in England before 1087. They were naturally in the possession of the king's friends and dependents whom he could safely trust to give him good advice and act as his administrative agents. It was long before the word came to signify more than intimacy with the king and acquired a technical and specialized meaning.

(d) The knights' fees

Although the Conqueror had limited himself to the creation of about five thousand such fees, it is very likely that many of his tenants-in-chief had, in the perils of the time, enfeoffed more than the quota he demanded. For the moment the knights' all-important asset was their fighting abilities, and it is not until the end of the twelfth century that a proportion of them had secured their social position and had established those county families which will be the indispensable factor in the royal control and direction of local government.

The strength of monarchical traditions remained, however, the basis of political unity. But no matter how strong the feeling for monarchy might be, it had to be stimulated constantly by a monarch of strong character and ability. The Anglo-Saxon and Norman dynasties were identical in their dependence upon this personal factor: the Norman Conquest made no difference in so vital a matter. Thus the success of the Conqueror was due in no small measure, not so much to originality or genius, as to his dominating personality and dynamic energy. We cannot ascribe to Rufus, any more than to his father, any high conception of the rights and duties of medieval kingship or any pre-visions of the triumphs to which it would attain. Rufus in his uncurbed violence, his unassuageable greed and flagrant immorality was in no way different from the most unruly of his barons. But, though he was tyrannical and ruled by a reign of terror so that his subjects hid at his approach, he kept the monarchy in existence unimpaired and even extended in its authority. That was his unwitting contribution for good. The twilight of Norman monarchy was attributable to the incapacity of Stephen. The assertion of Angevin monarchy was made possible only through the magnificent statecraft of Henry II.

Given an effective ruler, political feudalism in England upheld rather than menaced political order. It was an artifice of government, a means of ruling a medieval community which had not the resources of centralization and control which a modern state can command. Provincialism was always a strong force, for between the various parts of the country were barriers of geography, of dialects, of law, culture and traditions. The Scandinavian settlers had introduced one alien way of life, the Normans introduced another. The central government was compelled by circumstances to delegate authority to magnates in the localities. Nevertheless, a strong king could always prevent them from becoming too independent. The trump cards were in his hands: he could appoint those who would assist him as the chief crown tenants; he controlled the building of castles, the minting of coin, the granting of franchises; he could use the 'feudal incidents' like wardship, marriage and escheat to check the rise of over-mighty subjects.

Furthermore, the feudal order in England was no mere reproduction of Norman society, for English conditions had set their mark upon it: private war was deemed an offence, a difference from Norman practice which makes all the difference; military service was not exclusively feudal, for the fyrd could be mobilized; taxation and justice did not spring solely from a feudal source; even the *curia regis* itself had not a wholly feudal composition. And the king had inherited a paramount right to the allegiance of all his subjects, not simply the homage of his tenants-in-chief, and it did not need the Salisbury Oath of 1086 to secure his position as political sovereign as well as feudal suzerain. That event has been invested with too much significance in the history of feudalism. For it represents a practical measure of military preparedness, made necessary by political events abroad. Denmark, Norway and Flanders seemed likely to make common cause in an invasion of England: whether without the miraculous transportation of trained horses they could have prevailed against the Norman mounted knights with their high military technique is at least doubtful. In the event the scare came to nothing: the Danish fleet mutinied and the Danish king was murdered before the meeting at Salisbury took place at all. Indeed, William seems to have been far more perturbed by events in France where the hostility of the French king threatened his continental possessions, and he was determined to leave England for Normandy. In the circumstances he felt it wise to test and review the machinery of military feudalism he had established, and he summoned not only his tenants-in-chief but also all important sub-tenants of theirs to assemble on Salisbury Plain and took the opportunity to exact from them all an oath of fealty. Thereby he stressed publicly their loyalty to his person and impressed upon them the need for constant vigilance. His action was intended to solve a practical problem, and it is erroneous to believe that he was consciously propounding a new political theory and deliberately subordinating the homage to a lord to the fealty to a king. This fact was shown the very next year at the coronation of William Rufus when all men, irrespective of their feudal ties, swore a similar oath. Against such predominant monarchical feeling the feudal duty to a lord could not easily compete.

The paradox is that, whilst Norman feudalism was the means through which centralized monarchy worked, it was from such a feudalism that there came the only real check on the royal will when, by a long and scarcely noticed evolution, the medieval idea of contract nurtured the modern idea of limited monarchy. For the king's position as feudal suzerain complicated and reacted upon his position as political sovereign. And this combination of Norman and Saxon traditions can be traced henceforth throughout the history of the English monarchy. If the king did not observe the feudal contract, the resentment of his immediate tenants could be expressed in legal and tangible form, in a 'defiance' (*diffidatio*) in its early sense of breaking faith. The 'defiance' which dissolved the contract was only to be made after solemn efforts had failed to induce him to abandon what were deemed anti-feudal practices. Strictly speaking, a revolt against an irresponsible suzerain after a 'defiance' was neither rebellion nor treason, for homage had been renounced. The 'defiance' figures more than once in English history, notably before the sealing of the Great Charter, and, however crude in application, it did at least put opposition to tyranny within the framework of law where it had not been before.

THE OPERATION OF MEDIEVAL JUSTICE

It is well that we should carefully keep in mind and scrupulously distinguish the three types of medieval justice after the Norman Conquest.

(i) *Royal justice*

Until the turn of the century this was dispensed almost entirely in the king's court, the *curia regis*, or, as it was sometimes called, the king's council, the *concilium regis*, and it was restricted to great men and great causes. The Conqueror was in no position to become involved in the cares and expenses of administering justice at large, and this was left to the popular assembly courts, the seignorial courts, and the new ecclesiastical courts of the Church.

We have observed that the Anglo-Saxon witan was in essentials the king's creature and that its composition, in particular, was dependent on his will. The Norman Conquest introduced two changes: neither of them made much difference in practice, but in principle they were of great significance. (*a*) The composition of the court was feudalized. All its members no longer attended its sessions simply because the king chose to deem them 'wise' or thought it politic to discuss affairs of state with them. Most came because it was their feudal duty to do suit and service to the court of their overlord and to give him counsel. What therefore had been a public duty became in feudal fashion a private obligation, as it was in the ducal court of Normandy. This new principle did not entirely oust the Anglo-Saxon and far older conception that the king, as king, had the prerogative right to summon anyone he pleased and to take advice wheresoever he chose to seek it. Therefore there was always present a small group of royal officials, the men who were responsible for the routine work of government. It is true that many of them had often a double qualification, as tenants-in-chief and as royal clerks; nevertheless, the official element was clearly distinguishable and formed the important nucleus of the assembly by reason of its practical knowledge, experience and ability. (*b*) Though the *curia regis* was the court of the king as an overlord and was, therefore, his private court for the dispatch of his private business, it was also the court of his vassals to which they had a right to be summoned as well as a duty to attend. It was in their interests to see that it functioned, for only there could they get the judgment of their peers to which feudal law entitled them. Therefore, though after 1066 the old restraints of law and custom did not greatly curb the freedom of action of one who was a conqueror, yet the obligations of the king implicit in the feudal contract have now found an institutional expression. The barons have an instrument at their disposal to use against the king such as the members of the witan never possessed; once they have made certain of their security in a strange land, once their initial violence has quietened down and they have identified themselves with, broadly speaking, English interests, their feudal court can in time seek to turn itself, however slowly, into a quasi-national assembly and their feudal protests assume the character of quasi-constitutional opposition.

The most solemn meetings of the *curia regis* took place on the three great festivals of the Church when the king ceremonially wore his crown—Christmas, Easter and Whitsun—and we must bear in mind that these occasions were the important social events of the year for the upper classes and corresponded pretty much with what we mean by the 'Court' to-day. We have, unfortunately, information about only a few of its meetings under the first two Norman kings when problems of administration were discussed and the highest justice dispensed. Yet the relations of king and barons are clearly seen whenever it was thought advisable to make changes in the law. For, though the Conqueror wisely guaranteed to the English the practice and protection of the law as it stood under the Confessor, it was inevitable that he should make a few adjustments to ensure that that law did not conflict with feudal practices and operate to the disadvantage of the Normans themselves. Such enactments as he authorized—and they were not many, for though the Norman kings had entered into a tradition of law-making, none of them chose to maintain it—were not made solely on his own authority, especially if feudal law were involved, but with the 'counsel and consent' of the magnates. Along with the feudal knowledge, they had the feudal duty to advise their overlord and to co-operate with him in the business of his court, where changes in the law were little different in character from court judgments. What Henry I was to call his father's 'additions' to the Laws of the Confessor were not numerous. (*a*) A rule concerning trials between Normans and English to settle whose customary procedure should be followed, for the Norman innovation of 'trial by battle' had greatly complicated the issues. (*b*) The 'murdrum' fine: so many Normans were assassinated, presumably by Englishmen, that William decreed that every hundred, in which an unknown corpse was found without anyone being held responsible and produced for punishment, should pay this fine. This regulation worked capriciously, for many deaths were accidental. Eventually the hundreds managed to avoid the fine if they could prove by 'the presentment of Englishry' that the dead man was an Englishman, and by Edward III's reign the two races were so merged together that in 1340 the 'murdrum' and the 'presentment of Englishry' were both abolished. (*c*) Stern provisions concerning the royal forests. (*d*) Miscellaneous decrees prohibiting blood feuds; abolishing the tariffs of compensations for injuries which the recent social changes and the rise in prices made archaic and useless; preventing the export of slaves; and protecting highways, trade and commerce. (*e*) The decision which established independent courts for the Church.

(ii) *Popular justice*

Neither conquest nor feudalization destroyed the law and institutions and traditions of the native English. The shire and the
hundred courts still functioned alongside the seignorial courts,
though they did not maintain their position without trouble. The
manorial courts were more convenient to attend, for they were held
more frequently and they were usually nearer at hand; attendance
at the popular assembly courts was becoming territorialized, that
is, the duty to be present was attached to the holders of certain
prescribed tenements only and 'suit of court' was no longer the
concern of all; many hundred courts were losing their public
character and passing into private hands. Such 'private hundreds',
common in the twelfth century, had become by Edward I's reign
a half of the total number of hundreds in the country. Over them
the sheriff and his bailiff did not preside but the lord's steward;
not to the king but to the lord went the profits of jurisdiction. And
where the lords obtained the dearly cherished privilege of 'view of
frankpledge', the sheriff was even prevented from including these
hundreds in that regular inspection of his shire which took place
once or twice a year under the name of the 'sheriff's turn'.

Nevertheless, private jurisdiction got little higher than the level
of the hundred courts except in the palatinates: it stopped short
of the county courts in general, where the monarchy intervened to
prevent its encroachments there. On the Continent the courts
which had once been popular in basis and royal in patronage succumbed entirely to the insidious attacks of feudalism. The Anglo-
Saxons had built a stronger structure of local government, but even
it might have fallen into disuse but for the fact that the sheriff was
a royal officer and his office, with rare exceptions, did not become
feudalized: in consequence, the Norman monarchy was able to
adopt the same attitude as the Anglo-Saxon monarchy and compel
the people at large to continue the troublesome duty of attendance
and the administration of their own affairs. The preservation of
that tradition was of vital importance to the future: the way was
open whereby the king could get into direct touch with all his subjects, explain his needs, discover their grievances and bargain for
their support. So the crown kept its control over the local districts.

Since for many years after the Conquest the county courts were the
main vehicle of the king's will and of his jurisdiction in parts remote
from his court, it is little wonder that the sheriffs who presided

over them should have reached the highest point of their influence during the same period. The first two Norman kings saw the appointment as sheriffs of feudal barons who could ruthlessly keep the conquered in subjection and repress disorder. In their official capacity they were no longer answerable to earls and in the circumstances of the time they were allowed a wide authority: as military governors of their shires and financial representatives of the crown and royal agents in general. Baronial sheriffs were indispensable in exceptional times, but obviously they could become a menace: there was a danger that their office would become hereditary so that the fact that they were the nominees and servants of the king might be in danger of being forgotten; their extortion and corruption became too notorious to be ignored; they were occasionally taking part in rebellions against the king who appointed them. The locally-resident justiciars, who are found in office in Rufus's reign, had the sheriffs in subordination to them for at least some purposes. But this was evidently not enough. Therefore we shall find that Henry I no longer chose barons as his sheriffs but instead officials of his court and, as soon as the exchequer had got under way, he used that institution to call the sheriffs to account and keep them in order.

(iii) *Seignorial justice*

Alongside the unwritten customary law of the Anglo-Saxons was now placed another body of law, likewise unwritten and customary, the feudal law which had been slowly evolved in Europe for more than three hundred years. Seignorial justice, however, was not concerned solely with feudal law: it was made up of two constituent elements which were not at first kept distinct; and later the lords deliberately tried to keep them confused by continuing to telescope them together, whilst the kings for their part were determined to stress their fundamental differences. (*a*) *Feudal justice.* This was the consequence of the tenure of land: it was as it were rooted in the soil and was in no way the consequence of a royal grant. Lordship by feudal law carried with it jurisdiction over dependent tenants, and the trial of actions relating to land between their own tenants was obviously of serious moment. But the amount of such litigation dwindled as the twelfth century advanced to the legal changes of Henry II, and eventually the scope of feudal jurisdiction was not wide: petty offences like light assaults and larcenies, small debts, the infringement of the local bye-laws relating to agriculture. The manorial courts must be presumed to have been in existence shortly after the Conquest: they were small local courts to deal with the small affairs of peasants. The monarchy was quite content to leave feudal justice alone, for it performed a highly useful and, indeed, indispensable service. (b) *Franchisal justice.* The Norman Barons, however, were not likely to be satisfied with such limited jurisdiction. They would naturally expect to possess at least the rights they had enjoyed in Normandy and, since England was a country conquered by their swords, they might well expect even more. And in Normandy many of them had inherited powers of justice of an extensive kind, acquired by their ancestors long before the dukes of Normandy had asserted their supremacy. Therefore under William I it is evident that the Norman lords were exercising the highest judicial powers, even to the penalties of death and mutilation. When, however, his successors felt themselves seated more firmly on the English throne, they insisted that all jurisdiction which surpassed the limits of purely feudal justice did not result automatically from the tenure of land but issued from an express grant from the crown. It was a privilege, a liberty, a franchise: the king had delegated to the lords the exercise of his prerogative rights and the assumption was, therefore, that he could recall them. The king had two powerful supports for such an argument. The fact of the Conquest had placed the whole country in his hands. He could assert that all privileges, jurisdictional or otherwise, had thereby lapsed until he had chosen to renew them. Such a theory was applied to English landowners at once, and it was when it was applied to Norman lords under William Rufus and later monarchs that a stern struggle was precipitated between king and barons, on which great issues were to depend. Furthermore, the Norman kings had the prerogative rights of the Anglo-Saxon monarchy which had had no extensive franchisal jurisdictions to harass it severely. Therefore, though 'immunities' from royal control undoubtedly existed, for which their holders claimed the prescription of 'ancient seisin' or Anglo-Saxon charters, it was emphasized that such immunities represented franchisal and not feudal justice. Still, as we have observed, the first generation after the Conquest saw feudal courts as comprehensive, omni-competent and powerful institutions. The great tenants of the king exercised royal prerogative rights without any thought that thereby they were committing an act of usurpation.

Seignorial justice, popular justice, royal justice: these three will in the future interact upon one another. Royal justice as the basis of a wide administration of justice is historically the newcomer, yet in the long run it dominated its older companions. For though but a crude generalization, it is roughly true that popular justice was deliberately linked up with royal justice in an attack upon seignorial justice to deprive it of its privileges, its franchises. Only then could royal justice begin to assert a law that was common to all parts of the country and to all classes of the community, and on the foundation of that common law to construct a properly unified country.

II. The Impact upon Social Classes and Economic Organization

In political life feudalism signified a form of state in which political rights were to be held and duties performed through private contracts based on land. In social life feudalism tended in time to produce a sanctification of inequality: leaving qualifications on one side, we can roughly say that each man and his descendants after him were to enjoy the privileges and fulfil the obligations connected with their station in life and to remain contented with that status for ever. And social distinctions were permanently fixed through the hereditary nature of land tenure. The stratification of English society resulting from Norman feudalized conceptions did not on the surface appear to differ very greatly from the Anglo-Saxon social grades as depicted in the varied list of wergilds. In point of fact there was a significant difference. Whereas before the Norman Conquest social inequalities could still be expressed in terms of birth, after 1066 they were expressed in terms of tenure. Whereas the rank of thegn could be inherited without any need to inherit land as well, the knight eventually became clearly recognized as the hereditary lord of a fief with definite obligations to an hereditary overlord and definite rights over a group of hereditary tenants. Social status therefore came to depend upon the amount of land held and the nature of the services performed. The establishment of social relationships on the basis of tenure, and tenure alone, certainly made for simplification, and the insistence on uniformity helped to unify the social structure of medieval England. For English society in the early eleventh century had displayed a bewildering variety of social distinctions, not only as between Anglo-Saxon and Anglo-Scandinavian but also within each of the two main divisions of the country: there was a degree of fluidity and a confusing mixture of freedom and servility that was rarely to be found in continental society.

It is frequently argued that the unrestricted liberty to go with one's land to whomsoever one would at whatsoever time one pleased indicated an impending social anarchy; that the lack of rigidity and permanence in the relations between lord and man implied a social disintegration which could only be prevented by the cement of Norman feudalism. Since the government of the country depended in large measure upon the co-operative activities of lords, these lords had to know exactly where they stood, and therefore the personal relationships must be territorialized and thereby made immutable and permanent and the loose practice of 'commendation' must be discontinued. The feudalization of society as a deliberate and organized plan thus meant the increased stability of the state. This was to be bought presumably at the expense of making land and society static: the free alienation of land was to become impossible and a caste system was to be introduced. The diverse shades and confusions which existed in Anglo-Saxon England were to be standardized, and everyone was to be brought into a social scheme in which social status was determined by land tenure and became its simple reflexion. The country was to be put, as it were, into a strait-jacket, from which it would struggle long years to escape.

In criticism of this largely theoretical evaluation of the benefits of Norman feudalism it may be said at once that the history of the times has not led us to believe that the greater laxity of Anglo-Saxon life had in fact endangered the unity of the country or perilously weakened its social fabric. It is difficult to see why a society which had so magnificently, so uniquely, survived the terrors of the Dark Ages should collapse with the advent of more peaceful conditions. A high concept of social order had been reached before 1066 and, whatever alterations Norman feudalism may have introduced, it should not be argued that the fact that changes were made meant that changes were essential. Norman feudalism was a transient intruder upon a society whose basis was firmly laid in earlier centuries and remained substantially unaffected by what took place in the generation after the Norman Conquest. Indeed, in so far as military feudalism was intended to produce a society organized for war and to be primarily a safeguard against barbarian ravages, its introduction in 1066 was in a real sense unnecessary: the worst menace had assuredly passed by the end of William I's reign and the new arrangements were designed first and foremost to secure the safety of the king rather than of the king's new dominion. Fortunately, the excess of military skill and zeal found an outlet in military adventures abroad, yet it always tended to make for dispeace and even anarchy at home. Normandy after 1086 and England after 1135 are constant reminders that feudalism was potentially anti-social and the negation of social order.

To make such comments is not to deny but to reduce to its proper proportions the work of the Normans in unifying the social structure of England. The very fact that it was a conquest that had taken place caused so many changes in the ownership of land that the newcomers were presented with an excellent opportunity to remould Anglo-Saxon society according to their own ideas. But the new Norman society was itself confused and nothing like so stable and logical as the far older society into which it had entered, and it is not surprising that they found English society too sturdy a natural growth and too complex to be forced within any artificial framework. No social revolution took place, either immediately when the invaders had no desire to court trouble and disaster or later when they had security enough to work out their ideas. Thus, though Anglo-Saxon society was dominated by the conception of birth and Norman society by that of specialized service, though the one was freer and less organized than the other, yet society in general remained hierarchical and the main divisions to which King Alfred had referred between those who prayed and those who fought and those who laboured were in no way blurred. Nevertheless, the Norman Conquest bore hard upon a large proportion of the native English as individuals.

The most drastic change occurred in the upper stratum of society where the Anglo-Saxon earls and thegns, once so all-important, vanished remarkably rapidly as a class within twenty years to yield place to an alien aristocracy. The disintegration and ruin of the great English landowners was such that it has been estimated that not one per cent of the land held of the king in 1086 was in the hands of the families who owned it in 1066. The thegns remained merely as social anomalies with little to distinguish them from the higher peasantry save their wergild of 1,200 shillings which was rapidly becoming obsolescent. Yet the substitution of knights for thegns, however revolutionary it may have been in military affairs and the methods of government, did no serious violence to the evolutionary development of society: the transformation was made substantially easy through the favourable conditions found in England.

The peasantry, the vast bulk of the population, though naturally in no danger of displacement, were similarly depressed in status. Before 1066 they had formed a most heterogeneous non-noble class in society, either owning their own land like the sokemen and many of the ceorls or farming under a lord's economic control and direction, like the geneats, the geburs and cottars, to give the main divisions of the ceorl class in descending order of importance. Nevertheless, most peasants, even if they were not proprietors in their own right and were not economically free, were still legally free men with a high wergild of two hundred shillings, exempt from the degradation associated with serfs, paying rent for their plots of land in money or in kind or in labour-services, able to abandon the services of their lords and go elsewhere in the unlikely event of their wishing to do so. A deterioration set in when an alien aristocracy took control and, dominated by alien ideas and avaricious to get all they could, insisted strongly on the performance of labour-services. It seems likely that such were imposed in addition to and even in place of money rents previously paid. At all events, there was a considerable dislocation which brought disaster to many small free farmers who found their lands given without compensation to Norman warriors and themselves compelled to become tenants bound to a lord. Thus in Cambridgeshire the number of sokemen fell in the Conqueror's reign from over 700 to 213. The degraded middle classes were thrust into servitude along with the already dependent agricultural workers. And a servile theory was eventually worked out which covered the diverse Anglo-Saxon types of peasant under the name of villein, a word which, contrary to continental usage, came to have the meaning of unfreedom in England. No distinctions were made between the peasants in so far as they were all placed in the category of serfs. One distinction, however, which will be of great importance in future developments, seems to have been in the minds of the Domesday Commissioners, who apparently reserved the name of villein for those who had a share in the field system and that of cottar for those who had no such share and constituted an indispensable reserve of labour for miscellaneous needs, agricultural and otherwise. The test of social status was still economic, but the prevailing trend of thought and events was to be openly exhibited in the legal changes made a century later by Henry II, for the villeins, not yet deprived of their personal as distinct from their economic freedom, found that then a sharp distinction was made between free and unfree and that the line of personal liberty was drawn above them. Whatever the benefits of Henry's legal reforms might be—and they were un-doubtedly great—they were not for the villeins: they were left on one side as serfs who had no civil rights as against their masters. However much the villeins might take advantage of local conditions to remove the severities of economic repression, they could not escape the rigid definitions of the law. But for the Norman Con-quest it is unlikely that the peasantry in England would have fallen so low. The Anglo-Saxon slaves (*theows*) with the low wergild of forty pence, some 25,000 in number according to Domesday calcu-lations, had largely made it unnecessary to stress compulsory labour before 1066. Their economic usefulness must have given them a certain security and kept them free from gross abuses. Slavery was, however, an anachronism in a feudalized society, and the word disappeared for that reason and not through the application of any moral principles or kind-heartedness. The slaves themselves gained no material advantage and may, indeed, have been worse off when they joined the lowest level of the comprehensive villein class.

Nevertheless, the peasant substructure was not greatly altered. It was the ordinary villagers who constituted the essential and the really permanent England to an extent which our urban civilization to-day makes it difficult for us to realize, and it is likely that they found the Norman Conquest little more than a temporary and minor disturbance in the hard and merciless routine of wresting a living from the soil. It was a dislocation but not a break: rural England continued to be the England of Edward the Confessor, and Norman lordship made slight difference. Local customs were too securely founded on the traditions of centuries to be seriously affected by the Conquest and therefore the English 'folk-right', absorbed in the new term of the 'custom of the realm' (*consuetudo regni*), remained the firm and immutable basis of the English state. The peasants still attended their popular assembly courts of the shires and hundreds, they still used the legal procedure they had always known, and there still remained the doomsmen who decided how legal issues were to be tried. They were still obliged to take part in police measures like the hue and cry and frankpledge. They were still liable for military conscription for service in the national fyrd. This inherited complex of rights and duties remained as essentially unimpaired and unchangeable as the economic condi-tions which dominated their material existence.

So the Normans were unable in practice to iron out the tradi-tional distinctions between one peasant and another and thereby produce a uniform class. Particularly in the Danelaw, where ancient liberties strenuously resisted all encroachments, the relations between lord and man continued to be largely personal: the sokeman's bond with his superior was expressed in terms of money rents and suit of court rather than labour services; even villeins and cottars were not always forced to bear the grievous burden of weekly work which was the usual stigma of manorial discipline. Further to the north beyond the Danelaw those who undertook the stern task of reclaiming the 'waste lands' were left largely to their own devices and allowed to colonize them without interference. Furthermore, the Normans were far from successful in asserting a complete system of dependent tenures, for despite all difficulties there persisted all over England free men who knew nothing of either knight services or labour services. As peasant proprietors they formed an important element in society which was destined to bear a great responsibility in the routine administration of the country. We have only to remember the many twelfth-century charters they made in the course of buying and selling property to realize that, despite all feudalization, land continued to be transferable and society to be fluid.

As in social life, so in economic organization we must not exaggerate the contributions of the Normans. In spite of the shock of the Conquest economic life in England continued essentially the same as before. Rural communities living under a natural economy were still predominant. The Normans brought to agriculture no new technique and no new implements to change the methods of farming from the traditional system of the 'open fields'. The Anglo-Saxons had performed a miracle of patient, unspectacular and largely unrecorded labour in reclaiming forest land and fen and bringing the soil of England into cultivation. Though much undoubtedly remained to be done, it has been estimated that at the time of the Domesday Survey some five million acres were under the plough, that is nearly half as much as the land returned as arable in the census of 1879. The arrival of the Normans produced a sharp drop in agricultural prosperity, a natural reaction to events which was made unnecessarily severe by the merciless devastation of wide areas of the country and the enlargement of forest areas for the king's pleasure where special law was devised and imposed to preserve the royal hunting privileges—the Forest Laws which had as their evil descendants the 'bastard slips' of the

Game Laws. Fortunately agricultural recovery is never long delayed if sufficient numbers of stock remain alive, and already by the end of William I's reign the native English farmers had begun to make good the lost ground.

THE MANOR

It is not so very long ago since it was generally believed that the Norman Conquest covered England with innumerable manors of identical pattern, that most agricultural workers were villeins, that rent was usually paid by labour services according to the practice of natural economy. Furthermore, it was contended that the Anglo-Saxon villages had for the most part been included within the manors and largely become identifiable with them, whilst the villagers themselves had been degraded to the semi-servile tenants of a lord. Thus the manor became the basic unit of organized life, through which the bulk of the people gained its daily bread, and a coherent and uniform economic society had been formed immediately.

A normal manor had two main components. First, the lord's demesne. This was the home farm, often quite small in extent and usually, though not always, comprising a number of strips of land scattered here and there within the manor. Its cultivation was the first and foremost duty of the manorial tenants and all other activities on the estate were subordinated to it. The manor-house was the centre of administration, served by a competent staff under a steward and bailiffs, who worked in co-operation with the reeve as the representative of the tenants. The manorial court made the agricultural arrangements and regulations and saw that they were carried into effect. Secondly, the peasants' dependent holdings. Serfdom was the indispensable basis on which the manorial organization was founded. The manor therefore was a practical means of managing an estate through compulsory labour services. Its fundamental value was as an agricultural unit, for the main business of its inhabitants was to cultivate the soil so that they could live upon its produce. It was to be very largely self-sufficing and self-consuming.

The historians who gave us our first intimate knowledge of the manor and its workings so seriously overstressed its position in the social and economic structures of England that it seemed as though the Norman Conquest had caused a serious break with the past and introduced a new beginning. This it certainly did not do. The classic theory of the manor expresses what was thought to be the theories of the Norman mind as we see it at work, for example, in the Domesday Survey, but it does not correspond with the actual economic facts.

(i) The manor was no novel conception which broke with the tendencies of Anglo-Saxon society. It was established in all essentials but name before 1066 in the sense that great parts of the country were already being cultivated by the dependants of a lord, these dependants often holding their land by his favour and performing miscellaneous services in return. All the Normans had to do in such districts was to systematize a substantially older order of things.

(ii) The argument for the universality of the manor is based upon sources of information which are unsatisfactory because they are limited and biased. They are the records of the manorial courts which obviously speak only in terms of manors, and these manorial records are forthcoming only from part of the midland and southern districts of England and, even there, mainly from the great ecclesiastical estates where rigid conservatism and static conditions were maintained and encouraged. A truer perspective can be obtained only if there are included as well the unmanorialized estates (for which manorial records naturally provide no information), the lands of lay tenants, and the other parts of England. If we do that, the picture is completely altered. For intensive regional studies reveal that the manorial economy was by no means widespread or uniform. Northumbria scarcely conformed with the manorial pattern, in which the lord's demesne and serfdom were essential elements, but knew instead the presence of villages and villagers, who had a personal and not a tenurial tie with their lords and paid their rents often in money and in kind, and it drew no harsh dividing line between free and unfree. The south-western counties and the counties on the borders of Wales proved equally stubborn against any manorializing process, and this can be largely explained by the continued influence of Celtic traditions and Celtic methods and by the different requirements of pastoral rather than arable farming. It is surprising, however, to discover that in the east of England—in south Yorkshire, Lincolnshire and Norfolk—the 'ideal manor' was not the predominant institution. Furthermore, it was always the proud boast of Kent that, whatever Domesday might say to the contrary, villein tenure was unknown within its borders.

(iii) Not only has the area where the manor prevailed shrunk to the southern Midlands and the South but even there it is becoming increasingly clear that the conception of the manor is too artificial, too simplified, too static: the local variations are too many to admit of adequate generalizations. For there, as elsewhere, we come across lordless villages of independent freeholders, who were immune from manorialization, and freehold property, which did not form part of a manor and was not regarded as a manor by itself. We find manors which had no lord's demesne and therefore no manorial organization; or no courts; or no land held by villein tenure and no villeins; or no labour services. Furthermore, the manors which are more regular in their features often do not reveal themselves as essentially units, for some lords for various reasons had found it necessary to surrender part of their demesne land and rents and services to other lords, and sometimes the freeholders and even the villeins on one manor acquired lands in neighbouring manors and therefore acknowledged more than one lord. Therefore the manors themselves are more intricately connected and their organization more complex than has generally been understood. So the manor, even within the limited area of its main influence, was no more than a section, though an important section, of economic life two centuries after the introduction of Norman feudalism, centuries when manorialization was increasing rather than relaxing its hold upon the country. When there was such infinite diversity revealing manors at every possible point of development, it is impossible to invest the term 'manor' with a precise and technical meaning.

(iv) The village (or township) continued to be after the Norman Conquest exactly what it was before that event: the essential unit of rural organization and development. The word 'manor' is not to be found in Anglo-Saxon records. It is, however, used frequently by the Domesday Commissioners, though they never defined it, and it is difficult to be sure what exactly they meant by it: quite often it can mean no more than the chief residence, the manor-house itself. Nor was it a term that could be used intelligibly in the Danelaw and, indeed, it came as a comparatively late intruder there with a reconstruction of ecclesiastical estates on feudal lines. To essay a description in the most general terms, we may regard a manor as the estate, often small in extent, of a single lord which was worked as an economic entity and controlled by its own administration and which had a separate value attached to it: it was a unit of property, a unit of tenure or, from another angle, of seignorial jurisdiction. The village, on the other hand, was a block of territory with definite boundaries which might be divided up among many owners: it was a territorial unit, an agrarian unit, a unit of royal administration. Whereas the king did not interfere with the internal affairs of the manor, he continued to place administrative and fiscal duties upon the village and to keep it as a public institution, a part of the machinery of government. Thus, when personal taxation was introduced, the collectors dealt always with villages and not with manors. If the village and the manor happened to coincide, that was purely accidental, for quite often one manor contained all or parts of several villages and one village contained all or parts of several manors. For it has been calculated that, even within the manorialized area of England in the late thirteenth century when manorial organization reached its maturity, out of some six hundred and fifty villages more than half did not tally with manors in their territorial boundaries: it follows that there the manor was simply an artificial accretion which had little or no effect upon the unity of the village which reached back into the remote past. Elsewhere in the country it was certainly the village and not the manor that was the interest of the people at large.

It is increasingly evident that the 'manorial system' is becoming as vague a term as the 'feudal system' and that we cannot regard the manorial economy as an essential part of feudalism without at the same time denying the omnipresence of feudalism in Norman England. English social and economic organization was so firmly rooted and so complex that any attempt to make the manor universal and uniform was doomed to failure. The achievements of the Normans in this respect have been exaggerated, for their conceptions did not submerge the older traditions and habits to anything like the extent so often imagined. If this point is firmly grasped, it will assist us not only to understand many later developments, it will help us to estimate the true effect of feudalization and to say whether it struck its roots deeply or whether it was incapable of penetrating the 'cake of custom', to use Bagehot's phrase, to any serious depth.

THE BOROUGHS

The influence of the Normans upon the development of towns and the growth of commerce is comparable to that of their racial predecessors, the Danes: it is no less and it is no more. It is well to remember that England did not become an urban rather than an agricultural community until the Industrial Revolution of the eighteenth century and, indeed, that it was not until the close of the Middle Ages that a money economy can be said to have completely displaced the older economy based on payment in kind or labour services. In Norman England only London, York, Lincoln and Norwich could boast of more than five thousand inhabitants, and fully nine-tenths of the population of the country must have lived outside the towns altogether. Though the immediate effects of the Conquest were evil, bringing material ruin and disaster to many urban centres like Lincoln, where one hundred and sixty-six houses were razed to make room for a castle, eventually the impact of the Normans gave a natural stimulus to trade like that supplied earlier by the Scandinavians. There was, however, no revolutionary change, the process of development was all of one piece and can in no sense be dated from 1066. Had the Norman borough been a new creation, new in all its essential features, we should expect to find some evidence of this novelty. But the written records dealing with urban organization remain exasperatingly meagre for the next hundred years; the testimony of coinage provides no signs of a dynamic increase in trade before 1100 or of an altered attitude towards town life; the largest and wealthiest boroughs in the thirteenth century were still the same as the Anglo-Saxons had made pre-eminent; and London, for example, where the presence of so many foreigners might most readily have wrought drastic changes at once, saw Englishmen still prominent in civic affairs and her institutions still true to their native origin. The tremendous expansion in trade did not occur until the later twelfth century, and it came then from the general revival of commercial life all over Europe and would have affected England, whether a Norman Conquest had taken place or not.

The presence of two types of boroughs is seen under William I. (a) *The royal demesne boroughs.* By far the great majority of the old English boroughs were in the king's control, for he was the largest, though by no means the only, landowner there, and he appointed the port-reeves who ruled them and answered to him for that considerable part of his income he drew from them. The Conqueror made only one change in administration: demanding a higher return of profits, sometimes as much as double, he saw fit to treat the 'firma burgi' not as a separate and independent payment but as part of the 'firma comitatus' so that the sheriff was henceforward responsible for the collection of the borough revenues.

How precisely it came about that in two or three generations it was considered that *all* land in royal boroughs was held of the king is obscure, but presumably those burgesses who were tenants of feudal lords and could therefore claim feudal privileges found it an advantage to abandon them in favour of borough and gild privileges. Certainly by Henry II's time all were being required to pay tallage to the king without distinction. (*b*) *Seignorial* or *mesne boroughs*. Nearly all the boroughs which grew up under the protection of a lord rather than of the king were post-Conquest in origin, established as trading-centres under the influence of French ideas. A famous group was that on the Welsh Marches which comprised such places as Hereford, Shrewsbury and Rhuddlan: they were developed by Norman barons from the Breton Marches before the end of the eleventh century and their burgesses were granted the privileges of the 'Laws of Breteuil', a small and obscure Norman borough. The Breteuil 'Customs' in some form spread far and wide in the West Country, being applied to Haverfordwest in Pembroke and Bideford in Devon. To begin with, therefore, seignorial boroughs were quite numerous, though not greatly important, but they were not substantially different from others; and through escheat and forfeiture most of them sooner or later came into the king's hands, whilst few of the remainder managed to retain prominence.

III. The Impact upon the Church and Culture

We cannot hope to understand the true significance and to make a reasonable assessment of the Norman Conquest in this sphere of its influence unless we can place the developments in England against the background of those continental movements of which they always formed a part. In the first centuries of its history the Church had been inclined to look upon the world in which it lived as evil, to withdraw as much as possible from all contact with it, and to focus its gaze and to fix its hopes upon the world to come. It was this attitude of mind which had produced monasticism, and its appeal continued to be powerful. This insistence, however, upon independence and upon separation from the affairs of the world was not typical of the Middle Ages, which tried to look upon society as a unity and therefore not divisible. The phrase 'Church and

State', with its implicit recognition of a gap fixed between the clergy and the laity, was theoretically meaningless. However evil the world might be, it was the duty of the Church to work within it for its redemption and, inasmuch as the lay rulers of the world were pledged to govern by Christian principles and to enlarge the bounds of Christendom, the Church was willing to place itself under their patronage and churchmen to render them obedience. Kings therefore were given pre-eminence: they were the Lord's Anointed and more than mere laymen, they had a divine mission to convert the world, and their supreme authority was given recognition and support by popes and bishops. In consequence, they summoned councils of the Church, presided over them, settled the agenda, approved the acts and even influenced changes in doctrine. This conception of a royal theocracy prevailed beyond the middle of the eleventh century, and there can be no doubt that under it great results were achieved. But emperors and kings did not remain the only members of the laity to control the Church. For with the growth of feudalism their authority was curtailed, and much of it passed into the hands of lay lords, who built churches and chapels and founded monasteries, became their patrons, and in innumerable ways shaped the destinies of the Church.

There was the inevitable danger that the Church would find the world too much with it and be faced with a spiritual decline and, indeed, from the lay control of the Church there came three abuses which needed particular attention.

I. LAY APPOINTMENTS

Just as feudalism had obscured the unity of the State, so it obscured the unity of the Church, whose broken fragments became part and parcel of feudalized society. The possession of land turned churchmen into lay lords who must perform the lay services imposed upon land. All of them, from the pope himself down to the humblest parish priest, had a lay overlord, to whom they must do homage before entering upon their holy office if they were to obtain possession of the lands attached to that office. This meant in practice that, since they must be acceptable to their secular superiors, it was the latter who made the appointment. This fact was so well recognized that it was usual for them also to bestow the pastoral staff and ring which were the insignia of spiritual office. The Church came near forgetting that it had once had its appointments within its own control. Whatever rights a lay lord might have over church lands, it was clearly wrong that he should assume authority to grant spiritual functions. This, however, proved a desperately embarrassing problem: if the lord appointed someone who could do the services for the land adequately, there was no guarantee that he would be also a fit and proper person to be in the Church at all; on the other hand, if the Church appointed someone suitable for holy office, then there was equally no guarantee that he would competently fulfil his lay obligations to his lay lord. This dilemma was eventually to lead everywhere to the bitter struggle of the Investiture Contest.

II. SIMONY

This followed as an almost inevitable consequence of lay appointments. Spiritual office in the Church became a marketable commodity and was bought and sold without shame to the highest bidder. The papacy itself had since the early eleventh century become little more than the family possession of the House of Tusculum, and scandal reached its limit when a boy of twelve was elevated as head of the Church, sold his office as soon as he came of age to his godfather, and later sought to buy it back at the same price.

III. CLERICAL MARRIAGE

Since worldliness was the paramount evil, the remedy was obvious: the world must be renounced. Many of the clergy had entered the Church only to enjoy its wealth, and they continued to live as though they had not in some measure withdrawn from the world. So these men of the world, turned clerics, married and founded families, and bishoprics, abbacies and parish churches were apt to descend to their heirs like any lay inheritance. The ideals associated with monasticism condemned what the ardent Reformers in Western Europe also regarded as contamination, and it was felt that only by a strong insistence on the canons imposing celibacy could the Church escape from the mesh the world had thrown upon her.

For many generations, however, there was no break with long traditions and well-established customs, and the monarchic headship of the Church was taken for granted and received the approval of the Reformers themselves, who sought and obtained the sympathy and active assistance of princes in the work of regeneration.

This was set on foot in earnest early in the tenth century and for nearly a hundred and fifty years it had little or nothing to do with the papacy, which had become one of the spoils of aristocratic factions at Rome and fallen into grave disrepute. That is why the Reform movement had no central direction and was begun at different times in different places by different means: at Cluny in Burgundy in 910, shortly afterwards in Lorraine, and later in Italy.

The first signs of a change in attitude came with the totally unexpected appearance of a reformed Papacy, beginning with the accession of Pope Leo IX in 1048. No longer content with merely the consultative position hitherto assigned to the papacy, he summoned the famous papal council at Rheims in 1049 and, after condemning simony, clerical marriage and lay patronage in general, he insisted upon the primacy of the bishop of Rome within the hierarchy of the Church; reform, therefore, was no longer to be unorganized and concerned with the purification of first one and then another part of the Church: it was to be given a new meaning in that the Church in the West was to be purified under the supreme authority of the papacy. This led to a further demand for freedom of election to ecclesiastical office: in 1059 Pope Nicholas II took advantage of the tender age of the Emperor Henry IV to declare that the election of a pope was the responsibility of a college of cardinals and not of the emperor; his successor, Alexander II, refused to allow bishops appointed by the emperor even to be consecrated. It was not, however, until Cardinal Hildebrand became Pope Gregory VII in 1073 that reform became invested with yet another and a completely revolutionary meaning. No longer was it assumed that the conversion of mankind to a Christian life was to take place within the long accepted political and social order. Conversion was to come about through the creation of a new order of society in which priests were to be neither the assistants nor yet the equals of princes but their superiors: papal curia and ecclesiastical officials were to dominate royal court and royal ministers. The sacerdotal and anti-monarchical conception precipitated the greatest crisis in the history of the medieval Church. It is often asserted that it was the inevitable outcome of the attack on abuses, which made it imperative to elevate the papacy as a strong central executive and to remove lay control. This argument, however attractive by its simplicity and apparent logic, does not explain the fact that, so far as abuses were concerned, they could be and had been successfully fought under the patronage of princes, as the work of the reforming Emperor Henry III had quite recently shown, and the onslaught upon them was certainly not placed prominently by Gregory himself among the reasons for his extreme action. Nor is that action to be regarded simply as a continuation or culmination of the Reform movements that had gone before. His principles were by no means identical with those of the Cluniac reformers, for example, who concentrated their attention upon monasticism and were only incidentally interested in the Church which mixed with the world, accepted secular authority and lay patronage without misgivings, and showed no desire to intermeddle with politics.

Gregory, on the other hand, wished dominion over the world, but not because a struggle for the freedom of the Church meant simply a struggle for independence, which happened to resolve itself into a contest for supremacy. He took his stand upon the ancient and universally accepted premise that Christianity was the foundation on which the world and all its affairs rested. The consequent deduction was that the Church, far from freeing itself from the embrace of the world and seeking independence only, must itself embrace the world and rule it in order to fulfil its vocation of converting it. These ideas were not novel, for Gregory was by no means an original thinker. But never before had an attempt been made to translate them into practice. Believing that secular government must come into the purview of the Church and that the office of an emperor, king or prince must be assimilated to that of an ecclesiastic and subject to similar discipline, Gregory was logically compelled to enter political life, to overthrow the usurping domination of temporal rulers and to bring the laity into subordination. When, therefore, the Emperor Henry IV ignored his decree in 1075 which forbade princes to invest bishops with their spiritual functions, Gregory took the novel and astounding step of not merely excommunicating him from the Church but of deposing him from his throne. Therein lay the revolution which turned the existing order upside down. It met the bitter resistance of vested interests that any such profound reconstruction of society must expect: not only outside the Church but also within the Church, for many bishops disliked their subordination to a foreign pope in Rome and the sharp rupture of their traditional connexion with secular princes. So the tremendous questions at stake were crystallized in the single issue of the great Investiture Contest, which disturbed high politics for half a century before a compromise was reached in the Concordat of Worms in 1122.

With a knowledge of what had been taking place on the Continent we can properly appreciate the position of the Anglo-Saxon Church and the attitude adopted by William and Lanfranc after the conquest of England.

The enthusiasm for Christianity which became evident in Normandy about the time that Cnut ascended the English throne owed nothing to stimulus from Rome, for a reformed papacy was still a quarter of a century in the future. In particular, we should notice that no provincial church was more completely under secular control: the duke appointed and deposed bishops and abbots, tried them in his court for their offences, and demanded military service from them as from his knights. Though separate ecclesiastical courts were in existence, their jurisdiction was strictly limited and always subject to the duke's approval and control. William the Conqueror took these conceptions of his authority with him to England and found nothing there to contradict them, for there was nothing peculiar in the organization and point of view of the Anglo-Saxon Church. Therefore, like all contemporary rulers, he took his stand upon tradition and custom: what had been in the past should continue to be, and innovations were to be rigorously excluded. He would support the moral reform of the Church in England, but he would also remain its master.

The importance of the Norman Conquest in the history of the English Church turns upon the question of reform. For just as William's expedition to England was depicted by Norman monastic chroniclers in the light of later events as something in the nature of a crusade, undertaken in the name of the papacy against a country whose temporal head was a perjurer and whose spiritual head was a schismatic, so many historians of the present day have been led by a consideration of what was done after 1066 to believe that the Conquest marks an entirely new beginning. The contemporary view implies that the Anglo-Saxon Church needed to be completely reorganized and purified; the modern view implies that this was done by the Normans. Neither implication can be accepted, for the first does, as we have seen, less than justice to the pre-Conquest Church, and the second exaggerates and even misinterprets the reforms of the Conqueror and Archbishop Lanfranc.

Lanfranc was not a Norman but an Italian, born at Pavia in Lombardy round about 1010. A student of Lombardic, and probably Roman, law, he was in legal practice at Pavia in his early manhood. Only then did he turn his thoughts to theology instead and leave

Italy to teach in the cathedral school at Avranches in Normandy. About 1040–2 he took monastic vows: he entered the small monastery of Le Bec in Normandy, rose to be its prior, and three years before the Norman Conquest was transferred as abbot to William's new foundation at Caen. At both places he founded schools of instruction which attracted future popes and archbishops and abbots as their students. Lanfranc was rightly acknowledged as the foremost teacher in Western Europe, and it was almost entirely due to his efforts that Normandy became noted as a centre of scholarship which was to find its most famous representative in another Italian, St. Anselm.

The nature and versatility of Lanfranc's career profoundly affected his ecclesiastical policy in England. His life in the world had given him a breadth of view, a wide experience, a knowledge of men, that could not have been gained by one who lived solely within the cloister. His training in law was disclosed by the way in which he put forward documentary proofs in evidence of his claims as archbishop of Canterbury. His cosmopolitanism helped him to a sympathetic understanding of Anglo-Saxon ways and habits of thought. His reputation in the world of scholarship placed the Anglo-Saxon intellectuals on his side. Yet Lanfranc was first and foremost neither an original thinker nor a saint (he was not canonized): he was essentially the administrator, the practical organizer, who suited his methods to his means.

REFORMS IN THE SECULAR CHURCH

Lanfranc's work in the Church reflected that of William in the State in its pursuit of orderliness and unity: in that respect the close co-operation between the two men represented the political and ecclesiastical forces combining together to attain the same object.

(i) *The exaltation of the authority of Canterbury*

If reforms were to be made effective, they must be centrally directed, and therefore Lanfranc had to obtain unquestioned authority. For that reason he went almost out of his way to provoke an early quarrel with the Norman archbishop of York, and there was a stern struggle extending over two years before he obtained a recognition of the precedence of Canterbury for the duration of his own lifetime. Lanfranc found no difficulty in obtaining the Conqueror's support, for it was clear from past history, to which the legal-minded Lanfranc deliberately appealed, that ecclesiastical disunity was always an expression of political disunity: Mercia had marked its separatism by the archbishopric of Lichfield (787–803), the metropolitan see of York was fixed in the Scandinavianized parts of the country and what guarantee was there that its occupant might not follow the example of some of his predecessors and identify himself with Danish interests and support a Danish claimant to the throne? Lanfranc's action was, however, not new, for the same point had been stressed since the days of Theodore of Tarsus. Nor, unfortunately, was it permanent in its results, for an acerbity unknown before 1066 had been introduced into the relations between the two metropolitans, and the question of precedence was reopened under Anselm and troubled the Church for many generations to come.

(ii) *The system of church councils*

Lanfranc found in these a direct and expeditious method of spreading his influence and achieving his ends, and they helped him to keep a close eye upon the progress of reform. It was a council at Winchester in 1070 which deposed Stigand and other ecclesiastics, a council at Winchester in 1072 which settled the controversy over the primacy of Canterbury, a council at London in 1075 which carefully laid down the full programme of reform, a council at Winchester in 1076 which decided the Church's attitude towards clerical marriage. Here again there was no new beginning, for we can draw no hard and fast line between the assemblies which legislated for the Anglo-Saxon Church and those which directed the affairs of the Norman Church. It was the Conqueror who summoned and presided over the council of 1070, and ever afterwards the royal permission had to be obtained before a council of the Church could meet; lay magnates were so conspicuously present at the council of 1072 that it was impossible to distinguish it from a session of the king's court; other councils, meeting at the same time and in the same place and with apparently the same membership as the king's court, suffer from the same confusion.

(iii) *The normanization of the episcopacy*

The Conqueror knew quite well the value of the Church in reconciling the people to his rule and upholding his supremacy. Regarding matters from a strictly political point of view, he had no wish to antagonize the native English Church and create needless difficulties for himself: therefore, however much was later made of Archbishop Stigand's schismatic appointment, William did not choose to remove him until three years after the Conquest, and in allowing him to consecrate the bishop of Dorchester he permitted him to do what the Anglo-Saxon Church itself had never countenanced. Furthermore, eight out of the fifteen pre-Conquest bishops and many abbots were left in possession of their sees and abbeys as long as they lived. Nevertheless, it was natural that William should desire to work with people of his own stock, and the systematic appointment of Normans to all the high places in the Church was steadily pursued. William, in fact, appointed no Englishman to an English see. Of the thirteen sees which made up the province of Canterbury in 1066 and the two sees which formed the province of York, three were already ruled by Normans appointed by the Confessor, two fell vacant by death in 1069–71 and four more were rendered vacant in 1070 by the deposition of Stigand and three other bishops. By 1080 the government of the secular Church had been so successfully transferred into the hands of Norman prelates that only Wulfstan of Worcester remained a native English bishop. We may and must deplore the political prejudice which robbed the Church of the highest services of those who had built it up, and the self-seeking worldliness and greed of many of the Normans appointed. Fortunately it was not all loss. For Lanfranc could call upon his old schools at Le Bec and Caen to supply him with some of his episcopal assistants, who came as trained and competent administrators, 'spiritual drill-serjeants', to attempt to set the Church in orderly array.

(iv) *The reorganization of diocesan life*

Before 1066 the headquarters of the bishoprics had been often associated with country villages, whose importance was only gradually overshadowed by the growth of towns as a result mainly of trade. This stood in sharp contrast with the practice on the Continent where episcopal sees had normally been connected with ancient Roman cities. The process of transference to populous centres had already begun in 1050 and Lanfranc gave it a considerable acceleration: from Sherborne to Salisbury, Selsey to Chichester, Wells to Bath. The bishops were commanded to hold diocesan councils regularly for the discipline of their clergy, to visit their dioceses, and to submit their problems to Canterbury. As for the priests, they were not to wander about the country as they pleased but must obtain permission before leaving their diocese.

(v) *The improvement of clerical morals*

That the Anglo-Saxon Church needed a vigorous overhaul is without question. Fortunately England had remained free until 1066 from the type of political feudalism common on the Continent and had, in consequence, escaped from the worst infamies that disgraced other provincial Churches. Hence the reforms followed an unspectacular and well-beaten track, and none of them was in any way a novel consequence of the Conquest. If we refuse to accept without question the prejudiced and often incredible comments of Norman monks a generation or more later and allow the provable facts to speak for themselves, we shall discover that the specific accusations levelled against the Anglo-Saxon Church are seriously exaggerated. Thus, taking the Anglo-Saxon episcopate in 1066 as the obvious subject of examination, we find that no bishop was guilty of simony, only one bishop is known to have been married, and only Stigand was a pluralist in retaining the bishopric of Winchester, along with the archbishopric of Canterbury on which his hold was always at least precarious. It was with the higher clergy that the Normans were necessarily mainly concerned, and we have practically no evidence of the state of morality of the lower clergy. They were most seriously touched by the delicate question of clerical marriage. For though it had been constantly condemned by ecclesiastical councils in England in the tenth and eleventh centuries long before Gregory VII in 1075 ordered the clergy to put away their wives, the decrees had not been obeyed. Whatever the celibate scribes of the monasteries might say, there was no general feeling in Europe against marriage, save in the case of popes and bishops. The politic Lanfranc knew that to enforce the papal ban was impossible, and he made the humane and sensible compromise that the married clergy could retain their wives but all who entered the Church in future were to take a vow of celibacy. Yet, despite the fact that all abuses which it was believed good reformers should attack were attacked, their work cannot have made great headway in the Church as a whole. For the reign of William Rufus saw the Church fall into a degradation without precedent, during which abuses flourished as never before.

(vi) *Ecclesiastical building*

Nothing expressed the close alliance between the Normans and the Church more practically than the cathedrals which were founded in seven of the fifteen dioceses. As in Normandy, so in England, the Conqueror and his companions for conscience' sake made generous benefactions for building purposes, and Lanfranc, who had been responsible for the rebuilding of Le Bec Priory and the construction of Caen Abbey, set an example by erecting a cathedral at Canterbury within the short space of seven years to take the place of that burnt down three years before he arrived in England. Before he died he had the satisfaction of knowing that the foundations of nine others had been laid.

REFORMS IN THE MONASTIC CHURCH

Once again the political needs of William and the ecclesiastical aims of Lanfranc coincided to produce a happy co-operation and identity in methods. It suited them both to have the English abbeys placed directly under Norman control. Therefore the abbacies, like the episcopate, were normanized: thirteen out of the twenty-one abbots who attended the Council of 1075 were Englishmen, but by the time of Rufus twenty-seven out of the then thirty abbots were Normans, chosen mainly from Le Bec and Caen. It is indicative of the Norman predilection for monasticism that some fifty monasteries and nunneries, comprising less than a thousand members, enjoyed an income from landed property of over £10,000 a year, which was nearly as much as the king reserved from that source for his own private use and a quarter as much again as the secular Church had for its own maintenance.

Since Lanfranc was himself a monk, it might have been anticipated that he would endeavour to use the monastic Church in order to reform the Church as a whole. Fortunately, his long residence in the world had helped him to see that the revival of monastic life was only one part of a far greater movement. Therefore he reversed the process of events as they had been in Normandy and, like Theodore of Tarsus, he concentrated his attention upon the diocesan organization of the secular Church. Consequently he would not allow the monasteries to become too independent: their right to elect their own abbots was limited to a right to be consulted only, and they were kept subordinate to the bishops.

Though the first Cluniac priory in England was established at Lewes in 1077, no more were founded during the Conqueror's reign. The centre of interest, therefore, remained the old Benedictine monasteries of England, richly endowed by Norman patrons, vigorously reconstituted by foreign abbots and influenced by the reformed Cluniac version of the Benedictine Rule.

Thus, even if we judged the period before 1066 by the same standards as that after 1066, we are forced to the conclusion that the two differ in degree rather than in kind. The Norman Conquest marked an intensification of reforms already foreshadowed or actually undertaken. But, in fact, the two periods ought to be judged by different criteria of 'reform', for this word meant something different after 1073 from what it meant before the pontificate of Gregory VII. The Anglo-Saxon Church, as we have already seen, had always accorded the papacy a traditional reverence, but it had been given no precise standard wherewith to measure the papal claims. The papacy had begun to set its house in order only twenty years before the Conquest, and it was not to be expected that England, suffering from the political ill-effects of a feeble king and the anxiety of a doubtful succession and then from the ecclesiastical ill-effects of intrigues in Rome which had left the archbishop of Canterbury a schismatic, would make changes in her attitude to the papacy such as were not to be found elsewhere at the time. The position was different under the Conqueror, for his reign covered a generation in which the papacy had clearly and formally enunciated its claims to supremacy and had in unmistakable token thereof humbled the Emperor before the world. A standard had been fixed and the policy of William and Lanfranc must be measured by it. When we find, therefore, that their outlook was still the traditional outlook, that the archbishop resented papal interference in the affairs of his province no less than the king resented the pope's demand for fealty, and that neither was at all perturbed when Gregory VII was finally forced into exile by his imperial foe, we might well argue that the English Church after the Norman Conquest was no more inclined to follow European religious movements than before.

THE RELATIONS OF MONARCHY AND PAPACY

In the eyes of the ardent reformers William was the man who had invaded England under a papal banner and was therefore pledged to support the papacy and to espouse the reforms it was advocating. William, however, was no papalist. The reforming king could not be allowed to dominate the political king, whose main object was to found a strong monarchy in England. He could not countenance any project that might decrease his authority, and therefore it was to his mind unthinkable that the Church should be removed from his control. He knew what the assertion of a strong monarchy meant to his own fortunes, and the Church was knit too closely into the fabric of the State to be detached without doing serious damage. Hence he could not tolerate the development of the political prerogatives of the papacy. Indeed, a highly centralized Church under the pope was something outside his experience, it was an innovation that did not square with long-established custom either in Normandy or in England and therefore it had no basis in law. Not that he in any way repudiated the pope to whom he was always respectful, but he would have no dualism of authority within his realm. Therefore, in accordance with his declaration that he would have all the croziers in England in his hand, he went on appointing bishops and investing them with the spiritual insignia of office, a course of action which struck at the very heart of the reform movement at a time when the Investiture Contest was at its height.

His jealousy for his kingly position and kingly prerogatives and his firm insistence on the old ways were clearly revealed. (i) William came to England as the papal nominee to the throne. He had quite voluntarily submitted his claim to the papal curia and received a verdict in his favour. Gregory VII somewhat naturally assumed that the Norman Conquest had made England a papal fief, and about 1080 he demanded that William should do him homage as his vassal. This action on Gregory's part was in no way unique, for he had successfully sustained the same claims for homage from Spain and Hungary. If he could obtain recognition by kings of the supremacy of the papacy, he hoped to be able to use it to undermine the position of the emperor. But William made a point-blank refusal: homage had not been rendered by any of his predecessors, therefore it would not be rendered by him. (ii) He let the customs on which he relied be clearly understood. He insisted that, unless his consent had been obtained, no pope should be recognized in England, no papal letters should be received, no bishop should leave the country (and, it was implied, by going to Rome come under papal influence), no tenant-in-chief should be excommunicated. Such barriers to papal influence were unknown to the Anglo-Saxon Church, for they had never been found necessary, and William's insistence that he should have full cognisance of papal activities within his new kingdom was calculated to weaken rather than strengthen the ties with Rome.

The position of the papacy was the crucial point. For the reformers had gone far to confuse two issues: the reform of the Church and the exaltation of the papacy. They felt that they would never achieve the first without previously attaining the second. We can see from such a reign as that of William Rufus that they were not without justification in arguing that there must be some authority placed so high that it could override the acts of a lay ruler. But not all rulers were like Rufus. To men such as William the Conqueror it seemed perversely unnecessary to confound the two points. Therefore he resolutely opposed the interference of the papacy, declaring that the archbishop of Canterbury and his spiritual colleagues were fully capable of conducting the government of the Church in England. The only reason why Gregory did not try to prevent Normandy and England from continuing practices, like lay investitures, which he denounced elsewhere was because he knew that both William and Lanfranc were sincere in their devotion to the lesser factors of his reform programme, like the attack on simony and clerical marriage, and because he was fully occupied with the contest with the Empire.

The position of Archbishop Lanfranc, with his allegiance divided between pope and king, should have been one of great embarrassment and perplexity. In actual fact, he found little difficulty in deciding his policy. For, like the king, he let 'custom' settle the problem. His early life in Italy had coincided with the lowest degradation of the papacy, and this must have coloured his outlook: he was certainly never among the advanced reformers. Furthermore, in Normandy and in England the papacy had never been more than a distant tribunal, which could be called into action when wanted and which should not function on its own account. That it should take it upon itself to interfere in the internal affairs of provincial Churches was unheard of, and the practice of appeals to Rome was almost unknown. Therefore, though he reverenced the pope and frequently referred to him for guidance, Lanfranc himself was no papalist and in his time there was no papalist party in the country: the leaders of the English Church felt that the king, in taking his stand upon tradition, was acting well within his rights, and they gave him their obedience and their undivided support and in no way challenged the traditional conception that the temporal power had a divine mission to promote a Christian society.

THE RELATIONS BETWEEN CHURCH AND STATE

In these circumstances friction between State and Church was avoided. William and Lanfranc remained firm friends and peaceful collaborators. The safety of the State and the safety of the Church were regarded as interdependent, and William feared no danger in leaving England in the archbishop's keeping when he visited his Norman duchy. Nevertheless, all the foundations of future discord were already laid, for William and Lanfranc had unwittingly made innovations which helped materially to set Church against State.

(i) *The creation of separate church courts*

This was the most novel and the most lasting of his ecclesiastical measures. About 1072 he issued a writ which prohibited 'cases concerning the rule of souls' from being heard in the hundred courts and reserved them for adjudication by churchmen in church courts in accordance with church law and church procedure. Strictly speaking, the ordinance did not apply to the shire courts, where some bishops continued to preside until Henry I's reign. And, as in Normandy, the king's court paid little heed in practice to any limitations upon its judicial competence. Nevertheless, the momentous breach had been made. Ecclesiastics ceased to attend the popular assembly courts, which had once had jurisdiction over both laymen and clergy and over offenders against the law of God as well as the law of the State. For moral wrongdoing the church courts had jurisdiction over laymen as well as clergy, but William could never have imagined how the Church would enlarge that jurisdiction by interpreting an 'ecclesiastical cause' so that a wide field of law was covered, and by extending its cognizance from 'ecclesiastical causes' to 'ecclesiastical persons' so that clerics, who had perpetrated crimes like murder and robbery, were removed from the competence of the royal courts. So the church courts were to withdraw the most educated section of the king's subjects and a substantial number of offences, committed by laymen as well as clerks, from the royal jurisdiction, and the ideal of 'one people, one law' was not to be attained again until the sixteenth century.

Just when William gave courts of its own to the Church, Lanfranc for his part provided it with the material out of which a canon law favourable to papal claims could rapidly develop. For if papal authority were to be obeyed, it would have to prove that it had a basis in law, and it was this proof that Lanfranc himself provided in England. Under the influence of his early training in civil law in Italy he did not address himself to the task of reorganizing the Church in England without first methodically learning what the law of the Church was. For that purpose he made a summary of it from contemporary canonical collections, which were themselves not uninfluenced by the 'False Decretals', which had been compiled in the ninth century for the express purpose of exalting the pope's position. Lanfranc's version was multiplied, for most libraries of importance in England secured their own copies, and thus it became an authoritative manual of church law in England until the middle of the twelfth century. It was inevitable that the thoughtful members of the English Church should become aware of a great discrepancy between what was ordained by the Church and what was practised by the State. The practical result was to provide an instrument with which the barriers of 'custom', so carefully erected against the intrusion of papal authority in England, could be broken down, and to encourage churchmen to look to the pope rather than to the king as the source of law.

(ii) *The feudalization of the Church*

The second factor which disturbed the traditional harmony between Church and State was more fundamental. Although the immediate effect of Norman feudalism on the English Church was to identify it even more closely with the State than before 1066, that result, paradoxically enough, led to the first real split between them. For when the higher dignitaries of the Church became also tenants-in-chief of the king, their position at once became extremely delicate, unless they were prepared to ignore the claims of the papacy to their allegiance. That this was possible to the older generation of churchmen was shown by the smooth collaboration between William and Lanfranc. But as soon as papal influence gained expression through the new church courts and the new canon law, and as soon as the monarchy became less zealous for any kind of church reform, the loyalties of churchmen became irreconcilably opposed. And so the Investiture Contest came to England only a generation after its appearance in the Empire. Yet it must be remembered that the case for the State was as good as the case of the Church against it, for bishops and abbots were as vital to the State in their temporal capacity as they were to the Church in their spiritual capacity.

So, for the first time in the history of England, Church and State were brought into violent collision, and henceforward the relations between them have constituted a problem which has defied all solutions. At the present day it stands prominently in the forefront of politics in every country in Europe, not excluding Britain, and despite all changes in circumstances it remains fundamentally the same as that which perplexed the Middle Ages. There is no question of a struggle between right and wrong: it is one between two rights. The State primarily represents political order: therefore it cannot permit the existence of any group within it that holds opinions which in its view seem likely to upset that order. So it cannot afford to ignore the Church. But, unfortunately, any attempt by the State to control the Church is apt to reduce it merely to a government department. Naturally, no self-respecting Church can accept such a position, for its moral judgments must rise superior to political statecraft and often go directly counter to it, and the Church must surely have the right to give full expression to its views. In this respect it champions, or appears to champion, political liberty. But political order and political liberty, though both praiseworthy objects, are not easily reconciled. Such is the nature of the problem which confronted Norman and Angevin kings until so great a crisis was reached that an archbishop lay murdered in his cathedral and the strongest king in Europe submitted to humiliating penance for what was done.

It is difficult, and perhaps not of the first importance, to determine whether the momentous changes in the Church in England would have come about without the Norman Conquest. Two things seem clear, however. On the one hand, there is no reason to suppose that the reform movements of the eleventh century would not have reached England during that century, for the country was neither so isolated from the Continent nor its Church so independent of Rome that such powerful currents of thought would have failed to influence it. On the other hand, it is probable that, while English kings would have been no more willing than Norman kings to allow papal interference with the rights of the Crown, they would not have exercised the intimate control over the Church which Norman feudalism gave the succeeding dynasty, and therefore the conflict between Church and State might have come sooner than it did if the Normans had not set foot in England.

When William was succeeded by William Rufus in 1086 and the temporizing Lanfranc by the uncompromising Anselm in 1093, peace was no longer possible. In the event, the breach was first opened by the action of the monarchy itself. On the death of the Conqueror it not only ceased to be interested in the cause of church reform but became definitely obstructionist and thus laid itself open to a justified attack. The viciousness of Rufus's private life and of his court made it difficult for the Church to co-operate with him. And his insatiable greed led him to destroy the Church's work. For his policy of extortion induced him to use the Church as far as possible to produce revenue for the Crown. To that end he seized upon the property of deceased churchmen, and prolonged the vacancies to high ecclesiastical offices as much as possible so that the incomes attached to these offices could be diverted to himself: thus, when Lanfranc died in 1089, the Church was deprived of its leader, for the throne of Canterbury was not filled for four years. When Rufus died, he had in his hands the lands of the three sees of Canterbury, Winchester and Salisbury, and of eleven abbeys. Nevertheless, if a high enough bid was made, the king was willing to make an appointment, and thus the abuse of lay investiture was connected with the sin of simony as well. A similar spoliation of the Church was taking place at the same time in Normandy under the Conqueror's eldest son, Robert, and it is well to bear in mind that even the Conqueror's youngest son, Henry I, despite all the promises he made to gain favour at the beginning of his reign, made no appointment to Canterbury for five years after Anselm's death in 1109. When royal control meant a vested interest in old abuses, the spoliation of the Church and the destruction of its work, the reformers were left with no alternative but to transfer their allegiance and pin their hopes to the papacy.

It was only when Rufus lay in terror of death in 1093 that he agreed to appoint Anselm of Aosta, prior of Le Bec, to succeed Lanfranc. Anselm was another Italian scholar of European reputation whose original thought, especially in his *Cur Deus Homo,* fixed the channel of theological and philosophical speculation for many years; a saint in character and yet ruthlessly strong in his single-mindedness; a more and more ardent reformer as the years passed by: such a man had nothing in common with the king, and quarrels were inevitable.

(i) *The recognition of a new pope*

Gregory VII had died in exile from Rome in 1085 and the emperor had apparently triumphed. Pope and anti-pope made their usual appearances, and the choice between them had to be made just at the time of Anselm's appointment. After Rufus had seemed likely to give his support to the emperor's anti-pope, he eventually recognized Urban II and, though Anselm had anticipated that decision, he warned the king that this was not a matter for any lay ruler to decide alone.

(ii) *The right to visit Rome*

Because Rufus had not finally made up his mind which pope to acknowledge, he refused to allow Anselm to leave the country to go to Rome, as Lanfranc had done before him, to receive the pallium, which the popes had by a long tradition given to every occupant of the throne of Canterbury as a special mark of dignity for the primate of all England. In view of his father's list of vetoes Rufus was not acting in any capricious way. But Anselm had no intention of submitting tamely to the king's decision, and he had the question brought before a royal council of lay and ecclesiastical magnates at Rockingham in 1095. That council is not so much important for what it did; indeed, Anselm found himself so poorly supported by the bishops that he surrendered in the matter of the pallium and consented to receive it from the hands of a visiting legate. The council made history, however, inasmuch as it was the first occasion on which an open rupture had occurred, and the head of the Church had openly refused to regard himself as subject in all things to the head of the State, for Anselm had made it perfectly plain that in some things his prime allegiance lay with the pope and not the king.

In 1097 Anselm, irked by his powerlessness to fulfil his duties and desirous of consulting the pope, again asked permission to go to Rome and, despite the threat that his departure would mean the confiscation of his archiepiscopal lands, he went into voluntary exile and thereby registered a public protest against the caesaro-papism of the king.

So in 1100, with a vicious and ruthless despoiler of the Church upon the throne of England and no archbishop upon the throne of Canterbury, the hour of crisis in the relations of Church and State could not be long delayed.

THE EFFECT UPON CULTURAL DEVELOPMENT

The prevalent tendency to attribute to the generation after the Norman Conquest the achievements which more properly belong to the later part of the twelfth century should be avoided, not only in the study of political and social development but in that of the arts also. For there is nothing to indicate that the battle of Hastings was followed by the transplantation of any higher culture into England, whilst there is much to suggest that the advance of civilization was seriously retarded. We would not normally expect the arts of peace to flourish within a community which had comparatively recently been heathen in its religion and barbarous in its practices: in 1075 it was still struggling, not to suppress, but simply to impose restrictions upon blood-feuds and in 1091 upon the right of private warfare. The Normans were crude and of themselves had little to offer, but they had a remarkable faculty for appreciating and assimilating the higher civilizations in which they lived. Thus the fame of Le Bec as a centre of scholarship was due to the happy accident that brought the Italian Lanfranc to North France, and few of the abbeys in Normandy were in 1066 under abbots of Norman race. So in England the Normans came into contact with a civilization which was immeasurably older and finer than their own. The immediate result of the Conquest was undoubtedly destructive, but once the initial shock had passed, the conquered civilized their conquerors, and it was the fusion of the two peoples which made possible the Anglo-Norman civilization which triumphed in the twelfth century.

In the minor arts the Norman Conquest was directly responsible for the disappearance of a fine tradition of craftsmanship and for the substitution of inferior work: the illuminated manuscripts, which survive for the years 900–1066, are nearly ten times as many as those of the period 1066–1140, and none of the Norman manuscripts can, in the opinion of experts, compare in beauty with their Anglo-Saxon predecessors; the Norman coinage shows a very marked decline in skill and did not recover the level reached under Edward the Confessor until the first Angevin ascended the throne. In literature English poetry is lost to sight, and English prose, though it held its own manfully until the turn of the century, even in the official documents issued by the central government, and continued to be used for the Peterborough version of the Anglo-Saxon Chronicle until 1154, became of little more than antiquarian interest to most scholars when the civilization of France came to dominate the world of letters in the twelfth century. The English language obviously did not disappear. But it is plain that the Norman Conquest compelled England to fall into line with the

Continent and use Latin for the purposes of administration and law, whilst French became the vernacular for the upper and upper-middle classes. English remained the basic tongue of the great majority: the language of King Alfred and of Aelfric was degraded to be the speech of the illiterate and unlearned serfs; it drifted down to the status of a peasant patois. The inflexions and elaborate genders of a once developed language fell into disuse, and English was saved from a fatal impoverishment only by its resilience, its power of adopting and adapting from French whatever it needed in the way of syntax and vocabulary. The most permanent result of the impact of civilizations was, therefore, a change in the structure of the English language. Instead of Englishmen speaking a language not unlike modern Dutch, they came to have at their command that supple, graceful and ever-adaptable tongue which by Chaucer's time had firmly staked its claim to become even the language of society and was to produce the verse of Shakespeare and the prose of the Authorized Version of the Bible.

The suggestion is often made that, but for the Norman Conquest, architecture in England would have been poor and stunted. And the very phrase 'Norman architecture' implies that the Normans brought with them to England a new type of architecture peculiar to themselves. Modern expert opinion supports neither of these views. The Norman and Anglo-Saxon styles were local varieties of the widespread 'romanesque' architecture of the Continent, and there was nothing radically different between them: if England had known no Conquest, it would have yet produced architecture like that of the Rhineland. Nor is it clear that the Norman variety was at a higher stage of development, for early Norman buildings endeavoured to make up by crude massiveness for the ignorance of the principles governing the factors of stress and strain. And recent explorations have shown that the ground plan and dimensions of the Westminster Abbey of the Confessor's reign surpassed those of any contemporary church in Normandy. It is at least wise to remember that the Old English Age was marked by much architectural activity of distinction, and to propound the question whether the Norman Conquest opened a new, or simply continued an old, development.

IV. The Impact on Continental Relations

It is often asserted that the ties which connected England with Western Europe before 1066 were extremely tenuous, and that there was a danger that she would link her fortunes to the culturally backward Scandinavian north. For this view there is very little support. The whole series of migrations and conquests had shown that, far from being a barrier, the sea provided, when compared with the obstacles that travel by land had to overcome, an easy means of communication. As we have seen, the natural economic development that was already apparent was quite sufficient to ensure that the connexions with Western Europe were maintained, whilst her membership of the Church Universal guaranteed that England could not and would not remain uninfluenced by changes that took place within it. A closer connexion before the middle of the eleventh century might well have been calamitous, for Europe in general had little or nothing to offer her in the art of government, in social and legal development, in religious and cultural life, in advance of what she already had, and it was all to the good that she remained immune from the private warfare and anarchy, the flouting of law and legal process, and the excesses of ecclesiastical degradation which were rampant on the Continent. With the complete cessation of barbarian migrations into Western Europe in the eleventh century and a consequent revival of commercial and civilized life, it was inevitable that England should enter more and more fully into the religious and economic movements of Europe. The Norman Conquest, however, involved her in political developments as well and compelled her to become an intimate part of the European state system. It would be more accurate to say that the power which became of European account was not England— broadly speaking, England was not a European power until modern times—nor even Normandy, but the Anglo-Norman Empire and, after it, the Angevin Empire. It is altogether too provincial to regard these Empires as English dependencies just because their rulers were the kings of England. For they were both a congeries of states of which England was only one member, albeit the most important one, and it was as a member of these Empires that England participated in continental politics. Dreams of empire haunted the imaginations of all powerful medieval rulers, and the future kings of England were to prove no exception. Nor were they to be exceptional in finding imperialist projects expensive and illusory.

The continental problem of the future cannot be understood in all its implications without a previous knowledge, however summary, of the history of the monarchy in France and of the hindrances to its advance. Monarchy had been very much slower in establishing itself there than in England, simply because political feudalism had taken deeper root. Indeed, by 1066 monarchy in France was little more than the shadow of its former self: the processes of feudalism had deprived it of nearly all its lands so that its personal estates were little more than the district between Paris and Orleans, and these could not provide it with sufficient financial and military resources to enable it to enforce its will outside them. Future events for many centuries were to be conditioned by the great feudal fiefs which had made their appearance.

At one time it seemed likely that what is now called France would become the abode, not of one, but of two different civilizations, for the north and the south were, and still are, markedly distinct. Whereas north of the Loire was predominantly Germanic in its characteristics, dynamic and energetic but culturally backward, the country to the south exhibited the different ways of life and mentality of a 'Romance' (that is a 'Roman' or Latin) country, which enjoyed a warmer climate and became the cultured home of the troubadours and the best-known vernacular literature in France. Furthermore, the two parts had not the bond of a common language: their dialects of 'Romance', which was no longer Latin but not yet French, were so distinct that the north became known as the land of the 'langue d'oil' and the south of the 'langue d'oc' (Languedoc), 'oil' and 'oc' being the variant forms of what became, with the eventual predominance of the north, the modern 'oui'. Actually no such schism became permanent, nevertheless France split up into so many large feudal states that the socialist, Proudhon, could still speak in the nineteenth century of the 'thirty submerged nationalities' of France.

I. THE SOUTHERN FIEFS

The south had always aspired to independence, and its opportunity came with feudalism. That is partly the reason why many of the fiefs passed so readily and easily into the hands of the king of England. They included Poitou (taking its name from its capital town of Poitiers), Aquitaine (the district stretching east from Bordeaux, the term being the same as 'Guienne', itself simply an abridged dialect version of 'Aquitaine'), Gascony (the region between the Gironde and the Pyrenees where the strange Basque language was spoken), Toulouse, and Barcelona. Of these the first three had come together under the counts of Poitou, who were then accustomed to use Aquitaine as a comprehensive term for all their dominions. They had scarcely more than a nominal connexion with the Capetian royal house at Paris, and it was these lands which came to Henry II of England by marriage.

II. THE NORTHERN FIEFS

These included Normandy, where the Danish colonizers had with great rapidity become French and largely abandoned their own Scandinavian tongue; Brittany, where the Celtic settlers always kept their province something distinct from their neighbours' lands and continued the Celtic speech; Flanders, where the inhabitants spoke either the German dialect called Flemish or Romance; Champagne, which had little sense of unity and in time was united to Blois. Blois, though only a small fief on the middle Loire, had gained a disproportionate importance through the able rule of its lords: one of them, Stephen of Blois, played no small part in the first crusade and was the father of the English king Stephen; once it had acquired Champagne in the north-east, it had as it were a stranglehold upon the domain of the king of France. Maine lay like a buffer state between Normandy and Anjou: both had struggled hard to possess it, and it had been gained by William the Conqueror three years before his expedition to England, though it continued to be extremely restless under the Norman rule and remained a centre of Angevin intrigues. Anjou and Touraine did not make a very large fief territorially, but no rulers were more capable and more unscrupulous than its counts, and there was a long tradition of hostility between Angevins and Normans. Burgundy, the last great fief, had no natural or historical unity of any kind and was simply the creation of feudalism: only loyalty to a great reigning house was to keep it together until the middle of the fourteenth century.

Amidst the heterogeneity and independence of such feudal states it is little wonder that monarchy in France had well nigh disappeared from sight, and only their mutual rivalries saved it from extinction. The early Capetian kings from 987 onwards had done what they could to maintain the prestige of royalty inherited from the Carolingian past, especially by retaining a close connexion with the Church, which gave to them, and to them only, the divine unction at their coronation. But they were all apt to make the great mistake of concentrating their attention and frittering away what strength they had on outside matters before establishing their authority firmly within their own estates. Inside the Île de France were scores of brigand lords, who persistently and fiercely defied their feudal lord and royal sovereign, and, whilst the Capetians were asserting their claims to the homage of distant vassals, it remained a journey fraught with great peril to go from Paris to Orleans.

In such conditions Normandy had developed into an independent state, acknowledging only in the most formal way the position of the Capetian monarch. A fortunate concatenation of circumstances had placed the great wealth of the kingdom of England at the duchy's disposal. William the Conqueror could do no more than attempt to maintain his authority on a firm basis of consent in both England and Normandy. For almost immediately he was embroiled with all three powers which had been unwontedly at peace with him in the momentous year of 1066, and most of his later years had to be spent abroad repelling as far as possible their aggressions.

(i) *Flanders*

When Count Baldwin, his father-in-law, died in 1067, William was ill-advised enough to interfere in a consequent succession dispute on behalf of his nephew, and to send his old friend, William fitz Osbern, over to Flanders as guardian. In the course of the civil war fitz Osbern was himself slain, and the rival candidate won the day. Naturally enough, the alliance with the Conqueror was broken off and followed by a long period of bitter and dangerous hostility.

(ii) *France*

When Philip I came of age, his attitude was bound to be one of suspicion and fear of his reputed vassal, who now was his kingly equal and his superior in resources. He had many chances to build up a coalition against the Conqueror which might well have driven him out of France altogether, but he was not an ambitious man and such policy as he had was marred by recurrent fits of apathy. In 1076 he sent help to rebels in Brittany simply because William for his part had determined to assist its count to subdue them, and he compelled William to withdraw from the struggle. In 1078 he supported the rebellion of William's eldest son, Robert, who found it irksome that, having been made regent of Normandy and count of Maine, he was not given real responsibility and allowed to govern; Philip granted him the strong fortress of Gerberoy, where in 1079 a temporary reconciliation between father and son took place. In 1077 Philip resumed possession of the Vexin, a district which one of his predecessors had given to a duke of Normandy a generation earlier; for ten years William was in no position to retaliate, then he began a campaign against his French overlord, during which the burning of Mantes was the indirect cause of his own death.

(iii) *Anjou*

The dynastic feud had ended, and the Angevin rulers were once more free to give expression to their traditional policy of territorial expansion. An opportunity came during the disorders in the Norman county of Maine. This district had been annexed by William in 1063, but it had never been properly subdued, and in 1069 the local barons gathered to the support of one of the heirs of the old line of counts. This rising is given a peculiar interest because Le Mans, the capital, declared itself a 'commune', a city republic, which faintly anticipated the famous communes of the near future in North France and Flanders. Le Mans, however, was not strong enough to make good its claim and, on being overthrown, it made an appeal to Fulk of Anjou as the nominal overlord of Maine. There followed an expedition of Normans and English under William against Angevins and Bretons under Fulk. In the end a compromise was reached in 1081, whereby William retained Maine in his possession but promised to regard Fulk as his overlord. In such a relationship there lay many openings for the future renewal of hostilities, for it is evident that William never succeeded in subjugating Maine and was steadily losing influence to his Angevin rival.

The history of England would have followed a very different course if the eldest born of the Conqueror had succeeded him in his kingdom. However, the Norman monarchy, though it naturally upheld the principle of hereditary succession, paid no attention to any rigid principle of primogeniture: thus Rufus became king instead of Robert; Henry I by a *coup d'état* again excluded Robert;

Stephen of Blois, grandson of the Conqueror, ascended the throne in place of the husband of the late king's daughter. There was nothing materially different in this sequence from what had happened under the Anglo-Saxon monarchy: the succession was partly selective and dependent on a variety of circumstances, among which the wish of the preceding monarch and the safety of the kingdom were the most powerful. That a process of selection was a necessary protection against disruption in a continuous time of peril was readily recognized by the Conqueror who, far from endeavouring to keep his lands a unit, reverted to the Germanic practice of dividing his inheritance among all his children. Thus the feckless eldest son, Robert, had his hereditary rights in Normandy recognized, and it was the second son, William, who by the will of his father succeeded to his prize of war, England, whilst the third son, Henry, received his share in money. William II, therefore, was faced with the task of re-establishing the Anglo-Norman state. Robert's utter misgovernment of Normandy brought it not only to anarchy but to the verge of disruption: his brother, Henry, had purchased the district of the Cotentin, almost a third of Normandy itself, whilst Maine had been seized by Fulk of Anjou. Rufus determined to see if he could obtain a share of the province before it disappeared altogether, and made war in 1090. Out of the confused strife which followed between the three sons of the Conqueror—first Robert and Henry against William, then Robert and William against the luckless Henry—there emerged a peace by which Robert renounced his claims to the English throne, though his eventual succession rights were guaranteed, and William kept hold of the richest half of the duchy. In 1094 William was confronted with an alliance between Robert and Philip of France, but by this time Robert had grown tired of misgoverning Normandy and was eager to take part in the first crusade. Therefore in 1096 he pawned what was left of his duchy to William for 10,000 marks and left him in control there for the last four years of his reign. Thereafter William entered into schemes for the further extension of his power on the Continent by attacks upon the French Vexin and Maine, but his plans were too grandiose, too utterly beyond his means, to meet with more than partial success.

So far continental politics have shown no more than a desire to protect or re-acquire Norman territory. The problem of real interest is left to Henry I, for he had not only to conquer and safeguard the Anglo-Norman state but to devise ways and means of providing it with a framework, a common framework if possible, of government.

England had been committed willy-nilly to European politics. Her kings and her ruling classes had great continental interests, and therefore her people and her resources were long embroiled in the pursuit of their personal ambitions. The tradition of hostility, which was so mutually destructive to both France and England, had a further regrettable result. In some form or other the problem of the unification of the British Isles came to the forefront to demand attention, and probably no time was more suitable than the early Middle Ages for obtaining a permanent solution. Unfortunately, the obsession with the Continent meant that no wholehearted attempt was made to bring the island group into one organic whole, and events were to make this impossible later. As it was, William I made one reconnaissance in force into Wales in 1081, and William II a more ambitious expedition in 1097, but otherwise the conquest of Wales was left to the individual efforts of the Marcher earls, which saw North Wales first won and then lost again and South Wales permanently penetrated. The authority of the monarchy, however, was not thereby increased. Similarly in Scotland, slight advantage was taken of propitious circumstances. No opposition was offered by the Scottish king Malcolm Canmore to the Norman army, which marched as far north as Abernethy near Perth in 1072 and compelled him to expel Edgar the Atheling, whose sister he had married, and to promise a vague allegiance. Malcolm's raid across Northumberland as far as the Tyne in 1079 made it necessary to build Newcastle in defence, his second raid as far as Durham in 1091 was followed by a punitive expedition into the Lothians, which forced him to do homage to Rufus, and the following year by the incorporation of Cumberland and Westmorland, which had been part of the Scottish kings' dominions since 945, into the kingdom of England, the deliberate settlement of Englishmen in the Eden valley, and the fortification of Carlisle. Malcolm's last raid in 1093 resulted in his ambush and death at Alnwick, and eventually Scotland remained quiet under the rule of his son, Edgar, who stayed dependent for his throne on Norman support. Evidently the Norman kings were quite content to have the frontier fixed at the line of the Solway and reserved their main attention for the Continent.

So in conclusion it must be stressed that the coming of the Normans was not 'the beginning of English History'. The essential truth is contained in the words of Freeman, an historian who is disparaged too much by those who have not read his works but only the criticisms of them: 'William conquered neither to destroy nor to found but to continue.' To appreciate the full importance of what happened, we must look before as well as after 'the thin red line of the Conquest'. Only through a true interpretation of both the Anglo-Saxon and the Anglo-Norman ages can the influence of the Normans be faithfully traced. Much was taken over and preserved, yet there was not just a continuation of existing usages: English history would have been very different without the Normans. But if the final result had within it much that was new, the whole must be considered as 'a reorganization of existing usage' rather than as a completely fresh start, for the new developments, begun by a comparatively small body of alien adventurers amid perilous surroundings, would have been quite impossible save on the basis of past achievements, and contained more than the shadow and much of the substance of what was old. Estimates of the comparative contributions of Saxons and Normans to our modern civilization may well vary, but there can be no reasonable doubt that both contributed. The result at the end of the eleventh century was neither Anglo-Saxon nor Norman: it was Anglo-Norman. The interaction and complex blending of two different systems of government, two different structures of society, two different types of culture, had remodelled them all and produced a distinctive version. In what way it was distinctive is left for the remarkable twelfth century to disclose.

SELECT READING

Stenton, 546–52, 588–678; Stephenson and Marcham, 33–46; W. J. Corbett, 'Development of the Duchy of Normandy and the Norman Conquest of England' in *C. Med. H.*, v (1926), 481–520; Pollock and Maitland, i. chs. iii, iv; C. H. Haskins, *Norman Institutions* (1918), 3–61; F. M. Stenton, *First Century of English Feudalism* (1932), 1–40, 114–89; G. B. Adams, *Council and Courts in Anglo-Norman England* (1926), xi–xxxv, 1–98; J. Goebel, *Felony and Misdemeanour* (1937), 336–440; F. M. Stenton, 'The Scandinavian Colonies in England and Normandy' in *T.R.H.S.*, 4th Series, xxvii (1945), 1–12; Stenton, 'English Families and the Norman Conquest' in *T.R.H.S.*, 4th Series, xxvi (1944), 1–12; J. H. Round, 'Introduction of Knight Service into England' in *Feudal*

England (1895), 225–314; J. Tait, 'Map of England and Wales in 1086' in *Historical Atlas of Modern Europe* (1896–1900: ed. R. L. Poole).
Lipson, i (1937), 32–87; J Tait, *Medieval English Borough* (1936), 139–93, 339–58; C. Stephenson, *Borough and Town* (1933), 73–119; L. C. Lathom, *The Manor* (Historical Association Pamphlets, no. 8: 1931); E. A. Kosminsky, 'The Hundred Rolls as a Source of English Agrarian History' in *Econ. H. R.*, iii (1931), 16–44; H. C. Darby, 'The Economic Geography of England, 1000–1250' in *Historical Geography of England* (1936: ed. H. C. Darby), 165–229.
Brooke, 1–146; A. J. Macdonald, *Lanfranc* (1926); D. Knowles, *Monastic Order in England* (1940), 100–145.

CHAPTER XVIII

THE SOURCES OF HISTORY IN THE TWELFTH AND THIRTEENTH CENTURIES

BEFORE the close of this period the sources at the disposal of the historian are so numerous and so rich that often he can do no more than sample them: indeed, some have remained to this day practically untouched because few scholars are in a position to give the years of study required for their adequate examination. Thus, whilst the chroniclers and annalists provide a continuous narrative which reaches its most minute detail with Matthew Paris, the government itself has begun to make and keep a record of its routine activities in finance, administration and law, and is supplying dispassionate, objective and authenticated information. It is evident, therefore, that here we can do little more than direct attention to the main original authorities. We may be permitted one generalization. Many of the chroniclers can tell us little from personal knowledge, and their comments on contemporary affairs are often uninforming or wearisomely jejune. In fact, minor monastic chronicles, of which many survive from the thirteenth century onwards, so seldom contain matters of historical value that they have been left unprinted. By and large, the evidence of records is far superior to the chroniclers' accounts, and these are valuable in inverse proportion to the survival of records.

Literary Evidence

I. THE CHRONICLES

Though the Anglo-Saxon Chronicle was continued in English at Peterborough Abbey and gives some inkling of the point of view of the conquered until 1154, the writing of history was otherwise left after the Conquest to the Normans or those who, like Eadmer of purely Saxon origins or Ordericus Vitalis of mixed parentage, had identified themselves closely with the interests of the Normans. The study of the chronicles will cause much mental confusion unless it is carefully remembered that the writers, with scarcely an exception, felt it incumbent upon themselves to begin right from the beginning with the Birth of Christ or even the

Creation of the World. In consequence, they reproduced time and time again what had already been written, and they should not be loosely quoted as though their own statements, relating even to events in the recent past, possessed any independent historical value. It is only when they deal with contemporary or almost contemporary events and part company with their predecessors that they constitute themselves original authorities, and it is only with this part of their work that we should in general associate them, though they may incorporate earlier work that is otherwise unknown. To give one illustration: Florence of Worcester went back to the Creation, using for that purpose the general chronicle of Marianus Scotus which ends in 1082, and incorporating extracts from Bede, Asser and from at least one version of the Anglo-Saxon Chronicle that has not survived, to provide the account of English history; but it is not until after 1082, or more probably 1103, that his work has any claim—and the claim is dubious—to independent authority up to 1117. Simeon of Durham, who died about 1129, relied upon Florence as one of his sources from 887 onwards, and only for the years 1119–29 does he write at first-hand: he, however, used some northern annals no longer extant. Henry of Huntingdon, who died some time after 1157, similarly adopted earlier sources for his popular 'History of England' and became original only between 1129 and 1154.

Our knowledge of the Norman Conquest of England owes much to William of Jumièges, an obscure Norman monk, who noted the main events of the early years; to Ordericus Vitalis, a Shropshire man, who became a monk at St. Évroul in Normandy, and somewhere between 1123 and 1141 wrote a valuable account of the general history of both England and Normandy under the Norman dynasty; and to Eadmer, a monk of Canterbury who died after 1124, whose 'History' made Lanfranc and, more particularly, Anselm the centre of its discussion and gives us in a carefully considered and orderly arrangement the best detailed history of the Investiture Contest under Rufus and Henry I that we possess.

But William of Malmesbury, the son of a French knight and an English mother, who died about 1143, towers above his contemporaries so much that he is the first one to rival Bede in the quality of his historical thinking. For he conceived it to be his business, not simply to register facts, but also to explain them by stressing the connexion between cause and effect. To him history was more than a chronological summary of events, it approached the old classical definition of 'philosophy teaching by examples'. And though he had his prejudices, such as his bias against Stephen, his judgments were bridled with common sense, and his Latin style was worthy of the literary traditions of the old monastery of Aldhelm. Therefore, the last part of his 'History of the Kings of England' and his 'Modern History' constitute an indispensable survey of the first forty years of the twelfth century.

The writing of history languished during the anarchy under Stephen and in those early years of Henry II's reign which were fully occupied with the task of exorcising the spirit of disorder. Save for the Anglo-Saxon Chronicle and the facts supplied by Henry of Huntingdon and unfortunately embellished as a result of his literary pretensions, we are dependent on an anonymous 'History of Stephen', which champions the cause of that king without becoming too partisan.

So far, with the exception of Archdeacon Henry of Huntingdon who wrote at his bishop's instigation, it is the monastic chroniclers who have dominated the scene. And to some extent that remains true for the rest of the twelfth century. For William of Newburgh, an Augustinian canon who seems never to have gone beyond his native Yorkshire, wrote about 1198 the 'English History' which has earned him the description of the 'father of historical criticism'. Whilst relying in the normal manner upon earlier writers, he made selections of the important facts, cast them into a new arrangement, and used them critically to produce, not so much a chronicle, as a reasoned explanation of all phases of development in England during the twelfth century. Thus he was almost unique in his scathing repudiation of the myths and marvels with which Geoffrey of Monmouth had surrounded the ancient British kings and which were accepted as truth by his contemporaries. When he came to his own time, William could not hope to obtain information within the walls of his own Newburgh priory, which was a recent foundation and no social centre likely to attract distinguished visitors. But he was fortunately in close touch with a group of well-known Cistercian monasteries like Rievaulx and Byland, and it was, in fact, at the suggestion of the abbot of Rievaulx that he began his work.

Nevertheless, the chronicles of the late twelfth century were not solely the product of the monastic scriptorium. The administration of the Angevin kings depended in large measure upon the supply of educated and competent men from the Church, and such received their reward by appointment to high ecclesiastical office. From their ranks came a new type of historiographer, men who had served the king at home and abroad, witnessed and even participated in the events they described, and had official orders and diplomatic correspondence passing through their hands or easily available. Cosmopolitan in their outlook, under the influence of the intellectual renaissance of the time and of the continental provinces of the Angevin Empire, they reflected in the orderliness of their compositions the new spirit which animated the government they served. The 'Deeds of Henry II and Richard', attributed erroneously to Abbot Benedict of Peterborough for whom a transcript was written before 1193, is by an unknown author and forms the most important single account of that king's reign, especially after 1172. The presence of many documents, inserted in the narrative, may lead us to surmise that it came from the pen of a one-time clerical servant of the Crown. Whether this guess is imprudent or not, it is certain that Roger of Howden, whose 'Chronicle' is closely related to the 'Deeds of Henry II and Richard', strictly contemporary for the years 1192–1201, and fortified by unique transcripts of public records, was a royal clerk, a royal justice, and a colleague of the statesmen he discusses. And Ralph de Diceto, though he was apparently not used by the king as a civil servant, had lived at the heart of affairs as archdeacon of Middlesex and dean of St. Paul's, and was the close and trusted friend of the royal ministers; he also included important documents in his 'Outlines of History', in which he impartially surveys events from 1172, and especially 1188, until his death shortly after 1202.

It is curious that the thirteenth century saw no more of such secular clerks and royal officials, turned historiographers, and that, at the time when monasticism had begun its period of decline, the responsibility for narrative histories should have returned almost entirely to the lot of the monks to fulfil. There are exceptions, of course, like the 'History' of the 'minstrel' of Béthune, which is particularly valuable for John's reign, or the long 'History of William the Marshal', written in England shortly after the death of the great earl Marshal, which illumines for us the ideals of feudalized society before its imminent disruption, or the 'Chronicles of the Mayors and Sheriffs of London', compiled by Arnold fitz Thedmar, alderman of London, who stood alone in championing the cause of the king during the Barons' War. It was neither the Reformed Orders nor the new Mendicant Orders that undertook the work, though the first gives us the 'English Chronicle' of Abbot Ralph of Coggeshall, a Cistercian House not far from the great abbey of Bury St. Edmunds, who speaks with particular knowledge of the years 1187–1223, and the second provides the precious account by Friar Thomas of Eccleston 'Of the Coming of the Friars Minor to England'. The glory remains with the old Benedictine monasteries of pre-Conquest days. In some form or other, most of them, like Ramsey, Abingdon and Bury St. Edmunds, had long compiled their 'Annals' of private and local interest: the 'Chronicle' of Jocelin de Brakelond deserves special mention because it supplies a vivid and detailed picture of monastic life in the twelfth century at Bury St. Edmunds with its daily routine, internal economy and petty squabbles. And in the thirteenth century such monastic works are of particular value, for the 'Annals' of Dunstable, of Osney and Waverley have general history interwoven with them, and the 'Annals' of Burton contain an important collection of documents concerning the baronial programme of reform in and after 1258, including what was once thought to be the only text of the famous 'Provisions of Oxford'. The incomparable achievement, however, was the 'St. Albans Chronicle'.

It has long been debated whether this wealthy Benedictine abbey had an official historiographer in the twelfth century, whose work formed the basis on which the great thirteenth-century historians built. The latest authoritative pronouncement dismisses such a suggestion outright as a myth for which there is not a shred of evidence, and regards Roger of Wendover as the founder of that 'Chronicle' which in its final form was to extend from the Creation to the mid-fifteenth century. His 'Flowers of History' were culled from the writings of others until the opening years of John's reign, when he could no longer make use of Howden and Diceto. Then for thirty-five years he was forced into independence, and he set the tone of the 'Chronicle'. Thus, presumably writing some years after John's death, he accepted the growing legend of that king's diabolical character and presented it in his convincingly quiet style as sober history. We should not forget, however, that he must often have seen John at St. Albans. However, his successor, Matthew Paris, exercised his youthful literary ambitions in making the picture more dramatic. It followed as a corollary that Wendover should express the case for the barons, and again Paris fell into line and vigorously reiterated the theme of limited monarchy.

When Wendover's work finished in 1235, Paris remained as head of the scriptorium for a quarter of a century to reveal himself as the greatest of all medieval chroniclers. With his absorbing interest in humanity and all its concerns, he had ample opportunity to hear the news of the world at St. Albans, situated as it was just twenty miles from London on the Great North Road, and he set it down in graphic prose and lively style, irrespective of whether it was idle gossip about inconsequential trifles or first-hand information about critical events. Though a monk, he moved outside St. Albans, being on friendly terms with the king himself and knowing well the chief ministers and servants of the Crown, who were in a position to provide him with the historical documents he needed for his work. The personality of this 'hard hitter and good hater', with his extravagant prejudices against Scots and Jews and new-fangled ideas in religion and with his habit of grumbling and of being against the government, stands out from his pages the whole time. What he wrote he frequently rewrote in altered form and different language. The variant manuscripts have caused much confusion, both about his own contributions to the 'St. Albans Chronicle' and the 'St. Albans Chronicle' itself, and it is only recently that the position has been clarified. Paris was responsible for the 'Greater Chronicle' which incorporated, and in the process touched up, Wendover and continued his work (the *Liber Additamentorum* is his collection of papal bulls, royal writs and other official documents used in the writing of this chronicle); the 'English History', 1066–1253, which is an abridged version of the 'Greater Chronicle' with many of its highly coloured statements toned down by later reflexion ; the 'Flowers of History', which reproduces the 'Greater Chronicle' from the Creation to 1066 and thereafter gives a further altered version of the later portion of it; the 'History of the Abbots of St. Albans' up to 1255. When his occasional writings, such as his 'Life of Langton', are taken also into account, his patience and industry command the highest respect. If we are to single out the peculiar merit of Matthew Paris, it must be in the fact that for the first time we hear the voice of public opinion, mistaken or otherwise, on the great questions of the day.

II. BIOGRAPHIES, LETTERS AND SERMONS

We can do no more than refer to these categories of documents, on which so much critical work remains to be done. For example, we have the 'Lives' of Anselm by Eadmer, of Bishop Wulfstan of Worcester by the monk, Coleman, who wrote in Anglo-Saxon and had his work, now lost, faithfully reproduced in Latin by William of Malmesbury; of Thomas Becket by ten different authors within a few years of his murder, including John of Salisbury; of Bishop Hugh of Lincoln by Abbot Adam of Eynsham; of Langton by Matthew Paris. There is the correspondence, sometimes existing in a contemporary collected form but usually to be looked for in scattered places, of archbishops Lanfranc, Anselm, Theobald and Becket; of Bishop Foliot in the twelfth century and Bishop Grosseteste in the thirteenth; of philosophers and theologians, like John of Salisbury, Peter of Blois and the great Franciscan, Adam Marsh. There is homiletical literature, like the 'Sermons' of Ailred of Rievaulx, Stephen Langton and Robert Grosseteste.

III. THE 'DIALOGUE OF THE EXCHEQUER'

The author was Richard fitz Neal, the great-nephew of the famous minister, Bishop Roger of Salisbury, who was himself eventually bishop of London, and treasurer for some forty years until 1196. Liberally educated, as we should expect in the case of one who lived in the intellectual ferment of the late twelfth century, he was first and foremost the civil servant, and the 'Dialogue' forms his lasting monument. Written in the late 1170's and imperfectly revised some ten years later, it is cast in the form of a day's conversation between a senior officer of the exchequer and a junior seeking instruction, and it purports to describe the organization of the exchequer (the personnel and their various duties, the rolls and writs, the chessboard and counters, the tallies and scales) and its procedure (the sources of the royal revenue, the collection of the royal debts, the method of rendering accounts, the treatment of debtors). It is little wonder that such a treatise, composed so early in the history of the exchequer, should hold a unique place in the history of West European financial administrations.

IV. THE LAW TREATISES

Attempts had been made in the reign of Henry I to discover and state intelligibly the law of England, and even to make it conform to some kind of rational treatment: the Liber Quadripartitus translated the Anglo-Saxon laws into Latin; the 'Laws of Edward the

Confessor' provided another but less reliable Latin version and stressed the position of the Church, and this combination of patriotism and religious zeal helped to give this law-book a popularity which caused it to be still considered worth revising in the reign of Richard or John; the *Leges Henrici*, written about 1118 by a royal official, is the fullest expression of contemporary rules of law, and the author had clearly in mind the desirability of relating them to what he knew of continental practices. It was a brave but entirely unsuccessful effort, for the law still spelt something different in Wessex, in Mercia and in the Danelaw, tribal custom was intermingled with feudal custom so that the ordeal and compurgation existed alongside trial by battle, and the legal vocabulary was a hotch-potch of Anglo-Saxon and Norman terms. The growth and expansion of royal justice certainly made some rules general in their application and thereby cut a path through the legal confusion. But it was the overwhelming passion for the study of Roman law, which possessed all countries of Western Europe in the twelfth century, that was mainly responsible for producing a coherent and reasoned system of law. Before the close of the twelfth century the 'Treatise on the Laws and Customs of England' provided the first systematic exposition of the law of England as it was administered in the royal courts. It goes under the name of 'Glanville', the Justiciar of the last years of Henry II's reign, but it is doubtful whether it should be attributed to him, and a case has been made for the authorship of his kinsman, Hubert Walter. The question is one of academic interest only. What is important is that someone, versed in civil and canon law, has used his knowledge of general legal principles to write a book, which has as its preface an adaptation of the preface to the *Institutes* of Justinian though its substance is a clear and precise commentary on the English king's writs. Valuable as it was, it was dwarfed by Bracton's 'Laws and Customs of England', incomparably the most important of the law-books of medieval England. Bracton (*c.* 1210–68) entered the royal service in 1239 as a king's clerk, acted as a justice in eyre, and later became a justice of the king's bench, but he had previously received an academic training, probably in the law-schools at Oxford. For, despite his occasional blunders, it is evident that he had studied the *Institutes* carefully and had a more general acquaintance with the rest of the *Corpus Iuris Civilis*. He continued to consult the current text-books on Roman law while in the king's service and while writing his treatise. He was, in consequence, well prepared to let the 'gladsome light of Roman jurisprudence' shine upon and through the laws of England, and we must not underestimate the influence of Roman law upon his work, for it was not slight. Nevertheless, it was not a book of Roman law but of English law that he wrote. He had his 'Note Book' by him, in which were copied some two thousand cases extracted from the plea rolls, and it was on the basis of judicial decisions—decisions that he himself considered good without any thought that they should be regarded as binding on the future in the modern meaning of 'case law'—that he wrote his treatise round about 1256. The legal rationalism, learned from Rome, and equally the pioneer work of Glanville assisted him to make out of these isolated decisions a logical, defined and unified body of law. Theory worked hand in hand with practice to give us 'the crown and flower of English medieval jurisprudence'.

Record Evidence

Although we should not lose sight of the ecclesiastical records (such as the cartularies, which reach back almost to the Norman Conquest, and the episcopal registers, which survive from the early thirteenth century), or the manorial account rolls and court rolls or the borough records (which all begin in a thin stream in the thirteenth century), yet we would do well to consider principally the development of the 'records', using that term to denote documents prepared under government authority and kept continuously in government custody. In discovering why they were made at all, we shall go a fair distance towards understanding the manner in which the government functioned and the part played by the civil service in operating it.

I. DOMESDAY BOOK

It is probable that the motive of acquisitiveness was responsible for the compilation of such detailed financial statistics: as a contemporary chronicler expressed it, 'the king loved scheming to get gold and silver'. As soon as William discovered that he had inherited the right to a land tax, originating with the old Danegeld, he levied it immediately after his coronation, again the following year, and very heavily in 1084, to the undoing and depression of many of the peasantry. But he was evidently not satisfied with the result, and at Christmas 1085 a plan for an elaborate survey of the whole kingdom was discussed and sanctioned at Gloucester. The English counties were divided into apparently nine groups, and each group was visited by a set of royal commissioners who pursued their investigations at meetings of the shire courts. Each hundred, possibly each village, made its own individual replies to the questions laid before it, and the truth of their statements was vouched for by a jury composed half of Englishmen and half of Normans. Much discussion has taken place regarding the form in which the information was committed to writing, but there seems no question (a) that it was first arranged under hundreds or wapentakes and (b) that more information was supplied than it was thought necessary to include within the final digest. Domesday Book certainly does not simply copy the information as it was rendered by the commissioners. Instead, it rearranges the material, with many omissions and not without repetitions, inconsistencies, and superfluities. The final classification is under the principal classes of landholders, apparently because it was the tenants-in-chief who were expected to stand good for the geld: for each county there is given successively the estates of the king, of the ecclesiastical and the lay tenants-in-chief, of women, of English thegns, and of others of lesser importance. Domesday Book, so called since the twelfth century because from its verdict there could be no appeal, is in two volumes. The second is concerned only with the three eastern counties of Norfolk, Suffolk and Essex, and it is so much more detailed than its companion volume that it has been suggested that it was written first and on a scale that was found impossible to maintain for all the other counties. The first volume, therefore, covers all the rest of England, save for the four northernmost counties. Apart from minor omissions, there are some important ones: most unfortunately, we have no survey of London, Winchester or Bristol. It seems impossible to offer any other explanation than that Domesday Book was never finished.

The Domesday Returns were primarily financial documents which could serve a double purpose. (a) They informed the king of his present fiscal rights by disclosing the local distribution of the land tax. It was, however, evident that many of the old assessments were too low, therefore (b) the 'returns' went further to reveal also the full financial resources of the country. Each township was compelled to yield particulars of its arable, woodland and pasture, its plough-teams and its mills, the number of its cultivators who stood responsible for rents and services, and the names of its owners in the time of Edward the Confessor and again in 1086. Thus the real annual value of all land, whether it owed anything to the king or not, was ascertained. Domesday Book, therefore, was more than a geld-book, more than a book of rates: it was a valuation list, intended to be used to revise assessments, though there is no evidence that it was ever so used.

Whatever its intention, Domesday Book is an inexhaustible quarry of information about matters of other than financial interest. Its indispensability to the ecclesiastical and economic historian, to the topographer and the genealogist, is obvious: indeed, the history of the great families, their descent and their inter-marriage, seems likely to form a new approach to the study of the Norman age and for that work Domesday Book is essential. We must also note that it reflects quasi-judicial investigations in that the royal commissioners were at times puzzled by disputes over land, which were the inevitable sequel to the drastic changes in ownership produced by a violent conquest. That they could settle title, however, is a matter that is far from proved. It is, in the main, for its illumination of the structure of society in England that Domesday Book is most highly prized. For the most difficult task of the medieval historian is to find out what is happening in the countryside among humble folk, to learn about changes which will very rarely be set down in monastic chronicles or official documents. The historian of eleventh-century England is happy to possess a record unique in Europe: it will not save him from the perils of speculation but it does make that speculation possible. And he is fortunate to be able often to test his tentative deductions by reference to those 'satellite surveys'—the 'Exeter Domesday', the 'Ely Inquest', and the 'Cambridge Inquest'—which incorporate many of the original 'returns' more faithfully and completely than Domesday Book itself.

It is well to remember that the Norman clerks were aliens, describing in an alien language what was to them an alien society: we should not be greatly surprised if we are puzzled to understand what they were puzzled to understand themselves. Moreover, the Domesday Inquests were not planned as a feudal or social survey but as a review of financial arrangements. Therefore the people of England were regarded from an economic point of view and, in the process, social distinctions, as, for example, among the numerous class of ceorls, were ignored. When that has been said, we are, nevertheless, presented with the statistics of two periods, separated by twenty years, which exhibit a dynamic and not merely a static social order. The conditions of the old English society are described on the very eve of the Norman Conquest; the re-arrangement of that society in its higher ranks on a feudal basis shows exactly how Norman changes have worked out in practice. For that reason Domesday Book remains pre-eminent among the embarrassment of riches stored in English archives.

II. THE ROLLS OF EXCHEQUER AND CHANCERY

The magnificent series of enrolments, going back for the most part to the late twelfth century, did not owe their origin to any idea that it was the duty of the State to protect the interests of the subject by placing on permanent record the privileges and favours he had gained or the law-suits he had won. The ends to be served were those of the king and of his professional servants, and financial profit, probably not unmixed with higher motives, underlay them all. The story is a complicated one and can be only barely outlined, but it gives a meaning and significance to what would otherwise be a dreary recital of the contents of the public archives.

Let us begin with the royal interests. The king was concerned both with what was paid to him and with what he had to pay to others, and each of these two simple considerations was responsible for a group of related records. (i) *Payments to the king*. The financial activities of the exchequer produced the 'Receipt Rolls' and the 'Pipe Rolls'. The first record all sums paid into the exchequer; they are alluded to in the 'Dialogue of the Exchequer', and some fragments survive from the twelfth century, while they are extant as a series from 1219–20. On the 'Pipe Rolls' were entered the audited accounts of the sheriffs and other debtors: the earliest to survive belongs to the year 1130 and there is an almost unbroken series of them after 1156 for nearly seven hundred years. The 'Plea Rolls', as we have them, do not go further back than the reign of Richard: however, in the exchequer the word 'plea' was used to denote a pecuniary penalty, and there is good reason to believe that the 'Eyre Rolls' began, not in 1195–6, but in 1166 when there was a reorganization of judicial circuits, and that the justices were required to have them written for return to the exchequer so that it could hold the sheriffs to account for the fines and amercements it was their business to collect; similarly, the 'Common Bench Rolls', which give us their earliest example in 1194, were certainly being compiled long before the close of Henry II's reign; the 'King's Bench Rolls' appear in 1200 as soon as a court of justices is seen regularly attendant on the king in person. The 'Fine Rolls' were made in the chancery, not merely from the opening year of John's reign but in 1194–5, and possibly twenty years before that: they recorded, among other things, the promises of payment for favours granted. Therefore, since it was essential that the chancery should let the exchequer know about these debts, it made periodical transcripts of all items of financial interest, what were called the 'Originalia Rolls', of which the earliest surviving fragment comes from 1195–6, and sent them to the exchequer where the information was transferred to the pipe roll. If at any time a problem arose over the collection of debts which needed to be referred to the barons of the exchequer, then a note of the point and the conclusion reached was made upon the 'Memoranda Rolls', which are extant as a series from 1199 but were certainly being made in 1196, and probably even before Richard I's accession. (ii) *Payments by the king.* When the king granted land or made a grant of money outright or indirectly by an allowance against an outstanding debt, the chancery copied the writs (*brevia*) it issued and sent transcripts (*contra-brevia*) to the exchequer for its information. By 1200–1 the chancery was evidently enrolling such writs, 'closed' and sealed and addressed to the individuals concerned, on the 'Close Rolls'. The 'contra-brevia' are mentioned in the 'Dialogue of the Exchequer', and it is a reasonable surmise that, just as the fine rolls enrolled debts to the king from the later part of Henry II's reign, so the close rolls were soon afterwards in existence to enrol debts incurred by the king. The close rolls came to be increasingly used to record other matters as well, until the point was reached when it was found advisable in 1226 to place the 'writs close' for exchequer attention on the separate 'Liberate Rolls'. The 'Issue Rolls' of the exchequer, surviving from 1219–20, include the actual payments made in correspondence with the 'Liberate Rolls' of the chancery.

Turning to the financial interests of the royal ministers and clerks, we have to bear in mind the 'constitution' or charter, granted by John in 1199, whereby he abolished the extortionate sealing fees, charged by his brother, for charters and letters patent—that is letters left open with the seal pendant—and fixed the rates as they were to remain for a very long time. The fees for sealing were, of course, quite distinct from, and additional to, the 'fines' paid to the king for his concessions. These two types of documents represented privileges of some kind given to private persons, and the fees paid for them were a chancery perquisite, being distributed among the chancellor, the senior clerks, and the spigurnels or sealers. It was obvious that some kind of note would have to be taken of the grantee, the instrument he obtained, and the amount of the fee required from him. Reliable summarization was (and always is) beyond the capabilities of hack clerks, and it was an actual economy of time to let them copy the document in full. So it happily became usual to enrol the instrument as it stood: not in the interests of the grantee, who otherwise would have been asked to pay for enrolment also, but of the chancery staff. The 'Charter Rolls', surviving from 1199, thus constituted a fee-book and, to begin with, carried both charters and letters patent, but the great increase in the number of the letters soon resulted in the separate series of the 'Patent Rolls'.

The chancery, therefore, was not looked upon in the late twelfth and the early thirteenth centuries as a repository of public documents or a register office, and such a conception was slow to be realized. Still, the great reforming work of Henry II had led to a tremendous increase in litigation, and it was often both advantageous and convenient for private individuals to have their rights and privileges officially recorded on documents in the custody of the king's officers. Thus, the 'Cartae Antiquae' represent the enrolment in the exchequer, at the instance of private persons or churches, of charters issued in their favour, which made it unnecessary to produce the originals for inspection; the pipe rolls were likewise used for entries of purely private interest, such as court judgments; the 'Rolls of the Great Assize' contain particulars recorded in the chancery, of 'writs of peace', which enabled an action to be tried by jury instead of by battle in conformity with the grand assize, instituted in or before 1179. These three instances are all to be found in Henry II's reign and are all, it will be observed, concerned with actual or possible litigation, and in these cases the concession of recording was dependent on the payment of a suitable fee. It is to be expected that the plea rolls from Richard I's reign onwards should contain the record of private agreements and be called in evidence in later disputes. Nor is it surprising that in 1195 it was arranged that 'final concords', that is conveyances of property, should be made in triplicate, and the third copies, the 'Feet of Fines', as they were called, deposited in the treasury at Westminster.

The exchequer was, to begin with, the place where private persons had their deeds recorded because the exchequer was the seat of the justiciar's court and the centre of his activities in general, while the king's court was ambulatory and more often than not was abroad. In the later twelfth century the justiciar issued the great mass of writs required for litigation and not the chancery attached to the king. A great change resulted from the loss of Normandy. It became exceptional for the king to leave England, the justiciarship became superfluous and was suppressed in 1234, while writs were issued from a single chancery, that attached to the king. Gradually the chancery took the place of the exchequer as the department where private deeds were enrolled, the close roll being selected for this purpose.

SELECT READING

G. B. Adams, *Political History of England, 1066–1215* (1905), 448–56; *Cambridge History of English Literature*, i (1909), 156–82; R. M. Wilson, *Early Middle English Literature* (1939), 3–127; D. C. Douglas, 'The Domesday Survey' in *History*, xxi (1936), 249–57; V. H. Galbraith 'The Making of Domesday Book' in *E.H.R.*, lvii (1942), 161–77; V. H. Galbraith, *Roger Wendover and Matthew Paris* (1944); A. L. Smith, *Church and State in the Middle Ages* (1913), 167–79; C. Jenkins, *The Monastic Chronicler and the Early School of St. Albans* (1922), 1–90; T. F. Tout, *Chapters in Medieval Administrative History*, i (1920), 33–50; V. H. Galbraith, *The Public Records* (1934), 20–52; H. G. Richardson, *Memoranda Roll, I John* (Pipe Roll Society Publications: 1943), xi–lix.

CHAPTER XIX

ADMINISTRATION UNDER THE NORMAN MONARCHY

THOUGH it is subject, like all generalizations, to qualifications, it is substantially true to say that the English constitution, as it came slowly into shape during the remainder of the Middle Ages, was the product of three forces, represented by the king, the feudal overlords, and the subject people with their ineradicable traditions and way of life, implicit in what was comprehensively termed the 'custom of the realm'. Through their interplay and through their influence upon one another the future was to be decided. If monarchy were strong, then, as in the past, it was in a position to provide the prime impulse, and, fortunately, the first two Norman rulers had put it on a firm basis. It was left to their successors to face the problem whether they could translate their large but ill-defined power into the form of institutions and thereby give it a recognized and legalistic framework.

Henry I's first and imperative task, however, was to set the precarious crown firmly on his head, for his hold upon it was threatened from two directions. (i) His title to the throne was weak, for it was indisputably inferior to that of Duke Robert of Normandy. It was not so much that Robert was his elder brother the laws of succession were far, as yet, from being rigidly fixed, and Robert had already been passed over by his own father in favour of a younger brother. But Henry had himself once sworn an oath of fealty to Robert and acknowledged him as his liege lord: the sin of perjury would be all the more heinous if it were committed when Robert was not yet returned from fighting for the Cross in Palestine and whilst his affairs in the West lay under the special protection of the Church. What Henry thought of the legality of his claims was plainly shown in his actions after his brother's assassination: if Harold is to be indicted for indecent haste, for a 'managed' election, and for coronation by suspect hands, the same charges must be levelled against Henry. For within the first few hours, and in the face of outspoken remonstrance, he laid rough hold upon the treasure-hoard at Winchester; the approbation of an extremely small group of barons served the purpose of formal election; by the third day he was crowned by the bishop of London, though never before had *both* archbishops of the Church

been thus ignored. (ii) Henry was confronted by a Norman aristocracy which found its co-operation with the monarchy irksome.
Its irritation had been caused by the fiscal oppression of William
Rufus and his minister, Ranulf Flambard, for they had viewed the
position of king as one that lent itself to unlimited profit-making,
and they had increased the amounts and the occasions of 'feudal
incidents' beyond precedent and without mercy. Nevertheless, it
is misleading to speak as though the barons as a whole were on the
point of rebellion. They well recognized that their security hinged
upon that of the king, and only a small section of them saw advantage to themselves in the overthrow of law and order. And if
a choice was to be made, there could be no doubt where their
preference lay: Robert they hardly knew, and what they heard of
him could hardly arouse more than contempt; Henry had lived
among them for the last half-dozen years and was in main essentials the antithesis of his brother in his passion for orderliness, his
patience and his industry.

Henry sought at once to allay discontent and gather support
from all classes by imprisoning Flambard in the Tower and inviting
Anselm to return to England as an indication that he would dissociate himself from the practices of the previous reign. His very
necessary policy of conciliation was emphasized further by two
well-conceived acts.

I. THE PUBLICATION OF THE SO-CALLED 'CORONATION CHARTER'

Constitutional historians have read too much into this document.
It is said that it represents the first clear acknowledgment of the
contractual nature of kingship, whereby the monarchy deliberately
defined its position with regard to the feudal barons. This argument has it that William I's rule, though harsh, had not been
capricious: he had always respected the contract that was implicit
in feudalism and, provided his authority was unquestioned, he had
acted with a proper sense of his responsibilities. On the other
hand, William II had used the vague and ill-defined feudal contract
as an instrument for excessive private profit. Thus he was inclined
to regard the fiefs as life tenancies rather than hereditary estates,
and on that ground to demand from the heirs a sum which approxi-
mated more to the capital value than to a reasonable relief; he
extended his rights of marriage to the widow as well as to the
heiress; he left bishoprics and abbacies vacant so that his right of

'primer seisin' could continue indefinitely. To his resentful vassals this was a distortion of feudalism to the verge of tyranny. Therefore Henry I was at pains to declare his belief that, if he flouted and distorted the feudal contract as his brother had done, such misconduct must bring monarchy into discredit and cause it to be destroyed as an institution which could not keep faith. For that reason he renewed the contract straightway in 1100 and openly stigmatized his brother's acts as a violation of it, and assured the barons that henceforward he would observe it in a just and lawful manner: thus, heirs to fiefs were no longer to 'buy back' their inheritances but to pay for them only an equitable relief; marriage rights were not to be exercised over widows; until an appointment had been made to a vacant church, nothing was to be taken from its ecclesiastical estates. So Henry acknowledged that there were some things the king could not do and, by formally recognizing restraints, made a notable contribution to the genesis of limited monarchy.

However attractive this theorization may be, it cannot be supported by the 'coronation charter' itself or later events. For the document is not one drawn up between the king and the barons; it contains no reciprocal bargaining; it is furnished with no guarantees or sanctions for its fulfilment: instead it is plainly addressed to all the faithful subjects of the king; it avows the reasons for its promulgation to be his reverence for God and his love for his subjects; it assured his people in general that he would keep firm peace within his kingdom and give them back the laws of Edward the Confessor, with such amendments as William I had introduced; it was witnessed by no more than three bishops and six barons. Nor, once it had served its purpose, did Henry pay any further attention to it; already in 1103 he was appropriating the revenues of Canterbury while Anselm was abroad, and by the close of his reign fiscal oppression was undoubtedly far heavier. The charter should, therefore, be viewed for what it was: an election document, a manifesto, an open letter, inspired presumably by his ecclesiastical advisers at the time of his coronation, making as large a bid as possible for support in its promises to the Church, the barons, and the native English, and exercising as much immediate, and as much permanent, effect as most electoral addresses. Nevertheless, though the original has not come down to us, copies of it were sent into every shire to be read in the county court, and after ages did not forget its existence. It was confirmed by Henry II shortly after he was crowned, and it was circulating in both Latin and French in the opening years of the thirteenth century to provide legal grounds for the opposition to John.

II. THE KING'S MARRIAGE OF EXPEDIENCY

Henry's efforts to strengthen his position induced him to marry Edith, niece of Edgar the Atheling and sister of the king of the Scots, who adopted the Norman name, Matilda, on her marriage. Thereby he not only established friendly relations with Scotland, but he grafted the Norman house on to the stock of the West Saxon royal line. Scarcely a generation had passed since the Normans entered the country and, though inter-marriage between conquerors and conquered was more frequent than is generally supposed, yet it could hardly have gone far enough to prevent the majority of the Normans from retaining their pride of race and viewing the native English as inferiors and their property as a prize of war. The chronicler's story that Henry's marriage excited the resentment and ribald jibes of the Norman barons is often cited, but it is not above suspicion. And, at all events, the marriage signified dramatically that the age of exploitation was drawing to its end, and the king began the process of wiping out distinctions between Norman and English so successfully that the author of the 'Dialogue of the Exchequer', writing some seventy years later, declared that the races were so mixed that he could not distinguish Englishmen from Normans within the free classes of the community. Henry insisted that he was not so much a Norman king as an Anglo-Norman king, who meant to rule over a homogeneous people. This marriage symbolized the fact that the monarchy would continue to devote its strength to obtaining the unification of the country.

Just how far gestures of conciliation were necessary we are unable to estimate, but certain it is that, when the testing-time came less than twelve months later, the slightness of the opposition to Henry was fully apparent.

In the first half-dozen years of the reign the three problems, which are going to dominate the twelfth and thirteenth centuries, are clearly discernible. Although they react upon each other all the time, it makes for clarity if they are disentangled and studied separately.

I. The Continental Problem

Henry's seizure of the English crown had once again created a division between England and Normandy and, apart altogether from the king's obvious ambition to rule over no less a realm than his father had done, he could scarcely have remained indifferent to what was taking place across the Channel. The danger to his throne came from a comparatively small and irresponsible clique of barons, but Henry could not cope with it as a purely domestic problem, for these men had extensive estates in the Duchy and they had succeeded in persuading Duke Robert to let himself become the centre of their machinations. His claims to the kingdom could be used to bring about the displacement of the too competent Henry or, at least, suspended like the sword of Damocles, provide a check upon his activities. Henry soon realized that the peace he needed for developments at home would not be attained until he had cleared the breeding-ground of disaffection and placed Normandy under his direct control.

Before Henry invaded Normandy, however, it was Robert who invaded England in 1101. He might never have taken this step if he had not been urged to it by barons, like the notorious Robert of Bellême and his brothers of the great House of Montgomery, who saw greater power and profit to themselves in conditions of anarchy. Persuaded that he had only to appear in England to be universally acclaimed, Robert landed at Portsmouth and marched towards London. To his dismay he found that the majority of the barons had no intention of coming to his side and that the trial by battle might well go against him. Henry for his part had no desire to take risks and was willing to negotiate: he met his brother on his way to the capital at Alton, and promised to pay him £2,000 a year for life on condition that he renounced his claims to the throne, whilst each promised that he would give no help to any rebellious subject of the other. As soon as Robert had left the country, Henry addressed himself to punishing the deserted rebels with ruthless severity: all were, in accordance with feudal practice summoned to appear before the feudal court of the 'Great Council' and those who did so were heavily punished with fines and forfeitures. Others who proved recalcitrant and offered armed resistance were overcome by 1102, largely with the aid of the English fyrd: Robert of Bellême fled to Normandy, the House of

Montgomery was completely destroyed, and the only visible sign of the disorder was a marked increase in the royal estates and revenues. The very fact that Henry dared to take such stern proceedings against members of the Norman baronage, and was never again in his reign called upon to face rebellion, is itself sufficient indication that the Norman barons as a whole were loyal to the Crown and identified their interests with his own and not with separatism. Henry had so few apprehensions about their support that he did not hesitate to found the earldom of Gloucester, which dominated the south-west of England and was no whit less powerful than any of the creations of the Conquest. It was to be the completely altered circumstances of the weak reign of Stephen that produced a different attitude of mind in the barons.

Henry could not be satisfied so long as there was a possibility that he might be stabbed in the back from Normandy. Therefore he deliberately set to work to dispossess Robert. Those clauses in the treaty of Alton which he did not simply disregard, like the payment of the annuity, he twisted unscrupulously for his own purposes. He put the hapless duke in an impossible position until, on the allegation that Robert was assisting his enemies, Henry in turn invaded Normandy, and in September 1106 gained a decisive victory at the battle of Tinchebrai. The complete and unexpected triumph had a double significance. (a) It achieved the prime purpose of Henry's invasion by removing the threat to his monarchy. It was not merely that Robert was captured and removed from the political scene to end his days in honourable captivity in Cardiff castle nearly thirty years later. But the intractable barons had no longer a cloak beneath which they could hide their own private schemings: from henceforth it was clear that, if they rebelled, they were, indeed, rebels. (b) A chronicler of the time declared that, by defeating the Normans at Tinchebrai, the English had balanced their own defeat at Hastings exactly forty years before. Though he was referring only to the use of English levies in the battle, he spoke more truly than he realized, for it was principally on behalf of his English interests that Henry had made war upon Normans.

It was not until his reign that monarchy in France began its slow rise to pre-eminence with Louis VI (or Louis the Fat), 1108–37. This Capetian king was completely realistic in his policy and, unlike his predecessors, he determined to put first things first and become master in his own house. He destroyed the power of the brigand lords within the Capetian personal domain of the Île de France by sheer perseverance, for it took him twenty years to accomplish it. In consequence, it was only occasionally and in desultory fashion that he could look further afield and insist that he was more than suzerain and that, as sovereign, he had it as his duty to protect his subjects within the whole of France and guarantee them justice. In doing this he was inclined to concern himself particularly with his vassal states of Normandy and Flanders, for through them access to the sea was easiest from the Île de France. After Tinchebrai, Normandy presented a unique difficulty, for the great resources of the English kingdom could be used in its support. The obvious solution was to get them separated, and it was the French king's efforts to do this and the English king's steps to prevent it that constitute the foreign policy of Henry I's reign.

The struggle in Northern France had three episodes, marked by the triumphs of diplomacy rather than battle, and in all of them Louis was able to use as his catspaw Duke Robert's worthless and vicious son, William 'Clito' (i.e. the Atheling). (i) In 1111 Louis VI decided openly to support William's claims to Normandy. The warfare that resulted was protracted and tedious and it came to an end with Henry's first successful act in detaching the French king's vassals from his support. By the Treaty of Gisors in 1113 a marriage was arranged between Henry's son, William, and the daughter of Count Fulk of Anjou: as the terms of the contract arranged that the county of Maine should be settled on them as a marriage-portion, it provided a tactful way for Normandy to recover her hold upon that long-contested province. (ii) In 1116 Louis thought it an opportune moment to renew hostilities, again using the Clito's claims as a cover. This time he took the precaution to get the quite unscrupulous Fulk of Anjou on his own side and, to balance this loss, Henry made an alliance with the count of Blois, the inveterate foe of Anjou. Again the war dragged along an undistinguished course until Henry's diplomacy gained the day a second time: he managed to persuade the count of Anjou to transfer his support to him and drove home his advantage by the decisive victory of Brémule in 1119. (iii) In 1123 Louis took action for a third time in the Clito's name. On this occasion he received more active support from Norman barons, but they were not the important feudatories, and they had their estates mainly in eastern Normandy where they were more susceptible to the French king's intrigues. Henry's hold on Normandy was at no time seriously jeopardized, for most barons had found it inconvenient to have their lands on both sides of the Channel under different authorities and found the unified control of Henry a distinct advantage, and the rebellion was sternly suppressed. With the Clito's death in 1128, when he was being further used as the French king's tool, this time in Flanders, what chance there had ever been of separating Normandy from England passed away.

II. The Ecclesiastical Problem

As part of his initial policy of conciliation Henry carried out the promise he had made in his manifesto of 1100 that he would not make financial profit by keeping bishoprics and abbeys vacant. He straightway made appointments to them and, most important of all, he requested Anselm to return to his duties at Canterbury as head of the Church in England. The two men regarded each other with respect, but the times had changed too much to permit any co-operation between them, such as had existed between William and Lanfranc. Anselm had already in the previous reign protested vigorously against two of the 'ancient customs' on which the king took his stand, and asserted, on the contrary, the right of the Church to be consulted in the recognition of any new pope, and the right of ecclesiastics to visit Rome. Three others of these 'customs' came to be disputed under Henry I.

I. LAY INVESTITURES

The regulation of the relations between Church and State was a problem that could no longer be passed over, and Anselm during his residence at Rome had become a more enthusiastic reformer and papal supporter than before. Although he had done homage to Rufus and been invested by him with the insignia of his sacred office, he would not look upon the new king in the same light and refused to do him homage. Henry for his part took his stand upon the 'ancient customs' his father had stressed and, though he acted with commendable restraint, he would not abandon his control of appointments in the Church and thereby of the Church itself. Eventually the archbishop returned once more to Rome, where he excommunicated some of the English bishops for subserviently accepting nomination and investiture by the king and even threatened Henry himself with the same penalty. It was a position of stalemate, too unsatisfactory to either side to be allowed to continue indefinitely. Already in France a compromise was being worked in accordance with suggestions put forward by the French scholar, Ivo of Chartres, and this compromise was accepted by Henry and Anselm at Le Bec in 1106 and published at a council in London in the following year. The king lost the right to bestow the staff and the ring upon newly created prelates; the Church failed to remove the king's control of the appointments, for the prelates were permitted to do homage for their lands, and the king was shrewd enough to make sure that homage came before consecration. The compromise of Le Bec was a triumph for the Church in that it definitely repudiated the divine aspect of the king's authority in ecclesiastical matters and laid all the emphasis on his purely secular control. That was a noteworthy and vital principle, but in practice it made very little difference. It could not force the king to accept the Church's nominees, for by refusing to accept their homage and thereby withholding their temporalities he had a practical power of veto. Therefore the Church continued to select candidates known to be acceptable to him, and it is significant that the first bishop created under the new arrangements was the king's chaplain and treasurer, Roger of Salisbury. When bishops and abbots remained the creatures of the lay ruler, when the great bulk of the Church's property was openly recognized to be subject to burdens imposed by the State, when parish churches and chapels stayed under the control of lay patrons, it can hardly be contended that the ideas of Gregory VII had been seriously received in England.

II. APPEALS TO ROME

Though not unknown, they had until this time been very rare and in no way encouraged. There could be little objection to the practice so long as the subject of the appeal was restricted to Church affairs, but, if it concerned lay matters, it assumed an altogether different complexion. For, if Rome became a final court of appeal in all cases, then the king would cease to be the real fountain of justice, law would come from a source outside the kingdom, his judicial authority, on which so much was to depend, would be subordinated to that of the pope. A famous appeal to Rome occurred a few months after the Conqueror's death. The bishop of Durham had been implicated in the rebellion which marked

William II's accession to the throne, and he was summoned to the king's court to answer for his treason. He refused to attend on the ground that the law of the Church did not permit him, a churchman, to be tried elsewhere than in a Church court. This objection was swept aside with the argument that he was accused, not as a bishop, but as a baron. When his lands were put under distraint to enforce his appearance, he went further and laid his case before the pope. In the event nothing important resulted from his action, which was mainly a desperate attempt to save his own skin. Still, the pope had been publicly urged to review the process of the royal court for a lay offence like treason. And Anselm had persuaded Henry I to submit the question of investitures to the papal curia for its reconsideration. Though appeals are not as yet numerous, they are on their way to becoming a normal practice.

III. PAPAL LEGATES

These were not an innovation in England. They had first been seen in the country under Offa, and then again under Edward the Confessor. Three of them had visited England immediately after the Conquest on the express invitation of William I and been warmly welcomed. But Gregory VII later gave them a new significance. Hitherto they had been sent from Rome as *ad hoc* commissioners, that is for one particular piece of work only. But Gregory began to arm them, not with such limited power but with full papal authority. As soon as the legates appeared, they took precedence, no matter how humble their own social origins had been, over all archbishops and bishops and could remove them from their sees. They therefore constituted a powerful instrument in furthering the centralization of Church government in Western Europe in the hands of the papacy. In England they were heartily disliked by nearly all the bishops, and they were deemed highly dangerous by the king, who clearly saw that they could impair his hold upon the Church. In 1116, therefore, Henry refused a papal legate permission to enter his kingdom, but in 1125 another was allowed to enter and to hold a legatine council to discuss a programme of reform, though he departed soon afterwards in personal disgrace. The royal hostility was eventually placated by an arrangement, accommodating both parties and fairly constantly maintained in after years: the pope was to have a permanent representative in England, but he was to be the archbishop of

Canterbury, and not a foreigner who was immune from royal control.

It is evident that Henry remained completely the master of the Church: how completely is shown by the fact that, for five years after Anselm's death in 1109, he made no nomination to Canterbury and appropriated the revenues himself. Nevertheless, it is equally clear that he had not the undisputed position and authority of his father: the 'ancient customs' had been challenged by Anselm, and a group of prelates, strong in influence though small in numbers, was adopting papalist views.

III. The Feudal Problem

We must be careful not to attribute too lofty a conception of its 'mission' to the Norman monarchy in England: to do so is to misunderstand the primary reasons for its development and the whole burden of the complaints against its operations. For all three Norman kings were dominated by the spirit of acquisitiveness: their lust for wealth could only be satisfied by the exertion of the fullness of their power and its extension at every possible opportunity, even to the point of illegal practices. From the stern enforcement of royal rights, so that they would yield full profit to the royal treasury, resulted the framework of centralized government. To collect the existing sources of revenue efficiently made it necessary to establish a really competent civil service: to augment those sources meant an ever expanding civil service. The preservation of order, the evolution of a common law, the dispensation of justice, were accidentals, the superb consequences of a meaner motive. We must remember the fundamental truth of the medieval dictum: *justitia est magnum emolumentum*.

This truth is illustrated in the little-understood activities of Ranulf Flambard in the reign of Rufus. That king was intent on the accumulation of money, and to achieve that purpose he did not act in a casual and haphazard way. His unrelenting and unceasing insistence on his fiscal rights implied a conscious policy, and that in its turn demanded an adequate financial organization and full-time officials. It was Flambard's duty to be what a contemporary chronicler called him, 'the chief executant of the king's will'. Though there seems little reason to believe that he held the office of treasurer, or that his was the legal mind that produced a logical systematization of the 'feudal incidents', yet it is plain that he was meant to produce revenue by means of the operations of the law. The inter-connexion of finance and justice is exhibited in all he did. For it seems not only that the office of the exchequer with its methods of working was being foreshadowed, not only that there was even an attempt by Flambard to introduce a novel and heavier assessment of land taxes, but he was also constantly at work, improvising the administration of justice and extracting the fees, fines and confiscations which attended it. His writs of instruction went throughout the land, the shire courts were stimulated into activity to advance the king's interests in the country districts, and, on the two occasions when we know that tribunals of justices were sent on eyre from headquarters, Flambard was always a member of them. Much gold stuck to his fingers, but it was because his operations were only too effective that he earned his evil reputation for corrupt extortion. Actually Henry I could have seen little wrong in him: though as a political gesture he imprisoned him in the Tower, from which he soon escaped to Normandy, the two were reconciled in 1101, and Flambard, permitted to return to England, showed in his diocese of Durham during the next twenty-seven years the skill in administration which had formerly been placed at the disposal of Rufus.

Henry I, who came to be reputed the wealthiest king in Western Europe, was moved by avarice, as his brother had been, to devise machinery of control, but in his case another factor came into play, which was equally powerful in forcing him to address himself to the art of government. For it was not sufficient to recover Normandy, he must also administer it. This made it necessary for him to spend half his reign in residence there, and he might be absent from either the kingdom or the duchy for years together. Therefore, some means of ruling either country had to be invented so that he himself could be done without, and there began immediately a period of experimentation which caused a parallel development on both sides of the Channel. In this respect, therefore, we must not be too ready to think of the twelfth-century system of government in England as being the result of purely English conditions. England was now one part, albeit an important part, of an Anglo-Norman Empire, and she was soon to be part of a far greater Angevin Empire, and her government was largely a practical answer to the problem of ruling *in absentia*. But for that it is doubtful if the reign of Henry I would have been as productive in the organs of administration as it was.

Thus it came about that, just as Normandy for the first time reveals the presence of a co-ordinated system of government under the control of Bishop John of Lisieux, who was already by 1109 acting as the king's deputy, so in England there appeared at the head of the administration Roger, bishop of Salisbury (1107-39). As justiciar he issued writs in his own name to direct the conduct of affairs and, though we cannot attribute to him all the functions of the line of famous justiciars who were responsible for the tremendous developments in government from Henry II's reign onwards, yet it is hardly open to doubt that he outlined the plan. At the same time there came prominently into view an aristocracy of service, composed of men like the Le Poers (of whom Roger was one), the Bassets and the Clintons, whom the king 'raised from the dust' to be the agents of his will, and whom he honoured with dignities and privileges in return for their official competence. Not until half a century after the Norman Conquest had the monarchy ventured to make the first serious departure from that close collaboration with the great feudal barons which had previously been indispensable.

The unitary organ of government was the king's court or, if that term has been deprived of its full significance by a modern connotation, the *curia regis*. As we should expect, it was a term with great elasticity of meaning, and it was applied to assemblies which differed widely in their membership and in the work they were called upon to do. However, it is with its four main forms that we are particularly concerned.

I. THE GREAT COUNCIL

The chronicles supply us with a fair amount of information about its activities, and it is possible to list at least twenty-seven of its meetings in Henry I's reign. Its attention was given to the dispensation of feudal justice to the king's tenants-in-chief when occasion arose, and to the discussion of politics in general.

II. THE SMALL COUNCIL

This was constantly in attendance on the king and had, as its all-important nucleus, the officials of the king's household. Their concern, unlike that of the feudal nobility in the Great Council, lay not with spasmodic politics but with the supervision of everyday administration. They were not so much, as it were, amateur politicians as professional civil servants, interested and trained in government.

III.   THE EXCHEQUER

The routine of government, however, devolved upon the 'king's court of the exchequer', as it was later sometimes called. It was in effect the court of the justiciar on either side of the Channel. The justiciar was the king's *alter ego* when he was absent from England or Normandy, and his principal minister when he was present. The exchequer was, in Jeremy Bentham's phrase, omni-competent: there was not a single function of government—finan-cial, judicial, administrative or deliberative—that it could not and did not perform. It is a point that should not be forgotten that the exchequer was the mainspring of government in the twelfth century. The increasing pressure and the increasing complexity of work, however, made it impossible for it to go on dealing with all kinds of business indiscriminately, no matter what their nature, and it was compelled to make particular arrangements in finance. Each Easter and Michaelmas term it held special sessions, devoted to one particular purpose: the supervision of the king's financial interests and the work of the king's book-keeping. This speciali-zation occurred some time before 1118, it resulted in centralizing and making more businesslike the control of revenue and expendi-ture, and it provided the first great advance towards scientific government. The sheriffs brought up to headquarters the money they had collected and paid it into the Treasury, later called the Lower Exchequer, where it was counted and tested for weight and purity. Then their accounts were audited in the important Upper Exchequer or exchequer of account, which was the financial session of the omni-competent exchequer. It was presided over until the early thirteenth century by the justiciar, then by the treasurer who naturally came to the fore with the disappearance of the office of justiciar, and it was nominally attended by other ministers, such as the chancellor: he was probably almost always absent, even under Henry II, and he eventually appointed a deputy to act for him, who became known as the chancellor of the exchequer. A precise system of reckoning with counters on a 'squared' or 'checkered' table (hence the name 'exchequer') was based on the novel principle of the abacus, and the results of the calculations were carefully recorded in the pipe rolls. The earliest to survive, and the sole survivor from Henry I's reign, belongs to the year

1130. It was almost a century before any distinct financial institution emerged to appropriate the term 'exchequer' to itself and become the first of the separate departments of state in England.

IV. THE JUSTICES IN EYRE

The fiscal rights and private profits of the king inevitably raised many questions which could only be resolved by judicial means. We must avoid the anachronism of accrediting Henry I with the high conceptions which lay at the back of what his far greater grandson will achieve. There is no evidence that Henry I at any time intended his subjects at large to believe that they could look past their feudal and local lords to a royal court and a royal justice which would be the same for everyone. Nor did he ever assert that certain offences, such as murder, rape, robbery and arson, were to be reserved exclusively to the royal jurisdiction on the ground that they were particularly dangerous to the stability of society, of which he was the guardian, and must therefore be submitted to his judgment. As yet the king did not claim such 'pleas of the crown' all over his kingdom, and he was interested in his fiscal rights rather than in jurisdictional rights. Henry I did not, in fact, advance the organization of justice beyond the point where it could make sure that the rights he already had, not the rights he might have by theoretical development, were fully observed and honoured. Still, provided we do not attempt to read the future into the past, we can realize that, however selfish in motive and restricted in scope, Henry's efforts pointed in the right direction. Because it was the same direction as Henry II followed to attain amazingly successful results, it is perhaps natural to look upon one as the forerunner of the other. But, as we shall see, there was a difference between the conceptions of the Norman and the Angevin ruler, which was to make all the difference.

It was through the justices in eyre that the *curia regis* entered boldly into the sphere of justice. The first two Norman rulers had been occasionally prevailed upon to intervene in the trial of cases before the shire courts by dispatching there a writ of instructions. They might go further than that and send down to the country a member of the *curia* to preside as a special commissioner over the hearing of a particular plea. This is not a new procedure, an innovation of the Normans introduced by them from the Continent, for it was well known in England throughout the tenth and eleventh centuries. After the Conquest, however, it was given a far wider application in matters of administration: for example, the commissioners for the Domesday Survey in 1086 made their inquiries in the shire courts. It is not surprising that visits to the country districts by members of the *curia regis* should tend to become a normal and fairly regular part of the machinery of government. Twice under Rufus and three times under Henry I we have evidence that justices in eyre were touring the country before the fact of judicial circuits is plainly revealed by the Pipe Roll of 1130. The liaison between finance and justice is writ large in their work, for their judicial activities were less arduous than their administrative duties in seeing that the king's rights and privileges were upheld and any breach of them heavily compensated. When the royal justices sat in the shire court, their presence converted it for the time being from a popular into a royal court: the authority for its session was no longer traditional Anglo-Saxon custom but the king's writ, its business was under the direction of officials to whom the king had delegated his power. They could, therefore, do in the localities what the *curia regis* could do at headquarters, and it was as though the *curia* was opening up temporary country branches. What is particularly significant was the definite linking up of royal and popular justice.

Apart from the supervision of the *curia regis*, Henry sought to strengthen his authority over the country in general by the reform of two institutions of local influence.

1. THE POPULAR ASSEMBLY COURTS

After the Conquest these had had to face the competing claims of seignorial justice, and the amount of business they were called upon to do must have been appreciably diminished. Nevertheless, by Rufus's time the shire, or county, courts were being used to further the royal schemes of extortion and were naturally considered to be meeting far too frequently, if that was to be the purpose of their summons. And the baronial sheriffs, freed from such restraints as the presence of earl and bishop might impose, saw in them a ready means of enriching themselves also, and called them as they saw fit. About 1109–11 Henry I decreed that they were to assemble as they had done under Edward the Confessor at regular times and places, and that, whenever royal business of any kind was to be transacted, then the suitors were to be specially summoned. Moreover, county court jurisdiction was at the same time confirmed by a regulation which clearly settled the limits of feudal jurisdiction: if a dispute arose between the vassals of *different* lords, there was to be no doubt that henceforward it was to be decided in the county court as a neutral arbiter.

The hundred courts were a different proposition, for many of them had by this time passed into private hands. There was little that Henry could do except order them to meet at customary times.

In the local courts Anglo-Saxon customary law prevailed. That is one of the reasons why in Henry I's reign some six or seven treatises were written to explain to the Normans in language they could understand what it exactly was. In any case, it was imperative that they should obtain this knowledge, for they frequently claimed that their privileges were founded upon those of the Anglo-Saxon lords they had displaced: that is to say, that they were based on custom, not on royal grant. The most important of these legal text-books is the unfortunately named 'Leges Henrici', so called simply because it happens to begin with Henry I's charter of 1100. Written about 1118 by a royal justice, though not an official work, it set itself to explain in Latin the Anglo-Saxon law that was then enforceable.

II. THE SHERIFFS

Henry I was strong enough to break with the practice of appointing powerful barons as sheriffs. He was determined that they should be distinctly royal officials, obedient to orders and removable at will. Therefore he imposed restrictions on the freedom of action which so far it had been considered advisable to leave to them; they were chosen, whenever possible, from among his trained officials; the period of office was to be clearly understood as one year; they were subjected to rigorous control twice a year at the exchequer. The most interesting of all these developments was the increased subordination of their judicial authority to that of the local justiciars, who had been appointed for the first time apparently in the reign of Rufus, and remained resident in their respective counties, and there represented continuously the authority of the Crown. There can be little doubt that their presence constituted a check upon the sheriffs, but whether they had been created for that express purpose or whether they came to form part of some deliberate scheme of general organization by the king, it is difficult to say. Even with all these precautions Henry had to dismiss eleven sheriffs in 1129.

Henry I's signal contribution lay in the centralization of authority in the king's hands and the consequent preservation of social order so that 'in his day no man dared harm another'. But it is very doubtful if the position he had adopted could have been long maintained by any later occupant of the throne. What he did was a great achievement, but it meant little more than bringing the barons strictly to heel. He had created few earls; he had deprived the tenants-in-chief of much of the local power they had exercised in his father's time; the solitary pipe roll is sufficient to reveal the arbitrary acts and repressions of his ministers, who raised feudal exactions or fines to the utmost limit and administered the forest law with unprecedented severity. Monarchy, based more on force than ideas and ideals and dependent on the ruthless ability of its exponent for its maintenance, could not have lasted long and, Stephen or no Stephen, the explosion point would sooner or later have been reached. To use the word 'statesmanship' in proper and fitting manner we must wait till the reign of his incomparable grandson.

The threat of a disputed succession clouded the last years of the king. Henry's only legitimate son, William, the heir of the Saxon line, had been drowned in the tragic disaster of the 'White Ship' in 1120; his only legitimate daughter, Matilda, had become the wife of the Emperor in 1114, and it was impossible to imagine that he would be allowed to ascend the throne of England and Normandy. A vacant throne meant the breakdown of central control, the destruction of Henry's whole policy, and the outbreak of violence and disorder. Henry looked for a solution in two directions. First, he remarried in 1122, but the marriage proved childless. Then, since the death of the Emperor in 1125 left Matilda free to marry again, her father arranged that she should become in 1128 the wife of the count of Anjou's son, Geoffrey. Henry hoped thereby that Normandy would be immune from any Angevin intrigues and that, when the critical time arrived, she would have someone strong beside her in her support. For Henry had named Matilda as his heir, and twice, in 1128 and again in 1131, had compelled the English barons to swear to receive her as their future queen. In 1133 Matilda gave birth to the future Henry II of England.

This marriage brought two continental rivalries to a head. (*a*) The English kings and the Capetian kings. So far the French monarchs had been generally successful in playing on the mutual jealousies of the great fiefs and keeping them at loggerheads. Now the menace that the Capetians had so long dreaded seemed very close: a combination of Normandy and Anjou, Maine and Touraine and, what was the worst aspect of all, a combination controlled by a rival monarchy. (*b*) Anjou and Blois. For many generations they had been enemies, and now the edge of their hostilities was sharpened by dynastic considerations. For Count Stephen of Blois was the grandson of William the Conqueror and a first cousin of Matilda and her rival for the English throne.

Thus England was caught up in the vortex of continental politics, and the English succession question became one of European moment. Henry's answer to the problem, perhaps the best possible in the circumstances, was not likely to go unchallenged, for the Normans, in particular, could hardly view their proposed subjection to the hated Angevin without resentment. His forebodings were to be only too well fulfilled.

SELECT READING

W. J. Corbett, 'England: 1087–1154' in *C. Med. H.*, v (1926), 521–7; Pollock and Maitland, i. ch. iv; Stephenson and Marcham, 33–70; K. Norgate, *England under the Angevin Kings* (1887), i. 1–96; G. B. Adams, *Council and Courts in Anglo-Norman England* (1926), 99–126; C. H. Haskins, *Norman Institutions* (1918), 85–122; W. Morris, *Medieval English Sheriff* (1927), 41–109; R. W. Church, *St. Anselm* (1883); R. W. Southern, 'Ranulf Flambard and Early Anglo-Norman Administration' in *T.R.H.S.*, 4th Series, xvi (1933), 95–128.

CHAPTER XX

THE LESSONS OF ANARCHY

THE salient characteristic of William the Conqueror's reign had been the action of a strong monarchy which functioned according to a definite and practical plan; his two sons had maintained it in its essentials. But monarchy remained a very personal institution and was not yet a machine, which would go on running irrespective of the king himself. So, when the male line of descent came to an end, a critical moment arrived for the future of developments in England. The reign of Stephen was to show by sharp contrast the benefits that effective monarchy could confer on the body politic and all that its collapse could signify, and it was to bring into the open those forces in Church and State which were retarding the work of political unification and the establishment of law and order and to exhibit their strength.

For England saw the first and only appearance of a type of what is commonly called 'feudal monarchy'. We shall certainly do Stephen some injustice if we attribute to him personally all the inevitable consequences of a disputed election. But whatever the reasons, in practice he laid little or no emphasis upon the all-important royal prerogative, he showed no high conception of his responsibilities as the guardian of the state and the protector of his subjects' interests. Instead, he was content with a position which was little more in practice than that of *primus inter pares*. Feudal conventions and feudal law were ever present in his mind, and he virtually reigned as a contractual king. For example, when the Church came to assert that he had broken his contract, he sent a representative to its assembly to refute the accusation and plead his cause. The barons for their part came to debase the meaning of allegiance and looked upon it as implying a mere feudal relationship, which could be terminated if the king exceeded what they chose to interpret as the limits of his authority. In such circumstances, anarchy was a foregone conclusion.

Stephen's reign also brought into prominence at once a question of constitutional importance, for it clearly revealed the trend of contemporary thought upon the right of succession to the throne. The Norman kings, like their Anglo-Saxon predecessors, always stressed first and foremost the hereditary nature of their kingship, though they too saw fit to have their formal election countenanced by assemblies of a few notables, for every one of them succeeded to the throne in defiance of a rival candidate. Nevertheless, they would have scorned any suggestion that such an election in any way bound their hands or implied any corresponding right to depose them. But the case was far different with Stephen, who was evidently prepared to acknowledge the contractual nature of his authority as the price of his election to the English throne. Elective monarchy implied the danger that the work of a strong and beneficent ruler would be jeopardized at his death and an even and continuous development made more difficult. For her part Matilda took her stand upon strict hereditary right, and in her public acts she emphasized that she did what she did as the daughter of her royal father. In other words, the rules of Roman law, relating to private property, were to be equally valid in as it were public law, as though a kingdom were a kind of personal estate and the office of king could be regarded as a form of property. The issue between hereditary monarchy and elective monarchy was decided only by a disastrous civil war, which ended with the acceptance of Henry II as king by virtue of his parentage: thereafter, the principle of direct hereditary succession was rarely abandoned.

When Henry I died in Normandy, it was apparent to everyone that what he had devoted the statecraft of his last years to achieving would not easily come to pass. The succession was to be treated as an open question: there was to be no automatic acceptance of Matilda as his heir. That being the case, her position was not strong, and it had strength thrust upon it only through the weakness of her rival. (a) She was the direct heir, born the child of a crowned king. The force of this argument was reduced, however, at three points. The rule of a woman was quite unprecedented and hardly likely to be welcomed by the feudal nobility. It was not clear at first whether her claim was to be vested in herself solely or in her son, or whether it passed from her by feudal law to her husband in the same way as Henry II was, through his wife, to become duke of Aquitaine; in view of what actually happened in Normandy, it is practically certain that, if Matilda succeeded, then Geoffrey would become king of England, as, in fact, he became duke of Normandy, though he might resign in favour of his son. The difficulty was that Geoffrey's claim to England was entirely 'by right of his wife', and that 'right' was not generally admitted. And Matilda's character caused her to be disliked. Her first marriage in very early life to the German emperor had cut her off from contact with English traditions; her second marriage to the Angevin count had aroused the resentment of the Normans. Nor was she able to overcome these prejudices against her by any virtue in herself: overbearing, obstinate and petulant, she was extremely unpopular and, even in the hour of her triumph, she had neither ability nor tact with which to keep her own party united in her own support. (b) Her rights had been secured to her by solemn oaths, twice exacted by her father, from all his powerful subjects, including Stephen of Blois. To refuse homage was to commit the sin of perjury, which society as it was then established could not lightly condone. However, this charge could be avoided if papal approval of Matilda's rival could be obtained, and this was precisely what was done. (c) Henry had trusted that his daughter's claims would be firmly supported by her undoubtedly able husband, the count of Anjou. His hopes were not altogether belied, but it was clear that Count Geoffrey could do nothing for his wife in England unless a strong party rallied there to her assistance, and that otherwise he must concentrate his energies on the adjacent Normandy. In the event, he conquered the duchy by 1144 and was acknowledged by the French king to be holding it as rightful duke. The fate of Normandy, however, could by no means settle the issue in England. (d) Matilda could rely upon some support in England, even if it was immediately only from those unruly factions who saw profit in disorder. But it was not substantial until Stephen had proved his incapacity: though the forceful earl of Gloucester, an illegitimate son of Henry I, was plotting on her behalf from 1137, it was not until his half-sister landed in England in 1139 that he ventured to declare for her openly, to become her chief adviser, and to make his vast estates in the west of England the seat of her authority.

To begin with, therefore, Matilda had much less to recommend her than Stephen. (a) If she was the daughter of the Conqueror's son, he was the son of the Conqueror's daughter, Adela, who had been married to the count of Blois. Furthermore, he represented not only the Norman dynasty but in some measure the Anglo-Saxon royal house as well, for his wife was, like the Empress Matilda, a granddaughter of that Margaret, sister of Edgar the Atheling, who had married Malcolm Canmore, King of the Scots. Nevertheless, Stephen never stressed his relationship to the Conqueror. It was not simply that on this ground he could not counter the superior rights of Matilda. For in seeking the throne of England he was ignoring the claims of his elder brother, Theobald. It is little wonder, therefore, that he preferred to magnify the principle of election and omit all reference to hereditary right in his regnal titles. (*b*) Stephen was able to obtain the support of the Church. His legal right was more than questionable, his hurried election was at the best dubious. It was imperative that he should at once remove the obstacle of the oath he had sworn to do homage to Matilda and that he should be able to present himself to his subjects as the Lord's Anointed. Only the Church could absolve him from his oath and only the Church could crown him, and it was fortunate for him that another brother of his, Henry of Blois, was at the time bishop of Winchester and such a dominant figure in ecclesiastical circles that he was able to bring his colleagues, including the archbishop of Canterbury, over to Stephen's side. Just three weeks after Henry's death, he was crowned at Westminster in the presence of a small gathering, but the fact of coronation could not thereafter be challenged. Shortly afterwards the choice of the Church in England was given official cognizance by the pope, to whom both candidates stated their cases. For by refusing to give judgment he quietly absolved Stephen from the charge of perjury. (*c*) He was given the full assistance of Blois on the Continent. His brother, Theobald, at first pressed his own claims and was, in fact, considered by the barons of Normandy for the title of king of England. But when Stephen took the adventurer's chance, rushed across the Channel, and presented Theobald with a *fait accompli*, the latter laid aside his pretensions and came magnanimously to his brother's side. He could do nothing for him in England, but abroad he willingly revived the traditional hostility to Anjou, especially when there was a distinct danger that Anjou might otherwise secure a hold upon the resources of England. (*d*) The high government officials accepted Stephen because the peace of the king still died with him, and the outbreak of disorder could not be ended until the interregnum ceased. Someone must be placed quickly in control, and they were most likely to adhere to the candidate who showed the greatest resolution. And the majority of the feudal barons were agreeable to his kingship, for his character made a more sympathetic appeal to them than Matilda's. Stephen had been a favourite of Henry I, who gave him great estates and a high position of dignity in England, and he had therefore a knowledge of the country and its ways which was much more intimate than his rival's. And his courage, his generosity and his simplicity marked him as the true type of feudal chivalry. It was only later events that revealed his dangerous vacillations and his fatal lack of statecraft.

Stephen's title, therefore, was not weak when compared with that of Matilda or, what was perhaps a more important consideration at the time, the claims of Geoffrey, her husband. If he had had any strength of character at all, he would have found no insuperable difficulties in his way. That he failed was almost entirely his own fault. His weakness was fully exposed after a few months. He adopted a fatal policy of concessions and allowed the power of the monarchy to dwindle away until he was reduced to a mere figure-head. Though, to begin with, he was in a far stronger position than his rivals, he acted in precisely the same way as Matilda and her son were forced to act before 1154. The bargains he struck with his influential subjects read almost like contracts between equals, and eventually the absurd position was reached where the with-holding of concessions was followed by rebellion, which could be easily justified by a simple transference of allegiance to Matilda. A remarkable increase in the number of earls, a dependence on Flemish mercenaries, a frittering away of royal revenues and an attempt to make up for the loss by a debasement of the coinage: such things were the negation of all the objectives of his Norman predecessors. So, in spite of and by reason of his concessions, Stephen's authority grew rapidly weaker.

(i) It was plain from the start that he could not preserve order within the frontiers of his realm. As early as 1136, for example, the king's castle of Norwich was attacked and captured by the earl of Norfolk, and Exeter castle was pillaged by a local magnate on the mere excuse that the king was rumoured to be dead. These are early instances of private rebellions and, though they were not serious, they showed the unsettled ideas of the time and, since what was done was done with impunity, they set an example which was soon followed over the whole country.

(ii) Not even from perils outside his frontiers could Stephen defend his kingdom. Although the French king had, to begin with, confirmed the possession of Normandy to Stephen, yet, when he paid his only visit there in 1137, he behaved with such tactlessness that he aroused Norman hostility against himself and left things in a more perilous condition than he had found them. Early in his reign he bought off an attack from Scotland by giving Cumberland to Henry, son of King David, but that was simply an invitation to exploit his weakness further, and a demand was made that the earldom of Northumberland should likewise be bestowed upon Prince Henry. This would have allowed the Scottish frontier to move too far south for even Stephen's liking, and he refused. The inevitable reply came in the merciless harrying of the northern shires in the early months of 1138 and an organized invasion in the late summer. Nevertheless, it was not Stephen who beat back the enemy but the local forces of Yorkshire, under the guidance and inspiration of Thurstan, the aged archbishop of York. And yet in 1139 Stephen threw away the fruits of this 'Battle of the Standard', which he himself had not won, by granting the earldom of Northumberland to Henry after all, on the significant understanding that he would help his English overlord against his rebellious subjects or, in other words, withdraw assistance from Matilda.

(iii) Stephen alienated from his cause the only forces in the land which might have made up for his own deficiencies: the civil service, formed by Henry I, and the Church. Unable to overthrow his enemies and bring them into subjection, he seemed determined to parade his lordship over his friends. It was the action of a weak man in power. The first error occurred in 1139, when Stephen fell foul of the wealthy and influential family of Le Poer. Henry I's minister, Roger of Salisbury, had continued to act as justiciar under the new king; his son, Roger, was the chancellor; his nephew, Nigel, was bishop of Ely and treasurer; his nephew, Alexander, was bishop of Lincoln. Stephen was apparently persuaded that they were a dangerous clique and seized a trivial excuse to command them to surrender their castles into the king's hands. However right it was in normal times that the king should resume control of them, no one wished in these perilous days to be deprived of the means of defence when royal protection was not forthcoming. The resistance of the Le Poer family was followed by their imprisonment and quite needless humiliations. Stephen's attack was a most foolish policy, for it dislocated the administration of the country, jettisoned an accumulation of ripe experience, and removed one of the main supports of his throne. The Le Poer group found shelter behind their ecclesiastical privileges, they caused it to appear that the king had made an attack upon the Church, they had him cited before an ecclesiastical council at Winchester and threatened him with excommunication. So in the approaching civil war the bishop of Ely, for example, will be found among the king's enemies and will hold Ely castle against him.

By the second error, occurring in the same year of 1139, Stephen threw away the aid of the Church, which had done most of all to place the crown upon his head. Hitherto the Church had been the firm upholder of monarchical authority in its endeavours to assert political order. Nothing shows the persuasiveness and force of the Reform Movement in England so clearly as the fact that the Church was willing for a time to disregard the deep-rooted traditions of collaboration and to be as capricious as the feudal aristocracy in its support of the king. It no longer demanded simple reform, irrespective of the authority which carried it out: it enunciated a cry for freedom from lay control, and Stephen was not the man to withstand its pressure. The charter he granted in 1136 defined the privileges of the Church and involved a complete surrender of the monarchical position: in its own words, 'justice and power over ecclesiastical persons and all the clergy and their goods and the distribution of ecclesiastical property were to be in the hands of the bishops'. And the laity as well were to be subject to the Church's jurisdiction in actions concerning the sacrament of marriage and the probate of wills. When William the Conqueror had authorized the institution of separate ecclesiastical courts, he had decreed that they should hear ecclesiastical causes only; he had had no intention of letting ecclesiastical persons, who had committed a lay offence such as murder or robbery, be judged by them instead of by lay courts. But by Stephen's reign the Church had gone so far on the way to becoming a self-contained corporation that it claimed complete disciplinary powers over all its servants, and contended that its jurisdiction covered not merely ecclesiastical causes but ecclesiastical persons and ecclesiastical property without regard to what the questions at issue might be.

The royal grip being thus relaxed, the pretensions of the Church reached their highest point in England. The innovations were probably inevitable but, as elsewhere in Europe, their introduction was accelerated. For the first time it obtained full liberty to make its own appointments to bishoprics and abbacies, and the new prelates seem to have sworn fealty only and to have done no act of homage; ecclesiastical councils were held without the supervision of royal representatives. Furthermore, the vacancy caused by the removal of the king was inevitably filled by the pope: he appointed what legates he pleased and they, and not the king, controlled the Church; he welcomed English bishops to Rome.

The development of serious consequence lay in the indication that the political state was to be subjected to the directives of the papacy. This was a novelty which, if left unchecked, might have seriously endangered the position of the monarchy. As we have already observed, Stephen had placed his claims to the throne before the pope in order to get absolution from the oaths he had sworn to Matilda's cause. He was later to surrender, under the threat of an interdict, for daring to banish Archbishop Theobald in 1148 as a punishment for attending a papal council in obedience to the pope but in defiance of his king. He was to abandon the project for having his son, Eustace, crowned during his own lifetime when the pope forbade it, and Theobald left the country to avoid taking part in the ceremony. Whatever the future might hold, never again in the Middle Ages would the State be able to dominate the Church as it had done in the past. Papal authority had been opposed but in the end acknowledged, and a papal party had been formed inside the English frontiers.

It was natural that the new conceptions should produce a new type of churchman, sharply distinguished from the low-born royal servants, like the members of the Le Poer family who had been rewarded for their services with bishoprics. The commanding personality of the early years was Henry of Blois. Of the same princely house as the king himself, educated at the great monastery of Cluny, highly cultured and capable, he had been appointed bishop of Winchester in 1129. He chose to adopt to the full the belief of the advanced Reformers that the salvation of the State could only be achieved and, what was more important, permanently guaranteed if the Church were exalted above it and imposed its own rules and discipline upon it. He had, therefore, no hesitation in becoming involved in secular affairs and playing the part of an ecclesiastical politician. In doing so, he was very much swayed by his own personal ambition to become one of the leading princes of the Church. There seemed every reason why he should have secured his own translation from Winchester to the vacant archiepiscopal throne of Canterbury in 1139, but Stephen, his brother, who owed so much to him, was moved, perhaps by jealousy of his dominant influence, to obtain the appointment of Theobald, abbot of Le Bec. In his disappointment Henry sought to persuade the pope to carve for him a new archbishopric of Winchester out of the province of Canterbury, and, though nothing came of this, yet he obtained the powers of papal legate in 1139 which placed him above his own metropolitan and gave him the leadership of the Church in England. It was through this unprecedented legatine power that he summoned the council at Winchester in 1139 and on behalf of the dispossessed and imprisoned Le Poer family made an open attack upon the king.

It was at that very time that Matilda thought it propitious to land in England and begin the disastrous civil war. Amidst the resulting confusion it is upon the action of the Church that attention should be focused. For two years Matilda and the earl of Gloucester bided their time in control of the western half of the country, allowing feudal disaffection to develop and bring more adherents to their side and awaiting an opportune moment to strike a decisive blow. It came in 1141 when the well-nigh independent earl of Chester, angered to find that Cumberland could not be regained for him from the Scottish prince, rebelled in conjunction with his half-brother, the earl of Lincoln. Gloucester hastened to join forces with them, and Stephen was defeated and captured at the battle of Lincoln and imprisoned at Bristol. The political State had dismally collapsed, but the Church remained, still able to speak for the country as a whole in her ecclesiastical councils, the only deliberative assemblies left. It was in a position to hold the balance between the rival parties, and never again was it to wield such political power. Henry of Blois saw his chance to pose as a mediator and summoned a council of the clergy at Winchester just two months after Stephen's defeat, and he publicly announced that by breaking his compact with the Church the king had forfeited allegiance. Therefore Matilda was 'elected' to take his place upon the throne of England. Such action was completely without precedent. It was presumably argued that a king-elect was no king until he was crowned and, as coronation depended upon the Church, it had an implied right of veto, which itself carried an implied right of election. And what it had done once it could do again. For Matilda was no stronger and no wiser than Stephen, but very much more objectionable in character. Ignoring the counsels of either the earl of Gloucester or the bishop of Winchester, she pursued her tactless way until London expelled her from its midst and Henry of Blois, regretting the action he had taken on her behalf, changed sides again and rallied the forces of opposition against her. The unexpected capture of the earl of Gloucester, the main prop of Matilda's party, was followed by his exchange for Stephen, and by December 1141 Bishop Henry had convoked another legatine council at Westminster, where he denounced Matilda for not fulfilling her promises to the Church, urged the acceptance of Stephen as lawful sovereign, and excommunicated all those who remained loyal to his rival. From that point Henry saw the scope of his influence diminish: his colleagues distrusted one who was capable of such tergiversations, and the new pope in 1143 did not renew his legatine authority. So the position in 1142 was again that of 1139. Both claimants had tried to govern the country, both had been equally useless, and both found their parties growing weaker every year.

Desultory fighting went on for some years until it died away into a peace of exhaustion. Stephen dealt another blow at his pres- . tige when his inept nomination to the archbishopric of York aroused the opposition of Archbishop Theobald, drew against him the denunciations of the great St. Bernard of Clairvaux, and forced the pope to quash the royal appointment in 1147. To balance that, the Angevin party also declined: in 1147 the earl of Gloucester, its only able member, died; in 1148 Matilda left England for ever; in 1151 count Geoffrey of Anjou died, and his young son, Henry, to whom he had resigned the duchy of Normandy two years earlier, was no longer free to give full attention to purely English affairs. The stalemate endured for two years until Henry was able to come again to England to fight for his rights and forced Stephen to agree to the Treaty of Wallingford in 1153: Stephen was to have a life-interest in the kingdom and be guided in the government of the country by Henry's advice; Henry was to succeed him, as he did a year later. It was surrender on Stephen's part, but he was an old man, and there was no point in continuing the weary struggle, for the son, Eustace, whom he hoped would be his heir, was already dead.

The remarkably vivid pictures which the chroniclers have drawn of the horrors of nineteen years 'when Christ and His Saints were asleep' are apt to lead us to too easy conclusions and too simple generalizations: by contrast we extol too much the kingship of Henry I and we condemn too much the feudal barons as a class. For the governance of that king was identified with the elevation to authority of men of low estate and with legal and financial oppression, exhibited most clearly in the creation of vast areas of 'forest' which were subjected to special law and produced a regular income from the multitude of fines imposed for special offences. The rule of law, as imposed by one who 'made peace for men and deer' and 'with whom God alone could contend' was too capricious, too completely a profit-making device, to be indefinitely maintained on those lines. The monarchy was not yet popular in any sense of the word, and we should bear in mind that at least the early troubles of Stephen were not altogether his fault but expressed a burst of relief which was bound to come sooner or later. And yet anarchy was not universally desired by the baronage. It was not so much that they deliberately sought independence as that independence was thrust upon them. When there were rival claimants to the throne, when there was civil war, when monarchy could offer no protection at all, what else could the barons do but look after their own individual safety, build their castles, and administer their estates as far as possible as a self-contained domain? That they did this does not necessarily imply that they wished to do it but rather that the force of circumstances compelled them to do it. It was certainly a propitious time for such unscrupulous adventurers as Geoffrey de Mandeville: an Essex magnate who traded his support to Stephen in 1140 for the earldom of Essex; who deserted him in 1141 and got Matilda to make him sheriff and justiciar of Essex and constable of the Tower of London; who retransferred his allegiance to Stephen at the end of 1141 and was made the local justiciar of Essex, London, Middlesex and Hertfordshire, thus obtaining precedence over the sheriffs of these counties and full control of London; who began intriguing again with Matilda in 1142 with a view to getting a higher bid for his assistance and, though arrested by Stephen in 1143, was too powerful to be kept in captivity by his king and died only by accident in 1144. His treacheries denoted anarchic feudalism at its very worst, and, where such men were powerful, the land was wantonly devastated, agriculture came to a standstill, and famine and plague worked havoc among the peasantry. But civil war was not raging over the whole country, nor did all feudal barons see advantage in disorder. To many of them perpetual warfare meant a loss of rents and a steady decline in prosperity and, indeed, some are found negotiating treaties with one another to keep fighting away from their own estates. Anarchic feudalism did not vanish when Henry II became king: the rebellion of his sons in 1174 showed the same disruptive ideas at work. Still, there was support for Henry II in his determination to reintroduce strong monarchy; so after the civil War of the Roses three centuries later the dictatorship of the Tudors was to be no less welcome.

SELECT READING

W. J. Corbett, 'England: 1087–1154' in *C. Med. H.*, v (1926), 521–52; Brooke, 147–90; K. Norgate, *England under the Angevin Kings*, i (1887), 347–71; F. M. Stenton, *First Century of English Feudalism* (1932), 216–56; J. H. Round, *Geoffrey de Mandeville* (1892); H. W. C. Davis, 'The Anarchy in Stephen's Reign' in *E.H.R.*, xviii (1903), 630–41 (reprinted *H. W. C. Davis: Select Papers* (1933), 81–96).

CHAPTER XXI

THE NEW MONARCHY

IF the years of anarchy had taught any lesson, it was surely this: that all who desired peace and order, firm government and effective justice, must look for them not even in the Church but in the monarchy alone. It remains, therefore, the centre of interest. Everything turned on the character, aims and abilities of the foreigner who became king of England at the age of twenty-one. In the event this man, who was impelled by his restless energy to tackle resolutely the chief problems of government and to supervise carefully the actions of his ministers, who possessed a mentality remarkably legalistic in its bias, and who showed an intelligent interest in things intellectual and cultural, was to be responsible for the quickest and most splendid period of growth in the whole of the Middle Ages.

It is usual to compare the achievements of the Angevin, Henry II, with those of the Norman, Henry I, and to suggest that in the main he simply continued on the lines his maternal grandfather had laid down. He is certainly in the direct tradition of the Norman Monarchy in so far as he was determined that the king should be in no sense first among equals but without an equal, and that the king's court should function as more than a purely feudal court. In other words, there was to be the same centralization of power in the royal person. But the basis of that power was to be different. A new conception was born, a new tradition was founded, a new monarchy was established. For the first Henry scarcely advanced beyond the limited ideas of feudal monarchy: he used to the uttermost the high powers and privileges which were always inherent in that office, nevertheless it did not enter into his thoughts that he could maintain his authority by any other method than the sternly enforced submission to his will of his feudal tenants. In that sense he was looking backwards rather than forwards. The second Henry's policy was manifestly imbued with a different spirit which was in keeping with the developments of the future. He made his monarchy popular rather than feudal by securing for it the support, not only of the more responsible barons, but also of the free men of the realm, who were attracted to the royal person and the royal court by the inestimable benefits placed at their disposal. Therein lies the essential originality of his work. He was not merely making normal the practices which before had been exceptional, he was not simply systematizing rather than experimenting. Indeed, it is very evident that the reign was one long amazing period of experimentation, adaptation and adjustment, during which much was often jettisoned in favour of improved arrangements. The result was something new, and it represented a rapidity of development which will not find its equal again for the next three hundred years.

Henry attained his objects mainly through a deliberate extension of royal justice, yet it should not be forgotten that, though he had the lawyer's mind and the lawyer's methods, his interests were not primarily legal. What he did was prompted by political and financial motives. The primary cause of reform in justice, police, army and other spheres was the severely practical necessity of uprooting the violent habits of twenty years of misrule or no rule at all. That could not be accomplished unless the central government was strengthened and extended its control over the entire community, unless the rights of property were safeguarded, unless the sure discovery and punishment of crime guaranteed peace and order. And Henry was quite as well aware as his predecessors that to widen the scope of royal justice would be to increase judicial profits; the more perfect the machinery, the more certain it would be that royal rights would be protected and enlarged.

The legal instrument used by Henry in his constructive work was the royal prerogative. As we have already noted, it was well known and well used in Anglo-Saxon times, though it had not then to face the special problems inherent in the dual nature of monarchy in a feudal state. After the Conquest it became more and more imperative that the king should clearly show that there were powers attached to his office that were far older than feudalism and that lifted him out of the feudal world and freed him from the shackles of feudal law. And during the Intellectual Renaissance of the twelfth century, which reached its culmination under Henry II, there was a great revival of interest in Roman institutions and Roman law, which caused greater emphasis to be placed upon the supreme position of the king and the need for a uniform system of law and procedure. The king therefore stressed and extended the elastic prerogative. Whether used deliberately or not for the purpose, the prerogative was the weapon with which feudal arrangements were attacked as it were from outside; it provided the pressure from above which forced into unity the broken pieces which made up his realm.

A revolution took place which changed the modes and ways of thought and life. It would not, however, have come about if it had not been given general support. Fortunately, Henry II was the first king to rule without a rival since the Norman Conquest introduced a disturbing series of disputed elections: hence there was no dynastic strife which could be used, as in the past, by small but powerful sections of the feudal aristocracy to promote and ensure their independence and their position. The baronage in great part, the Church, the administrative classes, the bulk of the people: all were eager to see the reassertion of strong rule, and the extent to which the monarchy of Henry II had public opinion behind it was fully shown during the critical rebellion of 1174.

It is not surprising that we hear little or nothing of a reform programme during the first ten years of the reign. Obviously nothing could be done until the aftermath of anarchy had been removed and the governmental machinery, still discernible, had been brought clearly into operation. The work of pacification alone was a tremendous task, and the king addressed himself to it with promising vigour. He published a short Coronation Charter, in which there was no question of anything but hereditary right and in which he ignored Stephen's reign as an interregnum and declared his intention to maintain peace as his grandfather had done. He disbanded the large contingents of mercenaries whom Stephen and Matilda and he himself had brought into the country, in particular the notorious 'Flemish wolves'; he resumed the royal demesne lands and privileges that had been so recklessly granted away; he suppressed most of the earldoms of the anarchy so that their holders would be deprived of their too magnified position in the country; above all, he made it his settled policy to destroy the private strongholds, the 'adulterine' castles, of which well over a thousand were reputed to have been built. Severe fighting was required, especially on the Welsh borders, but the work went on rapidly and the crisis of this frontal attack on disorder was so safely passed that by January 1156 Henry felt it safe enough to depart from England and not return for fifteen months.

But much remained to be done before the work of construction could get fully into its stride. Three measures of reform helped to clear the field for action.

I. THE OVERHAUL OF MILITARY FEUDALISM IN 1166

It was not enough for the king to destroy the evidence of past disorders, he must make sure that there was no repetition of similar horrors. Therefore he was led to investigate the whole military arrangements of feudalism. Nevertheless, he was not primarily concerned with military organization as such: rather were his objects financial and political. Hitherto, as we have seen, the system of knight service had been founded on a very simple plan: the first Norman king had decided the size of the army he needed and then demanded so many knights from each of his tenants-in-chief. What arrangements these themselves made were regarded as no affair of his. In practice it was evident that the great tenants had either enfeoffed too few knights for economy's sake, hoping to make up their number with hired mercenaries whenever military service was demanded, or, which was more usual, enfeoffed more knights than had originally been required. Henry seized the chance, offered by this confusion, to establish a new feudal assessment in 1166. He asked for particulars from all tenants-in-chief, both lay and ecclesiastical, which would tell him, first, what was their accustomed service (*servitium debitum*) and, secondly, how many knights they had actually enfeoffed. Having acquired this information, he reached a simple solution of the problem: if too few knights had been enfeoffed, then the tenant of the fief was still assessed on the basis of the old 'accustomed service'; if too many had been enfeoffed, then the *servitium debitum* was correspondingly increased and the dangerous tenant-in-chief was saddled with a greater financial responsibility. Henry thus used the old assessment when it was worth his while but abandoned it when it would have turned to his loss. There was naturally a great outcry, especially from ecclesiastical tenants, but Henry was strong enough to gain his point. Furthermore, from the political angle he insisted that all those knights, who held their lands directly from lords other than himself, should yet do him homage as their liege lord, though he naturally made no claim upon them for 'feudal incidents' and the like. Henry left no room for doubt that feudal 'homage' was to be subordinated to the older Anglo-Saxon conception of 'fealty', and the notion of 'allegiance' came rapidly to reach its modern meaning.

And it may be added here that Henry reconstituted the fyrd by the famous Assize of Arms of 1181, which regulated the military equipment that must be possessed and maintained for use in the king's service by all his noble and free subjects. Moreover, the export of ships or the wood from which ships might be made was forbidden: the need to provide full means of communication between his dominions could not be overlooked, and it was about this time that the Cinque Ports on the south-east coast contracted, in return for unique privileges, to provide ships in time of war.

The idea of a national rather than a feudal force was thus brought once again into prominence, and the king had made it plain that he was not depending for support on his immediate tenants only but had the intention of relying on the help of all free men. However much a feudal army was still a 'military reality' in the following century, it was in Henry II's reign that feudalism lost in England its prime justification as the basis of military organization. The king had been irked by the limitation of service to forty days and the uncertainty whether it should be performed at home or overseas, and he knew quite well that no continental campaign of any value could be undertaken without the aid of full-time experienced foreign soldiery. The method of subsidizing it was already to hand. For there had developed within a single generation of the Conquest the practice of 'commutation', whereby military services were translated into cash payments. Scutage in its origin certainly goes back to the first year of Henry I's reign, and it is vaguely outlined even under Rufus. It was apparently restricted in application at first to church lands, for ecclesiastical tenants found themselves in an embarrassing position: by feudal law they had to serve the king in battle, by canon law they were forbidden to shed blood. The obvious escape from the dilemma was to pay someone else to do their service for them. It was inevitable that the same concession should be made to lay tenants, especially minors, heiresses and widows. Under Henry II seven scutages were raised at a fixed rate for each knight's fee.

II. THE SURVEY OF ADMINISTRATION IN 1170

The full significance of this ambitious undertaking is hidden under the misleading name of the 'Inquest of Sheriffs', for they alone were not involved. During the previous four years the king had been absent from the country, and numerous complaints had reached him concerning the wrongdoings and corruption of those responsible for local government. Therefore the country was divided into circuits, and commissioners were appointed to each of them and furnished with a long list of questions, which had to be answered in detail by representatives of shires and hundreds, concerning the conduct not only of sheriffs but of all officials, no matter whether they were the servants of the king or of the barons. They were also prepared to hear complaints at large against any other persons. Their reports were to be made to headquarters within the short space of two months. It is unfortunate that only a few fragments of the records of this visitation have survived. What most impressed contemporaries was the fact that many of the sheriffs were dismissed. The year 1170 can, in fact, be taken as marking the end of their decline and fall during the twelfth century. In Stephen's reign many sheriffdoms had once again come into the hands of local magnates, and there was a danger that they might become hereditary in certain families. To begin with, Henry II had to accept the situation he inherited, but the abuse of authority provided him with the opportunity to make the sheriff purely the executive agent of his will, an obedient middle-class official. As such he was made the link between central and local government, and he became so loaded with administrative duties that he formed the indispensable pivot of the new judicial machinery. Without him to serve writs, summon juries, arrest culprits and execute judgments, centralized justice would have been impossible.

III. THE REMOVAL OF THE LOCAL JUSTICIARS

As in the case of the sheriffs, Henry apparently continued the system he found working at his accession. But these resident officials, first appointed by Rufus, had so exalted their position under Stephen that even earls and bishops were solicitous to attain it. However, their interests were local when they were not personal, and it is presumable that the king found them a serious hindrance to his schemes. Certainly within a few years he had managed to suppress the office. But not until then did he begin to lay the foundations of that judicial structure which endured, modified but substantially unchanged, till the fourteenth century. For their disappearance made possible the development of the system of itinerant justices.

The three major problems which had appeared under the Norman kings had not been solved by them, and they had been handed down to the Angevin rulers in a more serious and perplexing form. Henry II set himself resolutely to find a solution to them, but his efforts were not an unqualified success, and the questions remained to harass his son, John, and in close association with one another to bring about his downfall.

I. The Feudal Problem

The new machinery of government was neither a single nor a sudden act of creation but the result of work spread over more than two decades. We ought not to regard that work as casual and haphazard, for there was evidently logical thought and careful planning at the back of it. What the king and his great ministers did should be looked upon as all of one piece, whether it is the development of a central court of general administration resident at Westminster, or the organization of eyres in the country districts, or the king's insistence on his right to deal with serious crime, or the writs withdrawing a mass of litigation from seignorial and local courts, or the expansion of the jury system.

The system of central government which had been instituted by the close of Henry II's reign owed its establishment to the same practical need as had influenced developments under his grandfather: the task of governing lands on both sides of the Channel. It became a far more urgent problem when the king of England had to rule, not merely Normandy, but a congeries of states covering the entire western half of France and differing widely in their political and social structures. To cope with a situation, the like of which was not to be seen elsewhere on the Continent, deliberate and conscious statecraft was essential. The king could not be in several places at once, and, as he spent more years of his reign abroad than he did in England, he had to make arrangements for the governance of his kingdom while he was away, often for several years at a stretch, and for the operation of as common a system of administration for his dominions as possible. So far as England was concerned, out of these necessities emerged a centralized government which had no parallel in Western Europe.

We shall leave a more detailed study of this achievement until the reign of Richard, when the almost total absence of the king left the machinery to function under its own power and without the complications arising from occasional royal supervision, and when records are at last extant to reveal its activities with reasonable accuracy. It is sufficient here to say that everything that was done was done by the *curia regis,* by the king's court, whether it was considered to be with him or with the justiciar. That is the simple contemporary view. Specialization there is and a growing tendency to departmentalism, but the fact is not clearly faced in the twelfth century. Our concern at the moment is not with the *curia regis* in its aspect as an intermittent 'great council'. Nor is it with the *curia regis* as a 'small council' in permanent attendance on the king's person, for it could not govern England when the king took it abroad with him. The effective and continuous government of the country remained in the hands of the justiciar, who worked through the exchequer. To him was delegated the royal authority when the king crossed the Channel, and by virtue of it he summoned and held deliberative councils and issued writs in his own, and not the king's, name. The exchequer, settled at Westminster since 1172, was still an office of general administration for the most multifarious tasks: a financial bureau, a court of law with an ever-increasing activity, the quarters of a staff of clerks busily engaged in writing writs, a place where decisions could be taken on perplexing points at any time. The king's return made no practical difference in the work that it was doing under the justiciar's direction: it remained the nerve-centre of government.

Our main theme must be the truly remarkable expansion of royal justice through the combined operation of writs, juries, and special courts.

I. THE WRITS

Before the accession of Henry II jurisdiction over criminals and over civil matters, such as rights of property, lay in the main with the old popular courts of shire and hundred or the new feudal and franchisal courts of the aristocracy: only in special circumstances did they receive any external stimulus or supervision from the court of the king. Thus, in particular, the seignorial courts were interested in questions of tenure of concern to the lord's tenants. When problems of tenure happened to be brought before the shire courts, even there the influence of the local lords was predominant. Furthermore, though the local courts exercised criminal justice, many of the hundred courts had fallen into private hands and were functioning as 'franchisal' courts. So, despite the royal nomination of sheriffs, the device of resident justiciars and the inauguration of eyres, the dispensation of justice throughout the country, particularly the punishment of crime and the protection of property, was not dependent on the king. Local justice was rarely royal: it was popular and it was feudal. There was, however, no reason why the king's court should restrict itself principally to protecting royal interests and resolving the differences of his immediate tenants. Indeed, there was much to be said against it. For it was the king's duty to ensure peace in the land, and he could not perform it unless he ensured justice, for the two things are inseparable. The coronation oath itself had enjoined him to see that justice was done to all, no matter what their social status might be, and his general right to intervene for that purpose could not be, and was not, disputed. Moreover, ancient custom as well as the general feudal right of the sub-tenant permitted all who felt themselves wronged to appeal to the king and bring their complaints to his notice. Thus, if the king chose to let his willingness to redress wrongs be widely known and thereby to expand the scope of his justice, there was nothing to prevent it.

The complaints addressed to the king lie at the back of all his prerogative writs, issued by him in ever-increasing numbers until they came to provide the motive force of nearly all the machinery of the law. Although writs of similar kind and purpose can be found before Henry II's time, they are but occasional and special: only after his great reforms was their issue made regular and systematic. To begin with, the writs were brief letters of instructions, sent out by chancery clerks, to make sure that proper justice was done by those responsible for it, with the proviso that disobedience would be construed as contempt of the king and would result in their being summoned to answer for it before the king's justices. Such was the ordinary 'writ of right'. It was a short step to issuing writs which removed actions peremptorily and immediately to the royal courts: such was the writ of right called 'praecipe', which was sent, not to the lord, but to the sheriff, instructing him to 'order' the lord to restore the freehold in question or appear in the royal court. And as the fountain of justice was inexhaustible, the writs multiplied as practice revealed improved methods and new wrongs.

II. THE JURIES

That Henry II and his ministers decided to make sworn juries a normal and essential part of the judicial machinery of government is, in the light of later events, a fact of supreme political and constitutional importance. Because the jury became eventually a symbol of English liberties, there has been a natural reluctance to abandon a native, a popular, an Anglo-Saxon, origin for it. If we take the definition of a jury to be 'a body of neighbours summoned by a public officer to answer questions upon oath', the problem is not easy to resolve. It had clearly no connexion with the doomsmen of the local courts, whose business it was, not to state the facts, but to declare judgment on facts already established; or with the compurgators, who were summoned to his aid by a litigant, and not by a public officer, and who were under no compulsion to give their services; or with the witnesses to the sale of property, who were likewise friends of the contracting parties. Since, with the exception of one awkward piece of evidence which is discussed below, there is nothing to suggest that the jury was known in England before the Conquest, it is at the moment accepted doctrine that it was in its beginnings continental and not Anglo-Saxon, a royal and not a popular institution.

The argument goes that, early in the ninth century, the Frankish kings decided to discover the facts about their various rights by placing groups of their subjects on oath and asking them questions. To us there is nothing extraordinary in this procedure. But those living at the time knew quite well that there was no sanction for it in their customary law and that it did, in fact, ignore the proof by the defendant's witnesses sanctioned by that law. Such 'inquests', that is inquiries, were allowable, therefore, only through the exercise of the royal prerogative and could not be authorized by any of the king's subjects. They played a regular part in Frankish government, were introduced into Normandy, and transported thence to England. We have seen how they were used as an administrative device: for example, in ascertaining facts for the Domesday commissioners and for itinerant justices. It was, however, when they were used in judicial procedure as well that their great future lay open before them. Henry II, copying the innovations made by his father, Geoffrey, in Normandy whilst the duchy was in his hands, brought 'inquests' into the sphere of justice, and by slow degrees they grew into the criminal and civil juries of the present day.

Apart from the fact that we know absolutely nothing about the use of a sworn inquest in Normandy before 1066, the even development of this thesis is roughly broken at one point, and a point remarkably early in time. An ordinance of Ethelred the Unready, published at Wantage about 997, declared that a court should be held in every wapentake (the hundred of the Danelaw), and there the reeve and the twelve senior thegns should undertake on oath to give information about criminals. This seems to anticipate the Assize of Clarendon of 1166, which arranged for the presentment of suspected evildoers by the hundred. But, as it seemed impossible from lack of evidence to bridge the gap of nearly two hundred years between Ethelred and Henry II, the Wantage decree has been explained away on the ground that it applied only to the Danelaw and was, in consequence, a Scandinavian custom which came to nothing. The argument is not altogether convincing. It would be equally valid and more probable to believe that Ethelred was extending to the Danelaw a practice that already held good in Wessex. And it is hard to imagine that the prosecution of criminals should have been left entirely and completely for several hundred years to the initiative of merely private persons. What if through fear and intimidation they refused to take action at all? We know, indeed, that king after king in both Anglo-Saxon and Norman times had issued regulations for the arrest and punishment of evildoers, in which official and communal, rather than individual, prosecutions were involved: thus, it was an acknowledged principle of Anglo-Saxon law that a man of notorious ill-fame should not be allowed to establish his innocence by getting compurgators to speak for him but must go to the ordeal; it was the duty of reeves to investigate offences in connexion with coinage and tolls; it was for Anglo-Saxon communities to give information about cattle-thieves, and this was quite sufficient to set the machinery of justice in operation and might well end in the death of the accused; communal reports of crimes, as in the 'presentment of Englishry', were being made in shire and hundred courts long before 1166. It is therefore in the local courts that we must look for the evidence that small groups, as groups, were being compelled to voice suspicions, tell tales, inform against the criminal. The kings used the procedure for the purposes of general supervision: they gave their instructions to the local courts, and it was left entirely to those local courts to carry them out. The revolutionary change, wrought by Henry II, was to transfer the work of punishing criminals to the royal courts instead and to place it under the direct control of the royal justices, whilst retaining a method of communal prosecution, known in the Anglo-Saxon local courts of the tenth century and carried over the Norman Conquest without a break. Then the criminal jury emerged from the obscurity of local courts and appeared openly on the royal records, which have been preserved, as though it were a novel institution.

It is well, therefore, to abandon the Norman and ecclesiastical origin of the jury which presented criminals. At a time when the Church was the great borrower in constructing her system of canon law and procedure, it is far from likely that the church courts had invented a novel process which it was worth while for secular courts to adopt, and we can discard the view that sees the jury of presentment first authorized in 1159 in the ecclesiastical courts of Normandy, and in 1164 in the ecclesiastical courts of England (the Constitutions of Clarendon of that year decreed that a church court was not to put a layman on trial before it on vague rumour alone but either by the definite accusation of an individual or by the sworn testimony of twelve men of the neighbourhood), and at last in 1166 its transference to royal and secular courts as well.

(i) *The Criminal Jury*

We have already observed that, before Henry II's reign, the 'king's peace' as a legal concept had been a highly exceptional privilege, the grant of royal protection to a specially favoured few, and that 'pleas of the crown' did not form a group of serious crimes which must be reserved for the king's jurisdiction alone, no matter when or where or by whom they were committed. The idea that acts of violence were essentially the concern of the king and came under his purview, and that of no one else, was the result of legal innovations brought in by the Normans. The first was the conception of 'felony', which was alien to the English and to the spirit of their laws: it was a shameful word, once applied to the treachery of a vassal and then extended in an obscure way to all heinous and depraved wrongdoings. The second was the 'appeal' of felony, whereby it was left to the victim's relatives to bring a criminal to justice. If the accused appeared for judgment when he was 'appealed', that is, called, the normal method of settling the dispute, if it lay between Englishmen, was by ordeal or compurgation but, if between Frenchmen, by the third novelty of 'trial by battle'. But no customary or feudal laws contained any ruling on what was to be done if the adversaries were one a Frenchman, the other an Englishman, and the problem was settled by the exercise of the royal prerogative by William I when he regulated the methods of proof. If the accused obstinately refused to appear, then he was subjected to outlawry, which could only be pronounced in the county courts, which were with rare exceptions never out of the king's control. If he appeared and failed to clear himself, he was not permitted to make a monetary compensation in accordance with the English scale of tariffs but was condemned to capital punishment and, a final novelty, the felon's property was 'escheated' or forfeited to the king. Therefore, with a system of royal courts in process of formation, with a prerogative right to control procedure, with a strong financial inducement in the way of judicial profits, there was every attraction to the king to enter the field of criminal jurisdiction and there was nothing seriously to bar his way. So at last, starting with Henry II, the 'king's peace' began to become a form of protection for all, a right to trial which could be easily obtained by simply alleging a breach of the king's peace, for this forced the case to come into a royal court, usually that of the justices in eyre. And once the 'king's peace' had the whole community within its care, the 'pleas of the crown' came to indicate 'crimes' in the technical sense of wrongs, committed against the State and punishable only in the courts of the king. The number of wrongs construed as crimes increased rapidly, and by John's reign the tendency was to leave nothing but misconduct of a petty kind to local courts and to those private courts which could not claim a higher 'franchisal' jurisdiction.

The great advance was made in the Assize of Clarendon in 1166, when Henry II ordered twelve men from every hundred and four men from every village to come before his sheriffs and his justices to state on oath whom they believed to be murderers, robbers, thieves and the harbourers of such. Those under suspicion were to be tried before the justices only, to submit themselves to compurgation or the ordeal by water, and, even though the decision was in their favour, they were to leave the country within eight days for being of ill-repute with their neighbours. In 1178 the Assize of Northampton added arson and forgery to the list of offences and increased the mutilations inflicted on the convicted: the great rebellion of the reign had just ended, and a ruthless policy was needed in putting down disorder.

The presentments, or indictments, of what came to be called the Grand Jury (it was not abolished until 1933) provided only a suspicion of guilt: that guilt remained to be proved. Trial by battle could not be used because the king himself was the prosecutor; compurgation was too open to lies and deceit to meet the king's purpose of rigorously suppressing violence; the ordeal alone was left, a pre-Christian practice which the Church had ceremonialized. But it was too crude and too barbarous a method to appeal to those of the twelfth century who were eagerly assimilating the refinements of Roman law. In 1215 the ordeal disappeared when the pope forbade the clergy to take part in the proceedings, for without religious rites it could not become the infallible judgment of God. The royal justices hardly knew what to do with the indicted persons: in 1219 they were instructed to imprison for major, banish for medium, and grant bail for minor crimes. The gap, left by the ordeal, was gradually filled when those indicted were asked to accept the verdict of another jury of their neighbours, which was termed the Petty Jury. Their consent was indispensable, for a jury was not considered as trustworthy as the old ordeal, which might reveal God on the side of the accused even though his neighbours condemned him. However, in 1275 notorious evildoers, who refused a jury, were forced to undergo 'prison forte et dure', and this in some strange way turned a few years later into the 'peine forte et dure', not abolished till 1712, whereby they were compelled, usually by being pressed by weights, to accept a jury. Some heroically died under the torture to escape a certain condemnation, which would have caused their property to escheat to the crown and left their families destitute.

For a long time the presenting or Grand Jury was not kept carefully distinct from the trial or Petty Jury: members of the first might be put on the second, sometimes the first was simply turned into the second. But public opinion hardened against allowing a man's accusers to be also his triers, and the two types of criminal juries were definitely separated by statute in 1352.

(ii) *The Civil Jury*

The king allowed the free members of the community, though not the villeins, the use of his prerogative: if they wished, they could establish their title to land by means of a sworn inquest. He had no intention at first of taking property rights under the protection of the crown. What he wished to do was to stop men taking the law into their own hands and making forcible evictions. The best prevention was to guarantee that anyone, thus dispossessed, would be given quick redress. A speedy remedy, however, was not to be expected from the traditional procedures of feudal and local courts; it could only be provided by an authority which could override the accustomed methods. The step was not taken without long and serious deliberation, for it meant curtailing the jurisdictional privileges of the feudal aristocracy, but there was no other way of bringing order out of the chaos of conflicting claims, created during the previous reign. It has, indeed, been suggested that for some ten years or more the justices in eyre were required *ex officio* to investigate cases of eviction and take appropriate action, altogether regardless of the parties concerned, and that it was only after the new procedure had proved its worth and litigants desired it to be available at all times that the king devised formal writs and put them up for sale.

It is well to point out that the word 'assize' is used in the Middle Ages with various meanings, often at the same time. Originally, an *assisa* indicated simply the 'session' of a court; then the word was transferred to the enactments of the court (e.g. the Grand Assize), or to the jurors who formed the essential part of that procedure, or to the itinerant justices who were appointed to try the actions. (*a*) *The Petty Assizes*. Because these assizes, though concerned with land, were not exclusively civil actions but had a criminal aspect in that dispossession was a wrong nearly always accompanied by violence and, therefore, a breach of the peace for which fine, damages and even imprisonment might be the penalty, it is better to jettison the misleading and too limited phrase of the 'possessory assizes'. The assize of novel disseisin, 1166, constituting one of the most momentous events in English history, allowed any freeholder, who had been recently dispossessed of his land, to obtain a writ from the king which would put the matter before a sworn inquest of his neighbours. Knowing the facts, they could give a verdict on this issue instantly, and if it was favourable to the plaintiff, he recovered his property at once. The assize of mort dancestor, 1176, protected an heir in the same way from eviction at the perilous time of inheritance. The assize of darrein present-ment, *c.* 1179, protected the patrons of churches by arranging for the immediate settlement of the question who had 'last presented' a parson to an ecclesiastical benefice. The remaining petty assize was the assize 'utrum' (1164) which decided 'whether' a property was lay fee or alms, that is, whether it belonged to a lay lord or to the Church, for on the answer to this question depended the important point whether the lay or the Church courts were to have further jurisdiction. It was convenient to place the matter before an inquest as a kind of disinterested third party. (*b*) *The Grand Assize*. The first three petty assizes were intended to be only temporary settlement of land disputes: they decided the recent fact of possession but they left untouched the ultimate *right* of ownership. The unsuccessful party might well have a better title. He could, therefore, obtain a writ of right to prove that title by the slower and more elaborate procedure of the 'grand assize', conceived and authorized in or before 1179. The curious fact is that, a generation later, an action by the 'grand assize' was comparatively rare. Since the assize of novel disseisin happened not to confine the parties to a short term of years but allowed them to range further and further back into the past until by Henry III's reign a long period of dispossession was open to scrutiny, it was for all practical purposes deciding proprietary, rather than simply possessory, rights, and it became, not a mere preliminary to an action on title, but a complete form of action in itself, with which the parties were generally content. Similarly, the assize 'utrum' ceased to be followed by any further proceedings in the ecclesiastical courts.

The jurors, of course, were not judges in the sense that they weighed the evidence. They were witnesses on oath to certain facts. Still, they were always a little more than witnesses in that what they said was regarded as a proof which both parties to the action accepted without any questioning. If, however, the sworn inquest was to become like the modern jury, its members had to become less like witnesses and more like judges. This came about slowly but quite naturally: if the jurors had not full knowledge of the facts, they were allowed to co-opt other witnesses, and these in time separated themselves off and a distinction was drawn between the two groups. The final discrimination came when it was at last agreed that a defendant could challenge jurors and have them removed but could not challenge the witnesses.

III.   THE CIRCUITS OF THE JUSTICES IN EYRE

Though eyres occurred before 1166, we know little about them, and it is evident that that year, which had seen such a changed attitude to crime and to property, saw also a complete overhaul of the eyre system to fit it for its working of the Assize of Clarendon. In the following twelve months pleas were held in at least seventeen counties, and plea rolls, whatever their contents, were kept for delivery to the exchequer. By 1170 there was almost a complete circuit system in operation. The arrangements for six circuits in 1176 and for four circuits in 1179 have received quite unwarranted emphasis simply because they happened to be mentioned by the chroniclers. They are, in fact, but two illustrations of a policy which was in constant process of adjustment and change till the end of the reign, and they fixed no definite circuits at all. As the justices who patrolled the country were mostly members of the court of exchequer, the general control of the central government was effectively increased. The work of the justices in eyre continued to be most diverse: they did not simply hear pleas of the crown and private litigation but performed an ever-increasing number of miscellaneous administrative duties, including the vital supervision of local government officials. It is to the credit of Henry II and his ministers that they developed the eyre into a smooth-working and indispensable organ of government.

IV. THE CENTRAL COURT

In the sphere of judicature it was no longer possible to limit the *curia regis* to mainly great men and great causes. When royal justice was expanding with such acceleration, it was obvious that there must be some central tribunal continuously at work to fill the time-gap between the eyres and to exercise a general supervision over what was being done. Therefore the king placed the services of the *curia regis* itself at the disposal of ordinary men. It is customary to regard the arrangements made in 1178 as creating all at once the court of common pleas: five members of the king's court, two clerks and three laymen, were detailed to hear the complaints of all free men, and for this purpose they were to remain constantly with the king wherever he might be. All problems too difficult for them to settle were to be referred to the king and the 'wiser men' of the kingdom. In fact, there was no sudden act of creation, for the arrangements of this year represented no more than one among many experiments both before and after that date. When the 'bench', the future court of common pleas, comes more clearly into light in the following reign, it will have little or nothing in common with the itinerant court as instituted in 1178 but result instead from specialization within the exchequer.

It would be unwise to imagine that Henry II was so much out of touch and sympathy with contemporary thought that he was aiming deliberately at the elimination of feudal jurisdiction. It had an essential part to play in the life of the community and, even if he had had the desire, the king had neither the organization nor the officials with which to displace it. For political reasons Henry had found it necessary to see that heinous crimes and property disputes came under his supervision. But, to begin with, the number of such crimes he dealt with was not large, and in civil matters he did not compel men to abandon the old ways and seek the royal court. He had to engage their support by offering them something superior to what they could obtain elsewhere. They soon recognized the advantages of speedy and rational methods as compared with the long delays, archaic barbarisms, and biased workings of feudal justice, and even the feudal lords appreciated the differences and themselves used the new procedures.

All the same, the feudal aristocracy realized and resented the reduction in their feudal rights and authority. The petty assizes had ignored their courts altogether and, indeed, the assize of mort dancestor was levelled almost straight at them, for it was they, in particular, who were tempted to keep an heir out of his property. The grand assize attacked their very right to do justice, for the king had laid down the principles that no freeholder need defend his title to his property unless called upon to do so by a writ from the king himself; that he could *if he so desired* have the case transferred from the lord's to the royal court; that in the king's court he could buy the privilege of trial by jury instead of having to submit his claims to the hazardous trial by battle. No one could fail to see that a violent and drastic breach had been made in seignorial jurisdiction. The victory was won once and for all, for that jurisdiction was never to regain its old position but to dwindle away more and more before the encroaching tide of royal justice. The king had made it plain that he was to exercise ultimate control, that anyone could make a complaint to him of injustice and expect to be protected by his court. The justices of the Norman kings had reserved their attention well-nigh exclusively to what was of direct interest to their royal master: the justices of the great Angevin king placed their services at the disposal of the free community of the realm in matters which had no direct interest for the king. That represents an advance without parallel at the time in Europe.

If such developments weakened the power of the aristocracy by producing an administration which no longer depended on feudalism for its support, they were certainly favourable to the middle classes. They lifted the free tenants out of their feudal surroundings and gained their support; they brought about a permanent liaison between royal justice and the justice of the local courts.

The magnificent result of these vast and unremitting labours was the foundation of the rule of law, a royal law and not customary or feudal law, a law which commanded respect all over the country and obedience in places where the king had no direct feudal authority. Criminal justice had begun to be the same for every-one: no privilege could evade the police regulations of the Assizes of Clarendon and Northampton. The use of common writs, common procedure and common courts forged a common law that was to obliterate the racial and provincial distinctions created by the variations of Anglo-Saxon—i.e. West Saxon, Mercian, Danish—law and of feudal custom. No other European countries in this century were to find it possible to sweep away the local customs which thwarted their unification. When within the domain of law men began to think the same thoughts and speak the same language and share the same experiences, a common consciousness was born which was bound to make a great contribution to common unity in other spheres as well. A legally united England preceded, and prepared the way for, a politically united state. The evolution of the common law of England, based on unwritten custom and judicial decisions, is fortunately revealed to us in the treatise attributed to Glanville and that of Bracton. It had a wonderful future before it: by the time of the Tudors it had become too sturdy, too tough, to bend before the rising popularity of Roman law, and not long afterwards it was to travel three thousand miles across the Atlantic to rule the destinies of North America.

II. The Ecclesiastical Problem

This problem had become increasingly difficult as the Church moved steadily forward from a demand for independence to a claim to supremacy over the secular state. During the twelfth century it organized itself so well that papal government was never to reach a higher point than that attained during the reign of the English King John. But papal monarchy was an unnatural development and doomed to failure in the course of things because it ran counter to the quite inevitable emergence of national states. And it was recognized, in England as elsewhere, as a serious threat to the foundations on which lay society rested.

It was most unfortunate that, through a quite excusable mis-calculation on the part of Henry II, the problem of Church and State should have come prominently to the fore in the early years of his reign before he had had time to show how supremely impor-tant the reassertion and the expansion of royal authority and royal justice were going to be: otherwise, he would have been able to deprive Archbishop Becket of one of the strongest arguments in his case. Henry's programme of reform was clearly intended to bring the clergy as well as the laity within its scope and to sweep away what, in the opinion of the king and of many others, were clerical abuses. He himself could hardly tolerate the free and unimpeded departure of prelates from England to deliberate side by side with those who were his continental enemies, the ignoring of his right to control the elections to high ecclesiastical office, the encroachments on the jurisdiction of the lay courts, particularly by the contention that cases of debt and all other contracts must come before the Church courts because they involved an oath to keep faith. The feudal lords were irritated by the more frequent use of the weapon of excommunication against them, the removal of peasants from their service when they were accepted for Holy Orders, and the flouting of their rights as patrons of churches. And it was plain that public order could not be restored unless crimes, committed by clerks, were properly punished. Henry's aim was to bring about a restoration of past conditions and thereby recover the ground lost. He looked back to the time of his grandfather and determined to reassert the practices which were then traditional and, above all, to exclude the independent action of the papacy: the connexion between England and Rome was not, of course, to be broken, but it must, as in the past, be through the king. Nothing must be allowed to hamper him in his work of destroying the lawlessness of the preceding reign. If feudal exemptions from the operation of his justice were to be removed, surely clerical immunities should be removed also. It was not only that they sheltered the section of the community which by its education and close touch with the people at large was highly influential. It was still more dangerous if the Church courts were to extend their jurisdiction over criminal offences. For it was openly recognized that the penalties they could impose were far too light for a violent age when stern justice was imperative. Canon law forbade the shedding of blood: therefore the penalty of death could not be inflicted. The heaviest sentence was unfrocking and imprisonment, and even this was not often pronounced, because the first contained a reproach to the Church and the second was a profitless expense. In consequence, a felon was only too likely to escape with simply penance and a fine if he was in at least sub-deacon's orders.

Henry could at first do little more than influence new elections to ecclesiastical office and demand homage before consecration. On the death of Archbishop Theobald in 1161, he contrived the appointment of his chancellor, Thomas Becket, as his successor, believing with good reason that the result would be as cordial and fruitful a co-operation in the work of reconstruction as that between William I and Lanfranc. This turned out to be a blunder, and it forced the king into an even greater blunder: the promulgation of the Constitutions of Clarendon in January 1164. Though concerned with the affairs of the Church, they were an integral part of his general reform programme and provided a reasoned statement by the king of his views on the whole problem of Church and State. There was little that was new in the document, for it expressly stated the 'ancient customs' which had held good under Henry I and which had been ascertained after the most careful inquiries. Nor was it an extreme document, for it was produced with the assent of the barons, the majority of the bishops found no difficulty in accepting its provisions, even Becket himself gave his approval to the draft proposals, and the shrewd and politic Pope Alexander III, though he did not accept it as it stood, did not hesitate to make it the basis of negotiations. The grave error lay in converting the unwritten customs into a written enactment. For this defined and forced the issues. The 'customs' might be a correct statement of fact; indeed, no one could well dispute that point. But the times had changed and it could not be taken for granted that what held good once ought to hold good for ever. The bishops found themselves put in the embarrassing dilemma of having to decide whether they would obey their temporal or their spiritual superior, the law of the State or the law of the Church. They appreciated the good intentions of the king but, unlike him, they for their part could not regard the reign of Stephen as a mere hiatus and ignore those developments of twenty years which had emphasized papal sovereignty. The pope could not prevent himself from being dragged by Becket into the conflict as it developed. The document could not be left in the English fashion for the lapse of time to produce a compromise.

The Constitutions consisted of sixteen clauses. Six of them were rulings which excited no controversy and were accepted by the pope: for example, that no peasant's son was to be ordained without his lord's consent, and no archdeacon was to summon a layman to his court without definite accusation by a private individual or a jury of presentment; four tried to fix a boundary line between the secular and spiritual jurisdictions, asserting that disputes over the right of patrons to present to benefices (ch. 1), over property which was alleged to be held by free alms (ch. 9: the assize 'utrum', in which the use of a jury was itself a sign of impartial moderation), and over debt (ch. 15), were to be settled in the royal courts, whilst criminous clerks were to receive the same punishment as criminous laymen (ch. 3); six were concerned with the burning question of royal, as opposed to papal, authority. These last clauses set down the 'ancient customs': without royal permission no appeals were to be made to Rome (ch. 8), no ecclesiastics were to leave the country (ch. 4), no tenant-in-chief or—and this was new—royal official was to be excommunicated (chs. 7, 10); the bishops and abbots were to do homage before consecration and thus have their feudal position as royal vassals emphasized (chs. 11, 12). In the event, Becket would accept none of these claims, but it was into the question, not of papal supremacy but of 'criminous clerks', that all the current disagreements between Church and State were telescoped.

Whether or not clerks had been tried for criminal acts in the royal courts during the early years of the reign, Henry showed his willingness to reach a reasonable compromise in the Constitutions: anyone who committed a crime was to be accused and made to answer in the royal courts; if his offence was there proved and if he pleaded 'benefit of clergy', he was to be sent for formal trial to a Church court where a royal justice would be present specially to represent the king; if he were convicted there, he was to be deprived of his orders, and thereby of ecclesiastical protection, and handed over to the royal courts to be given the same punishment as a layman would have received. Becket, however, would tolerate no such procedure: by canon law a clerk accused of crime must be tried in a Church court and, if guilty, be there sentenced and punished. He objected to the preliminary hearing in the royal courts, the presence of a royal representative in the ecclesiastical courts, and the principle of a double punishment for a single offence, namely, unfrocking by the Church, followed by capital punishment or imprisonment by the State. This last argument was refuted by later popes, but Becket himself clung to it with the 'obstinacy of a man who has found a slogan'.

It is no easier for us than it was for his episcopal colleagues to sympathize with Becket's views as a whole, though among many dubious claims he made one good point. He knew from practical experience the way in which temporal justice could be withheld or abused in a violent age: it was not for nothing that the so-called 'Inquest of Sheriffs' was to be held six years later. There must be no possibility of a return to the conditions of Stephen's reign. Indeed, it was probably the breakdown and defects of secular justice at that time that had attracted litigants to Church courts and stimulated the growth of ecclesiastical jurisdiction over broken contracts and debts. And it could at least be argued that by 1164 the justice of the Church was becoming superior to that of the State in that its canon law represented a reasoned and enlightened system, developed by the great Italian jurists of the Italian law-schools according to the principles of Roman law, and as such it stood in sharp contrast to the law of England, based as it was on the customs of a barbarous age. Therefore ecclesiastical law knew legal refinements and subtle distinctions and equitable considerations that were quite beyond the ruder justice of the lay courts. And, substantive law apart, ecclesiastical procedure was much more civilized than the antiquated and unreasonable formalities and barbaric proofs, like ordeal and battle, which were used by secular courts.

The struggle with the Church was, unfortunately, precipitated before the royal justice could reveal its benefits or prove its permanence. Yet with any common sense or good will a solution to the problems could have been found and the sharpness of the conflict dulled. But the personal animosities of two overbearing men had entered to make this impossible. It is difficult to like Becket or to withhold sympathy from the king. Becket, a *parvenu* coming from a middle-class business family, had been a student at Paris and Bologna, and had entered the service of Archbishop Theobald before Henry II had his merits pointed out to him in 1155 and made him chancellor. In that office he became the second man in the kingdom, the faithful and favoured agent of the king in diplomacy and war, the jovial and worldly companion of his royal master, and no careful respecter of the Church's laws or the Church's property. In 1162 he was Henry's own choice as archbishop of Canterbury to assist him in his general reform programme. Immediately, Becket made himself the uncompromising champion of the most extreme clerical pretensions, upholding the independence of the Church and the sovereignty of the papacy. He may have been neither hypocritical nor insincere, but a romantic actor playing a part he had visualized for himself as the perfect archbishop. Whatever the psychological explanation, he was certainly obsessed with the importance of himself and his office, impervious to advice and criticism alike, unbalanced, tactless and spiteful. Even his friends admitted this and, in fact, most of the bishops deplored his intransigence, especially the ascetic and scholarly Gilbert Foliot, bishop of London. By 1164 Becket must have known that Henry II was neither a despoiler of the Church, like Rufus, nor a nominal king, like Stephen, and that his actions must lead to bitter strife. It has been well said that Becket, in his relations with the king, took a positive delight in stressing points of difference, however small, instead of reserving his resistance for occasions when high principles were at stake. For example, even before the Constitutions were published, he had deprived royal clerks of benefices, bestowed on them by the king in the normal way as a reward for their services; he had excommunicated a royal tenant-in-chief without consulting with the king; he had opposed the king over the question of the sheriff's aid. This was a customary charge, based on land and paid over locally to the sheriffs as a perquisite of office. Henry decided to annex it to the royal revenues, and ordered it to be paid direct to the exchequer. Becket chose to espouse the sheriffs' cause on the ground that they would be driven to make good the loss by extortion, and he managed in a council at Woodstock in 1163 to force the king to abandon his intention. It is little wonder that Henry, possessing to the full the ungovernable Angevin temper and impatience of opposition, was enraged by the virulent attacks of one who owed his eminence entirely to royal patronage. After Becket's rejection of the Constitutions the king threw prudence aside and went much further than he had ever imagined would be necessary. He decided to break the archbishop: he provoked petty quarrels with him until at last he summoned him before his royal court to account for moneys which had passed through his hands as chancellor, and he had him amerced for failure to appear. Becket realized his peril and fled the country in November 1164, leaving the small papalist party, which had supported him, in the lurch. Save for the last few weeks, he spent the rest of his life in exile, losing any sense of proportion he ever had, opposing the king and threatening him and his ministers with excommunication, attacking those prelates who had agreed to accept the Constitutions, and generally disturbing the peace of Europe.

In exile the archbishop was more jealous for the papacy than the pope himself, who was engaged in mortal conflict with the Emperor and had no desire to offend the English king and thereby unite against him the two strongest princes in Europe. He could, however, do nothing else but condemn ten of the Constitutions of Clarendon. Thereupon papal supremacy, and not criminous clerks, became the major issue, expressed concretely in the problem of appeals to Rome.

Becket was apparently not greatly missed in England during his six years' exile, but special circumstances arose to demand his recall. The king wished to put the succession to the throne beyond dispute in case of his own untoward death, and therefore during his own lifetime he had his son, Henry, crowned in 1170. The ceremony, carried through in the archbishop's absence, directly infringed the rights of Canterbury. Becket protested vigorously, the pope supported him, and, as the matter was too important to be left in any doubt, Henry invited Becket to return, no mention being made of the Constitutions. It was, however, the same unbending man who came back: he showed no magnanimity in the hour of virtual victory, but at once excommunicated the bishops who had dared to usurp his prerogative at the coronation. It was then that Henry uttered the hasty words that led to Becket's death.

Becket was far more important after his death than before it, because this murder of the head of the Church by the head of the State made him throughout the Middle Ages the rallying-point round which ardent clericalists could gather. To appease an outraged public conscience Henry saw fit in time to do abject penance. And yet Becket's death did not make the relations between Church and State more difficult but far easier. For the archbishop had stood for his own opinions rather than for those of the clerical body in general in England. The Church was nothing like as aggressive as he, and it had no desire to make capital out of what had happened. Therefore it willingly accepted and welcomed the two concessions that Henry showed himself prepared to make. (a) He abandoned the claim to a preliminary trial of criminous clerks and let the Church courts have full jurisdiction over them: they were privileged to commit at least one felony before being punished as severely as laymen. (*b*) He allowed freedom of appeals to Rome, with the significant reservation that they must not result in harm to his crown or his kingdom. No longer was the connexion between the papacy and the English Church to be indirect through the king, and thus the essential purpose of the Constitutions of Clarendon was defeated. As a result the door was open for the admission of canon law into England. The pope's advice was sought, and his decisions obeyed, without questioning; indeed, Alexander III apparently sent more papal missives to England after 1170 than to the rest of Europe put together.

Nevertheless, Henry by no means made a complete surrender. Though the Constitutions became a dead letter, he had not repealed all the 'ancient customs' contained in them: the king still controlled the elections to high ecclesiastical office and, in fact, the next episcopal elections were all of royal clerks; he went on enjoying the revenues from vacant sees; he still forbade the excommunication of royal officials and the entry of papal legates without his previous assent. Although the Church courts retained a wide judicial competence for purely ecclesiastical affairs—ecclesiastical tenures (subject to preliminary investigation by the assize 'utrum'), marriages and wills, spiritual offences like adultery, usury, and defamation committed by laymen as well as clerks, and secular felonies perpetrated by clerks alone—yet they lost much for which they had contended. The rights of patrons of churches, bound up as they were with property in land, were confirmed, and, as they passed with that property, they could virtually be sold at will: England was unique in this in Western Europe, and it was destined to have important consequences. The lay courts secured their jurisdiction over contracts and debts, simply begging the question by the assertion that pledges of faith were not essential to them. Even the concession relating to criminous clerks was whittled down: treason and forest offences were excluded from the list of felonies cognizable by the Church courts; the precise nature of all other charges of felony had to be decided by an *ex officio* investigation by the lay courts before 'benefit of clergy' was allowed and, though this was ostensibly to let the king know at once his rights to the accused's property and though its conclusions had no binding force, it certainly influenced the findings in the Church courts; and finally, all other clerical offences below the level of felony, that is the innumerable misdeeds which will soon come to be classified as trespass and misdemeanour, remained under the jurisdiction of the lay courts and clerks were no more privileged than laymen. Indeed, even for the Church the limited victory in the matter of criminous clerks was not altogether desirable, for it encouraged private revenge.

The important point to notice is, therefore, that the liaison between the Monarchy and the Church was not broken. The clergy were still willing to supply the king with advisers and officials; he for his part made the bishops of the Church his trusted ministers and judges. But for the continuation of this collaboration between a reforming king and educated men, versed in Roman and canon law, it is difficult to see how there would have been devised the splendid framework of organized government and the even finer foundation of a rational and systematic 'common law' in England.

III. The Continental Problem

This problem assumed a disproportionate importance in the special circumstances which gave an empire to Henry II and imbued him and his successors with the ambitions that were to be but a snare and a delusion. Henry could not, however, give full attention to those continental possessions, which always meant more to him than England, until he had tranquillized his kingdom. It was not sufficient to provide her with a stable government. He had to go further and make certain that her frontiers were secure, for already in Stephen's reign Scotland had extended her border sixty miles down the west coast south of the Berwick–Carlisle line, and Wales had similarly made inroads into the Marches. His efforts to attain this object were all made in the first half of his reign, and they led him to an ambitious policy of feudal suzerainty over his immediate neighbours.

THE UNIFICATION OF THE BRITISH ISLES

(i) *Wales*

The first expedition into difficult terrain in 1158, directed against the king of North Wales, succeeded in recovering the territories lost under Stephen, but when a more ambitious campaign was launched in 1165, this time against the king of South Wales, for the conquest of Wales itself, Henry realized that the task would be too arduous and exhausting. Therefore he contented himself with obtaining a formal acknowledgment of his overlordship and constructing a strong barrier of fortresses along the frontier. Apart from that, Wales was left under the rule of her two native kings, and relations with England remained peaceable, undisturbed even during the critical years of the great rebellion of 1174.

(ii) *Scotland*

Early in the reign Henry persuaded the king of the Scots to surrender the northern counties of Northumberland and Cumberland, and took homage from him, not for his kingdom, but for his English earldom of Huntingdon. The foolish participation of William the Lion in the rebellion of 1174 and his defeat and capture at Alnwick in Northumberland provided Henry with the opportunity to extend his suzerainty over the northern kingdom as well. By the treaty of Falaise the Scottish king agreed to become his vassal and hold his kingdom as a fief of the English crown: in this instance it was no mere formality, for William fulfilled his feudal obligations, attending the court of his overlord and allowing the disputes of his tenants to be evoked there from his own court. And for security reasons English soldiers were permitted to garrison the five towns of Berwick, Jedburgh, Roxburgh, Edinburgh and Stirling. Scottish bishops, for their part, grew accustomed later to look to the archbishop of York as their primate.

(iii) *Ireland*

This country had been so completely disorganized by the raids and conquests of the Northmen that it had relapsed into isolation from Britain and the Continent, except for the trade connexion maintained with the Scandinavian settlements around the principal ports along its east coast. The individual rulers of the six kingdoms were entirely engrossed with their attempts to keep their family dynasties firmly on their thrones, none of them had real power, and Ireland had rarely risen above the anarchy of clan life. The Roman Church could do little to foster orderliness because it was baffled by the independence, amounting to indiscipline, shown by the Irish Church and by the variation in its practices, and it found restricted scope there for its activities. Ireland lay helplessly exposed to conquest but in its poverty excited no greed. In 1155 Henry II had contemplated conquering the island, but events elsewhere forced him to abandon his schemes. It was not until 1169–70 that the dispossessed king of Leinster obtained help in recovering his crown from a small body of Norman adventurers from Wales. Their leader, Richard 'Strongbow', earl of Pembroke, aroused the suspicions of his English king when he himself became 'king' of Leinster in 1171, and, though he hastened to render conciliatory homage, Henry II determined to embark in person on the conquest of Ireland. Following William I's example, he had some years before persuaded the pope to look upon any such expedition as a crusade against a schismatic country. He landed in 1171 in the south-east at Waterford, and, meeting hardly any resistance, made an easy progress to Dublin. During his six months' stay he received the submission of many Irish and Scandinavian princes and lords, distributed fiefs among the Normans, established a form of government under Hugh de Lacy as justiciar, which was deliberately on the same lines as that which functioned in England and in Normandy in the absence of the king, and held a council of the Church, at which a programme of ecclesiastical reform was drawn up. Although it would at this time have evidently been a simple task, no proper steps were taken to consolidate what had been achieved so easily. Henry was content to see that the coastal towns were adequately garrisoned, and otherwise Ireland was generally left to the mercies of adventurers. And Ireland was not to be subdued completely in later times: the English kings did not undertake the work themselves, and they were too suspicious and jealous to allow others to do it for them. So there appeared at the very beginning the curse of Irish history, that the problems of Ireland were never to be considered on their own merits but only as they affected English interests.

Though perhaps no time was to be so propitious for an attempt to unify the British Isles, it did not enter Henry II's mind that he should concentrate on this problem. For he was born, and he died, in Anjou, and he was first and foremost a French prince: for every year of his reign he spent in England, he spent nearly two in France and, though he was acquainted with Latin and its 'Romance' derivatives, he knew little or no English. We must, therefore, remember that England counted with him, and his sons and grandsons after him, as only one part of their dominions and, since it felt the repercussions of whatever developments took place abroad, we cannot, and must not, divorce its history from that of France or, indeed, of Western Europe as a whole.

THE CONTINENTAL EMPIRE

Though Henry had no imperial title, it is difficult to find a comprehensive term for his accumulation of territories without adopting the modern, though inaccurate, description of them as the Angevin Empire. For there had come into his possession a series of principalities which stretched from the Grampians to the Pyrenees and gave him control of almost both sides of the Channel and the Atlantic seaboard of France. This king of England and feudal overlord of Scotland, Wales and Ireland, also possessed through his mother Normandy, through his father Anjou, Maine and Touraine, and through his wife the district between the Loire and the Pyrenees, called Aquitaine. Nor was Henry satisfied with what had come to him mainly by inheritance, for he set to work to drive his way to the Mediterranean and even tried to add Italian lands across the Western Alps to his dominions.

As we should expect, the legalistic Henry II sought to attain his ambitions by stressing his legal rights whenever possible and by preferring diplomacy, revealing itself in marriage alliances, to war. At first he met with considerable success, largely attributable to the easy-going nature and general ineffectiveness of the French king Louis VII (1137–80), who added to his early blunders of departing from France to go on the Second Crusade and of divorcing Eleanor, the heiress of Aquitaine, who was to marry his most dreaded foe, the further mistake of taking no serious advantage of Henry's interminable difficulties with Becket or with his own wife and sons. For the Capetian monarchs were now face to face with the spectre which had haunted them for so long: one of their nominal vassals who had united so many fiefs of France under his control that he overshadowed the throne altogether. It must have seemed to contemporaries that the house of Capet was doomed. (a) *The Acquisition of Brittany*. He secured the betrothal of the Breton heiress to his eight-year-old son, Geoffrey, in 1166 and, though it took him three military campaigns to force the Breton nobles to recognize Geoffrey's rights of succession, his ambition was realized in 1171, and Brittany remained quiescent for the rest of his reign. (b) *The Acquisition of Toulouse*. Henry advanced a claim in 1159 through his wife that it was historically a part of Aquitaine. In this instance he met sterner resistance, led by the French king, and he was, as usual, unwilling to break the solemn feudal bond and make war upon his overlord. Therefore it was not till 1173 that bribery placed a ring of enemies round the unfortunate count of Toulouse and compelled him to abandon the unequal struggle and become the vassal of the Angevin king. Thus Henry's authority reached the shores of the Mediterranean. (c) *The marriage of his eldest surviving son, Henry, to the daughter of Louis VII of France.* By this typical instance in 1160 of his diplomatic methods Henry intruded a member of his family into the Capetian House itself, for no one could foresee what accidents or succession disputes might not occur to allow him by a short cut to reach the French crown itself. Incidentally, as part of the marriage-dowry, the district of the Vexin was reincorporated in Normandy. (d) *Marriage alliances with the Great Houses of Europe.* The eight children with which Eleanor provided him were all made the instruments of his diplomacy. One daughter was married to that Duke Henry the Lion who lorded it over North Germany as the leader of the Guelph party (1168); another to the king of Castile (1169); and another to the Norman king of Sicily (1177). It was his youngest son, John, whom he nearly succeeded in marrying to the heiress of Savoy (1173).

By such means Henry established the strongest feudal monarchy that Europe had seen, ruled by the most intelligent of kings and supported by the wealth of mainly England and Normandy. Yet within a generation the Angevin Empire had crumbled to pieces. The very rapidity of its decline indicates how slender were its chances of long surviving. The difficulties of physical geography alone were sufficient after some time to cause the empire to collapse, but its ruin was hastened by particular problems.

(i) *The lack of any community of interest*

The hotch-potch character of the Empire was reflected in the variety of titles under which Henry governed: a king in England, an overlord in Scotland, Ireland and Wales, a vassal in France. The single tie of common allegiance could not be sufficient to hold it together. For each of his dominions knew different systems of government and laws and customs. Even Henry, with his passion for centralization and orderliness, wisely did not try to introduce uniformity. All he could do was to use his officials, wherever they had been born, in any part of his empire where their services could best be employed, and there was, in consequence, much coming and going within it. This intercourse was especially seen between England and Normandy, a province which was different from the

13

rest of his continental possessions in so far as it had close affinities with the English kingdom in its knowledge of centralized government and its replication of the administrative machinery of justiciar, exchequer, eyres and assizes. For that reason Henry chose to make Normandy the basis of his continental power. Nevertheless, the Norman barons who resided in Normandy had not experienced the pervasive influence of centuries of disciplined obedience, and it was plain that they would throw off the control that irked them as soon as they found a chance. Aquitaine presented a picture of the anarchical side of feudalism at its worst: effective government was apparently out of the question, and Henry temporized with difficulties as they arose. Despite all his efforts, the barons of Poitou remained notorious for their treachery, and war was endemic in all parts and on all occasions. The times were as yet too early for Monarchy to find an ally in the commercial middle classes: the privileges that Henry gave were merely intended to turn towns into garrisons and burgesses into soldiers.

(ii) *The rebellion of Henry's sons*

As Henry could not be in several places at once to cope with problems, he adopted the device of appointing his sons to represent him in the various parts of his Empire. Geoffrey was to rule in Brittany, Henry in Normandy, Anjou and Maine, and Richard in Aquitaine. He expected them to be as docile servants of his will as any of his officials. As, however, he resolutely refused to allow them any authority commensurate with their high dignities, they refused to play the role their father had assigned to them. Thus the element of family strife was added to the feudal chaos. Abetted by their remarkable mother, who repaid her husband for his libidinous infidelities by plotting against him for the advantage of her children, the brothers promoted the rebellion in 1173-4 which first broke out on the Continent and set the whole Empire aflame. After its suppression they raised isolated standards of revolt: Henry died while fighting his father in order to get Aquitaine from Richard (1183); Geoffrey was on the point of insurrection when he died (1186); Richard, who had a morbid hatred of his father, rebelled in his turn and offered his homage to the French king (1189). By that time Henry II, though only fifty-six, was dispirited, listless and broken-hearted and, when he learned that his youngest and favourite son, John, was also secretly among his enemies, he lost the will to live.

(iii) *The accession of the formidable Philip Augustus of France*

He ascended the throne at the age of fifteen, largely through the assistance of Henry himself, who often paid punctilious respect to the obligations of the feudal contract, even to his own disadvantage, lest he should set a bad example to his own vassals. Nevertheless, Philip did not hesitate to assist Henry's rebel sons. It was this ruler who found his kingdom far behind Normandy and England in methods of government and, whether deliberately or not, reorganized his administration on parallel lines. It was mainly through his agency that the Angevin Empire perished in the course of the first great international war in the West. But its memory remained to misdirect the actions of the rulers of England for three hundred years and to divert their energies from less artificial and more profitable undertakings.

SELECT READING

D. M. Stenton, 'Henry II' in *C. Med. H.*, v (1926), 554–91; Brooke, 191–214; Stephenson and Marcham, 71–95; W. Stubbs, *Historical Introductions to the Rolls Series* (ed. A. Hassall: 1902), 89–181; G. B. Adams, *Council and Courts in Anglo-Norman England* (1926), 151–78; R. L. Poole, *The Exchequer in the Twelfth Century* (1912); T. F. T. Plucknett, *Concise History of the Common Law* (3rd ed: 1940), 102–143; H. G. Richardson, 'Richard fitz Neal and the *Dialogus de Scaccario*' in *E.H.R.*, xliii (1928), 161–71; N. D. Hurnard, 'Jury of Presentment and Assize of Clarendon' in *E.H.R.*, lvi (1941), 374–410; W. H. Hutton, *Thomas Becket* (1908: revised 1926); F. W. Maitland, *Roman Canon Law in the Church of England* (1898), 51–99, 132–47; Z. N. Brooke, 'The Effect of Becket's Murder on Papal Authority in England' in *Cambridge Historical Journal*, ii (1928), 213–28; Mary Cheney, 'The Compromise of Avranches and the Spread of Canon Law in England' in *E.H.R.*, lvi (1941), 177–97.

CHAPTER XXII

THE RELIGIOUS REVIVAL AND INTELLECTUAL RENAISSANCE

EUROPE as a whole was not yet to be free from the incursions of barbarian peoples and left unmolested to fashion its own future: the Mongol Empire was to be established on the Middle Danube in the thirteenth century and the Turkish Empire in the fifteenth century. But the immunity of the West from the shock and devastation of such assaults made possible the regularization of feudalism as the basic organization of society, the introduction of reforms in the Church and the enhancement of its authority, and the diversion of military strength to the Crusades which brought the West into closer touch with the thought and the wealth of the East. The sense of security made the twelfth and thirteenth centuries a period of remarkable advance. Some manifestations, such as the rapid development of urban life, are discussed later in connexion with their political implications. Here we must confine our attention to two broad aspects: the religious revival, which expressed itself in the foundation of new Orders, and the intellectual renaissance which saw a renewed interest in the classics, an altered attitude towards theology, a systematic study of Roman law in its civil and ecclesiastical forms, and the beginnings of the universities. If we seem to spend more time upon the European background than upon the English scene, it is because this is the great age of cosmopolitanism, and events in England are part and parcel of continental movements, from which they must not be divorced if they are to be understood.

I. The Religious Revival

I. THE BLACK MONKS

In the Middle Ages the strong religious emotion that urged men to seek their ideals by rejecting material values was always apt to reveal itself in a new form of monasticism. And as that emotion was in the nature of things bound to be transient, there was a constant alternation of decline and revival in monastic history. The reformed Cluniac version of the Benedictine Rule had done much to purge monastic life of its ills since the early tenth century, and it had influenced the Anglo-Saxon Benedictine houses in and after the Age of Dunstan, and particularly when they came under the control of Norman abbots who had been previously associated with Cluniac foundations across the Channel. Nevertheless, the Benedictine abbeys did not cease to be independent and self-contained, and they formed no part of the Cluniac Order with its hierarchical form of government and ultimate allegiance to a foreign superior. Indeed, the first Cluniac priory to be established in England was at Lewes in 1077, and by 1135 there were no more than eleven in existence. And by that time the Cluniac Order had itself become discredited: countless donations had brought it great wealth and, in the opinion of many, it thought more of finely-built abbeys and magnificent ritual than of the prime virtues of simplicity and poverty. It was to recapture these that two new Orders were instituted and quickly became distinct from what had gone before: as White Monks, wearing plain, undyed or 'white' robes, they were marked off from the Black Monks of the Benedictine and Cluniac Rules.

II. THE WHITE MONKS

(i) *The Carthusians*

Their founder, Bruno, was a German monk of Cologne, who had become head of the cathedral school at Rheims and the tutor of Pope Urban II. He retired in 1084 into the wild and desolate parts of Dauphiny and built an abbey at the village of Chartreuse near Grenoble. Since in his opinion it was too much of a common life, shared by too many, that had engendered luxury, he reduced it to a minimum by returning to a very early and pre-Benedictine form of monasticism in which a few monks lived as much as possible the lives of hermits. His abbey saw a collection of individual cells instead of the cloister: each monk prepared his own food and said the daily offices by himself, and he met his fellows for a common meal only on the great festivals of the Church. This life of solitude and silence was too severe to make the Carthusian (Chartreuse: Latin *Carthusia*) Order popular, and it was not fully organized and recognized until 1176, but, though it was not large, it retained its original strength and zeal and could proudly boast that it had never had to be reformed.

The Carthusians did not reach England until the last years of Henry II's reign when, about 1179, they founded Witham Abbey in

Somerset. The most famous Carthusian was its first prior, the Burgundian Hugh of Avalon, who became the saintly bishop of Lincoln (d. 1200), that close personal friend of Henry II, whom he did not hesitate to rebuke openly for his sexual immorality. Before the Reformation there were no more than nine Carthusian Houses or Charterhouses ('charterhouse' is a corrupt form of 'chartreuse') in England.

(ii) The Cistercians

A score of Cluniac monks, eager to give literal obedience to the old, original Rule of St. Benedict instead of its Cluniac revised form, had in 1098 founded a monastery at Cîteaux (Latin *Cistercium*) near Dijon in Burgundy. The Cistercians were never as ascetic as the Carthusians in their way of living but they also stressed austerity: plain and not over-plentiful food, undyed robes, simple churches devoid of gold and silver and bells. The recitation of the divine offices occupied six hours of the day; manual labour was stressed in order to render the monks economically independent and in a position to refuse corrupting gifts; meditation in silence on the scriptures and the commentaries of the Early Fathers of the Church occupied their leisure, and literary work was banned. An Englishman from Sherborne in Dorset, Stephen Harding, became the third abbot (1109–34), and he so meticulously regulated the Cistercian Order that he is regarded as its second founder. Nevertheless, this movement for reform might well have perished if the future St. Bernard, with thirty companions, had not chosen in 1112 to enter Cîteaux as a novice and, two years later, to found a daughter-house at Clairvaux, where he remained abbot for the rest of his life (d. 1153). This outspoken and fiery Burgundian reached such fame as a theologian, preacher and reformer that he was more influential than the pope himself. So powerful was his personality that Cistercian Houses multiplied with great rapidity all over Europe: from nineteen in 1122 to three hundred and fifty about 1150 and five hundred and twenty-nine by the end of the century, extending from Norway to Italy and from Germany to Portugal. It was early evident that a formal constitution was essential, and the Cistercians, like the Carthusians, chose the Cluniac system of a Congregation rather than the Benedictine practice of independent monasteries, for it provided a means of guarding against corruption and of enforcing discipline. Thus the *Carta Caritatis*, granted by the pope in 1119, laid it down precisely that all abbots were to be subject to the spiritual authority, but not temporal control, of the Great Abbot of Cîteaux and must come every year in person or by proxy to Cîteaux to attend the General Chapter. Should the Great Abbot himself become lax, then he was to be disciplined, even to the point of deposition, by the abbots of Clairvaux and the three other earliest-founded houses. An interesting feature of the Order came to be the use of lay-brethren or *conversi*, as they were called. At one time any man, however poor, could become a monk, but the monasteries were growing more and more middle-class, and how could anyone be a monk if he did not know Latin well enough to be able to recite properly the divine offices? Therefore unlettered peasants were permitted to become half-monks: they took the vows of chastity, poverty and obedience, but their sole task was to labour in the fields and leave the choir monks free to devote themselves to the paramount duty of prayer.

Though the first Cistercian abbey in England was founded in 1128 at Waverley in Hampshire, the south of England remained Benedictine and Cluniac in its sympathies, and it was in the north of England, where old-established monasteries were neither numerous nor influential, that the new Order became strong. It was, in any case, a cardinal principle with the Cistercians to set up their houses as far away from the corrupting haunts of men as possible, and the northern counties gave them the inhospitable wilds and solitude they desired. St. Bernard gave his assistance, for with him monasticism had a social value, and the more abbeys like Cîteaux and Clairvaux were instituted, the sooner the Church as a whole and the world in general would be brought back to simplicity and purity. Thus Rievaulx Abbey (1132) and Fountains Abbey (1132) were the offspring of Clairvaux, and they had themselves a large family of affiliated Houses. By 1152 some forty Cistercian abbeys had been established, all but four of them being colonies from Waverley, Rievaulx and Fountains. This year presents the high point of expansion, for then Cîteaux saw fit to veto any further foundations and, though the ban was not strictly enforced, only half-a-dozen more houses were set up before 1216. There was little ill-feeling between the Cistercian monks and the secular clergy, for the Cistercians made it a cardinal principle to establish friendly relations with the bishops and, indeed, Archbishop Thurstan, himself an intimate friend of St. Bernard, gave them every assistance. The history of the Cistercians presents a curious paradox. In the deserted regions where they deliberately fixed their homes, tillage on a large scale was out of the question and they turned to sheep-farming and, as the wool trade increased with the years, they had wealth thrust upon them. This fact contributed to their eventful corruption, but it was not the only reason for it: we must remember that the Cistercian Order declined in other countries where these special conditions did not obtain.

England produced an exclusively English, though not distinctively English, Order in the Gilbertines. A Lincolnshire priest, Gilbert, established at Sempringham about 1131 a community of pious women under his own administration. Then, in order that the nuns should not be left without proper religious ministration and instruction, he added to it a community of canons or secular priests. Afterwards, in order to provide for the heavy manual work that women could not do, lay-brethren were also associated. The principle of the 'double monastery', which had been known to Bede and later disappeared, was thus revived. This curious medley of observances, in which the nuns obeyed the Cluniac interpretation of the Rule of St. Benedict, the canons the Rule of St. Augustine, and the lay-brethren the Rule of Cîteaux, was popular in Lincolnshire, Nottinghamshire and South Yorkshire, and provided a necessary outlet for the spiritual fervour of women, for the Gilbertine Houses were, to begin with, essentially nunneries. Thirteen had been instituted before the aged founder of the Order of Sempringham died in 1188.

III. THE CANONS

The religious revival was not confined to the monasteries. It was, as always, far more important that it should reveal itself among the secular clergy. We have already seen how before the Conquest the Church in England had increasingly realized that, as a member of a Universal Church, it had incurred responsibilities and obligations. Since then the ties with the papacy had been drawn tighter and canon law developed and observed. And it was during these years that the Church began to increase and systematize its machinery of administration, as, for example, in the division of bishoprics into territorial archdeaconries and these into rural deaneries, and to bring the establishment of parishes to its culmination. Attempts continued to be made to impose celibacy upon the parish priests but with slight success: it is quite evident that the great majority of them had wives or concubines, brought up families, and lived their lives in much the same fashion as their parishioners. The position was far different with the higher clergy, especially those who served the cathedrals and great churches. As we have seen, under the influence of the religious revival associated with Dunstan and his fellow-reformers, a movement had begun to place the cathedrals in the charge of monastic communities, and it had received a further stimulus from the Norman Conquest: nine cathedrals came to be governed by monastic chapters, a not altogether happy arrangement which caused much confusion and set monks and bishops at variance. The others remained in the care of chapters of priests, but there was a feeling that they should become subject to a 'rule' and live a celibate life in common. In practice no such 'rule' could be enforced. Still, there was no reason why any church, which could afford to maintain several clerks in its service, should not be viewed in a similar light: such were the arrangements for King Harold's foundation at Waltham Holy Cross. When communities of regular canons were established for the perpetual worship of God, then there seemed very little difference between them and the equally autonomous Benedictine monasteries. The main distinction in the twelfth century was that the 'regular canons' were in priests' orders, though they had, for most practical purposes, renounced the world.

(i) *The Black Canons*

In this twelfth century the conception was seen in its full force, and before its close there had been founded some one hundred and thirty houses of Augustinian, or 'Austin', canons, believed to be obeying the rules observed by St. Augustine. Under Henry I and Stephen a large number of houses of Black Canons were set up in England, mostly in the country districts, and such institutions continued to be founded for more than a hundred years to come, for they could be established with little formality, they were not subject to supervision except by the bishop, they were freer to develop as they pleased without the restrictions imposed by a rigid monasticism.

A 'rule' such as this, which was elastic, could be adapted to other religious foundations, such as hospitals, and St. Bartholomew's in London (*c.* 1123) was among the earliest of such institutions. Similarly, the Military Orders of St. John of Jerusalem (1114) and of the Knights Templars (1128) came to adopt the canonical life, and their members, though laymen, regarded themselves as Austin Canons.

13*

(ii) *The White Canons*

Some of the communities of canons added special regulations of their own to the Austinian Rule, and the most famous of these versions was observed by the Premonstratensian Order of White Canons, which followed the ideals and the constitution of the Cistercian White Monks. It had been founded by a German priest, Norbert, in Champagne in 1120 at a place mystically revealed to him (*Pratrum Monstratum, Pré Montré*: 'a mede revealed'). Once again it was St. Bernard who gave the new Order the encouragement which probably saved it from extinction and without which it could not have spread so far. The first Premonstratensian House in England was set up at Newhouse in Lincolnshire in 1143, and a score of others were founded in the following half-century.

IV. THE FRIARS

It is to the twelfth century that the Christian Church in the West can look back with most satisfaction at what it did and meant for the world at large. Nevertheless, it failed, as it was then constituted, to keep pace with the needs of a rapidly progressing society, and, largely for that reason, heresy emerged. It must not be imagined that it was not until the intellectual renaissance of the twelfth century that heresies made their appearance in Western Europe. Religious speculation must exercise intelligent minds at all times. But for a long time it had remained academic and had not disturbed the life of the common people. However, many factors like the revival of learning and the growing importance of the middle classes had combined to produce a new and unsettled atmosphere. And there was a mysticism at large in Western Europe which could find no satisfaction within the orthodox Church. It caused the formation of many groups like the 'Poor Men of Lyons', more commonly known as the Waldensians or Vaudois after their leader, Valdo, a merchant of Lyons (d. 1173), who anticipated the Franciscans in so much of their attitude to life. They renounced their worldly goods and lived solely on alms, thus being able to devote their whole time to contemplation upon the soul, upon immortality, upon God. And it was apparently the play of Eastern thought upon the restless mood of the time that promoted the great heresy of the 'Cathari' (Greek: 'pure'), which was known throughout the West and gained a particularly firm hold upon Southern France and

Northern Italy. Its centre in Provence was the town of Albi: hence its alternative name of the 'Albigensian' heresy. The beliefs of the Cathari came to be, in effect, a denial of Christianity. For they argued in favour of a theistic dualism, the existence of two Personalities, a good God and an evil God. The first portrayed himself in the mind of man, the second in his material body. That the good God might conquer, the body must be brought sternly into subjection. So for the 'elders' or priests of this creed it meant a revulsion from carnal desires such as were denoted by property and marriage. Since it condoned suicide, the murder of the body, it was anti-social; and since it denied the resurrection of the body, even Christ's, and abhorred the idea of purgatory and rejected any transubstantiation of material bread and wine into the Body and Blood of Christ, it was heretical in thus repudiating the central doctrines of the Christian Church. So the Roman priesthood found itself confronted by the Catharine priesthood, preaching and administering sacraments and rapidly gaining ground. It was to meet this crisis that two novel Orders were instituted. So far the Rule of St. Benedict and the Rule of St. Augustine had sufficed as a basis for religious foundations, and they had stressed the need for withdrawing as far as possible from contact with the world, for the observance of fixed rules, and for stability of habitation. The new Orders were to follow quite different principles of conduct: they were to seek an accommodation with the lay world, to leave themselves as free as possible to act as the spirit moved them, and to become mobile, preaching and proselytizing and administering to the wants of lay society.

(i) The Black Friars or Dominicans

It was evident that it was no longer enough to enunciate religious dogmas and take it for granted that they would be unquestioningly received: the reasons behind them must be explained and upheld by argument. It might have been thought that the Cistercian monks would have proved themselves equal to this task and it was, in fact, entrusted to them. But by this time they had amassed great wealth, become superior-minded, and in their lives they could not stand comparison with the simple-living and austere heretics they denounced. In consequence, their campaign of propaganda bore little fruit and monasticism seemed a spent spiritual force. An Austin canon of Castile, Dominic (1170–1221), noticed the defect as he was passing through Provence on his way to Rome in 1201 and, obtaining permission to preach against the heretics, he was careful to meet them on their own ground by renouncing property, living simply and depending on alms. He gathered round him a group of like-minded men, who were known as the 'Preaching Brethren' or the 'Friars Preachers', and, as the refutation of heresy was their main duty, they had to be clerks, versed in theology and skilled in dialectic. When Pope Honorius III gave official recognition to the Dominican Order in 1216, it had only twenty-one members, but papal support made all the difference. The Dominican Order was confirmed in 1220; it had as its groundwork the Rule of St. Augustine with which Dominic was familiar, and by the time he died in 1221 some sixty houses, comprising some five hundred members, had come into existence.

The Dominicans reached England in 1221 and were given an enthusiastic welcome by Archbishop Langton. It was typical of their devotion to intellectual pursuits that they should immediately establish themselves at Oxford. By the end of Henry III's reign they had founded forty-five houses, thirteen others being added by 1348 to make the full complement.

(ii) *The Grey Friars or Franciscans*

They also sought to extirpate heresy, but their approach to the problem was different, for they stole the thunder of the Cathari by supplying an outlet for mystical exaltation *within* the Church of Rome. They laid no stress, as the Dominicans did, upon dogma and upon learning: therefore, unlike the Dominicans, they had no need to be clerks and included in their ranks lay men and women, married men as well as bachelors. Moreover, their call was not to the mind but to the heart. Believing that the ills of the Church sprang from its worldliness, they forsook the world and preached the virtues of self-surrender and self-sacrifice. As simple evangelists they appealed to the emotions for a return to Christian humility and the love of God. Not that they were austere: having made their peace with the world, they were free from its refined harassments, and their cheerfulness earned them the description of 'God's jesters'. The Order was founded by Francis (1181–1226), a member of a North Italian merchant family, who forsook the world of fashion to live a life as closely modelled on that of Christ as he could make it. At first he lived a solitary penitent, meditating upon and reproducing in himself the sufferings of Christ, but soon he attracted to himself a dozen companions, who built their first cluster of huts at Assisi. The numbers of St. Francis's 'Little Brethren', or 'Friars Minor', naturally grew far more rapidly than those of the Dominicans, and within half a century they were to be found all over Europe. Some organization was essential. St. Francis disliked the prospect of it, fearing that ideals would be lost when institutionalized: for example, it was impossible to administer the affairs of an Order without financial resources and that meant withdrawing in some measure from the vow of complete poverty. However, with genuine reluctance he allowed two of his followers, Elias of Cortona and Ugolino (the future Pope Gregory IX) to frame an organization of a highly centralized form, culminating in the Minister-General (*minister*: 'servant'). Soon afterwards fraternities or religious gilds of the Third Order, the 'Tertiaries', were attached: they comprised laymen who, though they did not take the vow of poverty and continued in their ordinary occupations, yet engaged themselves to give support to the Friars Minor in every possible way. The Franciscan Order was nurtured by the papacy and used in the work of spiritual regeneration.

The Franciscans came to England in 1224, a band of five laymen and four clerics which included three Englishmen; fifty priories had been founded a generation later, the final total being fifty-seven. The Franciscans have been likened to the Salvation Army: they were essentially democratic, they worked in the slums of the growing towns and among neglected classes of the community, they cared for the sick and the infirm; even though simple laymen, they preached the gospel in and out of season. In the thirteenth century they appeared to all as the real justifiers of religion.

II. The Intellectual Renaissance

The reawakening of intellectual interests occurred in Western Europe in the early decades of the eleventh century. It found expression at first in a passionate study of the classical literature of Rome and seemed likely to usher in a great age of humanism. But this 'Latin' resurgence was overwhelmed round about the middle of the twelfth century by a still more fervent devotion to philosophy, ultimately founded on the treatises on logic of Aristotle, and 'Greek' thought, in the limited form in which it was then known, diverted men's minds to scientific studies and, still more, to that attempt to reconcile the new learning with the Christian faith which produced the system of 'scholasticism' and made the thirteenth century predominantly the age of medieval theology. When that happened, the classics well-nigh disappeared from the arts courses of the universities.

I. THE CLASSICS

The Carolingian renaissance of the ninth century made its greatest and inestimable contribution to civilization when it caused copies to be made of the writings of Roman authors and thereby made sure that they would not be irretrievably lost. The study of Latin literature was taken up in North Italy and elsewhere, but it was with the cathedral schools of France at Orleans and Tours and, more especially, at Chartres that it was closely identified. We know few Latin authors now that were not known then; Virgil, Ovid and Martial among the poets, Cicero and Seneca among the writers of prose, Pliny as the standard authority on natural science: with these as their exemplars students were turned into men of letters, distinguished for the breadth of their interests.

Englishmen were no strangers to this intellectual atmosphere, and many of them had sought their education in the 'classic calm of Chartres'. They found their patrons in lay, quite as much as in ecclesiastical, circles: Earl Robert of Gloucester, the champion of Queen Matilda's cause, received the dedication of the very different histories written by William of Malmesbury and Geoffrey of Monmouth; Henry II had a score of works, written on such diversified topics as sport, science, government and romance, addressed to him; Archbishop Theobald made of Canterbury a place of literary activity which knew the presence of John of Salisbury, one of the most learned scholars of the century, and, later, of Peter of Blois, his pale reflexion; of Vacarius, the authority on Roman law; of Gervase the historian, who wrote a chronicle covering the reigns of Henry I to Richard I; of Nigel Wireker, the precentor of Canterbury, who satirized in verse the follies of the times, particularly in ecclesiastical life; of the writers of the specially valuable letters which make up the bulk of what is referred to generally as the Becket correspondence.

Classical culture was no superficial literary grace: it penetrated the thought of those who came under its discipline. Not much in the form of Latin poetry has come down to us, but the prose writings of Englishmen deserved and attained a wide recognition.

Here we are not concerned with professed historians, with whom we have already dealt. Among cultured writers in the widest sense, John of Salisbury (d. 1180) stands supreme. Trained in classical studies at Chartres, attending courses of lectures given at Paris by the great Abelard, entering the papal service at Rome to leave it six years later to become a member of the household of Archbishop Theobald and of his two successors at Canterbury, the friend of St. Bernard and Henry II, he wrote in Ciceronian Latin the *Policraticus*, the first philosophic treatise on the nature of secular government; the *Historia Pontificalis*, which illumines the relations of the papacy with the Empire and the Norman kingdom of Sicily during his stay at Rome; the lives of Anselm and Becket; and numerous valuable letters to distinguished men of his day. He knew no Greek and bits of Aristotle's writings only at second or third hand, but his *Metalogicus* showed that he could appreciate the mental attitude demanded by logic. He returned to the scene of his student days to die as bishop of Chartres. Peter of Blois (d. 1204), educated at Bologna and Paris, also serving an archbishop of Canterbury as well as Henry II and Queen Eleanor, published an interesting collection of letters, which, however, owed much of their erudition to deliberate borrowing from John of Salisbury. Walter Map (d. 1210), a Welsh student at Paris, who later stood in high favour with Henry II, serving him as itinerant justice, ambassador to France and envoy to a papal council, and ending his days as archdeacon of Oxford, published in his 'Courtiers' Trifles' an entrancing miscellaneous gathering of travellers' tales and personal reminiscences of society life at the royal court of England, in which his shrewd and satirical reflexions vindicate his contemporary reputation as the wittiest conversationalist in court circles. Geoffrey of Monmouth (d. 1152) produced out of a medley of Celtic fables and classical legends and fictions of his own a 'History of the British Kings' up to the death of Cadwallon in 689: a readable story of adventure disguised as genuine history, it was the medieval equivalent of a 'best-seller' and formed the basis of the great cycle of Arthurian romances. Gerald of Wales (died *c.* 1220), the son of a Norman baron and grandson of a Welsh princess, a student at Paris, the intimate friend of kings and princes, wrote in a colloquial and easy style two books on Wales and two on Ireland, a book of *Invectives* against his critics, a tract on 'The Education of Princes' in which he spoke caustically of Henry II and his sons, and an incomplete autobiography: he exhibited to the full the versatility and the insatiable curiosity of the age.

II. PHILOSOPHY AND THEOLOGY

In the twelfth century an intellectual revolution occurred which not only put an end to classical and humanistic developments but made imperative a new approach to theology. It was largely the consequence of the great intellectual activity which had been going on in the Arab world between 900 and 1200. For Islam by its expansion had embraced the inheritance of learning of the Eastern Mediterranean and Western Asia. The contributions made by the Arabs to the advancement of knowledge seemed to West Europe so great and so unique that there is perhaps a danger of exaggerating their originality. For they were really continuing the wisdom of antiquity: they showed such a remarkable ability to enter into the thought of Greece and Persia and India, to define it and deduce from it, that they seemed to be presenting to the West a completely new array of learning. Thus the writings, for example, of Plato, Aristotle and Euclid were turned first into Syriac and then into Arabic, and Bagdad in the early ninth century became a famous centre for the making of translations which were transmitted throughout Islam. Toledo in Spain had become its counterpart in Western Europe before it was captured from the Moors in 1085, and the various treatises were thereafter translated from Arabic into Latin. So through the close contact with Arab civilization in Spain, South Italy and Sicily, Egypt and Syria, Western Europe was introduced to the spirit of research in exact sciences like arithmetic and algebra and, more especially, astronomy and trigonometry, and in experimental sciences like medicine (for which a school had existed at Salerno since the ninth century), alchemy or chemistry, and physics, particularly optics. In the sphere of pure thought it was the increased acquaintance with Aristotle and his system of logic that had the most powerful and disintegrating effect. For Aristotle (384–322 B.C.) had remained unknown in the West except through Boethius, who translated into Latin part of his treatise on logic in the early seventh century. Not until the twelfth century was his thesis widely appreciated that the true approach to knowledge lay in beginning not with theories or a preconceived view of life but with the facts: first let them be collected and studied, and only then let a philosophy be formulated and the eternal verities be explained. That is why the Arabs, informed by this Aristotelian spirit, produced so many encyclopaedias of all branches of knowledge. The attitude of the West had been entirely different. With it the scientific mind was rare, and science meant little more than the 'Natural History' of Pliny. It had lived for centuries on the ideas expressed by St. Augustine of Hippo and the other Church Fathers or derived at second-hand from one work of Plato, the *Timaeus*, which could be easily accommodated to Christian doctrine. The only encyclopaedias it knew dealt with literature, pagan as well as Christian, but not with science. Whatever qualifications we may make, it still remains broadly true that St. Anselm summed up the mental attitude of his own and preceding ages in his famous aphorism, 'Believe that you may understand'; that is to say, revealed religion must come first and other knowledge would then be properly apprehended. Aristotelian logic twisted the saying round into 'Understand so that you may believe'. The result can be compared only with the consequences of Darwin's theory of evolution on the thought of the nineteenth century. No longer must a collision with revealed religion be avoided at all costs. Thus William of Conches declared that 'the forces of nature must be analysed and explained for themselves alone' and that 'men must no longer believe after the fashion of peasants without inquiring reasons'. Adelard of Bath asked 'what is authority but a halter?' Abelard argued that 'a doctrine is not to be believed because God has said it but because we are convinced by reason that it is so', and in his famous treatise, called 'Yes and No', he arranged discordant passages of scripture side by side and debated their truth in the Aristotelian manner. It is little wonder that this daring radical drew down upon himself the denunciations of the conservative St. Bernard, or that he attracted to his lectures at Paris so many eager students that his fame did much to make that city the seat of a future university renowned for theology. But we must take care not to place these thinkers out of time and circumstance. They were not launching an attack upon religious dogmas from outside but making a new approach to them from within; for they were clerics who had no desire to contradict the truths of revelation. Mysticism and science must be conciliated; theology must no longer rely for its proofs upon the traditional practice of simply citing authorities but must call to its assistance the new intellectual weapon of formal logic and prove that the Christian faith was in harmony with the conceptions of human reason. So the scientific spirit worked within the old framework to produce the 'science of the Schools' or scholasticism. The most famous synthesis was made by the Dominican Thomas Aquinas (d. 1274) in his *Summa Theologica*, and so well did he do his work that its study was revived in the late nineteenth century under the official papal designation of 'Thomism'.

English scholars absorbed the new learning with avidity. Robert of Chester (*c.* 1110–*c.* 1160) lived some six years in Northern Spain and produced a Latin version of an Arabic treatise on algebra which gave West Europe its first knowledge of that subject and, after he had made London his home, he calculated the longitude and latitude of the city by astronomical computations. Adelard of Bath (*c.* 1099–*c.* 1150) spent much of his life in Mohammedan lands and translated many scientific works from Arabic into Latin, notably Euclid. Michael the Scot (*c.* 1175–*c.* 1235) visited Toledo and North Italy and became so versed in biology and astrology that he gained the reputation of being a sorcerer. Alexander of Hales (d. 1245), an English Franciscan, became the most famous professor of theology of his day at Paris. Bishop Robert Grosseteste of Lincoln (d. 1253), scientific in his outlook and particularly interested in mathematics and physics, was well known throughout Western Europe for his experiments with lenses. It is fitting that the last to be mentioned should be his pupil, the Franciscan Roger Bacon (d. 1294). He insisted that philology must be studied: otherwise it would be impossible to obtain accurate translations from Greek to Hebrew and thus the Scriptures and Aristotle could not be properly read, much less rightly understood. He urged that judgment must be dependent on direct observation and not upon authority. Yet, with all his passion for truth reached by scientific methods, he did not depart from the essential medieval position: the attainment of knowledge was for the prime purpose of establishing religious truths.

III. The Revival of Roman Law

In the centuries after the barbarian settlements of the fifth century, scores of systems of law had been established here and there in Western Europe that were simply local in their scope and influence. By the eleventh century the confusion of legal systems was a definite deterrent to the expansion of trade and commerce in the more peaceful conditions of the time. However, the law of Rome and a legal profession of laymen to expound it had not completely disappeared. There were law-schools at Rome up to the time when the city was sacked by the Normans in 1084; texts of Justinian (527–65) had continued to be systematically studied in the old Imperial Exarchate of Ravenna, especially at Bologna, and the Emperors in the West had given legal research there a great fillip by requiring the legists to supply them with arguments from Roman law which they could use against the claims of the papacy. It was not until the twelfth century that the influence of Rome on West European society proved really effective. Then, the results of the critical examination of the texts of Justinian by Irnerius of Bologna (*fl.* 1113) and other Glossators (or commentators) were diffused rapidly throughout the West, and were not without their influence in training men's minds in the processes of thought.

Meanwhile the Church had also been producing throughout a thousand years numerous collections of rules and regulations of varied application: the decisions of ecumenical councils and provincial councils, the decrees of popes and archbishops and bishops. The 'Pseudo-Isidorian' or 'False Decretals', compiled about 850 by a Frankish clerk, which stressed the authority of the papacy, gained a wide popularity, and since that time some forty other collections had been made which, like it, had not been authorized by Rome itself. There was, therefore, in the canon law of the Church, as there had been in the Roman or civil law, a great confusion. It was natural that at Bologna and in the twelfth century this extensive canonical literature should be carefully studied, and there the great work, destined to become the foundation of the *Corpus Juris Canonici*, was written: the *Decretum* of the monk, Gratian, about 1140. It was not an official compilation: its avowed object was to harmonize discordant texts. To do this, he had to express his own views, which were not only papalist but also those of the party of reform. The result inevitably attracted a wide circle of sympathetic readers. What gave it special value, besides its vast learning, was the fact that it arranged its material, not chronologically, but by subject, and it was, in consequence, easy to consult. Furthermore, Gratian supported his arguments by citing his documents in full.

Naturally, England did not stand isolated from this resurrection of Roman legal thought. Her law was influenced at every turn by 'the imperial mother and her papal daughter'. Cathedral and monastic libraries eagerly sought for copies of the texts of Justinian and of the 'Decretum' of Gratian. The Italian lawyer, Vacarius, was brought to England by Archbishop Theobald in Stephen's reign to lecture on Roman law, and compiled a summary of it, called the *Liber Pauperum*, because it was intended for the use of the poor students, who could not afford more complete and expensive texts. We must, however, realize that all this was no mere intellectual curiosity without a very practical purpose underlying it. The acquisition of Roman law-books was a consequence of the development of canon law. This was not an entirely independent body of law, for canonists considered it natural and legitimate to use Justinian to solve legal problems and support legal arguments, and they did not hesitate to cite civil law where canon law was deficient. Archdeacons and others went to Bologna to learn canon law, but this implied the study of Roman law also, the authority of which was implicitly accepted. The influence of Justinian was inescapable. There is no doubt that in a sense his law-books were studied for their own sake, still England had no civilians properly so called: the ultimate object in view was canon, and not civil, law. And the new class of legal pamphlets and text-books that appeared in the twelfth century in considerable numbers were guides to procedure: what were styled 'Ordines Judiciarii' or some variation of that title. These were necessary because neither Justinian nor the 'Decretum' could give much assistance on this side. In England, where special conditions had been created as soon as a system of writs and assizes had been evolved, the *Ordines* indirectly affected civil procedure, but, though Glanville and Bracton were quite clearly inspired by Roman and romanesque models, the procedure and the substantive law of their books remained English.

IV. The Rise of Universities

The tradition of lay teaching never entirely vanished: schools survived in Italy where the masters and the pupils were not clerks, and this made it easier for that country to become associated with secular studies, such as law and medicine. But elsewhere in Western Europe instruction passed into the care of the Church. Until the early eleventh century the finest education was to be obtained in monastic schools, but we shall distort the picture if we do not bear in mind that the monasteries were never intended by their founders to be educational establishments in any general sense, and that they never became such, for the more they associated themselves with the affairs of the world, the further they removed themselves from the monastic ideal.   The monastic schools were provided for those who intended to become monks in order that they could take an intelligent part in the recital of the divine offices in Latin and, inasmuch as they also served as the literary workshops of adult monks, they produced scholars as well as teachers.   But they remained essentially isolated centres of culture like Fulda, Le Bec, and St. Gall and, in England, Glastonbury and Winchester, and it cannot be said that they had much influence on contemporary secular life. Early in the twelfth century the monastic schools were definitely in eclipse. St. Anselm was the last great monastic teacher, and his old priory at Le Bec, for example, fell into obscurity a generation after his death.   The intellectual leadership passed to the cathedral schools.   Under the Carolingian Empire it had been laid down that every cathedral church was to have a school attached to it.   At first instruction was given by the bishop in person within his private household, but soon he handed over his duties to the 'master of the scholars', who ranked in dignity after the bishop and dean of the chapter, and who began about the middle of the twelfth century to call himself the 'chancellor' and to restrict his attention to advanced students, leaving the others to the 'grammar master'.   In his hands lay the authority to issue the 'licence to teach', which was the medieval equivalent of the modern degree.   The cathedral schools of Rheims, Cologne, Paris, Chartres and elsewhere were the homes of a fine scholarship, but from the point of view of general education they had serious defects: they catered primarily for the needs of those who entered the Church and were of only incidental assistance to those who had no intention of taking Holy Orders; they found it awkward to keep abreast of the times and adapt themselves to the new knowledge and the new interests that were entering West Europe in the twelfth century.   Chartres, for instance, was deserted for Paris when logic supplanted the classics.

It was natural that it should be in Italy, where lay schools still flourished, that the first of the universities should slowly and imperceptibly come into existence: though the school of medicine at Salerno achieved the earliest fame, it was Bologna, the centre of legal studies, that was early organized to attract to itself the name of 'university'. Beyond the Alps the universities were the product of cathedral schools. The first of these was at Paris, where the teaching of Abelard (d. 1142) drew students from other centres of instruction and made the city celebrated for its philosophical and theological learning. The lecturers were induced in their own interests to form themselves into a gild before the close of the twelfth century, a gild which shortly afterwards was called a 'university'. Still, such a descriptive term was only gradually applied to such institutions specifically, for the word 'universitas' never ceased to be a quite general term for any association, and that of masters and students was but one among many. The early description was 'studium generale', and 'generale' stressed the cosmopolitan character of the students rather than the nature of the subjects studied. The universities, five of which can trace their origins to the twelfth century, came to be of two distinctive types. (a) *The Student University south of the Alps*. In Italy it was not the native Italian teachers who needed corporate protection but the students, who came from all parts of Europe and who formed themselves into a gild, which in time was given legal recognition as the 'university'. (b) *The Master University north of the Alps*. As at Paris, all teachers were required to seek formal admission into the teaching gild, and it was the association of masters at Oxford, for instance, which grew into a university.

The universities did not secure a distinct place for themselves in society without difficulty. It was partly to withstand attacks that the different schools teaching different subjects like Arts, Law, Theology and Medicine, came together as faculties inside a single institution. The obstacle to development, as at Paris, was the bishop and his chancellor, who had no wish to lose their control of education by abandoning the right to grant licences to teach. The papacy, however, championed the cause of the universities: in 1231 it ruled once and for all that, when the masters at Paris agreed that the licence to teach should be given, then the bishop could not refuse it. The pope was engaged in a struggle against heresy and wished to have the universities which professed theology under his own supervision and rallied to his support. It was essential that the activities of those who were able to think, and might think dangerously, should be directed into paths of orthodoxy.

Why it was at such places as Oxford and Cambridge that universities came to be established in England remains a puzzle. Certainly, lectures in theology and law had been delivered at Oxford from early in the twelfth century, but it was no better known for instruc-

tion than Northampton, nor did it enjoy the advantages of a
cathedral city like Lincoln, Winchester or Exeter. Although
Canterbury, the busy centre of literary activity at the time, was
dominated by a Benedictine monastery and was *ipso facto* unlikely
to become the seat of a university, it is strange that London should
not have done so. Under Henry II the schools of Northampton
were pre-eminent but the scholars came into conflict with the
townsmen and dispersed, and by the end of the twelfth century the
supremacy had passed to Oxford. Dispersions were not infrequent
at this period. There were no university buildings, no colleges, no
material ties, and the perpetuation of schools in any particular place
was uncertain. The essentials were teachers of note and the enjoyment of the immunities and privileges of self-government that
scholars arrogated to themselves. The university of Oxford was the
creation of the thirteenth century and, in its course, suffered many
vicissitudes. Cambridge, smaller and feebler, grew almost unnoticed
and did not rival Oxford until the fifteenth century.

Oxford had not the same difficulties in consolidating its position
as confronted Paris. The bishop of the diocese was not resident
there but two hundred miles away at Lincoln, and control gradually
passed to a chancellor, chosen from among the masters themselves.
The government of Oxford resembled that of Paris, but the Oxford
chancellor combined the functions of the Parisian chancellor and
rector. He was the resident ruler: he presided over the meetings
of the masters, granted licences to teach, and had his own court to
try actions in which students were involved. Power resided in the
masters of the Arts faculty and not the higher faculties. However
the faculty of Theology was made famous by the Franciscans, who
found it necesary to depart from their founder's injunctions and to
acquire learning. They entered Oxford under the patronage of
Grosseteste, who agreed to lecture to them himself. It was not long
afterwards, probably about 1248, that Adam Marsh was admitted
as the first of a long line of regent-masters in theology, including
Roger Bacon, Duns Scotus and William of Ockham, who made the
Franciscan convent at Oxford a brilliant centre of intellectual life.
And we may add that, though they were not members of any faculty,
there were masters at Oxford from John's reign onwards, who gave
utilitarian instruction in the principles and practice of English law
in the course of training students how to write formal letters and
draw up legal instruments.

In the days when there was no printing press to assist the

distribution and ensure the preservation of the new learning, the universities played no small part in guaranteeing that what had been so hardly won should not be forgotten.

SELECT READING

A. H. Thompson, 'The Monastic Orders' in *C. Med. H.*, v (1926), 658–96; G. G. Coulton, *Five Centuries of Religion*, ii (1927: 'The Friars and the Dead-weight of Tradition'), 1–144; D. Knowles, *The Religious Houses in Medieval England* (1940), 1–58; D. Knowles, *The Monastic Order in England* (1940), 208–267, 346–62, 375–91; Rose Graham, *S. Gilbert of Sempringham and the Gilbertines* (1903), 1–28, 48–77; A. G. Little, 'The Mendicant Orders' in *C. Med. H.*, vi (1929), 727–760; Little, *Studies in English Franciscan History* (1917), 92–122, 158–221; M. Deanesly, *The Medieval Church* (1925), 119–142, 154–178; J. R. H. Moorman, *Church Life in England in the Thirteenth Century*, (1945), 242–401.

K. Norgate, *England under the Angevin Kings* (1887), ii. 431–92; W. Stubbs, *Seventeen Lectures on Medieval and Modern History* (1900), chs. vi, vii; C. H. Haskins, *Renaissance of the Twelfth Century* (1927), 3–31, 93–126, 278–367; Haskins, 'Adelard of Bath' in *Studies in History of Medieval Science* (1924), 20–42; F. M. Powicke, 'Gerald of Wales' in *B.J.R.L.* xii (1928), 389–410; Walter Map, *De Nugis Curialium* (trans. M. R. James: 1923); C. Singer, *Short History of Science to the Nineteenth Century* (1941), 126–161; H. O. Taylor, *The Medieval Mind* (1919), ii. 133–75, 260–337, 368–431.

Pollock and Maitland, i. chs. v–vii; H. G. Richardson, 'Azo, Drogheda and Bracton' in *E.H.R.* lix (1944), 22–47.

A. H. Rashdall, 'Medieval Universities' in *C. Med. H.*, vi (1929), 559–601; Rashdall, *Medieval Universities* (ed. Powicke and Emden: 1936), iii. 1–48, 274–85; H. G. Richardson, 'The Schools of Northampton in the Twelfth Century' in *E.H.R.* lvi (1941), 595–606; Richardson, 'Letters of the Oxford *Dictatores*' in *Oxford Historical Society Publications* (1942), 331–45.

CHAPTER XXIII

ADMINISTRATION WITHOUT THE KING

THE twelfth century has been broadly termed the 'Golden Age of Monarchy'. Western Europe had ceased to be terrorized by the incursions of Northmen, Slavs, Magyars and Moors, feudalism was rapidly losing its main reason for existence when it was no longer needed to provide a means of local defence, and national monarchies had emerged triumphantly not only in England but in France and Germany as well. We could not hope to find a better proof of the greatness and permanence of Henry II's monarchical system than the successful working of the administration under Richard, when the head of the State, despising peace and the arts of peace and passionately loving war, spent within his English kingdom only five months of his ten years' reign and left the preservation of the royal prerogatives to royal officials. Fortunately, a governing class had been established with strong traditions of service, and their work continued to bear the imprint of their late master's mind. Their control during the reign of the absentee king was in the main exerted through two institutions.

I. THE OFFICE OF JUSTICIAR

Though this went back in its origins, as we have seen, to the early years of Henry I's reign and had been filled by great ministers, such as Roger of Salisbury and, in the early years of Henry II's reign, Robert, earl of Leicester (c. 1154–68), it was not until the last quarter of the twelfth century that it reached its unique and pre-eminent position. For at first it was evidently considered that only to another crowned head could the king entrust the full majesty of his power when he left his kingdom: thus the queen and the son of Henry I, the queen of Stephen during his period of imprisonment, the queen of Henry II and then his eldest son after his coronation as king-associate in 1170, all in their turn acted as regents. The routine of administration was, of course, not done by them but by a small group of royal ministers, including the justiciar, who shared the work and responsibility among them all. It was only after Henry II found that his wife and his sons were playing the traitor to him that he was forced to delegate complete authority during his visits abroad to one who was not of royal blood. Ranulf Glanville, appointed justiciar in 1180, was allowed to govern the country as vicegerent during the king's absences and to remain the head of the administration at other times. He was the first of a long line of distinguished justiciars (William Longchamp, 1190–1; Walter of Coutances, 1191–3; Hubert Walter, 1193–8; Geoffrey fitz Peter, 1198–1212; Peter des Roches, 1212–15; Hubert de Burgh, 1215–32), who could hold courts in the king's name, issue writs in their own name and seal them with their own personal seals, and concentrate in their own hands all administrative, financial and judicial functions. Theirs was a high office, burdened with multifarious duties and heavy responsibilities, and it was within this too neglected 'Age of the Justiciars' that England found herself subjected to a government of routine and became accustomed in the end to the routine of government. Even when the policy of John caused the land to lie under a papal interdict for five years and the king himself to be excommunicated, the work of government went on without serious interruption, the people remained docile and the barons quiescent. It may be well at this point to add that the treasurer was not of exalted status before the thirteenth century, and Nigel le Poer in the closing years of Henry I's reign seems to have been the first clerical treasurer and, of course, was very subordinate to his uncle, Roger of Salisbury. And the chancellor was not regarded as a high-ranking official until Henry II's time: even then Becket's position (1154–62) was as personal and exceptional as that of Geoffrey Plantagenet, the king's son and the most faithful of his children, when he held the office (1182–9).

II. THE EXCHEQUER

The exchequer continued to be what it had been in the past. But the work of its staff was multiplied many times over in the last half of the twelfth century by the rapid growth of the writ system and the wide extension of royal justice. The exchequer remained in contemporary thought the *curia regis*: that is why it retained the appearance and attributes of a court of law, no matter the business on which it was engaged, and why the fact was so slowly recognized that its diverse and heavy labours must make the introduction of departmentalism inevitable. For, though it kept the judicial and the financial sides of its work as distinct as possible, both were being carried through by the same group of men, and therefore everything was considered to be done in the 'exchequer' even though it was in fact transacted on the judicial side in what was sometimes called the 'bench'. It was only gradually in the following reign of John that the once interchangeable terms of 'exchequer' and 'bench' were clearly differentiated so that the first denoted the financial bureau and the second the court of law.

Not even the irresponsible acts of Henry's sons could destroy what their father had built. For example, since Richard I was simply interested in his forthcoming crusade and viewed his new kingdom solely as a source of supply and was totally ignorant of English developments, he saw no harm in selling positions in the government service to the highest bidders, and in placing local barons in charge of counties and, more ominously, of royal castles for money down, or in bestowing upon his brother John a palatinate, made up of the counties of Nottingham and Derby in the Midlands, Devon and Cornwall in the south-west, Gloucester, Glamorgan and Lancaster in the west, which he ruled absolutely through his own chancery and exchequer and kept exempt from all supervision by the king's ministers. This was the work of one who knew only the feudal arrangements and quasi-independent fiefs of Aquitaine, and, by weakening the authority of the central government and letting local government, especially in the north, slip out of the hands of royal officials, he was striking a blow at the very heart of his father's reforms. This retrograde step made it easy for John in a short time to plot against him, and it hampered at once the activities of William Longchamp, the first justiciar appointed. The resentment aroused by his foreign origin, his low birth and, still more, the tactless arrogance which led him to ignore all colleagues would not of themselves have created a rebellious spirit: it was John who actively fomented dissension. It was apparently at his instigation, and not through the initiative of the barons themselves, that they came together in London in 1191 and received, as they expected, the strong support of the prominent Londoners, who were apparently ambitious that London should reach the status of the French 'communes' by electing its own mayor, obtaining immunities from outside interference, and thus achieving self-government. The position was full of dangers and the crisis was not easily surmounted. Fortunately, Richard had sent over to England Walter of Coutances, archbishop of Rouen, to watch the situation on his behalf, and he saw fit at this juncture to make known his appointment as justiciar and to exercise his consequent overriding authority. Longchamp retired to the Continent; John was recognized as Richard's heir; London secured the recognition of its claims: thus the dissidents were kept from overt rebellion. Nevertheless, Walter of Coutances was still disturbed by John's disloyalty, for, when Richard was captured on his way home from the East and no one knew whether he was alive or dead, John at once claimed the throne and, failing to compel the justiciar to do more than acknowledge him as 'rector regni', he crossed over to France and obtained recognition by Richard's bitter enemy, Philip Augustus. It was an ugly situation until the fact of Richard's survival became known for certain and left John openly exposed as a traitor. Richard replaced Walter of Coutances with Hubert Walter, a strong and resolute justiciar, and he himself reached England early in 1194 for his last visit of a few weeks, and with surprising generosity forgave John and eventually restored him to some of his estates, though no longer with exemption from supervision by the central government, and he permitted London to continue to elect its own mayor.

The most remarkable of all the justiciars was Hubert Walter, appointed in 1193, who ruled the Church also as archbishop of Canterbury and papal legate. Trained in a legal way of thinking by his studies at Bologna and his upbringing in the household of his famous uncle, Ranulf Glanville, and perhaps himself the author of the remarkable treatise on the laws of England which goes under his uncle's name, he proved himself a bold and skilful administrator and imposed his authority on the whole country, even in the north. When we consider whom he chose as his associates, nearly all of them at one time connected in some way with Henry II, it is particularly noticeable that this was a period when England was under the governance not so much of barons as of bishops and bishops-to-be. The bureaucracy of officials and clerks had emerged triumphant from the test of rebellion led by the very heir to the throne, it stood four-square as a sure guarantee that law and order would be maintained, it even increased the royal authority itself. For, despite Richard's absence, his ministers were not simply content to keep things going: they set new schemes in operation which taxed the machinery of government to its fullest extent. They were compelled to act, in any case, by the imperative need to increase the revenues of the crown to meet the charge of Richard's ransom, equivalent to five years' annual revenue, and the heavy costs of financing a ceaseless war on the Continent.

(i) *The judicial inquiry of* 1194

Partly to catch up with arrears of business, partly to get a clearer picture of the revenue that could be expected from the king's private estates and financial rights, the justices in eyre were given a list of 'chapters of the eyre' and were sent into every part of the kingdom to ask the local jurors so many new questions that, as in 1170, it was tantamount to a fresh survey of how local government was working. One of these chapters discloses the definite establishment of four coroners in every county, elected in the county court to look after the profits of the crown, particularly as derived from criminal jurisdiction, for it was their special duty to investigate crimes as soon as they were committed, to record these 'pleas of the crown', and to present the accused for trial before the justices in eyre.

(ii) *The new fiscal assessment of* 1198

The land tax in the form of the old pseudo-Danegeld had ceased to be imposed, though a tax had been placed on land in 1194 for the special purpose of raising Richard's ransom. In 1198 Hubert Walter decided to reintroduce a land tax and to draw up new assessments to take the place of the out-of-date ones. These were to be based upon 'carucates', each roughly 100 acres of 'ploughland' or arable land, and local juries were given the task of determining their amount. The scheme was not fully worked out, taxes known as 'carucages' were raised only occasionally, and the principle of a general land tax was abandoned before the middle of the thirteenth century.

(iii) *The military reorganization of* 1198

What was left of the military basis of feudalism was menaced by a proposal to set on foot a standing army. It was suggested that all who held a knight's fee and owed forty days' service in person should agree to an alternative scheme, whereby they would provide funds sufficient to maintain 300 knights for service overseas for a whole year. The advantages in military efficiency were obvious, but many of the barons, under the lead of the bishops of Lincoln and Salisbury, vigorously opposed any change. They saw clearly that this was the thin end of the wedge, for scutage would be levied henceforward as a regular tax all the time and no longer as a mere alternative to personal service on the occasions when a military campaign happened to be waged. Furthermore, they contended that for their lands in England their service ought not to be done overseas. And they were alive to the danger of endowing a formidable force of mercenaries which the king might use to their own detriment. In the event this scheme also was dropped.

It was natural for a civil service to keep a record of its administrative activities, and it is in the 'Age of the Justiciars' that there begins the magnificent series of enrolments which form the richest and most continuous of the ancient archives of Europe.

It is well to pause at this point, when it is evident that Henry II had founded the strongest monarchy in Europe, to consider the attitude adopted towards it by the politically conscious elements in the community. What was their reaction towards its powers and prerogatives, its wealth, its rapidly increasing host of civil servants, its formulation and imposition of a new law, a common law to which all must pay obedience? The elevation and extension of monarchical authority had been essential to the restoration and preservation of peace and order. It inevitably followed that there had to be a corresponding fall and restriction in the authority of the Church and of the baronage, and this had been plainly exhibited in the serious encroachments upon their jurisdictions. But after the turn of the century it was arguable that the unchecked power of the king was no longer necessary, that it had been increased unduly, that he had been allowed to shake himself dangerously free from customary, feudal and ecclesiastical restraints, that he was well on his way to becoming virtually an irresponsible despot. Will the monarchy in England develop as the monarchy in France later on develops? Or can the Church or the baronage or both together put forward and enforce political concepts to bar the way to tyranny and bring the king to a sense of his duties as well as of his prerogative rights? If so, will the opposition be directed solely by class interests, or will it assume a wider significance and contain the germs, however small, of something that can be described as constitutional? England has reached the crossroads in her progress, and the path she was to take was settled for her in the crisis of 1215 which produced the Great Charter.

Concerning the nature of monarchy there was a great freedom and diversity of opinion. We shall miss the truth if we deceive ourselves by labelling it as absolute or limited, ecclesiastical or feudal, for it takes on a different appearance according to the text we happen to study.

I. THE OFFICIAL VIEW

The civil service of administrators and lawyers would have set no limits to monarchical authority. They shared the contemporary political belief that monarchy was a divine institution, that the king was 'a saint and the Christ of the Lord', whose actions expressed the working of God's will on earth. Already the famous maxim of the Institutes of Justinian was on their lips: 'what pleased the prince had the force of law'; and from 1173 onwards the phrase 'king by the Grace of God' became a regular part of the royal style of English kings. The argument that subjects cannot challenge the most arbitrary acts of their rulers could not be put more starkly than in the words of Henry II's treasurer, the author of the *Dialogue of the Exchequer*: 'though abundant riches may often come to kings, not by some well-attested right but perhaps by ancestral custom or by the secret counsels of their own hearts or even by arbitrary decisions made at their pleasure, yet their deeds must not be discussed or condemned by inferiors'.

II. THE ECCLESIASTICAL VIEW

The coronation oath, administered by the Church, indicated a restraint but only a moral restraint. A slightly more practical control was exercised for a brief time whenever there was a disputed succession, for the archbishop was needed to anoint and consecrate the approved candidate. The circumstances of the accession of William Rufus, of Henry I and, in particular, of Stephen had given a certain sanction to an ecclesiastical doctrine of election. It naturally found no favour in the eyes of Henry II, who sought to circumvent it, first by having his eldest son formally recognized as his successor as early as 1155 and, secondly, warned by his quarrel with the Church of possible dangers ahead to his dynasty, by having his son consecrated and crowned in 1170 during his own lifetime. This adoption of a Capetian practice proved unwise, for King Henry the Younger chose to act as the equal of his father and to make alliances with his father's enemies, and after his son's death in 1183 Henry II abandoned the dangerous practice of association in the crown. The death of Richard in 1199 provided another opportunity for discussion about the hereditary character of monarchy. For, if the rules of primogeniture had been strictly followed, then Arthur, son of that Geoffrey, count of Brittany, who was the fourth son of Henry II, had a better title to the throne than John, the fifth son of Henry II, and the archbishop of Rouen was disposed to support his claims. In the event he realized that Arthur was no desirable candidate, for he had been brought up in Brittany by his mother to detest the English, and he was betrothed to a daughter of the archfoe of the Angevin Empire, Philip Augustus of France. But once the king was on the throne, the Church could see no way to deal with him if he turned out to be vicious. Like marriage, a consecration was difficult to undo. The king might be excommunicated, but to go further than that and try to separate a king from his throne was far more serious. The views the Church held, and had held for many centuries, were perfectly summarized at this time by a great English scholar, John of Salisbury, in his *Policraticus*, published in 1159: it is the first book to appear during the Middle Ages which expounded clearly, coherently and systematically a philosophy of politics. In its reasoned account of the doctrine of the Church on the nature of government and the rights and duties of both governors and governed, there is nothing novel or revolutionary. Monarchy had never been essential *per se* and, though the king as God's agent was granted high prerogatives, he ought not to abuse his authority. He existed for the sake of the people, not the people for his sake; therefore, if he refused to recognize his responsibilities, he was no longer the vicar of God but the deputy of the Devil and must be removed: even assassination might in such circumstances be explained as an expression of God's Will. Not that John of Salisbury was enunciating any theory of popular sovereignty: his concern was the Church and its welfare, and it was if religion were assailed that extreme measures could and must be taken. If the Church and its liberties were safe, then it followed that all must be right with the State. In his restricted view, therefore, the restraints on the king were such as he placed upon himself in rendering his account to God and God alone, they were not political and provided no answer to the urgent problem of the very near future. His speculations envisaged no means of deciding when monarchy had overstepped its bounds and degenerated into tyranny, no notion of a political community of the kingdom which could develop political institutions alongside the king and independent of him, through which it could express its own will and bring a tyrant to book or remove him altogether.

III. THE BARONIAL VIEW

So far baron had co-operated with baron in resistance only on those few occasions when they had felt that their privileges and liberty of action were in jeopardy. Even in the great feudal rebellion of 1174 there was no united front: less serious in England than on the Continent where it began, made dangerous mainly through the support given to it by the queen, the king-associate and his brothers, it was waged by a minority, however powerful, among the barons, and it was suppressed before the king returned from abroad to deal with it. Indeed, the structure of feudalism was so weak and the feudal lords as a class so loosely organized and so slow to realize the significance of what the monarchy was doing that they were crippled before they knew it. In any case, a clash was by no means inevitable in the twelfth century, for no wilful attack was ever made upon them, the more enlightened of them desired peace and stability and often gave support to achieve that end. Thus there was no general desire to abolish the reforms of Henry II, from which they had themselves received a guarantee of title in their lands, as against the king, such as they had not previously possessed: in so far as they were willing to let themselves remain under that land-law which was to form so prominent a portion of the law of the land, the common law, to that extent opposition to the king would cease to be feudal and take the first step along the road to constitutionalism. It is noticeable that Henry II had no hesitation in convoking feudal courts frequently, for he anticipated no difficulty in obtaining their consent to his schemes. Despite such frequent meetings together, the barons revealed few signs that they were becoming politically conscious, they formed no traditions, they pressed no claim that they had a paramount right to advise the king, and, as they were apparently agreeable to allowing the king to take counsel exactly when he pleased, they did not try to give the feudal court a definite place in the government of the country by converting it into a regular and permanent institution. To the baronage as a whole the ideal king was not the frugal, unostentatious and diplomatic Henry II but the flamboyant and extravagant warrior, Richard I. Political speculation being utterly beyond most of them, they cared nothing for theories of Divine Right Monarchy, but they bore in mind the feudal oath and the feudal contract which bound them to the king and the king to them. And their political development was so tardy a growth that they raised little protest against the occasional extraordinary taxation levied by the king, although they often had to pay it themselves and could have made much play with the feudal doctrine of assent. Before 1200 opposition to taxation was made by individuals and only rarely: we hear nothing of collective refusal. If, however, the time should come when it was imperative to resist the king, they could take their stand upon the feudal contract and stress its bilateral obligations.

SELECT READING

F. M. Powicke, 'England: Richard I and John' in *C. Med. H.*, vi (1929), 205–18; Stephenson and Marcham, 104–9; K. Norgate, *Richard the Lion Heart* (1924); F. M. Powicke, *Medieval England* (1931), 152–246; G. O. Sayles, *Select Cases in Court of King's Bench*, i (1936), ch. i; H. G. Richardson, *Memoranda Roll, I John* (1943: Pipe Roll Society Publications), xi–xvi; lxxv–lxxxvii.

CHAPTER XXIV

THE CIRCUMSCRIPTION OF MONARCHY

IT was the policy of John which forced a clarification of the issues and compelled his opponents to think out their opinions. There has been a tendency, largely induced by the standard biography of the king, to vindicate his character as 'the ablest of the Plantagenets'. It is argued that it is modern politics alone that have blackened his character. The parliamentary pamphleteers of the seventeenth century and the democratic historians of the nineteenth century looked upon the Great Charter as the foundation stone of the British constitution, and its achievement seemed more heroic and pointed a greater moral when it was depicted as being extracted from a monster of iniquity. Thus Macaulay dismissed John as a 'trifler and a coward', and Stubbs regarded him as the worst of English kings, who found pleasure in deliberately choosing the path of evil. These statements are largely based upon the biased and untrustworthy statements of chroniclers, like Matthew Paris, who wrote after John was dead. But if we agree to condemn his private character as vicious, vindictive, sadistic and treacherous, we must remember that a bad man can make a successful ruler, and even failure does not necessarily mean incompetence. His supporters enter an ingenious plea on his behalf. It is taken as a tribute to his administrative ability that England 'kept silence' during the demoralizing years of the Interdict and that there were no rebellions. His diplomatic skill helped him to escape from a highly dangerous isolation in Europe and to turn the edge of his enemies' weapons so successfully that he could construct an alliance which came near to destroying the Capetian Monarchy; it was his misfortune that a royal diplomatist was the reverse of a hero in the eyes of his feudal vassals, who regarded it as unworthy of a king to stoop to conquer, contemptuously described him as 'soft-sword', and made him pay the usual penalty for being in advance of his age. And the most plausible of the apologies for John stresses the fact that he had inherited problems that his gifted father could not solve just at the time when they reached their climax and were inextricably entangled: the continental problem when France was governed by Philip Augustus, the formidable founder of the New Monarchy; the ecclesiastical problem when the Church was ruled by Innocent

III, the most powerful of medieval popes; the feudal problem when the passage of time and altered circumstances had at last aroused a corporate sense among the barons.

This *ex parte* evaluation of the character of John and of his reign must not be over-emphasized. This son of Henry II had certainly a shrewd intelligence and a nimble wit, he could evolve administrative plans, and for a time he was capable of tremendous exertions in carrying them out. There was never any doubt that he was master in his own house. He was, however, incapable for long of self-control and sustained effort to adhere to what he had chosen and to finish what he had begun. The intermittent fits of energy and apathy which marked every one of his continental campaigns, the incredible inertia in moments of crisis, the duplicity which marked his relations with his father, his brothers, his baronial supporters: these suggest a form of mental disease and remind us of the insanity among his Angevin forebears and the streak of madness in all members of the Angevin dynasty, manifesting itself with even Henry II in his ungovernable rages. The argument that John was periodically unbalanced would explain what is on other grounds completely inexplicable. For John inherited complete and undisputed authority: though, to begin with, he made a bid for support by issuing a 'constitution' or charter in which he pledged himself to reform the abuses committed by his brother, he was the first to have the legend 'King of England' instead of 'King of the English' placed upon his seal, and he soon made his policy of despotism plain for all to see. Yet in fifteen years he had let the Angevin Empire break in pieces, he had surrendered to the Church which he had challenged, he had bowed to the barons and placed his father's great achievements in dispute. Expelled by his own subjects from his own capital, he saw before he died the most important part of his English kingdom under the control of a French prince. Both his son and his grandson will be faced with crises which have been created by a combination of grievances arising out of foreign policy, the Church and feudal problems, but neither in 1258 nor in 1297 will the monarchy fall so low in England as it did with John.

I. The Continental Problem

When John ascended the throne in 1199, he found himself in the midst of the first of the International Wars in the West, which filled the years 1191 to 1214. Although in origin it was a feudal conflict, yet it occurred at a time when feudalism was on the wane and nationalism coming slowly into view, and it is largely because the old and the new are found side by side that the course of the struggle is hard to follow.   For example, the earl of Essex was count of Aumale in France, and the earl of Chester was the count of Avranches.   The constant intrigues of English and French and German overlords to withdraw vassals from their prime allegiances make for an appalling confusion.   The position of one of the principal barons involved, the count of Flanders, provides an excellent illustration: though he was the vassal of the French king for the greater part of his territory, he was the vassal of the Emperor for those highly important lands along the right bank of the great waterway of the Scheldt, but the economic prosperity of his rich and populous cities depended on the cloth trade so that he dared not offend England who supplied him with raw wool, and he was usually found in hostility to France.

It is therefore possible to give only a general outline of this great continental war.   On two occasions in the twenty-five years after Henry II's death the kingdom of France was within a hair's breadth of being removed from the map of Europe, and it was accidents beyond the control of Philip Augustus that saved him from destruction.   In both the early and the late years of his reign he was confronted by a powerful coalition, and it was fortunate for him that he was given a breathing-space in between to recover from the ravages of the first and to prepare for the onslaught of the second.

I.   THE FIRST COALITION AGAINST FRANCE, 1193

Three of its members, England, the Empire and Flanders, gave it its potentialities.   An Anglo-Flemish-German coalition of great strength had not been anticipated by the French king Philip Augustus.   The next five years fulfilled his worst apprehensions, for he was harried and defeated on all sides and Richard, in particular, recovered all the territory he had inherited from his father. It was mainly luck that helped Philip to escape the nemesis: in 1197 the emperor Henry VI died, leaving a child of three as his heir, and in the consequent strife around the German throne France was forgotten; in 1199 Richard himself died of a chance wound.

Philip had an intimate personal knowledge of both Richard and John, and it is not without significance that, whilst he feared the one, he had no hesitation in disregarding his previous heavy defeats and renewing hostilities against the other. The easiness of his triumphs must have exceeded his most sanguine hopes, for the Angevin Empire disintegrated in less than half-a-dozen years. He had no difficulty in finding pretexts for war. (*a*) He first of all championed the cause of Arthur, who had been already accepted in Brittany and Maine, and he occupied Anjou and Maine in his name. John offered little resistance and readily came to terms at the Treaty of Le Goulet in May 1200: in return for the French king's recognition of his rights to all the French possessions (with the exception of Aquitaine, for which the old and remarkably vigorous queen-mother, Eleanor, had already done homage in preparation for resigning her rights to her son), John clearly acknowledged Philip as his overlord, surrendered the Norman Vexin to him, paid him the enormous relief of 20,000 marks which were to be spent against him in the next war, recognized Arthur as duke of Brittany and restored him to Philip's guardianship. (*b*) In 1202 Philip was prepared to listen to the appeals of the Poitevin House of the Lusignans against John's arbitrary seizure of their lands. The belief that ill-feeling arose because John carried off Hugh de Lusignan's betrothed, Isabella of Angoulême, and married her himself in August 1200 is a contemporary misapprehension of the facts. As suzerain Philip frequently summoned John to answer before him; on his repeated refusal to appear, as a vassal should, at his overlord's court, his lands were declared in April 1202 to be in sequestration, and a French army began to occupy them as a legal means of enforcing the judgment of the court. It is, therefore, a myth that war was resumed as a result of John's cold-blooded murder of Arthur, for that did not take place until 1203 and merely provided additional justification for Philip's previous actions. Normandy simply slipped out of the grasp of the English king. The Norman barons had so far remained faithful to the English connexion through feudal reverence for a warrior-king like Richard, but John was a man of different calibre who could not retain their respect. When he ignored the caution his father had always shown and renounced his homage to his overlord, they felt themselves free to repudiate him. Once the personal tie was broken, all other considerations urged the Norman landowners to prefer a French to an English attachment if their fiefs and privileges were guaranteed. So not a single baron or a single town attempted to resist the French forces. The loss of Normandy in 1204 was a decisive factor in the history of both England and France: for one it meant that the barons who chose to be domiciled in England had to concentrate on English interests, and to this fact the Great Charter is partly due; for the other it meant that the Capetian monarchy had made Paris secure, become at last a maritime power, and cut the connexions between England and the possessions in the southwest of France which still belonged to her.

II. THE SECOND COALITION AGAINST FRANCE, 1214

The loss of Normandy did not mark the end of hostilities, and John tried unsuccessfully to recover the lost ground till the end of his reign. By 1206 Touraine and even Anjou had been irretrievably lost. Philip Augustus, however, left it to his son to annex that inferno of anarchy and intrigue, Poitou, and he very wisely made no attempt to conquer Aquitaine: the provinces he had so far acquired were all in the land of the *langue d'oil* and easily assimilated, whereas Aquitaine belonged to the *langue d'oc* and was still virtually alien territory.

Though John imposed an ever-increasing burden of taxation upon England to provide funds for the hiring of mercenaries on a grand scale and strove to knit together a league of all the powers on the northern and eastern frontiers of France, his long quarrel with the Church kept him really impotent. And eventually, instead of his invading the Continent, he was confronted with the imminent invasion of England. For Innocent III excommunicated him in 1209 and four years later threatened, but only threatened, to depose him. Philip Augustus seized the opportunity of John's embarrassment to prepare an armed expedition for the furtherance of his own ambitions. John saved the perilous situation by surrendering to the pope and offering him his homage, for thereby he shrewdly placed himself under the Church's protection and made it impossible for the French king to attack him without at the same time himself falling foul of the Church. Relieved from his isolation, John again brought the Anglo-Flemish-German alliance into existence, and again Philip stood alone and in danger of being crushed between an English army on the west and a German-Flemish army on the east. He was completely outnumbered and only the hopelessly dilatory and ineffective tactics of his enemies helped him to survive. After a promising beginning to his campaign John succumbed to inertia and allowed himself to be checked on the Loire when it was essential that he should advance towards Paris. As it was, Philip was freed from anxiety about his capital and concentrated the bulk of his forces on the north-east against the Emperor to overwhelm him at Bouvines in 1214. Thereon John abandoned all but La Rochelle and Aquitaine, and the French dynasty was left supreme in France, in Flanders and in Western Europe in general.

II. The Ecclesiastical Problem

The most prolonged and severe schism between Church and State in the whole of the Middle Ages was created when king and pope came into collision over the appointment to the see of Canterbury. The right of election was legally vested in the cathedral chapter, which was in this instance identical with the prior and monks of Christ Church priory. However, it was only recently that the efforts to produce an administrative unity in the Church had insisted that episcopal elections should no longer depend on the uncontrollable and capricious decision of the clergy and people in general but be made in chapters that were easily subjected to discipline. The bishops of the province of Canterbury were still loath to be excluded from any voice in the election of their metropolitan, and it was because the monks were afraid that their rights might be filched from them that, after they had accepted the candidate selected by the king on the advice of bishops, some of them chose to emphasize their privilege by secretly nominating their sub-prior and sending him to Rome for papal approval. It was the arrival there of two men claiming the see of Canterbury that gave Innocent III the right to judge the issues involved and set aside both elections as illegal. He had, however, no right to compel the few monks who had come to Rome to elect Stephen Langton instead. The king would not tolerate the new procedure of election which would have deprived him of any control over ecclesiastical appointments, and he took his stand, as his ancestors had done, on historical precedents and customs in opposition to the newly formulated law of the Church. He refused to allow Langton to come to England, and thereupon the pope retaliated by placing the country under an Interdict in 1208 and excommunicating John a year later. For five years the English Church lay defenceless against the spoliations of the king, and he took full advantage of his opportunities. Since the higher clergy could no longer perform their duties, it was argued that they no longer had any right to their incomes: therefore, ecclesiastical property passed to the king's custody, the clergy were paid subsistence pensions only and the rest of the ecclesiastical revenue was appropriated by the Crown to the extent of more than £100,000. The excommunication of the king placed the clergy in such a dilemma of loyalties that the higher churchmen found no answer save in voluntary exile: by 1209 only two bishops remained in the country and such an abbey as Waverley was deserted altogether. Despite the moral deterioration, of which the closing of churches and cemeteries and the silencing of bells was a practical sign, the people at large remained quiescent, and it is to be observed that the barons viewed with apparent equanimity the distress of the Church and of the clergy, who were soon to be their own allies.

Nevertheless, in May 1213 John surrendered to the papacy: he agreed to do homage to the pope, hold England as a papal fief, pay 1,000 marks a year in practical recognition of his vassalage, and accept Langton as archbishop of Canterbury, the first time that the will of a strong king had not prevailed in England in an episcopal appointment. There was nothing unique or necessarily humiliating in what John did: many other princes of Europe had done similar homage, and to have the spiritual head of Christendom as overlord could imply no indignity. As we have seen, his diplomatic purpose was achieved, and the second coalition, which might have destroyed France, was made possible.

III. The Feudal Problem

Since taxation was to form one of the crucial issues at stake in the reign of John and of his successors for many generations, it is well that we should have a clear idea at the outset where the royal revenue came from. The outcry against John's fiscal oppression was not the consequence of any novel forms of taxation devised by or for him: indeed, no sources were drawn upon throughout the whole of the thirteenth century which had not already been tapped at some time or another during the twelfth century. It was to John's excessive exploitation of these sources that exception was taken. And if we make a bare tabulation of his income, we cannot but be impressed by the wealth at his disposal. (*a*) The demesne or private estates were returning an ever larger profit with the growing general prosperity of the country. (*b*) The Forest lands, kept strictly as game preserves for the king's pleasure, were to be found in almost every county in England and at one time, for example, covered Essex completely. Whilst remaining under the common law, they were in addition subjected to a special 'law of the forest', which was largely an expression of the king's will and yielded him an arbitrary revenue in the shape of rents and fines. (c) The right to tallage royal demesne and royal boroughs, that is, the right to impose a tax either at will or by bargain, was exercised about once every three years. (d) The Jews were entirely at the king's mercy in return for the protection he gave them against others, and in 1210 alone a tallage of £44,000 was demanded from them. (e) Customs had been levied arbitrarily on trade and commerce by John's predecessors, and he himself in 1205 imposed a duty of one-fifteenth on all imported and exported merchandise, which provided £5,000 in two years. (f) Judicial profits continued to mount with the development of writs and eyres. (g) The Church was called upon to pay its *dona*, or so-called free gifts, and in 1207 came the first demand that its spiritualities, as distinct from its temporalities, should contribute to the royal exchequer. And during the Interdict almost the entire wealth of the higher clergy was at John's disposal. (h) A carucage on *landed* property was levied in 1200; a tax of variable rate was placed upon *movable* property at frequent intervals: the thirteenth imposed in 1207 brought in nearly £60,000. (i) Scutage derived its origin from the feudal contract but, as it could be raised without any need for previous consent, the barons had no legal right to try to bring it under their control. John not only increased its rate but he made its incidence more frequent so that it bade fair to be more than an emergency levy and seemed likely to turn into an unlimited and regular source of revenue with no connexion with military necessities. The great inquiry into tenures and the consequent liabilities of crown vassals in 1212 presumably had behind it the intention of squeezing every possible penny out of scutage, and it was the imposition of a heavy scutage in 1214 that provided the immediate cause of revolt. (j) The feudal incidents grew in value because escheat was exercised on flimsier pretexts, reliefs were fixed at the king's will, and the rights of wardship and marriage were flagrantly abused. It was the 'aids' (*auxilia*), however, which formed the main point of controversy. It was recognized in feudal practice that the vassal must assist his overlord, when in distress, even with his money. By John's reign it had become agreed that on three occasions an ordinary aid could be demanded without question: for the ransom of the king, the knighting of his eldest son, the marriage of his eldest daughter once. John, however, was imposing aids for other purposes, and the barons were determined that such extraordinary aids must first receive their consent. It was out of such 'gracious aids' that modern taxation was to arise and that control of taxation was to come into existence.

Though it was felt that the fiction of a feudal aid to an overlord was insufficient to cover such heavy and arbitrary levies, nevertheless the fear of war and of invasion for long induced the barons to acquiesce or, at least, refrain from impeding action. The growth of any opposition that can be properly designated as organized was slow and hesitant. We must be careful not to attribute to the barons virtues that they did not possess. As we have already remarked, resistance to the government had so far been individual, and no recognized policy and no recognized leader had emerged. The baronage denoted a class of all sorts of men: naturally its motives were mixed and its actions often inconsistent. Some barons acted only under the pressure of personal grievances and had no thought of doing more than secure the abolition of abuses affecting themselves alone. They could only look backwards and seek their ideals in the past: all would be well if feudal law and feudal conditions, which had been whittled away, could be re-established. That is why the Great Charter is saturated with feudalism. But we shall miss the important interest of the struggle if we associate it with solely feudal ideas. For the more responsible among the barons appreciated the art of good government for itself and had acquired valuable experience, not only in the administration of their own estates, but in the service of the king himself. And the loss of Normandy and other French possessions in and after 1204 influenced developments because it compelled the barons, however much they were to remain, like their kings, French in culture until the close of the fourteenth century, to concentrate on English interests. They would continue to think feudal thoughts and to work in feudal ways, but their problems were at last basically English, and English ways and traditions would sooner or later influence the manner in which those problems were settled. They recognized that the fundamental problem went beyond feudalism: it was a problem of government in new conditions. It is quite evident from the new recension of the 'Laws of the Confessor', made about 1200, that the relations of the king to the baronage and the place of the baronage in administration were exercising men's minds. We should no longer believe that it was Stephen Langton who 'discovered' a copy of the Coronation Charter of Henry I and drew the barons' attention to it, for it was widely available at the time in both French and Latin versions. And it is beyond doubt that John was consulting the barons frequently. The greater frequency is presumably explained by the fact that John spent most of his time at home in England: nevertheless, he was not backward in referring questions to their deliberation. Consequently, it is not surprising that many barons, skilled in the running of their own estates, versed in local government, accustomed to giving advice, should have awakened to an interest in the rights and duties of monarchy and begun to argue that administration was not solely the king's concern but their own as well.

The Great Charter was more than sponsored by the barons: it was essentially their work. The king himself regarded it as a treaty (*pax*) with them, and they would not have clung to it as they did if they had not regarded it in the same light. The representatives of the Church certainly gave their assistance, and the barons were never in any doubt that they had the sympathy of the bishops, and they were quite willing, after the Charter had been ratified, to accept them as the interpreters of any ambiguities it contained and as mediators between the king and themselves in the short-lived attempt at co-operative government. But it is wrong to attribute to Archbishop Langton the real impulse and driving-force behind the Charter, for the obedience he owed to the pope, who supported John through thick and thin, was sufficient to tie his hands. In the event, force was used by the barons against his advice. That consideration apart, Langton did all he could to restrain the king from his evil courses. The archbishop had only recently been admitted to the country after the lifting of the Interdict and, in spite of John's submission, he was hardly likely to feel that the Church was safe with such a king on the throne. Moreover, the isolated baronial revolts taking place suggested that the only alternative to tyranny might turn out to be anarchy like that of Stephen's reign. As early as August 1213 he summoned a select meeting of prelates and barons in St. Paul's to discuss ways and means of obtaining redress on specific points and outlined a programme of reform, and for two years afterwards he worked hard to find a formula that would please all parties and prevent war. The explosion point, however, was reached soon after John's complete defeat abroad. The barons formed a confederation, swore a common oath, made a formal 'defiance', marched on London and occupied it with their armed forces, and compelled the king to negotiate and seal the Great Charter in June 1215. In studying it we shall be reviewing the domestic history of John's reign.

IV. The Great Charter

The true meaning of the Charter has been distorted by the uncritical interpretation placed upon it in modern times. The opponents of Stuart despotism believed that in its vindication of the freedom of the nation from tyranny and of the civil rights of individuals it was the foundation stone of the English constitution. Nineteenth-century historians with their fervour for democracy simply underlined what had been written and continued to regard the Charter as the palladium of English liberties. It is quite impossible to stress the 'constitutionalism' of John's reign after this fashion and yet, as so often happens, what is not historically true can profoundly influence the course of history: the myth was greater than the reality in the conditions of a later age and, however much reduced to a caricature of its real self, the Great Charter was at least as powerful a weapon in the hands of the parliamentarians as it was to those who forged it. In the twentieth century there came the inevitable reaction to the old liberal views, and the conduct and motives of the barons met with harsh criticism: far from being reverenced as opponents of tyranny, champions of liberty and even founders of parliament, they were stigmatized as a faction of turbulent self-seekers, better equipped with ambitions than abilities, who had tried to thwart the orderly development of government. For the new interest in administrative history had compelled a fuller recognition of the importance of the part played by the king in medieval government and a truer appreciation of that intricate and yet adaptable machinery, which had begun to run the country from a private household and a counting-house. However, to ask whether the Charter represents 'a landmark of progress or a hall-mark of reaction' is to miss the essential truth for the sake of an epigram, for men of these days did not think in such terms.

Our concern is with the medieval applications and implications of the Charter, and it is well that we should remember at the outset that medieval folk gave it its adjective 'great' simply because of its length, and not for its importance, and to distinguish it from the complementary Charter of the Forest, issued in 1217. Indeed, it contains little that cannot be paralleled in the contemporary laws and even contemporary charters of France, Spain or Hungary. It contained no philosophic declaration of the Rights of Man, but was an eminently practical and highly technical document: by making use of the formulas, witnessing and sealing required in a feudal conveyance of land, it made this grant of concessions from the king to the community as binding as possible.

It is essential to look at the Charter from two points of view and to appreciate its double significance.

I.   A FEUDAL DOCUMENT

This is naturally the predominant aspect since the Charter was the product of a feudal age and of a feudal opposition. There can be no doubt that the self-interest of the barons dominated the negotiations. From a narrow point of view a good case can be made out on their behalf, for purely feudal law would have given a verdict in their favour. John had been twisting and distorting feudalism to his own advantage. He had broken his side of the contract and *ipso facto* left his vassals at full liberty solemnly and formally to repudiate their own obligations. A similar situation had arisen under Rufus, and as a result one of the first acts of Henry I had been to issue his coronation charter, in which he promised that the crown would exercise its rights 'in a just and lawful way'. Once again abuses were prevalent. The avarice of John was largely to blame, for he wrung the last penny out of the fiscal rights he inherited by flimsy and even dishonest pretexts.

Therefore, when we read through the sixty-three chapters of the Charter, we realize that it is mainly concerned with the detailed working of feudalism so that royal exploitation will in the future be impossible: the regulation of such matters as reliefs, for which there was now to be a fixed scale of charges quite unrelated to different capital values—£100 for any barony, 100 shillings for any knight's fee, and proportionately for smaller holdings; wardships, during which heirs were not to be given in marriage to their disparagement and their property was not to be so misused that it could not be returned as originally found; the rights of widows to dower and their freedom from compulsory remarriage; the restraints on the alienation of land, especially by collusive gifts to the Church, which might injure the rights of the landlord. The barons were primarily intent on removing the vagueness which surrounded feudal relations, on re-stating and reasserting the feudal law and compelling the king to acknowledge its authority. When they forbade an arbitrarily extended use of the writ 'praecipe' (ch. 34), it was probably not meant to be a deliberate attack on that royal policy which had impaired private jurisdiction over land, but rather a simple reassertion of feudal custom which had allowed land-lords to have cognisance of proprietary actions as between their own tenants; in practice this restraint was of slight effect. And the articles forbidding prerogative and unauthorized taxation must not be forced to carry a modern rather than a medieval significance. One of them (ch. 12) stated the three occasions when feudal aids could be lawfully demanded, thus indicating quite plainly that they were part and parcel of feudal relations and not to be regarded as levied by virtue of the royal prerogative, and it forbade the king to impose any other 'aids' without first obtaining 'general counsel'; another (ch. 14) outlined the procedure which had to be followed in order to obtain that 'general counsel' for an extraordinary aid: an assembly had to be convoked, to which the greater barons were to be summoned individually and the lesser barons collectively through the sheriff on forty days' notice and with cause shown, and the vote of the majority was to be binding upon any absentees. Such provisions were in accordance with general feudal conceptions and, though the emphasis upon the doctrine of consent was highly important, it asserted nothing new. It is possible that ch. 14, which is not to be found in the 'Petition of the Barons' on which the Charter was based, was inserted under pressure from those negoti-ating on the king's behalf, for none of the magnates would really wish to be committed to making arrangements for taxing themselves or to accepting any decision without being personally consulted, and, in fact, they insisted long afterwards that they could be bound only by their own individual act. However, the two articles were dropped from all later issues of the Charter and therefore never became part of the law of the land.

It has therefore been argued that the Charter was not essentially a revolutionary document but simply a definition and restoration of what was customary. It was so feudal in its significance and so limited in the scope of its appeal that it was little more than a result of class agitation, and thus the 'special' protection given to baronial 'liberties' or privileges was an implied check upon 'general' liberty. Its sole purpose was to set down feudal law as practised in England and to see that the king observed it, to prevent him from developing into more than a contractual ruler and becoming an irresponsible despot. And in so far as feudalism was in rapid decline, the Charter was a commentary upon the past rather than a programme for the future, and the importance of most of its clauses was accordingly transient.

II. A POLITICAL DOCUMENT

If the Charter had simply defined the usages of a society which was fast disappearing, it would not have become the symbol of the hopes and aspirations of large sections of the community who had yet to make their presence known and their influence felt. In fact, the Charter went beyond feudal considerations at three points.

(i) *Opposition to arbitrary monarchy*

The predominating idea was not to defy the law but to enforce it. Monarchy was considered to be no longer the safeguard of order and the promoter of public welfare. The reforms and innovations of Henry II had been accepted with very little demur, and it is quite clear, even from the Charter itself, that the barons had placed themselves irrevocably under the 'common law'. It was the acts of a king, who was irresponsible at times to the point of dementia, that precipitated a crisis and made it necessary to think out the true position of monarchy within the state. The paradox had risen that, whereas England had discovered its legal unity through the operations of monarchy, it was to find its political unity by reacting against those operations in curbing the abuses and excesses of royal power. The administrative machine built up by Henry II had become so efficient that there was a real danger of tyranny. And it was a constant irritant that the government servants should be found in all places and at all times: the better the royal administration did its work, the more oppressive and tyrannous it seemed to become. If Henry II's reforms, designed to protect individual rights, were abused, then individual rights would be in far greater peril than before. Actions upon property should normally originate with a royal writ, but what if that royal writ were made too expensive or even withheld? Royal courts had greatly ousted the seignorial and popular courts, but what if the royal courts should now be deliberately closed to litigants? Royal justice had smothered much Anglo-Saxon and feudal custom, but what if that royal justice should be manipulated out of all reason to gratify the personal ambitions of its royal creators? The time was critical, for all these dangers had been suggested by John's arbitrary acts: writs had been denied, courts had been suspended, justice had been withheld. It must be emphasized that the people at large were not seriously affected. It was simply to the limited class of greater barons that the basis of John's rule seemed to be not law but intimidation: the demand for hostages as a guarantee of future good conduct, arbitrary disseisins, capricious taxation. The quarrel was bound up with a good deal of personal animus, the details of which are difficult to recapture, and there is reason to believe that John was in great measure acting in self-defence—and from his point of view he may have kept within the law. But it cannot be denied that what he did was frequently impolitic.

Against John's notion of kingship was set a conception founded on feudal custom and moral law. The king must bear in mind that, however much he chose to govern his realm through his household and its officials, it was obligatory for him to consult all his tenants-in-chief in changing the law, passing judgments upon those tenants, and obtaining financial aid from them. Not to do so would be to violate the sanctity of contract, the feudal contract which bound them to him only as long as he for his part observed it. The renaissance of the twelfth century had put more sophisticated ideas in currency, especially among the higher clergy: John of Salisbury and other thinkers had all insisted that a king differed from a tyrant only through his obedience to law, that kingship was an office with solemn responsibility for establishing on earth a system of law and order which should be as close a replica as possible of the moral law ordained of God and revealed in the Scriptures. Although the Church taught subjection to the powers that be, it was a conditional subjection, and Archbishop Langton's insistence on this fact helped to transform the feudal right of resistance into a moral and even political duty whenever the king needed to be brought to a sense of his duties. The fateful question was being decided whether the king was to be the master or the servant of the law.

Whether deliberately or not, whether from selfish motives or not, the opposition had enunciated high principles of action and assumed a guise of constitutionalism. The administrative system of Henry II was carefully continued because its value was appreciated. For example, a demand was made that the court of common pleas should be held in some fixed place (ch. 17)—a protest against John's recent suspension of its activities, which had forced litigants to seek instead the ever-moving court attendant on the king's person; that royal justices should come to each county four times a year to hold the assizes in collaboration with four knights, elected by the county court, and thus provide a check on any violent dispossession of property (ch. 18); that royal writs 'concerning hatred and malice' (*de odio et atia*), which gave protection from a malicious capital charge, should be issued free of charge (ch. 36); that the dispensation of justice in general should not be sold, delayed or denied (ch. 40); that judicial amercements should be assessed by neighbours and be reasonable in amount (ch. 20); and other regulations concerning the choice of suitable officials, and restraints to prevent them from abusing the powers entrusted to them. In this connexion one clause, providing the greatest of all safeguards of personal liberty, is still open to somewhat different interpretations (ch. 39): that no free men were to be imprisoned or dispossessed of property or outlawed 'save by judgment of their peers and the law of the land' (*nisi per judicium parium suorum vel per legem terrae*). The 'judgment by peers' or social equals is a principle of remote antiquity and has nothing as yet to do with the idea of 'trial by jury', with which it came much later to be associated. The 'vel', therefore, is not sharply disjunctive to produce an antithesis between the new royal process of trial by jury and the old customary procedure of ordeal and battle; it may be, as often in medieval Latin, simply conjunctive. 'By the law of the land' is another way of saying 'by due process of law' and allows for local variations in practice.

It is evident that the object was not to destroy but to control, that the grievance was not the Angevin reforms so much as the misgovernment of John which had abused those reforms, that there was a willingness expressed to support the royal innovations if coupled with the safety-devices of the Charter against administrative misapplications. The Charter was a not unworthy effort to face the problem that has defied the ages: how to get private liberty and public order to exist amicably side by side.

(ii) *Concessions to other than the baronial class*

These form but a small part of the Charter and do not penetrate far down the social scale. The king himself had broadened the resistance against him by his misrule which bore heavily upon ecclesiastics, merchants and ordinary men, and it is not surprising that it was considered politic to go somewhat outside the narrow circle of the baronage and do something on behalf of classes which were looming larger in the common life. The first clause of the Charter guaranteed the English Church its freedom. There is no suggestion here of nationalism or anti-papalism: the 'English Church' was a *papal* phrase connoting, in Hubert Walter's words, 'that portion of the Western Church which the Most High has planted in England', and it was freedom to be under papal control and out of royal control, especially in the matter of elections to bishoprics, that was demanded. In practice, the boundaries between Church and State and between papal and royal authority remained ill-defined and controversial. In other directions the concessions were surprisingly niggardly and often reverted ultimately to the advantage of the barons. Little was done for the trading classes, despite the assistance that London, in particular, had given. All boroughs were to have their privileges confirmed (ch. 13), privileges that they had already by their own efforts toiled to acquire. Foreign merchants were to be allowed free entry into the country (ch. 41: repeating an order of 1200), an agreement which hardly squared with the Londoners' eager desire for a monopoly and benefited the general consumer rather than business interests: this was also the case when weights and measures were ordered to be the same throughout the country (ch. 35: repeating an assize of 1197), and no arbitrary tolls were to be placed on foreign merchandise (ch. 41). And, although overlords were required to extend the reforms to their under-tenants, the barons might well have been urged to this by self-interest, for whilst they were tenants-in-chief for some of their lands, they often held other estates as the tenants of other lords. The variety of their own tenures would compel them, whether they wished it or not, to champion the rights of *all* landholders. In any event, the concession could be no more than a vague gesture so long as there were no sanctions to enforce it. Except for the provision that the villeins were not to be so heavily amerced that they were deprived of their means of livelihood (ch. 20), the great mass of the peasantry was excluded from consideration, and even here it should be noticed that this stipulation was made for the sake of the barons and not of the villeins, who were regarded as a source of profit to be kept immune from crippling amercements by royal officials.

Evidently we must not make too much of the importance of these clauses, nor must we readily attribute to the barons altruistic motives. To say that is not to deny the growing importance of the country gentry and the city burgesses but to assert that that importance was not reflected in the Great Charter: as yet they were not politically vocal and the barons had no desire nor even thought to express their point of view for them.

(iii) *The endeavour to devise some machinery of control*

The most important single article in the charter for future developments is the 'security clause' (ch. 61). To obtain the Charter was nothing as compared with the task of enforcing it. The barons, only too well aware of this, set up a representative Council of Twenty-five of their number to supervise the king's actions in order to make sure that he obeyed the Charter; if he proved recalcitrant, then it was declared lawful and right for that Council to organize armed revolt. A step towards achieving limited monarchy had been taken, for whilst the Great Charter had resembled the Coronation Charter of Henry I in defining the position of the king in a feudal state, it had gone further in setting up machinery to control him. For the two months after Runnymede during which they co-operated with the king, the 'Twenty-five Kings', as John's friends called them, saw to it that John observed his promise to remove unsuitable officials from their positions as sheriffs and keepers of castles, and they arranged for the transmission of copies of the Charter to all parts of the country. Even after the rupture with the king, the Council endeavoured to hold officials and important personages faithful to the oath they had exacted from them and to rule the kingdom without the king. We may condemn this machinery as crude and rebellious, especially in its legalization of civil war, and dismiss it as a mere feudal device, embodying the feudal 'defiance' for the preservation of the feudal contract. But inasmuch as there was no thought of deposing the Lord's Anointed, nothing else was possible at this stage of political development. And it should be remembered that the clause was intended to prevent and not to provoke war, that it was regarded as a *legitimate* means of compelling the king himself to come under the common law and stop rebelling against the long-established customs of his realm, and that it limited itself to the sole task of enforcing the Charter and countenanced war only in the special case of a breach of the Charter. Otherwise, the executive power remained with the king.

The 'concord of Runnymede' proved to be no concord at all because John had never had the slightest intention of observing it. The surrender of the kingdom to the pope is the fact that explains the sequence of events. The barons had proceeded against John in the court of his feudal superior at Rome. The pope was willing to do justice, but he naturally objected to the barons' action in taking the law into their own hands and coercing his vassal. Indeed, the agreement made at Runnymede seems to have taken Innocent III by surprise, and, though his representative, Pandulf, had assented to it, he had no hesitation, at John's request, in stigmatizing the Great Charter as a 'shameful and iniquitous agreement' and declaring all who supported it excommunicate. What the pope did was done under the form of law, not feudal but ecclesiastical law. The repudiation of the Charter put the 'security clause' into operation, and the rule of the 'Twenty-five' as an alternative government began. Langton was quite incapable of grappling with the situation: he considered it unlawful to excommunicate the barons, was suspended from office, appealed to the pope and named the king as respondent, and left for Rome to plead his case. The 'Twenty-five' announced the suspension of John and invited the son of Philip Augustus of France to come to England to take his place. The pope could not prevent the French prince from accepting the offer of the crown of England. Civil war broke out in which the issue was at least doubtful: Louis held the all-important London and the south-east, whilst John was more than holding his own in the north and elsewhere. There was, in fact, a military deadlock until John unexpectedly died in 1216.

Magna Carta was the herald of a new age: for the first time the Government and the Opposition have been placed in something like a constitutional setting. On the one hand, it put down in black and white the fundamental medieval doctrine of kingship, which was no modern theory of Divine Right but the belief that the king existed to promote the welfare of his subjects and that, if he abused his power, he forfeited his authority and position. Here was to be found a practical illustration of the argument that he was under the law, for the Charter was a body of law which he must observe. On the other hand, it gave the opposition a lawful place in the scheme of government. Resistance to the Crown had been seen under the Anglo-Saxons, but there was nothing to save it from the stigma of treason; under the Normans resistance found legal warrant in the feudal custom which permitted a vassal to make a formal 'defiance'; under John it had obtained a written sanction, it had been authorized by the king himself. That is why during the thirteenth century, when continual and ineffective attempts were made to control the king, the opposition constantly appealed to the Great Charter and took its stand upon that document.

In comparison with these principles, the details of all the clauses are unimportant: as feudalism dies, and dies quickly, they die with it. But the contractual idea, whether originating in feudalism or morality, and however vague, remained as an elastic concept which could be adapted to suit the different circumstances of later ages until the time came in the fourteenth century when it found a permanent expression in parliament. Indeed, after 1215 the scene changes and we pass from the sphere of law, where monarchy had done its finest work, to the sphere of politics, where monarchy has a rival, intent on supervising its activities. On the issue of the struggle between them will depend the country's future.

SELECT READING

F. M. Powicke, 'England: Richard I and John' in *C. Med.H.*, vi (1929), 218–51; Stephenson and Marcham, 96–104, 109–26; Brooke, 215–29; W. Stubbs, *Historical Introductions to the Rolls Series* (ed. A. Hassall: 1902), 439–87; K. Norgate, *John Lackland* (1902); F. M. Powicke, *Stephen Langton* (1928), 75–161; F. M. Powicke, *Medieval England* (1931), 51–92; G. B. Adams, *Council and Courts in Anglo-Norman England* (1926), 251–81; Adams, *Origin of English Constitution* (1912), 144–313; W. S. McKechnie, *Magna Carta* (1905); H. G. Richardson, 'The Morrow of the Great Charter' in *B.J.R.L.*, xxviii (1944), 422–43, xxix (1945), 184–200.

CHAPTER XXV

THE STRIVINGS TOWARDS CONSTITUTIONAL OPPOSITION

The reign of Henry III (1216–72), the third longest in English history, has a unity of its own when it is viewed as a commentary upon the Great Charter. After all, that Charter had done little more than state a case, valuable though that proved eventually to be, and the fundamental problem of how to force the monarchy to realize and fulfil its responsibilities had only been faced: it had by no means been solved. In the stress of civil war it seemed to all appearances as though the Charter was stillborn. Yet right through the century it was to exercise a powerful influence upon thought and action.

I. The Accession of Henry III in 1216

This was, indeed, a most critical moment, for it was the first occasion since the Norman Conquest that the heir to the throne was a minor. The only occurrence of a similarly unprecedented character had been the nomination of Matilda as the first woman ruler of the country, and the sequel had been anarchy. This might much more easily be the result when already civil war was in progress and a foreign army on English soil. The death of John, however, had removed the sharpest cause of dissension, and the accession of a boy of nine allowed many, whose consciences were troubled by the thought of their rebellion against both monarchy and Church, to put aside their misgivings and join a royalist party under William Marshal, earl of Pembroke, as 'rector regis et regni'. He had already given proof of his wisdom and strength of character, and he was particularly acceptable to the barons because his previous career seemed to them an embodiment of the ideals of knightly chivalry. And he could rely upon the general support of the civil service, as represented by administrators like Hubert de Burgh, and of foreign mercenaries like Fawkes de Bréauté, who were experts in the art of war, ready to sell their services to the highest bidder. And the Charter was deliberately used in a bid for general loyalty: quite ignoring the fact that it was the fruit of rebellion and had been repudiated by both King John and Pope Innocent III, the regent and the legate re-issued it in November 1216 as a declaration of government policy, shorn of such clauses as chs. 12, 14 and 61, which were no longer needed when it was obvious that a boy-king must be under control. The government of the 'Twenty-five' and Louis had won the war: victory lay with the barons. The policy of conciliation and compromise had a speedy reward: barons who had done homage to Louis of France proved willing to acknowledge allegiance to John's son. The problem was how to get rid of Louis. The influence of the Church became effective only after the issue had been settled by trial by battle. For the legate, Guala, seems to have been quite ineffective as the representative of the papacy until Louis had been defeated. The rather lucky victory at Lincoln was decisive. The choice was between Louis and Henry, and everything depended upon Louis's military power. Otherwise there was little in his favour. The demonstration that militarily he was vulnerable turned the scale. Even so he was strong enough to exact good terms for himself and his supporters in the Treaty of Lambeth of 1217: he left the country with full indemnification for his expenses. Thereafter the new pope Honorius III could use his influence to secure the quick acceptance of his young ward. Henry III was in the future always to believe, and to remember with humble gratitude, that he owed his throne to the papacy. The departure of Louis was the signal for a second re-issue of the Charter as a guarantee that it was to be more than a politic gesture in time of war and would inform the actions of the government in time of peace also.

II. Government by Council, 1216–1232

The government of the country was carried on day by day by a small group of barons and officials with the co-operation of the legate, for the king was kept in tutelage until almost the end of this period. There is evidence that the *curia regis* or *magna curia,* as it was frequently termed, was afforced in numbers from time to time, and there were the usual large gatherings of notables at the great festivals of the Church. But, just as great deliberative meetings had been infrequent in the twelfth century and under John, so now it was only on rare occasions, especially when the need for money made it essential to respect the doctrine of consent, that a 'Great

Council' of magnates was convoked: the most noteworthy was in 1224, after it had been considered advisable to declare the king nominally of age and thus strengthen the authority of the monarchy, when the Charter was issued a third time and in the form finally accepted as law and, in significant association with its promulgation, a grant of a fifteenth was made. Unfortunately, the earl of Pembroke died in May 1219, and the direction of affairs was left in the hands of a triumvirate consisting of Hubert de Burgh, Peter des Roches, the Poitevin bishop of Winchester, and the new legate, Pandulf. Two years later Pandulf left the country, and shortly afterwards de Burgh had made himself predominant, much to the indignation of des Roches whom he eclipsed altogether, and ruled as the last of the justiciars who could issue writs in their own, and not the king's, name. All the same, his office had in reality been deprived of its former plenipotentiary nature, for the loss of Normandy meant that the king had no reason to be absent from his kingdom and a vicegerent there was no longer needed.

Hubert de Burgh was not one of the great justiciars, and he was regrettably self-seeking. His supersession by William Marshal had already been significant of that fact, and he had played second fiddle to the papal legate after the Marshal's death. When he did emerge as first minister, he did not reveal himself as of the same calibre as his predecessors in office. Still, he did useful work for England in reducing an appalling chaos to order. As soon as he felt that government was sufficiently stable, he resumed control of the castles which had passed from the custody of the king to that of local barons. He expelled the freebooters like Fawkes de Bréauté, who had spared not even monasteries in their greed for the spoils of war and dared to carry off a royal justice for passing sentence against them. He saw to it that the Crown recovered the lands and revenues which had been given indiscriminately away as bribes to appease the irresponsible opponents of the government at the beginning of the reign. And he could count on baronial support against Fawkes and, later on, against the intimidating actions of the king. For such men as the younger Marshal had power and effectiveness, and on the whole they stood for good government, though they might be stung into rebellion by arbitrary measures. But de Burgh was too rugged in character and too high-handed in action to remain immune from attack: he made personal enemies among the barons, he was accused of building up too independent an aggregation of lands on the Welsh borders, he was charged with bungling the conduct of war and finance, and he lost eventually the passive support of a king who was determined to rule as well as reign. In 1232 he fell ignominiously from office. Nevertheless, it had been demonstrated conclusively that the kingdom could be governed by a Council, in which baronial advisers worked alongside professional administrators. But all depended on the attitude the king adopted, for the Council had neither fixed personnel, stereotyped procedure, nor acknowledged functions: Henry III had only to insist on his right to take counsel where he wished and to change the membership of the Council to alter completely the complexion of the government.

III. The Personal Government of the King

If Henry had been possessed of average ability and shrewdness, it is by no means impossible that the claims of the barons to an effective voice in the councils of the realm could have been quietly ignored and the vital influence of the Charter sapped away. The king in the thirteenth century, as earlier, considered that it was the barons' *duty* to attend his councils: otherwise he could not, for example, have controlled the barons themselves. The issue really was whether the barons could impose a veto on certain of the king's acts or decisions and so exercise a measure of control which might lead to baronial rule. Still, for the time being the king had no reason to doubt the loyalty of his subjects, and rebellion was inconceivable if he played his cards well. And, in fact, he found no difficulty in gathering the reins of authority into his own hands. The increasing activity of the exchequer and the chancery had left a need for the king's household to retain an intimate staff and organization of its own to attend to the personal and immediate affairs of the king. Under Henry II, Richard and John the chamber was already constituted as an organ of government, separate from the English and Norman exchequers, with drawings from the treasury mainly, and had been the great spending department. Under Henry III, though the details differed, the chamber continued to occupy the same position as before. After 1232 Peter des Roches, the bishop of Winchester (returned to high favour on the fall of his enemy, Hubert de Burgh) and his nephew and protégé, Peter des Rivaux, very skilfully developed the wardrobe, a subordinate part of the chamber, into a more prominent part of the governmental machinery. Since the king's private wealth and the public revenue were quite indistinguishable, there was never any reason why the wardrobe should not be a private treasury, tapping the revenues from crown debtors and estates before they reached the treasury and demanding block grants from the exchequer. And since the king could issue writs as and when he pleased, the wardrobe was provided with a special privy seal to warrant its missives. But we shall err if we set the wardrobe in sharp antithesis at this time to the older departments, like the exchequer and the chancery, and look upon its staff as royal officials who had triumphed over baronial ministers. For the administration in its entirety remained subordinate to the king. The office of justiciar, once the pivot on which the whole government turned, fell into abeyance as early as 1234: the king needed no *alter ego* when his continental empire had largely vanished and he was compelled to stay at home. The chancery peregrinated with him and was personal to him, even so far as warranting expenditure was concerned, and the chancellors were of the same episcopal rank as their predecessors under Richard and John: to call them 'prelate chancellors' or 'baronial chancellors' is merely to mislead. And the treasurers were royal officials in Henry III's reign quite as much as in his grandfather's. We must not think that such offices were held by magnates who were ceasing to look upon themselves, as in the past, as the king's personal servants, and that departments were already too large to be either contained within the royal household or kept under its control. Nor did the king's advisers see the facts in that light and cunningly decide not to make a frontal attack on the baronial position and thus risk stirring up dangerous opposition. There was no need to side-step baronial invigilation by building up another organization which had its centre in the king's household, that is, the wardrobe, whereby the acts of the king, as it has been suggested, would escape supervision and the conduct of the government would come under the king's personal direction, the older departments, slowly deprived of initiative, falling subject to the king's will. For not yet can it be said that monarchy had cause to begin the practice, seen in much later times of crisis, of retreating within an inner circle of defences, whenever an outer circle had been stormed by the opposition, or that the dualism of, as it were, 'national government' and 'household government' had been already created which was to form a major subject of strife between king and barons in the next two centuries. The king undoubtedly wielded a tremendous power, and mere

conservatism on the part of the barons might not have been proof
against the establishment of a despotism. The king was God's
vicar, but what if he did wrong? Can his court control him?
Conservatism might argue that it could: it depends on whether the
barons of the period of the Great Charter are to be considered as
exercising their rights after a formal defiance or acting as rebels.
There is much to be said for the barons' point of view. Their
dangerous weakness came through John's surrender of the kingdom
to the pope, who thus became overlord and could decide the issues
between king and barons on appeal. But if John had never had
power to make that surrender, then there was no appeal and the
barons' position was juridically strong. And, fortunately, arbitrary
rule needed to be justified by success, and this Henry came nowhere
near achieving.

I. THE INCOMPETENCE OF THE KING

Henry was quite incapable of bearing the burdens and responsibilities of personal government: completely impractical, capable of
adopting the most hare-brained schemes, possessing the pettishness
and obstinacy that so often go with a weak character, he could
never stand upon his own feet but always had to find someone
stronger than himself on whom to lean. His personal life was
beyond reproach, if morality is confined to the narrow limits of
sexual purity which consorted with his type of piety, and that
piety impelled him to be blindly subservient to the papacy and
thereby to bring the Church in England and eventually himself
into great distress. His utter futility as a man of action was conspicuously evident in his conduct of military campaigns. The
continental problem had not disappeared on the field of Bouvines.
The relations between the English and the French kings had ceased
to be those of lord and vassal since 1202, when the sentence passed
against John by the court of Philip Augustus formally broke the
feudal tie. The disaster of Bouvines in 1214 had been followed by
a truce rather than a treaty, and it was open to Henry III to
attempt to recover the lost Angevin possessions if he so desired:
indeed, their abandonment had in some quarters been felt to be
a disgrace to the monarchy which could only be wiped out by their
recovery. In any case, if the English king made no move, it was
certain that the French king would, sooner or later take further
action and put the remaining duchy of Aquitaine in danger. Philip
Augustus had been in no position to begin operations against the

south and south-west of France, but events played into the Capetian hands. For these districts had embraced a heresy, the Albigensian heresy, which Pope Innocent III stamped out by encouraging
ruthless adventurers from Northern France, like Simon de Montfort, father of the leader of the baronial revolt in England, to
undertake a crusade against the south. They did for the French
king what otherwise he must have done for himself, and they
acknowledged him as overlord of the principalities they carved out
for themselves. He was, in consequence, brought closely up against
Aquitaine. The tragedy of France in the Middle Ages lay in the
clash of two rights. French policy demanded that the provinces
should be brought under the direct rule of the crown, for this was
necessary and inevitable if the French state was to survive.
English policy required the king, as in honour bound, to recover his
inheritance. Twice Henry III was persuaded to embark again upon
war on the Continent and reclaim his lost fiefs, beginning with
Poitou: on both occasions—in 1230 when he operated in the north
from, and in alliance with, Brittany; in 1242 when he operated in
the south from Gascony and met a humiliating defeat at Taille-
bourg—he achieved nothing but discredit and financial loss. With
Poitou irrevocably abandoned to the French monarchy, Aquitaine
proper and Gascony remained alone in uneasy allegiance to the
English king, and it was fortunate for Henry that the throne of
France was occupied by Louis IX, not so much because he was his
brother-in-law as that he was deservedly famous for his scrupulous
regard for the legal rights of others. Nevertheless, the position of
affairs in France was too unsatisfactory to be left as it was, and by
the Treaty of Paris, concluded in May 1258 though not proclaimed
until December 1259, the English king definitively renounced the
provinces already lost and became once more the vassal of the
French king for the fiefs in the south-west left to him.

II. THE FAVOURITISM TO STRANGERS

Though much of the 'Angevin Empire' had still remained to Henry
III on his accession, Poitou and Aquitaine and Gascony had never
formed part of the Anglo-Norman system of government, and Gascony continued to be ruled after 1259 in the old fashion. It was the
disruption of the Anglo-Norman system that was all significant.
The loss of Normandy had implied that at last the administration
of England was no longer to constitute but one part of the very

much larger problem of governing an Anglo-Norman state: England will use the machinery of administration which had been constructed for her very largely as the outcome of her participation in that state, but her governance will now be in right of herself. Barons and churchmen grew conscious, though very slowly, of their English heritage, and the slogan of England for the English could come readily to their lips when the occasion suited. And at this very time more foreigners poured into England than ever before in a time of peace. It was as though the king, debarred from going to the Continent, was determined to redress the balance by having the Continent come to England. Poitevins had insinuated themselves into high office: it is sufficient to point out that Peter des Rivaux was at one time Keeper of the Wardrobe and the Privy Seal, Keeper of the Forests, Guardian of all the ports of England, and sheriff of twenty-one counties, and that he possessed equally extensive authority in Ireland. The king's wife, Eleanor of Provence, brought in her train her Savoyard uncles who were given exalted positions in Church and State. The king's half-brothers, the Lusignans, were greedy parasites and nothing more. In addition, England saw the presence of Italians: papal legates and papal collectors and many priests, provided by the pope with English benefices.

III.   THE SUBSERVIENCE TO THE POPE

The fact that England had become a papal fief in 1213 and, three years later, saw a minor on the throne gave the popes a chance to turn the situation to their own profit. And when Henry came of age, he showed a quite unprecedented deference to Rome and allowed the papacy to secure a firmer hold on his kingdom than on any other part of Christendom outside Italy. In the event, the Church in England found itself facing merciless demands upon its wealth. The papal need of money was understandable. Innocent III had fought strenuously, and not unsuccessfully, to realize the ideal of the world as a Church-State, a theocracy, a papal monarchy: if the papacy was to govern the world, it had to construct and maintain a most elaborate machinery of government, and it must tax the world to provide the necessary running costs. The exactions of Gregory IX, however, knew no moderation. (a) *Papal Provisions.* The papacy, in its determination to control the affairs of the Universal Church and to resist the excessive influence of the king, ignored the recently hard-won freedom of elections to bishoprics by cathedral chapters and advanced to the position where it claimed the right to make direct appointments itself. Furthermore, the bishops were compelled to find benefices for papal nominees, often foreigners: thus in 1240 the bishops of Salisbury and Lincoln were ordered to 'provide' for three hundred alien churchmen, and it was said with the usual wild exaggeration of the time that 'provisions' to the value of 50,000 marks a year were being made by Rome. Indeed, we must guard against the common tendency to overstate the extent of papal provisions. Still, the strict rules of the great Lateran Council of 1215 against pluralities and absenteeism were flouted; the novelty was even introduced of conferring benefices before they had become vacant so that priests waited expectantly for their fellows to die. It is little wonder that a storm of protest was raised by lay patrons, who, though the king's court would always protect their legal claims, were often disturbed in the enjoyment of one of their most cherished and peculiar rights, and by native clergy, whose chances of promotion were taken from them by foreigners who drew incomes from English benefices in which frequently they did not reside. The best element in the Church was particularly incensed, for such papal practices, if abused, made it difficult for it to introduce and enforce measures of reform. (b) *Clerical Taxation.* The papacy never made good its claim to impose taxation directly upon the laity. The clergy for their part resisted taxation by the king, but he got his way with the aid of the pope. Thus in 1226 the pope gave the secular government full liberty to tax the 'spiritualities' of the clergy; in 1254 he granted Henry III a tenth of all clerical revenues for the expenses of his Sicilian adventure, without arranging for the clergy to be previously consulted in any way. If we consider that the Crown was right in the attitude it adopted, we must concede that the papacy had justification also in its claim to tax the clergy. For, if the pope was the symbol of ecclesiastical privilege and the head of a separate and self-governing community, then there was much to be said on his behalf.

It is not surprising, however, that in these circumstances the Church in England as a whole became articulate. Its fearless spokesman was Robert Grosseteste, the saintly Bishop of Lincoln (1235–53). He could not be blind to the disastrous results of the papal policy in England, and he did not hesitate to criticize sharply the corruption he saw in the papal curia. He was neither afraid to oppose the papal legate in England nor to address an open letter to the pope himself to rebuke him for his scandalous 'provisions'. Yet he was in no way anticipating the heresiarch, John Wycliffe, of the next century. His attitude was precisely the same as that of Stephen Langton: he thought it permissible for him to consider a case on its own merits and to draw the attention of the pope to any errors of judgment he might make, but he also conceived it to be his ultimate duty to obey the pope, even if his commands appeared to be contrary to scripture and canon law. He might protest but he would not disobey: the pope had the *plenitudo potestatis*, the fullness of power, he was above the law, his will must prevail.

IV. THE DISPUTE OVER LAY TAXATION

Henry III had inherited a heavy debt which had been greatly increased during the disorders of his own minority. But retrenchment and economy were unpleasant to him and his own irresponsible spending intensified the evil: lavish gifts to favourites, acquiescence in papal demands, indulgence to the full of his artistic pleasure in magnificent building, beautiful decoration and *objets d'art* (perhaps a reflexion of his hero-worship of Edward the Confessor who had similar tastes), which resulted in additions to Westminster Abbey and the adornment there of the Confessor's shrine. The difficulty was not really that England was impoverished, for she increased in wealth as the century advanced, but there was a need for an altered attitude to the principles of taxation. The costs of government were constantly mounting as it enlarged its influence over the country and grew more complex in its character. Warfare was becoming increasingly specialized. Nevertheless, the old sources of revenue were diminishing rapidly through a rise in prices, and some of them were becoming obsolete: the whole system of fiscal feudalism was breaking down. The king needed more money to carry on even the ordinary work of administration, and it was unreasonable to argue that he must remain content with what his predecessors had enjoyed. If the royal government was to be efficient, it must be adequately financed. The barons would not concede the point, and any attempt by the king to raise money in any extraordinary way was always met with a prompt resistance. Furthermore, they could always urge that the power of the crown was too great and that it would be folly to increase it further. Thus the barons refused an aid in 1232 for a war in Wales, and they resolutely opposed every demand for a subsidy between 1237 and 1270.

During these years of personal government the barons found themselves in an extremely awkward and embarrassing situation. It was taken for granted that it was the king's business to govern, that the only machinery for the purpose was largely his creation and his creature, that ordered life depended on that well-organized and competent civil service which was bound closely to him and to his interests. By contrast the baronage was a group without any real cohesion: the minor tenants-in-chief were in process of settling down as country gentry, whilst the greater tenants-in-chief were still far distant from the notion of 'peerage', which would make them more distinctly noble, exclusive and class-conscious. This heterogeneous body had not succeeded in producing strong leaders and it acknowledged no unswerving loyalties. It had often little thought of doing more than maintaining its own privileges. The great safeguard of its position was provided by the practice of collaboration with the king in accordance with feudal conceptions.

The habit of large gatherings at the principal Church festivals remained in force, and the king apparently showed no less disposition to consult the barons than had John or Richard or Henry II. Nevertheless, there was no guarantee that that practice would not be discarded. It is in this reign that we constantly see the manifestation of those jealousies of amateur politicians for professional experts which lie at the root of future developments, particularly in the history of parliament. And the rebuff was all the greater when Henry placed foreigners within the inner circle of his advisers. The barons were perforce driven into opposition. If the king would not listen to them of his own accord, could he be forced to consult them, and take advice from them as his 'natural counsellors' instead of from whom he pleased? And if so, what machinery could be devised by which the barons could exercise such control?

It could, however, be argued that, if monarchy were trammelled in any such way, it could not continue to govern well and to guarantee law and order, and this was the point that was naturally uppermost with the royal officials. And such problems greatly agitated the minds of contemporaries. It was not the theoretical relations between the king and the barons that caused bewilderment. The great jurist, Bracton, plainly stated that the king was under the law, that there was no king where 'will rules and not law', that changes in the law could not be wrought by the king alone but only with the counsel of the magnates of his realm. This was a direct

15

legacy from both traditional practices and from feudal law, which stressed the principle of contract and thereby implied limitations upon the power of the king. Indeed, both Norman and Angevin rulers had published charters, acknowledging restraints upon their will, and John had accepted the Great Charter. The crux was how to translate theory into practice. The view of the learned and experienced Bracton seems to be quite clear. The king could do wrong, and that wrong could be and should be redressed on a petition of right, heard in the *magna curia*, meaning the court of common bench, afforced as need be by members of the council and by magnates. There is in his mind a contrast between the *magna curia* and the Great Council, the court of earls and barons, which alone could authorize changes in the law.

The truth was that the feudal world was rapidly passing away as the thirteenth century advanced, and feudal considerations would no longer suit the new conditions. An approach, though only a very slight and tentative approach, was being made to the process whereby private and feudal rights and obligations to a personal king were to be converted into public and national services to an impersonal state. The baronial grievances came to have less and less of a feudal content, and therefore their feudal right to renounce their homage became inoperative as a justification for action against the king. But the baronial dissatisfaction did not cease, and it is evident that the movement in which they were engaged was wider than feudalism in its significance and that a fundamental change was taking place. The problem is being transferred from the narrow field of law to the extensive domain of politics: the nature of political government is at issue, and the barons will simply assume that they speak for the 'community of England'. It was imperative for the barons to emphasize at every turn the need for the 'counsel of the magnates' as the only practical limitation on a virtually irresponsible king. They refused to stand aside themselves or to be thrust aside by the king, they continued to regard themselves as an essential part of the machinery of government, as indeed they had been during the days of the king's minority when their political experience ripened. We may wonder how far this idea would have become blurred and vanished if Henry III had governed well and provoked no resentment. As it was, his misgovernment convinced the barons that the root of the evil was the independence of the royal administration, which could produce every conceivable kind of abuse in the hands of either a weak or an unscrupulous king.

By their conservatism, by their determination to preserve their own rights and privileges, they performed an invaluable service. But they were not aware of its great significance, they were not thinking 'constitutionally', they were not deliberately fostering a political spirit among the English people and consciously making themselves their leaders.

The all-important reform was to compel the king to listen to and accept his barons' advice. Their demand was moderate and by no means revolutionary, and they had no thought of precipitating a civil war. If, however, the king refused to co-operate with them, then there was no legal means, no legal machinery, to compel him to do so: he could only be restrained by the threat of rebellion, and an appeal to arms was in the final course of things logically inevitable. But before the arbitrament of the sword was invoked, proposals at least had been put forward in the tradition of ch. 61 of the Great Charter. In 1237 the last extraordinary aid to be granted for a generation was conceded in return for the fourth solemn reconfirmation of the Charter and the admission of three barons among the king's counsellors. In 1244 (a case has been made for 1238) a more ambitious scheme was adumbrated, which may have owed something to the inspiration of Bishop Grosseteste. The disgrace and heavy expenditure of the recent military campaign in Gascony had caused the king to make a desperate demand for money. In reply the barons and prelates appointed a committee of twelve of their number to consider the matter. Their recommendations are significant: they declared that, though the Charter had often been confirmed, it had consistently been evaded, and they demanded that a revised edition should be published; they insisted that officials, like the justiciar and the chancellor, should be appointed from their own class; and they urged the establishment of a small council of four of their nominees who should be in constant attendance on the king to watch over the observance of the Charter, give advice, and remove all abuses in administration. The scheme was crude and not likely to have much influence upon the complex organism of government which had by this time been devised, and nothing apparently came of it. Nor did further protests in 1248 cause any change. However, these proposals did face the crucial question by trying to find a place within the scheme of government for the barons, and, in doing that, they pointed back to the Great Charter and forward to the Provisions of Oxford.

IV. Baronial Reform and Government, 1258–1265

The crisis of 1258 was very largely precipitated by the folly of the king in committing himself to the 'Sicilian Adventure'. Marriage ties had always bound the ruling dynasties of Europe closely together, and Henry III proved no exception to the rule: he himself had married Eleanor of Provence; Edward, his eldest son, Eleanor of Castile; Isabella, his sister, the Emperor Frederick II. Furthermore, his younger brother, Richard, had been nominated king of the Romans and, by implication, Emperor-designate. In 1254 Henry accepted the crown of Sicily on behalf of his second son, Edmund, and thus made himself the catspaw of the papacy in its determination to wrest the Sicilian kingdom from the heirs of the Hohenstaufen line of emperors and thereby secure itself from attack from the south. The king of England agreed to stand surety for the debts of the papacy, some 135,000 marks, and as a result became virtually responsible for financing a far-distant war, carried on by papal troops, over which he had not the least control. The pope mortgaged Henry's credit mercilessly and met his protests with a threat of excommunication if he did not fulfil his obligations. The barons were in no mood to give him financial assistance and, in any case, the severe winter of 1257 and the hard frost in the following spring put further taxation out of the question. As in France in 1789, famine and bankruptcy quickened the advent of revolution.

In the parliament which met at Oxford in 1258, the king made a full surrender. He agreed that his Poitevin favourites should be expelled from the country and that a committee of twenty-four, representing equally the royal and baronial interests, should be appointed to reform the government. Its proposals were debated and converted into the resolutions of the Oxford parliament and have come down to us in the memoranda called the 'Provisions of Oxford'. (a) A Council of Fifteen was to be appointed jointly by the king and the baronage. It was entrusted with a wide mandate, for it was to advise the king on every aspect of policy and make itself responsible for the redress of all abuses of government. (b) So that its work could be regularly supervised and, if necessary, stimulated, the Council was to meet a Committee of Twelve, appointed from their own ranks by the barons alone, three times a year when parliaments were to be convoked. (c) The great central offices of state were to be made independent of the king's household, their occupants were to hold office for one year only and then give an account of their stewardship to the Council. The resurrection of the office of justiciar was intended to provide a permanent check on the king's authority, but it had really become an anachronism after the loss of Normandy: no longer could the justiciar issue writs in his own name, no longer were all functions of government centred in his hands. Though a leading member of the council and, as such, responsible for general administration, he was, in particular, a judicial agent, responsible for the execution of a heavy programme of legal reforms. The chancellor was not to seal other than routine writs without the Council's permission. The treasurer was to see that revenue was henceforth paid only into the exchequer and not diverted elsewhere. (d) In local government it was decided that the sheriffs were to be landowners in the counties they served and remain in office for one year only, the custodians of castles were to be carefully scrutinized, other local officials placed under control, whilst a careful investigation was to be made into all complaints of official misconduct. (e) A Committee of Twenty-four was to consider the question of an extraordinary aid. In the event, nothing further was heard about its activities.

Three points of general interest, arising out of the negotiations and decisions of these momentous summer months of 1258, should be observed.

(i) The continued influence of the Great Charter

The petition of the barons, presented to the king at the Oxford parliament and containing a statement of their complaints, is still concerned with feudal grievances. And, before the parliament ended, it had been decided that copies of the Charter were to be sent to every shire and publicly read at the county courts. The vital connexion, however, between the opposition movements of 1215 and 1258 rests in the fact that both endeavoured to devise a system of government which would bring the king and his policy under effective control. The Provisions of Oxford, though tinged with feudalism, reveal the progress that 'constitutionalism' had taken in the intervening period: in particular, the barons have become completely reconciled to accepting the monarchical framework and organization of government. The difficulty, faced in ch. 61 of the Charter, had been faced again: the problem of how to keep the king in control, and at the same time keep the machinery of government, which was largely his creation, functioning properly, had received yet another solution.

(ii) *The baronial control of the executive*

The primary aim was not simply to draw up series of suggestions for the reform of government and leave it to the king to give them practical force. Such an attitude would have been altogether too ingenuous. The barons were fully aware that the crux of the matter was the question of sanctions, the guarantee that reforms would be implemented: they dared not withdraw from their task without that guarantee. Therefore, the power of the crown was put into commission, the council was dominated by the magnates and, though ruling in the king's name, referred so little to him that it cannot be said that this was in the regular line of development of the *curia regis*. The effective government was the justiciar and the Council of Fifteen, and that represented something new and something revolutionary.

(iii) *The normal functioning of the civil service*

Though the drive was to be supplied by the barons rather than the king, though council and parliament had as it were been captured by them, nevertheless the ordinary administrative and judicial institutions went on without interruption. The Council of Fifteen itself was not composed solely of baronial nominees, for the methods of electing it had allowed for the presence of those who could represent the king's interests, like the famous clerk, John Mansel, whilst the archbishop of Canterbury and the bishop of Worcester were also included in its personnel. Furthermore, there is no doubt that the Council included more than the Fifteen themselves: the justiciar was not of their number, but he could hardly have been absent from its deliberations, and the heads of departments and the prominent justices remained members as before. Similarly, the three parliaments which met every year were not simply occasions when the Council of Fifteen met the Committee of Twelve. That Committee had been devised in order to secure the representation at parliament of those prelates and magnates who were not members of the Fifteen, and, since parliaments were frequent and the burden of attendance heavy, this arrangement made it unnecessary for all magnates to attend regularly. But come they might and did, if they so desired or were specially summoned. And ministers and judges attended its sessions as they attended those of the Council. The significance of future events will escape us entirely unless we remember that, though the magnates over-shadowed the officials, they did not remove them and continued to draw upon their experience, listen to their advice, and use their technical skill and services in the work of government and reform.

The Council, thus controlled by the barons, governed England for some two years, authorizing the use of the great seal, managing the finances, conducting foreign policy, as in finally repudiating the Sicilian commitments and approving the definitive treaty of peace with France in 1259. The king was completely in their hands and accepted the Provisions willy-nilly, even submitting to the bitter humiliation of having his personal household reorganized for him—a precedent for the similar, but much more drastic, over-haul by the barons in the Ordinances of 1311. Since the king could command little respect and less support, the magnates could have consolidated their claims to be the 'natural' advisers of the king and real, even major, participants in the work of government, pro-vided they could maintain an unbroken front. And, to begin with, they exhibited an unwonted unanimity and vigorously introduced measures of reform, especially in local government, where four knights of every shire drew up lists of unjust practices and griev-ances, which were considered by specially appointed tribunals of judges on circuit. Yet unanimity was preserved only so long as it was a question of bringing down the royal government and prosecuting reforms at the expense of the king. So far there was neither hypocrisy nor insincerity. And many of those magnates, who were at the heart of affairs and nearest the king, remained faithful to the interests of good government. But, viewed as a group, the barons, numbering some one hundred and fifty in all, naturally approached all problems from the angle of their own class. As the months went by, events got beyond them, and they found that they had set a ball rolling which they could not stop. The full implications of the reform programme were not seen until it broadened out during its application. When the demand was made that all should permit an investigation into the abuses com-mitted by their own officials within their own estates, the crisis was reached. Since they had not rebelled in order to give up their privileges, therefore they came to view with fear and suspicion the instrument of government they had themselves brought into exist-ence. The position was worsened by personal feuds. Already in March 1259 Simon de Montfort and Richard of Clare, the powerful earl of Gloucester, had quarrelled violently before it was agreed that judges should inquire into injustices within baronial franchises. And there was little enthusiasm among Clare and his friends when the reformers began to look to the middle stratum of society for support and introduced its representatives into the central government. Still, in October 1259 the Provisions of Westminster were carried through, which assembled and published all together the decisions and changes in law and administration of the previous eighteen months.

In the circumstances the scheme of government, drawn up in 1258, could not long survive. And, in any case, the mechanism devised at Oxford was too elaborate and complicated: so far as we can judge, no one knew how long the appointments to the various councils and committees were to last or how vacancies were to be filled, and the relations between them were left too ill-defined. In 1260 the defection of Gloucester and his friends allowed the king's son, Edward, to form a royalist party again, liberal enough in its outlook to attract the moderates and leave the reformers crippled. In 1261 the king was absolved by the pope from his promise to observe the Provisions, and shortly afterwards he annulled them by royal ordinance, and the Council of Fifteen and the Committee of Twelve disappeared. The spirit of reform, however, did not disappear with its governmental expression, and Montfort obtained an unexpected accession of strength in 1262, when Gloucester died and his young son threw in his lot with the reformers. It was plain that the country was again on the verge of civil war, for the problem, raised by the refusal of the king to co-operate and the reformers to surrender, could only be solved by recourse to armed conflict. An effort was made to avoid it by submitting the matters in dispute to Louis IX of France, a ruler with an acknowledged reputation for wisdom and impartiality, but it failed completely. The Mise of Amiens which contained his award, whilst declaring that the king ought to observe the Great Charter he had so frequently confirmed, freed him from the need to adhere to the Provisions of Oxford on the ground that they flouted the sacred and inherent rights of kingship and forced him into virtual abdication. This judgment, however correctly based on law and political theory, took little or no account of local conditions and could not be accepted, and civil war broke out, to end in the victory of Simon de Montfort at the battle of Lewes in May 1264.

For a few troubled months Montfort had a chance to reveal how genuine a reformer he was at heart, for he wielded almost dictatorial powers. Although in his early years his interests had centred in the south of France where his father had played a prominent part in the crusade against the Albigensian heretics, it is a serious anachronism to think that he was regarded in any way as a foreigner by the French-speaking upper circles of society in England. He was shown considerable favour by the king as soon as he landed in 1230, and so approved himself that by 1238 he had been granted his father's old estates in Leicester with the title of earl and the hand of the king's sister in marriage. It is evident that he was generally recognized as a man of great administrative skill and strength of character, and he was given the hopeless task of administering Gascony between 1248 and 1253. He was, however, little likely to agree with his royal brother-in-law: he had little tolerance, especially for misgovernment, and personal differences took him over to the opposition. Though a prominent member of it, he was not its head as long as discontent could find a centre in Richard, earl of Cornwall, the king's brother. But when Richard succumbed to the fatal lure of the imperial dignity in 1257, then the barons gathered round Montfort quite as much because he too was within the circle of royalty as because of his own abilities. Whether or not his ideas had been influenced by his friendship with Bishop Grosseteste and other intellectuals, he showed himself the ardent champion of reforms and exhibited an uncompromising hostility to those 'traitors and perjurers' who stood in the way of their development and extension. His victory at Lewes did not solve his problems: he had to govern a kingdom with a captive king, he could rely upon the assistance of only a minority of the barons, he found that government by normal means was impossible and that, as was done in 1216, he had to rule through the organs of local rather than central government. He faced the situation squarely and frankly. (*a*) Since a form of aristocratic government was out of the question, he established an oligarchy. In 1264 he propounded a new form of government, the *Forma Regiminis*, whereby three Electors were to be nominated, then these were to nominate and control a Council of Nine, appointed to advise the king in the choice of his ministers and keepers of castles and on all other affairs of state. The triumvirate at first comprised Montfort, Gloucester and the bishop of Chichester. (*b*) Though everything Montfort did was animated by the current conceptions of the feudal aristocracy

15*

to which he belonged, though otherwise he would have been born out of his time—and that proposition cannot be established by the testimony of either Simon or his friends—he was an exceptionally able man, and he recognized the existence and the growing importance of new social groups within the community and appealed openly for their assistance. In 1264 he summoned knights of the shire to parliament, presumably to obtain their formal ratification of his proposed executive government. In 1265 he summoned town representatives for the first time to parliament. It is true that this parliament was simply an assembly of his own supporters, writs being issued to only five earls and eighteen barons, though to well over a hundred prelates. It was, at all events, an open expression of the support on which he relied. His great contribution was that he broadened the basis of the reform movement by the public inclusion of the middle classes in country and town which had made their voices heard by the barons in and after 1258 in their support of the Provisions of Oxford. A new development within society was taking place: it needed a leader, and Montfort was prepared to play the part. He became, therefore, a protagonist of the principle of popular representation. But popular representation was to be found before and long after 1265 at all kinds of central assemblies that were not parliaments: Montfort was making no conscious and deliberate contribution to the development of parliament as an institution and has no claim to be regarded as one of its founders.

When we come down to the details of his work, we must avoid excessive praise. In the little time in which he had to work, his schemes showed no new conceptions of political statecraft and, indeed, he had placed himself in a hopeless position. Since Henry III had refused to co-operate with the reformers among the barons and could not be trusted to rule justly himself, they could plead moral justification for rebellion and oligarchy, especially as they had previously made sincere efforts to devise machinery which should prevent recourse to armed conflict. Nevertheless, they had been forced to attempt the impossible. The institution of kingship was firmly established in the thirteenth century. A king, deprived of the exercise of his traditional prerogatives and held accountable to his own barons, was hardly conceivable. A revolution, which resulted in oligarchy based on middle-class support, could not provide a permanent solution to the complicated problem of constitutional opposition, and it soon collapsed when the young Gloucester, antagonized by Montfort, deserted to the king's side, and when the Lord Edward escaped from captivity to make himself the centre of resistance. Still, we may judge the widespread discontent and the firm determination not to return to the old ways by the fact that civil war continued for two years after Montfort was killed at the battle of Evesham in 1265. For resistance was made, not only by those of his supporters who had lost their lands by forfeiture, but by abbots and priors, small landowners in the counties and the lower bourgeoisie in the towns.

V. The Restoration, 1265–1272

Edward was left as the effective ruler of the country, and he soothed dissension by conciliation and compromise. The Charter was again confirmed to signify that monarchy recognized limitations, however vague and indefinite they might be. The major reforms of the Provisions of Oxford and Westminster, initiated by the barons, were adopted by the royal government and re-enacted in the Statute of Marlborough of 1267; thereby the importance of the middle strata of society was acknowledged, for it made so many concessions to small freeholders that in effect it destroyed the hold of feudalism upon them. Representatives of the boroughs were again summoned in 1268 to attend a meeting of the king's council. Even the 'Disinherited', those adherents of Montfort's who had lost their lands and been excessively victimized by the royalists after Evesham, were allowed by the Dictum of Kenilworth to buy back their estates at a sum judicially assessed to correspond with their guilt. And monarchy and monarchical institutions and agencies remained essentially unimpaired, and Edward found no difficulty in restoring them to their full activity.

The Provisions of Oxford and the succeeding events mark the conclusion of one epoch and introduce another, in which we can hardly use the word 'feudal' without essential qualifications which deprive it of its old and vital significance. A new society has revealed itself which does not recognize the old forms of life or admit the old restraints. We are on the threshold of the modern age. Yet, though new conditions will demand different attitudes and different methods, the old problems remain. Thus, the question raised openly by the Great Charter was still unanswered: how can monarchy be prevented from developing into tyranny? The barons had little to show in the way of political achievement for their sustained efforts to fetter the king's liberty of action. For, though they made progress, they had progressed in the wrong direction: oligarchy was alien to the traditions of English political development and could not be the alternative to absolutism. The true solution of a limited monarchy was still very far in the future. The importance of the baronial movement lay, therefore, not so much in what it did as in the spirit which informed it, for in curbing the king it had deliberately sought to work within the framework of the law. The barons did not enunciate abstract principles or talk of precedents for the future; their measures were often opportunist, experimental and without vision, but their inspiration to make arbitrary government impossible had remained the same throughout the century. They had naturally the limited aims of a limited class, but only they were in a position to conduct the government in the event of royal incompetence. However, lower sections of society were working their way into prominence, and it was becoming advisable and in some respects essential to consult them. The act of consultation carried with it the implication of control, however great or little it might be, and the dilemma of placing limitations on the monarchy without rendering it powerless to fulfil its essential functions was to be resolved by slow degrees in the metamorphosis of parliament from what was first and foremost a royal court into a political assembly.

SELECT READING

E. F. Jacob, 'Henry III' in *C. Med. H.*, vi (1929), 252–83; F. M. Powicke, *King Henry III and the Lord Edward* (1947), chs. 1–4, 7–8, 10–13, 16; Stephenson and Marcham, 129–53; M. A. Hennings, *England under Henry III* (1924: translated documents); K. Norgate, *Minority of Henry III* (1912); A. L. Smith, *Church and State in the Middle Ages* (1913), 101–179; G. Barraclough, *Papal Provisions* (1935), 1–18, 153–77; J. R. H. Moorman, *Church Life in England in the Thirteenth Century*, 1–241; C. Bémont, *Simon de Montfort* (trans. E. F. Jacob: 1930), 129–244; E. F. Jacob, 'What were the "Provisions of Oxford"?' in *History*, ix (1926), 188–200; R. F. Treharne, 'The Significance of the Baronial Reform Movement, 1258–67' in *T.R.H.S.*, 4th Series, xxv (1942), 35–72; H. G. Richardson and G. O. Sayles, 'The Provisions of Oxford' in *B.J.R.L.*, 17 (1933), 291–321.

CHAPTER XXVI

SOCIAL AND ECONOMIC DEVELOPMENTS IN THE TWELFTH AND THIRTEENTH CENTURIES

BEFORE we turn to examine that middle stratum of society which provided representatives to attend the parliaments of the king, it is well at this point to say something about the great bulk of the people of England who were occupied in the work of agriculture.

The Peasantry

The social status of a peasant in England was settled by the kind of work he had to do. We may with advantage concentrate our attention principally on the villein and on his relationship with his lord, for therein lies the crux of the agrarian problem of the Middle Ages. If we look at the villein from the angle of strict feudal law, he seems to be completely unfree, to possess neither property rights nor personal freedom. What he did with his land-holding was dependent on his lord's authorization and approval, and there was nothing to prevent that lord from ejecting him if he so pleased. Furthermore, his services to his lord were indefinite and he could not say from day to day what he would be required to do: he knew only that some part of every week must be spent on his lord's demesne (week-work), that extra heavy duties were demanded at the spring and autumn sowings and at harvest-time (boon-days), and that extraordinary levies on his time and work might be made at other times (love-days). In addition to his labour, he had to contribute regular payments in kind or in money-dues and to pay petty fees for permission to do this or that. And since his person was also subjected to his lord's will, he had no liberty of action: he was 'ascripted' to the soil on which he was born and could be brought back in chains to his 'villein's nest' if he ran away; he could not apprentice his son to a trade or arrange for him to enter the Church; he could not give his daughter in marriage without paying the 'merchet' fee; he could acquire no property that was not liable to tallage, that is, taxation at the arbitrary will of his lord. Only towards the close of the twelfth century did the law take cognisance of the villein, and its notice was brief: his murder or the mutilation of his body became an offence triable in the king's courts, whilst the Great Charter assured to him his 'wainage' or means of subsistence. But the royal writs and the royal justice were not made available to him as against his lord in any civil action.

Legal technicalities, however, did not square with economic facts. It did not pay the lord to oppress the agricultural labourers on whom the agricultural economy depended, and in practice they had substantial economic security. Their holdings in the 'open fields' were handed down as an indivisible unit by the ordinary laws of inheritance to their heirs on payment of the 'heriot', usually the best beast, and they had their share in pasture and in common. The extent of their services was regulated by custom. And ascription to the soil implied little or no hardship, for few were likely to want to leave the land that guaranteed them more or less a living.

Nevertheless, we ought not to imagine that conditions were static and to stress unduly the self-sufficiency of medieval estates. As towns and markets and trading and the use of money as means of exchange developed, the lords were led naturally to exploit the resources of their land, and the sale of produce brought them much profit. Therefore there was in the twelfth and thirteenth centuries a perceptible increase in the burdens laid upon the agricultural workers. So far as the freehold peasants were concerned, it is evidenced by their constant litigation in the royal courts to prevent their lords from exacting more than their customary services. But, since the royal courts of justice were denied to villeins, the result in their case was a long and painful struggle, the details of which are hard to ascertain, to get their rights and obligations committed to writing and protected by customary law instead. It was not easy for the peasants to make their voices heard, for the lord had the very considerable advantage of being backed by the full force of the law, and he could dominate the situation through his feudal court. No known limitations hedged his will about in these days, and it prevailed far more than has been thought. Therefore each 'manor' was the scene of considerable unrest before the indefinite and unwritten traditions which came to regulate its life were agreed to by both sides and carefully recorded. It is significant that we know nothing of such written customs before the second half of the thirteenth century.

By that time the peasantry of England stood divided into its three main groups, though it must be remembered that there was a great diversity within each section. (*a*) *The freeholders*. They figured larger in society than was once acknowledged. If we think simply of the region where the manor was mainly to be found and ignore the rest of England where a far greater measure of freedom existed, we shall yet find that even there the land held in freehold is not much less than that held in villeinage. The proportion has been roughly estimated as 4:6. The class of freeholders over the whole of the country was, therefore, considerable, and its numbers received a small, though steady, increase from above—the younger sons of knightly families, who did not inherit knightly rank—and from below—the villeins who by some means or other managed to escape from their serfdom. (*b*) *The villeins*. No social grade exhibited a greater range from prosperity to poverty. Obviously a villein with thirty acres—and not a few had much more than that—might be much better off than many freeholders. Most villeins, however, stayed at a bare subsistence level: that is the inescapable conclusion to be drawn from contemporary literature. For, though the population increased slowly, it did increase. In order to fix the responsibility for services to the lord, each villein tenement was regarded as an indivisible holding, but, though the strips seem never to be broken up, this was merely a convenient fiction, for they had often to support the families of several generations. The practice of sub-division could not go on indefinitely, and the time was bound to come when there was a land shortage. For example, though the sixty-eight tenants of a Norfolk manor at the time of the Domesday Survey had increased ostensibly to only one hundred and seven by 1291, there were nine hundred and thirty-five separate holdings, and these were divided into some two thousand strips. For this reason it is well to place in a separate category those villeins who, though not completely landless labourers, yet had not sufficient land to support themselves and their families. (*c*) *The cottars*. Presumably they once included within their ranks the slaves recorded in Domesday Book, but they mainly represented the younger sons of villeins who often had no inheritance, no share in the cultivation of the 'open fields'. Some left the family tenement and obtained a small croft on the lord's home farm. Their obligations were often lighter with their smaller holdings—ditching, carting and the like: in one instance they were termed 'lundenarii' because they were required to work only on Mondays. This by no means meant greater comfort, for they of all men were stalked by hunger. Others presumably became the village craftsmen—the smiths, carpenters, bakers and tailors. Others certainly provided labour for hire, which could be called upon whenever necessary. There was, indeed, always present in England some form of that wage-earning class which was to become the future economic basis of society.

It has already been observed that the peasantry at large paid their rents partly in money and partly in labour-services, and it is a serious error to under-estimate the money-payments which, we are informed, actually predominated in the thirteenth century even among the obligations of the villeins. In the main the money-payments come from two sources: first, the ancient and customary payments which had continued to be paid to lords since before the Norman Conquest; secondly, the more recent payments in the place of labour-services, which arose from the practice known as the 'sale of works'. Many lords had a right to more labour services than they could conveniently utilize: therefore they began to put a monetary value upon them and to 'sell' them back to the peasants at, for example, the rate of a penny for a day's work in the autumn or a half-penny in the winter. This 'sale of works', however, was quite variable in its application, a temporary expedient entirely dependent on the will of the lord, and therefore it was by no means commutation in the technical sense.

The peasants had, therefore, from the very start been rendering at one and the same time both labour-services and money-rents, and these came eventually to be regarded as alternatives. It was not a difficult step to commutation proper. This offered practical advantages to both sides. So far as the lords were concerned, very much the same reasons as urged the kings to commute military services for scutage induced them to commute labour-services for a money-rent: the system of compulsory labour was too clumsy, too inelastic in arrangements, too expensive in management, and it is plain that the services were often rendered in a grudging and inefficient way. To permit commutation and to use the money-rent for the hiring of labour meant a considerable simplification in estate-management. Furthermore, the lords were not unaffected by the changed outlook which the growing use of money entailed: a variety of causes like personal extravagance, royal taxation, the luxuries of life which the growth of trade and commerce introduced, all such things produced a need of ready money. If the lords were willing to commute, then there were peasants who had prospered enough to pay the heavy sum demanded.

For co-operative husbandry could not suppress individual enterprise. Freeholders apart, even villeins who had ability, energy and vision had no need to fly to the towns to improve their position and gain their freedom. They had in their families more than a sufficiency of labour to do the services they owed their lords and yet till their own holdings profitably. When their rents and services became fixed by the 'custom of the manor', they were presented with an unearned increment, for the thirteenth century onwards was an age of rising prices, and the change in the value of money meant not only that they were paying a progressively uneconomic rent but receiving a growing profit from their surplus produce. Thus they began to accumulate household goods, livestock and capital, to buy permission to exchange strips in order to make their own holdings more compact, to take on the responsibility for holdings outside their own manor, even to employ cottars as hired labourers. Such men as these were in a position to pay highly for full commutation. Indeed, it was not unknown for whole communities of villeins to join together to purchase it. Commutation might cover much or little and did not necessarily result in manumission, that is, the full status of a free man. In such cases the villeins, despite all economic concessions, remained personally in servitude as what were called 'moll men'.

Now, though commutation can be traced back to the twelfth century and became more common as the years went by, it did not work evenly in operation in all parts of the country. Curiously enough, though the increased use of money was bound to act as a powerful solvent on the existing social and economic structure, the situation was apparently not regulated simply by the amount of coined money available. For commutation was more frequent in the poorer districts and much less common in the well populated and prosperous eastern districts where advanced agriculture, trade and commerce made money more plentiful. This paradox is to be explained by the fact that both the lay and the ecclesiastical lords of great estates realized quite as well as the peasants that farming, if commercialized, could produce great profits and, therefore, far from commuting labour-services which would have to be replaced by hired labour costing more and more as prices rose, they sought to increase and exploit those services. Thus, roughly from Lincolnshire southwards, the main part of the work on the large estates was still being done on the basis of labour-services, and it is noticeable that it is precisely this region which bore the brunt of the Peasants' Revolt.

Before the Black Death, therefore, the movement towards commutation in the country as a whole was countered by a contrary movement in certain districts towards emphasizing labour-services. Like the French peasantry before the Revolution of 1789, the English agricultural labourers had more than a glimpse of better things, which in places were being deliberately withheld. It is only against this background that the Black Death and the Peasants' Revolt can be viewed in their proper perspective. For it is then beyond argument that neither introduced a change. What they did was to increase the pace of something which had begun many generations earlier.

The Emergence of Local Communities

Under the Anglo-Saxon dispensation the strength of Germanic customary methods of government, in combination with the royal directive legislation which created the shires and hundreds, had produced in England a system of local government depending for its practical success mainly upon the ability of local people to look after their own affairs. It survived the Norman Conquest of 1066, nevertheless that year saw the introduction of a rival whose unchecked development might have fatally weakened it. For upon the Anglo-Saxon system, resting primarily upon the conception of the community, was superimposed the system of feudalism, based upon the possession of land. It is true that the creation of franchises and the alienation of hundreds in favour of a privileged Church had begun before the Conquest, but the process was afterwards greatly accelerated. Every county saw large stretches of its territory withdrawn from its control by the construction of feudal franchises; many of the hundreds passed into private hands. It was, indeed, implicit in feudalism that government should be carried on by co-operation between the king and his vassals, and it was only through such collaboration that the early Norman rulers maintained and tightened their precarious hold upon the country in which the invaders were a small minority. The emphasis upon tenure, and through it upon the individual rather than the community, permitted, for example, the tenants-in-chief to speak for under-tenants in matters of taxation. This was not a new principle, for the Conquest seems to have made no appreciable difference in the incidence and levying of geld, but it was given a greater prominence. Once, however, the monarchy had established itself and could deliberately begin to stress its sovereign rather than its feudal rights, it emphasized its connexion with subjects rather than vassals, it founded its rule upon local communities and revitalized them, and it removed tenure from a too prominent position in the scheme of government. The reforms of Henry II decided the lines of future development. The feudal enclaves in every county lost whatever exclusiveness and measure of autonomy they had possessed: thus the Assize of Clarendon laid it down that all men, whether living within the bounds of a feudal franchise or not, were to come before the royal justices to assist them in their inquiries into wrongdoings. The crown began to impose upon the counties through the county courts an ever-growing number of duties which it had no intention of asking its vassals to fulfil and for which it had itself no adequate machinery. The great land-owners chose to hold themselves aloof and apparently did not attend the meetings of the county courts at which so much local government work was being done; in John's reign they were still insisting that they should remain responsible as individuals for the taxation of their own estates and their own villeins. The earls had always formed an exclusive group, and presumably there was always a rough and ready distinction between the magnates and the general mass of tenants-in-chief. But under John the great land-owners were singled out by the style of 'greater barons', they were given as a special mark of recognition individual writs of summons to the king's council, and they were allowed to restate their claim to speak alone on behalf of the 'community of the land'.

But by this time, the time of the Great Charter, the monarchy had weakened, though by no means removed, that claim by the responsibilities it had placed on other classes in society.

I. THE SHIRES

The administration of affairs fell into the hands not of a noble caste but of lesser men, the knights and freeholders, and no distinction was made between those who held their lands from great feudal lords and those who held them from the king. All of them were compelled to take an ever-increasing part in the work of government. Thus in judicial matters the country gentry attended the courts of eyre, county and hundred; they saw that litigants received a proper summons to be present; they acted as jurors in connexion with a lengthening list of criminal and civil actions, and carried to Westminster a 'record' of litigation when required; they had as their first great electoral function to choose the coroners; they came in time to be entrusted with the functions of justices of assize. In administration they investigated and reported upon local abuses of every kind, enforced the Assize of Arms, assessed taxes and eventually collected them, whether carucages, scutages or levies upon movable property; they acted as sheriffs, escheators and coroners.

In all that was done the lead was taken by the knights. In many cases they were minor direct tenants of the king but that relationship did not entail regular attendance at the king's court. Their position was openly revealed in 1215: the Great Charter complied with feudal theory in summoning the minor tenants-in-chief to councils, but showed that it did not expect them to be present by arranging for them to receive a general summons through the sheriff only and not, like the greater barons, an individual summons. Such knights settled down on their estates and became indistinguishable from other landowners of solid income and independence, and all came in time to be known as the 'knights of the shire' with complete disregard of any diversities created by feudal tenures.

The monarchy had acted in its own interests: though often desirous of ruling well, it had no completely unselfish motive in broadening the basis of government. The gentry for their part had no wish to have burdens imposed upon them: nevertheless, they obeyed tradition and acted as unpaid local government officials. Thereby generation after generation of them learned to assume greater and greater responsibilities and received a severely practical training in methods of administration. It must, however, be emphasized that this was not self-government. That view, derived ultimately from the imaginative misconceptions of the Germanic school of historians, has lingered on, when so much else has been rejected, to distort the true outline of development, and it should be discarded. What was done was done in obedience to instructions from the king, and nothing was done in the sphere of local government by county courts, hundred courts, knights of the shire or borough officials without his direct order or ultimate sanction. Self-government at the king's command is a contradiction in terms and, if intentionally paradoxical, may none the less be seriously misleading.

II. THE BOROUGHS

As we have previously noted, the only common factor to all boroughs of whatever kind and age, the one indispensable characteristic, was burgage tenure whereby property was held by a fixed money-rent in quittance of all services, was heritable, and could be disposed of easily. It differed from feudal tenure because it involved no feudal services; from free socage tenure because there was no bar to full right of alienation by sale, mortgage, or gift; from villein tenure because there was no demand for labour services. This tenure, therefore, bestowed a special social and legal status upon those who enjoyed it.

Another peculiar privilege, which was not, however, found in all boroughs, was also brought into existence by the peculiar needs of communities of men living through trade. Whether or not the merchant gilds of the pre-Conquest age had a monopoly of retail trade within the boroughs, they certainly acquired it soon afterwards, and it provided the dynamic of town life: for example, at Oxford in the late eleventh century and at York under Henry I. At a time when the boroughs were not permitted to manage their own affairs and were directly under royal or seignorial administration, the gilds frequently provided an outlet for local energy and initiative until the beginning of Richard I's reign. Composed of influential men for the purpose of regulating trade affairs in the gild-house, they could exercise a powerful, albeit unofficial, influence upon the formal borough government. So at times a practical advance towards autonomy was achieved. There is a striking parallelism between the gild alderman, the gild association and the gild common purse on the one hand, and the mayor, the borough assembly and the borough treasury on the other. Yet the similarities are deceptive, for the gilds were not the progenitors of the later municipal constitutions: many boroughs like London, Norwich and the Cinque Ports knew nothing of them, in others they failed to make much impression, whilst even important gilds temporarily lost their importance during the thirteenth century. The old borough organization—universal, firm-rooted and wider in scope and appeal—was to form the basis of the self-governing communities.

In a much quoted dictum, Maitland declared that the history of boroughs could not be written: so varied were their stages of development that only a history of individual boroughs was

possible. To some extent his statement is an exaggeration. Over a
hundred charters were granted by the kings of England before 1216,
and double that number by lords. The 'Laws of Breteuil' were
common to many boroughs in the west of England; the customs
contained in Henry I's charter to Newcastle were extended to Alnwick, Hartlepool and elsewhere, and were adopted by the four
boroughs of Scotland—Berwick, Roxburgh, Stirling and Edinburgh
—as the basis of urban government in that kingdom; the London
charter was copied by Oxford and many other boroughs throughout
England; the charter of Henry II to Bristol provided the model for
Dublin and other Irish towns. Many general franchises, therefore,
were common. Royal policy, however, was not consistent during
the century and a half after the Conquest. Though Henry I had
been willing to allow borough communities a measure of independence, his grandson adopted a policy of repression, for his general
programme of reform was not in sympathy with the separatist
spirit which any strivings towards autonomy suggested. Therefore, though he gave extraordinarily wide privileges to Wallingford
in recognition of the assistance its inhabitants had given him in
his victory over Stephen, this charter is misleading unless its
uniqueness is recognized, and in no way does it indicate his usual
attitude. Thus he allowed only five towns to collect and pay over
the compounded 'firma burgi', and he permitted none to compound
as a perpetual right; he would let no borough elect its own
justices as soon as they could be replaced by his itinerant justices,
though that could not take place until some years after his accession. But the movement could not long be held in check. The
accession of Richard, an absentee king who was in desperate need
of ready money, opened the way to the ambitions of the trading
classes. Indeed, it is the period covered by the reigns of Richard
and John that shows the greatest number of royal charters to
boroughs, for thereafter Henry III made few grants until just
before the Barons' War when he too was in urgent need of money,
whilst Edward I, somewhat surprisingly, made still fewer. We
should, however, be chary of generalizing about the royal attitude
to boroughs on the basis of figures: the king could give no charters
if there were no applications for them, and the fluctuating number
of grants may mean no more than a fluctuating demand. The
question can only be properly settled when evidence is produced to
show that the crown refused such applications.

Our interest lies not so much in the acquisition of economic advantages, like freedom from tolls and the right to hold markets. It is the advance towards rights of self-government that is all-important and, viewed broadly, it is made in four main stages. (*a*) *The privilege of farming the revenues.* When the citizens of Lincoln and London were allowed by Henry I to account direct to the exchequer, and not through the sheriff, the first real evidence of the trend towards self-government is revealed. A communal spirit had been manifested which desired to get rid of outside interference and, incidentally, of the middleman's profits and extortions. It is possible that this concession carried with it the complementary right to elect the reeves. Owing to Henry II's disapproval, little further progress was made in this direction until under Richard and John a perpetual grant of the 'firma burgi' was freely made, more than a score of towns obtaining it before 1216. (*b*) *Exemption from pleading outside the borough.* This guaranteed to burgesses the right to establish a court of their own within the walls of their town and the privilege of suing or being sued only there in civil and minor criminal actions. They became exempted from attendance at the shire and hundred courts, and even before the justices in eyre their representatives appeared as a distinct group. The borough courts dispensed a special law which had its own idiosyncracies, partly explainable by the fact that the charters to the boroughs incorporated and confirmed many early customs which the common law, when it evolved later, failed to recognize. Thus land in boroughs could be bequeathed by will, a right that common law had seen fit to reject elsewhere. (*c*) *Election of magistrates.* This most essential of all attributes of self-government was present long before the agitation in London in 1191, which is usually considered to be its originating force. There was nothing startlingly revolutionary in what was done then, and the 'grant of a commune' to London made little practical difference. The fashion of electing mayors, however, did spread by imitation, and by 1216 a dozen or more towns had been given permission to elect their own officials. The gild organization fell into the background, and the borough community came into its own. The process of incorporation had thus begun: the mayor represented the community and was also the executive officer of the king; councils of twelve or twenty-four were normally assisting him before the close of the thirteenth century and becoming rapidly oligarchic in character; seals appeared early as a visible symbol of a quasi-corporation, although it does not always follow that a seal connotes a municipality. (d) *The return of writs*. Henry III from 1252 to 1257 allowed some twenty towns to see to it themselves that his orders were executed and his writs returned. But only when the town was granted permission to elect sheriffs of its own could it exclude the 'foreign' royal official completely.

Until quite recently it was a generally accepted doctrine that the royal taxation of boroughs was made possible only through the insistence of Henry II, in particular, that they should be regarded as part of his own demesne lands so that their inhabitants became subject, like the villeins, to arbitrary feudal tallage. This view was always hard to square with the growing prosperity and dignity of the commercial class, and fortunately it can now be discarded. For Henry I and Henry II, considering that the antiquated land tax did not produce from the boroughs a sufficient tax on their increasing wealth, demanded 'aids' (*auxilia*) and 'gifts' (*dona*), either as an addition or as an alternative: business men, who had no secure place in the scheme of government and needed protection and guarantees of their trading privileges, were willing enough to contribute. Such borough aids were arranged and assessed by negotiation with each borough separately; they were non-feudal and highly remunerative, for, though they were only occasional in their incidence, they were heavy. By the close of Henry II's reign the practice had been extended downwards to simple villages within the ancient demesne of the crown—that is, the land in its possession in the time of Edward the Confessor— and was generally described as 'tallage'. Hence this royal *prerogative* tallage had no connexion with the *feudal* tallage of villeins. Because they were tallaged, the boroughs were exempted under Henry III from having to contribute to the tax on movables which fell on the rest of the country. Edward I experimented with both methods, sometimes including the boroughs in the tax on movables (1283, 1284, 1295, 1296) and at other times reverting to tallage (1304). Under his son tallage appeared for the last time, but it left traces of its influence in the higher rate of parliamentary taxation on the boroughs.

Until Edward I's reign the name of 'borough' was applied indiscriminately to all places, no matter whether they were great or small, old or comparatively recent foundations, royal or seignorial, provided they possessed 'burgage' tenure. The privileges they enjoyed, however, varied enormously, and towards the end of the thirteenth century an attempt was made to differentiate between them.   On two occasions, in 1275 and 1283, the sheriffs were ordered to send representatives from boroughs and from merchant towns (*villae mercatoriae*), and within the lower grade of 'merchant towns' were included undoubted boroughs. Unfortunately, this useful line of distinction was not maintained, and later writs referred again only to boroughs.   Indeed, in 1295 and later years there was an increase in the number of what were considered boroughs which ought to send representatives to parliament, presumably because the king had no wish to lose the greater return of taxation from them.   Nevertheless, there was much confusion: the taxers of subsidies frequently included more places as 'boroughs' in their lists than were contained in the lists of the sheriffs, and yet it has been calculated that they ignored twelve per cent of the boroughs recognized as such by the sheriffs.   The problem was left to settle itself: the small boroughs and most of the seignorial boroughs proved unable or unwilling to bear the heavier burdens imposed upon them in that capacity; their small privileges were no compensation for the greater costs of police measures, such as were made necessary by the statute of Winchester of 1285, for the payment of parliamentary representatives, for the heavier taxation.   So by the middle of the fourteenth century the number of boroughs decreased and there came to be substantial agreement between the lists of the sheriffs and the lists of the taxers.

It follows from what has already been said that social and economic developments were almost sufficient in themselves to ensure that representatives of the middle sections of society should be summoned sooner or later to attend central assemblies, convoked by the king to give advice or some kind of support. It is convenient to discuss briefly at this point, not the history, but the significance of the idea of popular representation, for this is commonly associated and confused with the growth of parliament, despite the fact that for well over half a century they did not pursue the same course at all.

There is no need to discuss the origins of popular representation. The idea was ancient and widespread in application throughout Europe and, if an illustration is needed, it can be found in the representative institutions formed for the government of towns. For its own purpose the monarchy found a particular use for it in the sphere of law and administration. To take instances commonly adduced, the reeve, priest and four men of each village attended the hundred court 'on behalf of all' early in the twelfth century, and by its close popularly elected juries were being required to present cases of wrongdoing and maladministration before the king's officials. Representative knights were summoned to headquarters to report there on law-suits brought in county and manorial courts, and whether or not the assembly ever met, there was nothing out of the way in John's action in 1213 in summoning four knights from each shire to a conference at Oxford. Similarly, representatives of the boroughs were compelled to appear before the justices in eyre and had appeared before the council for specific purposes long before Simon de Montfort's ascendancy. So far, however, we have nothing more than an extended use of the jury system whereby all that was required was information on precise points. So long as that attitude prevailed, a mere concentration together of juries of knights and of burgesses at Westminster or elsewhere would have contributed little or nothing to the establishment of representative government. For political representation, in the sense that one man has authority to act on behalf of others and to bind them to the decisions he makes, is of an entirely different order.

Its distinguishing characteristic was not the command from above but the mandate from below, and this does not make its appearance until the thirteenth century is half over. In 1254 the sheriffs were ordered to consult the shire courts about an aid to assist the king's expedition to France, and to have knights elected to report the decision to the council at Westminster. Though they were to represent 'all and sundry' of their counties, there was obviously no need and therefore no demand that they should have full powers of attorney. Nor was this required of them in the years succeeding the Provisions of Oxford, such as 1264 and 1265, when their summons was the result of party politics rather than financial need. The stipulation occurs, however, in nearly every writ ordering the election of knights and burgesses under Edward I and had become common form long before the end of his reign. The paramount reason for its insertion was the government's determination to obtain supplies. Most of the feudal sources of revenue were rapidly drying up and the king was driven to depend upon extraordinary aids. In feudal law he had a right to demand assistance from his vassals in time of stress, but he could not arbitrarily impose taxation upon them. He had, as the Great Charter had emphasized, to obtain their consent: thus Henry III never tried to levy an extraordinary aid without permission. The form that such an aid took was coming to be the taxation of movables, of personal property, because it was most likely to result in an ever-growing yield as public wealth increased. The doctrine of consent, however, presented serious legal problems. (*a*) It was thought at first that consent could only be personal and individual, that the decision of those who were present could not bind those who were absent, even that the majority could not pledge a minority: traces of such beliefs linger on throughout the thirteenth century. English custom which had insisted on unanimity, for example, in the jury and refused to allow it to speak with two different voices gave way slowly, however, before the principles of Roman law and the practices of the Roman Church: the cardinal rule that the consent of the majority can bind the rest had been already enunciated in the Great Charter, and it gradually won acceptance and removed the awkwardness and hotch-potch character of private bargainings with individuals. (*b*) The extraordinary aids concerned the tenants-in-chief only, and any vague theory that the barons could speak for their own tenants or even for the community at large was not likely always to meet with approval in the conditions of the thirteenth century. We have already noticed that even the tallage on towns had long been arranged by negotiation direct, and their consent was implicit. For many years, indeed, the question had not cropped up because there was an unprecedented refusal of extraordinary aids between 1237 and 1270. Edward I was, however, made of sterner stuff than his father, though it is clear that he also fully realized that the corporate consent of any council of magnates was not of sufficient authority to allow him legally to tax directly the free-holders of the shire and the townsfolk and that their own consent was essential.

The problem, first, of obtaining consent and, secondly, of making sure that that consent was recognized as binding every subject in the kingdom, was resolved by the quite deliberate policy of summoning popular representatives, armed with full powers of attorney, to meet the king in council to do 'what shall be ordained by common counsel'. Whilst it is natural to concentrate attention on the representatives' mandate, it should not be overlooked that their summons depended entirely on the king, and he had no thought either of allowing them to share his authority or to curb his power. His hand was forced by political necessities, particularly the lack of money, and this itself compelled him to find ways and means of obtaining that consent of all parties which was legally essential.

In addition, it was practical expediency to discuss with the tax-payers all together the burden they were to be asked to carry, for it made administration simpler and the work of collection easier. All the same, Edward could have had little vision of the future when in 1275 he surrendered his prerogative right to impose indirect taxation on trade, and fixed the customs on wool and leather with the assent of the representatives of boroughs and merchant towns. He and his successors were to regret a mistake which they vainly sought later to amend.

There was no ordered plan behind the practice of popular representation in the thirteenth century, and it was piecemeal and haphazard in its application. Knights and burgesses might be asked to attend parliament, but they were summoned there infrequently and not always in company with one another: only thirteen out of some fifty parliaments of Edward I knew their presence. Furthermore, though their summons to parliament usually indicated a demand for taxation, a fiscal motive was not the only one at work: on some half-dozen out of the few occasions when they came to Edward's parliaments no grants were made at all. It is only from the view-point of the modern age, however important in itself, assumed a significance in the early history of parliament that it never actually possessed, for their association was the product of administrative adjustments rather than of necessity. Knights and burgesses could be equally well summoned to assemblies that were not parliaments, and do there equally well all that they did in parliament: indeed, they came in 1283 to consider taxation in different assemblies according to whether they lived in the north or the south of England. Again, they could be, and were, consulted as separate classes in special meetings. Nor for many years was it definitely settled how many representatives should be summoned to parliaments and other assemblies. It was an age of constant and not always happy experimentation, and this is nowhere more clearly apparent than in the history of parliament itself.

SELECT READING

G. Lapsley, 'Some Recent Advances in English Constitutional History' in *Cambridge Historical Journal*, v (1936), 119–61; F. M. Stenton, 'The Changing Feudalism of the Middle Ages' in *History*, xxiii (1938), 289–301; H. M. Cam, *Liberties and Communities in Medieval England* (1944), 205–22; Lipson, i (1937), 88–132; W. Morris, *Early English*

County Court (1926), 89–146; H. M. Cam, *The Hundred and the Hundred Rolls* (1930), 1–33, 221–3; G. G. Coulton, *The Medieval Village* (1925); H. S. Bennett, *Life on the English Manor: A Study of Peasant Conditions, 1150–1400* (1937); G. C. Homans, *English Villagers in the Thirteenth Century* (1942); A. L. Poole, *Obligations of Society in the Twelfth and Thirteenth Centuries* (1946); N. Neilson, 'England' in *Cambridge Economic History of Europe*, i (1941), 438–66; E. A. Kosminsky, 'Services and Money Rents in the Thirteenth Century' in *Econ. H. R.*, v (1935), 24–45.

M. V. Clarke, *Medieval Representation and Consent* (1936), 247–76; A. B. White, *Self-Government at the King's Command* (1934); M. McKisack, *Parliamentary Representation of English Boroughs during the Middle Ages* (1932), 1–23; C. H. McIlwain, 'Medieval Estates' in *C. Med. H.*, vii (1932), 664–715; J. G. Edwards, 'The *Plena Potestas* of English Parliamentary Representation' in *Oxford Essays . . . to H. E. Salter* (1934), 141–54; Edwards, 'The Personnel of the Commons in Parliament under Edward I and Edward II', in *Essays . . . to T. F. Tout* (1925), 197–214; G. O. Sayles, 'Representation of Cities and Boroughs in 1268' in *E.H.R.*, xl (1925), 580–5; C. Stephenson, 'Taxation and Representation in the Middle Ages' in *Anniversary Essays . . . to C. H. Haskins* (1929), 291–312; Stephenson, 'Beginnings of Representative Government in England' in *The Constitution Reconsidered* (1938).

CHAPTER XXVII

THE MEDIEVAL PARLIAMENTS OF ENGLAND

IT is probable that England will be remembered *sub specie aeternitatis* for that experimentation in the art of government which ultimately produced the English parliament. Yet its history in the formative period of its growth is only now in process of being written. For its outline has been seriously distorted under the democratic and liberal bias of a modern age. The root cause of confusion has lain in the assumption that the history of parliament is identical with the history of popular representation, whereas it is the crux of the problem to understand why these two currents of development, once separate and separable, should have found their way eventually into a single channel. For at first they had little to do with one another: for example, between 1258 and 1300 some seventy parliaments were convoked, and only at nine of them were popular representatives summoned to be present, and we must accept the fact that during the thirteenth and early fourteenth centuries the presence of the commons was not regarded as essential to parliament, whose work was as effectively accomplished without them as with them.

What then is a parliament? When medieval men are permitted to supply their own answer, it is plain that all the emphasis is being placed upon the reform of administration and law and the dispensation of justice as the essential work of parliament, and that parliament was valued by the people at large because it provided a means of obtaining relief which for some reason or other could not be obtained elsewhere. The presence of the commons, the granting of taxes, the issue of legislation, are non-essentials: parliament can exist and do its work irrespective of them. If they are found associated with it, that arises from the convenience of the moment and not from any obligation, for they are found associated equally well with other types of assemblies, which made no formal provision for the righting of wrongs and which were not termed parliaments by contemporaries.

We have already remarked that the English constitution was the product of three forces, represented by the king, the feudal barons and the subject people: long at work in the past, they combined to produce the parliament of the thirteenth century.

I. THE KING'S DESIRE TO EXPEDITE THE PROCESSES OF ADMINISTRATION AND LAW BY THE PROVISION OF MEANS FOR RESOLVING DIFFICULTIES

In this sense parliament was the child of the monarchy and reared by the civil service. It was an instrument, devised by kings and operated by their ministers, for the sole purpose of making it simpler to run the government. It was the inevitable result of the way in which effective centralized government had evolved for nearly a hundred and fifty years. No opposition proved strong enough to check its development, and administrative expedients went on multiplying.

By Henry III's time England was already a much-governed country. The exchequer, the chancery, the wardrobe, the two benches and many lesser departments and courts had been more or less fully developed: they were staffed very largely by professional civil servants and lawyers; they had each of them a well-marked routine and they kept abundant records. At times matters came before them which seemed beyond their competence: the civil servants and the judges concerned either feared that there might be personal difficulties if they came to a decision on their own responsibility, or were convinced that the advice of other civil servants and judges and possibly of nobles, if their interests were involved, was indispensable before a final decision could be made. Therefore there was a tendency, growing into a habit, to refer difficulties and perplexities to the group of advisers attending the king's person. But problems might arise which even this group hesitated to deal with, and it became more and more usual to hold them over until a specially full meeting of the king's council happened to be held. In the nature of things, as the work of government grew more complicated, problems became more numerous and such specially full and specially solemn meetings of the king's council more frequent. From the 1240's onwards the word 'parliamentum' came to be used of them in a technical sense in the official records of exchequer, chancery and law-courts, though as vulgar Latin it had a long struggle before it overcame the competition of the classical 'colloquium' and found admittance to the political vocabulary of *all* royal clerks. The imperative need to speed up the machinery of government by settling problems and removing doubts provides one of the main reasons for the emergence of the institution known as parliament.

II. THE BARONIAL DESIRE TO CONTROL THE GOVERNMENT BY THE ESTABLISHMENT OF A METHOD OF PROPER CONSULTATION

This constituted another factor, not resulting wholly from royal policy and initiative, which made for frequent and regular parliaments. In this sense parliament represents an inheritance from a more remote past, and in this sense only it may be considered to have existed as an institution long before the name of parliament was given to it with a technical meaning. We have seen the doctrine of counsel and consent at work in the Anglo-Saxon witan and in the Norman 'Great Councils' which exhibited the feudal policy of collaboration between the king and his immediate vassals. Henry II's great legal reforms, though initiated by the king, were sponsored by the barons. Nevertheless, though Henry II was not so impolitic that he did not consult his tenants-in-chief on such matters as feudal custom and feudal taxation which touched their interests and their pockets, he chose his own time and place for doing so, and the 'Great Councils' were without any defined position in the scheme of government. It was the reign of John which forced the issues, the reign of a king who, being compelled to stay at home, concentrated his thoughts on the affairs of England. The events leading up to the rebellion in 1215, especially the fiscal oppression of the king, made it essential to regularize the position, and the Great Charter settled the composition of the 'Great Councils' and assigned to them the specific function of authorizing extraordinary financial aids. It was important that the right of attendance should be formally recognized, but otherwise the composition was in accordance with normal feudal practice.

The misgovernment of Henry III exasperated his barons and stimulated the demand to be consulted. The king, of course, had constantly with him a number of councillors, some of whom were civil servants and others nobles of his choice. With the advice of these men the day-to-day administration of the country was conducted. The king was not bound to act on the advice of these councillors: he was not a constitutional monarch in the modern sense. Nevertheless, he could not do without their assistance. For the amount of business which the king was supposed to transact personally was so great that, unless the greater part of it had been delegated, the government of the country would have come to a standstill, and, indeed, much of the business on which the king was, in fact, personally consulted was of so severely technical a character that professional advice was indispensable. However, a weak, vain and extravagant king like Henry III desired above all things to gratify his own whims and he could not brook opposition: therefore he looked for counsel only from his own friends and from subservient civil servants. The result was not a lapse into hopelessly bad government: the administration of the country went on much as before. Still, mistakes were bound to be made and they were bound to be attributed to the ill-effects of a clique of self-seeking men. Criticism grew in volume and, since protests did not lead to reform, the obvious scheme was to control the king through councillors who could be trusted to give salutary, if unwelcome, advice. The barons' opportunity came at Oxford in 1258 when they arranged for the king to be constantly attended by a council, chosen for him and not by him. Nevertheless, that council could not be left without control, and it was unthinkable that 'Great Councils' should be convoked frequently and as a matter of routine: the burden of attendance would have been so heavy that any such plan would have defeated its own purposes and come to nothing. So the barons, appreciating the value of the king's 'parliaments', gave them a definite place in their scheme of government and provided that three were to assemble every year to supervise the policy of the permanent council. These parliaments were, as usual, in no sense popular assemblies but meetings of earls, barons, bishops, judges and civil servants: they were large councils, such as the country had been accustomed to see, composed of much the same men, but meeting on an ordered plan instead of being summoned as necessity arose or the king thought fit. And, to prevent attendance being troublesome, an arrangement was made for the less important barons to be represented by twelve of their number. Thereby parliament came to be associated, not simply with the technicalities of government but more closely with what may be comprehensively termed politics.

III. THE POPULAR DESIRE TO GET ABUSES REMOVED AND GRIEVANCES REMEDIED THROUGH READY ACCESS TO AN INSTITUTION WHICH COULD GRANT THE HIGHEST JUSTICE

This third great factor in the evolution of parliament had made itself fully felt before the beginning of Edward I's reign. A hundred years earlier Henry II had let it be well known that no landlord would be immune from interference if he trespassed on the free-hold of his sub-tenant, for on the complaint of that sub-tenant the king would issue a writ to redress his wrong. But though in course of time writs grew in number and in range, yet the system of writs was a rigid and inflexible one: their invention and issue met with much opposition in conservative circles. Hence there was by no means a writ for every wrong. Yet the king by reason of his office must do justice to all men, and happily the fountain of justice was inexhaustible. Therefore the writ system was supplemented by another form of action, action by plaint or petition, which allowed all who were wronged to bring complaints to the king's notice easily and without cost and expect to have them redressed. The Inquest of Sheriffs of 1170 saw a vast inquiry by means of informal plaints into the misconduct of the local officers of the king, of the servants of the barons, and of every wrongdoer who had not been brought to justice. The same procedure came to be attached to the general eyres, but the eyres were not frequent, and there was no organized system in the first half of the thirteenth century for hearing complaints at headquarters. The result was that a great many grievances were not obtaining redress, and there was much unchecked oppression. When, therefore, discontent with the misgovernment of Henry III came to a head in 1258 and an attempt was made to reform the administration from top to bottom, the relief of the oppressed was made a principal item in the reform programme. It was decided to send tribunals of justices into every county to hear all grievances, and to revive the office of justiciar and place on him the obligation to see that all wrongs were put right. This action constituted a momentous and far-reaching revolution. For though the reformers did not themselves tie up the system of hearing complaints with that system of three parliaments a year they inaugurated, yet the presentation of written complaints to royal judges in royal courts was so well known and so well established that it was easy to extend the practice to parliament, and very soon the intimate connexion between parliament and the redress of grievances had been created. From almost the beginning of Edward I's reign petitions, which we can positively say were presented in parliament, survive to this day in considerable number. It will be upon the development of the system of parliamentary petitions, upon the way in which they were handled, that the whole organization of parliament will come to depend.

If we were to look for a more precise explanation for the

association of parliament with the redress of individual wrongs than is provided by normal developments at home, we should do well to examine contemporary developments across the Channel. In 1247 and 1248 Louis IX had made detailed inquiries into administrative abuses throughout his kingdom and had been aghast at the extent corrupt practices had reached. Determined to control his feudatories and to afford some definite means of relief from oppression, he came from about the year 1250 onwards to hold four special sessions of his court called parliaments, where the bulk of the business was judicial and very largely consisted of hearing complaints of injustice in feudal courts. Louis was doing therefore for France in the thirteenth century what Henry II had done for England in the twelfth and, whereas in England the result had been the creation of the courts of the eyre, the common bench and the king's bench, in France their functions were largely performed by the parliaments. It is not unlikely that the barons took over the idea of frequent and regular sessions of parliament from France, and, in fact, between 1258 and 1272 at least thirty-one parliaments had been convoked in England.

The abundant records which exist for the reign of Edward I enable us to get a clear and detailed picture of parliament at that time. During the first half of his reign there was obviously a deliberate scheme for holding parliaments at Westminster twice a year, at Easter and at Michaelmas: thus eighteen parliaments were in session between 1275 and 1286. Between 1290 and 1307, when the king's time was greatly occupied with affairs in Scotland, Wales and Gascony, parliament had to meet when convenient opportunities arose, and it assembled on twenty-seven occasions. Since parliament was a court placed above other courts and devised to dispense the highest justice in the land, it was covered by the special peace which attached to all such institutions: the place in which it assembled was sacrosanct and no one must come there possessed of arms; those who attended must not be interfered with either in coming or departing, nor must their property or their household be molested during their absence; those responsible for the conduct of affairs, like councillors and clerks, were immune from the ordinary process of law for wrongdoing so long as parliament remained in session. Indeed, if we seek the origins of the parliamentary privileges of later times, like freedom of speech and freedom from arrest, it is in the peculiar sanctities, accruing to a court of law, that we must look for them.

We can classify the business of parliament under seven heads: (i) the discussion of affairs of state, more especially foreign affairs; (ii) legislation; (iii) taxation or supply; (iv) the audience of petitions; (v) judicial business, such as the determination of causes, criminal and civil; (vi) administrative matters of difficulty; (vii) feudal ceremonial, such as the taking of homage.   Not all of these kinds of business were transacted at every parliament, and little of the time of parliament was taken up with politics—with debating state affairs or questions of supply or public grievances.   The surviving parliament rolls of Edward I are in overwhelming measure occupied by entries about the hearing of large numbers of private petitions. Indeed, if we took out of these rolls all the passages relating to petitions and pleas and other legal processes, the remaining entries would be found to fill but a small space and to provide relatively little information.   The history of parliament is not made up of great monuments of legislation or of dramatic political incidents: these have their place, but they take up little of parliament's time and are given little space upon its records.   If the king so willed it, high politics could be, and very often were, transacted elsewhere than in parliament, and no one objected. What concerned the ordinary man was that his personal grievances and requests should receive attention, and to him it was parliament as the dispenser of the highest justice available to him that was most essential.   For there was a general understanding that a petition, presented in parliament, should receive an answer before the session came to an end and, though this understanding was not always faithfully observed, a breach of it was resented. As for the subject-matter of parliamentary petitions, it fell into two broad categories: those which prayed for relief which the common law of the land did not for some reason or other afford, and those which solicited special favours not touching law at all, pure matters of grace.

The fact that parliament was an institution open to every man in the land inevitably determined the structure of the parliamentary machine.   Parliament was an afforced council—that is to say, a council strengthened both in numbers and ability.   But, sitting as a single body, it could not get through the vast amount of trivial business to be transacted, even if it had been proper to assemble so many important people in one place to do so much that was unimportant.   So experiment after experiment was made to obtain workmanlike arrangements.   The first business of the petitioners was with receivers of petitions, who performed a preliminary

weeding-out and rejected such as need not have been brought to
parliament. Those they accepted were then passed to a tribunal of
auditors or triers, to whom the receivers acted as clerks. The
auditors might deal with the matters out of hand: their directions
would then be written briefly on the back of the petitions. But
if they did not feel competent to give a final decision, the petition
went to a yet higher tribunal, a body which was technically the
council, though that might mean only a select number of its
members. And there, if the subject-matter of the petition in some
way affected the king's interests, it was reserved for the attention
of persons who could act on the king's behalf and who perhaps
received his personal instructions. Already by 1290 the tribunals
of receivers and auditors were overburdened with work and had
to be divided into panels so that one group of receivers and a corresponding group of auditors could concentrate on the English
petitions, another on Irish petitions, and a third on Gascon petitions.
In ascending scale, therefore, a petition might pass before four
tribunals. The replies given were rarely final. There was no time
during a parliamentary session for thorough investigations. But
a favourable reply would secure a remedy or accelerate a decision
in the appropriate court or government department. But this was
not the end of refinements in organization. For, although the
creation of special tribunals to deal with petitions relieved the
council of much detailed work, although its time was carefully
reserved for important matters, even then it was often found necessary to refer various items of council business, including litigation,
to specially constituted committees. Only in this way could the
work of parliament be dispatched. The occasions on which the
full body of councillors met—ministers and magnates—were few
and only for very solemn and formal business.

The men who arranged the business of each parliament and who
composed its tribunals were mainly men in the service of the king:
they were predominantly clerks, trained in the various branches of
the king's administration, and justices employed on one of the
benches or on eyre, though there were lesser barons and knights
among them who were regularly employed by the king in positions
of trust. It is rare to find barons, whose relationship to the king
was essentially feudal and not ministerial, and whose appearance
in parliament hinged upon their responsibility to do suit at the
king's court, achieving anything of consequence save in quite
unusual circumstances. And there are few signs of any activity on

the part of popular representatives on the few occasions when they were summoned to be present. It is true that sometimes the assent of the magnates and the 'community' was required to taxation or legislation, or their support was wisely solicited in the prosecution of foreign policy; that homage was rendered or royal marriages discussed or services in war rewarded in parliament: parliament has sprung in part, as we have seen, from a feudal court and may bear the guise of a feudal court from time to time. But the important element of parliament was the official element, and the important aspect of the business of parliament was the dispensation of justice and the expedition of matters of administration. Under Edward I parliament was an institution staffed by men trained in English and even Roman and canon law, men who were in every way professionally competent to cope with the kind of business which took up nearly the whole time of parliament. Their contribution was immeasurably greater than that of any other body of men represented there regularly or intermittently—barons, knights, or burgesses.

It may seem strange that so little has been said so far about the representatives of the shires and towns who figure so prominently in the usual discussions of the rise of parliament. In fact, under Henry III and Edward I their presence was rarely required. Though between 1258 and 1286 nearly fifty parliaments were convoked, the commons were summoned to less than half-a-dozen; between 1290 and 1310 they attended only thirteen out of thirty-four parliaments; between 1311 and 1327 seventeen out of nineteen parliaments; after 1327 they were invariably present at the forty-eight parliaments of Edward III's reign of fifty years. The tendency was evidently towards an increasingly regular attendance of the commons. Still, it is evident that parliaments, at which they were present, had no more authority than those from which they were absent: for example, the revolutionary parliament of 1310, which authorized the establishment of the Lords Ordainers to reform the administration of the country, contained no popular representatives. We can, therefore, attach no constitutional importance to the presence of the commons in parliament before 1327. And even subsequently their presence was far from being thought the criterion of a parliament, for after 1327, as before it, they were summoned to meetings which were not called parliaments but 'Great Councils' instead, their purpose apparently being to save parliament from its congestion of business by relieving it of its political work and freeing it for its normal judicial functions.

The part played occasionally by the commons in the parliaments of Henry III and Edward I is not easy to understand. That it was thought essential to consult them regarding legislation we can dismiss, for some of the most important legislation of the Middle Ages was carried through at parliaments at which they were not present. Nor were popular representatives summoned officially to present petitions which would reveal to the king the defects and abuses of local government, and there was at this time no question of any bargain on the lines of redress before supply. If any motive predominates, it is that of finance, for, as we have already observed, popular representation and taxation went often hand in hand, and knights and burgesses were, indeed, consulted in parliament when some forms of taxation were proposed. On the other hand, they were sometimes summoned when, so far as we know, no questions of taxation were raised at all. We may in such instances suspect a political motive, for it is plain that the reality or appearance of popular support was worth having, and such support would presumably have greater value in the troubled times of Edward II.

It is very evident that parliament was the subject of many experiments by men who planned only for their own time and generation. Those experiments were not always wise or even intelligent, and many had to be discarded. We can find an excellent illustration if we consider the relations of the clergy to parliament. The higher clergy always had a position in parliament simply because the king was recognized to have the right to summon them to his councils if he so desired. Just as in the case of the nobles, there were some of the higher clergy whom the king clearly could not ignore, and many others who might or might not be summoned; but the tendency in the fourteenth century was to restrict the 'spiritual peers' to some twenty bishops and the heads, roughly thirty in number, of only the greatest religious houses. There was no difficulty in absorbing these prelates into the future house of lords. There is no problem here. But the case is different when we have to explain the motive behind the summoning of representatives of the lower clergy to parliament in 1297, when the addition of the 'praemunientes' clause to the writs of summons to the bishops required them to see that deans and archdeacons attended in person and the cathedral chapters by one proctor and the diocesan clergy by two proctors. For the clergy were already effectively organized in their own provincial councils. If there was any idea of dealing in parliament with the English Church as a whole for the purpose of consultation about taxation and thereby avoiding delays in a year when the king needed help urgently, that idea was hopeless from the start. The Church throughout the Middle Ages stood against the State as an independent and, indeed, a rival power. If the Church had grievances against the king and his ministers—and throughout the Middle Ages this was usually the case—the grievances were formulated in the provincial councils and presented to the king in parliament by the prelates. The Church also made good the claim that subsidies should be voted in the provincial councils or convocations. As a matter of convenience, the convocation of the province of Canterbury met about the same time in London as parliament met at Westminster. But the only effective voice of the clergy in parliament was the voice of the archbishop and his suffragans. Proctors of the lower clergy attended certain other parliaments of Edward I, and apparently some later parliaments in the fourteenth century. What they did there is still a mystery, but it was certainly so little that before long they stayed away entirely, and their summons became a mere formality. The work of parliament went on the same whether they were there or not. Evidently the adjustment of parliamentary procedure and practice to the needs of the country was a long and difficult process of trial and error.

It must be re-emphasized, therefore, that the vital force in parliament was the council with all its subordinate committees and tribunals. The presence and activities of popular representatives and clerical proctors and the host of private petitioners, who sought parliament for their own purposes, cannot be explained apart from the council. Parliament could exist without any of these: it could not exist without the council.

We have now to face the question why parliament became separated into king, lords and commons, and concentrated on politics rather than the dispensation of justice. There is nothing like it at the end of the thirteenth century: it is evident in the second half of the fourteenth century.

Throughout the period of the three Edwards there was no change in the functions of parliament, but there was a gradual and important change in emphasis. As we have seen, politics did not at first occupy much of the time of parliament and could always be discussed apart from it. But in the difficult times of Edward II they assumed a more prominent place in what was done there:

thus the Ordainers placed upon parliament the responsibility of controlling the council, appointing ministers and granting taxes. This tendency was greatly accelerated in the following reign with the concentration on war measures in diplomacy, taxation, legislation and the like. A direct result was apparent under Edward II: the ministerial class became outweighed by the baronial class in the various tribunals and committees for every matter that was not one of the strictest technical law. This was no accident: it makes its appearance after the Ordinances of 1311 and was a deliberate plan to restrict the authority and minimize the importance of the royal ministerial group in parliament. It represents a feudal or—as we should now begin to term it—an aristocratic reaction whereby the nobles were determined to gain effective control of parliament and, through it, of the government. Although the Ordinances were declared null and void in 1322, the barons succeeded in their main object: the official class never regained its old prestige and power. This involved a revolutionary change in the conception of the council in parliament. Previously it had included all those who were expected to be present because they held some office under the crown and all those who received an individual writ of summons. For a long time it had been a body of very fluctuating composition. Occasionally very few magnates would be summoned at all, though the bishops, the greater abbots, the earls, the most important barons, would normally be certain to be required to attend. Beyond this rather narrow circle there was a wider circle with a very vague circumference, for the king summoned whom he willed, sometimes a larger number, sometimes a smaller. But under Edward II a different conception gained ground. The nobles began to regard summons as a right, as something not subject to the whim of the king, and, borrowing an idea from the Continent, they began to call themselves 'peers of the realm' who had a right to be consulted. Others, and particularly the lesser abbots and priors, were glad not to be summoned to parliament and sought to escape. It is then that the 'great council in parliament' emerged to insist that important questions must be laid before it. When such ideas gained ground, the practical effect under a weak king was to sap the authority of the ministerial element in parliament and delay the dispatch of public business. The position of the professional councillors—the ministers, the judges, the masters in chancery, the other civil servants—became anomalous. Whereas under Edward I they had performed nearly all the work of parliament, under Edward III they were quite obviously much less important people in parliament than the nobles. The results were conspicuous. Of necessity parliament could no longer function as of old: the private petitions presented to parliament grew fewer and fewer in number, and judicial work fell into the background. But if the ministerial element became weak in parliament, it remained strong and efficient in the chief departments of government, and the causes which led to the development of parliament in its modern form brought about the transfer, particularly to chancery, of much of the work which had once been performed by parliament. Politics became the main, though still not the exclusive, concern of parliament, and the judges and other officials, relegated to the position of mere assistants, gave their advice when they were asked to do so and only then. So, as the professional element dropped gradually to a subordinate position, a 'house of lords' emerged. To give a date for it is impossible. All we can say is that the writ of summons tended to be hereditary in certain families, being attached to persons and not, as originally, to lands. The consolidation of this noble group of about fifty men in Edward III's reign, achieved largely through the doctrine of peerage, was increased by a new development, begun by Richard II in 1387 and seen frequently in the fifteenth century, whereby hereditary baronies were created by royal letters patent and carried a writ of summons to parliament with them. So by the close of the Middle Ages an Upper House was well on its way to being an exclusive house of hereditary peers, and by the sixteenth century this it finally became.

Meanwhile the commons remained as they had begun, outside the council in parliament. If they had been originally summoned to give a formal assent to measures, fiscal or political, propounded to them, such subjects came up for discussion far too intermittently and irregularly to give them a sense of coherence and integration. For example, out of the twenty-one parliaments which met in the first ten years of Edward III's reign, only five voted supplies. Their corporate development cannot therefore be explained from such an angle. It resulted from the fact that they came to exercise a new function, a function which could have had no existence apart from the judicial character of parliament. For the principal of their duties was conceived to be to petition as a body, to bring to the fountain of justice the complaints of the people at large, and by 1327, when popular representatives came to attend every parliament, they had assumed the responsibility for presenting petitions which claimed to be of public interest. All over Europe at this time popular representatives were being called for consultation to the headquarters of government: that in England they should have been permanently associated with so technical an institution as parliament was to have immense consequences for the future. It was the result of a necessary adjustment in procedure. Hitherto the barons had claimed the right to speak on behalf of the 'community of England' and present petitions in its name to the king's council in parliament. But they had promoted themselves and turned that council into the 'great council in parliament'. Having now become judges instead of petitioners, they had to see that their former role was filled, and it was an obvious step to let the representatives of the commons bring forward the requests and supplications of the community for baronial consideration. Therefore the presence of the commons in parliament became indispensable, but nevertheless they remained of slight political importance, for the barons continued to dominate the parliaments of the fourteenth and fifteenth centuries. In such circumstances a special procedure was followed: petitions from the commons as a body were not delivered to the ordinary receivers and considered by the ordinary auditors. Instead, they were handed direct to the clerk of parliament and heard in the first instance by the great council. This procedure is of the highest significance, for it determined the separate identity of the commons from that of the lords and regulated and stereotyped the relations between them and, by doing so, it settled the structure of parliament as the bicameral institution we know to-day.

Such an altered conception of legislative authority was revolutionary, far beyond the vision of any of the unknown architects of parliament. For until the commons became an inseparable component of parliament, the usual form of legislation was legislation from above, drafted by the king's professional advisers and not necessarily submitted to the council in parliament. But thereafter, upon the lengthy petitions submitted to the council by the commons there was founded a series of statutes, a form of legislation which became usual throughout the fourteenth century and which has gradually developed into the modern legislative system. Nevertheless, it presented a sad declension from the days of the first Edward, when statutes as the expression of government policy were well ordered and well drafted. For the commons' petitions gathered together haphazardly a number of quite unrelated requests and, when those unacceptable to the government had been abstracted, the typical statute followed closely, chapter by chapter, the order and language of the remaining articles. Simply because they had to be a direct answer to the demands put forward in writing by unskilled men, they could not fail to be clumsily drawn. The problem afterwards was to secure an exclusive right in legislation for parliament, to confine legislation to the subject-matter of parliamentary petitions, and this was slowly achieved through the control by the commons of taxation. By insisting wherever possible on the principle that redress must precede supply, they very largely obtained their way.

But not only did the commons present public grievances. They gradually assumed the function of presenting private grievances as well. For they were willing to sponsor petitions affecting the interests of but one section of the community, like single counties, single towns, groups of merchants, or even of private individuals. This itself called for serious deliberations, and they were careful to disavow all individual petitions, which pretend to contain matters of national interest and to be put forward on behalf of the community, if they had not passed their own scrutiny. In consequence, though common petitions ought to have been always of general interest, private petitions began to be presented to the commons in the hope that they would support them and pass them to the lords. The commons constituted, in fact, a tribunal co-ordinate with that of the auditors. A petitioner, therefore, had the choice of two avenues of approach to parliament: it might well seem to him, or to his professional advisers, the better course to bring his case in suitable form before the commons with the intent that it should become one of the articles embodied in the bill finally laid before the 'great council in parliament'. The practice of approaching the commons went on unimpeded, and by Richard II's time petitions were often openly addressed, not to the king and council or the council, but to the commons, and were accepted, considered and adopted by them. This meant no more, of course, than a *prima facie* case for obtaining a remedy in the common interest: the effective examination of the petition fell to the council to perform. But gradually it came to be thought that every parliamentary decision, even on a private petition, should receive the assent of the commons as well as of the lords. Here we have the origin of private acts of parliament as distinct from public and general acts of parliament, although it was not until the fifteenth century that such a conception became possible.

The house of commons of the future was, therefore, born and bred in the judicial atmosphere of an essentially judicial institution. That this important period in the development of the commons should have coincided with the years when the crown was desperate for money was important because it placed an essential weapon in their hands. Yet their efforts to control taxation and to introduce administrative reforms were quite spasmodic. Not so their consideration of public and private wrongs, and they owed their real consolidation to the common consciousness produced by long deliberations and debates upon the grievances of the community at large and the complaints of all who gained their ear. And they set them down in 'common petitions' and presented them in an ancient and traditional way for judgment to the tribunal of the 'lords'.

When once we have appreciated the real interests and functions of the commons, we can understand why it was that constant demands were made for annual parliaments and why there was little unwillingness to serve. Knights of the thirty-five shires allowed themselves to be elected again and again: even sheriffs, who had every opportunity to avoid service if they wished, accepted parliamentary duties until they were excluded by statute in 1372. Similarly, the representatives of roughly eighty boroughs did not cavil at re-election, and by the close of the fourteenth century there were few instances of default. There was, in fact, always present a fair proportion of members who were not newcomers to parliament. Certainly, there were excellent opportunities for a lawyer, who had got himself returned, to do some private practice in parliament by pleading his clients' cases and getting them accepted for inclusion in a commons' petition, and it was mainly as a protest against this that an attempt, largely unsuccessful, was made to disqualify practising lawyers from acting as representatives of shires or boroughs.

We have spoken of the commons as though the attitude of the knights and that of the burgesses were completely identical. Yet Edward III's reign was far advanced before these two groups showed any signs of coalescing. It was not enough to draw them together that they were all summoned through the sheriff and, at least ostensibly, elected by the communities they represented. For 'a delicate balance of repulsion as well as attraction' always existed between country and town. Whilst the burgesses had deliberately withdrawn themselves from the administrative affairs of the shire, so the knights, conscious of their social superiority to those engaged in trade and of their closer affiliation with the baronial class, remained aloof from the burgesses. Even in taxation they were divided, for the boroughs paid tenths and the counties fifteenths. It was not surprising, therefore, that often the knights were referred to in association with the nobles, or consulted by themselves as a separate 'estate', or even contrasted with the 'commons' in the sense of the burgesses. That the two classes were telescoped together, a development peculiar to English political life, was not due to their own inclinations, but partly because a growing emphasis was being laid on peerage which separated the nobles sharply from the knights, partly because it was a natural thing for them to be associated with each other as petitioners in the public interests, and partly because there was, especially in the fifteenth century, a transformation in the character of borough members through the creation of 'pocket boroughs', which allowed the infiltration into their ranks of landed gentry. Nevertheless, the knights continued to dominate the proceedings of the commons as a whole and to keep the more numerous, and possibly wealthier, burgesses in so subordinate and insignificant a position that they produced no prominent personalities, no Speaker for the commons before Henry VII's reign, and on no occasion took a line of action of their own.

The commons represented a mode of procedure. If they had had independent control over it, there would be no doubt about the tremendous power they could have exercised. It is generally stated that, because the commons included within their ranks many county gentry, trained in unpaid public services, lawyers, business men, and experienced parliamentarians, they exerted a great influence in parliament. Yet this is a mere assumption: if it were true, then we should expect to find it borne out by the evidence. But, on the contrary, the facts point to the subservience rather than the independence of the commons. For in all questions of high politics the direction came from the lords. The late fourteenth and fifteenth centuries constituted a period of patronage, of 'bastard' feudalism, when the knights were attached by personal and territorial ties to the nobles and sought to advance their own fortunes through a good connexion: even Peter de la Mare, the famous Speaker in the Good Parliament of 1376, was the steward of the earl of March. So the aristocracy got their dependents elected, sent members of their own class to assist the commons in their deliberations, and took command of the petitionary procedure of the commons whenever they thought fit. In no other way can we explain the curious revulsions of Richard II's time when the commons, without any radical change in personnel, seem to initiate one revolutionary policy only to follow it up shortly afterwards by another diametrically opposed to it. How far parliament and its procedure could be made the tool of aristocratic factions the fifteenth century was more fully to disclose.

The medieval parliament provides an epitome of the way in which the various elements in the state have acted and reacted upon one another until in the fullness of time they could compound into an organic whole. The three traditions we have seen at work since the Norman Conquest—royal, seignorial and popular—have slowly produced the three estates of the realm—king, lords and commons—and at last brought the trinity into the unity of a single institution.

SELECT READING

F. W. Maitland, 'Introduction to Memoranda de Parliamento, 1305' in *Selected Essays* (1936), 1–72; C. H. McIlwain, *High Court of Parliament* (1910), 109–256; J. F. Baldwin, *The King's Council* (1913), 1–68, 307–44; A. F. Pollard, *Evolution of Parliament* (1920), chs. ii, iii, vi; H. L. Gray, *Influence of Commons on Early Legislation* (1932), 118–378; C. Petit-Dutaillis and G. Lefèbvre, *Studies Supplementary to Stubbs*, iii (trans. 1929), 305–55, 406–505; T. F. T. Plucknett, 'Parliament' in *The English Government at Work, 1327–1336* (1940), 82–128; H. G. Richardson and G. O. Sayles, *The Early Statutes* (1934), *Select Cases of Procedure without Writ under Henry III* (1941), chs. ii–vi, ix, and their articles in *T.R.H.S.*, xi (1928), 137–83, xxviii (1946), 21–45; *E.H.R.* xlvi (1931), 529–50, xlvii (1932), 194–203, 377–97; *Bulletin of Institute of Historical Research* v (1928), 129–54, vi (1929), 71–88, 129–55, viii (1930), 65–82, ix (1931), 1–18; *B.J.R.L.* xxii (1938), 3–50.

INDEX

Printed by Jarrold & Sons, Ltd., The Empire Press, Norwich, England